STANDARD LESSON COMMENTARY
1994-95

International Sunday School Lessons

published by

STANDARD PUBLISHING

Eugene H. Wigginton, *Publisher*

Richard C. McKinley, *Director of Curriculum Development*

James I. Fehl, *Editor*   Hela M. Campbell, *Office Editor*

Forty-second Annual Volume

In This Volume

Artists

TITLE PAGES: James E. Seward

Cover design by Listenberger Design Associates, Indianapolis

Lessons based on International Sunday School Lessons © 1991 by the Lesson Committee.

Index of Printed Texts, 1994-95

The printed texts for 1994-95 are arranged here in the order in which they appear in the Bible.
Opposite each reference is the number of the page on which it appears in this volume.

Cumulative Index

A cumulative index for the Scripture passages used in the STANDARD LESSON COMMENTARY
for the years September, 1992—August, 1995, is set forth below.

Worry Is for the Birds!

by Bob Russell

ON A NUMBER OF OCCASIONS I've asked people in Christian audiences to raise their hands if they struggle with worry. Almost always, about two-thirds of those present will raise their hands and snicker a little about their open admission of worry.

Christians are willing to admit worry openly because they regard it as a "respectable" sin. It's a "weakness" that we're willing to confess, not a sin we keep hidden.

Jesus, however, saw it differently. Ten verses in the Sermon on the Mount (Matthew 6:25-34) are given to the subject of worry. Jesus made it clear that worry is a serious sin that needs to be properly diagnosed and cured.

The Causes of Worry

Why is worry such a common problem today? Some of it has to do with *temperament.* Some persons are melancholy temperaments who, by nature, are perfectionists. They are sticklers for detail and agonize over small mistakes. Melancholy temperaments are wonderful administrators and are a blessing to any organization, but they are chronic worriers.

Another cause of worry is the *affluence* of our age. Solomon said, "The sleep of a laborer is sweet, whether he eats little or much, but the abundance of a rich man permits him no sleep" (Ecclesiastes 5:12).* It is erroneous to assume that the more material goods one has, the more secure he will feel and the less he will worry. Just the opposite is true: the more one possesses, the more he has to protect, insure, and worry about.

Another contributing factor to anxiety is *media hype.* We worry about matters to which people a century ago were oblivious. The media brings global problems right into our living rooms every night.

It's good to be informed, but one needs to remember that the media is in the business of improving ratings and selling advertising. In order to captivate attention, media personnel have to make whatever happens during the course of the day sound as threatening and crucial as possible, because if people don't watch, they don't sell ads; then they're out of business!

Another factor that creates anxiety is *experience.* One might assume that the older we get, the less we worry. But the opposite is true: anxiety often increases with age because we have witnessed tragedies occur and we know terrible things can happen.

Another factor contributing to anxiety is our *rapid pace of life.* Advanced travel, FAX machines, cellular telephones, and other modern "conveniences" have made our schedules so hectic that we seldom relax. It's doubtful that God designed our nervous systems to cope with the kind of artificial pressures we place on ourselves.

The primary cause of worry is *lack of faith* in God. Jesus said, "O you of little faith." Man wants to be in control of everything. He's not willing to surrender significant areas to the providence of God. The Bible says, "Cast all your anxiety on him because he cares for you" (1 Peter 5:7). But too many people are not willing to take their burden to the Lord and leave it there. They want to be in charge themselves. So they spend a good portion of their time fretting over things that are beyond their control.

The Command: "Do not Worry"

Three times in this section Jesus commands, "Do not worry." What exactly does that command mean? I think there is a difference between *concern* and *anxiety.* Concern focuses on probable difficulties and results in action. Anxiety focuses on uncontrollable difficulties and results in inaction. Worry is always asking "What if?" "What if there is an earthquake?" "What if I get cancer?" Anxiety frets but takes no action; it focuses on problems that are beyond our control. Jesus said, "Don't be anxious."

But we need to be concerned. We need to give attention to real problems and seek to resolve them. Jesus said, "Look at the birds." I was watching a flock of birds one day. They were having a meeting in mid-October. Do you know what they were discussing? They were planning their upcoming trip to Florida! They sensed that winter was coming, and they were concerned enough to get ready to migrate. Jesus did not suggest a total disregard for tomorrow's potential problems. See 14:28-30. So it's not a sin to save for your children's education, to buy insurance, or to plan ahead.

But we are commanded not to be anxious. Jesus said, "Who of you by worrying can add a single hour to his life?" (Matthew 6:27). Instead of increasing our life span, it decreases it. Worry is so futile—it accomplishes nothing.

The Cure for Worry

How can one win over worry? It's unrealistic to think that there is an easy cure. But Jesus said, "Look at the birds of the air" (Matthew 6:26). Several important lessons can be learned by observing the birds—lessons that will help to overcome anxiety.

Develop an Eternal Perspective

"Look at the birds of the air; they do not sow or reap or store away in barns, and yet your heavenly Father feeds them. Are you not much more valuable than they?" (Matthew 6:26). People are more important than birds because they have been created in the image of God, and God breathed into man "the breath of life." We have been promised eternal life.

This world is the primary focus of birds. But human beings are made for a higher purpose. We are special. We are spiritual beings. We should live with eternity in view.

Pagans who do not know God live for this world only. They chase after all these "things." But those who know the Lord should be constantly aware that "life [is] more important than food, and the body more important than clothes" (Matthew 6:25). By worshiping God regularly, we are reminded of these vital truths.

Learn to Trust the Providence of God

A second lesson that should be learned from birds is to trust God's providential care.

Some birds eat two or three times their weight in food every day! But birds are created to trust God's provision for their needs.

Birds do two things that humans would do well to emulate. They trust God to supply their need, and they work hard to assist Him. Birds don't sit in their nests all day and expect God to drop food in them. Early in the morning they start looking. They are diligent in searching for their needs to be supplied.

Trusting God doesn't mean laziness or indifference. It does mean realizing God is taking care of us. God has promised to provide for our needs. It's a matter of believing His promises and being content with what He has supplied.

That's what makes worry a serious sin. It is accusing God of being a liar. God says, "I will meet all your needs according to my riches in Christ Jesus" (cf. Philippians 4:19); worry says, "I don't believe He will supply my needs.

Maintain Proper Priorities

Birds focus every day on the things of this world. Since humans are more valuable than birds, we are to "seek first [God's] kingdom and his righteousness" and then the things of this world will be added to us. The Christian's priorities are God, people (with a special emphasis on family), job, and self. When one keeps these priorities in order, God promises to supply every need. But worry inverts priorities. The job becomes more important than family; self becomes more important than others. As a result, our responsibilities seem greater than our resources, and our energy is sapped by anxiety.

When we trust God, we keep our priorities in order. We don't just say it; we do it. We go to church every Sunday even though it would be nice to have a weekend with the family on the lake. God comes first. We tell the truth, even though it would be to our financial advantage to lie. Others matter more than self. We put our work aside and listen to a spouse or child who wants to talk. Family matters more than the job. When we keep priorities in order, God supplies those things we need—especially peace of mind.

Live One Day at a Time

Birds don't store up food in barns. They live one day at a time. "Therefore do not worry about tomorrow, for tomorrow will worry about itself. Each day has enough trouble of its own" (Matthew 6:34). The Lord didn't say, "Don't worry about tomorrow because nothing bad will ever happen to you." He was very realistic. He said there will be trouble tomorrow.

Bad things do happen in this world. The birds die. Our parents get Alzheimer's. Our children have accidents. Our health breaks.

We are not promised exemption from problems, but we are promised enough spiritual resources to cope with them. If today's problems measure a 6 on the pressure scale, he will supply six reinforcements. If they measure a 10 tomorrow, he will reinforce us with ten resources. But if we waste three of today's six resources worrying about tomorrow's ten pressures, we aren't able to stand up under the stress of today. We have to master the art of living one day at a time.

Indeed. "God is faithful; he will not let you be tempted beyond what you can bear. But when you are tempted, he will also provide a way out so that you can stand up under it" (1 Corinthians 10:13). Therefore, trust God to provide, and live one day at a time. Let the words of the psalmist be your motto: "This is the day the Lord has made; let us rejoice and be glad in it (Psalm 118:24).

This article is adapted from pages 75-86 of the book *When Life Is a Zoo God Still Loves You* by Bob Russell, copyright ©1992. The Living Word, Inc. Used by permission.

*Scripture quotations in this article are taken from the *New International Version*.

Autumn Quarter, 1994

Theme: From the Conquest to the Kingdom

Special Features

Lessons

Unit 1. The Conquest of the Land

Unit 2. The Rule of the Judges

Unit 3. The Beginning of the Kingdom

Unit 4. The Kingdom Under David and Solomon

About these lessons

This study focuses on the history of the people of Israel from their conquest of the promised land to the later years of Solomon's reign. Significant achievements and failures of the people and of their first three kings are noted.

The Complete Picture

Of WHAT VALUE to Christians is a knowledge of the Old Testament? Isn't it just ancient history? One of the values of these writings is precisely that—they relate to the history of an ancient people, Israel. More specifically, however, they contain the record of God's working through that people to accomplish His purpose in the human arena.

In time, God's purpose was brought to light in the life, death, and resurrection of Jesus and in the establishment of the church. An understanding of the historical background of these events, along with the prophecies regarding them, helps to establish the certainty of one's faith in Jesus Christ as Lord and Savior.

The Autumn and Summer quarters this year are courses of Old Testament history. It can be seen that the latter quarter takes up the story where the former leaves off. All of the Old Testament historical studies in this lesson cycle are in chronological sequence in order to give a clear and comprehensive view of Israel's history.

Of course, the New Testament is emphasized in this lesson cycle. The Winter quarter examines the life of Jesus, focusing on His fulfillment of the Old Testament promises. Paul's letters to the Corinthians, the subject of the Spring quarter, provide guidance for the church today, as they did for the church in Corinth in the first century.

International Sunday School Lesson Cycle
September, 1992—August, 1998

YEAR	AUTUMN QUARTER (Sept., Oct., Nov.)	WINTER QUARTER (Dec., Jan., Feb.)	SPRING QUARTER (Mar., Apr., May)	SUMMER QUARTER (June, July, Aug.)
1992-1993	Old Testament Personalities (Old Testament Survey)	Good News for All (New Testament Survey)	Believing in Christ (John)	Following God's Purpose (Ephesians, Philippians, Colossians, Philemon)
1993-1994	The Story of Beginnings (Genesis)	The Story of Jesus (Luke)	Good News for God's People (Romans) Set Free by God's Grace (Galatians)	God Redeems a People (Exodus, Leviticus, Numbers, Deuteronomy)
1994-1995	From the Conquest to the Kingdom (Joshua, Judges, 1 and 2 Samuel, 1 Kings)	Jesus the Fulfillment (Matthew)	Christians Living in Community (1 and 2 Corinthians)	A Nation Turns From God (1 and 2 Kings, Amos, Hosea, Micah, Isaiah)
1995-1996	The Story of Christian Beginnings (Acts)	God's Promise of Deliverance (Isaiah) God's Love for All People (Jonah, Ruth)	Teachings of Jesus (Matthew, Mark, Luke)	A Practical Religion (James) God Is With Us (Psalms)
1996-1997	God's People Face Judgment (2 Kings, Jeremiah, Lamentations, Ezekiel, Habakkuk)	New Testament Personalities	Hope for the Future (1 and 2 Thessalonians, Revelation)	Guidance for Ministry (1 and 2 Timothy, Titus) A Call to Faithfulness (Hebrews)
1997-1998	God Leads a People Home (Major Prophets, Minor Prophets, Nehemiah)	God's People in a Troubled World (1 and 2 Peter, 1, 2, 3 John, Jude)	The Gospel of Action (Mark)	Wisdom for Living (Job, Proverbs, Ecclesiastes)

Experiments in Government

by Orrin Root

WHEN WE SEE the many kinds of governments in the world, it is almost a shock to read that "the powers that be are ordained of God" (Romans 13:1). Is God experimenting with all those governments to see what kind will work the best? No, God does not experiment in order to learn. He already knows. But within limits He lets us experiment so that we may learn.

When God called the people of Israel from Egypt to be His own, He gave them a law. If all of them would live by it, and if all the parents would teach their children to live by it, they would be governed in the ideal way. But those people were not prepared for the responsibility of ordering their lives by the law. God made Moses a virtual dictator, and backed him by such evidence of divine power that resistance was overwhelmed.

When Joshua took Moses' place, the people seemed to have learned their lesson. With few aberrations they followed the new leader and lived by the law while they conquered the promised land and settled down in it.

Then it was time for each person to accept his own responsibility, but the people failed miserably. Through greed and malice and laziness and love of pleasure, they disobeyed the law of God. Thus they became so weak and spineless that they were easy prey for bandit gangs or national armies of heathen who invaded the land. Through all the time of the judges they showed that only with powerful leadership would they behave as God's people ought.

Since strong leadership seemed to be needed, the people decided to have a king. God knew that was not the answer, but He let the people experiment and learn. Kings are only human. They too can be motivated by greed and malice and laziness and love of pleasure.

Would Israel—would any nation—ever learn the infallible way to national stability, prosperity, and happiness? It is for each person to do right by preference, not by compulsion—and to look to God's Word to see what is right.

In past lessons we have read of Moses' troubled dictatorship that was able to succeed because it was supported and directed by the Almighty. In the lessons before us we shall see the times of Joshua and the judges and the first three kings of Israel. Our studies of the next three months are divided into four units as follows:

Unit I. The Conquest of the Land

September

Lesson 1. From the camp of Israel east of the Jordan, Joshua sent two daring spies across the flooded river to learn what they could about Jericho. They found that the city walls were strong, but the people were frightened.

Lesson 2. The river was a raging torrent overflowing its banks. But God said it was time to go, so the people loaded their donkeys and shouldered their packs and marched toward the swollen stream. As the first feet splashed into the shallows, the flow swiftly receded. Far upstream the water piled up in a heap, leaving an empty river bed for the people to cross.

Lesson 3. Defenders on the walls of Jericho watched and wondered as the Hebrew warriors marched around the city and then went back to their camp. Day by day they repeated the march, once around the city and back to camp. On the seventh day they circled the city seven times. Then the trumpets sounded and the walls fell down flat. Thousands of Hebrew soldiers scrambled over the tumbled stones to destroy everybody and everything in town.

The war went on for about seven years, but everywhere God gave His people victory. When they had taken as much land as they could use, they settled down to farming. For a long time they had peace and prosperity. Our lessons begin near the end of Joshua's life.

Lesson 4. More than a hundred years old, Joshua called the people together to hear his last message. They had a choice, he said. There were the gods their fathers had served centuries ago by the Euphrates; there were the heathen gods of the land they had taken; there was the Lord who had led them from Egypt and given them this land. Which God would they serve? Loudly the people declared they would serve the Lord.

Unit II. The Rule of the Judges
October 2, 9

For a long time the Hebrews kept their promise to serve the Lord. But, one by one, death took the valiant warriors who had won the land. They were replaced by a softer generation, a generation blessed by rain and sun and good harvests instead of mighty miracles and victory in battle, a generation not so acutely aware of the Lord among them (Judges 2:10).

Lesson 5. Envy grew, and dishonesty, and violence, and murder. People even began to join in the feasts of pagan gods. God's punishment came in the form of heathen invaders who stole livestock and harvest, killing anyone who stood in their way. Hungry and afraid, the people thought again of the Lord, stopped worshiping other gods, and began pleading for help. Mercifully, God provided a leader (judge) to rally them and defeat the invaders. But when peace and prosperity were restored, all too soon the people began to forget God again. This happened over and over through a period of about three hundred years. We call this time the period of the judges.

Lesson 6. This lesson brings one example of the repeated process described in lesson 5. This time Midianites from the desert occupied Israel. When the suffering people again turned to the Lord, He called Gideon to rescue them. Gideon raised an army of thirty-two thousand, but the Lord reduced it to three hundred. With that handful the Lord chased the innumerable host of invaders back to the desert. Convinced of the Lord's power, the people again were loyal to Him—but not for very long.

Unit III. The Beginning of the Kingdom
October 16, 23, 30

Samuel was the last of the long line of judges. He rallied the people to drive out the Philistines who had oppressed them, and then he led the nation in righteousness. But in his old age he made his sons judges, and they were greedy and crooked (1 Samuel 7:3—8:3).

Lesson 7. Leaders of the people asked Samuel to give them a king. Samuel and the Lord did not approve of that. The Lord was the proper king of Israel. The people had only to obey Him to have peace and prosperity forever, but that way had failed to work. The people had turned away from the Lord again and again. The leaders persisted in their request for a king, and the Lord said to let them have their way.

Lesson 8. The Lord chose Saul to be the first king of Israel, and the people gladly acclaimed him.

Lesson 9. Saul began his reign with a brilliant victory over Ammonites who threatened a city of Israel (1 Samuel 11). But soon he faced a greater test of his trust in the Lord. When Philistines in force invaded Israel, the Lord told Saul to hold his troops at Gilgal till Samuel would come to offer sacrifice and direct the campaign. Saul waited about a week, but the situation was so threatening that he finally went ahead with the sacrifice before Samuel came. For that he was told that his family would not continue on the throne of Israel.

Unit IV. The Kingdom Under David and Solomon
November

The Lord chose David to be the next king, but Saul continued to rule for many years while David was maturing and being prepared to rule a nation. When Saul was killed in battle, David became king and established his capital at Jerusalem. He brought the ark of the covenant there and proposed to build a temple for the Lord. Nathan the prophet brought God's answer: David was not to build the temple, but God promised that people of David's line would continue to rule forever (2 Samuel 1:1—7:17).

Lesson 10. Humbly David accepted God's will and gave thanks for His promise. But even David was not immune to temptation. He committed adultery with a neighbor's wife, and then had the neighbor killed in battle (2 Samuel 11).

Lesson 11. God sent Nathan to denounce David's sin, and David humbly confessed his guilt.

Solomon was the next king. At his request, God gave him special wisdom. God also gave riches and honor that Solomon did not ask. The new king improved David's empire, and built the temple that David was not allowed to build. His reputation spread far and wide.

Lesson 12. The queen of Sheba was one of many who came to see if Solomon lived up to his reputation. She found that he did, and more.

Lesson 13. Having everything his own way, Solomon neglected to give enough attention to God's way. For political purposes he brought heathen princesses to Jerusalem as his wives. They brought their heathen religions, and Solomon built places of worship for their heathen gods. The Lord's rebuke was plain, and His punishment was severe. Solomon's glorious empire would be lost; his kingdom would be divided; his son would rule only one tribe of Israel's twelve.

This series of lessons proclaims the power of God and the weakness of men. Showered with God's blessings, people turn away from Him. The people of Israel did it over and over in the time of the judges. Their kings did it too. Elevated by God's power and blessed by His favor, Saul and David and Solomon all disobeyed Him. Their failure is the common failure of mankind. Who among us will not say with David, "I have sinned against the Lord"? (2 Samuel 12:13).

So all history unites in proclaiming this truth: People need a Savior. Praise the Lord, He has provided one—Jesus Christ His Son. By His gracious forgiveness we sinners can have "the righteousness which is of God by faith" (Philippians 3:9). There is no other hope for mankind.

The Subject of Our Lives

by Gary E. Weedman

POLITICAL REVOLUTIONS, changing national boundaries, and uprootings of ethnic peoples are not unique to the latter part of the twentieth century; they also make up much of the narrative of the book of Joshua in the Old Testament. The political changes in central and eastern Europe and in the former Yugoslavia have monopolized our headlines in recent months without much understanding from western observers. Yet one of the clear messages of Scripture is that similar events described in the book of Joshua have meaning that we are able to know from the revelation of God himself.

There is some temptation to view the Israelite conquest of Canaan under the leadership of Joshua from a narrow political or national or military perspective; in other words, to think that God "blesses" the nation that honors Him by enhancing their military might, their expansionist interests, or their national stature. Coming to the book of Joshua with this world view will cause one to misunderstand the events recorded in it as well as affect any meaning this book holds for our own times.

God, the Subject of Joshua

Joshua is an intriguing character. He led the Israelites across the Jordan River with its waters "piled up in a heap," even though it was at flood stage (Joshua 3:16).* Fearlessly he led the priests, the ark of the covenant, and the armed men around the city of Jericho. He asked God to stay the sun over Gibeon to give the Israelites the needed time for victory. Finally, near the end of his life he stood before the Israelites and delivered one of the famous addresses of all history—one that revealed a great faith and a single devotion.

Yet, Joshua is not the subject of the book that bears his name; God is the subject. Note the following reverences with my emphases. God told Joshua, *"I* will give you every place where you set your foot, as I promised Moses. . . . *I* will never leave you nor forsake you" (1: 3, 5). After Joshua sent two men across the Jordan on a spy mission and they were befriended by Rahab, they returned to Joshua with this report: *"The Lord* has surely given the whole land into our hands" (2:24). As the Israelites made preparations to cross the Jordan and claim the covenant made to Abraham, God told Joshua, "Today *I* will begin to exalt you in the eyes of all Israel, so

they may know that *I* am with you as I was with Moses" (3:7).

Joshua knew who the subject of the narrative really was. After the people crossed the Jordan and set up the stones as a memorial at Gilgal, Joshua told them, *"The Lord your God* dried up the Jordan before you. . . . *The Lord your God* did to the Jordan just what he had done to the Red Sea" (4:23). At Jericho it was not merely a clever strategy that provided a victory for the Israelites. Even before the battle, God spoke to Joshua, "See, *I* have delivered Jericho into your hands, along with its king and its fighting men (6:2). Joshua's cry on the seventh day, after the army marched around the city seven times, was, "The *Lord* has given you the city" (6:16). And so goes the narrative of Joshua. It is the narrative of God working with Joshua. God said, "For *I* have delivered into your hands the king of Ai" (8:1). In the campaign against the southern cities, the Israelites were victorious because "the *Lord, the God of Israel,* fought for Israel" (10:42). Neither the intelligence nor the courage, nor the power, nor the resourcefulness of Joshua or the Israelites are the subject of this book. They may have been wise and courageous and resourceful. The subject, however, is God himself.

What About Us?

When the narratives of our lives are written, who will be the subject? In our western, enlightened, and increasingly secular society, one does not expect God to be made the subject of life; it is common for humans, or events, or other things to occupy that position. It is tragic, however, to see this secularist tendency creeping into the lives of believers. The examples are many.

When a crisis occurs in the lives of others, we hear believers say to them, "You're in our thoughts," or "We're remembering you," or, "You have our sympathy." These well-intentioned responses reflect the impact of secular society even into the life of the church. How hard it has become for many believers to say, "We'll pray to God for your difficulty"!

A local congregation finished a much-needed education wing for their building. During the celebration reception, many of the members were observing how many persons had worked, sacrificed, and given to the project. A local minister associated with another fellowship came through the reception line and noted, "It looks like the Spirit of God has been at work here!" God's Spirit had been at work in that congregation, and still is at work; why is it so difficult for those good people to say so?

In an Austrian village not far from Haus Edelweiss, the European headquarters of the mission agency TCM International, there is a small hotel named *Die Auge des Gott* ("The Eye of God"). When asked about this unusual name, the proprietors explained that they were so aware of the presence of God throughout their lives, they wanted to affirm that faith by such a name for their hotel; the name seemed natural to them. The very fact that I regarded this name as "strange" is evidence of the effect that this secularist trend can have on those of us living in the western world.

This attitude, a reluctance to make God "the subject of our narratives," has at least two causes. First, I suspect that many do not want to appear to be religious zealots in the same mold as the religious cults, who attribute the events of their own history, as extreme and bizarre as they are, to the acts of God. The world remembers the fanaticism of Jim Jones and David Koresh, persons who seemed obsessed by the idea of God in their lives.

Second, the scientific world view has influenced us all more than we may know. During the eighteenth century a movement known as "The Enlightenment" emerged. It was a movement that set the stage for the modern world view—an understanding of all that happens from a purely human perspective. The leaders of this movement not only believed that one could understand the world from a purely secular perspective, they also believed that human effort could control the events of the world. Persons did not need God to understand the world or to control its events. Humans, they believed, had the capacity to solve their own problems, whether social, material, physical, or "spiritual" by the application of the same kind of inventiveness used in scientific advances. Joshua, however, had a different viewpoint.

A Heavenly Perspective

The perspective from which one sees any object or event greatly affects the understanding of it. While living in England, my sons and I watched cricket matches as baseball-loving Americans. What we "saw" was very different from what cricket-loving Englishmen saw. It was only when we began to see the game as they saw it, to understand cricket separate from the perspective of baseball, that we had any real understanding of what was going on.

So it was with the man, Joshua. God is the subject of the book of Joshua because Joshua saw his world from the perspective of God himself.

Joshua saw God fulfilling His eternal purpose of keeping His covenant with Abraham, Isaac, and Jacob. He saw God giving the land of Canaan to the people of Israel, the descendants of those patriarchs (Genesis 12:1, 7; 15:7, 18). Joshua saw God making of them "a great nation" (Genesis 12:2). Joshua knew as surely as if it had already happened that in the Israelites, "all peoples on earth [would] be blessed" (Genesis 12:3). He saw God's hand in those events, a divine involvement elaborated upon by the apostle Paul nearly fifteen hundred years later when he wrote, "For I do not want you to be ignorant of the fact, brothers, that our forefathers were all under the cloud and that they all passed through the sea. They were all baptized into Moses in the cloud and in the sea. They all ate the same spiritual food and drank the same spiritual drink; for they drank from the spiritual rock that accompanied them, and that rock was Christ" (1 Corinthians 10:1-4).

God is working in the world today through Christ, bringing to fulfillment His great plan of redemption. May we all, like Joshua, be aware of God's eternal purpose and make Him the center, the subject as it were, of our lives.

----

*All Scripture quotations in this article are taken from the *New International Version*.

Answers to Quarterly Quiz
on page 8

Lesson 1—1. two. 2. in the house of Rahab, the harlot. 3. true. **Lesson 2**—1. priests. 2. stand still. 3. rose up in a heap. **Lesson 3**—1. six. 2. the seventh. 3. they were to be put into the treasury of the Lord. **Lesson 4**—1. Shechem. 2. serve. **Lesson 5**—1. anger. 2. judges. **Lesson 6**—1. ten thousand. 2. the way the men drank water from a stream. 3. three hundred. **Lesson 7**—1. Samuel was old, his sons didn't walk in his ways, they wanted to be like all other nations. 2. His people. **Lesson 8**—1. Benjamin. 2. the Philistines. 3. false. **Lesson 9**—1. he offered a burnt offering. 2. heart. **Lesson 10**—1. sat. 2. true. **Lesson 11**—1. Nathan the prophet. 2. to die. 3. David. **Lesson 12**—1. Sheba, hard. 2. half. **Lesson 13**—1. seven hundred, three hundred. 2. heart.

Who's at the Hitching Post?

by Jeffrey A. Metzger

I LEARNED ABOUT the aggressive nature of evil when I was ten or eleven years old. I was playing with some of my friends when one of them noticed a hole in the old siding of a locked building. The hole appeared large enough to go through it. "Let's go in," someone said.

On my own I never would have considered entering a locked building. With the urging of my friends, however, I joined them.

We were in the building for only a few minutes, but I was uncomfortable every second. My discomfort increased when one of my friends picked up two spark plugs and encouraged me to do the same. I didn't even know what spark plugs were, but I knew that what I was doing was wrong. For the first time in my life I had deliberately done something that my conscience told me I should not do.

Why did I do it? Because I wanted to be part of the group. Within two years I was using profanity and sneaking an occasional cigarette while with my friends. They made it easy for me to do what I knew I shouldn't do.

I'm very grateful that just before I entered high school Jesus found me, and I found some new friends, Christian friends.

I discovered that God called me to live according to standards that are different, higher, than those adhered to by worldly persons. To followers of Christ Peter wrote, "But you are a chosen people, a royal priesthood, a holy nation, a people belonging to God. . . . I urge you, as aliens and strangers in the world, to abstain from sinful desires, which war against your soul. Live such good lives among the pagans that, though they accuse you of doing wrong, they may see your good deeds and glorify God on the day he visits us" (1 Peter 2:9-12, *New International Version*).

God always has wanted His people to live distinctive lives, lives that give testimony to His holy character. To Israel, chosen to be a people for God's own possession, God said, "Ye shall be holy; for I am holy" (Leviticus 11:44). Nothing less is demanded of us who are Christians: "Be ye holy; for I am holy" is still God's call (1 Peter 1:16).

Do We Have a Problem?

God established Israel in the land of promise and warned His people not to have close relations with the pagan nations that surrounded them. God knew that His people would be morally and spiritually corrupted by associating with those peoples. But Israel disobeyed repeatedly. In time, Israel clamored for a king so they could be just "like all the nations" (1 Samuel 8:5). What a mistake!

In the early years of the church the Corinthian Christians succumbed to the same temptation. They were maintaining such close ties with unbelievers that they were becoming just like them. Recognizing the problem, Paul instructed them, "Be ye not unequally yoked together with unbelievers: for what fellowship hath righteousness with unrighteousness?" (2 Corinthians 6:14). *Today's English Version* puts it this way: "Do not try to work together as equals with unbelievers, for it cannot be done. How can right and wrong be partners? How can light and darkness live together?"

Why? What's the problem with Christian people having close associations with people of the world? It is simply this: Close associations have profound influence. To the Corinthians the apostle Paul said also, "Do not be misled: 'Bad company corrupts good character'" (1 Corinthians 15:33, *New International Version*).

Do we have the proper respect for the power of evil? Are our relationships everything that they should be?

Check Your Environment

We remember the tragic explosion of the space shuttle *Challenger*. Do you remember that the cause of that tragedy was related to an environmental factor? The O-rings of the rocket booster had functioned well time after time when the temperature was above freezing. But on the occasion when the temperature dropped below thirty-two degrees, they malfunctioned, and disaster resulted.

Even so, sinful desires that are restrained in a godly environment may be unleashed when one is in the company of the ungodly. It is for our protection, therefore, that Paul cautions us not to be "unequally yoked together with unbelievers." Israel ignored this warning again and again and suffered disastrous consequences. Are you any wiser?

Someone said, "If you put on white gloves and play in the mud, the gloves always get muddy. The mud never gets glovey." So, watch who's at the hitching post of your life. Getting yoked with the wrong crowd is dangerous indeed.

Quarterly Quiz

The questions on this page may be used in several ways: as a pretest at the beginning of the quarter; as a review at the end of the quarter; or as a review after each lesson. The questions are based on the Scripture text of each lesson (King James Version). **The answers are on page 6.**

Lesson 1

1. Joshua sent (two, seven, twelve) men to spy out Jericho. *Joshua 2:1*
2. Where did the spies stay when they came to Jericho? *Joshua 2:1*
3. The spies agreed that Israel could easily overcome Jericho. T/F *Joshua 2:24*

Lesson 2

1. Who bore the ark of the covenant when the Israelites crossed the Jordan River? *Joshua 3:8*
2. What were those who bore the ark to do when they stepped into the river? *Joshua 3:8*
3. When the Jordan River was stopped, what did the waters from upstream do? *Joshua 3:16*

Lesson 3

1. For how many days were the Israelites to march around Jericho once each day? *Joshua 6:3*
2. On which day did the Israelites march around Jericho seven times? *Joshua 6:15*
3. What was to be done with the precious things captured at Jericho? *Joshua 6:19*

Lesson 4

1. Where did Joshua deliver his farewell address to the people of Israel? *Joshua 24:1*
2. In his farewell address to Israel, Joshua exhorted the people to choose whom they would _____. *Joshua 24:15*

Lesson 5

1. By worshiping the gods of the people who were round about them, the Israelites provoked the Lord to _____ *Judges 2:12*
2. The Lord raised up _____ to rescue Israel from those who spoiled them. *Judges 2:16*

Lesson 6

1. Gideon's army was made up of how many men at first? *Judges 7:3*
2. Gideon's army was reduced to its final size on the basis of what? *Judges 7:5, 6*
3. God enabled Gideon and his army of how many men to defeat the Midianites? *Judges 7:7*

Lesson 7

1. What three reasons did the elders of Israel give Samuel for their request that he appoint a king over Israel? *1 Samuel 8:5*

2. Israel sinned in wanting a king; but the Lord would not forsake them, because it had pleased Him to make them what? *1 Samuel 12:22*

Lesson 8

1. Saul, the first king of Israel, was a member of which tribe? *1 Samuel 9:16*
2. God told Samuel that Saul would rescue Israel from what people? *1 Samuel 9:16*
3. When his selection as king was made public, Saul was eager to serve. T/F *1 Samuel 10:22*

Lesson 9

1. What did Saul do at Gilgal causing Samuel to say that he acted foolishly and that his kingdom would not continue? *1 Samuel 13:12, 13*
2. Samuel told Saul that he would be replaced as the ruler of God's people by a man after God's own _____. *1 Samuel 13:14*

Lesson 10

1. Learning that his house would endure forever, David went in and (stood, knelt, sat) before the Lord and prayed. *2 Samuel 7:18*
2. David marveled that one of such humble beginnings as he would be so greatly blessed by God. T/F *2 Samuel 7:18*

Lesson 11

1. Who told King David a story about a rich man who provided a meal for his guest by taking a poor man's only lamb? *2 Samuel 12:1*
2. What did David say the rich man deserved? *2 Samuel 12:5*
3. The rich man stood for whom? *2 Samuel 12:7*

Lesson 12

1. The queen of _____ heard of the great wisdom the Lord had given Solomon and came to test him with _____ questions. *1 Kings 10:1*
2. Overwhelmed by the wisdom of Solomon and the magnificence of his kingdom, the queen admitted that the _____ was not told her regarding them. *1 Kings 10:7*

Lesson 13

1. How many wives and how many concubines did Solomon have? *1 Kings 11:3*
2. When Solomon was old, his wives turned away his _____ after other gods. *1 Kings 11:4*

Spying Out Jericho

DEVOTIONAL READING: Joshua 1:1-9.

LESSON SCRIPTURE: Joshua 1, 2.

PRINTED TEXT: Joshua 2:1, 8-14, 22-24.

Joshua 2:1, 8-14, 22-24

1 And Joshua the son of Nun sent out of Shittim two men to spy secretly, saying, Go view the land, even Jericho. And they went, and came into a harlot's house, named Rahab, and lodged there.

. . . .

8 And before they were laid down, she came up unto them upon the roof;

9 And she said unto the men, I know that the LORD hath given you the land, and that your terror is fallen upon us, and that all the inhabitants of the land faint because of you.

10 For we have heard how the LORD dried up the water of the Red sea for you, when ye came out of Egypt; and what ye did unto the two kings of the Amorites, that were on the other side Jordan, Sihon and Og, whom ye utterly destroyed.

11 And as soon as we had heard these things, our hearts did melt, neither did there remain any more courage in any man, because of you: for the LORD your God, he is God in heaven above, and in earth beneath.

12 Now therefore, I pray you, swear unto me by the LORD, since I have showed you kindness, that ye will also show kindness unto my father's house, and give me a true token:

13 And that ye will save alive my father, and my mother, and my brethren, and my sisters, and all that they have, and deliver our lives from death.

14 And the men answered her, Our life for yours, if ye utter not this our business. And it shall be, when the LORD hath given us the land, that we will deal kindly and truly with thee.

. . . .

22 And they went, and came unto the mountain, and abode there three days, until the pursuers were returned: and the pursuers sought them throughout all the way, but found them not.

23 So the two men returned, and descended from the mountain, and passed over, and came to Joshua the son of Nun, and told him all things that befell them:

24 And they said unto Joshua, Truly the LORD hath delivered into our hands all the land; for even all the inhabitants of the country do faint because of us.

GOLDEN TEXT: Truly the LORD hath delivered into our hands all the land.—Joshua 2:24.

Lesson Aims

After this lesson a student should be able to:

1. Retell the story of Israel's spies in Jericho.
2. Explain why the people of Israel were confident as they prepared to invade the promised land.
3. Confidently undertake some needed service for the Lord.

Lesson Outline

INTRODUCTION
    A. The Birth of a Nation
    B. Lesson Background
I. DANGEROUS MISSION (Joshua 2:1)
    A. Information Needed (v. 1a)
    B. Bold Beginning (v. 1b)
II. MAKING A DEAL (Joshua 2:8-14)
    A. Fear (vv. 8-11)
        Recognizing God's Power
    B. Deal (vv. 12-14)
        Unlikely Heroes
III. MISSION ACCOMPLISHED (Joshua 2:22-24)
    A. Return (vv. 22, 23)
    B. Report (v. 24)
CONCLUSION
    A. Jericho's Confidence
    B. Israel's Confidence
    C. Our Confidence
    D. Prayer
    E. Thought to Remember

Visual 1 of the visuals packet illustrates thoughts in the conclusion of this lesson. The visual is shown on page 12.

Introduction

"I will make of thee a great nation." So said the Lord, and Abraham believed it. Depending on that promise, he set out for a country unknown (Genesis 12:1-4; Hebrews 11:8).

Abraham was a hundred years old before he had a son to inherit the promise. When his son Isaac was sixty, he had two sons; but only one of them inherited the promise. So in the third generation the nation-to-be was only one man.

Then expansion began. Jacob had twelve sons, and all of them were heirs of the promise.

Jacob was 130 years old when he led the family to Egypt, and it numbered about seventy people. In a few centuries it grew to perhaps three million. Jacob's other name, Israel, became the name of the nation.

A. The Birth of a Nation

Those years in Egypt may be called the prenatal period of Israel. There was growth in numbers, but not in independence. The growth alarmed Egypt's king. What if the people of Israel would join some outside enemy and overthrow him? He made slaves of them and tried to work them to death, but they thrived on hard work.

Then came the time for the infant nation to be delivered. The birth was difficult, but Israel was free—free, but feeble and fearful. For forty years God nurtured it in the desert, till it became mature enough to inherit the land He had for it—the land of Canaan at the east end of the Mediterranean Sea.

B. Lesson Background

From the southern desert, God led His people northward east of the country of Moab that lay along the east shore of the Dead Sea. When they turned west toward the Jordan, the Amorites opposed them with deadly force; but Israel quickly vanquished those opponents and took over their country. Moving north on the east bank of Jordan, they captured Bashan as well.

Israel camped in the eastern plain, looking across the flooded Jordan toward Jericho. Moses died, and Joshua became the nation's leader.

I. Dangerous Mission
(Joshua 2:1)

Winter was giving way to spring as the new leader prepared to take his people across the river and conquer the tribes in Canaan.

A. Information Needed (v. 1a)

1a. And Joshua the son of Nun sent out of Shittim two men to spy secretly, saying, Go view the land, even Jericho.

Israel's camp was in *Shittim*, an area of indefinite size a few miles east of the Jordan. Its name

VISUALS FOR THESE LESSONS

The *Adult Visuals/Learning Resources* packet contains classroom-size visuals designed for use with the lessons in the Autumn Quarter. The packet is available from your supplier. Order No. ST 192.

means acacias, so we suppose those trees grew abundantly there. Across to the west, Jericho lay in the narrow plain between the river and the mountains beyond. Obviously it would be the first place to be captured. Joshua sent two daring young men to see what they could learn about the place: the lay of the land, the strength of the walls, the number of people, the kind of weapons they had. No less important was the morale. Were the people of Jericho confident and resolute, or were they frightened?

B. Bold Beginning (v. 1b)

1b. And they went, and came into a harlot's house, named Rahab, and lodged there.

As the rainy season was just ending, the Jordan was deep and wide, overflowing its banks (Joshua 3:15). But probably the Israelites had captured some boats along with the land of the Amorites. Crossing the river was not very difficult, even if the spies did it at night.

On the west bank, apparently the spies thought a bold approach would be best. Perhaps they hoped people would think they were ordinary travelers, not men from the camp of Israel. They simply walked into Jericho and found lodging in *a harlot's house*. It may seem strange that men of Israel would stop in such a place. Only a short time before, some had died for their sins with sexy women of Moab (Numbers 25:1-5). But perhaps all the hotels in Jericho were of the same kind. Some think the Hebrew word *zonah* means primarily a hostess or innkeeper, and that Rahab may not have been a prostitute. Gesenius, the famous lexicographer, rejects that thought; but others hold it strongly. It would not be surprising if every lodging house in town was a house of prostitution. The people of that land were corrupt beyond any hope of reformation. The Lord ordered them to be destroyed—men, women, and children (Deuteronomy 20:16-18).

If the spies hoped to find safety in their boldness, they were disappointed. Someone knew or guessed where they came from and why they were there. The king was told of it, and he sent his men demanding that the harlot turn in her guests. Rahab put on an innocent face. "Why, yes, some men were here," she said, "but I had no idea where they came from. They left just before the gates were closed for the night. Hurry after them! Surely you can catch them."

If the officers were suspicious enough to search the house, they found no men of Israel. Rahab had hidden them under a pile of flax on the roof. So the king's men raced toward the Jordan, and the gate was locked behind them so the spies could not escape if they were hidden somewhere in the city (vv. 2-7)

II. Making a Deal
(Joshua 2:8-14)

Rahab was wise as well as wily. Protecting her guests was not just a matter of good business, hoping they would come again or recommend her place to their friends. The woman had sized up the situation accurately, and she meant to save her own life by saving the spies.

A. Fear (vv. 8-11)

8. And before they were laid down, she came up unto them upon the roof.

Before her guests bedded down for the night, Rahab came up to the roof to make a deal with them.

9. And she said unto the men, I know that the LORD hath given you the land, and that your terror is fallen upon us, and that all the inhabitants of the land faint because of you.

If the spies wanted to learn about the morale of Jericho's defenders, they had come to the right place. Rahab's eyes and ears had been open. She was convinced that *the Lord*, the God of Israel, had given her country to His people, and they would surely take it. She knew that God by name, for *the Lord* here represents the personal name that has come into English as *Jehovah*. She knew her fellow citizens were terrified by the approach of the fearsome Israelites, and that all the inhabitants of the land were fainting with fear. To *faint* is not to lose consciousness; it is to lose strength of body and mind, to be paralyzed with fright.

10. For we have heard how the LORD dried up the water of the Red sea for you, when ye came out of Egypt; and what ye did unto the two kings of the Amorites, that were on the other side Jordan, Sihon and Og, whom ye utterly destroyed.

Forty years had passed since the LORD had *dried up the water of the Red sea* for Israel. Perhaps that great event happened before Rahab was born; but news of it had come across the miles to Jericho, and it had not been forgotten.

Recent events were no less alarming. Just *on the other side Jordan*, and in recent months, *the two kings of the Amorites* had opposed Israel; and Israel had *utterly destroyed* them. Those were

---

How to Say It

AMORITES.   *Am*-uh-rites.
BASHAN.   *Bay*-shun.
RAHAB.   *Ray*-hab.
SIHON.   *Sye*-hun.

strong and warlike kings. Not long before, Sihon had taken some of the territory of Moab (Numbers 21:26). Probably they could muster more troops than Jericho could. What would happen when the destroyers of the Amorites came across the Jordan to Jericho?

11. And as soon as we had heard these things, our hearts did melt, neither did there remain any more courage in any man, because of you: for the LORD your God, he is God in heaven above, and in earth beneath.

Morale in Jericho was not just low; it was missing. There were no strong hearts there, no courage. There was no hope of victory, and therefore no will to fight. The people were convinced that the Lord ruled both Heaven and earth; and He was for Israel and against Jericho. The hearts of the spies must have soared at the news. This town would be a pushover!

RECOGNIZING GOD'S POWER

Sometimes it seems one can point to the time when a major shift in culture or history takes place. The year 1948 is an example. When the year began, there were nineteen television stations broadcasting in the United States, and Americans owned 186,000 TV sets. By year's end the number of stations had more than doubled and a million sets had been sold. We had entered the video age, and nothing could turn back the clock. Few people could have guessed the amazing changes—for both good and bad—that would take place in American culture because of television.

Rahab seems to have had an insight about the changes that would take place in her land when Israel invaded Canaan. She told Joshua's spies that the reputation of their God had preceded them. He was feared as the One who had miraculously delivered Israel from slavery and had led them in conquering the Amorites. Rahab could see that only those who were on the side of Israel's God had hope for survival.

We naturally desire to be on the "winning" side in life's great battle. Just as important, however, is that we recognize that God has been at work in history and that we take part in the redemptive work He is doing through His people at this moment in time.   —C. R. B.

B. Deal (vv. 12-14)

12, 13. Now therefore, I pray you, swear unto me by the LORD, since I have showed you kindness, that ye will also show kindness unto my father's house, and give me a true token: and that ye will save alive my father, and my mother, and my brethren, and my sisters, and all that they have, and deliver our lives from death.

The deal was simple. Rahab had saved the lives of these two spies. She asked them to guarantee her safety and the safety of her whole family in the coming destruction of Jericho. And she meant the entire family with no exceptions: *father* and *mother* and *brethren* and *sisters*, and *all that they have*—all their wives and husbands and sons and daughters.

Rahab wanted the spies to agree to this deal and to give her *a true token*. Perhaps that means she wanted them to specify some sure sign by which she and other members of her family could be recognized and spared in the rightful confusion when the city was being destroyed.

14. And the men answered her, Our life for yours, if ye utter not this our business. And it shall be, when the LORD hath given us the land, that we will deal kindly and truly with thee.

Promptly the spies agreed to the deal. Rahab had saved their lives, and more. She had saved their mission, and now they saw how important that was. News of the terror in Jericho would give courage to the warriors of Israel. If the spies had failed to come back, that would have generated doubts and fears. So the men promised safety to their hostess, but only if she would continue to keep their movements secret.

UNLIKELY HEROES

Matewan, West Virginia, is a little mountain town with a checkered past and a difficult present. In 1878, the famous Hatfield-McCoy feud began there for reasons no one is sure about today. In the 1920s, Matewan's bloody "coal wars" occurred. That labor rebellion has been called by some America's largest armed insurrection since the Civil War. Since 1957, the Big Sandy River has flooded thirty-three times destroying much of the town.

In light of this, Matewan's hope for the future is especially interesting. The leaders of the town have decided to revive their community by attracting tourists, capitalizing on the feud between the Hatfield and McCoy clans. If their plans succeed, people who share the blame for the town's infamy will become the unlikely "heroes" bringing a brighter future to Matewan!

visual 1

God has used many unlikely heroes to accomplish His will throughout history. Rahab, a prostitute in Jericho who recognized the power of God, protected the Israelite spies. The lesson for us is that none are so disreputable or so evil that they cannot further God's cause today if they will acknowledge His power and His rightful place in their lives.   —C. R. B.

III. Mission Accomplished (Joshua 2:22-24)

Verses 15-21 supply additional details. Rahab's house was on the city wall. From her window she lowered a rope outside the wall so the men could climb down in the darkness. The king's men were searching the plain, so she told her guests to hide in the hills for a few days. They could go back to their camp in safety after the search was over.

The red rope by which the spies escaped became the "true token" Rahab requested (v. 12). She was to tie it in her window where it could be seen by Israel's warriors as they approached the city. It would mark the only safe house in all Jericho. Rahab must see that all her relatives were in that house when the attack came. Any found outside would die with the rest of the inhabitants.

A. Return (vv. 22, 23)

22. And they went, and came unto the mountain, and abode there three days, until the pursuers were returned: and the pursuers sought them throughout all the way, but found them not.

Following Rahab's advice, the spies went west *unto the mountain* instead of east to the river. Rugged mountains rise steeply only a little way from Jericho. Rocky ravines provided good hiding places. The rainy season was near its end, but water could be found in little streams and pools. Perhaps Rahab had given the fugitives enough food for a few days. In the mountains they rested comfortably while the king's men scoured the plain between the Jordan and Jericho. If the searchers found a boat the spies had used, that encouraged them to think the intruders had not escaped across the river. So they searched diligently, but within three days they gave up trying to find them!

23. So the two men returned, and descended from the mountain, and passed over, and came to Joshua the son of Nun, and told him all things that befell them.

Probably in the darkness of night the spies came down *from the mountain, and passed over* the river, *and came to Joshua* with their report.

B. Report (v. 24)

24. And they said unto Joshua, Truly the LORD hath delivered into our hands all the land; for even all the inhabitants of the country do faint because of us.

Of course the spies had not talked with *all the inhabitants of the country*, but they may have talked with a number of them before they stopped at Rahab's house for the night. Even Rahab was not in touch with *all the inhabitants*; but she entertained guests from various places. She said the whole country was terrified, and the spies believed her. She thought *the Lord*, the God of Heaven and earth, was giving the land to the Israelites; and the spies thought so too.

Conclusion

Athletes and coaches are aware of two dangers: overconfidence and the lack of confidence. The overconfident competitor, sure of victory, may lose because he trains halfheartedly and competes carelessly. The one who lacks confidence may lose because he is too tense to do his best.

These dangers are not confined to the world of sports. The overconfident student may fail a test because he neglects his homework; the one lacking confidence may fail because anxiety paralyzes his mind. One businessman overextends himself and goes into bankruptcy; another fails because he is too timid to take advantage of his opportunities. One candidate loses the election because he does not campaign seriously; another loses because in his anxiety he resorts to wild exaggeration or outright lying.

A. Jericho's Confidence

To say the people of Jericho lacked confidence would be an understatement. Rahab said they were terrified—and not only the people of Jericho, but the people of the whole country.

Those people had good reason for their terror. Rahab put her finger on the heart of the problem. It was not the people of Israel alone. It was the Lord, the God of Israel, the God of Heaven and earth. He had brought Israel through the Red Sea. He had showered them with manna from Heaven. He had refreshed them with water from the arid rock. He had given them victory over the Amorites east of Jordan.

Now those people favored of the Lord were looking across the river at Jericho, and the sinners of Jericho were trembling behind their walls. Westward and northward and southward the rest of the people of Canaan were trembling too. It was not only the people of Israel that scared them; it was the God of Heaven and earth.

B. Israel's Confidence

Israel's confidence was built by the same events that shattered the confidence of Jericho. Israel walked through the sea on dry ground; Israel followed an unfailing pillar of cloud and fire; Israel lived on manna from Heaven and water from the rock. Israel defeated the Amorites with the sword, but not without the support of the Lord.

Now, poised to invade the main part of the promised land, Israel seemed confident. Moses was dead, but he and the Lord had appointed Joshua to take his place. The pledge of three tribes may well have been the pledge of the whole nation to Joshua: "All that thou commandest us we will do, and whithersoever thou sendest us, we will go. According as we hearkened unto Moses in all things, so will we hearken unto thee" (Joshua 1:16, 17). We wonder if Joshua's own confidence wavered a little. After forty years in a subordinate position, he was suddenly thrust into the position of leadership at a critical time. It was an awesome responsibility. The first nine verses of Joshua record the Lord's repeated encouragement to him: "Be strong and of a good courage. . . . Be thou strong and very courageous. . . . Be strong and of a good courage." The Lord repeated also the reason for confidence: "As I was with Moses, so I will be with thee: I will not fail thee, nor forsake thee. . . . Be not afraid, neither be thou dismayed: for the Lord thy God is with thee whithersoever thou goest." The promise of success also was repeated: "Every place that the sole of your foot shall tread upon, that have I given unto you. . . . There shall not any man be able to stand before thee all the days of thy life. . . . Unto this people shalt thou divide for an inheritance the land, which I sware unto their fathers to give them."

Such assurance from the Lord provided all the support Joshua's confidence needed. Firmly he gave the order for the people to advance (Joshua 1:10, 11).

C. Our Confidence

There may be Christians who are overconfident. Those brethren who take poisonous snakes to church to prove that God will keep the promise of Mark 16:18—perhaps they should remember that Jesus quoted, "Do not put the Lord your God to the test" (Matthew 4:7, *New International Version*). The church that "steps out on faith" to construct a building bigger, more ornate, and more expensive than it needs or can pay for—perhaps it should recall what Jesus said about counting the cost (Luke 14:28-30). But lack of confidence handicaps more of us than overconfidence does.

Consider your own congregation and community. Have you been noticing something that *they* ought to do? Have you been saying sadly, "Oh, no, *I* couldn't do it"?

Maybe you can, if you approach it with confidence, with prayer, with thoughtful study and preparation, with training, with eagerness, with the help of friends and the help of God.

Can you be present, alert, attentive, and happy in all the meetings of the church?

Can you participate thoughtfully in those meetings where participation is invited?

Can you help with the cleaning and maintenance of the church building and property?

Can you teach a class or lead a group in discussion?

Can you contribute more than ten percent of your income to the Lord's work?

Can you talk to a neighbor about your faith as freely as you talk about baseball?

Or whatever you see that ought to be done—can you do that? Maybe you can.

D. Prayer

Our Father in Heaven, You have given us some wonderful abilities, physical, mental, and spiritual, and we are grateful for every one of them. Even more we are grateful because You have abilities far more marvelous than ours, and You are with us as truly as You were with Joshua. May we have wisdom enough to know what You want us to do, and confidence enough to do it. In Jesus' name we pray. Amen.

E. Thought to Remember

"So do not throw away your confidence; it will be richly rewarded" (Hebrews 10:35, *New International Version*).

Home Daily Bible Readings

Learning by Doing

This page contains an alternate lesson plan emphasizing learning activities. Classes desiring such student involvement will find these suggestions helpful.

Learning Goals

As students participate in today's class session, they should:

1. List the risks that Joshua, Rahab, and the spies undertook for God.

2. Choose at least one risk they believe God wants them to take for Him soon.

Into the Lesson

Before class, write each of the following words, scrambled, on your chalkboard for class members to see as they arrive: IKRS (risk), TRVOCIY (victory), DEECEIBON (obedience), VRESCIE (service).

Distribute pencils and half sheets of paper, and ask your students to unscramble the words. To begin the class, let volunteers share their unscrambled words. Then ask class members to write sentences about the Christian life and use these words in the sentences. After about three minutes, let volunteers read the sentences they have written.

Discuss with the class, "Which word suggests to you the biggest challenge to your Christian life? Why?"

Mention that each of these words summarizes the theme of one of the four lessons in the first unit of this quarter's study. For those who chose *risk* as the most challenging word, today's lesson will be the most challenging, for "risk" is the theme of this lesson.

Into the Word

Use the material in the "Introduction" section on page 10 to establish the background for this lesson. If you have time, do both of the following Bible-study activities. If you have time for only one, do the second one.

Before either activity, have a volunteer read today's printed text aloud. As he or she does so, have the students listen to decide why "risk" is the key word in this account.

And I Quote! Write the following quotes on index cards, one quote per card. Make enough of the "quote" cards so that half of your students can each have one. If you repeat quotes, that's OK. Give each of the other half of your students a card with one of the following names on it: Joshua, Spies, Rahab. Ask class members to stand. Each one with a quote card should find a student with a matching name card. When all

have done this, they can be seated. Then check to see if the matches are correct. (Correct answers are indicated after each quote for the teacher's convenience.)

"Go, look over the land, especially Jericho." (Joshua)

"I don't know which way they went." (Rahab)

"The Lord dried up the water of the Red Sea when you came out of Egypt." (Rahab)

"Give me a sure sign that you will spare the lives of my family." (Rahab)

"Our lives for your lives!" (spies)

"The Lord surely has given the whole land into our hands." (spies)

After this activity, discuss the following questions: What adjectives would you use to describe Rahab? What motivated her to act as she did? What did the spies learn about Jericho from their visit there? Why did they respond to Rahab as they did? What can we learn about God from this account?

Take a Risk! Divide the class in half. The first half should form groups of three to five. Examining today's text they should answer the following questions about Joshua and the spies:

What risks did Joshua and the spies take? Why did they take them? Were they foolish or wise to take these risks? Why? What was the outcome? How would the outcome have been different if they had been unwilling to take the risks?

The second half also should form groups of three to five and answer the same questions about Rahab.

Into Life

Ask, What does this passage seem to teach about risk-taking? Is risk-taking something God may approve? When and why?

Ask the students to pair off, and have each pair think of three situations in which God may require Christians to take risks today. After three minutes, write their suggestions on the chalkboard.

Ask, "When was the last time you took a risk for God? What happened? Did it make you more or less willing to risk for Him again?"

Challenge class members to look at the list on the chalkboard and to decide if it contains an area where God might want them to take a risk for Him this week. Then conclude with a time of prayer.

Let's Talk It Over

The questions on this page are designed to encourage review of the lesson Scriptures and to promote discussion of the lesson by the class. The answers provided are only discussion starters. Let your class talk it over from there.

1. What comparison can we draw between Israel's sending out the two spies before invading the land of Canaan and the church's surveying, planning, and evaluating before undertaking a major project?

Nothing in the book of Joshua suggests that the mission of the two spies represented a lack of faith in God's power to conquer. The spies' report did, however, strengthen the confidence the Israelites already possessed. In the same way a church undertaking a bold new evangelistic outreach, a building project, or a program to increase missions support can combine firm faith in God's guidance and power with careful planning. The plans will show how the people who need to be evangelized can be reached and how the money can be raised for the building or missionary projects. In this way the congregation will develop an increased level of confidence and enthusiasm which, combined with their assurance of God's blessing, will produce powerful results.

2. Rahab lied about her knowledge of the two spies, and the Bible does not speak disapprovingly of her act. What shall we say about this?

The Bible does not speak disapprovingly of many recorded actions that are contrary to its laws. In this regard, the checkered career of Samson is one example that comes to mind. So the Bible's silence in the present case cannot be taken as justification for the use of falsehood to advance a good cause. Like Samson, Rahab is mentioned in Hebrews 11:31, 32 among Old Testament exemplars of faith. We recognize, however, that many Old Testament worthies fall far short of being models of Christian faith and lifestyle. For our models we look to Jesus Christ himself and to New Testament teaching. In Colossians 3:9 we are told, "Lie not one to another, seeing that ye have put off the old man with his deeds." Revelation 21:8 and 22:15 state that liars will be excluded from Heaven.

3. In Joshua 1:6-9 we find the Lord's repeated exhortation of Joshua to be strong and courageous. How does such exhortation help all of us to be more confident?

At Moses' death, the awesome responsibility of leading Israel fell to Joshua. He could have given in to feelings of inadequacy and fearfulness, but at God's urging he chose instead to focus on faith and to lead with courage and confidence. We have that same challenge. It is easy to allow the negative emotions of fear, doubt, and faintness of heart to rule us. But we have the capacity to believe, to be confident, and to envision victory, and the Lord calls on us to utilize this built-in source of strength. Jesus frequently urged His disciples to "take courage" (Mark 6:50, *New International Version* or "take heart" (John 16:33, *New International Version*). And Paul often exhorted his readers to "be strong" (1 Corinthians 16:13; Ephesians 6:10; 2 Timothy 2:1).

4. How is the church hindered by members who lack confidence?

Church members who lack confidence fail to recognize and acknowledge the talents they possess. Work that they are capable of doing in the church may be neglected because they do not put their talents to use. Their timidity may also cause them to pass up opportunities to share their faith in Christ. Thus the growth of the church and the enriching of the fellowship suffers. If lack of confidence persists in one, it may be that that person will feel so unworthy to worship God that he or she may eventually cease participation in the church altogether.

5. What can be done to promote a healthy level of confidence within our church?

An excellent beginning would be to read in our worship services Scriptures such as those cited in the answer above. While Joshua 1:6-9 is an Old Testament passage and deals with challenges different from what we face, it nevertheless has the power to stir Christians today. We could also transform negative statements into positive ones. If members lament over empty pews, a deficit in the church budget, etc., let us urge them to envision boldly what they can do to fill those pews or to increase the offerings. One more approach is to give members who lack confidence small, simple tasks to complete instead of loading them down with responsibilities for which they are not ready. By successfully executing these "faith-sized" chores, they can build confidence for taking on greater challenges.

Acting on Faith

September 11
Lesson 2

DEVOTIONAL READING: Hebrews 11:23-31.

LESSON SCRIPTURE: Joshua 3, 4.

PRINTED TEXT: Joshua 3:7-17.

Joshua 3:7-17

7 And the LORD said unto Joshua, This day will I begin to magnify thee in the sight of all Israel, that they may know that, as I was with Moses, so I will be with thee.

8 And thou shalt command the priests that bear the ark of the covenant, saying, When ye are come to the brink of the water of Jordan, ye shall stand still in Jordan.

9 And Joshua said unto the children of Israel, Come hither, and hear the words of the LORD your God.

10 And Joshua said, Hereby ye shall know that the living God is among you, and that he will without fail drive out from before you the Canaanites, and the Hittites, and the Hivites, and the Perizzites, and the Girgashites, and the Amorites, and the Jebusites.

11 Behold, the ark of the covenant of the Lord of all the earth passeth over before you into Jordan.

12 Now therefore take you twelve men out of the tribes of Israel, out of every tribe a man.

13 And it shall come to pass, as soon as the soles of the feet of the priests that bear the ark of the LORD, the Lord of all the earth, shall rest in the waters of Jordan, that the waters of Jordan shall be cut off from the waters that come down from above; and they shall stand upon a heap.

14 And it came to pass, when the people removed from their tents, to pass over Jordan, and the priests bearing the ark of the covenant before the people;

15 And as they that bare the ark were come unto Jordan, and the feet of the priests that bare the ark were dipped in the brim of the water, (for Jordan overfloweth all his banks all the time of harvest,)

16 That the waters which came down from above stood and rose up upon a heap very far from the city Adam, that is beside Zaretan; and those that came down toward the sea of the plain, even the salt sea, failed, and were cut off: and the people passed over right against Jericho.

17 And the priests that bare the ark of the covenant of the LORD stood firm on dry ground in the midst of Jordan, and all the Israelites passed over on dry ground, until all the people were passed clean over Jordan.

GOLDEN TEXT: The priests that bare the ark of the covenant of the LORD stood firm on dry ground in the midst of Jordan, and all the Israelites passed over on dry ground, until all the people were passed clean over Jordan.—Joshua 3:17.

From the Conquest to the Kingdom

Unit 1: The Conquest of the Land

(Lessons 1-4)

Lesson Aims

After this lesson students should be able to:

1. Tell how the people of Israel crossed the Jordan River in time of flood.

2. Tell of some other events that helped the Israelites to believe in God's power and goodwill.

3. Mention some things that give strength to their own faith in God, Christ, and the Bible.

Lesson Outline

INTRODUCTION
 A. Everyday Faith
 B. Faith and Action
 C. Lesson Background
 I. PROMISE TO JOSHUA (Joshua 3:7, 8)
 A. Promise of Greatness (v. 7)
  Humility and Exaltation
 B. An Order to Be Passed On (v. 8)
 II. PROMISE OF A SIGN (Joshua 3:9-13)
 A. Call to Listen (v. 9)
 B. Sign of Success (vv. 10-13)
 III. THE PROMISED SIGN (Joshua 3:14-17)
 A. Forward Into the Flood (vv. 14, 15)
 B. A Heap of Water (v. 16)
 C. The Crossing (v. 17)
  Acting on God's Word
CONCLUSION
 A. More Faith-Building Facts
 B. How Is Our Faith?
 C. Acting on Our Faith
 D. Prayer
 E. Thought to Remember

Visual 2 of the visuals packet illustrates thoughts in the conclusion of this lesson. It is shown on page 21.

Introduction

"Now faith is being sure of what we hope for and certain of what we do not see" (Hebrews 11:1, *New International Version*).

A. Everyday Faith

We live by faith day by day, in the most practical affairs of life.

We set the alarm clock and go to sleep, "being sure" it will wake us as we hope it will; and it does, usually.

We sit down at the table with calm faith in our breakfast cereal. Oh, yes; we know perverted people have slipped into stores and poisoned stock on the shelves, but we are "certain" that our cereal is wholesome and nourishing, having all the vitamins and minerals announced in small type on the box.

We hurry to the car, confident that the engine will start. One time we found the battery dead, but we don't get up half an hour early to check it today.

Fearlessly we drive to work, trusting the cross traffic to stop when our light is green.

Workplaces have burned down in a night, and employees have arrived to find themselves fired; but we are confident that both workplace and job will be there when we arrive.

In faith we work all week, expecting to be paid. On payday we take a check, confident that it will be good at the bank.

B. Faith and Action

James 2:20 says, "Faith without works is dead." That applies to everyday faith as well as to religious faith. What happens if we trust the alarm clock, but fail to set it? What if we have faith in our breakfast cereal, but do not eat it? How far can we go by faith in an automobile if we never get behind the wheel and drive? Can we live on faith in an employer if we never go to work? Will faith in a paycheck sustain us if we keep the check in our pocket? So our lesson title is "Acting on Faith," and our text gives some examples.

C. Lesson Background

Reading the opening chapters of Joshua, we soon see that they are not organized as modern writers are taught to organize their material. Perhaps the inspired writer made notes at various times, and later put the notes together without caring that some things are mentioned more than once and that the chronological order is not always clear.

Here we suggest a possible order of events leading up to those recorded in our lesson text.

1. After destroying two kingdoms on the east bank of Jordan, Israel camped in the plains of Moab opposite Jericho and a few miles east of the river (Numbers 22:1).

2. Joshua was appointed to take Moses' place as the leader of Israel (Numbers 27:18-23).

3. Moses died in the land of Moab, and God buried him in a sepulchre unknown to man (Deuteronomy 34:5, 6).

4. Israel remained in camp for a month of mourning for Moses (Deuteronomy 34:8).

5. Joshua sent two spies to investigate Jericho and its vicinity, as we saw in last week's lesson.

They must have been gone at least five days, perhaps several days longer (Joshua 2).

6. The people of Israel moved their camp close to the river (Joshua 3:1).

7. Three days were allotted for preparation to cross the river (Joshua 1:10, 11).

8. At the end of three days the people were alerted to follow the priests who would carry the ark of the covenant (Joshua 3:2, 3).

9. Joshua gave the signal, and the priests began the march (Joshua 3:6).

I. Promise to Joshua
(Joshua 3:7, 8)

God's promise and directions to Joshua are recorded more fully in Joshua 1:1-9. The promise was that God would be with him and that he would be successful in capturing the land west of the river. The directions were in two parts. First, Joshua must be strong and very courageous. Second, he must remember and teach and obey all the law that had been given earlier. Now we see a simpler summary of the promise.

A. Promise of Greatness (v. 7)

7. And the LORD said unto Joshua, This day will I begin to magnify thee in the sight of all Israel, that they may know that, as I was with Moses, so I will be with thee.

The Lord was going to *magnify* Joshua, make him greater, *in the sight of all Israel.* That enlargement would begin that very day. Joshua would promise a safe passageway across the river, and it would appear. Later on, Joshua's reputation would continue to grow as every campaign he would direct would be successful. The purpose of this was not just to exalt the new leader; it was to let everyone know God was with Joshua as He had been with Moses.

HUMILITY AND EXALTATION

When Prime Minister Margaret Thatcher of England was reelected to her third term of office, she promised that she would continue her work of leadership with, in her words, a sense of "great humility." In her speech, she quoted from Rudyard Kipling's poem, "Recessional":

> The tumult and the shouting dies;
>   The Captains and the Kings depart:
> Still stands Thine ancient sacrifice,
>   An humble and a contrite heart.

Kipling, writing when Britain ruled a worldwide empire, had an insight into the fleeting nature of earthly pomp and circumstance, and he emphasized the quality that every leader should possess.

Joshua was exalted by God to become Moses' successor in leading the nation of Israel and being God's spokesman to His people. Joshua did not—indeed, he could not—exalt himself to that position.

Those who are great in God's eyes are the humble. Knowing themselves to be weak, they trust in the strength of the Lord, and find His strength becoming their own.   —C. R. B.

B. An Order to Be Passed On (v. 8)

8. And thou shalt command the priests that bear the ark of the covenant, saying, When ye are come to the brink of the water of Jordan, ye shall stand still in Jordan.

The priests were to lead the way to the river, but not to lead all the way across. They were to *stand still in Jordan* while the people would pass them and go on to the west bank. The people would see that even the priests obeyed Joshua as Aaron had obeyed Moses, and so the new leader would seem greater in their sight.

Here again it seems probable that the events are not recorded in the order in which they occurred. Perhaps God gave this command to Joshua and Joshua passed it on to the priests before they picked up the ark of the covenant and led the march (v. 6).

II. Promise of a Sign
(Joshua 3:9-13)

Now we come to Joshua's promise to the people. It would begin to be kept that very day, and therefore Joshua would be greater in the eyes of his people.

A. Call to Listen (v. 9)

9. And Joshua said unto the children of Israel, Come hither, and hear the words of the LORD your God.

Joshua had sent officers through the camp to tell the people to get ready (Joshua 1:10, 11). Now the people were ready and massing for the march. It seems that Joshua stood up and shouted to the whole three million. What a voice!

B. Sign of Success (vv. 10-13)

10. And Joshua said, Hereby ye shall know that the living God is among you, and that he will without fail drive out from before you the Canaanites, and the Hittites, and the Hivites, and the Perizzites, and the Girgashites, and the Amorites, and the Jebusites.

Israel was not moving into empty country west of the Jordan. Seven powerful tribes lived there. Forty years earlier, their tall men and strong city walls had intimidated ten of the twelve scouts Moses had sent to spy out the land (Numbers 13, 14). Tall men and strong walls were still there. If the men of Israel considered only their human resources, they might again decide the land could not be taken. But God was among the people of Israel. He had determined that those tribes west of the Jordan were too evil to be tolerated any more. He was going to use Israel to wipe them out, and He would do it *without fail*. Joshua said God was about to give the people of Israel a sign by which they could know He was among them and was able to do whatever He determined to do.

11. Behold, the ark of the covenant of the Lord of all the earth passeth over before you into Jordan.

The ark of the covenant was a symbol of God's presence among His people. When they were in camp, it rested in the Holy of Holies in the tabernacle. When they were on the march, it was carried by the priests. It was a wooden chest covered with gold and holding the stone tablets engraved with the Ten Commandments, the basic part of God's covenant (Deuteronomy 10:3-5). God was and is *the Lord of all the earth;* not only the people of Israel, but also those doomed tribes west of the Jordan were subject to Him. That ark leading the way *into Jordan* meant that God was leading.

12. Now therefore take you twelve men out of the tribes of Israel, out of every tribe a man.

These representatives of the twelve tribes were to take stones out of the Jordan for a memorial monument on the west bank. As future generations of the people of Israel would pass the monument, children would ask about that structure of twelve stones, and parents would tell again how God had helped His people across the river (Joshua 4:1-7).

13. And it shall come to pass, as soon as the soles of the feet of the priests that bear the ark of the LORD, the Lord of all the earth, shall rest in the waters of Jordan, that the waters of Jordan shall be cut off from the waters that come down from above; and they shall stand upon a heap.

How to Say It

AMORITES. *Am*-uh-rites.
CANAANITES. *Kay*-nan-ites.
CEPHAS. *See*-fus.
GIRGASHITES. *Gur*-ga-shites (*G* as in *get*).
HITTITES. *Hit*-ites or *Hit*-tites.
HIVITES. *Hi*-vites.
JEBUSITES. *Jeb*-yuh-sites.
PERIZZITES. *Pair*-iz-zites.

Carrying the ark, the symbol of God's presence, the priests would walk into the shallow water at the edge of the flooded stream. The water then would be *cut off* from its supply up the river. The water in front of Israel would run on down to the Dead Sea; the water up the river would be piled up in *a heap* instead of flowing past the waiting people. The bed of the river would be empty so the people could walk across. This control of the stream would demonstrate that God himself was there as truly as the symbol was, and the people would be assured of His help in all their battles (v. 10).

III. The Promised Sign
(Joshua 3:14-17)

What did the people think of the promise Joshua gave them? Some of them had been teenagers when they had crossed the Red Sea forty years before. They had seen the water standing like a wall to the right and the left (Exodus 14:22). But after forty years, could they expect to see another such miracle? All the people under forty years of age, of course, had lived all their lives in the desert. They had never even seen such a flood of water as they were seeing now. But they had seen little streams after desert storms, and copious springs flowing from dry rock (Numbers 20:11). They knew water runs downhill, and now Joshua said it would rise up in a heap. We can imagine some of the hearers may have said, "No way!" But whatever doubts they may have had, they had faith enough to act. They loaded their donkeys and picked up their packs and followed the priests toward the river.

A. Forward Into the Flood (vv. 14, 15)

14. And it came to pass, when the people removed from their tents, to pass over Jordan, and the priests bearing the ark of the covenant before the people.

Carrying God's symbol on their shoulders, the priests marched toward the river. The people followed half a mile behind (Joshua 3:4), probably spread out in a wide front so all of them could see what would happen.

15. And as they that bare the ark were come unto Jordan, and the feet of the priests that bare the ark were dipped in the brim of the water, (for Jordan overfloweth all his banks all the time of harvest).

The river was out of its banks and spreading over the plain, so it was shallow at the edge. Boldly the priests walked into the shallow water as if they were going to walk all the way across the river—as indeed they were, but not without stopping till all the people crossed it.

B. A Heap of Water (v. 16)

16. That the waters which came down from above stood and rose up upon a heap very far from the city Adam, that is beside Zaretan; and those that came down toward the sea of the plain, even the salt sea, failed, and were cut off: and the people passed over right against Jericho.

As Joshua had promised, the water of the stream stopped flowing past. It just piled up in a heap somewhere up the river. The water in front of the people of Israel kept running down to the sea, leaving a stretch of empty riverbed many miles long. As to the place where the heap of water rose, the *American Standard Version* and the *New International Version* follow a different reading that probably is better. The heap of water was *very far* from the place where the Israelites were, and *at the city of Adam.* However, no one now can be sure where that city was or where *Zaretan* was, so we don't know where the heap was either. The Jordan in flood carries a lot of water, and the flow must have been stopped for hours, so the heap of water must have been a very big one. Artists sometimes picture the people walking in a thin column no wider than a sidewalk, but the people may have moved in a mass five miles wide, so the crossing could have been done quickly. So they crossed the river westward toward Jericho.

C. The Crossing (v. 17)

17. And the priests that bare the ark of the covenant of the LORD stood firm on dry ground in the midst of Jordan, and all the Israelites passed over on dry ground, until all the people were passed clean over Jordan.

From verse 8 some students conclude that the priests with the ark stood at the spot near the east side where they first waded into the water, but verse 17 sounds as if they went on to the middle of the riverbed. In either case, the point is that God's symbol stood there like a barrier in the bed of the river, and God's will made the water stop far up the stream, allowing the people to cross safely to the west side.

The travelers laid down their burdens at a new campsite on the plain between the river and Jericho. The twelve selected men (v. 12) carried twelve stones out of the river to be built into a monument (Joshua 4:1-8). The crossing was complete. At God's command, Joshua called to the priests to bring the ark of the covenant to the bank beyond the reach of high water, the piled-up water was released, and the flooded river flowed by as before.

Some scholars imagine that a huge landslide blocked the whole channel of the Jordan at a

visual 2

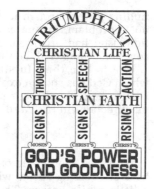

narrow place some miles north of Jericho. This made a dam, they suggest, north of which the water spread out to form a lake till it was high enough to run over the top of the dam. Then the dam was swiftly eroded, and the river flowed on as before. But if the water was spread out in a lake, would it be called a heap? (vv. 13, 16). The record seems to indicate a mound of water. That would defy the law of gravitation as we know it, but every miracle shows that God knows some laws we do not know.

Even if we suppose a landslide stopped the water, we must recognize a marvelous miracle in the timing of the events. Joshua assigned three days for preparation (Joshua 1:10, 11), and the stoppage came promptly at the end of those days. Just at the moment when the priests with the ark marched into the edge of the stream the water started to go down. The riverbed was empty just long enough for the people to cross, then promptly it was full again. This was no accident of nature; it was a miracle of God. It was provided not only to get the people across the river, but to assure them that God was with them and would give them success (Joshua 3:10).

ACTING ON GOD'S WORD

In 1986 an iceberg—fifty miles wide and seventy miles long—broke off the Antarctic ice shelf. Moving northward, by early 1991 the iceberg was approaching the shipping lanes near the southern tip of South America.

As it drifted into warmer waters, it "calved" numerous smaller icebergs to litter the sea lanes with dangerous obstacles. Its cliffs towered two hundred feet above the ocean and created its own weather system around it. The fog that surrounded the giant iceberg made it difficult for navigators to locate it. It was a dangerous, forbidding obstruction.

Israel confronted an imposing deterrent to their goal of reaching the promised land: the Jordan River in flood stage. They had no trouble seeing the obstacle, however; their problem was finding a way through it. But the problem was not a problem. Joshua gave Israel the instructions God had provided, Israel followed God's commands, and God did the rest.

Life is like that. In situations concerning which God has spoken explicitly, we may expect Him to help us with our problems if we follow the directions in His Word.   —C. R. B.

Conclusion

With awe the people of Israel stood looking back at a roaring torrent where they had walked a little while before. That torrent had stood aside to let them pass! They knew it was no accident, for Joshua had told them exactly what was going to happen. God could do and did do the impossible, and He was with them! It is small wonder that they were ready to act on faith again. Resolutely they advanced to Jericho.

A. More Faith-Building Facts

This mighty miracle was one of many in Israel's memory. Older people could remember the night when they left Egypt. The sound of wailing was around them, for in each Egyptian household was one dead; but there was no death in Israel that night. Those older ones could remember walking through the Red Sea; they could remember seeing the pursuing Egyptians dead on the seashore. Younger ones had lived all their lives with a pillar in the sky to guide them. They could remember water gushing from the rock at the tap of Moses' rod; and even yet each morning brought new manna for their daily bread. It is no wonder that they moved with powerful faith; the marvel is that their faith could sometimes fail.

B. How Is Our Faith?

"All these things that happened to them were symbolic, and were recorded for our benefit" (1 Corinthians 10:11, *New English Bible*). The stopping of the Jordan built the faith of Israel; can it do any less for ours? The God who did impossible things is our God. How is our faith?

John the Baptist was in jail because he told the truth. Wondering, he sent a question to Jesus: "Art thou he that should come, or do we look for another?" Jesus answered with facts, not philosophy: "Go and show John again those things which ye do hear and see: the blind receive their sight, and the lame walk, the lepers are cleansed, and the deaf hear, the dead are raised up, and the poor have the gospel preached to them" (Matthew 11:2-5). The facts were enough to establish John's faith; are they not enough to establish ours?

Paul summarized the good news he proclaimed in Corinth: "How that Christ died for our sins according to the Scriptures; and that he was buried, and that he rose again the third day according to the Scriptures: and that he was seen of Cephas, then of the twelve: after that, he was seen of above five hundred brethren at once. . . . After that, he was seen of James; then of all the apostles. And last of all he was seen of me also" (1 Corinthians 15:3-8). On those facts the Christians in Corinth stood (1 Corinthians 15:1). Do we stand as firm as they?

C. Acting on Our Faith

"What shall we do then?" Listeners asked John the Baptist, and he told them to share with people in need. Read more in Luke 3:10-14.

"Men and brethren, what shall we do?" Listeners asked the apostles, and Peter told them to repent and be baptized. Read more in Acts 2:36-42.

Without a specific question, Paul told Christians to be transformed so as to demonstrate what is God's will. Read some details in chapters 12 to 15 of Romans. Add those in 1 Corinthians 12, and see chapter 13 for what is even better. For more rich thoughts about acting on our faith, read the whole New Testament. And "be ye doers of the word, and not hearers only." Otherwise you're only fooling yourself when you talk about your faith (James 1:22).

D. Prayer

Thank You, Father, for giving us solid reasons for our faith. We do believe in You; may we have grace and power to act on our faith. Amen.

E. Thought to Remember

How firm a foundation, ye saints of the Lord, Is laid for your faith in His excellent Word!"

Home Daily Bible Readings

Monday, Sept. 5—They Acted by Faith (Hebrews 11:23-31)
Tuesday, Sept. 6—Instructions to Follow the Ark (Joshua 3:1-6)
Wednesday, Sept. 7—The Jordan Will Stop Flowing (Joshua 3:7-13)
Thursday, Sept. 8—Israel Crosses Over the Jordan (Joshua 3:14—4:7)
Friday, Sept. 9—Twelve Stones Carried With Them (Joshua 4:8-14)
Saturday, Sept. 10—Stones for Remembering the Crossing (Joshua 4:15-24)
Sunday, Sept. 11—God Offers Restoration and Protection (Isaiah 43:1-7)

Learning by Doing

This page contains an alternate lesson plan emphasizing learning activities. Classes desiring such student involvement will find these suggestions helpful.

Learning Goals

As students participate in today's class session, they should:

1. Discover how little the Israelites needed to do in order to enter the promised land and how much, by contrast, God did to make the entrance possible.

2. Identify God's magnificent responses to our small steps of obedience.

3. Choose one significant step to take soon in obedience to God.

Into the Lesson

Write these two open-ended sentences on your chalkboard: "Obeying God is *easy* because—" and "Obeying God is *difficult* because—"

Divide the class in half. Have the students in each half pair off with a classmate sitting nearby. The pairs in the first half are to complete the first sentence; those in the second half are to complete the second sentence.

After three minutes, let volunteers share what they have decided. Tell your class, "The key word in today's lesson is *obedience*. We'll look at a Bible story that can help us decide how obedience is easy and how it is difficult.

Into the Word

Connect this lesson with last week's lesson by giving a brief lecture based on the material presented in the "Lesson Background" section on page 18. Begin today's Bible study by having three volunteers read Joshua 3 to the class, following these verse divisions: 1-6, 7-13, and 14-17. Then ask class members to tell everything that Joshua and his people did as recorded in this chapter. Write them on the chalkboard.

Then, beside that list, write what God did in response to what Joshua and the people did.

Discuss with your class members, "Who did more in this incident, God or His people? Who did the more difficult thing, God or the people?"

There may be some difference of opinion on these questions; if so, don't press for the differences to be resolved yet. That can come later.

Ask your students to complete the following comparative Bible study. Distribute copies of the Bible-study chart shown at the top of the right column. The answers, which are given in italics, are for the teacher's convenience and should not be given to the students ahead of time.

Person and Scripture	How God Was Obeyed	What God Did in Response
Shadrach, Meshach, Abednego (Daniel 3)	*Refused to worship Nebuchadnez-zar's idol*	*Saved them from harm in the fiery furnace*
Elijah (1 Kings 18:20-40)	*Preached against Baal and challenged his prophets*	*Consumed Elijah's offering with fire*
Abraham (Genesis 22:1-19)	*Showed willing-ness to sacri-fice Isaac*	*Miraculously provided an offering*

If you have time, have students explore Joshua's feelings during the events described in Joshua 3. Write these verse headings on the chalkboard: 1-6; 7, 8; 9-13; 14-17. For each paragraph students should jot a word, phrase, or sentence to describe what they think were Joshua's feelings at each time.

Allot five minutes for this. Then, for each paragraph, let volunteers share what they have written. Discuss, "What do you suppose Joshua learned from these events? What about the people? What can we learn from their experience?"

Into Life

Write this sentence on your chalkboard: "If we will take the first step, God will do the rest." Discuss: "How true was this principle in the examples we have studied today? Can you think of other Bible stories that show the truth of this principle? (Possibilities: Noah, Joseph, Moses, the apostle Paul.)

Ask class members to think of this principle in relation to their own lives. Have there been times when God has provided magnificently in response to their obedience? Possible examples would be as a result of tithing, confessing a sin, saying "no" to an unethical business practice or some other temptation.

Discuss this with the class: Why are we sometimes so hesitant to take the first step?

Ask, "Is there a step in obedience to God that you should take before the end of this year?"

If any students will share what they are thinking, make special mention of their goals in your closing prayer. Otherwise, lead them to pray silently about how they need to obey God.

Let's Talk It Over

The questions on this page are designed to encourage review of the lesson Scriptures and to promote discussion of the lesson by the class. The answers provided are only discussion starters. Let your class talk it over from there.

1. The lesson writer goes into some detail in describing how we all exercise faith daily in mechanical devices and in other human beings. What can we do to appreciate better this regular exercise of our faculty of faith?

Perhaps it would be helpful to keep a log of our daily activities for a week or two and note how faith is required in connection with them. In a Bible school class or a study group in someone's home, this topic could stimulate discussion from each person present. The benefit of such an emphasis is to remind us that we are not the self-made, self-sufficient individuals we sometimes imagine ourselves to be. In virtually every activity "we walk by faith, not by sight" (2 Corinthians 5:7). The Christian differs from other people by focusing this faith on God and His principles and promises.

2. The Lord magnified or exalted Joshua in the sight of all Israel. What lesson lies in this statement for modern Christian leaders who achieve a measure of fame and exaltation among men?

Any Christian preacher, musician, writer, etc., who attains a high level of human recognition must be careful about taking credit for his or her success. The Lord's part in it must not be overlooked. Recognizing God's hand in one's success should serve as a safeguard against excessive pride or a tendency to harbor contempt for those in less prominent positions. It is obvious that God had a purpose in magnifying Joshua. Israel needed a strong leader as Moses' successor, someone who could hold the nation together through the approaching years of conquest. In raising up leaders today, God surely has a purpose to be worked out, for His own glory and not that of the leader.

3. The priests were to set an example of faith by carrying the ark into the water of the flooded Jordan. How can leaders in the church set examples of faith for the membership?

The members of a church need to see their leaders act on their faith by boldly supporting the Lord's work with their time, energy, and finances. When a call is issued for prayer supporters, door-to-door callers, workers for vacation Bible school, people to assist with building and grounds maintenance, etc., leaders should be prominent among the volunteers. Of course, leaders cannot do all the work themselves, and so they must recruit other workers. But they must do enough of the little jobs to demonstrate the willingness, enthusiasm, and commitment that should characterize each worker.

4. How can reading and studying Old Testament miracles strengthen our faith?

Scoffers claim that these accounts of miracles are myths or exaggerations. They cannot prove such claims, but neither can we offer unassailable proof that these events happened as recorded. We can point out, however, that the miracles fit in well with the historical narrative of the Old Testament. Somehow a nation of slaves was able to gain freedom from Egypt after several generations of bondage. The biblical account of the ten plagues and the crossing of the Red Sea provide a credible explanation as to how that happened. That nation was then able to conquer a land of mighty peoples living in walled cities. The miracles that are recorded in the book of Joshua, such as the crossing of the Jordan River and the destruction of the walls of Jericho, tell us how this crusade was accomplished. In this same way all the Old Testament miracles are woven into the fabric of historical narrative.

5. How can reading and studying New Testament miracles strengthen our faith?

John made it clear that his purpose in writing about Jesus was to stimulate faith: "These are written, that ye might believe that Jesus is the Christ, the Son of God; and that believing ye might have life through his name" (John 20:31). Like the other Gospel writers John recorded some of Jesus' miracles, including the most significant miracle of all: the resurrection. And like the other Gospel writers John showed how Jesus' miracles were consistent with His character and His claims. He claimed to be the Son of God; His sinless character gave evidence that that was true; and His power over the elements of nature, sickness, and death provided the final, compelling link of evidence. It is a faith-building experience to read the Gospels and examine how these strands of evidence are bound together.

Winning the Battle

DEVOTIONAL READING: Psalm 149.

LESSON SCRIPTURE: Joshua 6.

PRINTED TEXT: Joshua 6:1-5, 15-20.

Joshua 6:1-5, 15-20

1 Now Jericho was straitly shut up because of the children of Israel: none went out, and none came in.

2 And the LORD said unto Joshua, See, I have given into thine hand Jericho, and the king thereof, and the mighty men of valor.

3 And ye shall compass the city, all ye men of war, and go round about the city once. Thus shalt thou do six days.

4 And seven priests shall bear before the ark seven trumpets of rams' horns: and the seventh day ye shall compass the city seven times, and the priests shall blow with the trumpets.

5 And it shall come to pass, that when they make a long blast with the ram's horn, and when ye hear the sound of the trumpet, all the people shall shout with a great shout; and the wall of the city shall fall down flat, and the people shall ascend up every man straight before him.

. . . .

15 And it came to pass on the seventh day, that they rose early about the dawning of the day, and compassed the city after the same manner seven times: only on that day they compassed the city seven times.

16 And it came to pass at the seventh time, when the priests blew with the trumpets, Joshua said unto the people, Shout; for the LORD hath given you the city.

17 And the city shall be accursed, even it, and all that are therein, to the LORD: only Rahab the harlot shall live, she and all that are with her in the house, because she hid the messengers that we sent.

18 And ye, in any wise keep yourselves from the accursed thing, lest ye make yourselves accursed, when ye take of the accursed thing, and make the camp of Israel a curse, and trouble it.

19 But all the silver, and gold, and vessels of brass and iron, are consecrated unto the LORD: they shall come into the treasury of the LORD.

20 So the people shouted when the priests blew with the trumpets: and it came to pass, when the people heard the sound of the trumpet, and the people shouted with a great shout, that the wall fell down flat, so that the people went up into the city, every man straight before him, and they took the city.

GOLDEN TEXT: Joshua said unto the people, Shout; for the LORD hath given you the city.—Joshua 6:16.

From the Conquest to the Kingdom

Unit 1: The Conquest of the Land

(Lessons 1-4)

Lesson Aims

After this lesson a student should be able to:

1. Retell the story of the fall of Jericho.

2. List at least five attitudes and activities that are included in God's plan for His people today.

3. Find at least one way to follow God's plan better this week.

Lesson Outline

INTRODUCTION
    A. Peaceful Passover
    B. Lesson Background
I. PROMISE OF VICTORY (Joshua 6:1, 2)
    A. Anxiety (v. 1)
    B. Promise (v. 2)
II. BATTLE PLAN (Joshua 6:3-5)
    A. Six Circuits (v. 3)
    B. Marching Music (v. 4a)
    C. The Seventh Day (vv. 4b,c, 5)
III. VICTORY (Joshua 6:15-20)
    A. Seven Circuits (vv. 15, 16)
    B. Devoted City (vv. 17-19)
      The Most Significant Reward
      The Wealth Belongs to God
    C. Triumph (v. 20)
CONCLUSION
    A. Knowing God's Plan
    B. Following God's Plan
    C. Prayer
    D. Thought to Remember

Visual 3 of the visuals packet relates to the thoughts included in the Conclusion section. The visual is shown on page 28.

Introduction

D day—do you remember it? Men and munitions and material had been massing for months in Britain. The world waited on tiptoe, and defenders in Europe waited in anxiety. Few people knew just when the great day would be; but when the word was given, the response was swift. Waves of boats and aircraft swept across the English channel; thousands stormed the beaches of France and plunged into conflict.

Israel's D day was that famous day when Jordan's water rose up in a heap and a nation of people walked dry-shod through the river. But unlike the invaders of Europe, the people of Israel did not plunge into instant combat. No troops were massed to meet them on the west bank. The defenders were scared. They had heard how these invaders had walked through the Red Sea forty years before, and how they had trodden down two nations on the east bank just recently (Joshua 2:10, 11). Now in addition they knew how the Jordan had stopped to let these people cross (Joshua 5:1). Obviously someone more than human had these invaders in His care. No one came to fight them. No doubt anxious sentinels watched and worried on the wall of Jericho as the people of Israel made their camp in the nearby plain. No doubt scouts of tribes farther west were perched in the mountains above Jericho. But in that plain beside the Jordan no one was seen coming to meet the men of Israel.

A. Peaceful Passover

The day Israel crossed the Jordan was the tenth day of the first month (Joshua 4:19). That was the very day when each family was to select a lamb to be eaten in its Passover feast four days later (Exodus 12:1-8). Just forty years after the first Passover in Egypt, Israel celebrated its first Passover in the land of promise (Joshua 5:10). The next day the Israelites ate some of the grain grown on the west bank, and manna came no more. The wanderers were in their homeland now, but they still had to vanquish the people who lived there.

B. Lesson Background

Then one day a stranger came with sword in hand, and Joshua hurried to confront him. "Are you for us or for our enemies?"

"Neither," he replied, "but as commander of the army of the Lord I have now come."

No doubt Joshua got the message. The Lord's army was in the field and ready, but it was on the Lord's side rather than any human side. It would fight against any who opposed the Lord; it would fight for any who obeyed Him. This was both an encouragement and a warning. Joshua and Israel had better take care to be on the Lord's side too (Joshua 5:13-15, *New International Version*).

I. Promise of Victory (Joshua 6:1, 2)

Digging in the plain of Jordan from 1930 to 1936, John Garstang thought he found the ruins of Joshua's Jericho. The small city was protected by a double wall about thirty feet high. The outer wall was six feet thick, the inner one twelve feet. Both walls had tumbled down, and ashes showed that the town had been burned. Later diggers thought that that town was destroyed before Joshua's town, but they found much less evidence of a later one. Whether Joshua saw that particular town or not, we know he saw a town protected by a wall.

A. Anxiety (v. 1)

1. Now Jericho was straitly shut up because of the children of Israel: none went out, and none came in.

With that horde of Israelites camping near by, the people of Jericho were taking no chances. They went inside the walls and barred the gates. Their cisterns were full of water, for the Passover came at the end of the rainy season. No doubt they had stored food enough to last for a long time. There were quantities of charred wheat and barley in the ashes of that city Garstang found. Well supplied with food and water, and seeing no battering ram in that huge camp of Israel, the anxious men of Jericho may have felt safe behind their well-built wall. But none can be safe when they are godless.

B. Promise (v. 2)

2. And the LORD said unto Joshua, See, I have given into thine hand Jericho, and the king thereof, and the mighty men of valor.

The Lord had His own army in the field (Joshua 5:14), and He would deliver the city to Joshua. Neither the king nor his soldiers would be able to keep it safe. That did not mean Joshua and his men would have no part in the capture; it meant that success was certain.

II. Battle Plan
(Joshua 6:3-5)

God himself gave Joshua the plan of battle; and that was well, for surely Joshua never would have thought of such a plan. And if he had devised it, it would not have worked without God's help. God both planned the work and worked the plan; and yet the fighting men of Israel had a part in it, and the plan would have failed if they had not done their part.

A. Six Circuits (v. 3)

3. And ye shall compass the city, all ye men of war, and go round about the city once. Thus shalt thou do six days.

Imagine the puzzled surprise of the watchers on the city wall. Israel's entire fighting force came out and marched once around the city, then went back to camp. The next day they did it again, and every day for six days. Some of the

---

<table>
<tr><td colspan="2">How to Say It</td></tr>
<tr><td>GETHSEMANE.</td><td>Geth-sem-uh-nee.</td></tr>
<tr><td>RAHAB.</td><td>Ray-hab.</td></tr>
</table>

marchers may have been puzzled too. What could be the purpose of this daily hike? But at least the marchers had a sound reason for doing what they did. God told them to do it.

B. Marching Music (v. 4a)

4a. And seven priests shall bear before the ark seven trumpets of rams' horns.

More details of the procession are given in verses 6-14. Imagine yourself on the wall of Jericho watching the parade. A feature that catches your eye is the ark of the covenant, carefully shrouded from view (Numbers 4:5, 6), supported on long poles, and carried on the shoulders of priests. Seven priests go ahead of the ark, blowing on trumpets made of rams' horns. Are they playing a lively march, or a somber dirge for the doomed city? On that point we have no information. Part of the armed men march ahead of the trumpeters, and the rest follow behind the ark. The fighting men of Israel number six hundred thousand (Numbers 26:51). It has been estimated that they could march seventy-five abreast in a column long enough to surround the city completely while staying out of reach of an arrow shot from the wall. Quite an impressive sight to the defenders of a small city!

C. The Seventh Day (vv. 4b, c, 5)

4b, c. And the seventh day ye shall compass the city seven times, and the priests shall blow with the trumpets.

On the seventh day the procession was to move out as it had done on the other six days. But this time it was not to stop after one circuit. It was to march on around the city seven times.

5. And it shall come to pass, that when they make a long blast with the ram's horn, and when ye hear the sound of the trumpet, all the people shall shout with a great shout; and the wall of the city shall fall down flat, and the people shall ascend up every man straight before him.

After the seventh circuit, the trumpeters would stop their marching music and give the signal with *a long blast.* At that signal, all the marching troops would *shout with a great shout.* At the shout, *the wall of the city* would *fall down flat.* The procession of Israel's fighting men would be stretched out all around the city. With the wall out of the way, every man of the six hundred thousand would charge up the slope and into the city *straight before him*.

Such was the plan God gave to Joshua. Verses 6-14 tell how it was carried out through the first six days of the marching.

III. Victory
(Joshua 6:15-20)

Verses 4 and 5 describe the plan of action for the seventh day. Now we are to see how that plan was carried out.

A. Seven Circuits (vv. 15, 16)

15. And it came to pass on the seventh day, that they rose up early about the dawning of the day, and compassed the city after the same manner seven times: only on that day they compassed the city seven times.

The marchers got up early because they had much to do that day. First, they would walk around Jericho *seven times*. Of course we do not know how far they walked or how long it took. For example, suppose their path around the city was three miles long, making a circle somewhat less than a mile in diameter around the city. Then seven circuits at an unhurried pace would take about seven hours. The time needed to destroy the city would be added to that, making a long day for Israel's warriors. If they made a smaller circle around the city, of course the time would be less. The ruined city that Garstang described was small and compact, having only six or seven acres inside the wall.

16. And it came to pass at the seventh time, when the priests blew with the trumpets, Joshua said unto the people, Shout; for the LORD hath given you the city.

Again we see that the writer does not always record events in the order in which they happened. The seven trumpets could be heard all around the circle, even if it was a mile wide. That was the signal for the people to shout (v. 5), so we cannot suppose Joshua took time after the

trumpet call to give the instructions in this verse and those that follow. And we need not suppose he shouted to the troops spread out in a mile-wide circle. He must have given these instructions before the march began that morning. At that special long blast of the trumpets, the men were to "shout with a great shout," trusting the Lord to break down the walls so they could take the city as His gift.

B. Devoted City (vv. 17-19)

17. And the city shall be accursed, even it, and all that are therein, to the LORD: only Rahab the harlot shall live, she and all that are with her in the house, because she hid the messengers that we sent.

This continues the instructions Joshua gave before the troops started their march on the seventh day. Other versions give the thought better by saying *the city shall be devoted . . . to the Lord* rather than *accursed . . . to the Lord*. Jericho was the first city to be taken in the campaign west of the Jordan. It must be given to the Lord, as were the firstfruits of the harvest (Deuteronomy 26:1-11). People of Israel might live in towns taken later, but all Jericho must be destroyed. Stores of food must be burned, along with clothing and household goods. Animals and people must be killed. Only Rahab and her family were to be spared, because she had saved the lives and the mission of Israel's spies. That was the subject of our lesson two weeks ago. Apparently one bit of the city wall would not collapse with the rest, for Rahab's house was on the wall (Joshua 2:15), and all her people were to gather there (v. 18). The spies whom Rahab had saved were appointed to see that she and her family were kept safe (Joshua 6:22-25). Probably the whole family was accepted in Israel along with her. Rahab has an honored place among the faithful (Hebrews 11:31).

THE MOST SIGNIFICANT REWARD

At dawn on April 15, 1865, two men on horseback came to the home of Dr. Samuel Mudd, asking him to set the broken leg of one of them. After doing so, he gave them food and a place to rest. Dr. Mudd might have lived his whole life in obscurity were it not that the man whose leg he treated was John Wilkes Booth, "on the run" after assassinating Abraham Lincoln.

Mudd was convicted of conspiracy in the assassination and sentenced to life imprisonment. (Some legal experts today feel the evidence presented was insufficient to prove Mudd's guilt.) While in prison, he saved the lives of fellow inmates and soldiers during a yellow fever epidemic. For this, President Andrew Johnson pardoned Mudd after only four years in prison.

SUCCESS
NEXT RIGHT

Learn and follow God's plan

visual 3

Rahab, a prostitute, would have been forgotten long ago but for one thing: when Joshua's spies came into Jericho, she hid them and then helped them escape to freedom. For her act of kindness (and faith, as Hebrews 11 tells us), her life and the lives of all in her household were spared when the Israelites took the city.

Sometimes other people reward us in significant ways for the good we do; at other times they ignore it entirely. Nevertheless, *God* knows, and that is the most significant reward for the person who loves God. —C. R. B.

18. And ye, in any wise keep yourselves from the accursed thing, lest ye make yourselves accursed, when ye take of the accursed thing, and make the camp of Israel a curse, and trouble it.

Any wise means *any way.* If a man should be tempted to take something from Jericho for himself, he must say, "No way!" A soldier might enrich himself with spoil from other cities, but not this one. Jericho was *accursed,* devoted to the Lord, a sacrifice, and therefore to be destroyed. Anyone who would steal from that sacred sacrifice must be likewise *accursed,* and therefore destroyed. Worse than that, such theft from the devoted city would make the whole *camp of Israel a curse.* Chapter 7 gives an example. One man did steal some of the spoil of Jericho, and all Israel was shamefully defeated until that man was detected and destroyed.

19. But all the silver, and gold, and vessels of brass and iron, are consecrated unto the LORD: they shall come into the treasury of the LORD.

Metal things would not be destroyed but neither would they be taken for private property. They must be put in *the treasury of the Lord.*

THE WEALTH BELONGS TO GOD

George Walker filed an affidavit in Pretoria, South Africa, in July, 1886, staking his claim for gold, and then sold his claim for fifty dollars. Thus began one of the greatest gold rushes in history. Within three years, people bitten by the gold bug had swarmed into the shantytown of Johannesburg from all over the world. No one knows what happened to George Walker.

This story has parallels among the "forty-niners" of the California gold rush and among those who braved the frigid dangers of the Alaskan frontier in the rush of 1898. The prospect of fabulous wealth has lured many people to their destruction, either physical or moral.

God warned the Israelites against taking for themselves any of the wealth they might find in Jericho. He sought to protect them from the moral destruction that sometimes accompanies great wealth gained with too little expenditure of personal effort. But more than that, this city and everything in it was devoted to the Lord. Israel was to recognize that and see that all the precious things were put into His treasury. We today do well to remember that all our riches really belong to God. —C. R. B.

C. Triumph (v. 20)

20. So the people shouted when the priests blew with the trumpets: and it came to pass, when the people heard the sound of the trumpet, and the people shouted with a great shout, that the wall fell down flat, so that the people went up into the city, every man straight before him, and they took the city.

This was just what the Lord had promised (v. 5). The *trumpets* sounded their long blast, *the people shouted with a great shout,* and *the wall fell down flat.* Many scholars have suggested that the united shout of six hundred thousand men might generate sound waves powerful enough to shake a wall apart; others doubt that any number of human voices could do that. We must remember that an unseen army of the Lord was there too (Joshua 5:13-15). No doubt that army could demolish a wall with ultrasound, or by some method entirely unknown to us.

If this was the city described by Garstang, it was built on the top of a knoll. The outer wall tumbled down the slope; the inner one collapsed into the space between the walls. More than half a million fighting men of Israel were surrounding Jericho. With the wall out of the way, they *went up* the sides of the knoll, over the fallen bricks, and *into the city* from all sides. Imagine the surprise of the people in the town. Paralyzed by shock and fear, they made no effective resistance. The invaders slaughtered them all—men, women, and children (v. 21).

If such a massacre seems revolting, we need to remember that it was ordered by the Lord, not by the men who carried out the order. "The Lord is merciful and gracious, slow to anger, and plenteous in mercy" (Psalm 103:8). But when He determines that people are too evil to live, He is not squeamish about killing them. Remember the destruction of Sodom (Genesis 19:24, 25) and the flood that destroyed most of mankind (Genesis 7:21, 22). Innocent children died, yes; and for them it was far better to die in innocence than to grow up and die in sin.

So the Lord's battle plan worked perfectly, for the Lord and His people worked it together. Israel *took the city,* but no one in Israel was richer because of the taking. Like the firstfruits of harvest, this first-captured city was a sacrifice, an offering to the Lord.

Conclusion

How can we win life's battles? By accepting God's plan and following it. We all know that. But that is not so simple as it sounds. We long for day-by-day instructions such as God gave to Joshua, instructions simple, detailed, and complete. God gives us principles and leaves us to work out details in our own lives. But God gives us minds to work with. Can we learn to accept our responsibility and find joy in it?

A. Knowing God's Plan

God's plan for us is in the Bible. We all know that. But do we spend more time with the Bible than we do with TV, which often presents lifestyles that are contrary to God's plan?

Bible study seems so indirect. We look for step-by-step instructions like those in a cookbook; God gives us life-guiding principles. If we really want to follow God's plan, we can figure out how to apply His principles.

Bible study seems so slow. We would like to have each guiding principle stated in ten words or less. But we learn about faith from the lives of Abraham and Rahab and Stephen. We learn about sacrifice from Abel and Jesus on the cross. We learn about prayer from Hannah and Elijah and Jesus in Gethsemane. We learn about fortitude from Joseph and Jeremiah and John the Baptist. Do we care enough about right principles to learn them in this way?

Bible study seems so impractical. We want to know how to make the mortgage payment, and God tells us how Joshua took Jericho. But Joshua took Jericho by following God's instructions, and we know we had better not make the mortgage payment by stealing or cheating.

Really, we know how to make that payment. We do it by getting along with one car instead of two or three, by preparing meals at home instead of dining out, by wearing old clothes longer, by taking long walks instead of playing golf. But we don't like self-denial, even if it is a sound principle. Following God's plan may be harder than knowing it.

B. Following God's Plan

The Israelites didn't take Jericho the day after they crossed the river. The Passover was at hand, and they took time to celebrate it properly. Following God's plan involves taking time for reverence, time for worship, time to be holy. It takes time to absorb Bible principles from the lives of heroes and from the teaching of Jesus and the apostles. Do you have time for Sunday school and church, other group Bible studies, and your own daily study at home?

God's plan includes sincerity, honesty, truth (Ephesians 4:25). Did you try to fool anyone last week?

God's plan includes self-control (Ephesians 4:26). Did you get through the week without "blowing up"?

God's plan includes clean talk (Ephesians 4:29). Did you lapse into any "corrupt communication"?

God's plan includes wholesome thinking (Philippians 4:8). Are you ashamed of any of your thoughts?

God's plan includes kindness, consideration, compassion (Ephesians 4:32). How did you do with those?

God's plan includes helpfulness (1 Corinthians 10:24; read *good* instead of *wealth*). Did you go out of your way to help someone last week?

God's plan includes humility (1 Peter 5:5). Are you happy when someone gets ahead of you?

God's plan includes sacrifice, self-denial (Hebrews 13:16). What did you do without last week for the sake of some good cause?

God's plan includes doing good to your enemies (Luke 6:27). Did you manage that?

Don't stop now. List some other things that you know are included in God's plan for you.

C. Prayer

Father, how wonderful it is that You have a faultless plan for us! How good it is to know that Your plan is revealed in Your Word! In gratitude we promise that we will try to know Your plan and follow it. In Jesus' name, amen.

D. Thought to Remember

Any life lived by God's plan is a successful life.

Home Daily Bible Readings

Monday, Sept. 12—Joshua's Preparation for Battle (Joshua 5:10-15)
Tuesday, Sept. 13—The Lord Is Near (Psalm 145:14-20)
Wednesday, Sept. 14—God's Promise to Joshua (Joshua 6:1-5)
Thursday, Sept. 15—Beginning the March Around Jericho (Joshua 6:6-11)
Friday, Sept. 16—The Fall of Jericho (Joshua 6:12-21)
Saturday, Sept. 17—Rahab's Family Is Spared (Joshua 6:22-25)
Sunday, Sept. 18—God Gives Victory (Psalm 98:1-6)

Learning by Doing

This page contains an alternate lesson plan emphasizing learning activities. Classes desiring such student involvement will find these suggestions helpful.

Learning Goals

Students in today's class should:

1. Summarize the facts in the story of Israel's battle against Jericho.

2. List some principles for achieving spiritual victory today.

3. Choose one principle to put into practice more fully in their own lives.

Into the Lesson

Write the following words on your chalkboard: *risk, obedience, victory*. Class members may remember that the word *risk* summarized lesson one of our current unit, and *obedience*, lesson two. Today's lesson focuses on *victory*.

To begin today's session ask the class members to work individually and to write a sentence or two in which all three of the words are used to express a truth concerning the Christian life. Here are some possibilities:

Those who *risk obedience* to God will enjoy spiritual *victory*.

Obedience to God brings *victory*, but it may require *risk*.

One doesn't really *risk* anything when one knows that *obedience* to God ultimately brings *victory*.

Allow class members two minutes to write their sentences; then ask for volunteers to share what they have written. Tell the class, "Today's study lets us look at a victory Israel experienced under Joshua's leadership. We'll see how many of your statements seem true in light of our discussion of today's text."

Into the Word

Divide your class into four sections and assign each section a different portion of Joshua 6 according to the verse divisions that follow. Within each section, class members should work in pairs or groups of three. Each small group should write a one-sentence summary of the group of verses assigned to its section. Allot five minutes for this.

1. Promise of victory (vv. 1, 2)
2. Battle plan (vv. 3-5)
3. Prelude to victory (vv. 6-14)
4. Victory (vv. 15-21)

As students are working, write the four headings on the chalkboard or an overhead projector transparency. When time is up, ask for volunteers to share their summaries. Write at least one summary under each heading.

Ask class members, "What do you find interesting or surprising about this story? Why? What does it teach about victory? About risk-taking? About obedience?"

Option. Some of your students could do a Bible study about the subject of victory. (If you wish, divide the class into five sections instead of four. Four of them could do the study described above, while the fifth does the study of victory as described in the following paragraph.

For each of the following Scriptures, students should jot down an answer to the question, "What does this verse teach about spiritual victory?" The verses are Psalm 44:5; John 16:33; Romans 8:35, 37; 1 John 5:4; Revelation 3:5.

Into Life

Use the material in the "Conclusion" section of the first lesson plan to apply this lesson to life today. Read aloud the first paragraph, which begins, "How can we win life's battles?" Discuss with your class, "Why hasn't God given us day-by-day, step-by-step instructions as He did Joshua in the event recorded in our lesson text? What role does Bible study have in helping us to find spiritual victory?"

Proceed to section A, entitled "Knowing God's Plan." Introduce it, then read aloud the topic sentences ("Bible study seems so indirect." "Bible study seems so slow." "Bible study seems so impractical.") You may even want to write these on the chalkboard. Ask students to decide how each of these sentences is true and in what sense they may be false.

Then ask, "How, then, can we hope to get God's guidance for our lives? How can we find victory?"

Read to the class section B, "Following God's Plan." Ask, "Which of the principles suggested here seem most challenging to you? Why?"

Write the word *victory* down the center of your chalkboard. Ask students to suggest principles for achieving spiritual victory in their lives; each principle should begin with a word that begins with a letter in *victory*. Write some of these on the chalkboard as students suggest them. Ask volunteers to share which of these principles could most effectively promote their spiritual growth.

End with sentence prayers for victory.

Let's Talk It Over

The questions on this page are designed to encourage review of the lesson Scriptures and to promote discussion of the lesson by the class. The answers provided are only discussion starters. Let your class talk it over from there.

1. Why is it important that we recognize the distinction between being on the Lord's side and having Him on our side?

People have been known to claim God's sanction and approval for all kinds of atrocious actions. A biblical example is Saul of Tarsus (later Paul). In recounting his career as a persecutor of Christians he later said, "I verily thought with myself, that I ought to do many things contrary to the name of Jesus of Nazareth" (Acts 26:9). He assumed God was on his side, but he eventually learned otherwise. We need to begin by committing ourselves to being on God's side, of discovering what that means, and of adhering to that principle when we are tempted to give divine sanction to our opinions or prejudices. Like the sons of Levi, who responded to Moses' call, "Who is on the Lord's side? let him come unto me" (Exodus 32:26), we should commit ourselves to doing the will of God.

2. The Lord said, "I have given into thine hand Jericho." But Joshua and the people of Israel had to make an effort to take what was given. How does this illustrate the way by which we appropriate God's gifts?

It is clear that God would not have permitted the Israelites to defeat Jericho had they not followed God's directions. So today God gives His people victories and blessings, but they are not appropriated by those who have only an "armchair faith." We must follow God's directions and act upon our confidence that He wants us to achieve victories in His cause. In the book of James we are warned that "faith without works is dead" (James 2:20). A faith that consists of mere feelings and good intentions is lifeless and fruitless. But when faith in our hearts is combined with the efforts of our hands and feet, we can lay hold of the rich resources God offers.

3. God, who is the giver of life, had the right to order the complete destruction of Jericho and its citizens. God also has a right to everything we possess, because He has enabled us to possess it. Why is it important that we stress this?

The fact that Jericho was devoted to God and that the spoil of the city was to come into the treasury of the Lord was an indication that everything the Israelites later possessed in the land was theirs through God's provision. They, therefore, could be expected to receive such blessings thankfully and to use them in such a way as to please the Giver. We who are Christians must likewise acknowledge the divine source of all we enjoy (see 1 Timothy 6:17). That will help us use our blessings wisely and benevolently, especially in supporting the work of Christ's church.

4. What is involved in using the Bible to discern God's plan for our lives?

As James 1:22-25 indicates, the Bible is a kind of mirror that shows us ourselves as we are and as God means us to be. The Bible records the experiences of many persons, and their moral errors as well as their positive character traits are open to our view. As we consider their lives, we should pray for help in avoiding their errors and in emulating their good traits. The New Testament also includes listings of godly characteristics, such as in Matthew 5:1-12, Galatians 5:22-26, and Colossians 3:12-17. It is vital that we meditate on these, pray over these, and strive to reproduce them in our own character. Since God's plan for us also involves our service for Him, we should give careful attention to passages that speak of service, such as Romans 12:3-8 and 1 Peter 4:10, 11. And we must pray that we will be guided into that area of service where God wants us.

5. What is involved in putting into action God's plan for our lives that is revealed in the Bible?

In the preceding answer we referred to James 1:22-25 and its comparison of the Bible with a mirror. In that passage James points out how easily we can forget what a mirror reveals, if we do not act upon what is revealed. This reminds us of how vital it is for us to follow through promptly when our study of the Bible impresses us with the need for some specific action. If we delay, we will soon forget that impression, and that work for the Lord will be left undone. Some Bible students have found it helpful to keep a journal or log of their personal study. In this way they can keep a record of passages studied, of insights gained, and of actions taken in response to those insights.

Choosing to Serve God

DEVOTIONAL READING: Psalm 116:12-19.

LESSON SCRIPTURE: Joshua 24.

PRINTED TEXT: Joshua 24:1, 2, 11-16, 22-25.

Joshua 24:1, 2, 11-16, 22-25

1 And Joshua gathered all the tribes of Israel to Shechem, and called for the elders of Israel, and for their heads, and for their judges, and for their officers; and they presented themselves before God.

2 And Joshua said unto all the people, Thus saith the LORD God of Israel,

· · · · · · · · · · · · ·

11 And ye went over Jordan, and came unto Jericho: and the men of Jericho fought against you, the Amorites, and the Perizzites, and the Canaanites, and the Hittites, and the Girgashites, the Hivites, and the Jebusites; and I delivered them into your hand.

12 And I sent the hornet before you, which drave them out from before you, even the two kings of the Amorites; but not with thy sword, nor with thy bow.

13 And I have given you a land for which ye did not labor, and cities which ye built not, and ye dwell in them; of the vineyards and oliveyards which ye planted not do ye eat.

14 Now therefore fear the LORD, and serve him in sincerity and in truth; and put away the gods which your fathers served on the other side of the flood, and in Egypt; and serve ye the LORD.

15 And if it seem evil unto you to serve the LORD, choose you this day whom ye will serve; whether the gods which your fathers served that were on the other side of the flood, or the gods of the Amorites, in whose land ye dwell: but as for me and my house, we will serve the LORD.

16 And the people answered and said, God forbid that we should forsake the LORD, to serve other gods.

· · · · · · · · · · · · ·

22 And Joshua said unto the people, Ye are witnesses against yourselves that ye have chosen you the LORD, to serve him. And they said, We are witnesses.

23 Now therefore put away, said he, the strange gods which are among you, and incline your heart unto the LORD God of Israel.

24 And the people said unto Joshua, The LORD our God will we serve, and his voice will we obey.

25 So Joshua made a covenant with the people that day, and set them a statute and an ordinance in Shechem.

GOLDEN TEXT: Choose you this day whom ye will serve; . . . but as for me and my house, we will serve the LORD.—Joshua 24:15.

From the Conquest to the Kingdom

Unit 1: The Conquest of the Land

(Lessons 1-4)

Lesson Aims

After this lesson a student should be able to:

1. List at least three great things the Lord did to help Israel.

2. Tell what the people of Israel promised to do in response to God's help.

3. State his or her choice to serve the Lord.

4. Consider God's will in every choice he or she makes.

Lesson Outline

INTRODUCTION
    A. Moving In
    B. Lesson Background
  I. GOD'S WORD (Joshua 24:1, 2, 11-13)
    A. The Meeting (v. 1)
    B. The Speaker (v. 2)
    C. God's Help (vv. 11-13)
 II. JOSHUA'S WORD (Joshua 24:14, 15)
    A. Serve God Only (v. 14)
    B. Choose (v. 15a)
    C. Joshua's Choice (v. 15b)
      The Mark of Greatness
III. THE PEOPLE'S PLEDGE (Joshua 24:16, 22-25)
    A. Prompt Pledge (v. 16)
    B. Witnesses (v. 22)
    C. Repeated Pledge (vv. 23, 24)
      The Importance of Pilots
    D. Formal Covenant (v. 25)
CONCLUSION
    A. Our Choices
    B. Prayer
    C. Thought to Remember

Display visual 4 of the visuals packet and let it remain before the class. The visual is shown on page 37.

Introduction

Looking eastward from their highland pasture, Abraham and Lot saw the valley of the Jordan. It was "well watered every where . . . as the garden of the Lord." Lot thought it would be a fine place to live (Genesis 13:10, 11).

That valley must have looked even better to the people of Israel some centuries later, when they came in from the desert and looked westward from the plains of Moab. Many of them had never seen a river; now they saw the Jordan overflowing with life-giving water. For most or all of their lives they had walked among pale gray desert shrubs; now they saw Jericho lying in a valley green with springtime, for spring comes early in that garden spot eight hundred feet below the level of the sea. Like Lot of old, the Hebrew people thought that verdant valley would be a good place to live—and God had said it would be their own. So they moved in.

A. Moving In

Lessons 1-3 have told us how the Hebrews moved into the valley. Lesson 1 told how the spies of Israel ventured into Jericho and escaped with the help of their hostess, Rahab. Lesson 2 told how the overflowing waters of the the Jordan were built into a mountain so the newcomers could walk across a dry riverbed. Lesson 3 told how the wall of Jericho fell down flat, and how half a million fighting men raced across the fallen bricks and wiped out the city.

From Jericho the fighting men went on to capture more of their promised land. They lost one battle when one man of Israel was guilty of outrageous sin; but the sinner was detected and destroyed, and then the others went back to fight and win (Joshua 7, 8). They were tricked into a treaty by crafty men of Gibeon (Joshua 9). With these exceptions, the men of Israel went from victory to victory, for the Lord was with them. He had decreed destruction for those depraved tribes of Canaan, and destroyed they were.

It was a war of infantry, slogging on slow feet from place to place. The Lord had said, "Every place that the sole of your foot shall tread upon, that have I given unto you" (Joshua 1:3), and their feet did tread on all the land they conquered. So it was about seven years before they could stop fighting. They distributed among their tribes the land they had conquered. The division is recorded in chapters 13-22 of Joshua.

B. Lesson Background

The goodness and power of God were evident in the help He gave to Israel in the invasion and conquest. The people of Israel were so deeply impressed that they were faithful in their worship and obedience. The heathen around them were impressed too. None of them wanted to attack those fearsome newcomers who had wiped out so many heathen. So Israel lived in peace in the new land for a long time, while Joshua grew old (Joshua 23:1). But Joshua could not live forever, and he knew it. With more than a hundred years behind him, he wanted to impress his people once more with God's power and their duty. So He called a meeting.

I. God's Word
(Joshua 24:1, 2, 11-13)

It is puzzling to see that chapters 23 and 24 of Joshua are so much alike. The explanation seems to be that chapter 23 records Joshua's meeting with leaders of the nation, while chapter 24 records a mass meeting of all the people. As the president of the United States consults leaders of Congress before he announces a policy publicly, Joshua made his presentation to leaders of the nation and gained their support before he talked to the whole nation. Our lesson goes straight to his talk to all the people.

A. The Meeting (v. 1)

1. And Joshua gathered all the tribes of Israel to Shechem, and called for the elders of Israel, and for their heads, and for their judges, and for their officers; and they presented themselves before God.

Joshua gathered all the tribes, plus the leaders he had gathered before. Shechem was a central place located between two mountains. It was a good place to speak to a big crowd. Perhaps that was why it had been chosen for a reading of the law soon after Israel arrived in the promised land (Joshua 8:33-35). It was also the place where God had spoken to Abraham when that patriarch arrived in the promised land (Genesis 12:6, 7). Now Joshua called the millions of Abraham's descendants to hear God's message to them. They did not just meet with Joshua; *they presented themselves before God.*

B. The Speaker (v. 2)

2. And Joshua said unto all the people, Thus saith the Lord God of Israel.

It was Joshua's voice the people heard, but the words he spoke were the words of God. Speaking as a prophet, Joshua quoted the words God gave to him. In the verses that follow, *I* is not Joshua; it is God. The Lord began by recounting the history of His people from the time of Abraham. The Lord had brought Abraham from Mesopotamia to the land of promise, and later had brought Abraham's descendants from Egypt to that same land (vv. 2-10). The next part of our printed text takes up the story as these emigrants from Egypt crossed the Jordan.

C. God's Help (vv. 11-13)

11. And ye went over Jordan, and came unto Jericho: and the men of Jericho fought against you, the Amorites, and the Perizzites, and the Canaanites, and the Hittites, and the Girgashites, the Hivites, and the Jebusites; and I delivered them into your hand.

Last week we considered the battle of Jericho, the first city the Israelites took when they crossed the Jordan. *The men of Jericho fought* as well as they could; but their fighting was futile because God had already terrified them by many miraculous kinds of help to Israel, and because God demolished their wall and let the army of Israel take them by surprise.

The other tribes mentioned in verse 11 were not in Jericho, but they all fought against Israel one or a few at a time through the next seven years. Their fighting was as futile as the fighting of the men of Jericho. Israel won victory after victory, not because the men of Israel were such fierce fighters, but because God *delivered* each enemy to them.

12. And I sent the hornet before you, which drave them out from before you, even the two kings of the Amorites; but not with thy sword, nor with thy bow.

The Hebrew word for *hornet* appears only three times in the Old Testament. Each time it is used as it is here, meaning an instrument God used to drive out the enemies of Israel. Some students think it is to be taken literally, meaning that God sent such a plague of hornets that the heathen enemies were forced to leave the area. However, the historical record in the book of Joshua does not record such a plague. It indicates rather, as does verse 11 of our text, that each tribe fought the Hebrews, though feebly and futilely. Some students suggest that *the hornet* may be a figure of speech for the fear that tormented the heathen when the Hebrews came near. In our text for September 4 we saw how Rahab described that fear (Joshua 2:8-11). The Hebrew word for *hornet* comes from a verb that means to hit, strike, or smite. Possibly it means that the enemies were so terror-stricken that they could not fight effectively, or possibly it refers to an epidemic of disease that struck down the enemies. In any case, the point is that the defeat of

---

How to Say It

Amorites.   *Am*-uh-rites.
Canaanites.   *Kay*-nan-ites.
Euphrates.   U-*fray*-teez.
Girgashites.   *Gur*-ga-shites (*G* as in *get*).
Hittites.   *Hit*-ites or *Hit*-tites.
Hivites.   *Hi*-vites.
Jebusites.   *Jeb*-yuh-sites.
Perizzites.   *Pair*-iz-zites.
Shechem.   *Shee*-kem or *Shek*-em.
Sihon.   *Sye*-hun.
Terah.   *Tee*-ruh.

Israel's enemies was due to the Lord more than to the *sword* and *bow* of Israel. This began even before Israel crossed the Jordan. *The two kings of the Amorites,* Sihon and Og, were routed on the east bank (Numbers 21:21-35).

13. And I have given you a land for which ye did not labor, and cities which ye built not, and ye dwell in them; of the vineyards and olive-yards which ye planted not do ye eat.

The victorious Israelites were not pioneers in a wild, rough land. They took over fields already cleared of brush and stones, terraced on the hillsides, plowed and planted without any work by those who now possessed them. The Israelites had lived in tents for forty years; now they took over whole cities of houses furnished and ready to be lived in. They took over fruit trees and grapevines mature and bearing fruit. All of these were gifts from God.

II. Joshua's Word (Joshua 24:14, 15)

In verses 2-13, Joshua quoted the words of God as God gave them to him. The *I* in those verses means God, not Joshua. But in verses 14 and 15, Joshua spoke in his own person. The *me* in this paragraph means Joshua, not God. But still Joshua was God's prophet, speaking as God directed him.

A. Serve God Only (v. 14)

14. Now therefore fear the Lord, and serve him in sincerity and in truth; and put away the gods which your fathers served on the other side of the flood, and in Egypt; and serve ye the LORD.

To *fear the Lord* is not to run away from Him and try to hide, as guilty sinners sometimes do. It is to seek His presence and His will with reverence and awe; it is to be afraid to do wrong. To *serve him* is to worship and obey Him. Joshua appealed to the people to do this *in sincerity and in truth*: not with formal ceremonies only, but willingly and gladly in all the acts of daily living. God's power is plain in verses 11-13, giving ample reason to regard Him with reverence. His goodness to His people is no less plain in those verses, leading good people to obey Him with gratitude and love.

The Lord is the only real God there is. Other so-called gods are not gods at all. Terah, Abraham's father, was among the *fathers* who served other gods (Joshua 24:2). He lived in Ur, where the moon was worshiped along with many imaginary gods. The location of Ur is described as the *other side of the flood,* but the word for *flood* is literally *river.* In the Bible the Euphrates sometimes is called simply "the river." The Hebrew term for *other side* is used loosely. In the book of Joshua it is sometimes translated *this side.* Here the meaning seems to be simply that Terah and other *fathers* lived beside the Euphrates. Now Joshua urged his people to have nothing to do with the non-gods that were worshiped long before in that faraway place. Furthermore, he urged them to renounce the non-gods the older ones had lived among *in Egypt.* Nowhere in the world or out of it is there any other real God, so *serve ye the Lord!*

B. Choose (v. 15a)

15a. And if it seem evil unto you to serve the LORD, choose you this day whom ye will serve; whether the gods which your fathers served that were on the other side of the flood, or the gods of the Amorites, in whose land ye dwell.

Joshua acknowledged that the people were free to choose. The Lord was the only real God, and these people were indebted to Him for freedom from slavery in Egypt, guidance and provision through the desert, and victory in the promised land. Both good sense and gratitude would lead them to worship and serve the Lord "in sincerity and in truth." But the Lord demanded that His people obey His law, that they live upright and moral lives, that they be good and do good. If that seemed *evil* to anyone, he was free to choose another way. There was the moon worship of faraway Ur, and there was the Baal worship of the nearby Amorites. Neither of these put any restraint on greed and cheating, booze and promiscuous sex. Make up your mind!

C. Joshua's Choice (v. 15b)

15b. But as for me and my house, we will serve the LORD.

Joshua and his family had made their choice. They had chosen good sense and gratitude. They had chosen truth and right. They had chosen upright, moral living. They had chosen *the Lord!*

THE MARK OF GREATNESS

Dave Dravecky's life is one of the great heartbreak stories in modern major league baseball. Dravecky, who is a Christian, was pitching for the San Francisco Giants when his career was cut short by cancer. In October, 1988, he had surgery to remove a tumor from his pitching arm.

Amazingly, ten months later Dravecky pitched and won a game. In his next game, however, his arm broke as he made a pitch in the sixth inning. After his arm was broken accidentally two months later, his "miraculous" comeback had to be abandoned. Eventually, doctors would have to amputate his arm in order to save his life. When asked about his faith in the face of the cancer that destroyed his career, Dave Dravecky said, "My focus is not just on how I can become healed, but how I can serve God through all this."

Real greatness is seen in the decision stated by Joshua in our lesson today, and expressed in similar words by Dave Dravecky: "Regardless of what may happen to me, I will serve God."

We may be unable to control history, our health, or the actions of others, but each of us can decide to serve God regardless of circumstances or consequences. This is true greatness.

—C. R. B.

III. The People's Pledge
(Joshua 24:16, 22-25)

We are left to imagine how the whole huge assembly of Israel expressed its answer to Joshua. Perhaps some well-known leader took it on himself to speak for the nation, or perhaps a group of leaders conferred together and put forward one of them to say what all were thinking. When the spokesman made his statement, the people could express their assent by shouting, "Amen!" In some such way an answer came from the huge assembly, and it is recorded for us.

A. Prompt Pledge (v. 16)

16. And the people answered and said, God forbid that we should forsake the LORD, to serve other gods.

Forsake the Lord? Serve other gods? Such ideas were utterly abhorrent to these people, and their spokesman said so in the plainest terms. He went on to give reasons for being faithful to the Lord: He had set them free from Egypt; He had preserved them in the wilderness; He had secured the promised land for them (vv. 17, 18). These were the same reasons the Lord had given through Joshua (vv. 5-13).

Perhaps Joshua perceived that the answer was too quick and easy, not thoughtful enough. Instead of accepting it with thanks and approval, he hurled back an unexpected challenge: "Ye cannot serve the Lord" (v. 19).

Now certainly the people stopped to think. Joshua had been urging them to serve the Lord. They had promised to do it, and now he said they couldn't. What could he mean?

Joshua explained. These people could not serve the Lord because He is holy and He is jealous. He will not accept halfhearted service or worship shared with imaginary gods. He will not tolerate sin. If the people would violate their

pledge and do wrong, He would hurt them instead of helping them (vv. 19, 20).

More thoughtfully the people reaffirmed their promise: "Nay; but we will serve the Lord" (v. 21).

B. Witnesses (v. 22)

22. And Joshua said unto the people, Ye are witnesses against yourselves that ye have chosen you the LORD, to serve him. And they said, We are witnesses.

When an important contract is made, disinterested parties are called to witness the signing of it. In this case there were no disinterested parties present, so Joshua called the people themselves to be witnesses of their pledge. If they would break the pledge, they would be condemned by their own words. Solemnly the people accepted the responsibility. If the promise should be broken, they would testify against themselves.

C. Repeated Pledge (vv. 23, 24)

23. Now therefore put away, said he, the strange gods which are among you, and incline your heart unto the LORD God of Israel.

It seems that the pledge was already being broken in some degree: some *strange gods* were *among* the people. Joshua urged them to get rid of every god that was *strange*, or foreign, whether Mesopotamian, Egyptian, or Amorite (vv. 14, 15). The people of Israel should give their hearts completely to *the Lord God of Israel*.

24. And the people said unto Joshua, The Lord our God will we serve, and his voice will we obey.

The people reaffirmed the pledge they had made twice before (vv. 16-18, 21). They said they would without fail be loyal to *the Lord*.

THE IMPORTANCE OF PILOTS

Air traffic controllers lost radio contact with a Royal Air Force jet fighter while it was flying five hundred miles an hour at thirty-one thousand feet over Salisbury, England. An American

"I"

Prayer of
COMMITMENT

The dearest idol
I have known,
Whate'er that idol be,

Help me to tear it
from Thy throne,
And worship only
Thee.

WILLIAM COWPER

visual 4

pilot flying in the area was asked to make a visual inspection of the fighter. He discovered the fighter's cockpit canopy to be missing, as were the pilot's seat and the pilot.

The American pilot flew his plane alongside the fighter for seven hundred miles until it ran out of fuel and crashed into the sea. The British pilot's body was later found near Salisbury, where radio contact had first been lost.

Some persons are like the pilotless plane, moving along through life apparently quite well, generally staying on course, but with no controlling spirit to guide them safely to their destination. As long as no obstacle gets in front of them or no unforeseen crisis develops, they seem to function normally. Ultimately, however, such persons will crash-land with disastrous results.

The people of Israel committed themselves to serve the Lord, and to obey His voice. Those today who seek God's guidance, and who thoughtfully decide to submit to His control, will be able to avoid "mid-air collisions" as well as the final "crash-landing."   —C. R. B.

D. Formal Covenant (v. 25)

25. So Joshua made a covenant with the people that day, and set them a statute and an ordinance in Shechem.

We cannot be sure of the precise meaning of the words *statute* and *ordinance*, but the main thought of the verse is clear. Joshua put the people's pledge into a formal *covenant*, an agreement or contract, and put it in writing (v. 26). The covenant reaffirmed the one made at Sinai by the fathers of these people (Exodus 19:8).

Joshua erected a monument as a permanent reminder of the covenant reaffirmed. The meeting adjourned. The people went home, pledged anew to be faithful to the Lord (vv. 26-28).

Conclusion

The people of Israel kept their promise as long as Joshua lived, and longer. They were faithful to the Lord as long as they were guided by men who remembered the mighty miracles that brought them into the promised land (Judges 2:7).

In next week's lesson we shall see how later generations abandoned the sacred covenant.

A. Our Choices

We who are Christians have made our choice to serve the Lord, but keeping our pledge to Him brings us to smaller choices day by day.

Now that the children are away, you're getting rid of that second car. You can tell a buyer that it runs all right, which is true; or you can add that

it uses an outrageous amount of oil, which also is true. What do you choose to say?

You hear a very ugly rumor about the woman next door, whom you don't like very well. You can say you don't believe it; you can say nothing; you can repeat the rumor to a few close friends. What do you choose?

Some very good friends invite you on a Sunday trip to see some beautiful autumn foliage. Will they stop for church along the way? No, no; they really don't have time for that. What do you choose?

The PTA is planning some gambling games for its carnival. Such games are illegal in your state, but the authorities will look the other way. You can help with the planning; you can say nothing; you can protest against teaching children that it's OK to break the law if you can get away with it. What do you choose?

People are asking to have the Bible removed from the school library. They are influential people; probably your voice would have no effect. Besides, who ever reads the Bible in a school library? You can ignore the matter; or you can talk with the librarian, the principal, the school board. What do you choose?

Perhaps you will not face any of these choices this week, but you will face others. Choose thoughtfully.

B. Prayer

Long ago we pledged our loyalty to You, our Heavenly Father; and now we promise anew to seek Your will in every choice we make. In Jesus' name we pray. Amen.

C. Thought to Remember

"We will serve the Lord."

Home Daily Bible Readings

Monday, Sept 19—Praise for God's Care (Psalm 116:12-19)

Tuesday, Sept 20—Joshua's Reminder of God's Protection (Joshua 23:1-8)

Wednesday, Sept. 21—Joshua's Charge to Remain Faithful (Joshua 23:9-11, 14-16)

Thursday, Sept 22—Joshua's Recall of Their Deliverance History (Joshua 24:1-10)

Friday, Sept 23—Joshua's Call for Commitment (Joshua 24:11-15)

Saturday, Sept 24—The Promise to Serve God (Joshua 24:16-23)

Sunday, Sept 25—The Stone of Witness (Joshua 24:24-31)

Learning by Doing

This page contains an alternate lesson plan emphasizing learning activities. Classes desiring such student involvement will find these suggestions helpful.

Learning Goals

As students participate in today's class session, they should:

1. List the spiritual choices that were presented to the Israelites, and some that Christians confront today.

2. Recommit themselves to their choice to serve God only.

Into the Lesson

Ask class members to mention areas of everyday life, regarding which many choices are open to us. (Examples may include markets for grocery shopping, malls where we can buy clothes, gas stations for the purchase of fuel, places for dining out, etc.) Are all of these choices good for us? Have your students ever been in a situation where the choices open to them were bewildering or bad instead of good?

Tell your students that today's session explores the spiritual choices that the ancient Israelites faced, and those that God's people face today.

Into the Word

Once again write this unit's summary words, one under the other, on your chalkboard: *Risk, Obedience, Victory, Service*.

Beside *Risk* write "Lesson One" and ask a volunteer to tell what that lesson taught about risk.

Write "Lesson Two" beside *Obedience* and ask someone else to summarize that lesson.

Write "Lesson Three" beside *Victory* and have a student summarize that lesson.

Then use material under the heading "A. Moving In" in the "Introduction" section (page 34) to connect Lesson Three with this one. Briefly mention the events recorded in the book of Joshua that occurred between the fall of Jericho and the event in today's lesson.

Tell the class that today's lesson emphasizes "service." (Write "Lesson Four" beside *Service*. Have a student read Joshua 24:1-27, and instruct the others to listen for what this text teaches about serving God.

Next, distribute the questions listed below. You may want to discuss these with the whole class in the order shown. Or you may choose to divide the class into groups of five to seven and have each group discuss a different question. After about six or eight minutes, reconvene the class into one large group and hear answers to all the questions.

1. Why did Joshua remind the people of the great heroes from their past? What could be learned from remembering the stories of the patriarchs (vv. 2-4), Moses (vv. 5-7)? Their own possession of the promised land (vv. 8-13)?

2. What choices did Joshua present to the people (vv. 14, 15)? How did the people respond to this challenge (vv. 16-18)? Why?

3. Why did Joshua seem to reject their initial response (vv. 19, 20)? How would you summarize this challenge to the people?

4. As recorded in Joshua 24, how many times did Joshua prompt the people to proclaim their faithfulness to God? Why did he make them repeat their vows so often? By what physical signs did Joshua summarize their commitment? What was the value of these?

5. What clues about the people's faithfulness to God do you see in Joshua's comments (vv. 14, 20, 23)? Given the many ways God had worked among them and their forefathers, how could they still have a problem with making Him Lord? What does this teach you about faithfulness? Peer pressure? Sin and temptation?

Into Life

Discuss these questions with the class:

1. Why do you suppose Joshua said, "Choose this day whom you will *serve*"? Why didn't he say, "Choose whom you will *believe*"? Or "Choose whom you will *worship*"? What is significant about the idea of service?

2. In a sense, it may be said that each of us is serving someone or something. What are some choices available to people in our culture as to whom or what they will serve?

Perhaps you should list on the chalkboard the answers to this second question. Keep prodding the class for responses until you have a couple of dozen. Then, if you have time, ask class members to decide on the six or eight that are most chosen by people today. Put a star beside each of these items on the board.

Ask class members if they have been tempted to choose these starred items instead of God. How have they been able to choose God instead?

End with a time of sentence prayers, during which class members will reaffirm their commitment to serve God only.

Let's Talk It Over

The questions on this page are designed to encourage review of the lesson Scriptures and to promote discussion of the lesson by the class. The answers provided are only discussion starters. Let your class talk it over from there.

1. The land the Israelites were given was settled, prepared, and cultivated for human habitation and use. In what ways is the spiritual heritage we receive upon becoming Christians similar to the Israelites' experience?

We are heirs of the accumulated knowledge, religious liberty, and spiritual victories provided by nearly two thousand years of Christianity. We have access to the Bible, which has been preserved, translated, and explained by generations of believers before us. The theological treatises, devotional writings, and hymns of godly men and women of the past enrich our faith. On a different level, we have inherited blessings in our local congregation. Previous generations of members labored to establish the congregation, erect its building, faithfully conduct its programs of teaching and worship, and keep it going through difficult times. We have come, as young Christians, to benefit from their labors.

2. Joshua's challenge to the people to choose whether they would serve the Lord or the imaginary deities of the heathen is a challenge that needs to be sounded in the church on a regular basis. Why is this so?

The Israelites were not to think they could divide their loyalties between the Lord and heathen deities. If they were to choose to serve the Lord, that would mean breaking off their devotion to other gods. Today there are members of the church who want to hold on to heathen practices such as astrology, or maintain an idolatrous and futile attachment to money, or continue a sexually immoral life-style. These persons are deluded if they believe that God will accept such diluted discipleship. They must understand that God places an exclusive claim on their allegiance, and that such "friendship of the world is enmity with God" (James 4:4).

3. Some may think it a bit presumptuous for Joshua to have said, "As for me *and my house*, we will serve the Lord." Many parents today back away from imposing religious values on their children. But how is Joshua's declaration one that modern parents would do well to imitate?

We recognize that children must come to the point of making their own decisions as to whether or not they will follow Jesus Christ. But we certainly should not hesitate to influence them for Christ while they are young. They will be subjected to other philosophical influences in school, through entertainment media, and by friends. Our influence must not be imposition; our encouragement must not be coercion. Instead, by exposing them to the Word of God, the power of prayer, and the witness of our own Christ-centered behavior, we should aim to demonstrate to them the superiority and desirability of the Christian life.

4. Why must we not give prospected Christians the impression that taking Christ as Savior and Lord is an easy choice?

When the Israelites proclaimed that they would serve God, Joshua made it plain that serving God demanded their absolute commitment to Him, which required the forsaking of other gods. When we urge people to accept Jesus Christ as Savior, we dare not neglect telling them that that decision will of necessity involve their turning away from certain habits and practices. Of course, we should place strong emphasis on the blessings that accompany such a commitment, but we do them a disservice if we fail to call them to absolute allegiance to Christ. We could say that Joshua urged the Israelites to "count the cost" of vowing their allegiance to God. This is what Jesus urged the people to do as they considered becoming His disciples (see Luke 14:25-33). And it is what we also must do.

5. Joshua told the people that their promise to serve the Lord made them witnesses against themselves. Could we say that our public confession of faith in Christ makes us witnesses against ourselves? If so, how?

This may seem a rather negative way of viewing our confession of faith, but it does demonstrate the seriousness of that act. The biblical references to the public confession of faith in Christ (Matthew 10:32, 33; Romans 10:9, 10) indicate the significance of the act. Thereby we are identifying ourselves with Jesus Christ and committing ourselves to His cause. We need to keep that in mind during those times when we are tempted to disloyalty toward our Lord. Since we have confessed Him, let us live in consistency with our confession.

Israel's Tragic Pattern of Life

DEVOTIONAL READING: Psalm 81:6-16.

LESSON SCRIPTURE: Judges 2:6—3:6.

PRINTED TEXT: Judges 2:11-19.

Judges 2:11-19

11 And the children of Israel did evil in the sight of the LORD, and served Baalim:

12 And they forsook the LORD God of their fathers, which brought them out of the land of Egypt, and followed other gods, of the gods of the people that were round about them, and bowed themselves unto them, and provoked the LORD to anger.

13 And they forsook the LORD, and served Baal and Ashtaroth.

14 And the anger of the LORD was hot against Israel, and he delivered them into the hands of spoilers that spoiled them, and he sold them into the hands of their enemies round about, so that they could not any longer stand before their enemies.

15 Whithersoever they went out, the hand of the LORD was against them for evil, as the LORD had said, and as the LORD had sworn unto them: and they were greatly distressed.

16 Nevertheless the LORD raised up judges, which delivered them out of the hand of those that spoiled them.

17 And yet they would not hearken unto their judges, but they went a whoring after other gods, and bowed themselves unto them: they turned quickly out of the way which their fathers walked in, obeying the commandments of the LORD; but they did not so.

18 And when the LORD raised them up judges, then the LORD was with the judge, and delivered them out of the hand of their enemies all the days of the judge: for it repented the LORD because of their groanings by reason of them that oppressed them and vexed them.

19 And it came to pass, when the judge was dead, that they returned, and corrupted themselves more than their fathers, in following other gods to serve them, and to bow down unto them; they ceased not from their own doings, nor from their stubborn way.

GOLDEN TEXT: The children of Israel did evil in the sight of the LORD, and served Baalim: and they forsook the LORD God of their fathers, which brought them out of the land of Egypt, and followed other gods, of the gods of the people that were round about them, and bowed themselves unto them, and provoked the LORD to anger.—Judges 2:11, 12.

From the Conquest to the Kingdom
Unit 2: The Rule of the Judges
(Lessons 5, 6)

Lesson Aims

After this lesson students should be able to:

1. Recall at least one improvement in their own Christian living during the past year.

2. Specify at least one improvement to be made in the coming year.

Lesson Outline

INTRODUCTION
    A. Israel's Climb
    B. Israel at the Top
    C. Preparing to Plunge
  I. THE PLUNGE (Judges 2:11-13)
    A. Evil and Idolatry (v. 11)
    B. Provoking the Lord (v. 12)
    C. Mrs. Baal (v. 13)
      Trying to Live in Two Worlds
 II. DISASTER (Judges 2:14, 15)
    A. The Spoilers (v. 14)
    B. A Promise Kept (v. 15)
III. SUMMARY OF THREE CENTURIES (Judges 2:16-19)
    A. Deliverance (v. 16)
    B. Downhill Again (v. 17)
    C. The Lord's Loving Help (v. 18)
    D. Another Plunge (v. 19)
      After Other Gods
CONCLUSION
    A. Which Way?
    B. The Goal and the Way
    C. Prayer
    D. Thought to Remember

Display visual 5 of the visuals packet, and refer to it specifically when considering verse 19. The visual is shown on page 45.

Introduction

Going downhill is easier, but going uphill is safer. On the climbing road we use more energy, but control is easy. On the downward slope we gain speed but lose control. The runner is more likely to stumble and fall; the wheeled vehicle may leave the road on a curve.

This is true in the moral realm as well. It takes effort to be upright and noble; but on the downhill side one coasts easily from small lies to big lies, from minor cheating to major fraud.

A. Israel's Climb

Israel's journey from the land of Egypt to the promised land was uphill all the way. The generation that started the journey lacked the courage and stamina to complete it quickly. Fearful and faltering at the border of the promised land, the people of Israel were turned back and made to live the next forty years in the desert (Numbers 13, 14).

The Israelites who grew up in the desert were toughened by their rugged life. Better than that, they learned to depend on the Lord, who supplied manna from Heaven and water from the rock. Trusting in the Lord, they advanced boldly into the promised land and destroyed nations much greater and stronger than they were (Deuteronomy 9:1-3).

B. Israel at the Top

In about seven years the people of Israel captured as much of the promised land as they were ready to use. Heathen tribes still surrounded them, but they divided the land and settled down to farming (Joshua 13—19). The people worshiped God and obeyed Him faithfully for a long time (Joshua 23:1). Joshua's farewell address exhorted them to continue their faithfulness, and they promised that they would (Joshua 24). They kept their promise even after Joshua was dead (Judges 2:7). Peace and prosperity prevailed. Israel lived on the summit for possibly sixty years or more after the long climb ended and the land was theirs.

C. Preparing to Plunge

Two things conspired to prepare Israel for a plunge from the happy summit of righteousness, prosperity, and peace.

First, the people failed to finish the job. They had been told to destroy or drive out all the heathen in their new land (Deuteronomy 7:1-5). But when Israel was firmly in control, it seemed unnecessary to kill the defeated people. Certainly it was more profitable to let them live and make

How to Say It

ASHTORETH.   *Ash*-toe-reth.
ASHTOROTH.   *Ash*-ta-roth.
BAALIM.   *Bay*-uh-lim.
CANAANITES.   *Kay*-nan-ites.
MIDIANTIES.   *Mid*-e-un-ites.
MOABITES.   *Mo*-ub-ites.
OTHNIEL.   *Oth*-ni-el.
PHILISTINES.   Fi-*liss*-teens or *Fil*-iss-teens.

them pay tribute. So many of the Israelites became accustomed to heathen neighbors and heathen ways (Judges 1:21—2:5).

Second, the passing of years brought the passing of all the people who remembered how God had helped them in the long climb from slavery in Egypt to victory in the promised land. A new generation grew up in the land, and they knew only peace and comfort and the support of tribute from heathen neighbors. Accustomed to easy living, these Israelites lacked the strength of their fathers and grandfathers. Worse, they lacked their fathers' steadfast trust in the Lord (Judges 2:10).

I. The Plunge
(Judges 2:11-13)

It seems that human beings are designed to be moving. Spiritually and morally, if we stop going forward, we begin to go backward; if we stop climbing, we start descending. We have guessed that Israel may have been at the top for sixty years, but that is only a guess. Whether that time was longer or shorter, it was far too short. Then came the downward plunge.

A. Evil and Idolatry (v. 11)

11. And the children of Israel did evil in the sight of the LORD, and served Baalim.

Of course the change was not so abrupt as it sounds in this verse. There must have been a very gradual change in attitude. Perhaps it began with a few rebellious teenagers who kept on sowing wild oats when they grew up.

How could such a slide get started? The following scenario is purely imaginary, but it illustrates what may have happened.

Waking at midnight, an eighteen-year-old Hebrew heard faint sounds of music and happy shouting from a heathen festival a mile away. The next week he took his flock to a water hole just as a heathen boy arrived with his sheep. Curious, the Hebrew asked about the festival.

The answer told of things that certainly would not be done in worship of the Lord. The Hebrew boy could hardly believe they were done in any worship. "You're kidding!" he charged.

The heathen boy shrugged. "Why don't you come and see?"

Perhaps not at the very next festival, but in time the Hebrew got one or two other daring young men to go with him. What they saw was more shocking than what he had heard. The beef was good, the wine was plentiful, the fun was uproarious, the entertainment was X-rated, and the women were seductive. The boys left with their minds in a whirl, but they went back

to another festival and took some other fellows along. Not wanting to be freeloaders, they took a calf from somebody's father's herd to be sacrificed. And after several such festivals, they got drunk enough to join in the sex orgy.

In some such way, the downward slide began in various places around Israel. After such festivals, the worship of the Lord not only seemed dull, but also made the boys feel guilty—so they dropped out. Those were the days when every man did what was right in his own eyes (Judges 17:6). No one disciplined the defectors, and the downward slide gained momentum.

Baalim is the plural of *Baal,* a name given to various idols and imaginary gods of the heathen of Canaan. Each tribe might have its own Baal. Ceremonies of worship might vary, but none of the Baalim had any regard for the Lord's standards of honesty, decency, and morality. Those who *served Baalim* also *did evil in the sight of the Lord* in other ways as well.

B. Provoking the Lord (v. 12)

12. And they forsook the LORD God of their fathers, which brought them out of the land of Egypt, and followed other gods, of the gods of the people that were round about them, and bowed themselves unto them, and provoked the LORD to anger.

Those who joined in heathen rites did not feel comfortable in meetings to worship the Lord, especially if God's law was taught and sin was rebuked. Increasingly *they forsook the Lord God of their fathers,* forgetting that they were indebted to Him for their freedom and their prosperity. The first of the Ten Commandments proclaimed, "Thou shalt have no other gods before me" (Exodus 20:3). By ignoring this basic rule, the Israelites *provoked the Lord to anger.* As Joshua had reminded his people, the Lord is holy, and He is jealous (Joshua 24:19).

C. Mrs. Baal (v. 13)

13. And they forsook the LORD, and served Baal and Ashtaroth.

The *Ashtaroth* were imaginary goddesses supposed to be associated with the Baalim. One of the Ashtaroth would be called an Ashtoreth. As each heathen tribe had its own Baal, it had also its own Ashtoreth. Each tribe might represent her by a different idol; but all the heathen tribes regarded her as a very sexy deity.

TRYING TO LIVE IN TWO WORLDS

In tropical American waters lives a strange species of fish, the *Anableps.* It is known as the "four-eyed fish," due to the unusual construction of its eyes. Each of its two eyes has an upper and a lower part, each part functioning independently of the other. As the fish swims at the surface of the water, the upper part of its eyes project above the water. This enables the fish to search for food and watch for enemies. At the same time the lower part enables it to survey its underwater environment. In a sense, the *Anableps* lives in two worlds, something few of God's creatures are able to do.

Some persons try to live in two worlds, spiritually speaking. Wanting to enjoy all this world offers, they conduct their business and daily affairs as if God did not exist. By occasionally "looking up" and acknowledging God, however, they convince themselves that they are maintaining a vital relationship with Him.

If, after the death of Joshua's generation, Israel practiced similar self-deception, in time they completely *forsook* the Lord to serve Baal. Let us not be deceived into thinking we can live safely in two worlds. "Set your affection on things above," Paul said, "not on things on the earth" (Colossians 3:2).   —C. R. B.

II. Disaster
(Judges 2:14, 15)

As God revealed himself to Moses, He is "merciful and gracious, long-suffering, and abundant in goodness and truth, keeping mercy for thousands, forgiving iniquity and transgression and sin" (Exodus 34:6, 7). We do not know how long He tolerated Israel's defection, or how complete that defection was. But with all His mercy, God "will by no means clear the guilty" (Exodus 34:7). Sooner or later, those who persist in guilt must face the anger they have provoked.

A. The Spoilers (v. 14)

14. And the anger of the LORD was hot against Israel, and he delivered them into the hands of spoilers that spoiled them, and he sold them into the hands of their enemies round about, so that they could not any longer stand before their enemies.

The Lord's method of punishment was simple. He had been supporting Israel against all enemies; now He simply switched His support to the other side.

Of course this was due in part to natural causes. The Israelites of this generation were soft. They had lived all their lives in peace and comfort. They knew nothing of war. They had no military organization or leaders. When armed marauders swept into their land, what could they do but run for the hills, leaving their homes and fields to be spoiled? So the marauders drove off sheep and cattle, took away wheat and barley

from threshing floors and granaries, helped themselves to ripened fruit. When they were gone, the people came back from the hills to find themselves destitute.

The statement that God *sold them into the hands of their enemies* does not mean the enemies made any payment to God. It says merely that God handed them over to the enemies as if they had been sold. The natural weakness of the Israelites may have been enough to accomplish this. If not, God used other methods as they were needed. It is not recorded, however, that He did for the heathen any such mighty miracles as He had done for the people of Israel.

B. A Promise Kept (v. 15)

15. Whithersoever they went out, the hand of the LORD was against them for evil, as the LORD had said, and as the LORD had sworn unto them: and they were greatly distressed.

Not always did the people of Israel run for the hills when enemies approached. Sometimes they *went out* to battle. But as *the hand of the Lord* had been with them in the conquest of their land, now it was *against them*. As they had won before, now they lost. The Lord's hand is the decisive factor in any struggle in which He takes a part. The people should have known that God would be against them when they had turned against Him. Defeat by enemies was one of many ways He had promised to punish their disobedience (Leviticus 26:14-25).

III. Summary of Three Centuries
(Judges 2:16-19)

These four verses summarize the history of Israel for almost three hundred years. It can be done thus briefly because basically the same events happened over and over, only with wide variations. Many different times Israel turned away from God and was troubled by "spoilers" (v. 14). The spoilers were different groups with different ways. Verse 14 seems to speak of raiding parties that came and went, taking spoil with them; but at one time the Canaanites dominated a part of Israel for twenty years (Judges 4:1-3). Seldom if ever did a spoiler gain control of the whole country. The Canaanites dominated the north part; the Philistines harassed the south; the Midianites came across the Jordan to strike at Israel's heartland. Periods of oppression and periods of peace are recorded separately as if one had followed another, but some of them may have overlapped. There may have been different oppressors in different parts of Israel at the same time; or there may have been different judges at the same time in different areas.

A. Deliverance (v. 16)

16. Nevertheless the LORD raised up judges, which delivered them out of the hand of those that spoiled them.

When spoilers brought them to poverty and misery, the people of Israel remembered who had helped them before. Again they appealed to the Lord, and He provided a leader to help them get rid of the spoilers. These leaders are called *judges*, but they were very different in their personalities and their methods. Gideon was a distinguished military leader who turned down the invitation to rule Israel when victory was won. Deborah was more like what we call a judge. She held court under a palm tree (Judges 4:4, 5). Shamgar was an individual hero who brought relief by his single-handed conquest (Judges 3:31). There were many more judges in three hundred years, and no two of them were alike.

B. Downhill Again (v. 17)

17. And yet they would not hearken unto their judges, but they went a whoring after other gods, and bowed themselves unto them: they turned quickly out of the way which their fathers walked in, obeying the commandments of the LORD; but they did not so.

The people listened to their leaders till the spoilers were gone, and perhaps for some years longer. But all too soon they lapsed again into idol worship and wickedness instead of going on in the godly way of *their fathers* who had lived in the time of Joshua. Then the Lord sent spoilers again. Israel's forsaking of the Lord to worship idols is compared to infidelity in a marriage.

C. The Lord's Loving Help (v. 18)

18. And when the LORD raised them up judges, then the LORD was with the judge, and delivered them out of the hand of their enemies all the days of the judge: for it repented the LORD because of their groanings by reason of them that oppressed them and vexed them.

"This hurts me worse than it does you." So said the old-fashioned father as he applied the paddle or switch. The paddled child never believed it, of course—till he grew up and became a parent. Then he knew it was true. Likewise the Father in Heaven was grieved by the pain of His children on earth, though He himself sent the spoilers to inflict the pain. When the punished children in their groaning turned to the Lord, admitting their sin and pleading of relief, the Lord raised up a judge to lead in defeating the spoilers. *The Lord was with the judge* to help defeat the enemies, and to exert a godly influence on the people when the oppression was ended.

visual 5

Chapter 3 gives an example. Idolatrous Israel was punished by an invasion from Mesopotamia, and oppressed for eight years. When the suffering people cried to the Lord, He raised up Othniel not only to lead in defeating the invaders, but also to lead in loyalty to the Lord after the invaders were gone. So Israel was true to the Lord and at peace for forty years, till Othniel died (Judges 3:7-11).

D. Another Plunge (v. 19)

19. And it came to pass, when the judge was dead, that they returned, and corrupted themselves more than their fathers, in following other gods to serve them, and to bow down unto them; they ceased not from their own doings, nor from their stubborn way.

Look again at the example in chapter 3. After forty years of peace and prosperity with Othniel, the people of Israel lapsed into sin and idolatry again. This time the Moabites and some allies moved in, and for eighteen years the Israelites had to give up produce and livestock in tribute to Moab (Judges 3:12-14).

Would the people of Israel never learn? No, not in three hundred years. When God blessed them with peace and plenty, in time they pursued pleasure rather than righteousness. Pursuing pleasure, they fell into immorality and idolatry. Then came the spoilers, bringing oppression and misery. Misery brought the sinners to grieve over their sin and turn away from it, appealing to the Lord for relief. So the gracious Lord provided a judge, a leader to rally the penitent people and defeat the spoilers. Victory brought the people of Israel to another era of peace and plenty. Why couldn't they stay there?

AFTER OTHER GODS

Israel had a hard time learning that unfaithfulness to God brought them only pain and suffering. Time and again they turned from God to paganism, and each succeeding generation was more corrupt than the one before it.

The United States of America has traditionally been thought of as a "Christian" nation. Whether God considers this to be so is open to question, of course. Some of the founders of the nation were Deists, not Christians; nevertheless, they came to their conclusions about government and society within the context of a culture that was based on Christian principles.

So it is somewhat surprising to most of us to read about the advance of paganism in modern American culture. The evidences are many: In Los Angeles, a coffeehouse is billed as "a meeting place for pagans"; multitudes convene in the desert to be part of "harmonic convergences" of the "spiritual" powers of the universe; "New Age" believers, astrologers, psychics, and dabblers with crystals mix their paganism with small portions of Christian teaching; Eastern religions are building temples all across America.

As America moves from one spiritual aberration to the next, are we different from ancient Israel? It's a question we need to ask.   —C. R. B.

Conclusion

People of our time are moving too. Are we climbing up or coasting down?

As young people we advance automatically. We grow taller and stronger. We get our permanent teeth. We advance in school. We go out and get jobs. As adults we tend to level off. Easily we get into a comfortable rut, and we start downhill before we know it.

A. Which Way?

Which way are you going? Think of yourself as you were a year ago and as you are now.

Are you taking better care of yourself physically? What improvement have you made in diet, exercise, habits of work, recreation, and rest? What improvement can you make now?

Have you grown mentally? What important things have you learned? What do you need to learn now?

Are you kinder, more sympathetic, more forgiving? Do you see some room for improvement?

If you are married, are you more attentive to your mate? Do you see how you can do better?

How about your job? Are you doing it better and more happily, and improving your relationship with fellow workers? Is there some improvement you need to be planning?

Has your praying become more meaningful and more satisfying? Do you need to give it more time and more thought?

Are you finding Bible study more helpful, and doing more of it? Could you get more out of it if you would put more in?

Have you taken any new responsibility in the work of the church? Do you think of one you can take now?

Have you increased your contribution to the Lord's work? You know church expenses are going up just as yours are.

You can think of other ways to compare you as you are with you as you were. Do you think you are climbing up, staying still, or coasting down? What will you be doing from now on?

B. The Goal and the Way

Where are we going? What lies at the end of our upward way? Is it worth the climb?

We are moving toward "the measure of the stature of the fulness of Christ" (Ephesians 4:13-15). Our aim is to be like Jesus; and yes, it is worth all the effort we can make. All the effort we can make is not enough, of course; our transformation depends on the grace of God. But at His bidding, we press on in the upward way. So "when he shall appear, we shall be like him; for we shall see him as he is" (1 John 3:2).

The way to the top is not to exalt ourselves. That is the way down (Luke 14:11). The way to take is the way Jesus took. He "took upon him the form of a servant"; He "humbled himself, and became obedient unto death" (Philippians 2:5-11).

C. Prayer

Father in Heaven, how wonderfully You care for us! With all our failings, Your love will never fail. With praise and gratitude we pledge anew to continue in the upward way, bringing honor and glory to You and Your Son. Amen.

D. Thought to Remember

Keep on climbing.

Home Daily Bible Readings

Monday, Sept. 26—God's Goodness Calls for Faithful Response (Psalm 81:6-16)

Tuesday, Sept. 27—After Joshua's Death, Israel Forsook God (Judges 2:6-12)

Wednesday, Sept. 28—God Sent Judges to Help Israel (Judges 2:13-19)

Thursday, Sept. 29—A Time of Testing (Judges 2:20—3:6)

Friday, Sept. 30—Another Cycle of Apostasy and Deliverance (Judges 3:7-15)

Saturday, Oct. 1—Again God Rescues a Wayward People (Judges 4:4-10)

Sunday, Oct. 2— Israel Known as "a Rebellious People" (Isaiah 30:8-14)

Learning by Doing

This page contains an alternate lesson plan emphasizing learning activities. Classes desiring such student involvement will find these suggestions helpful.

Learning Goals

As students participate in today's class session, they should:

1. Describe the cycle of sin, suffering, and deliverance that characterized the experience of the Israelites in the time of the judges.

2. Compare and contrast this cycle with the experience of Christians today.

3. Determine how to get out or stay out of this cycle of behavior.

Into the Lesson

Divide the class members into groups of from five to seven members each. One half of the groups should discuss the following statement to decide on reasons that prove it to be true:

When we disobey God, we put ourselves in peril. God always punishes disobedience.

The other half of the groups should discuss the following contrasting statement to prove it is true:

Although our sins grieve God, He never gives up on us. As a merciful God, He always provides His children with a way back to Him.

Write the two sentences on your chalkboard or duplicate them onto sheets of paper for distribution to the groups. Allot five minutes for the groups to discuss their statements. When they have come up with their "proofs" (they may use common sense reasons as well as biblical examples), lead the whole class in a discussion along the following lines of thought: "The two sentences seem to contradict each other. Is one right while the other is wrong? Are they both wrong? Is there a sense in which each is correct?"

Tell the class that today's Scripture text shows both the wrath and the mercy of God in relation to His people when they sin against Him.

Into the Word

Use material from the "Introduction" section on page 42 as the basis for a brief lecture that connects the book of Joshua with the book of Judges, and last week's lesson with the lesson for today.

After you have given the lecture, ask students to summarize the sections of Judges 2 indicated by these verse divisions: verses 6-9; 10-13; 14 and 15; 16 and 17; 18; and 19. Let students choose one of the following four ways to summarize each verse or group of verses:

- a *color* to characterize the section
- a *word* to summarize the section
- a *song* to depict the meaning of the section
- a *weather report* to portray the mood of the section

Write the verse sections and the italicized words above on the chalkboard. Have the students work individually or in pairs to do a single summary. You may find it better, however, to have your students work in the same groups that were formed for the introductory activity. If so, ask each group to choose at least three of the four options for their summaries of the text. After about ten minutes, ask class members to share what they have written.

Then lead the class in discussing these questions: "What was the cycle of behavior that characterized the Israelites during this time of their history? Why do you suppose they behaved as they did?"

If you have time, ask class members to browse through the rest of the book of Judges to see illustrations of this pattern.

Into Life

Discuss the following five questions with the whole class:

1. In what sense is it surprising to know that the Israelites repeated this cyclical pattern of behavior so many times? In what sense is it understandable?

2. What similar cycles of behavior have you seen in the lives of Christians you know?

3. Think of contemporary counterparts to each of the following elements in the Israelites' experience:

- gods other than the Lord God (vv. 11-13, 17)
- powerful enemies that win victories against God's people (v. 14)
- judges (vv. 16, 18, 19)

4. Why do God's people sometimes refuse to "give up their evil practices and stubborn ways"? (v. 19, *New International Version*).

5. What can we learn from the experience of the Israelites in the time of the judges? How can we get ourselves out of their cycle of despair and keep ourselves out of it?

Close with sentence prayers from volunteers who will thank God for the lessons learned from the portion of His Word we have studied today.

Let's Talk It Over

The questions on this page are designed to encourage review of the lesson Scriptures and to promote discussion of the lesson by the class. The answers provided are only discussion starters. Let your class talk it over from there.

1. Failure to complete the task of destroying the inhabitants of Canaan was one reason for Israel's downfall recorded in Judges. What is the effect when church members fail to complete tasks they have agreed to do in the church?

Often tasks undertaken in the church are only half completed. A calling program enlists many volunteers at the outset, but it falls short of completion when those volunteers gradually slip away. A person agrees to be a teacher or youth leader and soon resigns after seeing how much work or patience will be required. These situations and others like them can cause confusion and discouragement in the church. The church needs workers who will see their jobs through to a successful conclusion, who will not merely *fill* an office, but *fulfill* all the responsibilities thereof. Focusing on the joys and rewards of service, and the positive impact we can have on others for Christ, will help us do that.

2. What can one do to counteract the dangers inherent in easy, comfortable living?

The abundance of material possessions can cause a person to trust in those riches and to become blind to the more important spiritual dimension of life. We would do well to contemplate the prayer contained in Proverbs 30:8, 9: "Give me neither poverty nor riches; feed me with food convenient for me: lest I be full, and deny thee, and say, Who is the Lord?" There is no sin in having the means to live comfortably, but we need to recognize the danger such wealth poses. Setting spiritual goals and pushing ourselves to achieve them is essential. Giving generously of our time to serve people in and out of the church, and of our money to support the local church and other worthy causes, will help us to avoid the trap of self-satisfaction and to remain alert and disciplined for the Lord.

3. What can a Christian do if he or she begins to regard the Christian life and Christian worship as dull?

Israel was lured to worship the idols of their heathen neighbors because of the carnal pleasures associated with that worship. The result was Israel's moral and spiritual collapse. It is still true today that there are life-styles and forms of worship that may appeal to bored believers and entice them away from "sincere and pure devotion to Christ" (2 Corinthians 11:3, *New International Version*). If we should find that the Christian life and Christian worship are becoming dull, we should respond to that in a positive way. By putting more of ourselves into our worship and discipleship we can experience more of the excitement inherent in following Christ. Reading God's Word again, to remind ourselves of the glorious future that awaits the faithful, will surely renew our enthusiasm for serving Christ.

4. The Israelites' cycle of blessing, sin, suffering, repentance, deliverance, and restoration to blessing has been reproduced in the lives of many believers. How can a person keep such a cycle from beginning?

A glance at this cycle reveals that the key is how we respond to God's blessing. We can take such blessing for granted; we can assume that it has come through our own efforts; and we can lose sight of the fact that it is indeed *God's* blessing. The alternative response is to be genuinely thankful and to demonstrate such thanksgiving by obedience to and trust in the great Giver. If we had to depend on our strength alone, we would surely fail. But because we have God's Spirit dwelling in us, and we enjoy access to God's Word, we have the power to keep this cycle from starting.

5. What are some specific ways in which we can measure our growth in Jesus Christ?

Our attitude toward the Lord's Supper is one standard of measurement. If we find it easy to be absent from the Lord's table, we have some growing to do; if we keenly anticipate Communion with our Lord, that is a definite sign of growth. Another standard is the quality of our spirit of servanthood. The Christian who is most interested in being served is clearly immature, while the believer who takes delight in serving others is becoming more like His Master. Our readiness to share our faith in Jesus Christ with others is one more standard. If we feel a consistent inner yearning to win others to Him (see 1 Corinthians 9:16-23), then we are approaching the biblical ideal.

Deliverance by God's Hand

DEVOTIONAL READING: Psalm 33:10-22.

LESSON SCRIPTURE: Judges 6:1—8:21.

PRINTED TEXT: Judges 7:2-7, 19-21.

Oct
9

Judges 7:2-7, 19-21

2 And the LORD said unto Gideon, The people that are with thee are too many for me to give the Midianites into their hands, lest Israel vaunt themselves against me, saying, Mine own hand hath saved me.

3 Now therefore go to, proclaim in the ears of the people, saying, Whosoever is fearful and afraid, let him return and depart early from mount Gilead. And there returned of the people twenty and two thousand; and there remained ten thousand.

4 And the LORD said unto Gideon, The people are yet too many; bring them down unto the water, and I will try them for thee there: and it shall be, that of whom I say unto thee, This shall go with thee, the same shall go with thee; and of whomsoever I say unto thee, This shall not go with thee, the same shall not go.

5 So he brought down the people unto the water: and the LORD said unto Gideon, Every one that lappeth of the water with his tongue, as a dog lappeth, him shalt thou set by himself; likewise every one that boweth down upon his knees to drink.

6 And the number of them that lapped, putting their hand to their mouth, were three hundred men: but all the rest of the people bowed down upon their knees to drink water.

7 And the LORD said unto Gideon, By the three hundred men that lapped will I save you, and deliver the Midianites into thine hand: and let all the other people go every man unto his place.

. . . .

19 So Gideon, and the hundred men that were with him, came unto the outside of the camp in the beginning of the middle watch; and they had but newly set the watch: and they blew the trumpets, and brake the pitchers that were in their hands.

20 And the three companies blew the trumpets, and brake the pitchers, and held the lamps in their left hands, and the trumpets in their right hands to blow withal: and they cried, The sword of the LORD, and of Gideon.

21 And they stood every man in his place round about the camp: and all the host ran, and cried, and fled.

GOLDEN TEXT: Arise; for the LORD hath delivered into your hand the host of Midian.
—Judges 7:15.

From the Conquest to the Kingdom

Unit 2: The Rule of the Judges

(Lessons 5, 6)

Lesson Aims

After studying this lesson a student should be able to:

1. Tell how the Lord drove the Midianites out of Israel.

2. Mention one victory of the Lord that the student has participated in.

3. Mention a present or future struggle that the Lord can win with the student's help.

Lesson Outline

INTRODUCTION
    A. Down to the Depths
    B. Lesson Background
  I. DISMISSING THE FEARFUL (Judges 7:2, 3)
    A. Too Many (v. 2)
    B. Swift Reduction (v. 3)
 II. DISMISSING THE OVERCONFIDENT (Judges 7:4-7)
    A. Still Too Many (v. 4)
    B. Strange Test (v. 5)
    C. The Chosen Few (vv. 6, 7)
III. ROUTING THE FOE (Judges 7:19-21)
    A. Ready? (v. 19a)
    B. Now! (v. 19b)
    C. Response (v. 20)
    D. Terror (v. 21)
      The Power of One
CONCLUSION
    A. Mopping Up
    B. The Lord's Victory
    C. More of the Lord's Victories
    D. God Is Calling
    E. Prayer
    F. Thought to Remember

Display visual 6 of the visuals packet throughout the class session. You will want to refer to it in reference to points B, C, and D of the Conclusion section. The visual is shown on page 53.

Introduction

Three hundred years is a long time in the life of a nation. The Roman Empire lasted longer than that, but the Babylonian Empire not nearly so long. The Constitution of the United States is only 207 years old. Three hundred years ago the British had taken New York from the Dutch, but were contesting with the French for Nova Scotia and debating the boundary of Florida with the Spanish. Three hundred and two years ago, nineteen alleged witches were hanged in Massachusetts. Three hundred sixty-one years ago, the authorities compelled Galileo to retract his bold announcement that the earth moves.

In Israel, the time of the judges lasted about three hundred years. During this time there were great and momentous changes, but the most notable feature about this period was that the people of Israel repeated the same pattern over and over. At ease and affluent, the people cared more about getting rich and having fun than about doing right. Consequently they resorted to dishonesty and idolatry. Punishment came by means of invaders who took away their riches and their fun. In poverty and misery, the people turned to the Lord, and He provided a leader to rally them and defeat the enemies. Peace and prosperity returned.

This repeated cycle was the subject of our study last week. This week we are to study one example of it.

A. Down to the Depths

In forty peaceful and prosperous years, the people of Israel more and more "did evil in the sight of the Lord" (Judges 5:31—6:1). This time the invaders came across the Jordan River from the east.

The Midianites and other tribes were nomads. In the desert country east and south of Israel, they had to keep moving to find pasture for their sheep, cattle, and camels. Now they just moved across the Jordan into Israel. The fields of growing wheat and barley were lush pasture for flocks and herds used to the sparse growth of the desert. The invaders fanned out over the country all the way to the Mediterranean coast and south to Gaza. The land was utterly devastated. Probably the nomads then went back to the desert, to come again the next year when the fields were green with a new crop. This went on for seven years.

Intimidated by the huge number of invaders, the Israelites fled to the hills and became cave dwellers. The record in Judges 6:1-6 sounds as if whole tribes of desert people moved in, bringing women and children as well as livestock; but the next chapter seems to describe a military camp. Perhaps the people and animals spread out over a wide area, while corps of tough fighting men camped together, ready to go swiftly to any place where there seemed to be a threat of attack.

Now the hungry people of Israel cried unto the Lord (Judges 6:6). His first response was to send a prophet to remind them of His former benefits, which they seemed to have forgotten (Judges 6:7-10). Then He summoned Gideon to raise an army and drive out the invaders (Judges 6:11-14).

B. Lesson Background

Gideon undertook the task reluctantly, but moved energetically to get it done. Thirty-two thousand volunteers responded to his call. They camped on the north slope of Mount Gilboa with the widespread camp of the Midianites below them on the floor of the valley. Then came a surprise.

I. Dismissing the Fearful
(Judges 7:2, 3)

The invaders were innumerable as a plague of grasshoppers (Judges 6:5), but an estimate of their number emerges later in the story. Fifteen thousand were left after a hundred and twenty thousand were killed. There must have been at least a hundred and thirty-five thousand in the camp that Gideon and his men saw before the fight began. It would be natural to think that thirty-two thousand were far too few to attack that multitude, but God said they were far too many.

A. Too Many (v. 2)

2. And the LORD said unto Gideon, The people that are with thee are too many for me to give the Midianites into their hands, lest Israel vaunt themselves against me, saying, Mine own hand hath saved me.

Outnumbered though they were, the thirty-two thousand men of Israel still made an impressive army. If they would rout the Midianties, they might think they had done it by their own strength and heroism. The Lord wanted all of them to understand that the victory was due to Him, not to them.

B. Swift Reduction (v. 3)

3. Now therefore go to, proclaim in the ears of the people, saying, Whosoever is fearful and afraid, let him return and depart early from mount Gilead. And there returned of the people twenty and two thousand; and there remained ten thousand.

"Anyone who is afraid may be excused." That was a sure-fire way to reduce the size of an army in sight of the enemy. More than two-thirds of the troops took Gideon at his word and dropped out. Only ten thousand were left. If Gideon himself began to be afraid, who can blame him? But the reduction was not yet complete.

It is surprising to see the name *Gilead* here, for that is best known as the name of an area east of

the Jordan. Perhaps some spur or hump of Mount Gilboa also had that name. Some students think an ancient scribe copying the record may have made a mistake, writing *Gilead* for *Gilboa*. At this late date, there seems to be no way of proving either of these theories.

II. Dismissing the Overconfident
(Judges 7:4-7)

Ordinary human thinking would conclude that ten thousand men had no chance to defeat that horde of invaders in the valley. It would be better to give up the dream of freedom and go back to their caves in the hills. But ordinary human thinking does not include the Lord in the equation. A handful of men plus God would utterly overwhelm all the myriads of Midian. God had called these men to conflict, and He would give them victory; but God would not win the victory by himself. The men of Israel must do their part, and do it heroically; but they must not think their heroism could win without the Lord.

A. Still Too Many (v. 4)

4. And the LORD said unto Gideon, The people are yet too many; bring them down unto the water, and I will try them for thee there: and it shall be, that of whom I say unto thee, This shall go with thee, the same shall go with thee; and of whomsoever I say unto thee, This shall not go with thee, the same shall not go.

Wisely Gideon had assembled his men at a place where there was an adequate supply of drinking water. Their camp was beside the well of Harod, or the spring of Harod, as the *New International Version* has it (v. 1). This was a large spring on the north side of Mount Gilboa, and it supplied a little stream. Gideon was to have his ten thousand men go down to the spring and the stream to get a drink of water before the battle. There the Lord would point out, one by one, the men to be excused and those to stay with Gideon.

B. Strange Test (v. 5)

5. So he brought down the people unto the water: and the LORD said unto Gideon, Every one that lappeth of the water with his tongue, as a dog lappeth, him shalt thou set by himself; likewise every one that boweth down upon his knees to drink.

The next verse makes this a little clearer. One lapping with his tongue would not lap directly from spring or stream, but would cup a little water in his hands and drink from that. One bowing on his knees would kneel at the edge of stream or pool, bend forward, and put his lips to the surface of the water to drink. People who have camped by unpolluted streams know what a satisfying way that is to drink one's fill. But soldiers and athletes and hard workers know it is unwise to drink one's fill just before going into vigorous action. Encamped in the valley below, the Midianites certainly saw the Hebrews assembled on the hillside. The Midianites might come out to battle at any time. Those who scooped up water with their hands would drink less and be more ready for combat. Each of them was to be set on one side; each one who bowed down on his knees was to be set on the other side.

C. The Chosen Few (vv. 6, 7)

6. And the number of them that lapped, putting their hand to their mouth, were three hundred men: but all the rest of the people bowed down upon their knees to drink water.

When the division was complete, only *three hundred men* stood on one side. *All the rest* of the ten thousand were on the other side.

7. And the LORD said unto Gideon, By the three hundred men that lapped will I save you, and deliver the Midianties into thine hand: and let all the other people go every man unto his place.

Gideon may have been hoping to keep the larger group; but no, the Lord assigned the three hundred to him. Along with the little group, however, He gave a very big promise. He, the Lord, would use that little group to bring the whole huge horde of Midian under the power of Gideon. So the rest of the ten thousand were told to go home. Verse 8 seems to indicate that the departing men left enough supplies so each of the three hundred had food. Besides, every man of the three hundred had a trumpet.

Gideon may have been getting nervous as his band was getting smaller. Verses 9-14 tell how one more bit of encouragement was given to him. After nightfall the Lord sent him and his servant down to the camp of Midian. In the darkness they sneaked close enough to hear two Midianites talking.

One Midianite was telling about a dream. He had seen a loaf of barley bread come tumbling into the camp to crush a tent. The Hebrew text says *the* tent, perhaps meaning the commander's tent, the army's headquarters.

How to Say It

GILBOA.   Gil-*bo*-uh.
GILEAD.   *Gil*-e-ud.
MIDIANITES.   *Mid*-e-un-ites.

The other Midianite was quick to interpret the dream. He said the barley loaf represented Gideon, who was about to tumble into camp with his troops to crush it.

Obviously the Midianite intelligence division had done its work well. The men not only knew about the nearby Hebrews, they even knew the name of the commander. They had seen thirty-two thousand men assemble on the hill, and they had seen most of them go away. Where were those men going? It would be natural to suppose they were going to encircle the Midianites and attack them from all sides. So the men of Midian were nervous, uneasy. They would be easy victims of Gideon's plan.

III. Routing the Foe
(Judges 7:19-21)

Gideon and his servant went back up the hill to waken their men. Quietly they distributed equipment and gave instructions. Each man had a trumpet. Each one also had a torch, which he probably lighted at the campfire before he covered it with a clay jar to hide it till the proper moment. Then the three hundred formed three companies and moved out in the darkness. Silently they surrounded the camp of Midian and waited for Gideon's signal (vv. 15-18).

A. Ready? (v. 19a)

19a. So Gideon, and the hundred men that were with him, came unto the outside of the camp in the beginning of the middle watch; and they had but newly set the watch.

Gideon and the men with him crept as close to the enemy camp as they could without alerting the sentries. They timed their arrival between ten and eleven o'clock, just after the changing of the guard. The new sentries, wakened from their early sleep, were nervous but still sleepy. Smothering his impatience, Gideon waited till the other two companies had ample time to get into their positions.

B. Now! (v. 19b)

19b. And they blew the trumpets, and brake the pitchers that were in their hands.

Suddenly the sound of a hundred trumpets blasted the silence. Suddenly a hundred torches flared in the darkness. It was a startling signal.

C. Response (v. 20)

20. And the three companies blew the trumpets, and brake the pitchers, and held the lamps in their left hands, and the trumpets in their right hands to blow withal: and they cried, The sword of the LORD, and of Gideon.

Like twin echoes, a hundred trumpets blasted from this side, and a hundred more blasted from that. Two hundred more torches flared. Between trumpet blasts the battle cry rang out. The name of Gideon was alarming, for the Midianties knew he commanded those gathering Hebrews. The name of the Lord was even more alarming, for the Midianties had heard from their grandparents what terrifying things the Lord had done in years gone by.

D. Terror (v. 21)

21. And they stood every man in his place round about the camp: and all the host ran, and cried, and fled.

The Israelites did not rush the camp; they just let the trumpets and the torches do their work. The Midianites woke to the sound of trumpets and the sight of a ring of fire. Normally one bugler is enough for a battalion, or perhaps a regiment. How many vengeful Hebrews were massed behind three hundred trumpets? Bewildered and befuddled, groping in darkness for shoes and swords, the Midianties *ran, and cried, and fled*. Their terrified minds could think of nothing but getting away from the camp and the pursuing army.

Panic and confusion must have been fatal to many of the Midianties, for "the Lord set every man's sword against his fellow" (v. 22). We can imagine the result. Stumbling out of his tent with sword in hand, a man saw a running figure bearing down on him and struck it down—but it was one of his comrades. Or perhaps the runner struck first, and the other died. There may have been hundreds or thousands of such deaths as comrades fought each other "throughout all the host" (v. 22).

THE POWER OF ONE

Several computer networks—one of them involving sixty thousand computers—were rendered useless in November 1988. A "virus" attack began to rapidly infect computers across the nation. As word of the epidemic spread, operators of thousands of computers not yet infected "quarantined" their systems by disconnecting them from the networks.

This relatively benign virus didn't destroy any files; it merely duplicated "garbage" so rapidly that the computers' memory banks were filled up so they could not operate. The crisis was caused by only one person, a graduate student in computer science, who thought his experiment would be harmless. Because the system his virus attacked was one used by the U. S. Defense Department, the FBI found the case *very* interesting!

visual 6

Gideon and his select band of soldiers had their part in routing the huge Midianite army, but they, more than anyone else, would know that they could not take credit for the victory. It was God's victory alone—beginning with the winnowing down of Gideon's army from thirty-two thousand to the plan for surprising the Midianties. It is said that "one person and God make a majority." Actually, God is a majority without anyone else. Wisdom dictates that we align ourselves with Him.

—C. R. B.

Conclusion

So with torches and trumpets and three hundred men, the Lord put an army to flight. The Midianites ran southeast toward the Jordan River and their homeland beyond it (v. 22), but their troubles were far from over.

A. Mopping Up

Thousands of Israelites started for home before the trumpet blast (vv. 2-8). Now runners caught up with them, inviting them to turn back, and join the pursuit (v. 23).

Spread far and wide over Israel, Midianite families with flocks and herds soon learned what was happening. They too started for home, but they could not move swiftly with their livestock. Gideon called on the tribe of Ephraim to intercept them as they fled. The men of Ephraim captured and killed two princes of the enemy. There is no record of how many more they killed, or how many cattle and sheep were captured (vv. 24, 25).

Meanwhile the remnant of Midian's fighting men escaped beyond Jordan to a place where they felt secure. But Gideon and his three hundred followed, surprised them, and defeated them again. The two kings of the Midianites were captured, and later they were slain (Judges 8:10-12, 18-21).

Again loyal to the Lord, Israel was at peace for forty years (Judges 8:28).

B. The Lord's Victory

Thirty-two thousand men were too many, the Lord said. Even ten thousand were too many for the Lord's army. If the Lord would win the victory by so many, they might think they did it by themselves. So the Lord's army was cut down to a mere three hundred. No one could possibly think such a tiny handful would defeat that huge army in the valley.

Gideon saw the Lord's angel and heard the Lord's voice to give him courage, but the three hundred saw no angel and heard no voice but Gideon's. Still, in faith they moved out to surround and destroy an army four hundred and fifty times as big as theirs. They trusted the Lord.

The Lord won the victory through men of faith, but He did it in such a way that faithless persons still could say the Lord had nothing to do with it. An unbeliever could scoff—in fact, unbelievers do scoff—saying the three hundred simply used a clever strategem of their own to scare the enemies out of their wits. But people of faith know the Lord won the victory.

C. More of the Lord's Victories

Early in the fourth century special coins of the Roman Empire were struck to celebrate the extermination of Christianity; but only about a decade later, a Roman coin displayed Chi-Rho, a symbol of Christ. Let credit be given to hundreds of Christians who gave their lives to keep their faith, and let credit be given to the emperor who made Christianity legal; but the Lord won the victory.

Next month our Thanksgiving celebration will call to mind the Pilgrim fathers who survived a bitter winter on the stern New England coast, who toiled hard through the summer, and who paused in the autumn to give thanks. Let us honor their courage and fortitude and hard work; but they knew the Lord won the victory, and they gave Him thanks.

In 1992 a Florida church building was demolished by a hurricane. Promptly the members set about rebuilding, though they had their own homes to rebuild too. Give credit to their devotion and sacrifice, and give credit to Christians all over the land who sent funds to help; but the Lord won the victory.

Mr. Chumbley was ninety-three years old when he gave his life to Christ. For seventy years his wife had been telling him he ought to be a Christian. At least a dozen Christian ministers through the years had tried to teach him the way of the Lord. Christian friends at work had tried to win him, and later his associates in a Christian retirement home had made like efforts. Perhaps he never would have been won without such efforts, but still the victory belonged to the Lord.

In these instances and many more, no one saw the Lord or heard His voice; but He was there. No earth-shaking miracle proclaimed His presence, but He was at work. From the human point of view the odds against Him seemed long, but He won.

Take a few minutes to think about your own life. In how many of God's victories have you had a part? What victory is He now about to win through you?

D. God Is Calling

"Moses," called the Lord. "Moses."

"Here I am," said Moses, before he knew who was calling.

After Moses learned who was calling, the Lord said, "I will send thee unto Pharaoh, that thou mayest bring forth my people the children of Israel out of Egypt" (Exodus 3:10).

Then Moses said, "Who, me?"

But Moses took his life in his hands and went to Pharaoh, and through every difficulty and danger he "endured, as seeing him who is invisible" (Hebrews 11:27). Through Moses, God won a mighty victory.

You may not hear God's call with your ears, but you will hear it with your faith. Will you answer "as seeing him who is invisible"? God can win through you.

E. Prayer

"Now unto the King eternal, immortal, invisible, the only wise God, be honor and glory for ever and ever. Amen" (1 Timothy 1:17).

F. Thought to Remember

The Lord can do wonders—through you.

Home Daily Bible Readings

Monday, Oct. 3—A Faithless People Cry for Help (Judges 6:1-10)

Tuesday, Oct. 4—Gideon's Call to Lead the Israelites (Judges 6:11-18)

Wednesday, Oct. 5—A Sign to Reassure Gideon (Judges 6:19-24)

Thursday, Oct. 6—Gideon Destroys the Altar of Baal (Judges 6:25-32)

Friday, Oct. 7—Two More Signs Affirm God's Call (Judges 6:33-40)

Saturday, Oct. 8—The Selection of Gideon's Army (Judges 7:2-14)

Sunday, Oct. 9—The Enemy Flees From Gideon's Army (Judges 7:15-21)

Learning by Doing

This page contains an alternate lesson plan emphasizing learning activities. Classes desiring such student involvement will find these suggestions helpful.

Learning Goals

As students participate in today's class session, they should:

1. List what God did and what Gideon did in Israel's victory over the Midianites.

2. Discover ways God's methods for bringing us victory may be surprising or unusual.

3. Decide one way to accept God's surprises for their own lives.

Into the Lesson

After all the class members have arrived, ask them to pair off. In their pairs, have each student tell a two-minute story about himself or herself relating to one of these topics:

"A time when victory was particularly sweet."

"A time when God surprised me."

"A time when I worried for nothing."

After four minutes (two minutes for each partner's story), ask for three volunteers to share their stories with the class, one for each heading. Then tell your class, "As we look at how God worked in Gideon's life, decide how your stories relate to the themes in today's study."

Into the Word

Use the material in the "Introduction" on page 50 to remind class members of last week's study and to connect it with this week's. Then read all of Judges 7 aloud to the class.

A dramatic way to do this is to have a *dialogical reading*. One person reads all the words of God in this passage. Another reads everything that Gideon said. A third person reads the words of the first Midianite (v. 13), and another reads the second Midianite's words (v. 14). All of the remaining words are read by the narrator.

Divide the class in half and instruct one half to listen for "everything that God did." The other half is to listen for "everything that Gideon did." When the reading of the text is finished, ask the students in each half of the class to arrange themselves in groups of three and to list under their respective headings the actions they detected. Then ask volunteers to share with the class as you write the items under each heading on your chalkboard.

Optional activity. If you have time, divide your class into groups of from four to seven members each. One person from each group should volunteer to deliver a monologue before the whole class. The other class members in each group are to help the speaker prepare his or her monologue.

The monologues are to be no longer than two minutes in length and are to begin with one of the following statements:

"I am Gideon—"

"I am the Lord—"

"I am Phurah, Gideon's servant—"

"I am a soldier in the Midianite army—"

"I am one of Gideon's three hundred warriors—"

If you have five or fewer small groups, make certain that each group selects a different topic. Students are to prepare their monologues by studying and discussing chapter 7 of Judges.

After either or both of these Bible-study activities, lead a class discussion based on the following questions: "Why did God command Gideon to limit his army as He did? What might Gideon and his forces have learned from this experience? What did it teach the rest of the Israelite nation? What can we learn from it?"

Into Life

Ask the students to arrange themselves into groups of from four to seven members each (the same groups they were in for the Bible study above. As they do so, write this statement on your chalkboard: "God's ways are not man's ways." Each small group should list as many examples as they can think of that show that this statement is true.

After five minutes, ask volunteers to share some of the examples they have noted. Discuss with the class, "How have you been surprised by the way you have seen God work in your world? Has your response to God's actions matched Gideon's? Has God's work in your life matched what He did for Gideon? What happens when we ignore God's commands and insist on doing His work in our own way instead of His? How can we become more willing to follow His methods instead of insisting on taking our own approach?"

Ask class members to reflect privately for a moment on this question: "What is the situation in your life where you most need God to provide the victory?"

Perhaps volunteers will share what they are thinking. Then ask several to pray sentence prayers to close today's session.

Let's Talk It Over

The questions on this page are designed to encourage review of the lesson Scriptures and to promote discussion of the lesson by the class. The answers provided are only discussion starters. Let your class talk it over from there.

1. Why must the church be wary of putting too much confidence in large numbers?

The Lord wants the church to grow, both numerically and spiritually. In the beginning, additions in large numbers were made to the church (see Acts 2:41; 4:4). In our quest for greater numbers, however, we must not forget that God can work mightily through comparatively smaller groups, as He did in Gideon's time. Small congregations can waste energy by lamenting their smallness, or they can let God work through them to accomplish such worthy enterprises as supporting a young missionary family, sending young men and women of faith to Bible colleges, or developing an exemplary program of evangelistic outreach in their own community. God can do similar works through small groups within the church, if the members will commit themselves to His use.

2. What would happen in our church if we were to announce, "Any member who is afraid to serve Christ is excused from service in the church"?

Such an announcement might well result in the loss of many of the church's workers. On the other hand, it might lead some members to engage in self-examination and help them see that their tendency to fearfulness in regard to Christian service is groundless. Perhaps they would feel ashamed for allowing fear to keep them silent when they should be speaking up for Christ, or permitting fear to keep them inactive when they should be shouldering responsibility for the Lord. One wonders if any of the twenty-two thousand who left Gideon's army because they were afraid later wished they had stayed and become part of the victorious three hundred. Allowing fear to rule us can rob us of the joy of sharing in victories for the Lord Jesus.

3. Gideon's three hundred may have been chosen on the basis of their demonstrating readiness for action. How can we demonstrate our readiness for action in the cause of Christ?

"Therefore, prepare your minds for action; be self-controlled; set your hope fully on the grace to be given you when Jesus Christ is revealed" (1 Peter 1:13, *New International Version*). This verse indicates that personal discipline is a key to readiness. Gideon's three hundred were physically and mentally alert, and so must we be. If our minds are cluttered with the images, values, and allurements of the world, and if our bodies are flabby because of poor life-style habits, we will be ill-prepared to win victories for our Lord. From a positive standpoint our readiness depends upon a consistent contact with God through study of His Word and prayer.

4. An unbeliever may look at the account of the Midianites' defeat by Gideon's band and say that God had nothing to do with it, and that it was simply the result of a very clever plan of attack. How shall we answer this?

We can understand that an unbeliever would want to explain the event in such a way. But when one considers that three hundred men were able to put to rout an army 450 times its size, it is only sensible to acknowledge the involvement of a power greater than man. On other occasions God intervened in battles with miraculous power to give His people victory, but with Gideon's army He chose to use a method that brought confusion and panic to the enemy. The record clearly indicates God's role from the selecting of Gideon as the leader to the reducing of the army to a size that could effectively employ the chosen strategy.

5. Why should Christians have a spirit that anticipates victory in their own lives and in the life of the church?

Some followers of the Lord are inclined to take a defeatist view regarding the church and their own discipleship. We hear them say, "I don't think this church will ever grow," or, "There's no way we can get enough in offerings to pay our bills," or, "I've had that bad habit so long that I doubt I'll ever be able to get rid of it." Such attitudes are incongruous with the fact that we serve a risen, victorious Christ. We should be imbued with the spirit of 1 Corinthians 15:57: "But thanks be to God, which giveth us the victory through our Lord Jesus Christ." In any undertaking within the church or in connection with our Christian walk, we should expect to succeed. And when we do not, we should show resilience and launch out on a fresh undertaking with renewed hope.

Israel Demands a King

DEVOTIONAL READING: Psalm 47:1-9.

LESSON SCRIPTURE: 1 Samuel 7:15—8:22; 12:19-25.

PRINTED TEXT: 1 Samuel 8:4-9, 19; 12:19-25.

1 Samuel 8:4-9, 19

4 Then all the elders of Israel gathered themselves together, and came to Samuel unto Ramah,

5 And said unto him, Behold, thou art old, and thy sons walk not in thy ways: now make us a king to judge us like all the nations.

6 But the thing displeased Samuel, when they said, Give us a king to judge us. And Samuel prayed unto the LORD.

7 And the LORD said unto Samuel, Hearken unto the voice of the people in all that they say unto thee: for they have not rejected thee, but they have rejected me, that I should not reign over them.

8 According to all the works which they have done since the day that I brought them up out of Egypt even unto this day, wherewith they have forsaken me, and served other gods, so do they also unto thee.

9 Now therefore hearken unto their voice: howbeit yet protest solemnly unto them, and show them the manner of the king that shall reign over them.

. . . .

19 Nevertheless the people refused to obey the voice of Samuel; and they said, Nay; but we will have a king over us.

1 Samuel 12:19-25

19 And all the people said unto Samuel, Pray for thy servants unto the LORD thy God, that we die not: for we have added unto all our sins this evil, to ask us a king.

20 And Samuel said unto the people, Fear not: ye have done all this wickedness: yet turn not aside from following the LORD, but serve the LORD with all your heart;

21 And turn ye not aside: for then should ye go after vain things, which cannot profit nor deliver; for they are vain.

22 For the LORD will not forsake his people for his great name's sake: because it hath pleased the LORD to make you his people.

23 Moreover as for me, God forbid that I should sin against the LORD in ceasing to pray for you: but I will teach you the good and the right way:

24 Only fear the LORD, and serve him in truth with all your heart: for consider how great things he hath done for you.

25 But if ye shall still do wickedly, ye shall be consumed, both ye and your king.

GOLDEN TEXT: Make us a king to judge us like all the nations.—1 Samuel 8:5.

From the Conquest to the Kingdom	
Unit 3: The Beginning of the Kingdom	
(Lessons 7-9)	

with overeating and overdrinking, idol worship and adultery.

Or one's own eyes may foolishly conclude that what is profitable is right. Then one may approve of lying and cheating and stealing because they make him or her rich.

Lesson Aims

After this lesson students should be able to :

1. Explain how Israel got a king, and what was wrong with that.

2. Accept responsibility for what they do.

3. Specify one way they can follow God's leading more perfectly.

Lesson Outline

INTRODUCTION
  A. Again and Again
  B. The Last Judge
  C. Lesson Background
  I. CALL FOR A KING (1 Samuel 8:4-8)
  A. Troubled Elders (v. 4)
  B. Problem and Solution (v. 5)
  C. Reluctant Permission (vv. 6-8)
 II. WARNING IGNORED (1 Samuel 8:9, 19)
  A. Solemn Warning (v. 9)
  B. Repeated Request (v. 19)
III. REASSURANCE AND WARNING (1 Samuel 12:19-25)
  A. Prayer Request (v. 19)
  B. Reassurance (vv. 20-23)
      Antidote to Fear
  C. Final Warning (vv. 24, 25)
CONCLUSION
  A. Do It Yourself
  B. Looking Ahead
  C. The Way That Works
  D. Prayer
  E. Thought to Remember

Display visual 7 of the visuals packet and refer to it when appropriate in the lesson. The visual is shown on page 61.

Introduction

"Every man did that which was right in his own eyes." This is the repeated description of Israel's conduct in the time of the judges (Judges 17:6; 21:25). In deciding between right and wrong, one's own eyes are not a safe guide unless they are enlightened by God's Word.

Without that light, one's own eyes may mistake what is pleasant for what is right. So luxury and laziness may be perceived as right, along

A. Again and Again

Such blunders were the bane of Israel in the three centuries of the judges. When things were going well, people ran wild in pursuit of pleasure and profit. Doing what was right in their own eyes, they did what was evil in the sight of the Lord. God's way of correcting their eyesight was to bring in a heathen tribe to steal their profits and end their pleasures. In poverty and misery the people could see their mistake. They began again to obey God, and then He provided a leader to drive out the invaders. Obedient Israel found the way back to prosperity. This cycle rolled on and on for three hundred years.

B. The Last Judge

Samuel was the last of the judges. Dedicated to the Lord before he was born, and brought up by a godly priest, he became a godly man and a prophet. But in his youth the people of Israel again were doing what was right in their own eyes and evil in the sight of the Lord.

This time God's punishment came through the Philistines who lived in the coastal plain. They continued to dominate and oppress Israel for twenty years (1 Samuel 4:1—7:2)

Then Samuel sounded a call to repentance, and the people responded. They got rid of their idols and gave their worship and obedience to the Lord. Samuel summoned them to a big prayer meeting in Mizpeh (1 Samuel 7:3-6).

Seeing the nation gathering for prayer, the Philistines thought an army was assembling to rebel against their rule. Quickly mustering their own troops, they marched to put down the insurrection. This time the Lord fought for Israel. He upset the Philistines with a terrific thunderstorm, and the Israelites chased them back to their plain. (1 Samuel 7:7-14).

With peace restored, Samuel moved to maintain righteousness. He became a circuit judge, going from place to place so people could more easily come to him with cases to be decided according to God's law (1 Samuel 7:15-17).

C. Lesson Background

Even before Samuel died, the oft-repeated slide into corruption began again. Samuel's own sons led the way.

When Samuel was growing old, he sent his sons to be judges in the south part of Israel. That would have been an excellent move if the sons had been like their father. But those young men cared nothing for justice or God's law. They "took bribes, and perverted judgment" (1 Samuel 8:1-3). With the courts of justice so corrupted, how could another national disaster be avoided?

I. Call for a King
(1 Samuel 8:4-8)

The elders of Israel were disturbed, as they should have been. They could remember how they had suffered under Philistine rule, and how God had helped them with a thunderstorm at just the right moment. But in a few years these elders would die, and so would Samuel. The new generation would not have the same memories to warn them against evil; and if justice could not be found in the courts, soon it would not be found anywhere in Israel. How could the nation be saved from another slide into evil and idolatry and disaster? The elders were right to be concerned about the problem, but the solution they suggested was wrong.

A. Troubled Elders (v. 4)

4. Then all the elders of Israel gathered themselves together, and came to Samuel unto Ramah.

Something had to be done for the safety of their children and grandchildren, and Samuel was the man to do it. He was the undisputed leader of the nation, the one who had guided them to freedom from the Philistines, the one who had blessed them with equal and exact justice in his court, the one they trusted. So the huge group of elders came to his home in Ramah.

B. Problem and Solution (v. 5)

5. And said unto him, Behold, thou art old, and thy sons walk not in thy ways: now make us a king to judge us like all the nations.

The elders stated the problem very simply. First, Samuel was *old*. He would not be there to dispense justice much longer. Second, his sons were not walking in his ways: there was no prospect that they would dispense true justice.

How to Say It

AMMONITES. *Am*-un-ites.
PHILISTINES. Fi-*liss*-teens or *Fil*-iss-teens.
JABESH-GILEAD. *Jay*-besh-*gil*-e-ud (strong accent on *gil*).

Some kind of change was needed, and the elders suggested a change that looked good to them: *Make us a king to judge us like all the nations.* All the nations around Israel had kings. Monarchy seemed to work. It was simple and effective. The king was the head: everybody did what he said to do—or if anyone was disposed to object, the king had a standing army to keep him in line. Not being under a king themselves, the elders did not see the many abuses that arise in that kind of government. Apparently they expected Samuel to find them a king like himself, godly and wise and incorruptible.

C. Reluctant Permission (vv. 6-8)

6. But the thing displeased Samuel, when they said, Give us a king to judge us. And Samuel prayed unto the LORD.

The reason for Samuel's displeasure is not explained. Perhaps he thought the request reflected dissatisfaction with him personally (v. 7). But no doubt there was more than that. With his wisdom and inspiration from the Lord, Samuel must have known the proposed solution would not work. Where would he find a man as capable and upright and unselfish as himself? Such men are not numerous in politics. And if such a man could be found, who could guarantee that his sons would not be as bad as Samuel's sons turned out to be?

A lesser man might have denounced the elders' plan instantly and loudly, but Samuel was too wise for that. He took the matter to a higher judge: he *prayed unto the Lord.*

7. And the LORD said unto Samuel, Hearken unto the voice of the people in all that they say unto thee: for they have not rejected thee, but they have rejected me, that I should not reign over them.

The Lord gave consent, but not approval. Samuel should listen to the elders and do what they asked. It would not solve their problem, but it would show them and their children that such a solution would not work.

God said Samuel should not feel hurt by the elders' request. They were not rejecting him; they were well pleased with his leadership. Their problem lay deeper than that. The Lord said, *They have rejected me, that I should not reign over them.*

God was the proper king of Israel. He made His will known in the law given through Moses. In the law itself He promised blessing and help to Israel when Israel obeyed His law; He promised disaster when the law was ignored. He did not provide a king on earth to make the people obey the King in Heaven; instead, He made all persons responsible for their own obedience and for teaching their children to obey. Whenever the people did not obey, they were rejecting the Lord, that He should not reign over them. Regardless of what they said, they were in fact rejecting Him when they disobeyed.

It was not impossible for the people to keep God's law well enough to receive His blessing and help. They did it as long as Joshua led them, and for years after he died (Judges 2:7). They did it for forty years after God and Gideon rescued them from Midian (Judges 8:28). They did it for years after God and Samuel rescued them from the Philistines (1 Samuel 7:13-17).

Now the elders saw the beginning of another slide into disobedience and disaster, and Samuel's sons were leading the way. Why didn't those elders assume the responsibility of teaching obedience to their families and clans? Why didn't they resolve to establish the reign of God so fully that no one would ever feel a need to appeal to those rascally sons of Samuel?

In our own communities, do we take upon ourselves the responsibility of teaching God's Word and will so thoroughly that no one will ever disobey? No, we banish God and His Word from our classrooms, and we establish police and courts and jails to restrain the disobedience of the untaught. The elders of Israel wanted a king to do that for them.

8. According to all the works which they have done since the day that I brought them up out of Egypt even unto this day, wherewith they have forsaken me, and served other gods, so do they also unto thee.

The people of Israel had a long history of pledging their loyalty in words but rejecting God in fact. If they now were rejecting Samuel and his advice, it was just what they had been doing to the Lord for centuries.

II. Warning Ignored (1 Samuel 8:9, 19)

The Lord let His people in Israel have their own way, but He told Samuel to explain the perils of it.

A. Solemn Warning (v. 9)

9. Now therefore hearken unto their voice: howbeit yet protest solemnly unto them, and show them the manner of the king that shall reign over them.

Samuel was to let the people have their way; he was to help them get the best king that was to be had. But he was to let them know that being ruled by a king was no bed of roses. The king would draft their young people for military service, and civilian service too. He would requisi-

tion fields and vineyards, slaves and livestock, for his officials. He would levy a ten percent tax. The people would find all of this to be oppressive (vv. 10-18).

B. Repeated Request (v. 19)

19. Nevertheless the people refused to obey the voice of Samuel; and they said, Nay; but we will have a king over us.

Samuel's protest made small impression on the elders. They had been thinking about this matter, and their minds were made up. The injustice of Samuel's sons was a clear and present danger. They repeated their request for a king.

The following verse records the elders' three reasons for their insistence:

1. No one could tell them a monarchy wouldn't work. All the other nations had kings, and they seemed to be doing all right.

2. They needed a king to judge them as Samuel had been doing. He would settle their disputes, he would tell them what to do, he would enforce the law. The elders would be relieved of the responsibility of learning and teaching and enforcing that long and wordy law.

3. The king would be responsible for national defense. It would be his job to muster an army and repel any invasion of Israel, and to lead any necessary invasion of another country.

Again Samuel took the matter to the Lord, and again he was told to go ahead with plans for a king. So the meeting adjourned (vv. 21, 22).

III. Reassurance and Warning (1 Samuel 12:19-25)

The elders went home, and Samuel waited for the Lord's leading. First he was led to a man named Saul, whom he anointed privately to be the king of Israel (1 Samuel 9:1—10:1). Then he called a mass meeting for the purpose of choosing a king by lot. The lot fell on Saul, thus confirming the choice already made in private and letting all the people see that the choice was made by the Lord, not by Samuel. Saul was tall and handsome, a fine figure of a man. With a few exceptions, the people acclaimed him with enthusiasm (1 Samuel 10:17-27).

Soon came the first test of the new king. Ammonites from the east threatened Jabesh-gilead, a city on the east bank of Jordan. Saul quickly recruited an army and soundly defeated the Ammonites. Samuel led the people to Gilgal to celebrate the victory and confirm the establishment of the kingdom (1 Samuel 11).

To the crowd at Gilgal, Samuel reviewed the great help that God had given to Israel through centuries. Plainly he told the people they had sinned by asking for a king instead of obeying the Lord as their king. It was wheat-harvest time, a time when it never rains in Israel. But Samuel asked God to confirm his statement by thunder and rain, and God responded. Thus convinced of their sin, the people were frightened.

A. Prayer Request (v. 19)

19. And all the people said unto Samuel, Pray for thy servants unto the LORD thy God, that we die not: for we have added unto all our sins this evil, to ask us a king.

Freely the people confessed not only former sins but also the sin of asking for a king instead of recognizing God as their king and obeying Him. Now they begged Samuel to pray that they would not die for their sin.

B. Reassurance (vv. 20-23)

20. And Samuel said unto the people, Fear not: ye have done all this wickedness: yet turn not aside from following the LORD, but serve the LORD with all your heart.

Samuel did not make light of the people's sin, nor did he withdraw his accusation. Rather, he repeated it with emphasis. Still he said, *Fear not.* The important thing was what they were going to do, not what they had done in the past. From now on, they had better not turn aside from the straight line of wholehearted service to the Lord.

21. And turn ye not aside: for then should ye go after vain things, which cannot profit nor deliver; for they are vain.

If God's people would turn away from God, to what would they turn? To idols or imaginary gods. These are *vain things*, empty, worthless things, things that really are nothing. They *cannot profit* their followers by giving rain and sunshine and good crops as the Lord does. They cannot *deliver* their followers from enemies as the Lord does.

ANTIDOTE TO FEAR

Peter Ilyitch Tchaikovsky was one of the world's greatest composers, but fear and depression clouded his life. When he was ten, his mother left him in a Saint Petersburg preparatory school. He so feared being left alone that he ran after her carriage, trying to grab its wheels to stop her departure. His mother died four years later, and he became obsessed with his misery.

Finally, in music he found some consolation. In time he taught harmony at the Conservatory of Moscow. During a brief, unhappy marriage he attempted suicide. Thereafter he suffered from frequent depressions. Toward the end of his life, he sank into extreme depression and thought he was going mad. During this period he wrote

visual 7

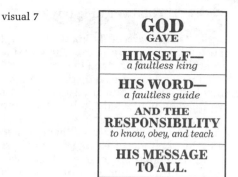

GOD
GAVE

HIMSELF—
a faultless king

HIS WORD—
a faultless guide

AND THE
RESPONSIBILITY
to know, obey, and teach

HIS MESSAGE TO ALL.

what many regard as his greatest composition, the "Symphonie Pathetique." He conducted its premiere, which was not well received, and a week later Tchaikovsky was dead.

Sometimes, like Tchaikovsky, our troubles come from the way others have treated us or from a temperamental disposition to gloominess that seems beyond our control. More often, discouragement and fear are the natural consequences of bad choices we have made.

Samuel told the Israelites that their request for a king was wrong, but he urged them neither to fear nor turn away from serving the Lord. That would lead only to futility. Repentance of sin and wholehearted obedience to God were the keys to their spiritual health. It is so even today.
—C. R. B.

22. For the LORD will not forsake his people for his great name's sake: because it hath pleased the LORD to make you his people.

To many other sins the people of Israel had added the sin of demanding a king. That was what they said (v. 19), and it was true. They did not deserve the Lord's favor and help, but He was going to help them anyway for the sake of His great name: His reputation, His honor, His position as the one and only God who can do great things. Back in the time of Abraham He had chosen this particular family of people for a great purpose. Through them He was going to bring a blessing to all families of the earth (Genesis 12:3), for through them He would send His Son to redeem the lost and offer salvation and eternal life to all mankind.

23. Moreover as for me, God forbid that I should sin against the LORD in ceasing to pray for you: but I will teach you the good and the right way.

The people had asked Samuel to pray for them (v. 19). That he would do; it would be a *sin against the Lord* to stop his praying. But he would also continue to denounce their sins and to teach them *the good and the right way.*

C. Final Warning (vv. 24, 25)

24. Only fear the LORD, and serve him in truth with all your heart: for consider how great things he hath done for you.

The people had asked for a king, and now they had one. In spite of past sins, all would be well if they now would hold the Lord in reverence and give Him wholehearted obedience. Samuel already had assured them of that (v. 14). Now he reminded them again that their well-being depended on their wholehearted obedience. God had done *great things* for them all through their history. They ought to remember all those things and serve God both out of gratitude and in the hope that He would continue to do great things for them in the future.

25. But if ye shall still do wickedly, ye shall be consumed, both ye and your king.

The people had thought a king would solve all their problems. Not so! Their problems could be solved only by doing right. If they would do wrong in the future, disaster would come to them and their king together.

Conclusion

"Righteousness exalteth a nation: but sin is a reproach to any people" (Proverbs 14:34). Israel was not alone. Doing right is beneficial everywhere, and doing wrong is disastrous.

A. Do It Yourself

The righteousness that exalts a nation is a do-it-yourself project. You are responsible for what you do; I am responsible for what I do. Neither of us can escape responsibility by blaming parents or spouse or associates, government or society or the system.

In our modern society we need police and courts and jails to deal with people who do not accept their responsibility; but a frequent complaint about our justice system is that it does not make bad people good. Criminals who go into our jails and prisons are still criminals when they come out. They remain criminals till they themselves decide to change.

God can help us do right, of course; and we can help one another do right or wrong. But all who do wrong do it themselves, and none do right without doing it themselves.

B. Looking Ahead

One of the responsibilities of our generation is to teach God's way to the next generation. Our public schools give us no help in this; it is our own responsibility. We are not only to teach God's way when we are sitting at home; we are also to show how the teaching is applied in all our going and coming, all the activities of daily living (Deuteronomy 6:6, 7).

Our failure to teach the next generation does not excuse its failure to obey the Lord, but neither does its failure to heed our teaching excuse our failure to teach.

C. The Way That Works

We cannot become good unless we desire in our hearts to be good, but we cannot become good by our effort alone. It takes a greater power than ours.

"All have sinned" (Romans 3:23), and "the wages of sin is death" (Romans 6:23). If we do nothing but good from now on, that cannot atone for the sins of the past. The only way to escape from sin and death is to be justified by God's grace "through the redemption that is in Christ Jesus" (Romans 3:24). The only way to become good is to have our sins forgiven; and we have our sins forgiven when we give ourselves to Jesus: believing in Him, trusting Him, obeying Him (Acts 16:30-33; 2:37-42; 22:16). Thus we become good with a righteousness not our own, "the righteousness which is of God by faith" (Philippians 3:9).

D. Prayer

How gracious You are, dear Heavenly Father! Out of Your goodness You have provided both forgiveness of sin and a faultless guide to righteous living. In love and gratitude we pledge ourselves anew to do Your will. In Jesus' name we pray. Amen.

E. Thought to Remember

"The Lord will not forsake his people" (1 Samuel 12:22)

Home Daily Bible Readings

Monday, Oct. 10—Peace Under Samuel's Leadership (1 Samuel 7:12-17)
Tuesday, Oct. 11—Israel Asks for a King (1 Samuel 8:1-9)
Wednesday, Oct. 12—God Reigns Over All the Earth (Psalm 47)
Thursday, Oct. 13—Rejection of Samuel's Warning About a King (1 Samuel 8:10-22)
Friday, Oct. 14—Samuel Defends His Own Leadership (1 Samuel 12:1-5)
Saturday, Oct. 15—Samuel Pleads for God's Kingship (1 Samuel 12:6-18)
Sunday, Oct. 16—Samuel Appeals for Faithfulness to God (1 Samuel 12:19-25)

Learning by Doing

This page contains an alternate lesson plan emphasizing learning activities. Classes desiring such student involvement will find these suggestions helpful.

Learning Goals

As students participate in today's class session, they should:

1. Decide why God did not want the nation of Israel to have a king, and why He allowed them to have one anyway.

2. List practical steps they can take to make their nation more pleasing to God.

Into the Lesson

Write the following sentences on your chalkboard for students to see as they arrive:

• Our job is to make our nation a Christian nation.

• Our job is to live like Christians in our non-Christian nation.

To begin, ask class members which sentence they agree with the most. Ask for a show of hands and tell class members they must vote for one or the other of the two sentences.

Ask class members to form groups of two or three. Each group must have at least one person who chose the first sentence and one who chose the second. In their groups students should tell each other why they chose as they did. Allow five minutes for them to do this. Then lead a brief class discussion of the sentences.

Into the Word

Connect this week's lesson with last week's lesson. The material under the "Introduction" heading (page 58) will provide the information that you need. Ask your students to open their Bibles and look at the chapter and section headings for the first eight chapters of 1 Samuel. As they read the headings to you, review the events in those chapters and the significance of each. Then ask a volunteer to read today's printed text aloud while the class listens for these three things:

1. What did the people want?
2. What did Samuel want?
3. What did God want?

You may want to divide the class in thirds and have each third listen for the answer to a different one of the questions as the Scripture is read. Then answer each question by leading the whole class in discussing them.

Next, give each class member a copy of the following Bible-study questions. If you have time, divide the class into groups of from five to seven students each, and ask the groups to answer the questions. After several minutes lead the whole class in discussing them.

1. Why did the elders of Israel want a king? (1 Samuel 8:5).

2. How did Samuel react to their request? Why? (v. 6). What does Samuel's response to the elders show about his character?

3. What was wrong with the elders' request for a king? Why did God allow what He did not approve?

4. What was God's assessment of the Israelites? (v. 8). Give some examples to substantiate God's assessment of His people.

5. What warnings did God tell Samuel to give the people regarding having a king rule them? (vv. 9-18).

6. Read verse 20 and list the three reasons the elders gave for wanting a king. Does their rationale seem reasonable? How may one account for their insistence upon wanting a king to reign over them?

7. According to 1 Samuel 12:19-25, how did Samuel respond when the people finally saw the error of their request? Would God bless them, even though their having a king was against His will? On what conditions? What did Samuel regard as a valid reason why Israel should obey the Lord wholeheartedly?

Into Life

Ask a volunteer to read Proverbs 14:34 aloud to the class. Then read to the class only the first paragraph under the heading "A. Do It Yourself" in the "Conclusion" section on page 62. Then lead the class in discussing the following questions: "Is our nation more or less righteous today than it was ten years ago? How about twenty years ago? What evidence can you give for your answer? Are Christians more or less visible today than a generation ago?"

To make personal application of this lesson, ask class members to consider this question: "What can you do to make our nation more righteous this week?" Distribute slips of paper and ask each student to write down at least one answer to the question. Collect the slips and read them back to the class. Then let several volunteers close with sentence prayers for the nation, for the class, and for the specific ideas noted on the slips of paper.

Let's Talk It Over

The questions on this page are designed to encourage review of the lesson Scriptures and to promote discussion of the lesson by the class. The answers provided are only discussion starters. Let your class talk it over from there.

1. Samuel, a very godly man, had sons who were morally corrupt. How can we explain this?

"Train up a child in the way he should go: and when he is old, he will not depart from it" (Proverbs 22:6). If Samuel adhered to this principle, his sons should have become godly persons. It is possible, however, that Samuel became so busy with his duties as a judge that he failed to give his sons proper training. Today, too, some godly ministers and elders spend so much time in the work of the church that they neglect the spiritual nurture of their own children. On the other hand, it may be said that Proverbs 22:6 is a general rule, to which there can be exceptions. No matter how thorough the spiritual and moral instruction they receive as children, all human beings must take responsibility for their own decisions and conduct. Samuel's sons chose a lifestyle opposite from that of their father.

2. In asking for a king the elders of Israel were looking for what must have seemed an easy solution to their problems. What can be said about seeking easy solutions to church problems?

Sometimes easy solutions are legitimate and workable. Often, however, what appear to be easy solutions are merely "quick fixes" that fail to address the real problems. Any time the church faces a problem for which there seems to be an easy solution, we must ask, "Does this solution deal with the actual problem? Are we merely delaying the time when we must handle a deeper problem? Are we allowing the real problem to grow worse by choosing the easy solution?" Church leaders should pray for wisdom and courage to adopt the right solutions, whether they are easy or difficult.

3. The Lord told Samuel to warn the people regarding the negative aspects of having a king rule over them. What are some decisions people make today, which have negative aspects they need to know?

Marriage is ordained by God, and is designed to bring joy and fulfillment to those who enter it. Trials and pressures accompany that relationship, however, and those couples who are planning marriage need to be made aware of them. The fact that so many marriages today fail suggests that couples approach their wedding day unprepared for the kind of patience, compromise, forgiveness, perseverance, and the like, which they must exercise. To go a step further, parenthood is a responsibility that must not be undertaken lightly. A couple planning to have a child should be made aware of the sacrifice of time and money and the vast amount of patience such a decision will require. Before one takes a job, matters such as the degree of stress involved and amount of time required to be away from family should be carefully considered.

4. How may it be a sin not to pray for someone?

Various biblical passages contain the command for God's people to pray (see Luke 18:1; Philippians 4:6; 1 Thessalonians 5:17). In general, therefore, failure to pray is disobedience to God's will for us. If we were to refuse to pray for anyone who asked for our prayers, would that not reveal our hearts to be seriously out of tune with the Spirit of God? The people of Israel asked Samuel to pray for them. Since they had insisted on a king, and in a sense had rejected his leadership, he may well have been tempted to refuse their request. Had he done so, he felt he would have sinned against God. We may have difficulty praying for people who have wronged us or who have foolishly enmeshed themselves in troubles. But Christian love and mercy dictate that we pray for them.

5. Why must we be careful not to expect too much from human government?

While civil authorities "are ordained of God" (Romans 13:1), they are still human beings. We are to honor them and obey them, and we may enjoy the benefits they provide. As human beings, however, they are prone to spiritual shortsightedness and moral corruption. So we must be discriminating in our support of political leaders. Furthermore, we recognize that human government is limited in what it can accomplish. No laws or government programs can solve the basic problem of man, which is his sinful rebellion against God. What we offer as messengers of the gospel of Jesus Christ goes far beyond what any political leader can give.

Saul's Opportunity as King

DEVOTIONAL READING: Psalm 106:40-48.

LESSON SCRIPTURE: 1 Samuel 9:15—10:1a, 20-24.

PRINTED TEXT: 1 Samuel 9:15-17; 10:1a, 20-24.

1 Samuel 9:15-17

15 Now the LORD had told Samuel in his ear a day before Saul came, saying,

16 Tomorrow about this time I will send thee a man out of the land of Benjamin, and thou shalt anoint him to be captain over my people Israel, that he may save my people out of the hand of the Philistines: for I have looked upon my people, because their cry is come unto me.

17 And when Samuel saw Saul, the LORD said unto him, Behold the man whom I spake to thee of! this same shall reign over my people.

1 Samuel 10:1a, 20-24

1 Then Samuel took a vial of oil, and poured it upon his head.

· · · · · · · · · · · · · · · ·

20 And when Samuel had caused all the tribes of Israel to come near, the tribe of Benjamin was taken.

21 When he had caused the tribe of Benjamin to come near by their families, the family of Matri was taken, and Saul the son of Kish was taken: and when they sought him, he could not be found.

22 Therefore they inquired of the LORD further, if the man should yet come thither. And the LORD answered, Behold, he hath hid himself among the stuff.

23 And they ran and fetched him thence: and when he stood among the people, he was higher than any of the people from his shoulders and upward.

24 And Samuel said to all the people, See ye him whom the LORD hath chosen, that there is none like him among all the people? And all the people shouted, and said, God save the king.

Oct 23

GOLDEN TEXT: Then Samuel took a vial of oil, and poured it upon his head,
and kissed him, and said, Is it not because the LORD hath anointed thee
to be captain over his inheritance?—1 Samuel 10:1.

From the Conquest to the Kingdom
Unit 3: The Beginning of the Kingdom
(Lessons 7-9)

Lesson Aims

After this lesson a student should be able to:

1. Tell how God's choice of a king was made known to God's prophet and God's people.

2. Outline the qualifications of a king of Israel, and compare the qualifications of a citizen of God's kingdom today.

3. Find a way to improve his or her understanding of and obedience to God's will.

Lesson Outline

INTRODUCTION
    A. Change
    B. Lesson Background
  I. INFORMING THE PROPHET (1 Samuel 9:15-17; 10:1a)
    A. Announcement in Advance (vv. 15, 16)
    B. Identification on Arrival (v. 17)
    C. Anointing the King (10:1a)
  II. INFORMING THE PEOPLE (1 Samuel 10:20-24)
    A. Selecting the King (vv. 20, 21)
    B. Finding the King (vv. 22, 23)
      A Reluctant Hero
    C. Accepting the King (v. 24)
      The Measure of a Person's Worth
CONCLUSION
    A. The Manner of the Kingdom
    B. God's Kingdom Today
    C. Prayer
    D. Thought to Remember

Refer to visual 8 of the visuals packet as you discuss the thoughts in the conclusion of this lesson. The visual is shown on page 69.

Introduction

Last week we read that the people of Israel demanded a king, and the Lord consented to give them one. This week we shall see how the Lord let the prophet and the people know about the king He chose for them.

A. Change

Change was brewing in Israel. The people were going to have a king, and they were optimistic. Samuel had been their chief judge for a long time, and they had prospered. Samuel was old now, and he would not be with them much longer. Furthermore, his sons were greedy and crooked. Greed and crookedness had grown in Israel several times before, and big trouble had followed every time. The people wanted a king to banish greed and crookedness, to manage the economy so everyone would prosper, to vanquish all foreign foes.

Samuel warned the people that a king would bring new problems instead of solving the old ones. With or without a king, doing right brings prosperity and doing wrong brings disaster. But the people were not listening. All the other nations had kings, didn't they? Obviously that was the kind of government that worked. Good old Samuel would find a good king for Israel, and all would be well.

God agreed to give them a king without giving His approval to their request. God himself chose the king, but neither the prophet nor the people knew who he was.

B. Lesson Background

Kish was a prosperous man of the tribe of Benjamin. Somehow his donkeys got out and wandered away. So Kish told his son Saul to take one of the servants and go out to find the strays.

Saul was not a mere boy on the farm. He was a man in the prime of life. His son Jonathan was an adult; not much later he commanded a thousand fighting men (1 Samuel 13:2).

Saul and the servant tramped over a lot of territory in the next three days, but found no donkeys. They were about to give up and go home when they thought of Samuel. They happened to be near the town were he was. Samuel was God's prophet, and he often gave God's messages to the people. Surely God knew where the donkeys were. If He would tell His prophet, the prophet could tell the searchers (1 Samuel 9:1-13).

I. Informing the Prophet
(1 Samuel 9:15-17; 10:1a)

Saul and the servant hurried to the town where Samuel was. At the gate they met the prophet himself, who was going out to give his blessing to a sacrifice and feast at a nearby high place (1 Samuel 9:14).

A. Announcement in Advance
(vv. 15, 16)

15. Now the LORD had told Samuel in his ear a day before Saul came, saying.

The Lord not only knew where the donkeys were; He also knew where Saul and the servant were and just when they would come to see Samuel. So *a day before Saul came,* the Lord foretold his coming. He gave this information to Samuel privately, *in his ear.*

16. Tomorrow about this time I will send thee a man out of the land of Benjamin, and thou shalt anoint him to be captain over my people Israel, that he may save my people out of the hand of the Philistines: for I have looked upon my people, because their cry is come unto me.

Years earlier, the Philistines had oppressed Israel for a long time. Samuel had rallied the Israelites to drive them out with the help of a thunderstorm from the Lord, so at that time "they came no more into the coast of Israel" (1 Samuel 7:3-14). But the Philistines were watchful and persistent. They meant to come back. Through the years they probably saw signs of weakness in Israel. Now they were beginning to step up their pressure, and had established at least one outpost in Israel's territory (1 Samuel 10:5). Israel, however, had not turned so far away from God that He was willing to let the Philistines subdue them. This time He wanted the new king to take the lead in defeating those enemies, and Saul was to be the new king. Samuel was to designate him as king by anointing him. All this the Lord confided to Samuel the day before Saul and the servant met him.

The Hebrew word translated *captain* is not a military term for an officer in the army. It means the one in charge. In the Old Testament it is most often translated *ruler;* sometimes *prince* or *leader.* Here, of course, it refers to the king.

B. Identification on Arrival (v. 17)

17. And when Samuel saw Saul, the LORD said unto him, Behold the man whom I spake to thee of! this same shall reign over my people.

When Samuel saw Saul, the Lord plainly told His prophet that this was the one to be king. Samuel took Saul to the feast and seated him in the place of honor, then gave him lodging for the night. The record centers on Saul, but no doubt the servant remained with him. As the two were leaving in the morning, Samuel went a little way with them. He asked Saul to tell the servant to go on ahead so the prophet could speak privately with Saul (vv. 18-27).

C. Anointing the King (10:1a)

1a. Then Samuel took a vial of oil, and poured it upon his head.

From time immemorial there has been a custom of anointing a king to induct him into office or to indicate his dedication to that office. David, for example, was anointed three times: once long before he actually became king, once when he became king of Judah, and once when he became king of all Israel (1 Samuel 16:1-13;

> ### How to Say It
>
> MATRI.   *May*-tri.
> PHILISTINES.   Fi-*liss*-teens or *Fil*-is-teens.
> THUMMIM.   *Thum*-im (*th* as in *thin*).
> URIM.   *You*-rim.

---

2 Samuel 2:4; 5:1-3). In Israel, priests were anointed for their office long before there was a king (Exodus 28:40, 41). There is one mention of the anointing of a prophet (1 Kings 19:16). Some students think that among God's people the anointing oil signified a special gift of God's Spirit (1 Samuel 16:13). But of course God's Spirit comes as He will, with or without anointing (Judges 3:10; 6:34; Acts 8:14-17; 10:44).

Anointing was used to dedicate things as well as people to sacred uses. Jacob anointed a stone, making it a monument in memory of God's appearing to him (Genesis 28:18). The tabernacle in the wilderness was anointed, along with the things in it (Exodus 30:22-29).

So the first king of Israel was chosen by the Lord and anointed by the Lord's prophet, but no one knew it except the Lord, the prophet, and the king.

Certainly Saul was not seeking or expecting any such honor and responsibility. In his own view, he was a member of the most unimportant family in the most unimportant tribe of Israel (1 Samuel 9:21). After he left Samuel, do you suppose he might begin to wonder if it was really true? Could it be possible that he was to be the king? Samuel had a way to quiet any such doubts. He told Saul exactly what was going to happen to him as he was going on his way, and each thing happened just as Samuel had foretold. So each event became added evidence that Samuel was a true prophet (1 Samuel 10:2-12).

II. Informing the People (1 Samuel 10:20-24)

Now that the king was chosen, the next step was to let all the people know about the choice. For that purpose Samuel called a national meeting and told the people to present themselves before the Lord (1 Samuel 10:17-19). The Lord was going to select a king from among them, and apparently some way of casting lots was to be used to show the choice to the people.

When we flip a coin to decide a matter, we expect the result to be entirely by chance. But when the Hebrews cast lots to decide a matter of national importance, they confidently expected God to decide the outcome, and He did.

The Scripture does not give a description of how lots were cast. We do know that part of the high priest's equipment was the mysterious Urim and Thummim by which questions were decided. (See Exodus 28:30; Numbers 27:21) Some scholars speculate that these were two pebbles of the same size and shape, but of different colors. To answer a question, the priest would reach into his pouch without looking and take out a pebble. The white one meant yes and the black one meant no.

In this way or some other, the people expected God to let them know whom He had chosen to be king. So they began to present themselves before the Lord, first by tribes and then by thousands, the smaller family groups within a tribe (1 Samuel 10:19).

A. Selecting the King (vv. 20, 21)

20. And when Samuel had caused all the tribes of Israel to come near, the tribe of Benjamin was taken.

For a tribe to *come near* before the Lord, it was not necessary for the whole tribe to step forward. One man could simply mention the name of the tribe, and wait for an answer. To each tribe the answer was no, till *the tribe of Benjamin* was mentioned. Then the answer was yes. The king was a man of that tribe.

21. When he had caused the tribe of Benjamin to come near by their families, the family of Matri was taken, and Saul the son of Kish was taken: and when they sought him, he could not be found.

After the tribe of Benjamin was taken, the next step was to name the *families* within that tribe. These were presented one by one, and the Lord said yes to *the family of Matri*. Possibly there was another step, not specifically mentioned, by which the sub-family of Kish was chosen from among those of his brothers in Matri's family. But at last the members of a family were presented one by one, and *Saul the son of Kish was taken*. And now we see that it was not necessary for a man even to be present to be presented before the Lord. Someone merely put forward Saul's name, and the Lord said yes. Now all the people knew who was their king, and *he could not be found*.

B. Finding the King (vv. 22, 23)

22. Therefore they inquired of the LORD further, if the man should yet come thither. And the LORD answered, Behold, he hath hid himself among the stuff.

If the Lord was giving yes or no answers, then a series of questions must have been needed as *they inquired of the Lord further:*

Is this man Saul going to arrive later?
No.
Is he already here in camp?
No.
Is he in his tent?
No.
Is he taking care of the animals?
No.
Is he in the baggage area?
Yes.

So some of the people raced to the place where baggage was stored, and found Saul hidden *among the stuff*.

A RELUCTANT HERO

Victor Frisbie was for many years one of the most quoted persons in Los Angeles, although he was never seen in public! His opinions on numerous matters were often seen in the *Los Angeles Examiner*. His obituary appeared in the January 6, 1962, issue of the *Examiner:* "Victor Frisbie, well-known sportsman and traveler, died today."

The cause of death for Victor Frisbie was that the *Examiner* "died" that day also. Frisbie was the fictitious creation of bored copy writers on the newspaper's staff, who used Frisbie's "quotes" to enliven articles concerning recurring events such as the New Year's Day Rose Parade. Apparently, the editors never caught on to the ruse, but when the paper stopped publication, Frisbie died with it.

Saul really did exist, but when the time came for him to be presented as God's choice for Israel's first king, he was nowhere to be seen. Saul preferred anonymity to public acclaim.

Was it humility or lack of self-confidence that caused Saul to hide? We may never know. But for one to have a bit of reticence when faced with a task of great importance is far better than to be filled with braggadocio. An assignment of great responsibility calls for humble reliance on God, not boastful posturing.   —C. R. B.

23. And they ran and fetched him thence: and when he stood among the people, he was higher than any of the people from his shoulders and upward.

Reluctant Saul was brought to the meeting, and he was a head taller than the crowd. He was good-looking too (1 Samuel 9:2). Of course the Lord did not choose him for that reason, for "the Lord looketh on the heart" (1 Samuel 16:7). But the outward appearance made a fine impression on the people.

Saul, with all his height and good looks, was not arrogant or aggressive at this time. He was modest, even bashful. He described himself as

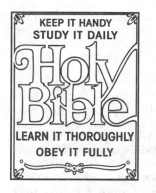

visual 8

the most insignificant man in Israel (1 Samuel 9:21). When he heard that he was to be king, he told no one (1 Samuel 10:15, 16). And when he knew the secret was about to come out, he hid instead of stepping forward to claim his place. But when it was time for action, he proved to be bold and capable (chapter 11).

No doubt both Saul's noble appearance and his modesty helped to make him acceptable to the people. Added to these was the fact that the Lord chose him.

C. Accepting the King (v. 24)

24. And Samuel said to all the people, See ye him whom the LORD hath chosen, that there is none like him among all the people? And all the people shouted, and said, God save the king.

The new king looked more kingly than anyone else in the crowd, and he was the Lord's choice. Samuel was quick to point out both these facts, and the people responded with a great shout of acclamation. Literally, the shout is "Live the king!" The *New International Version* aptly translates it as "Long live the king!" But King James' men interpreted it with the more pious acclaim they gave to King James: *God save the king!*

THE MEASURE OF A PERSON'S WORTH

In 1931, the 1, 250-foot Empire State Building in New York City became the world's tallest building. In 1972, New York's World Trade Center grabbed the honors at 1,350 feet. Then, in 1973, the Sears Tower in Chicago became the world's tallest building at 1, 454 feet.

Another member of the "world's tallest" club is "Bullwinkle," a 1,615-foot off-shore oil drilling rig in the Gulf of Mexico. One would never guess it to be that tall, since only 262 feet of it is above water!

We are fascinated with things and people of gargantuan proportions. From basketball players to national leaders, tall people seem to have an advantage. So it was that Saul's height was something for everyone to remark about as he was designated king of Israel.

However, Saul's later behavior demonstrated that there is more to the measure of a person than height. Like the oil-drilling rig, "Bullwinkle," what is beneath the surface may be far more significant than what can be seen at first glance. What is in one's heart—moral character and spiritual sensitivity—is far more vital than how tall a person is or any of the other physical standards the world uses to measure a person's worth.

—C. R. B.

Conclusion

Let's conclude our study with 1 Samuel 10:25, the verse that follows our lesson text: "Then Samuel told the people the manner of the kingdom, and wrote it in a book, and laid it up before the Lord."

A. The Manner of the Kingdom

The Lord was the proper king of Israel. When He gave His law, about four hundred years before Saul's time, He neither commanded nor encouraged the people to have any other king. Still He foresaw the time when Israel would have a human king, and He set down regulations for the king and the kingdom (Deuteronomy 17:14-20). No doubt these were the regulations Samuel told the people about. Let's consider them.

1. The king must be one chosen by the Lord.

2. He must be an Israelite, not a foreigner.

3. He must not have many horses. Horses were not used for plowing; they were used for war. Israel was to be a peaceful nation.

4. The king was not to have many wives.

5. He was not to have much silver and gold.

6. The king must make a copy of God's law, keep it with him, and read from it every day. Thus he would learn to fear the Lord and obey His law.

Notice how Saul fitted the legal description of a king:

1. He was chosen by the Lord. The Scriptures make that very plain.

2. He was an Israelite.

3. Probably he had no horses at all. Donkeys fitted his style of life.

4. Second Samuel 12:8 seems to indicate that Saul had more than one wife, and that David took Saul's wives along with his kingdom. Apparently monogamy was not recognized as ideal in those days.

5. As to silver and gold, it seems that Saul's family was moderately wealthy; but certainly it was not among the idle rich. Saul was put on foot in search of lost donkeys.

6. Without having any definite information, we may suppose Saul took home a copy of the law. Humble as he was at this time, perhaps he read it diligently and learned much. Next week we shall see that his obedience faltered at a critical time. Before we condemn him, let's consider our own Bible study, assess our own learning, and check our own obedience.

As God designed it, Israel was to be an absolute monarchy with himself as its king and with every citizen obedient to His law. Still there were to be judges and officers in every community to lead the way, to teach all the people to know the law and obey it, and to rebuke and punish when it was necessary (Deuteronomy 16:18).

On the other hand, Saul's kingdom was a limited monarchy. The king himself must obey God's law as strictly as the lowliest citizen did. The king must not issue any decree contrary to God's law. The Lord was still supreme.

This was the manner of the kingdom. Samuel told the people in the presence of the king so both king and people would understand. He put it in writing so it would be available for reference at any time. He laid it up before the Lord so it would be preserved for posterity.

B. God's Kingdom Today

The kingdom of God as we know it is not the kingdom of Israel. One striking difference is that God's kingdom now is not limited to the descendants of Israel, or Jacob, as he is more often called. It is open to anyone who chooses to be ruled by God. Nevertheless the kingdom of God is similar to Israel in several ways.

One came into the kingdom of Israel by being born to parents who were Israelites. One comes into the kingdom of God by being born again, born of water and the Spirit (John 3:3-5).

Home Daily Bible Readings

Monday, Oct. 17— Saul Seeks Help From a Seer (1 Samuel 9:1-10)
Tuesday, Oct. 18—Saul Comes to Samuel (1 Samuel 9:11-21)
Wednesday, Oct. 19—Samuel Anoints Saul to Be King (1 Samuel 9:22—10:1)
Thursday, Oct. 20—Signs to Confirm Saul's Appointment (1 Samuel 10:2-8)
Friday, Oct. 21—Saul's Heart Is Changed (1 Samuel 10:9-16)
Saturday, Oct. 22—Saul's Kingship Affirmed by Israel (1 Samuel 10:17-26)
Sunday, Oct. 23—Saul's Victory Over Israel's Enemy (1 Samuel 11)

Like the old kingdom of Israel, God's kingdom is designed to be an absolute monarchy with God as its king. If we say Christ is its king, that also is true, for God and Christ are one (John 10:30).

Like those in Israel, each person in God's kingdom is responsible for his own obedience to God. Many people, especially beginners, need help with this responsibility. Israel had judges and officers to keep the people in line; God's kingdom has elders to help and guide those who need their help. All of us in the kingdom should respect and follow those leaders (Hebrews 13:17), but only as long as they lead in God's way. No one has a right to overrule the Lord God Almighty.

Since there is no human king and each person is responsible for his own conduct, the regulations set down for the king of Israel may well be applied to each person in God's kingdom.

1. The king of Israel must be chosen by the Lord, and all those in God's kingdom also are chosen by Him (1 Peter 2:9, 10).

2. The king of Israel must be an Israelite, and each person in God's kingdom must be reborn as a child of God (1 John 1:12, 13).

3. The king of Israel must not have many war horses, and the citizen of God's kingdom must keep the peace if he can (Romans 12:18).

4. The king of Israel must not have many wives. An overseer in the church must be a one-woman man (1 Timothy 3:2). Is that not standard for those he oversees as well?

5. The king of Israel must not have much silver and gold, and people of God's kingdom are urged to lay up treasure in Heaven, not on earth (Matthew 6:19-21).

6. The king of Israel must have a copy of God's law and read from it daily, reading carefully and learning to fear God and obey Him. Every citizen of God's kingdom needs to be a diligent Bible student with the steadfast purpose of knowing God's will and doing it. How much time have you spent with God's Word in the past week? What have you learned about His will for you? How will you do God's will better this week?

C. Prayer

Our Father and our King, with the psalmist we pray, "Open thou mine eyes, that I may behold wondrous things out of thy law" (Psalm 119:18). Among other things, may we see a wondrous vision of what we ought to be doing in the work of Your kingdom, and by Your grace may we be doing it with joy and determination.

D. Thought to Remember

"The Lord your God was your king" (1 Samuel 12:12).

Learning by Doing

This page contains an alternate lesson plan emphasizing learning activities. Classes desiring such student involvement will find these suggestions helpful.

Learning Goals

This lesson should help students:

1. List Saul's qualities and potential for success as a leader.

2. Decide how God may be calling them to leadership today.

Into the Lesson

Ask students to complete one of the following sentences and to share their completion with a friend:

I most want a leader to be—

When I'm asked to lead, I usually—

My example of a good leader is—

Tell class members that today's lesson is about leadership. The lesson text focuses on the choice of Saul as Israel's first king, and you will want them to consider Saul's leadership potential.

Into the Word

Before class write the following phrases on slips of paper, one phrase per slip. Make enough slips so each class member may have one:

How God chose the leader

How Samuel felt about the new king

How Saul felt about being king

How the people felt about the new king

To begin today's Bible study, explain the background of today's text. Then put all the slips face down in a basket so the students cannot see what is written on them. Ask them to take a slip from the basket as it is passed to them.

Next, read today's printed text aloud to the class. As you do so each student is to listen for information about the topic on the slip he or she has drawn.

After the Scripture has been read, have your class members stand and ask each other what is written on their slips. Each is to find a partner whose slip matches his or her own. Once everyone is paired, give students five minutes to discuss their topics. Then lead the whole class in a discussion of the four topics.

Option. Make enough copies of the following instructions for each class member to have one:

Pick your activity. Decide which of the following Bible-learning activities you would like to complete. Then find at least one other person who will work with you on that activity. Your group will have six minutes to complete the activity. Then the teacher will ask several volun-teers to share what they have prepared. Pencils, paper, and drawing materials are on a table in the front of the room.

Choice one: Suppose you are Saul talking to your son Jonathan about the events of the day preceding your coronation, and the coronation day itself. What do you say to him? Be ready to have this conversation in front of the whole class. One person will need to be Saul, and the other Jonathan.

Choice two: Suppose you are a member of the nation of Israel writing a diary entry on the events of the days mentioned in our lesson text. How do you feel about the new king? Write down your impressions.

Choice three: Suppose you are an artist who wants to depict the historical events described in today's lesson text. How would you picture them? Draw one picture, or perhaps a series of pictures, to tell the story.

Encourage students to work together to complete these projects. Not everyone needs to do the actual acting, writing, or drawing. But members of the groups can give ideas to the ones actually completing the "creative" part of the project. If you choose the "Pick-your-activity" option for the Bible-study activity, try to see that all three choices are selected by different groups.

Into Life

Lead the whole class in discussing the following questions.

1. How might the events of 1 Samuel 10 have been designed to equip Saul for leadership? Consider each following verse or group of verses individually in this regard: verse 1, verses 2-8, verses 9-13, verses 20-24, and verse 27.

2. How do you think Saul felt about being chosen to be king of Israel? Consider especially 1 Samuel 9:21; 10:14-16; and 10:22, 23.

Perhaps one or more students will share their responses to these questions: Have you ever been tapped for some service in the church that you didn't feel qualified to perform? How did you react? How did you decide whether or not God wanted you to do it?

As you ask the following questions, have the students reflect on them privately: Are you more of a leader or a follower? Are you sure? If God were going to use you as a leader in some situation today, what would it be?

Let's Talk It Over

The questions on this page are designed to encourage review of the lesson Scriptures and to promote discussion of the lesson by the class. The answers provided are only discussion starters. Let your class talk it over from there.

1. When a church selects its leaders or makes any decision that affects the life of the church, it has no infallible method by which to determine God's will. How can a church ascertain as well as possible what God's will is in such matters?

Of course, divine guidelines for selecting candidates for the offices of elder or deacon are available in 1 Timothy 3:1-13. If members are given the opportunity to choose from among apparently qualified individuals, however, they still may have questions in their minds about the readiness of one or more candidates. It is obvious that the process of selecting such officers must be undergirded with prayer from start to finish. The candidates and the entire congregation must join in prayer for divine guidance. Similarly, when making a decision regarding a change in schedule or the repairing or remodeling of the building, the church must take into account any relevant Scriptures and then pray for God to lead them in doing what is best.

2. Why is modesty an important characteristic for one who seeks a position of leadership?

The opposite of modesty is boastful pride. We read in Proverbs 16:18, "Pride goeth before destruction, and a haughty spirit before a fall." When a leader falls, the lives of those whom he or she leads are adversely affected. For this reason a person's character and personality should be scrutinized carefully before that person is put in a position of leadership. From a more positive viewpoint, the leader who is genuinely modest will seek to help others rather than to exalt himself or herself. A modest person will be more likely to enlist the aid of others and to appreciate their contribution to the work. And, even better, such a person will be more likely to depend on the guidance and strength of the Lord instead of smugly assuming he or she can handle the challenge alone.

3. The kingdom of God is to be a kingdom of peace. How can we contribute to that peace?

"For the kingdom of God is not a matter of eating and drinking, but of righteousness, peace and joy in the Holy Spirit" (Romans 14:17, *New International Version*). Since the Holy Spirit is the author of peace in the church, Christians should cooperate with Him. If one sincerely studies the Spirit-inspired Word and follows its teachings, the Holy Spirit will produce His special fruit in that person—love, joy, peace, and other such spiritual characteristics (Galatians 5:22, 23). If every member is engaged in this same quest, peace and harmony will prevail in the church. Unrest and disharmony result when God's Word is set aside in favor of human opinion.

4. The people of God's kingdom are to value heavenly treasures above earthly treasures. What can we do to keep this priority in mind?

Heaven is a popular topic for sermons and Bible discussions. Most Christians want to know what we will do in Heaven, how we will recognize one another there, and various other matters. Christian teachers should take advantage of this interest in Heaven by pointing out that we need to begin now to develop heavenly values, heavenly attitudes, and heavenly habits. Whatever may be ours in Heaven in the way of "a mansion, a robe, and a crown," it is clear that the greatest treasures of heaven will be our personal fellowship with our Father, with Jesus Christ, and with our fellow saints. Since we are already citizens of Heaven (Philippians 3:20, *New International Version*), we should begin now to demonstrate our appreciation of Heaven's greater treasures.

5. The people of God's kingdom are to be diligent students of His Word. What does this mean and how can we accomplish it?

The purpose of having a Sunday school class is to give Christians the opportunity to study God's Word. But if this is the only time one studies the Bible, can that person be called a diligent student of God's Word? The Bible is a vast storehouse of wisdom, given by God to help us live forever in Heaven. Each Christian should be challenged to dig into his or her Bible to learn what God has to say about faith, holiness, Christian fellowship, and a host of other topics. We should become familiar with study helps such as Bible dictionaries, concordances, and commentaries for the enlightenment they can give. It is surely not an exaggeration to say that a well-equipped library should be among a church's highest priorities.

King Saul Disobeys God

DEVOTIONAL READING: 1 Samuel 15:22-26.

LESSON SCRIPTURE: 1 Samuel 13.

PRINTED TEXT: 1 Samuel 13:5-14.

1 Samuel 13:5-14

5 And the Philistines gathered themselves together to fight with Israel, thirty thousand chariots, and six thousand horsemen, and people as the sand which is on the seashore in multitude: and they came up, and pitched in Michmash, eastward from Bethaven.

6 When the men of Israel saw that they were in a strait, (for the people were distressed,) then the people did hide themselves in caves, and in thickets, and in rocks, and in high places, and in pits.

7 And some of the Hebrews went over Jordan to the land of Gad and Gilead. As for Saul, he was yet in Gilgal, and all the people followed him trembling.

8 And he tarried seven days, according to the set time that Samuel had appointed: but Samuel came not to Gilgal; and the people were scattered from him.

9 And Saul said, Bring hither a burnt offering to me, and peace offerings. And he offered the burnt offering.

10 And it came to pass, that as soon as he had made an end of offering the burnt offering, behold, Samuel came; and Saul went out to meet him, that he might salute him.

11 And Samuel said, What hast thou done? And Saul said, Because I saw that the people were scattered from me, and that thou camest not within the days appointed, and that the Philistines gathered themselves together at Michmash;

12 Therefore said I, The Philistines will come down now upon me to Gilgal, and I have not made supplication unto the LORD: I forced myself therefore, and offered a burnt offering.

13 And Samuel said to Saul, Thou hast done foolishly: thou hast not kept the commandment of the LORD thy God, which he commanded thee: for now would the LORD have established thy kingdom upon Israel for ever.

14 But now thy kingdom shall not continue: the LORD hath sought him a man after his own heart, and the LORD hath commanded him to be captain over his people, because thou hast not kept that which the LORD commanded thee.

Oct 30

GOLDEN TEXT: Now thy kingdom shall not continue: the LORD hath sought him a man after his own heart, and the LORD hath commanded him to be captain over his people, because thou hast not kept that which the LORD commanded thee.—1 Samuel 13:14.

From the Conquest to the Kingdom

Unit 3: The Beginning of the Kingdom

(Lessons 7-9)

Lesson Aims

After this lesson a student should be able to:

1. Tell how King Saul disobeyed the Lord's command, and what sentence was pronounced by the Lord's prophet.

2. Explain how the Lord's commands come to us.

3. Give more attention and better obedience to God's Word.

Lesson Outline

INTRODUCTION

    A. A Job for the King

    B. Confirming the Kingdom

    C. Lesson Background

I. DANGER IN ISRAEL (1 Samuel 13:5-7)

    A. Fearsome Invaders (v. 5)

    B. Fearful Israelites (v. 6)

       Fighting Fear With Faith

    C. Flight and Fear (v. 7)

II. DISOBEDIENT SACRIFICE (1 Samuel 13:8, 9)

    A. Scary Waiting (v. 8)

    B. Frightened Sacrifice (v. 9)

III. EXCUSES (1 Samuel 13:10-12)

    A. Caught in the Act (v. 10)

    B. Frightening Situation (v. 11)

    C. Desperate Need (v. 12)

IV. SENTENCE (1 Samuel 13:13, 14)

    A. Foolish Disobedience (v. 13)

    B. Severe Penalty (v. 14)

CONCLUSION

    A. God Is Unseen

    B. God Is Unheard

    C. Concluding the Conclusion

    D. Prayer

    E. Thought to Remember

The places mentioned in this lesson are included on the map identified as visual 9 of the visuals packet. The map is shown on page 76.

Introduction

What is a king supposed to do? Saul must have wondered about that. He was snatched suddenly from the farm to the throne, with no training or experience in politics. There was no former king to set an example, no government organization. The law said the king should study it and obey it; but specifically it said more about what the king should not do than about what he should do. Samuel was still the chief judge. As God's spokesman, he gave instructions to the nation. So what was a king to do?

What Saul did was to go back home to the farm (1 Samuel 10:26; 11:5). There he received news from the east, and suddenly he knew what the king ought to do.

A. A Job for the King

A strong force of Ammonites from the desert besieged Jabesh, a town on the east bank of Jordan. Hopelessly outnumbered, the men of Jabesh offered to surrender and pay tribute; but the arrogant Ammonite king wanted to humiliate them further by gouging out the right eye of every man. At that, the besieged people of Jabesh sent messengers throughout Israel to beg for help.

Saul's response was fully worthy of a king. He sent out an urgent demand for volunteers, and 330,000 men responded. With superb generalship, Saul led them to surround the Ammonite force and cut it to bits (1 Samuel 11:1-11).

B. Confirming the Kingdom

Samuel then called the people to meet in Gilgal to celebrate the victory, confirm the kingdom, and give thanks to the Lord. Though Saul had been a magnificent leader, Samuel at last convinced the people that they had done wrong in asking for a king. Nevertheless, Samuel assured them that peace and prosperity could be had exactly as before. With or without a king, they must simply obey the law of God (1 Samuel 11:14—12:25).

C. Lesson Background

Saul then dismissed most of his army, keeping only three thousand men. He deployed two thousand of them in the high country at Michmash and Bethel. Saul's son Jonathan took command of the other thousand and led them to Gibeah, his hometown. The Philistine outpost at Geba was between these detachments of Israelites.

It was Jonathan who began hostilities. With his thousand men he "smote the garrison of the Philistines that was in Geba." Whether any Philistines escaped alive or not, the news soon reached the Philistine homeland down by the Mediterranean Sea.

It seemed certain that the Philistines would be out in force to avenge the crushing of their outpost in Israel. Saul sent a call to all the land, and the men he had recently dismissed began to assemble again at Gilgal, down in the Jordan Valley (1 Samuel 13:1-4).

I. Danger in Israel
(1 Samuel 13:5-7)

The Philistines had a number of city-states, but they had remarkable success in stifling rivalries among them and acting together. Now some of them remembered a former defeat in Israel (1 Samuel 7:10, 11). Intending to be successful this time, they put together all the armed forces they could muster.

A. Fearsome Invaders (v. 5)

5. And the Philistines gathered themselves together to fight with Israel, thirty thousand chariots, and six thousand horsemen, and people as the sand which is on the seashore in multitude: and they came up, and pitched in Michmash, eastward from Beth-aven.

Without doubting the truth of the Bible, many scholars think the number *thirty thousand* must be viewed with suspicion here. Usually the horsemen in an army are many more than the chariots (2 Samuel 10:18; 1 Kings 10:26; 2 Chronicles 12:3). It is hard to believe that the Philistines had *thirty thousand chariots* and only *six thousand horsemen*. Besides, students find no other record of as many as thirty thousand chariots. Therefore many students think some uninspired scribe in ancient times must have made a mistake in copying the number from the inspired original. Some ancient versions and some modern versions have recorded *three thousand* instead of thirty thousand. Some students think it is more likely that the original number was *one thousand*.

In any case, it was a fearsome army that swept their way into Israel. There were at least a thousand chariots and six thousand horsemen, plus foot soldiers so numerous that the reporter did not even venture to estimate their number. It is probable that the Israelites had no chariots or horsemen at all. If they could recall the 330,000 men who had gone to Jabesh (1 Samuel 11:8), we can only guess how that number compared with the uncounted horde of Philistines now camped at Michmash. Saul and his two thousand men had been at Michmash not long before (v. 2), but they had withdrawn to Gilgal in the Jordan Valley to wait the arrival of the rest of their army (v. 4).

B. Fearful Israelites (v. 6)

6. When the men of Israel saw that they were in a strait, (for the people were distressed,) then the people did hide themselves in caves, and in thickets, and in rocks, and in high places, and in pits.

The sheer size of the Philistine army was frightening. Israelites living near the invasion route hid in the hills, leaving their homes and farms to be pillaged by invaders in search of grain, meal, and animals for food.

FIGHTING FEAR WITH FAITH

A phobia is an exaggerated and often disabling fear. There are names for literally dozens of phobias. For example, there is hydrophobia (fear of water), claustrophobia (fear of closed-in places) and its opposite, agoraphobia (fear of open spaces).

A phobia recently come to light is shared by tens of thousands of persons who formerly drove automobiles. They now have an uncontrollable fear of getting behind the wheel of a car. It seems that long bridges trigger the phobia. A police dispatcher in the area around the Chesapeake Bay Bridge in Maryland says that on some days there are as many as ten drivers who cannot make it across the bridge. These drivers "freeze up" on the bridge and come to a halt, making it necessary for someone to come out and drive their cars the rest of the way across the bridge.

When the Philistine forces invaded the land, the Israelites were overcome with fear, and they hid themselves in caves, in thickets, in high places or anywhere else they could seclude themselves from what seemed like sure disaster. At times our fear of what lies in the future threatens to undo us. Sometimes those fears are unreasonable, exaggerating the danger we face. But whether our fear is reasonable or not, like Israel we need to find our refuge in God, who holds both us and the future in His hands.

—C. R. B.

C. Flight and Fear (v. 7)

7. And some of the Hebrews went over Jordan to the land of Gad and Gilead. As for Saul, he was yet in Gilgal, and all the people followed him trembling.

Instead of hiding near their homes, *some of the Hebrews* looked for safety farther away. Hoping the war would be confined to the west side of the Jordan, they crossed to the other side of the river.

How to Say It

AMMONITES. *Am*-un-ites.
GEBA. *Gee*-buh (*G* as in *get*).
GIBEA. *Gib*-e-uh.
JABESH. *Jay*-besh.
MICHMASH. *Mik*-mash.
PHILISTINES. Fi-*liss*-teens or *Fil*-iss-teens.

visual 9

Saul stayed *in Gilgal* on the west side of the river, but *all the people* who joined him there were *trembling* with fear.

II. Disobedient Sacrifice (1 Samuel 13:8, 9)

Waiting may be harder than fighting, especially if the waiting people are scared. So it was with Saul and his soldiers at Gilgal. We can readily imagine they were too nervous to sleep well, their appetite failed, and fear grew bigger day by day.

A. Scary Waiting (v. 8)

8. And he tarried seven days, according to the set time that Samuel had appointed: but Samuel came not to Gilgal; and the people were scattered from him.

This looks back to the day when Samuel anointed Saul to be king. At that time Samuel had told what was going to happen in the near future, and it had happened just as he had predicted (1 Samuel 10:2-6). Samuel also had said that Saul then should do what he would see occasion to do (1 Samuel 10:7). Saul had seen occasion to rescue Jabesh, and he had done that (1 Samuel 11:1-11). He had seen occasion to smash a Philistine outpost, and Jonathan had done that with a detachment of the army (1 Samuel 13:2-4). We do not know how much time it took to do all that; but afterward the time came to obey the last part of the instruction Samuel had given on that anointing day. (See 1 Samuel 10:8).

While Saul was at Michmash, Samuel may have reminded him of those instructions. With or without such a reminder, Saul remembered. He went down to Gilgal (1 Samuel 13:4). Hard as it was to wait there idly, *he tarried seven days, according to the set time that Samuel had appointed.* He knew Samuel was a prophet who relayed God's commands, and he needed the prophet to tell him what to do next (1 Samuel 10:8.)

But the seventh day came, and Samuel did not. It must have seemed to Saul that the waiting was becoming unendurable. His situation grew worse day by day, for *the people were scat-*

tered from him: that is, his soldiers were deserting. Each morning the army was smaller, and in seven days the loss seemed ominous. Saul felt that he could wait no longer.

B. Frightened Sacrifice (v. 9)

9. And Saul said, Bring hither a burnt offering unto me, and peace offerings. And he offered the burnt offering.

We need not suppose Saul usurped the place of a priest and made the sacrifice with his own hands. There were priests in his camp, enough of them to carry the ark of the covenant (1 Samuel 14:3, 18). Probably they conducted the sacrifice with the proper ceremony (Leviticus 1). But the king had been told to wait till Samuel arrived (1 Samuel 10:8). That was the Lord's command given through His prophet, and Saul had disobeyed it.

III. Excuses (1 Samuel 13:10-12)

Like most of us who disobey a command of the Lord, Saul had reasons that he thought were compelling. But were they?

A. Caught in the Act (v. 10)

10. And it came to pass, that as soon as he had made an end of offering the burnt offering, behold, Samuel came; and Saul went out to meet him, that he might salute him.

How often we disobedient ones are embarrassed by being caught in the act! We ought to be embarrassed whether anyone sees us or not, for we know the Lord sees every disobedience.

Some students think it is unfair to condemn Saul for his act. They say he waited seven days according to his instructions. They say Samuel broke his promise by failing to come in seven days, and therefore Saul was no longer bound to obey the command. Other students think Saul did not wait till the seven days were ended, but only till the seventh day began. They think Saul made his offering on the seventh day, and Samuel came on that day as he had promised.

We can leave that difference of opinion unsettled. In any case, the command to Saul was not only to wait seven days, but also to wait till Samuel came. That he failed to do.

B. Frightening Situation (v. 11)

11. And Samuel said, What hast thou done? And Saul said, Because I saw that the people were scattered from me, and that thou camest not within the days appointed, and that the Philistines gathered themselves together at Michmash.

What Saul had done was plain enough. The fire was still blazing on the altar. Saul had violated God's command by offering the burnt offering instead of waiting for Samuel to arrive. So Saul did not answer the question by telling what he had done. Like a guilty child caught in the act, the king began to tell why he had done it. He gave three excuses:

1. His troops were deserting. Every day made his army less capable of conflict.

2. Samuel did not come *within the days appointed*.

3. The Philistines at Michmash were poised to strike. They might strike any day.

If Saul had put more trust in God and less in human resources, he could easily have seen the fallacy in his reasoning.

1. It would be better to lose his whole army than to lose the Lord's help by disobeying Him.

2. Samuel's delay called for more trust in God, not for disobedience.

3. The gathering of Philistines provided a perfect opportunity for the Lord to defeat them.

C. Desperate Need (v. 12)

12. Therefore said I, The Philistines will come down now upon me to Gilgal, and I have not made supplication unto the LORD: I forced myself therefore, and offered a burnt offering.

"I had no choice." How often we hear that excuse, or make it ourselves! So Saul said, "I didn't want to do it, but I just had to." The imminent danger demanded immediate action. The Philistines might swoop down at any time, and it was unthinkable to go into battle without asking for the Lord's help.

Here Saul displayed a mixture of good thinking and bad. It is wise to seek God's help in any crisis, yes; but it is foolish to think His help can be gained by disobeying Him.

IV. Sentence
(1 Samuel 13:13, 14)

We may feel inclined to sympathize with Saul. The man was in a critical situation, and it was getting worse. After all, he did wait a week, and then all he did was to seek the Lord's help. What's wrong with that? But Samuel pronounced the sentence of the Lord, and His word is more reliable than our feeling.

A. Foolish Disobedience (v. 13)

13. And Samuel said to Saul, Thou hast done foolishly: thou hast not kept the commandment of the LORD thy God, which he commanded thee: for now would the LORD have established thy kingdom upon Israel for ever.

It is foolish to disobey *the commandment of the Lord thy God*. No matter how critical the situation, no matter how urgent the need, no matter how plausible the excuses, it is foolish to disobey the Lord. If Saul had been as wise as he was valiant, he would have been obedient. Then the Lord would have established his kingdom *for ever:* his descendants would have been rulers in Israel through all the generations, and the Messiah would have come from his line. But now there was no chance of that, for Saul had *done foolishly*.

B. Severe Penalty (v. 14)

14. But now thy kingdom shall not continue: the LORD hath sought him a man after his own heart, and the LORD hath commanded him to be captain over his people, because thou hast not kept that which the LORD commanded thee.

Thy kingdom shall not continue. This does not mean Saul was finished ruling Israel as of that moment. It means his kingdom was not to continue through the generations of his descendants, as it would have done if Saul had been wise and obedient (v. 13). To head that lasting line of kings the Lord now had chosen someone else, *a man after his own heart*. We know that man was David, but perhaps only God then knew who he was. Even Samuel may have learned at a later time, and certainly David himself did not yet suspect that such a destiny awaited him.

As for Saul, God did not cast him off after that one disobedience. The Lord used him and his daring son Jonathan to win a victory over those fearsome Philistines at Michmash (1 Samuel 14:1-23). He used them to defeat other enemies as well (1 Samuel 14:47, 48). Later disobedience brought rejection of Saul (1 Samuel 15), but even then he continued to rule for years. Meanwhile, through danger and hardship and valor, David was being prepared to become king. Chapters 16—30 of 1 Samuel tell about it.

Conclusion

Thou hast done foolishly. When all our explanations are made and all our excuses are offered, the word of God's prophet still rings through the centuries at every misdeed of ours: "Thou hast done foolishly." That same word comes to all mankind: to Adam and Eve in the garden, to the many who drowned in the great flood, to those burned up in Sodom, to the disobedient ones who died in the destruction of Jerusalem in A.D. 70, to you and me and every sinner of today, for "all have sinned, and come short of the glory of God" (Romans 3:23). It's foolish.

A. God Is Unseen

Saul's failure was a failure of faith, and so is ours. He could see the threat of the Philistines, but the Lord was hidden from his sight. So he yielded to the visible threat and disobeyed the invisible Lord. That was foolish. In like manner we yield to the pressure of circumstances and tell a lie, or join in malicious gossip, or turn away from a brother in need. It's foolish.

God has chosen to be invisible so we may walk by faith (2 Corinthians 5:7). Yet the invisible God is not without a visible witness. Rain and sun and harvest speak of His power and His love (Acts 14:17). The heavens declare His glory (Psalm 19:1), and the whole earth is full of it too (Isaiah 6:3). The testimony of earth and sky is so conclusive that there is no excuse for any who fail to believe in God and obey Him (Romans 1:20-22).

B. God Is Unheard

Saul heard Samuel speak; but when Samuel was not present, Saul did not hear the voice of God. Still Saul had good reason to be sure the voice of Samuel spoke the message of God. Samuel told him what was going to happen, and it did happen. Saul should have kept the word of the prophet in mind.

God has chosen to be unheard by most of us, but He has not left us without His Word. He spoke to His prophets and gave them His message for us. "For the prophecy came not in old time by the will of man: but holy men of God spake as they were moved by the Holy Ghost" (2 Peter 1:21).

God spoke to a few prophets. Each prophet spoke to a few people, or a few hundred, or a few thousand. But some of the prophets also wrote their messages, and some of their writings have been collected in a book, the Bible. The book speaks to the whole world. Specifically, it speaks to you. It speaks to me. This is the Word of God that we need to carry in our minds so we will not disobey it. "Thy word have I hid in mine heart, that I might not sin against thee" (Psalm 119:11).

To hide God's Word in your heart is not to conceal it or to keep it away from anyone. It is to treasure it, to love it, to know it, and above all to obey it. Of course the one who thus treasures God's Word will be more than eager to share it with others.

The king of Israel was charged to have his own personal copy of God's law in a time when copies were few. He was not only to have it, but also to read from it every day. And he was not only to read from it, but also to learn to fear God and obey Him (Deuteronomy 17:18, 19).

When Israel decided to have a human king, this was God's law for him. Now we have decided to have no human king. The kingdom of God is nearer to its original plan. God is the only king, and each one of us is personally responsible to Him. Then each one of us had better have his own copy of God's Word, and read it, and learn to fear God and obey Him.

C. Concluding the Conclusion

"Let us hear the conclusion of the whole matter: Fear God, and keep his commandments: for this is the whole duty of man" (Ecclesiastes 12:13).

So wrote Solomon, one of God's prophets—or so his writing is translated in the *King James Version*. Note that the word *duty* is in italics, indicating that it is not in the original writing. The Hebrew reads simply, "This is the whole of man." This is the essence of humanity; this is what God designed each person to do; this is the way to be truly human: "Fear God, and keep his commandments."

D. Prayer

How good You are, our Father: how precious, how kind, how loving! Not only have You given us Your faultless Word to guide us in Your way; You also have given Your faultless Son to atone for the foolish failures in which we have turned away from Your Word. We thank You, Father; and in gratitude we pledge ourselves anew to read Your Word and follow it. In Jesus' name, amen.

E. Thought to Remember

"Fear God, and keep his commandments."

Learning by Doing

This page contains an alternate lesson plan emphasizing learning activities. Classes desiring such student involvement will find these suggestions helpful.

Learning Goals

Today's session will help students:

1. Understand Saul's situation while he waited for Samuel to come and offer the prescribed sacrifice.

2. Compare Saul's situation with that of Christians today who are waiting for God to answer a prayer or provide direction in their lives.

3. Name one situation in their lives in which they will continue to wait on God.

Into the Lesson

The foundation for today's discussion is a series of multiple-choice statements printed here and in the next section, "Into the Word." Make a copy for each student, or read the statements to the class as you conduct your discussion.

To open today's session, ask your students to complete the following three multiple-choice statements (more than one completion may be chosen).

1. When I think my prayers are unanswered, I
    a. quit praying
    b. pray harder
    c. change my prayer
    d. ask a Christian friend for advice

2. When I wonder what I should do in a specific situation, I usually
    a. pray
    b. read the Bible
    c. go to church
    d. do what seems best at the moment

3. When I realize I've done something wrong, my first reaction is usually to
    a. make excuses
    b. ask forgiveness
    c. get down on myself
    d. ask if it was really so wrong after all

Tell your class that in the event recorded in today's text, King Saul faced situations similar to those listed above. As you study today's Scripture, your students should decide how their responses compare with Saul's.

Into the Word

Use the material in the "Lesson Background" section to connect last week's lesson with this lesson. Then have a student read today's text aloud to the class. The multiple-choice statements below may then be used as an outline for your discussion of today's text.

1. The Israelites were afraid because
    a. the Philistines were strong
    b. they didn't trust God
    c. they didn't trust Saul
    d. anyone would have been afraid under the circumstances

2. Saul offered the burnt offering himself because
    a. he was afraid he would lose the battle
    b. his army was deserting him
    c. he didn't trust Samuel
    d. he was obeying the spirit of the law, if not the letter of it

3. Samuel asked Saul, "What have you done?" because
    a. he didn't know what Saul had done
    b. he couldn't believe what Saul had done
    c. he wanted Saul to admit what he had done
    d. he was hoping to hear a good reason for what Saul had done

4. Saul's response to Samuel showed that
    a. Saul ignored what God had commanded
    b. Saul tried to make himself look good
    c. Saul trusted God
    d. Saul trusted himself

5. Samuel's response to Saul proved that
    a. Samuel was displeased with Saul
    b. God was displeased with Saul
    c. Saul would no longer be king
    d. God had another king in mind for Israel

Into Life

Distribute copies of the following five incomplete statements. For numbers 1, 2, and 3, have students write down their answers, share their answers with a neighbor, or discuss them with the whole class.

1. When I think about "waiting on God," I remember the time when—

2. The hardest thing about waiting on God to act or direct is—

3. It's always a good idea to keep waiting on God, because—

Ask volunteers to read these Scriptures at this time: Psalm 27:14; 37:7; Proverb 20:22; Isaiah 40:31; Lamentations 3:25.

Then ask students to respond privately to these two open-ended sentences:

4. I am presently waiting on God to—

5. I will continue to wait on God because—

Let's Talk It Over

The questions on this page are designed to encourage review of the lesson Scriptures and to promote discussion of the lesson by the class. The answers provided are only discussion starters. Let your class talk it over from there.

1. "I was afraid." Even Christian adults will sometimes use this or a similar statement to excuse their failure to do God's work. What does the Bible indicate regarding this?

While Saul himself may not have been afraid of the huge Philistine army, many of his people were, and that affected his decision to disobey the Lord's command. It is clear that neither Samuel nor the Lord himself accepted that fearfulness as an excuse for Saul's disobedience. Other biblical examples may be cited in which fear caused a person to be disobedient. Moses' series of objections when God commanded him to deliver Israel from Egypt is an obvious example (Exodus 3, 4). The wicked servant in Jesus' parable of the talents (Matthew 25:14-30) provides us a New Testament example. In each instance, the person's fear was rejected as being a legitimate reason for disobedience.

2. Saul explained to Samuel, "I forced myself therefore, and offered a burnt offering" (1 Samuel 13:12). In the *New International Version* this is rendered, "So I felt compelled to offer the burnt offering." What can we say about occasions when we feel compelled to disobey a command of the Lord?

We should ask ourselves what the source of such compulsion is. Are we being drawn away of our own lust? (See James 1:14.) Is another human being pressuring us to do what is wrong? Can we detect the working of the devil in the force that assails us? Whatever the source of the compulsion, let us remember that no person nor thing can compel us to disobey God. We have the power to resist, and we have the Lord's promise of help in overcoming. In 1 Corinthians 10:13 we are told that "God . . . will not suffer you to be tempted above that ye are able; but will with the temptation also make a way to escape, that ye may be able to bear it."

3. Why may one be inclined to sympathize with Saul? Why must we be careful about sympathizing with those who disobey God under confusing circumstances?

One may read 1 Samuel 13 and conclude, "It's not fair!" The matter of fairness is stressed in our time. We expect to be treated fairly by other human beings and by God, and we become upset when we feel that we are receiving unfair treatment. Therefore, one may be quick to jump to Saul's defense. It is true that Saul was in a difficult situation, and he did wait for Samuel during a long and trying week. But Saul had clear instructions to await the arrival of God's prophet, who would offer the appropriate sacrifices to God. By disobeying, Saul revealed a weakness in his character that made him unfit to rule. This account is a reminder to us that we must be wary of judging God's commands and judgments by our standards of fairness. Instead, we must yield to His unfathomable wisdom and justice and respond to Him with humble trust and obedience.

4. Samuel accused Saul of acting foolishly. If someone were to accuse us of foolish behavior, how should we react?

While Jesus warned of the danger in calling someone a fool (Matthew 5:22), on occasion He addressed His hearers with that term (Matthew 23:17; Luke 11:40; 24:25). Obviously Jesus was not intending to insult or belittle His hearers, but to stir them to repentance and deeper awareness of truth. If we are accused of foolish actions, let us use that as a prod to search our hearts and lives to see if there is any truth to the charge. If there is, let us change our ways and seek more diligently for the wisdom God offers us (see James 1:5).

5. Solomon's conclusion in Ecclesiastes 12:13 provided a sound principle for life under the Old Testament law: "Fear God, and keep his commandments: for this is the whole duty of man." As New Testament believers, how might we view this principle?

We could say that the whole duty of man is to respond to Jesus Christ's offer of salvation and eternal life, or to live in the light of God's grace. But once we adjust Ecclesiastes 12:13 from a New Testament perspective, we find it a very worthwhile principle. It is vital that we fear, reverence, and honor the heavenly Father who sent His Son to be our Savior. And it is equally important that we obey His commandments. We could express the principle this way: "Fear God, and live as Jesus Christ would have you live: for this is the whole duty of Christians."

David Claims God's Promise

DEVOTIONAL READING: Psalm 86:1-12.

LESSON SCRIPTURE: 2 Samuel 7.

PRINTED TEXT: 2 Samuel 7:18-29.

2 Samuel 7:18-29

18 Then went king David in, and sat before the LORD, and he said, Who am I, O Lord GOD? and what is my house, that thou hast brought me hitherto?

19 And this was yet a small thing in thy sight, O Lord GOD; but thou hast spoken also of thy servant's house for a great while to come. And is this the manner of man, O Lord GOD?

20 And what can David say more unto thee? for thou, Lord GOD, knowest thy servant.

21 For thy word's sake, and according to thine own heart, hast thou done all these great things, to make thy servant know them.

22 Wherefore thou art great, O LORD God: for there is none like thee, neither is there any God besides thee, according to all that we have heard with our ears.

23 And what one nation in the earth is like thy people, even like Israel, whom God went to redeem for a people to himself, and to make him a name, and to do for you great things and terrible, for thy land, before thy people, which thou redeemedst to thee from Egypt, from the nations and their gods?

24 For thou hast confirmed to thyself thy people Israel to be a people unto thee for ever: and thou, LORD, art become their God.

25 And now, O LORD God, the word that thou hast spoken concerning thy servant, and concerning his house, establish it for ever, and do as thou hast said.

26 And let thy name be magnified for ever, saying, The LORD of hosts is the God over Israel: and let the house of thy servant David be established before thee.

27 For thou, O LORD of hosts, God of Israel, hast revealed to thy servant, saying, I will build thee a house: therefore hath thy servant found in his heart to pray this prayer unto thee.

28 And now, O Lord GOD, thou art that God, and thy words be true, and thou hast promised this goodness unto thy servant:

29 Therefore now let it please thee to bless the house of thy servant, that it may continue for ever before thee: for thou, O Lord GOD, hast spoken it: and with thy blessing let the house of thy servant be blessed for ever.

GOLDEN TEXT: O LORD God, the word that thou hast spoken concerning thy servant, and concerning his house, establish it for ever, and do as thou hast said.
—2 Samuel 7:25.

From the Conquest to the Kingdom

Unit 4: The Kingdom Under David

and Solomon (Lessons 10-13)

Lesson Aims

After this lesson a student should be able to:

1. Recall the main thoughts of David's prayer that is recorded in our text.

2. Mention two or three of God's promises that are precious to the student.

3. Identify one way of doing God's will more perfectly this week.

Lesson Outline

INTRODUCTION

  A. David the Shepherd-Musician

  B. David the Hero

  C. David the Fugitive

  D. From Fugitive to King

  E. David the King

  F. Lesson Background

  I. GOD AND DAVID (2 Samuel 7:18-20)

    A. Who Is David? (v. 18)

    B. Divine Promise (v. 19)

    C. Divine Knowledge (v. 20)

  II. GOD AND HIS PEOPLE (2 Samuel 7:21-24)

    A. The Greatness of God (vv. 21, 22)

      Alone in the Universe?

    B. The Greatness of God's People (vv. 23, 24)

  III. GOD AND HIS WORD (2 Samuel 7:25-29)

    A. Prayer for David's House (v. 25)

    B. Prayer for God's Name (v. 26)

    C. Prayer Based on Promise (vv. 27-29)

CONCLUSION

  A. Prayer of God's People

  B. Precious Promises

  C. Prayer

  D. Thought to Remember

Display visual 10 of the visuals packet. The Lesson Background and Conclusion sections refer to the truth it illustrates. The visual is shown on page 86.

Introduction

Saul couldn't wait. The job facing him was dangerous as well as difficult—he had to drive out a big army of well-armed Philistines. He wanted to get on with it, but the Lord said to wait till Samuel would come with instructions. So Saul waited, but not quite long enough. Disobedience was still disobedience, even after seven days of obedience. Last week's lesson told about that.

A later disobedience was even worse. Off to the south was a tribe of people who had attacked Israel repeatedly. The Lord decided that that tribe had become too wicked to live. So the Lord told Saul to take his army and destroy the tribe of Amalek, every man, woman, and child. This was an expedition for punishment, not plunder. Sheep and cattle and other property were to be destroyed along with the people.

Again Saul obeyed, but not quite enough. He took his army and destroyed most of the tribe, but he caught the king and brought him back alive. He also saved some of the best of the cattle and sheep—for a sacrifice to the Lord, he said. You can read about this in 1 Samuel 15.

That was when the Lord announced that Saul was rejected. Saul continued as king the rest of his life, and his doings are recorded in the first book of Samuel; but now David took center stage.

A. David the Shepherd-Musician

God sent Samuel to Bethlehem to anoint David as the next king. Not many people were allowed to know about that, however. Saul once had been modest and unselfish, but now he was an arrogant and egotistical tyrant. He would kill both Samuel and David if he knew about this anointing (1 Samuel 16:1-13).

David was a shepherd, and he also was such a fine musician that his fame had spread far from Bethlehem. When King Saul was troubled by an evil spirit, his advisers thought he might be calmed by music. David was recommended, and brought to the king (1 Samuel 16:14-23).

David then became a frequent traveler between the pastures of Bethlehem and the palace of the king. He was a shepherd at home till he was called to play for the king (1 Samuel 17:15).

B. David the Hero

The Philistines invaded Israel again. Their army and Saul's army faced each other across a valley, and a Philistine stepped out with a challenge. Why should whole armies fight? That was his question. Let the Hebrews send a man to fight him in single combat. Whoever lost, his side would concede the victory to the other.

This Philistine was over nine feet tall. No man of Israel volunteered to meet him, till David came to the camp. When he saw the situation, he promptly volunteered to fight the giant. He said the Lord would deliver the big man into his hand, and that was what happened (1 Samuel 17:1-54).

With that victory to his credit, David came into the army. Soon he was its commander. His troops were so successful that David was the hero of the victory celebration. But Saul was furious. He could not stand to see the general more celebrated than the king (1 Samuel 18:5-9).

C. David the Fugitive

The jealous king decided to assassinate his popular general. His crude efforts were frustrated, however, and David escaped to the desert. There he was joined by members of his family and others who were out of favor with the king (1 Samuel 18:10—22:2).

Instead of resorting to robbery, this outlaw band protected people of Judah against raiding Philistines. Probably the grateful men of Judah responded by providing them with supplies. So they moved about in the desert, while Saul and his army tried to catch them. For a while they tried to find refuge with the Philistines, but that did not work out very well. So David and his band went on living in the desert, defeating Saul's enemies and dodging Saul's army. This went on till Saul died in a battle with the Philistines (1 Samuel 22:3—31:13).

D. From Fugitive to King

David belonged to the tribe of Judah, and he had won the gratitude of his tribe by defending its people against the Philistines and other raiders. So when Saul was dead, the men of Judah soon made David their king (2 Samuel 2:1-4).

Meanwhile Ishbosheth became king of the other tribes. He seems to have had no ability as a leader, but he was Saul's son, and he was backed by Abner, capable commander of Saul's army (2 Samuel 2:8-11). There was spasmodic war between David's troops and Abner's, and the advantage was with David (2 Samuel 2:12—3:1).

When both Ish-bosheth and Abner were dead, their tribes had no strong national leader. Abner already had suggested to them the idea of joining David's kingdom (2 Samuel 3:17, 18). Now they were ready to do it. Tribal leaders went to David and anointed him as king of all Israel (2 Samuel 5:1-5).

E. David the King

Now united under an able king, Israel prospered. Soon David captured Jerusalem. The tribe of Judah had taken that town centuries before (Judges 1:8), but the heathen Jebusites had reoccupied it and had lived there for a long time. Now David made it his capital (2 Samuel 5:6-10).

David wanted to bring the ark of the covenant to his new capital. Years earlier the Philistines had captured it and taken it to their country, but

---

How to Say It

AMALEK. *Am*-uh-lek.
ISH-BOSHETH. Ish-*bo*-sheth.
JEBUSITES. *Jeb*-yuh-sites.
PHILISTINES. Fi-*liss*-teens or *Fil*-iss-teens.

---

soon they had returned it. Since that time it had been kept in a private house (1 Samuel 4:1—7:2). From there David moved the ark to Jerusalem, where a special tent became its new home (2 Samuel 6:1-19).

F. Lesson Background

The immediate background of this lesson is seen in 2 Samuel 7:1-17.

King David relaxed in a fine house built by artisans from Tyre, and the ark of the covenant rested in a tent. That ark represented the presence of God among His people. David thought the ark should have a finer house than the king had, and he proposed to build such a house.

Nathan the prophet promptly approved, but he did it without waiting to hear from the Lord. When God spoke, Nathan had to retract his approval. With all good intentions, David was running ahead of the Lord's plan. God would have His house, but David would not build it. The reason is not recorded at this point in the record, but the Lord explained it to David at this time or later. It was because David was a warrior, a man of blood (1 Chronicles 22:7-10). This does not mean David's wars were wrong. God expressly directed many of his battles. But the battles were fought to make peace. God's kingdom is properly a peaceful kingdom, and it was more fitting for God's house to be built by a man of peace, David's son.

David must have been disappointed because he was not allowed to build a house for the Lord, but the message in 2 Samuel 7:5-16 softened the disappointment in several ways:

1. The house was David's idea, not the Lord's. The Lord had never had a house, He had never asked for one, and He was not asking for one now (vv. 5-7).

2. The Lord's favor to David was clear in the shepherd's rise from farm to palace (vv. 8, 9). Being so blessed and favored, David should accept God's will concerning the house.

3. God was going to provide a permanent place for His people Israel (vv. 10, 11). That was reassuring to David, who had been fighting to secure such a place.

4. God's house would be built, though David would not build it (vv. 12-15).

5. Though David would not build a house for the Lord, the Lord would build a house for David. This is seen in the end of verse 11 and in verse 16. God would not build a house of stone and wood, but a household, a family, that would continue to rule forever. We do not know how fully David understood that promise; but with inspiration of the Holy Spirit he was able to sing of the king eternal, the Christ, whose kingdom has no end (Psalm 16:8-11; Acts 2:25-36).

I. God and David
(2 Samuel 7:18-20)

Surely the message from the Lord brought disappointment to David; but it brought also such reminders of past favors and such assurance of future favor that disappointment was lost in humble gratitude and praise and hope. Out of an overflowing heart David uttered the prayer that we read in our text.

A. Who Is David? (v. 18)

18. Then went king David in, and sat before the LORD, and he said, Who am I, O Lord GOD? and what is my house, that thou hast brought me hitherto?

David found a private place for his prayer. Some students think he went into the tent where the ark of the covenant was kept (2 Samuel 6:17). But it was not necessarily so. He could go into a private room of his own palace and sit before the Lord, for he understood that God was with him everywhere. It was David who sang the beautiful assurance of Psalm 139:8-10:

If I ascend up into heaven,
  thou art there:
If I make my bed in Sheol,
  behold, thou art there.
If I take the wings of the morning,
And dwell in the uttermost parts of the sea;
  Even there shall thy hand lead me,
  And thy right hand shall hold me.
                    —*American Standard Version*

David could sit before the Lord in any private place, and so can we.

Who am I? David was a shepherd boy, the youngest of eight sons. That boy had not elevated himself to the throne of Israel; the Lord had lifted him (2 Samuel 7:8, 9). Humbly David admitted that the Lord did not owe any such favor either to him personally or to his *house*, his family. God's own will and God's own power had made the shepherd boy a king. All this is true, but David's modesty does not conceal from us the fact that God lifted this particular boy because He looked at David's heart and saw that it was like God's own (1 Samuel 16:7; 13:13, 14).

B. Divine Promise (v. 19)

19. And this was yet a small thing in thy sight, O Lord GOD; but thou hast spoken also of thy servant's house for a great while to come. And is this the manner of man, O Lord GOD?

To be lifted from sheepfold to throne was no small thing in David's sight, and it is no small thing in ours. But the Lord went on with something else beyond the power of human wisdom: He foretold the future of David's *house*, his family. Members of that family would continue to rule forever (vv. 12-16). Such prediction for eternity is not *the manner of man;* only God can do it. David could be sure the divine promise would be kept, and so can we. Jesus, the son of David, is the king eternal.

C. Divine Knowledge (v. 20)

20. And what can David say more unto thee? for thou, Lord GOD, knowest thy servant.

David was feeling very humble, unworthy of the great help God had given him and of the great promise given for the future. He had expressed his feeling in the words we read in verse 18. Now he saw no need to say any more about it, for he was sure God understood his heart. In the opening lines of the psalm quoted above, David wrote:

O Jehovah, thou hast searched me,
  and known me.
Thou knowest my downsitting
  and mine uprising;
Thou understandest my thought
  afar off.

It is good to realize that we too are helpless without God, and unworthy of His help. But dwelling too much on these thoughts may keep us from doing what we really can do with God's help. We need to remember that He does help His people even if they are not worthy.

II. God and His People
(2 Samuel 7:21-24)

From thoughts of himself, small and weak, David turned to thoughts of God, who is great and powerful. Our thinking may well follow the same pattern. We are unable to do much, but God is able to do wonderful things through us.

A. The Greatness of God (vv. 21, 22)

21. For thy word's sake, and according to thine own heart, hast thou done all these great things, to make thy servant know them.

It was not for David's sake alone that God made him king; it was for the sake of God's word. God had promised a man after His own

Home Daily Bible Readings

Monday, Oct. 31—David Becomes King and Captures Jerusalem (2 Samuel 5:1-10)

Tuesday, Nov. 1—God's Covenant With David (Psalm 89:1-8)

Wednesday, Nov. 2—God Will Exalt David (Psalm 89:19-27)

Thursday, Nov. 3—David's Line Will Endure Forever (Psalm 89:28-37)

Friday, Nov. 4—David Wishes to Build a Temple (2 Samuel 7:1-7)

Saturday, Nov. 5—David's Son Will Build the Temple (2 Samuel 7:8-17)

Sunday, Nov. 6—Prayer for Blessing on David's House (2 Samuel 7:18-29)

heart (1 Samuel 13:14), and David was that man. It was not according to the wish of David's heart that he was made ruler of Israel; it was according to the wish of God's own heart. By the great things He had done, God made His servant David not only to know those great things, but also to know the great God who did them. David then could be sure God would do the great things He promised for the future.

22. Wherefore thou art great, O LORD God: for there is none like thee, neither is there any God besides thee, according to all that we have heard with our ears.

Wherefore, because of the great things God had done, David could say with assurance, *Thou art great*. God not only is great; He is the greatest: *There is none like thee.* and not only is there no other God like the Lord; there is no other God at all. That was proved by all that David had seen in his lifetime, and also by *all that we have heard with our ears*. The stories handed down through generations confirmed the conclusion drawn from David's own experience. The Lord had rescued His people from Egypt; He had kept them in the desert for forty years; He had brought them into the promised land in spite of the opposition of bigger and stronger nations. There was no one else in all the universe who could do such things.

ALONE IN THE UNIVERSE?

On October 12, 1992, the five hundredth anniversary of Columbus's discovery of the New World, NASA scientists turned on an extremely powerful computer to begin an intensive "Search of Extraterrestrial Intelligence." The computer is connected to huge radio telescopes in the Mojave Desert and Puerto Rico. It will listen for radio signals that might indicate the existence of other civilizations.

There are those who are fervent proponents of the idea that numerous intelligent civilizations exist throughout the star systems of the cosmos. Many people believe "UFOs" represent some of these civilizations trying to contact (or at least, observe) us. Among scientists, opinions vary. A Vatican representative visited the NASA experiment, and after studying the project he made this telling observation: "They are looking for God." It is likely that he was right.

Whether *we* are unique in the universe is probably irrelevant. What is important is that our (and Israel's) *God* is unique. David said there is none like Him, and there is no God other than our God. All who worship Him can be assured that they have a place in the will of the God who alone rules the universe.   —C. R. B.

B. The Greatness of God's People
(vv. 23, 24)

23. And what one nation in the earth is like thy people, even like Israel, whom God went to redeem for a people to himself, and to make him a name, and to do for you great things and terrible, for thy land, before thy people, which thou redeemedst to thee from Egypt, from the nations and their gods?

In all the world there was no nation like *Israel*. However, Israel's unique greatness was not due to the goodness or strength of the people. It was due to the Lord. In His relationship with Israel He set out to do three things:

1. He set out *to redeem . . . a people to himself*, to rescue Israel from every peril and make it His own nation. He did save Israel *from Egypt*, and then *from the nations and their gods* in the promised land.

2. The Lord set out *to make him a name*, to create a reputation for himself, to let many nations know there is no god to compare with Him. The kind of reputation He built is seen in Joshua 2:9-11. The people of Canaan were convinced that the Lord was God of Heaven and earth.

3. The Lord set out to do *great things and terrible* for His people and for His land. With great miracles He rescued His people from Egypt, led them and fed them in the desert, gave them victory in the land of promise.

24. For thou hast confirmed to thyself thy people Israel to be a people unto thee for ever: and thou, LORD, art become their God.

Confirmed means set in place, established. Not by any merit of Israel, but by the Lord's own will and power He set up Israel as His own nation and placed himself as Israel's God. That was what made Israel unique.

III. God and His Word
(2 Samuel 7:25-29)

David proposed to build a house for God; but that was not what God wanted, so David gave up his wish. The Lord proposed to build a house for David; and that prospect was so magnificent that David now prayed that God would do according to His own will and keep His promise.

A. Prayer for David's House (v. 25)

25. And now, O LORD God, the word that thou hast spoken concerning thy servant, and concerning his house, establish it for ever, and do as thou hast said.

God had said David's *house*, his household, his family, would continue to rule forever. Now David merely said amen—so let it be.

B. Prayer for God's Name (v. 26)

26. And let thy name be magnified for ever, saying, The LORD of hosts is the God over Israel: and let the house of thy servant David be established before thee.

One thing God set out to do was to make a name for himself (v. 23). Now David prayed that God's name would be magnified forever by people acclaiming Him as God over Israel. His name would be the more famous as He would keep His promise about the house of David.

C. Prayer Based on Promise (vv. 27-29)

27. For thou, O LORD of hosts, God of Israel, hast revealed to thy servant, saying, I will build thee a house: therefore hath thy servant found in his heart to pray this prayer unto thee.

David would hardly dare to ask such a future for his family if God had not promised it. But God did promise it, and with all confidence David prayed that God would do as He said He would.

28. And now, O LORD GOD, thou art that God, and thy words be true, and thou hast promised this goodness unto thy servant.

visual 10

Thy words be true. David was sure of that, so he did not hesitate to ask for what the Lord had promised.

29. Therefore now let it please thee to bless the house of thy servant, that it may continue for ever before thee: for thou, O LORD GOD, hast spoken it: and with thy blessing let the house of thy servant be blessed for ever.

Once again David prayed that the Lord would do just what He wanted to do, what He had said He would do. So good was His promise that David could ask nothing better.

Conclusion

The house David wanted to build was built by his son, Solomon. It was a magnificent temple of stone and cedar lined with gold. For more than three hundred years it stood in Jerusalem, but it has been gone for two thousand years.

The house God built for David is standing today, and it will stand for eternity.

A. Prayer of God's People

Disappointed in his wish to build a temple, great David prayed that what God proposed would be done. Facing death on the cross, great David's greater son prayed, "Not my will, but thine, be done" (Luke 22:42).

How many followers of the Master have echoed that same prayer! In disappointment or loss, in grief or in pain, this is the prayer of God's people: "Thy will be done."

B. Precious Promises

Not only to David and to Israel, but also to you and me God has given "exceeding great and precious promises" (2 Peter 1:4). "He that believeth and is baptized shall be saved" (Mark 16:16). "If we confess our sins, he is faithful and just to forgive us" (1 John 1:9). "The dead in Christ shall rise first: then we which are alive and remain shall be caught up together with them in the clouds, to meet the Lord in the air: and so shall we ever be with the Lord" (1 Thessalonians 4:16, 17).

What other precious promises are you cherishing today? They will be kept. Praise the Lord!

C. Prayer

Eternal Father, we rejoice in the long record of Your promises that have been kept, and we rejoice in the many precious promises You have given us. We trust You, Lord; and we promise You our faithful service.

D. Thought to Remember

"Thy will be done."

Learning by Doing

*This page contains an alternate lesson plan emphasizing learning activities. Classes
desiring such student involvement will find these suggestions helpful.*

Learning Goals

In this lesson, lead your students to:

1. Consider the fact that great men of God have sometimes failed to obey Him.

2. List the attitudes of David, the deeds of God, and the requests of David as seen in David's prayer recorded in 2 Samuel 7.

3. Thank God for keeping all His promises.

Into the Lesson

Read the following agree/disagree statements to your students. If they agree with a statement, they should raise their hands after it is read. If there is significant difference of opinion concerning any statement, pause to let the students explain why they responded to the sentence as they did.

1. A spiritually mature person is less likely to displease God than an immature Christian.

2. The longer one lives for God, the *easier* it is to please God in one's life.

3. The longer one lives for God, the *more difficult* it is to please God in one's life.

4. When God has a special task for a special leader, He provides that leader with special protection against sin.

5. God may forgive any sin, but the consequences of that sin cannot be removed. Discuss these ideas as much as your class time will allow. Just make sure that you don't take time that you need for Bible study and life application later.

Tell class members that today's lesson begins the last unit in this quarter's lessons, and in this unit you will be studying the lives of David and Solomon.

Ask class members if they can discern what these agree/disagree statements have to do with David and Solomon. After brief discussion remind them that both David and Solomon were great men of God, and that both fell to great sins against God. In this unit we will look at both the promise and the failure of each of these men. And we will try to see how we can avoid the same failures in our lives.

Into the Word

Begin the Bible study by reminding class members of the latter days of Saul's reign, of how David became king, and how he prospered as king early in his reign. This information is summarized in the "Introduction" section on page 82. You may want to give this material to a class member during the week before class so that he or she can present this review for your class.

However you conduct your review, make sure it also includes the summary of 2 Samuel 7:1-17 from the "Lesson Background" section of this Introduction. Then you'll be ready for the inductive Bible study suggested below.

Write on the chalkboard the three column headings indicated by the bold lettering below. Then ask your class members to examine today's printed text and to make lists under each heading. Have them work in groups of from five to seven students. Provide pencil and paper for each group.

Allow ten minutes for the groups to do their work. As you discuss the results of their study, record their answers under the headings on the chalkboard. (The answers given in each paragraph below are for the teacher's convenience.)

Attitudes of David: humility, gratitude, awe (vv. 18, 19, 22, 23); faith (vv. 25, 26, 28, 29); courage (v. 27); submission (vv. 28, 29).

What God Did: raised David from humble beginnings to the throne of Israel (v. 18); made great promises to David (vv. 19, 21); redeemed Israel as a people for himself (v. 23); redeemed Israel from Egypt (v. 23); performed great and mighty wonders to establish and protect Israel (v. 23); established Israel as His own nation forever (v. 24).

David's Requests to God: Keep Your promise concerning the future of David's "house" (vv. 25, 26); bless the house of Your servant so that it may continue forever (v. 29).

Into Life

Ask half of your students to decide, "What does this lesson teach us about David?" and the other half, "What does this lesson teach us about God?" Have class members pair off to discuss their assigned question for three minutes. Then discuss with the whole class.

End the class session with sentence prayers of thanks and praise to God for (1) His plan to establish a people unto himself, for (2) including Christians among them, and for (3) His faithfulness to keep this and all His promises from generation to generation.

Let's Talk It Over

The questions on this page are designed to encourage review of the lesson Scriptures and to promote discussion of the lesson by the class. The answers provided are only discussion starters. Let your class talk it over from there.

1. David was concerned about the fact that he was living in a fine house, while the ark of the covenant remained in a tent. How should Christians feel about the relative condition of their own homes and the church building in which they worship?

Since the church building speaks to many of the presence of God in the community, its condition and appearance should be a matter of concern for every member. If we keep our homes in good repair, clean, and presentable, should we not do the same for the church building? And if we neglect the church building, doesn't that reflect unfavorably on the church and the Lord of the church? We could carry this further and speak about the furnishings of both home and church. Every family enjoys having appliances and devices that enable them to do household duties effectively and conveniently. The church building also needs to have the kind of equipment that will enable it to fulfill its divinely given duties.

2. Why is it helpful periodically to ask ourselves humbly the question, "Who am I?"

Many experiences tend to feed our pride. We feel the satisfaction of accomplishment when we successfully complete a job. We are warmed by words of praise in the expressions of others' esteem. We receive promotions, advancements, and pay raises that move us ahead of our peers in terms of authority or economic status. Especially on such occasions we should echo David's question, "Who am I?" Then we can trace the movements of God's favor that have enabled us to reach our present level of achievement, and, like David, praise God for His goodness. It is well for us to acknowledge also the errors we have made along the way and to thank God that He has permitted us to escape the full consequences we could have suffered from these.

3. To praise God for His superiority over all that are called gods may seem pointless, since He alone is God. What are some of life's experiences that should lead us to praise God for His greatness?

When we consider what we regard as great, it may help us to appreciate the superior greatness of God. As we view the heavens and ponder the vastness of space, we experience a sense of awe; how much more should we be in awe of the One who created the universe! A mountain may be majestic in appearance; how much greater the majesty of God who brought forth the mountains! (Psalm 90:2). An airplane soaring into the heavens may leave us breathless in the wake of its power, but it should lead us to say with David, "O Lord our Lord, how excellent is thy name in all the earth! who hast set thy glory above the heavens" (Psalm 8:1).

4. In his prayer recorded in our lesson text, David reminded God of the promise He had made regarding David's household, and asked that it be fulfilled. How is it helpful to mention God's promises in our prayers?.

God certainly does not need reminders of what He has promised. It seems sensible, however, to feel that He enjoys hearing His promises repeated in prayer, because He wants us to learn His Word, to honor it, and to believe it. Perhaps the greatest benefit of including biblical promises in our prayers is the effect it has on our faith. Sometimes our prayers are offered with a measure of uncertainty, because we do not know what the will of God is in regard to the matter about which we are praying. But when we repeat a biblical promise and then say, "Lord, let this be accomplished in my home or my church or my personal life," we can be assured that our prayer is in line with God's will.

5. Why should the petition, "Thy will be done," be a regular part of our prayers?

One answer to this question is found in the Lord's Prayer (Matthew 6:9-13; Luke 11:1-4). In it the accomplishing of God's will on earth occupies a prominent place. A major purpose of prayer is that we who pray will learn God's will and adopt it as our own. God did not give us the privilege of prayer so that we could obtain what we want without regard for His will. When we say, "Thy will be done," we prepare ourselves for whatever answer God may give. If the answer is no, we can learn to accept that as His will. If we receive the blessing we have requested, then we can know that God wants us to use that blessing in a way that will honor Him and further accomplish His will.

David Sins Against God

DEVOTIONAL READING: 1 John 1:5-10.

LESSON SCRIPTURE: 2 Samuel 11:1—12:19.

PRINTED TEXT: 2 Samuel 12:1-10, 13.

2 Samuel 12:1-10, 13

1 And the LORD sent Nathan unto David. And he came unto him, and said unto him, There were two men in one city; the one rich, and the other poor.

2 The rich man had exceeding many flocks and herds:

3 But the poor man had nothing, save one little ewe lamb, which he had bought and nourished up: and it grew up together with him, and with his children; it did eat of his own meat, and drank of his own cup, and lay in his bosom, and was unto him as a daughter.

4 And there came a traveler unto the rich man, and he spared to take of his own flock and of his own herd, to dress for the wayfaring man that was come unto him; but took the poor man's lamb, and dressed it for the man that was come to him.

5 And David's anger was greatly kindled against the man; and he said to Nathan, As the LORD liveth, the man that hath done this thing shall surely die:

6 And he shall restore the lamb fourfold, because he did this thing, and because he had no pity.

7 And Nathan said to David, Thou art the man. Thus saith the LORD God of Israel, I anointed thee king over Israel, and I delivered thee out of the hand of Saul;

8 And I gave thee thy master's house, and thy master's wives into thy bosom, and gave thee the house of Israel and of Judah; and if that had been too little, I would moreover have given unto thee such and such things.

9 Wherefore hast thou despised the commandment of the LORD, to do evil in his sight? thou hast killed Uriah the Hittite with the sword, and hast taken his wife to be thy wife, and hast slain him with the sword of the children of Ammon.

10 Now therefore the sword shall never depart from thine house; because thou hast despised me, and hast taken the wife of Uriah the Hittite to be thy wife.

. . . .

13 And David said unto Nathan, I have sinned against the LORD. And Nathan said unto David, The LORD also hath put away thy sin; thou shalt not die.

Nov
13

GOLDEN TEXT: David said unto Nathan, I have sinned against the LORD.
—2 Samuel 12:13.

Lesson Aims

After studying this lesson a student should be able to:

1. Tell the story of David's sin, Nathan's parable, and David's response to the parable.

2. From his or her own observation, recall at least one of sin's consequences that forgiveness did not remove.

3. Be alert to avoid sin.

Lesson Outline

INTRODUCTION
    A. Building an Empire
    B. The Big War
    C. Lesson Background
  I. PARABLE (2 Samuel 12:1-6)
    A. Rich Man, Poor Man (vv. 1-3)
    B. Robbery (v. 4)
    C. Punishment (vv. 5, 6)
 II. REALITY (2 Samuel 12:7-10)
    A. Guilt (v. 7a)
    B. Favor (vv. 7b, 8)
    C. Ingratitude (v. 9)
      To See Ourselves
    D. Punishment (v. 10)
III. PARDON (2 Samuel 12:13)
    A. Confession (v. 13a)
      Big Enough to Admit It
    B. Forgiveness (v. 13b)
CONCLUSION
    A. Consequences
    B. Run Away
    C. Prayer
    D. Thought to Remember

Visual 11 of the visuals packet illustrates an important truth found in the lesson text. The visual is shown on page 93.

Introduction

Last week during the study of our lesson we saw how powerfully David became king of all Israel, and how humbly he gave up his wish to build a house for God and accepted the will of God. Now we shall see how nobly he built the empire of Israel, and how tragically he ignored God's will.

A. Building an Empire

David soon moved to subdue the heathen nations that had troubled his country. King Hiram of Tyre gladly became a friend, sending men and materials to build David's palace (2 Samuel 5:11). King Toi of Hamath gratefully sent rich presents to thank David for defeating Toi's chief enemy (2 Samuel 8:9, 10). The other nations around Israel were defeated and forced to pay tribute. Thus David's empire came to include most of the land promised to Israel much earlier (Joshua 1:4).

While extending his rule abroad, David also attended to domestic affairs. He organized the government for effective control, and established justice in the land (2 Samuel 8:15-18).

B. The Big War

David's wars came to their climax when the Ammonites and Syrians joined forces against him. After some hard fighting the Syrians gave up and agreed to pay tribute, but the Ammonites were harder to subdue. Apparently winter brought a temporary end to the campaign against them. In the spring, Joab took the army to besiege a chief city of the Ammonites, while David stayed in Jerusalem to manage the domestic affairs of the kingdom (2 Samuel 10:1—11:1).

C. Lesson Background

From the roof of his palace, David saw a woman taking a bath—a beautiful woman. On inquiry he learned that her name was Bath-sheba and that her husband Uriah was away with the army. So David brought her to his palace and his bed. Then he sent her back home (2 Samuel 11:2-4).

How did the woman feel about this? Was she a virtuous wife, dragged to the king against her will? Or was she a lonely lady, pleased and flattered by the royal invitation? Or did she deliberately entice the king by exposing herself in his sight? These questions are not answered. The lady was indiscreet at least, but we have no clear indication of her moral character.

In any case, the king was responsible. We cannot excuse him with a plea that he was starved for love. The record indicates that he had a number of wives. Though David was a man after God's own heart, he certainly was far from the Creator's ideals of love and marriage. He must have known that adultery was forbidden by law and punishable by death (Leviticus 20:10).

In due time David learned that Bath-sheba was pregnant (2 Samuel 11:5). That would be embarrassing to the king as well as to her. Could Uriah and the neighbors be led to think her husband was the father of her child?

David called Uriah to Jerusalem to report on the siege, then told him to go home for the night. But Uriah was a dedicated soldier. He thought it would not be fair to enjoy a night with his wife while his comrades had to stay in the field. He spent two nights with the king's servants, and then went back to the battle (2 Samuel 11:6-13).

David's next plan was more sinister. He ordered Joab to see that Uriah died in battle, and Joab did. The widow mourned for the customary time, then became the wife of David (2 Samuel 11:14-27).

I. Parable
(2 Samuel 12:1-6)

David himself was a prophet (Acts 2:29-31), but sometimes God spoke to him through another prophet. We saw an example in the background of last week's lesson (2 Samuel 7:1-17), and now we see another.

A. Rich Man, Poor Man (vv. 1-3)

1. And the LORD sent Nathan unto David. And he came unto him, and said unto him, There were two men in one city; the one rich, and the other poor.

The Lord sent Nathan. In chapter 7 we saw that Nathan gave his own opinion and then had to correct it after he heard from the Lord. Now the record makes it clear that Nathan came as the Lord's messenger.

Two men in one city. The prophet began as if he were presenting a case for the king to judge.

2. The rich man had exceeding many flocks and herds.

Flocks are sheep; *herds* are cattle. *The rich man* may have had stores of gold and silver too, but the story focuses on livestock.

3. But the poor man had nothing, save one little ewe lamb, which he had bought and nourished up: and it grew up together with him, and with his children; it did eat of his own meat, and drank of his own cup, and lay in his bosom, and was unto him as a daughter.

The poor man had no livestock for market. He had only one lamb. Poor as he was, he *had bought* it for a family pet. Quite literally, the lamb was like one of the family.

B. Robbery (v. 4)

4. And there came a traveler unto the rich man, and he spared to take of his own flock and of his own herd, to dress for the wayfaring man that was come unto him; but took the poor man's lamb, and dressed it for the man that was come to him.

The duty of hospitality was taken seriously in that time and place. It would be unthinkable not to have a good dinner for a traveling friend who stopped at one's house. But even a rich man had no freezer in his house. The only way to keep fresh meat was to keep it alive. An unexpected guest had to wait for his dinner till an animal was slaughtered and cooked.

Rich as he was, this host was too stingy to use one of his own lambs. He stole the poor man's pet and prepared it for his guest.

C. Punishment (vv. 5, 6)

5. And David's anger was greatly kindled against the man; and he said to Nathan, As the LORD liveth, the man that hath done this thing shall surely die.

That rich man might well be called "the meanest thief." With plenty of lambs in his own flock, he stole a beloved pet and left a family bereaved. *David's anger* flared at that.

The man that hath done this thing shall surely die. The *New International Version* says it better: *The man who did this deserves to die!*

Literally, David said the man was *a son of death.* That means he *ought to die* rather than he *will* die.

6. And he shall restore the lamb fourfold, because he did this thing, and because he had no pity.

Now the *King James Version* is accurate: *He shall restore the lamb fourfold.* That was the legal penalty for stealing a sheep (Exodus 22:1). With strict justice, David pronounced the sentence the law required, though special circumstances in this case made the theft so heinous that the thief deserved the death penalty.

II. Reality
(2 Samuel 12:7-10)

Months had passed since David's sin. Bathsheba was now his wife, and the child of their adultery had been born (2 Samuel 11:26, 27). Through all those months David had been tormented by conscience, as he reveals in Psalm

32:3, 4. Still he did not suspect that Nathan's story had anything to do with his own sin. The prophet's next words must have come as a total surprise.

A. Guilt (v. 7a)

7a. And Nathan said to David, Thou art the man.

"Who, me?" David must have thought. "Me? That heartless wretch who stole a poor man's pet, that miserable thief who deserves to die, me?" Perhaps he was shocked and insulted by Nathan's charge, but he must have been puzzled even more. Before explaining the charge, the prophet paused to recall what wonderful things the Lord had done for David.

B. Favor (vv. 7b, 8)

7b. Thus saith the LORD God of Israel, I anointed thee king over Israel, and I delivered thee out of the hand of Saul.

Very clearly David must have remembered that day when he had been called from the pasture to be anointed as king (1 Samuel 16:1-13). No less clearly he recalled the years when Saul's army had combed the desert to catch him and kill him, but still he had been safe. David well knew he had been highly favored by the Lord.

8. And I gave thee thy master's house, and thy master's wives into thy bosom, and gave thee the house of Israel and of Judah; and if that had been too little, I would moreover have given unto thee such and such things.

It seems that it was customary for a new king to take over the former king's wives along with his palace. The record names one wife of Saul (1 Samuel 14:50), but this verse suggests that there were more—probably the choicest ladies in the land. The Lord had given David everything that belonged to Saul, including the kingship of Israel and Judah. The Lord was willing to give more, but what else could David want?

C. Ingratitude (v. 9)

9. Wherefore hast thou despised the commandment of the LORD, to do evil in his sight? thou hast killed Uriah the Hittite with the sword, and hast taken his wife to be thy wife, and hast slain him with the sword of the children of Ammon.

It was wrong for anyone to break God's commandment; but it was doubly wicked for David to disobey after the Lord had done so much for him. He was guilty of the sin of ingratitude along with his other sins.

The Lord had said, "Thou shalt not kill," and "Thou shalt not commit adultery" (Exodus 20:13, 14). Moreover, the Lord had said that either of these crimes should be punished with death (Exodus 21:12; Leviticus 20:10). Surely stealing the one wife of a loyal soldier was worse than stealing the pet lamb of a poor man, a crime for which David had said the thief deserved to die. But to the theft of a wife David had added the murder of a husband. He had earned the death penalty twice.

TO SEE OURSELVES

O wad some power the giftie gie us
To see oursels as others see us!
It wad frae monie a blunder free us,
An' foolish notion.

The eighteenth-century Scottish dialect of Robert Burns's poem, "To a Louse," sounds a bit strange to our ears, but we can understand its message: If we could just see our lives through the eyes of other people, we might be saved from entertaining many foolish ideas and from the sinful actions that result from them!

Perhaps most of us have been tempted to do something foolish or worse, thinking, "No one will ever know; surely, I can get away with it! It would be so enjoyable, and besides, what could it possibly hurt?" In those moments, we are blessed if we have a friend who knows what we are contemplating and says, "Don't be foolish!"

Unfortunately, King David did not have such a friend to prevent him from the arrogant use of his royal power. As a result, he committed adultery with Bath-sheba. Then, compounding his sin, David arranged to have her husband murdered in battle so David himself could marry her.

God, however, would not be mocked. By means of a simple parable, His prophet Nathan confronted David with the enormity of his sin. Finally, David saw himself as God saw him, and (as the saying goes) it was not a pretty picture!

—C. R. B.

D. Punishment (v. 10)

10. Now therefore the sword shall never depart from thine house; because thou hast despised me, and hast taken the wife of Uriah the Hittite to be thy wife.

The Lord announced punishment to fit the crime. Read the first part of verse 10 with the last part of verse 9: *Thou . . . hast slain him with the sword of the children of Ammon. Now therefore the sword shall never depart from thine house.* David had murdered Uriah with violence; through the rest of his life David would be grieved by violent deaths in his family. Then read the last part of verse 10 with the first part of verse 11: *Thou . . . hast taken the wife of Uriah the Hittite to be thy wife. Thus saith the Lord . . . I will take thy wives before thine eyes, and give them unto thy neighbor.* The

Hebrew word for *neighbor* is sometimes translated *another*. Later chapters reveal that the one who took David's wives was his own rebellious son, Absalom.

Conscious of his own adultery and murder, David failed to deal sternly with his sons when they committed similar crimes. Partly because he failed to deal sternly, such crimes multiplied.

David's son Amnon raped his half sister, Tamar. David was angry, but apparently did not punish Amnon. Two years later, David's son Absalom, full brother of Tamar, had Amnon killed. Absalom then fled the country, but after a while he was allowed to return. Perhaps encouraged by David's leniency, Absalom gathered followers and staged a revolt to take his father's throne for himself. David had to flee from Jerusalem, and Absalom made a show of taking his father's wives as his own. David soon gathered his forces and put down the revolt, but Absalom was killed along with many others in the civil war. (See 2 Samuel 13—18.)

In David's last years, his son Adonijah also plotted to take the throne. This time the plot was nipped in the bud; but soon after David died, Adonijah was executed for his continuing ambition to be king (1 Kings 1, 2). So to the end of David's life and beyond, the sword did not depart from his house.

III. Pardon
(2 Samuel 12:13)

Throughout the Bible David is honored as a hero and a prophet, the sweet singer of Israel, and a man after God's own heart. Yet no effort is made to hide his sin. His wicked acts are exposed in all their horror.

This emphasizes the goodness of God. He is "merciful and gracious, long-suffering, and abundant in goodness and truth" (Exodus 34:6). Such a sinner as David was not beyond the reach of His grace, and neither are we.

A. Confession (v. 13a)

13a. And David said unto Nathan, I have sinned against the LORD.

David offered no excuses. He did not say that the woman tempted him, or that the one he killed was a Hittite and not a man of Israel, or that the death of a soldier is a small matter, or that a king has rights that others do not have. He was not angry with Nathan for denouncing him. In the plainest language he declared the awful truth: *I have sinned against the Lord.*

This thought was not new to David. It had burdened his secret mind for a long time. In his penitential song he wrote, "My sin is ever before

visual 11

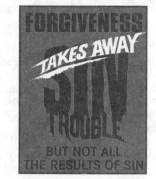

me" (Psalm 51:3). It had been to him like the searing heat of a dry summer (Psalm 32:3, 4). Now at last he made open and honest confession, not only to Nathan, but also to the Lord. This is the way to pardon (Psalm 32:5). So it is for us: "If we confess our sins, he is faithful and just to forgive us our sins, and to cleanse us from all unrighteousness" (1 John 1:9).

BIG ENOUGH TO ADMIT IT

Rudy Ruiz came home from work and discovered his wife sick in bed. His two teenage sons had not done their chores. Rudy told the boys how important their mother was to him after helping him recover from two heart attacks. His unfortunate "parting shot" was, "I love you boys, too, but I don't need you—not the way I need your mother." His fourteen-year-old son, John David, was especially stung by the remark.

Several weeks later Rudy, John David, and a friend were fishing on a rain-swollen river when the current sucked their rubber raft into a culvert beneath a concrete bridge that was under a foot of water. John David was thrown onto the bridge, but Rudy could only grab the edge of it. His foot was caught in a rope on the boat, and he was being pulled under. John David grabbed his dad, and he and their friend held on desperately until help came. Through his son's courage and strength, Rudy survived. After his rescue, Rudy said to his son, "I'll never say 'I don't need you' to anyone again."

When confronted with his sin, David showed how "big" a person he was by facing the truth and admitting his guilt. To be able to admit, "I was wrong," may be the best evidence there is of the maturity of spirit that leads to repentance and restoration. —C. R. B.

B. Forgiveness (v. 13b)

13b. And Nathan said unto David, The LORD also hath put away thy sin; thou shalt not die.

So David was forgiven. Like the rich man of the parable he deserved to die, but he did not die. He lived for many years to build up the empire of Israel. Exultantly he sang, "Blessed is he whose transgression is forgiven, whose sin is covered. Blessed is the man unto whom the Lord imputeth not iniquity" (Psalm 32:1, 2).

Yet how often the joy of forgiveness was marred! Forgiveness takes away sin, but it does not take away all the consequences of sin. David was forgiven, but he prayed in vain for the life of the child born of his sin. The child died (2 Samuel 12:14-23). David was forgiven, but the dire prophecies spoken by Nathan were not withdrawn. David seethed with anger when his daughter was raped (13:21); but with his own adultery in mind, how could he chasten the rapist? Though forgiven, David grieved when one son killed another and fled to a foreign country (v. 37). David had to flee from Jerusalem (15:14-17) while his rebel son stole his wives (16:20-22). David agonized in grief at the death of that rebel son (18:33). He had to put down another rebel, a scoundrel named Sheba (chapter 20). Feeble with age, he had to rouse himself and act vigorously to thwart the plotting of his son Adonijah (1 Kings 1). Truly, through all his life, the sword never departed from his house.

Conclusion

If God's forgiveness is sure, why should we worry about our sin? Why not trust Him to forgive us, and sin whenever it seems convenient or pleasant? Strongly Paul warns against that silly notion: "How shall we, that are dead to sin, live any longer therein?" (Romans 6:1-4).

A. Consequences

A city councilman was detected in adultery. He said he was sorry, and loyal constituents forgave him and elected him to another term. But when he ran for a higher office he suffered a humiliating defeat. Many voters thought a man who would cheat on his wife might cheat the taxpayers as well.

After an angry quarrel at work, Joe was driving furiously when he was maimed in a wreck. He may be forgiven, but he is still maimed. And an innocent motorist killed in the accident is still dead.

Angered by a snub, Mabel told a vicious lie about the woman who snubbed her. When her anger cooled, Mabel apologized. The other woman forgave her, and probably the Lord did too. But the falsehood is still being whispered all over town.

A usually decent man got drunk and beat his wife. When he became sober he repented and was forgiven, but the wife is still scarred.

Tempted by hard times, Frank stole some money he was taking to the bank. He said he had been robbed, and robberies were so frequent that he was not suspected. But his conscience tormented him till he told the truth. His employer is a good-hearted man, so Frank is forgiven—but he is no longer trusted.

B. Run Away

How many times David must have regretted that day when he watched a woman at her bath! Joseph had a better idea. When a woman tried to seduce him, he ran (Genesis 39:7-12).

"Flee fornication" (1 Corinthians 6:18). Get away from it. Turn off the TV programs that encourage it. Avoid the pornography that flourishes everywhere. Pray, "Lead us not into temptation"; and don't go where the Lord doesn't lead.

"Finally, brethren, whatsoever things are true, whatsoever things are honest, whatsoever things are just, whatsoever things are pure, whatsoever things are lovely, whatsoever things are of good report; if there be any virtue, and if there be any praise, think on these things" (Philippians 4:8).

C. Prayer

Lord, we are overwhelmed by Your goodness. Like David we confess that we have sinned against You, and like David we rejoice in Your forgiveness. Today and tomorrow and all the days of our lives, so lead us that we will not need to be forgiven so often. This we pray in the name of Jesus our Redeemer. Amen.

D. Thought to Remember

As we hope to go to Heaven
    And our Lord's "well done" to win,
It is good to be forgiven,
    But it's better not to sin.

Home Daily Bible Readings

Monday, Nov. 7—David's Sin (2 Samuel 11:1-13)

Tuesday, Nov. 8—David Causes Uriah's Death (2 Samuel 11:14-25)

Wednesday, Nov. 9—Nathan Rebukes David (2 Samuel 11:26—12:9)

Thursday, Nov. 10—God's Judgment and Forgiveness (2 Samuel 12:10-15a)

Friday, Nov. 11—A Prayer of Repentance (Psalm 51:1-14)

Saturday, Nov. 12—Thanksgiving for Forgiveness (Psalm 32:1-7)

Sunday, Nov. 13—Death of the Child (2 Samuel 12:15b-23)

Learning by Doing

This page contains an alternate lesson plan emphasizing learning activities. Classes desiring such student involvement will find these suggestions helpful.

Learning Goals

As students participate in today's class session, they should:

1. Review the story of David's adultery with Bath-sheba and his plotting to cover his sin.

2. Paraphrase the parable of Nathan.

3. Understand that sin may produce unpleasant consequences in this life, even though the sin is forgiven.

Into the Lesson

Write the following scrambled sentence on the chalkboard, or display it on a poster that you have prepared before class:

sure will out your find be sin you.

Ask class members to unscramble the sentence ("be sure your sin will find you out"). Ask them to think of examples from their own lives, or from history, or from current events to prove the truth of this divine pronouncement found in Numbers 32:23.

Ask how the sentence applies to the lives of David and Solomon, the two great kings we are studying in this unit of lessons. Some students may refer to the Bible story that is the text of this lesson. Tell the class that today we will look at this story in depth to see what we can learn about how God feels about our sin.

Into the Word

Before class, write the following ten headings and Scripture references on notecards:

David's Sin (2 Samuel 11:1-5)
David's Ploy (2 Samuel 11:6-13)
David's Plot (2 Samuel 11:14-17)
The Messenger's Report (2 Samuel 11:18-24)
David's Response (2 Samuel 11:25-27)
Nathan's Parable (2 Samuel 12:1-4)
David's Reaction (2 Samuel 12:5, 6)
Nathan's Rebuke (2 Samuel 12:7-12)
David's Punishment (2 Samuel 12:13-15)

Distribute the cards to different class members. They are to look up the references and read the assigned Scripture verses aloud to the class in the order given here. Ask your class members to listen for ideas under the following four headings as the Scriptures are read (write these on the chalkboard):

1. What surprises you about David.
2. What you learn about Nathan.
3. What surprises you about God.

4. A question you would like to ask about this story.

Have each volunteer read aloud the heading on his or her card before reading the assigned text to the class.

After all the Scriptures are read, discuss with the class their ideas under the four headings suggested above.

Following this discussion divide your class members into groups of four to six students. Ask each group to write a modern-day paraphrase of Nathan's parable in 2 Samuel 12:1-4. Each paraphrase should be in a contemporary setting, with twentieth-century counterparts to each element in the story.

After ten minutes, let volunteers read their paraphrases. Comment on their insights. Then ask class members to list the punishments that God said would follow David's sin (vv. 10-12, 14). Discuss: "Why was the Lord so angry at David's sin? (vv. 7-9, 14).

Into Life

Continue your discussion with the following questions:

1. Why do you think God insisted on punishing David, even after David had repented and God had forgiven him?

2. Does repentance and forgiveness blot out the need for punishment of an infraction?

Ask class members if they can remember the consequences that David suffered because of his great sin involving Bath-sheba and Uriah. Ask them to share specific examples. Then, referring to the list under "B. Forgiveness" beginning on page 93, remind them of incidents they omitted. Discuss, "Do such dire consequences always follow our sin?"

Then ask class members to share examples, hypothetical or real, of how consequences often follow a sin, even after it has been forgiven. Possibilities are suggested under "A. Consequences" in the "Conclusion" section on page 94.

Discuss: "What should we learn from the story of David?" Possible answers:

"God forgives the one who repents sincerely, but the consequences of one's sin remain."

"It is a blessing to be forgiven, but it is better not to sin in the first place."

"One should think twice before sinning; sin never delivers what it promises."

Let's Talk It Over

The questions on this page are designed to encourage review of the lesson Scriptures and to promote discussion of the lesson by the class. The answers provided are only discussion starters. Let your class talk it over from there.

1. What can we learn from Nathan's method of confronting David with his sin?

To some readers it may seem that Nathan was "beating around the bush," but his approach proved effective in causing David to face his sin and to come to repentance. This is a reminder that one must plan carefully the manner in which one confronts someone who has sinned. Some people may be reached best by a blunt, direct approach; others, like David, may respond better to a more tactful method. In the New Testament this element of caution is demonstrated in Paul's counsel: "Brethren, if a man be overtaken in a fault, ye which are spiritual, restore such a one in the spirit of meekness; considering thyself, lest thou also be tempted" (Galatians 6:1).

2. People often judge most harshly those sins of others that resemble their own. Why is this true?

David was indignant over the injustice and heartlessness of the man Nathan described. At the same time he must have been aware of the unjust and heartless treatment he had given Uriah the Hittite. Likewise those who are proud are often quickest to condemn pride in others; those who are prone to lose their tempers may be most unforgiving toward those whose fits of anger have brought them trouble; those who indulge in uncharitable gossip are often horrified by the looseness of other persons' tongues. Paul was on target in Romans 2:1 when he noted that "wherein thou judgest another, thou condemnest thyself; for thou that judgest doest the same things." Perhaps this tendency is one device we use to blind ourselves to our own sins. It is a tendency that reminds us of our need for regular self-examination.

3. David's sins were shown to be particularly bad in view of all the good things God had done for him. How can this observation be helpful to us?

Our gratitude for the evidences of God's favor should deter us from sinning against Him. We should be able to say, "How can I sin against God, when He has given me a wonderful family, a satisfying job, a fine home, many precious friends, and best of all forgiveness of sins and hope of eternal life through Jesus Christ?" What God gave to David appears insignificant in comparison to what He has given us. He made David king over Israel, but He has made us heirs of an eternal kingdom. He delivered David out of the hand of King Saul, but He has delivered us from sin, condemnation, and the devil. He gave David temporal power and authority, but He gives us spiritual power in order to serve Him effectively in His church. We have many reasons to avoid sin.

4. Why should the fact that God was willing to forgive David be an encouragement to the worst kinds of sinners who seek God's forgiveness today?

The sins of adultery and murder are bad enough in themselves, but what made David's deeds even more heinous was that he sinned against a strikingly loyal servant. A close examination of this account reveals the depth of Uriah's faithfulness to his king and his fellow soldiers. One cannot help feeling a sense of outrage that such a man should be callously sentenced to death in battle and his wife taken away. Sinners today often lament what they have done to a parent or a spouse or someone else who has loved them. In the final analysis, however, David's confession in Psalm 51:4 holds true for every sinner: "Against thee, thee only, have I sinned, and done this evil in thy sight." All sin is ultimately against God, and God is willing to forgive anyone who repents and turns to Him.

5. David's experience raises a question about the extent of God's forgiveness: if God is willing to forgive our sins, why does He not also take away the consequences of our sins?

In the midst of the severe family-related trials he had to endure in his later years, David may well have been tempted to ask, "Did the Lord really forgive me of my sins in the matter of Uriah the Hittite? If so, why am I suffering so much heartbreak?" Similarly, Christians who sin, seek forgiveness, and then suffer severe consequences may wonder about their forgiveness. David, of course, was warned about the consequences that would result from his sin, and we know that in the Christian era sin, though forgiven, may still bring dire consequences. Perhaps one reason God allows this to happen is to keep before our minds the dreadful seriousness of sin.

Solomon's Glorious Reign

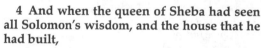

DEVOTIONAL READING: Proverbs 3:5-15.

LESSON SCRIPTURE: 1 Kings 9:1-9; 10:1-24.

PRINTED TEXT: 1 Kings 9:1-3; 10:1-7, 23, 24.

1 Kings 9:1-3

1 And it came to pass, when Solomon had finished the building of the house of the LORD, and the king's house, and all Solomon's desire which he was pleased to do,

2 That the LORD appeared to Solomon the second time, as he had appeared unto him at Gibeon.

3 And the LORD said unto him, I have heard thy prayer and thy supplication, that thou hast made before me: I have hallowed this house, which thou hast built, to put my name there for ever; and mine eyes and mine heart shall be there perpetually.

1 Kings 10:1-7, 23, 24

1 And when the queen of Sheba heard of the fame of Solomon concerning the name of the LORD, she came to prove him with hard questions.

2 And she came to Jerusalem with a very great train, with camels that bare spices, and very much gold, and precious stones: and when she was come to Solomon, she communed with him of all that was in her heart.

3 And Solomon told her all her questions: there was not any thing hid from the king, which he told her not.

4 And when the queen of Sheba had seen all Solomon's wisdom, and the house that he had built,

5 And the meat of his table, and the sitting of his servants, and the attendance of his ministers, and their apparel, and his cupbearers, and his ascent by which he went up unto the house of the LORD; there was no more spirit in her.

6 And she said to the king, It was a true report that I heard in mine own land of thy acts and of thy wisdom.

7 Howbeit I believed not the words, until I came, and mine eyes had seen it; and, behold, the half was not told me: thy wisdom and prosperity exceedeth the fame which I heard.

. . . .

23 So king Solomon exceeded all the kings of the earth for riches and for wisdom.

24 And all the earth sought to Solomon, to hear his wisdom, which God had put in his heart.

Nov
20

GOLDEN TEXT: King Solomon exceeded all the kings of the earth for riches and for wisdom. —1 Kings 10:23.

From the Conquest to the Kingdom

Unit 4: The Kingdom Under David

and Solomon (Lessons 10-13)

Lesson Aims

After this lesson a student should be able to:

1. Tell why the Queen of Sheba visited Jerusalem and what she learned about Solomon and his kingdom.

2. Explain why Solomon was wiser and richer than other kings of the world.

3. Resolve to seek God's kingdom and His righteousness.

Lesson Outline

INTRODUCTION
 A. Strong King
 B. Godly King
 C. Wide Empire
 D. Great Buildings
 I. THE LORD'S APPROVAL (1 Kings 9:1-3)
 A. Occasion (v. 1)
 B. Appearing (v. 2)
 C. Approval (v. 3)
     Consecrating the Temple
 II. A QUEEN'S HOMAGE (1 Kings 10:1-7)
 A. Arrival (vv. 1, 2a)
 B. Conference (vv. 2b, 3)
 C. Observation (vv. 4, 5)
 D. Homage (vv. 6, 7)
     Telling the Other Half
 III. THE WORLD'S HOMAGE (1 Kings 10:23, 24)
 A. Comparison (v. 23)
 B. Homage (v. 24)
CONCLUSION
 A. The King's Devotion
 B. Righteousness Exalts
 C. Prayer
 D. Thought to Remember

Visual 12 of the visuals packet illustrates the thoughts found in the conclusion of this lesson. The visual is shown on page 101.

Introduction

Old King David turned over the kingdom to young King Solomon, and gave two bits of advice along with it. The first was, "Be thou strong." The second was, "Keep the charge of the Lord thy God" (1 Kings 2:1-3). Young Solomon took both bits of advice seriously.

A. Strong King

Solomon's half brother Adonijah had tried to steal the throne for himself; but David had learned of it, and the plotting had been interrupted by the sound of trumpets announcing that Solomon was king. Adonijah's plotters had swiftly deserted him then (1 Kings 1:5-49).

Solomon tried to be lenient with Adonijah. He said, "If he will show himself a worthy man, there shall not a hair of him fall to the earth" (1 Kings 1:50-53). But Adonijah did not show himself worthy. At the first sign that he was still plotting, Solomon showed himself strong. He executed both Adonijah and the tough old army general who had supported him (1 Kings 2:13-25).

B. Godly King

Following his father's second bit of advice, "Solomon loved the Lord, walking in the statutes of David his father" (1 Kings 3:3). He went to Gibeon, the nation's chief place of worship, and offered a thousand burnt offerings. There the Lord appeared to him in a dream. The Lord said, "Ask what I shall give thee." Solomon asked for wisdom and understanding to rule the nation well. Pleased with that request, the Lord not only granted what was asked, but promised riches and honor as well. And if Solomon would continue to obey the Lord, he would have a long life too (1 Kings 3:4-14).

C. Wide Empire

Following his father's advice to be strong, Solomon built a formidable military force (1 Kings 4:26). This secured his hold over the wide empire David had built, reaching from the river, the upper Euphrates, in the north to the border of Egypt in the south. The kings of that area paid tribute, and Israel lived in peace and safety (1 Kings 4:21, 24, 25).

D. Great Buildings

Mindful of David's wish for a temple for the Lord, Solomon set about building it. He enlisted the king of Tyre to procure timber from the famous cedars of Lebanon (1 Kings 5). From Tyre came also a master craftsman to supervise the construction. His name was the same as the king's name, Hiram (1 Kings 7:13, 14). Actual building of the temple began in the fourth year of Solomon's reign, and was finished seven years later (1 Kings 6:37, 38).

It took another thirteen years to build Solomon's own house (1 Kings 7:1). This was a magnificent palace for the nation's headquarters as well as for Solomon's home. Second Chronicles 8:1-6 tells briefly of other building projects that Solomon undertook "throughout all the land of his dominion."

Tyre was noted for seamen and traders as well as builders. King Hiram and his people helped Solomon build a fleet of ships on the Red Sea, and Israel became a power in world commerce (1 Kings 9:26-28).

Voyages of the trading ships helped to spread Solomon's reputation for wealth and power, and above all for wisdom. The king of Israel was world famous as the outstanding authority in many fields, "and there came of all people to hear the wisdom of Solomon" (1 Kings 4:29-34).

I. The Lord's Approval
(1 Kings 9:1-3)

At this time in his career, Solomon loved the Lord and obeyed Him (1 Kings 3:3). The Lord's approval was more important to him than all the tributes of kings and all the accolades of scholars, and the Lord did express His approval.

A. Occasion (v. 1)

1. And it came to pass, when Solomon had finished the building of the house of the LORD, and the king's house, and all Solomon's desire which he was pleased to do.

Two phases of Solomon's activity were completed: the temple and the royal palace. Probably *all Solomon's desire* means all he wanted to do on those buildings, not all he wanted to do throughout the whole land. Temple and palace together took twenty years to build (1 Kings 6:38; 7:1; 9:10). When they were done, the Lord took that occasion to give additional revelation to the king.

B. Appearing (v. 2)

2. That the LORD appeared to Solomon the second time, as he had appeared unto him at Gibeon.

The earlier appearing at Gibeon has been mentioned in section B of the introduction above. The Lord had appeared in a dream and had promised wisdom, riches, and honor. Now He appeared again.

C. Approval (v. 3)

3. And the LORD said unto him, I have heard thy prayer and thy supplication, that thou hast made before me: I have hallowed this house, which thou hast built, to put my name there for ever; and mine eyes and mine heart shall be there perpetually.

Chapter 8 of 1 Kings records the dedication of the temple, including Solomon's long prayer on that occasion (8:22-53).

How to Say It
ADONIJAH. Ad-o-*nye*-juh.
ETHIOPIA. E-thee-*o*-pee-uh (*th* as in *thin*).
EUPHRATES. U-*fray*-teez.
GIBEON. *Gib*-e-un.
MESOPOTAMIA. Mes-uh-puh-*tay*-me-uh.
SHEBA. *Shee*-buh.
YEMEN. *Yem*-un.

What we are reading in the third verse of chapter 9 is clearly God's answer to that prayer. God said He had heard the prayer, that He had hallowed the house to put His name there forever, and that His eyes and His heart would be on that house perpetually.

This presents a slight puzzle. Solomon offered his prayer when God's house was completed. Why did God answer it thirteen years later, when the king's house also was completed? Various explanations have been suggested, but we will give only the one that seems to be most widely accepted:

When God's house was completed, Solomon prayed that God would accept it as His. This is recorded in chapter 8. God did accept it, and made His acceptance plain by filling the house with a visible cloud of His glory (8:10, 11). But the king's house was finished thirteen years later. By that time there were some signs that Solomon was becoming more worldly and less godly. Therefore the Lord took that occasion to remind Solomon of his prayer. He had asked God to accept the house, and God had done so. But now, thirteen years later, God added a warning that His acceptance was conditional. If king and people would continue to obey the Lord, the temple would continue to be honored as God's house (9:4, 5). But if they would turn away from the Lord, He would reject both them and the temple they had built (9:6-9).

CONSECRATING THE TEMPLE

Eighty-three years after President Theodore Roosevelt laid its cornerstone in 1907, the Washington National Cathedral was formally dedicated (although it will take another thirty years before it is completed). It is built in the classic manner of many European cathedrals: Gothic in style and intricately decorated with the work of craftsmen skilled in wood and stone.

The National Cathedral is like some others in that it is taking several generations to complete. The most extreme example may be the Protestant Cathedral in Ulm, Germany, which was begun in 1377 and not completed until 1890!

When Solomon had completed the most exquisite house of worship ever built for God, the Lord announced that He had consecrated it to himself "for ever." There is a sense, however, in which the dedication of any house of God is not a once-for-all matter. Some buildings that were dedicated to God in years past became cultural relics, or museums devoted to secular purposes, or unused shells that were finally torn down. Indeed, the temple Solomon built was in time destroyed. Regardless of its beauty or cost of construction, a house of worship remains consecrated to God only by the faithfulness of God's people who worship Him there. —C. R. B.

II. A Queen's Homage (1 Kings 10:1-7)

The location of ancient Sheba has long been disputed. Many students have thought it was Ethiopia, on the east coast of Africa; but now the prevailing opinion seems to be that it was Yemen and some surrounding territory in southwestern Arabia. Ethiopia and Yemen face each other across the Red Sea. Both were in easy reach of Solomon's merchant ships (1 Kings 9:26-28).

A. Arrival (vv. 1, 2a)

1. And when the queen of Sheba heard of the fame of Solomon concerning the name of the LORD, she came to prove him with hard questions.

Solomon was famous both for wisdom and for wealth (1 Kings 4:22-34). It is to his credit that his fame was connected with *the name of the Lord*. Apparently he let it be known that his wisdom and wealth were God's gifts (1 Kings 3:3-14).

The queen of Sheba was not one to believe everything she heard. She may have doubted both that Solomon was wiser than her scholars and that the Lord was greater than her gods. She meant to find out for herself instead of trusting the tales told by sailors and travelers.

We are not told what *hard questions* the queen brought. Some students think they were riddles. Indeed, the Hebrew word is the one used of the riddle that Samson invented to challenge the guests at his wedding (Judges 14). But apparently our translators thought the lady brought more serious problems. She may have collected *hard questions* in science, philosophy, religion, commerce, government, and other fields.

2a. And she came to Jerusalem with a very great train, with camels that bare spices, and very much gold, and precious stones.

The queen had learned what things were valued in Jerusalem—*spices, and very much gold, and precious stones*—and she brought them in abundance. She had no fleet of ships at sea to match Solomon's, but perhaps she had more *camels* than he had. We are not told how many of them were in her *very great train*, but surely there were enough to make an impressive entrance.

B. Conference (vv. 2b, 3)

2b. And when she was come to Solomon, she communed with him of all that was in her heart.

Communed could be translated *talked* or *spoke*. Solomon gave the queen a royal welcome and spent as much time in conference as she wanted to spend. *All that was in her heart* seems to indicate that she brought real problems rather than clever riddles or in addition to clever riddles.

3. And Solomon told her all her questions: there was not any thing hid from the king, which he told her not.

Here is clear evidence that Solomon was specially gifted with wisdom from above. An ordinary man cannot even answer all the questions of an ordinary person, much less those of a head of state burdened with all the affairs of a nation.

C. Observation (vv. 4, 5)

4. And when the queen of Sheba had seen all Solomon's wisdom, and the house that he had built.

As we have mentioned, Solomon was famous for two things: his wisdom and his wealth. Great wisdom was plain in his answers; great wealth was plain in the size and splendor and masterly craftsmanship of *the house that he had built*. The next verse adds some details of what the queen saw in that magnificent palace.

5. And the meat of his table, and the sitting of his servants, and the attendance of his ministers, and their apparel, and his cupbearers, and his ascent by which he went up unto the house of the LORD; there was no more spirit in her.

Solomon's *table* required a lot of fine food for his family and officials and guests, plus even more food, not quite so fine, for a multitude of servants. See 1 Kings 4:22, 23 for his daily grocery list: more than five hundred bushels of flour and meal, thirty beef cattle, a hundred sheep, plus wild game and poultry. No wonder the queen was surprised.

We have no such clear picture of the other things that won the queen's admiration. Evidently two classes of attendants are called *servants* and *ministers*. No doubt the queen was impressed by the huge number of them as well as by their fine *apparel*. The *cupbearers*, waiters at the table, may have been impressive too; but some students think the Hebrew word here refers to the drinks that were served and not the waiters.

The *King James Version* mentions also *his ascent,* meaning an elaborately decorated path or ramp or stair *by which he went up unto the house of the Lord.* The *New International Version* gives a different meaning to the Hebrew words: "the burnt offerings he made at the temple of the Lord."

It is not necessary to know exactly what all these details were. Together they made a profound impression on the visiting queen. She had come in a high-spirited way; hoping her long camel train loaded with precious things would make an impression on Solomon. But she found her glory eclipsed so completely that *there was no more spirit in her.* As the *New International Version* put it, "she was overwhelmed."

D. Homage (vv. 6, 7)

6. And she said to the king, It was a true report that I heard in mine own land of thy acts and of thy wisdom.

The queen was convinced. The reports she had heard back in Sheba were not myths, not exaggerations, not the bragging of sailors far from home. They were sober truth.

7. Howbeit I believed not the words, until I came, and mine eyes had seen it; and, behold, the half was not told me: thy wisdom and prosperity exceedeth the fame which I heard.

Seeing was believing. The reports heard in Sheba were true, but only half the truth. Solomon's wisdom and prosperity far surpassed the reports. His wisdom was proved by his ready answers to all questions (v. 3). Verses 14-22 tell something of his prosperity. For example, in one year Solomon received 666 talents of gold. A footnote in the *New International Version* estimates that to be about twenty-five tons.

Read the rest of the queen's tribute in verses 8-10. Notice that she gave homage to the Lord as well as to Solomon. She even gave the Lord credit for Solomon's high position. No doubt Solomon himself had assured her that God had made him what he was.

TELLING THE OTHER HALF

While Communism still held sway throughout Eastern Europe and much of Asia, it was common for the Communist press to present current events with a propagandized slant in opposition to the Western world. History books were rewritten to remove from the historical record whatever was embarrassing to the Communist leaders.

Then Mikhail Gorbachev gained power in the Soviet Union. As a part of his widely hailed *glasnost* (openness) policy, censors no longer peered over the shoulders of historians. A new high school history book was published in 1989,

visual 12

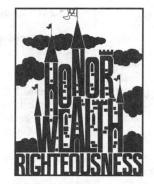

telling much of the truth that had been falsified for decades. But even its authors admitted that so much new information about past lies was coming to light that they had to begin immediately to write another, still more accurate, version of history. Perhaps more than half the truth about Soviet history was yet to be told to its citizens and to the world!

When the queen of Sheba visited Solomon, the "half that had not been told her" was not covered over by lies. On the contrary, the truth of how God had blessed Solomon far exceeded even the truth about him that the queen previously had heard.

It has often been said that truth is stranger than fiction. God's blessings are not fiction. The truth about how He blesses those who are faithful to Him would be difficult to exaggerate.

—C. R. B.

III. The World's Homage (1 Kings 10:23, 24)

The queen of Sheba was one of many who came to Jerusalem to see if the reports they heard were true, to admire Solomon's splendor, and to learn from his wisdom.

A. Comparison (v. 23)

23. So king Solomon exceeded all the kings of the earth for riches and for wisdom.

In other times, when the Lord was not properly honored, little Israel was overshadowed by great empires in Egypt and Mesopotamia. Heathen kings exceeded faithless kings of Israel in riches and wisdom. But in Solomon's time both Egypt and Mesopotamia were weaker. Israel was the dominant nation, and Solomon was famous far and wide *for riches and for wisdom.* Note again the indications of wealth in this chapter, verses 14-22 and 26-29. Review the praise of his wisdom in 1 Kings 4:29-34. And remember that both wisdom and wealth were the Lord's special gifts to a king who honored Him (1 Kings 3:3-14).

B. Homage (v. 24)

24. And all the earth sought to Solomon, to hear his wisdom, which God had put in his heart.

All the earth, of course, means that part of the earth that heard about Solomon: Mesopotamia and the countries bordering on the Mediterranean Sea and the Red Sea. From all of these, the wisest seekers of truth came to learn from Solomon; and again the historian pauses to give credit to God, who gave Solomon his wisdom.

Conclusion

Solomon's wealth and wisdom are extolled again and again, but let it never be forgotten that his devotion to the Lord preceded them and accompanied them. The king began his reign by following the parting advice of David: "Keep the charge of the Lord thy God, to walk in his ways, to keep his statues, and his commandments, and his judgments, and his testimonies, as it is written in the law of Moses, that thou mayest prosper in all that thou doest" (1 Kings 2:3). Solomon did keep God's law, and he did prosper in everything. His was no lip service or conforming to tradition; "Solomon loved the Lord" (1 Kings 3:3).

A. The King's Devotion

The king's devotion is seen in the thousand offerings he made early in his reign (1 Kings 3:4) and in his humble prayer for wisdom to rule the people of God (1 Kings 3:9). It is seen in the magnificent temple he built for the Lord, and in the prayer he offered when the temple was completed (1 Kings 8:22-53). "Three times in a year" Solomon continued his sacrifices, probably cele-brating the three annual feasts established by the law (1 Kings 9:25; Exodus 23:14-17).

Solomon made no secret of his devotion and his indebtedness to the Lord. Plainly the record says his wisdom and wealth were special gifts (1 Kings 3:12, 13). The queen of Sheba acknowledged it (1 Kings 10:9), and so did the king of Tyre (1 Kings 5:7). It seems that all who came to hear Solomon's wisdom heard also that God had put it in his heart (1 Kings 10:23, 24).

The Lord himself acknowledged Solomon's devotion by appearing to him twice with great promises (1 Kings 3:5; 9:2), by granting him wisdom and riches and fame (1 Kings 3:12, 13), and by accepting the completed temple and filling it with glory (1 Kings 8: 10, 11).

B. Righteousness Exalts

"Righteousness exalteth a nation" (Proverbs 14:34). Never was Solomon's proverb illustrated more clearly than in Solomon's Israel. A country smaller than half of New Jersey ruled an empire eight times as big, and received honor from all the world.

More remarkable still, it seems that "all the earth" responded as the queen of Sheba did, with respect and admiration rather than envy and enmity. Apparently Solomon in all his glory was so modest about his accomplishments and so persistent in giving God the glory that he made friends instead of foes. In his wisdom he illustrated what David's greater descendant was to say centuries later: "Do not worry, saying, 'What shall we eat?' or 'What shall we drink?' or 'What shall we wear?' For the pagans run after all these things, and your heavenly Father knows that you need them. But seek first his kingdom and his righteousness, and all these things will be given to you as well" (Matthew 6:31-33, *New International Version*). Solomon sought God's righteousness. He asked for wisdom to lead God's people in God's way, and riches and honor were given to him along with what he asked.

C. Prayer

Father in Heaven, we are thankful for Your Word, which teaches us to know what is right. We are thankful also for the Savior, through whom we are forgiven and we have the righteousness that is from You by faith. As we seek Your kingdom and Your righteousness, may we have wisdom to understand the Word and grace to follow the Savior. Amen.

D. Thought to Remember

"Seek ye first the kingdom of God, and his righteousness" (Matthew 6:33).

Home Daily Bible Readings

Monday, Nov. 14— Solomon Is Made King (1 Kings 1:28-40)

Tuesday, Nov. 15—God's Blessing and Promise (1 Kings 9:1-9)

Wednesday, Nov. 16—Solomon's Building, Use of Forced Labor (1 Kings 9:10-22)

Thursday, Nov. 17—Solomon's Prosperity (1 Kings 9:23-28)

Friday, Nov. 18—The Queen of Sheba Visits Solomon (1 Kings 10:1-7)

Saturday, Nov. 19— Praise and Gifts From the Queen (1 Kings 10:8-13)

Sunday, Nov. 20—Solomon's Greatness in Riches and Wisdom (1 Kings 10:14-29)

Learning by Doing

This page contains an alternate lesson plan emphasizing learning activities. Classes desiring such student involvement will find these suggestions helpful.

Learning Goals

As students participate in today's class session, they should:

1. Discover that God's blessing was the foundation for Solomon's wisdom and wealth.

2. Decide how to make their nation wealthier, wiser, or more righteous so as to please God.

Into the Lesson

Before class write the words *Wisdom* and *Wealth* on your chalkboard. To begin today's session, distribute slips of paper and ask class members to write a sentence that includes the two words. Collect the slips and read the sentences back to the class.

As you read each sentence, or after you have read them all, analyze them. Do class members agree with all of them? Why or why not? Are the ideas of wisdom and wealth mutually exclusive? Is it possible for the same person to enjoy both wisdom and wealth?

Tell class members that this lesson is the first of two about Solomon, perhaps the wisest man who ever lived, and one of the wealthiest. Like his father, David, Solomon brought great glory to God and also failed before Him. Today's lesson looks at the glory, and next week's study examines the failure.

Into the Word

Ask class members to share what they know about Solomon. Write on your chalkboard the headings in the introduction section on page 98 (Strong King, Godly King, Wide Empire, Great Buildings). Use these headings as an outline for a brief lecture to explain how Solomon became king and what he had accomplished already before the events recorded in today's text.

Ask two volunteers to read the following Scriptures aloud to the class: 1 Kings 3:4-15 and 1 Kings 9:1-9. Then divide the class into groups of about six or eight to compare and contrast the two passages. What is different about the two visions from God? What is the same about them?

Discuss with the class: What is present in the second vision that was not in the first? Why do you suppose God added warnings that He had not mentioned when He first spoke with Solomon?

Ask another volunteer to read 1 Kings 10:1-7, 23, 24 aloud. Then ask your class members to work in the same small groups to examine all of chapter 10 for (a) Evidences of Solomon's Wisdom and (b) Evidences of Solomon's Wealth. (There is room for listings under these two headings in the student book.) Allow about ten minutes for the groups to study; then put the headings on your chalkboard and let class members suggest what to list under each one.

Ask class members, "Why was Solomon so prosperous?" Have one member look up and read aloud 1 Kings 3:9, 12, 13 and another 1 Kings 10:9, 23, 24; then discuss the question fully. Help class members to see that God was the source of Solomon's success, and that Solomon and the surrounding nations readily acknowledged God's blessing in Solomon's kingdom.

Into Life

Ask a class member to read aloud Proverbs 14:34 for Solomon's own analysis of how God responds when a nation acknowledges Him.

Once again write the word *Wisdom* on your chalkboard. Beneath it write *Wealth;* then write *Righteousness* beneath both words. Next, put the following series of numbers beside each word:

-3 -2 -1 0 +1 +2 +3.

Ask your class members to decide if their nation has more or less wisdom, wealth, and righteousness than it had ten years ago. They should use the above numbering system to quantify their answers. For example, if they feel their nation has much less wisdom now than it did a decade ago, they should put a -3 beside *Wisdom.* If they feel the country is about as righteous now as it was a decade ago, they should put a 0 beside *Righteousness.*

Ask students to write the words and their number/vote on slips of paper. Then poll the class for each word. If you have time, you may want to write a cumulative number score on the board beside each word.

Which of the three elements did your class decide their country needs most? How would the presence of the other two help the third one to increase? Lead the class in discussing how individual Christians can make a country more righteous, wiser, or wealthier. What steps could they as individuals or your class as a whole take this week or this month to improve the character of their country?

Let's Talk It Over

The questions on this page are designed to encourage review of the lesson Scriptures and to promote discussion of the lesson by the class. The answers provided are only discussion starters. Let your class talk it over from there.

1. Why is it important that we pray for and sincerely seek the wisdom God offers?

Solomon wrote, "Wisdom is the principal thing; therefore get wisdom: and with all thy getting get understanding" (Proverbs 4:7). The supreme value and desirability of wisdom is one of the most prominent themes in the book of Proverbs. We should pray for wisdom (James 1:5), but it would be foolish for us to pray and then neglect our chief source of wisdom, the Bible. Furthermore, it would be foolish for us to seek wisdom prayerfully through study of the Bible and at the same time keep our eyes and ears open to a full range of worldly values. When we read God's Word, let us pray, "Lord, make me wise in Your ways, and help me to choose Your wisdom exclusively." Then, seeking His wisdom wholeheartedly, we should shut out as much of the world's influences as we can.

2. People knew that Solomon's fame was associated with the name of the Lord God of Israel. How can we make sure that whatever fame we achieve is connected with the name of the Lord?

Not many of us will become nationally or internationally famous, but it is possible for us to become famous in our community or among a wide circle of friends. Fame can build up our pride and make us think more highly of ourselves than we ought to think (see Romans 12:3). We should make it our goal instead that anyone who comes to know us or to know of us will be aware that we are firmly committed to the cause of Jesus Christ. Without giving the impression that we think we are better or holier than others, we need to show people that Jesus Christ is the most important reality in our life.

3. Solomon was able to answer the queen of Sheba's hard questions. What are some hard questions Christians are capable of answering?

The most basic questions human beings ask pertain to who we are, where we came from, and where we are going. The wisdom of the world offers unsatisfying answers to these questions. We who are Christians can explain that we are God's creation, made in His image, made to honor Him, and given the opportunity to enjoy eternal fellowship with Him. We can answer the question, "What is man's fundamental problem?" by pointing out the biblical doctrine of sin. And it is also our privilege to proclaim Jesus Christ as the solution to mankind's sin. The gospel of Jesus Christ provides answers to the most vexing and frustrating questions with which human beings grapple.

4. The queen of Sheba was overwhelmed by Solomon's wisdom and the splendor of his kingdom. Is it legitimate for a church to aim to make visitors to its services feel overwhelmed by what they observe?

If it takes the trappings of wealth and splendor to overwhelm visitors, the answer obviously is no. However, if they can be led to catch a glimpse of the majesty of God through the quality of a church's worship and fellowship, then the answer would surely be yes. Such worship would be infused with thoughts of God's love and mercy and grace. It would focus on the atoning death of Jesus Christ and His triumphant resurrection as dramatic realities. In regard to a church's fellowship, we might recall the famous exclamation of an observer of the early church: "Behold how these Christians love one another!" The love and caring that Christians demonstrate toward one another can make a significant impression on outsiders.

5. How can we profit from the example of Solomon's early devotion to the Lord?

It may be difficult for us to relate to Solomon's devotion. He offered sacrifices in abundance to the Lord, but we may not possess an abundance of gifts to offer. He built a splended temple for the worship of the Lord, but its splendor is beyond anything we could imagine doing for the Lord. However, when we give willingly of our money and our labors, using what we have for God's glory, we demonstrate a devotion equal to that of Solomon. Solomon's animal sacrifices were pleasing to the Lord, but our financial sacrifices to support the local church, missionaries, and benevolent efforts are just as pleasing. The temple Solomon built brought honor to God. However, we build even more wonderful temples, the kind referred to by the poet who wrote, "But the temple the teacher builded . . . was a child's immortal soul."

Solomon Turns From God

DEVOTIONAL READING: Proverbs 16:1-7.

LESSON SCRIPTURE: 1 Kings 11.

PRINTED TEXT: 1 Kings 11:1-13.

1 Kings 11:1-13

1 But king Solomon loved many strange women, together with the daughter of Pharaoh, women of the Moabites, Ammonites, Edomites, Zidonians, and Hittites;

2 Of the nations concerning which the LORD said unto the children of Israel, Ye shall not go in to them, neither shall they come in unto you: for surely they will turn away your heart after their gods: Solomon clave unto these in love.

3 And he had seven hundred wives, princesses, and three hundred concubines: and his wives turned away his heart.

4 For it came to pass, when Solomon was old, that his wives turned away his heart after other gods: and his heart was not perfect with the LORD his God, as was the heart of David his father.

5 For Solomon went after Ashtoreth the goddess of the Zidonians, and after Milcom the abomination of the Ammonites.

6 And Solomon did evil in the sight of the LORD, and went not fully after the LORD, as did David his father.

7 Then did Solomon build a high place for Chemosh, the abomination of Moab, in the hill that is before Jerusalem, and for Molech, the abomination of the children of Ammon.

8 And likewise did he for all his strange wives, which burnt incense and sacrificed unto their gods.

9 And the LORD was angry with Solomon, because his heart was turned from the LORD God of Israel, which had appeared unto him twice,

10 And had commanded him concerning this thing, that he should not go after other gods: but he kept not that which the LORD commanded.

11 Wherefore the LORD said unto Solomon, Forasmuch as this is done of thee, and thou hast not kept my covenant and my statutes, which I have commanded thee, I will surely rend the kingdom from thee, and will give it to thy servant.

12 Notwithstanding, in thy days I will not do it for David thy father's sake: but I will rend it out of the hand of thy son.

13 Howbeit I will not rend away all the kingdom; but will give one tribe to thy son for David my servant's sake, and for Jerusalem's sake which I have chosen.

GOLDEN TEXT: Solomon did evil in the sight of the LORD, and went not fully after the LORD.
—1 Kings 11:6.

From the Conquest to the Kingdom
Unit 4: The Kingdom Under David and Solomon (Lessons 10-13)

Lesson Aims

After studying this lesson a student should be able to:

1. Tell about Solomon's folly and explain how it could have been avoided.

2. Tell how we can keep ourselves from similar folly.

3. Find more time for Bible study.

Lesson Outline

INTRODUCTION
    A. Power Corrupts
    B. Wealth Corrupts
    C. Does Wisdom Corrupt?
 I. FORBIDDEN WIVES (1 Kings 11:1-3a)
    A. Many Wives (v. 1)
    B. Heathen Wives (v. 2)
    C. The Number of Wives (v. 3a)
 II. IMPORTED SINS (1 Kings 11:3b-8)
    A. Imperfect Heart (vv. 3b-5)
    B. Evil Doings (vv. 6-8)
III. SEVERE PENALTY (1 Kings 11:9-13)
    A. Anger of God (vv. 9, 10)
    B. Loss of Kingdom (v. 11)
    C. Modified Penalty (vv. 12, 13)
       Far-reaching Consequences
CONCLUSION
    A. Getting Wisdom
    B. Testing Wisdom
    C. Too Busy?
    D. Prayer
    E. Thought to Remember

Display visual 13 of the visuals packet and let it remain before the class throughout this session. The visual is shown on page 109.

Introduction

Solomon was the wisest man in the world. The Lord said, "I have given thee a wise and an understanding heart; so that there was none like thee before thee, neither after thee shall any arise like unto thee" (1 Kings 3:12).

Solomon was the richest man in the world. The record says he "exceeded all the kings of the earth for riches and for wisdom" (1 Kings 10:23). Gold abounded in the temple (6:20-22), and scarcely less in the palace (10:14-21). Silver was plentiful as stones in Jerusalem (10:27).

Solomon was the most powerful man on earth. His military machine was fearsome (1 Kings 4:26). He stationed strong forces in fortified cities "in all the land of his dominion" (9:17-19). So "Judah and Israel dwelt safely . . . all the days of Solomon" (4:25).

A. Power Corrupts

Power corrupts. That saying has been illustrated so many times that few will doubt its truth. In recent lessons we have seen that Saul was humble and modest in his youth, but as king he became a tyrant without conscience. He disobeyed God (1 Samuel 15), and he tried diligently to kill his best supporter (19:1). David was a man after God's own heart (13:14), but with the power of a king he became an adulterer and a murderer (2 Samuel 11, 12).

Solomon was the most powerful man on earth. Could he escape the corruption of power?

B. Wealth Corrupts

How many small businessmen, honest and industrious, have become big businessmen and then crooks! Some wealthy entrepreneurs of Wall Street multiply their riches by illegal "inside trading." Millionaire bankers and financiers find it easy to defraud customers and investors. Sadly Jesus commented, "It is easier for a camel to go through the eye of a needle, than for a rich man to enter into the kingdom of God" (Mark 10:25).

Solomon was the richest man on earth. Could he escape the corruption of riches?

C. Does Wisdom Corrupt?

The Lord approved Solomon's wish for wisdom, and Solomon's proverbs praise wisdom over and over. But Paul reminds us that not many wise after the flesh are called to God's kingdom (1 Corinthians 1:26). He also warns,

---

How to Say It

AMMONITES.	*Am*-un-ites.
ASHTORETH.	*Ash*-toe-reth.
CHEMOSH.	*Kee*-mosh.
EDOMITES.	*Ee*-dum-ites.
HITTITES.	*Hit*-ites or *Hit*-tites.
MOABITES.	*Mo*-ub-ites.
MOLECH.	*Mo*-lek.
MOLOCH.	*Mo*-lock.
PHARAOH.	*Fair*-o or *Fay*-ro.
ZIDONIANS.	Zye-*doe*-nee-uns.

"Be not wise in your own conceits" (Romans 12:16). Isaiah notes that "the wisdom of their wise men shall perish" (Isaiah 29:14). Is it possible that wisdom can corrupt the wise as power can corrupt the powerful and wealth can corrupt the wealthy? If so, could Solomon escape the corruption of wisdom?

Whether we can blame power or wealth or wisdom, Solomon's glory was terribly corrupted in his later years. The Lord's favor depended on Solomon's obedience. The Lord made that plain more than once (1 Kings 3:14; 6:11-13; 9:4, 5). A man as wise as Solomon should have remembered. But the time came when Solomon trusted his wisdom more than he trusted God's law.

I. Forbidden Wives
(1 Kings 11:1-3a)

Solomon's writings seem to approve lifelong faithfulness to one wife (Proverbs 5:18, 19; Ecclesiastes 9:9). But Solomon also wrote, "Whoso findeth a wife findeth a good thing" (Proverbs 18:22), and it seems that he himself found one as often as possible.

A. Many Wives (v. 1)

1. But king Solomon loved many strange women, together with the daughter of Pharaoh, women of the Moabites, Ammonites, Edomites, Zidonians, and Hittites.

Early in his reign, Solomon made a peace treaty with Egypt and strengthened the alliance by marrying the daughter of Pharaoh (1 Kings 3:1). Then Solomon proceeded to strengthen ties with other nations in the same way. *Strange women* means foreign women, not women of Israel. The nations named were subject to Solomon. After the custom of the time, he left them free to manage their own affairs as long as they paid tribute to him regularly. Women of these royal families could serve as hostages as well as wives. When a princess of Moab, for example, was in Jerusalem, the king of Moab would hesitate to offend Solomon. That might mean his daughter in Jerusalem would lose favor with the king, and might be mistreated?

Long before Israel had a king, the Lord made specific laws for the king who would come in the future (Deuteronomy 17:14-20). Among other things, the law said the king should not "multiply wives to himself" (Deuteronomy 17:17). David ignored that law, and Solomon ignored it even more outrageously. It seemed wise to take all those wives for political reasons, and Solomon chose to follow political wisdom rather than divine law. The wisest man in the world acted foolishly.

B. Heathen Wives (v. 2)

2. Of the nations concerning which the LORD said unto the children of Israel, Ye shall not go in to them, neither shall they come in unto you: for surely they will turn away your heart after their gods: Solomon clave unto these in love.

The law allowed no one in Israel to marry a heathen from the other nations (Deutereonomy 7:3, 4). A heathen wife or husband would turn the Israelite's heart away from the real God. So Solomon violated the law in two ways: his wives were many, and were heathen.

C. The Number of Wives (v. 3a)

3a. And he had seven hundred wives, princesses, and three hundred concubines.

Special mention is made of the princess of Egypt (1 Kings 3:1; 7:8), but some nations must have contributed whole groups of *princesses* to Solomon's harem. We cannot count seven hundred different nations near Israel. Perhaps Solomon thought he needed a princess from each of the influential families or clans within a nation.

Concubines were second-class wives, not so important as the princesses. Still they may have been the most attractive ladies in the harem, chosen for beauty and charm rather than for political reasons; and so they may have enjoyed more of the king's attention. Even the wisest man on earth could hardly find time to give much personal attention to each of a thousand wives. Some humorist has reckoned that if Solomon spent a one-month honeymoon with each of the thousand, that was eighty-three solid years of honeymoons—and Solomon reigned only forty years (1 Kings 11:42).

II. Imported Sins
(1 Kings 11:3b-8)

The law forbade marriage with heathen, "for surely they will turn away your heart after their gods" (v. 2). Solomon may have smiled at that: "Not me! Nobody is going to turn away my heart."

Who is wise enough to know his own heart and his own weakness? Have you ever caught yourself doing something you had thought you would never, never do?

A. Imperfect Heart (vv. 3b-5)

3b. And his wives turned away his heart.

How could that be? Wasn't Solomon wise? Yes, he was wise, and he was strong. But the wise man acted foolishly when he ignored God's Word and took those heathen wives, and the strong man acted weakly when lovely ladies begged to be allowed to worship their own gods.

4. For it came to pass, when Solomon was old, that his wives turned away his heart after other gods: and his heart was not perfect with the LORD his God, as was the heart of David his father.

Solomon did not deny the Lord. The Lord still had his heart, or maybe ninety-nine percent of it. He just made a bit of room for phony gods. A man can make a few concessions to get along with his wives, can't he?

So Solomon 's heart *was not perfect*, not complete, not entire, *with the Lord his God*. Perhaps only a small percent of it was given to phony gods to please seven hundred wives. But God's demand is firm, uncompromising, intolerant: "No other gods" (Exodus 20:3).

5. For Solomon went after Ashtoreth the goddess of the Zidonians, and after Milcom the abomination of the Ammonites.

Two phony gods of contrasting types are mentioned as examples. *Ashtoreth* was the love goddess worshiped in Zidon (or Sidon) north of Israel. *Milcom* was the brutal king-god of the Ammonites east of Israel. Sometimes he is called Moloch or Molech (v. 7). Our text calls him an *abomination*, a detestable thing.

How much did Solomon have to do with the worship of these imaginary gods? Scholars debate that question. Some think *went after* means he himself joined his wives in worshiping. Others think he did not join in the worshiping, but only permitted it and provided places for it. In either case, Solomon was at fault. If his heart had been perfect, he would not have tolerated the worship of any other god.

B. Evil Doings (vv. 6-8)

6. And Solomon did evil in the sight of the LORD, and went not fully after the LORD, as did David his father.

When one's heart is not perfect with the Lord (v. 4), soon what he does is imperfect too. "For from within, out of the heart of men, proceed evil thoughts, adulteries, fornications, murders, thefts, covetousness, wickedness, deceit, lasciviousness, an evil eye, blasphemy, pride, foolishness" (Mark 7:21, 22). Solomon's imperfect heart did not lead him into all of these, but it did at least lead him into some foolishness. He should have followed his own advice: "Keep thy heart with all diligence; for out of it are the issues of life" (Proverbs 4:23).

7. Then did Solomon build a high place for Chemosh, the abomination of Moab, in the hill that is before Jerusalem, and for Molech, the abomination of the children of Ammon.

A high place is a place of worship. *The hill that is before Jerusalem* is the Mount of Olives. Not in Jerusalem itself, but just across a narrow ravine to the east, Solomon built a place of worship for Chemosh. *Moab* and *Ammon* were kindred nations descended from two sons of Lot (Genesis 19:36-38). Their imaginary gods, *Chemosh* and *Molech*, were supposed to be similar in nature. Possibly both could be worshiped in the same place. If not, Solomon built two high places for them.

8. And likewise did he for all his strange wives, which burnt incense and sacrificed unto their gods.

Of course the Moabites and Ammonites could not be favored above the rest of the wives. All of them had to have suitable places to worship their gods. Some have supposed that every hill near Jerusalem was crowded with places of heathen worship. Probably, however, dozens of the wives worshiped the same god, so huge numbers of high places were not needed.

III. Severe Penalty (1 Kings 11:9-13)

Part of Israel's mission in the promised land was to destroy all the idols and altars and places of heathen worship (Exodus 34:13; Deuteronomy 7:5; 12:2, 3). When Solomon built what he ought to destroy, the Lord's response was severe.

A. Anger of God (vv. 9, 10)

9. And the LORD was angry with Solomon, because his heart was turned from the LORD God of Israel, which had appeared unto him twice.

It was wrong for anyone to turn away from the Lord, but it was worse for Solomon to turn away after the Lord *had appeared unto him twice* with special favor and promises. Though Solomon did not turn away very far, *the Lord was angry*.

10. And had commanded him concerning this thing, that he should not go after other gods: but he kept not that which the LORD commanded.

Besides the commandments given to all Israel and written in the law, Solomon had God's word given to him personally. Plainly the Lord had warned him that turning away would have terrible results (1 Kings 9:6-9). In spite of that, Solomon *kept not that which the Lord commanded*.

B. Loss of Kingdom (v. 11)

11. Wherefore the LORD said unto Solomon, Forasmuch as this is done of thee, and thou hast not kept my covenant and my statutes, which I have commanded thee, I will surely rend the kingdom from thee, and will give it to thy servant.

Solomon had been ignoring God's commandments more and more. In violation of the law he took heathen wives, and he took many wives. He also acquired many horses contrary to the law, and he got them from Egypt (Deuteronomy 17:16; 1 Kings 10:26-29). But when he gave some recognition to phony gods, that was the last straw. God had given him a glorious empire, and God was going to take it away from him.

C. Modified Penalty (vv. 12, 13)

12. Notwithstanding, in thy days I will not do it for David thy father's sake: but I will rend it out of the hand of thy son.

The punishment was modified, not for the sake of Solomon, but for the sake of David. This was not done as a personal favor to David, who had died years before; it was done so God's promise to David would be kept. Concerning Solomon, the Lord had said to David, "My mercy shall not depart away from him, as I took it from Saul" (2 Samuel 7:15). Deprived of God's mercy, Saul had died in bloody defeat (1 Samuel 31:1-6). But by God's mercy, Solomon's glorious empire would remain intact till Solomon would die of natural causes. Then the kingdom would be taken swiftly from his son.

13. Howbeit I will not rend away all the kingdom; but will give one tribe to thy son for David my servant's sake, and for Jerusalem's sake which I have chosen.

The punishment was modified in a second way. One of the twelve tribes would be left for Solomon's son to rule. This would not be done for the sake of Solomon or his son, but for the sake of David and Jerusalem. This too must be understood in the light of God's promises and purposes. God had chosen David's family to continue on the throne forever (2 Samuel 7:12, 13, 16), and God had chosen Jerusalem as the special place of His presence (1 Kings 9:3). Neither of these choices would be nullified by Solomon's misdeeds, but Solomon's glorious empire would end. Only David's own tribe, the tribe of Judah, would still be ruled by men of David's family.

FAR-REACHING CONSEQUENCES

Galena, Illinois, was once the commercial and cultural center of the Midwest! In the middle of the nineteenth century, it was a progressive city on the American frontier. Its setting on the Galena River was just a short distance from the Mississippi.

The produce of the surrounding region and the ore from local mines could be traded for goods brought upstream from the South and other parts of the country on the great inland

visual 13

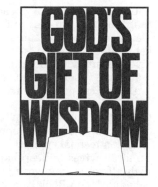

waterway formed by the Mississippi and Ohio Rivers. The "city fathers" were so sure of their future as a riverboat town that when the railroad wanted to build a terminal there, they said they didn't want it.

In those days, Chicago was just a small town that also had access to water transportation. But Chicago's leaders said yes to the railroads, and the rest is history. Galena's mines gave out, the population dwindled, and the town declined. A decision on the part of a few had far-reaching consequences for many.

Solomon had his rationalizations for marrying foreign women: we know it was considered good international politics; he may also have thought it made Jerusalem a more cosmopolitan city. But Solomon's unwise decision was in direct opposition to God's specific command. The price to be paid was the decline and destruction of a whole nation. Sin still has its price today.   —C. R. B.

Conclusion

How could such a wise man be so foolish? It wasn't hard at all. Solomon began to trust his wisdom too much, and failed to check it by God's Word. While we mourn over his folly, let's give a bit of thought to our own. Our wisdom is less than Solomon's, but do we always live by the wisdom we have? How many times have you said, "I should have known better," or "Why did I do that?" or "How could I be so stupid?" With the good sense we have now, all of us can do better than we have been doing. Can't we? At the same time, all of us can be growing wiser.

A. Getting Wisdom

Solomon's wisdom was a gift from God (1 Kings 3:12), and so is ours. "If any of you lack wisdom, let him ask of God, that giveth to all men liberally, and upbraideth not; and it shall be given him" (James 1:5). But that does not mean we receive His gift without any effort on our part.

God gives our daily bread, but we work for it too. With the muscles and minds God gives us we work with the materials He gives, and so we get the food He gives. With the same minds God gives we study the Scriptures He gives, and thus we get the wisdom He gives.

Do you suppose Solomon neglected his homework? The law said he should have a copy of God's Word and read from it every day (Deuteronomy 17:18-20). But Solomon had a nation to rule, a big commercial enterprise to manage, and seven hundred wives to keep happy. Do you suppose daily Bible reading was crowded out of his busy schedule? The Book said he shouldn't multiply horses (Deuteronomy 17:16). But what if he hadn't seen that part of the Book for ten years? Could that explain why he ignored it?

Are there some parts of the Bible that you haven't read for ten years? Maybe you do not have as much wisdom as God wants to give you.

B. Testing Wisdom

The devil is no fool. He tries to deceive us with wisdom that is as phony as the gods of Moab and Zidon.

Eve thought it would be wise to eat from the forbidden tree. If she became wiser, she became sadder too. She lost her home in Eden (Genesis 3).

Solomon thought it would be wise to take hundreds of heathen wives. The strategy seemed to work: he had little trouble with their fathers. But his kingdom was split in two when he died (1 Kings 12:1-20).

King Herod thought it was wise to kill anyone who might possibly take his throne, including a baby who was called King of the Jews (Matthew 2). But Herod died, his kingdom was split four ways, and Jesus still is King.

Communist dictators thought it was wise to destroy all dissenters and ultimately to take charge of the whole world. But they made their downfall sure when they decreed that God did not exist. Their country is split more ways than Herod's.

Eve could have had a very simple way to test her thinking. She knew what God said: "Don't eat from that tree." That settled it.

Solomon could have checked his thought just as simply if he had kept up his homework. God's law said, "Not many wives; no heathen wives; no other gods."

Herod knew how to find out where the Christ was to be born. He called the Bible students, and they gave him the information from Scripture (Matthew 2:4-6; Micah 5:2). If Herod had pursued the matter further in the same way, he could have learned that Christ's kingdom cannot be destroyed (Daniel 2:44).

Russian Communists may have been misled by corrupt church officials who misrepresented God, but they could have bypassed the officials and read God's Word for themselves. It gives no support either to church corruption or Communist tyranny.

How do you think you and I can test our thinking to see whether it is wise or not?

C. Too Busy?

If anyone could claim to be too busy for Bible study, Solomon could. Some of us make that claim while our responsibilities are far less than his. But an empire was lost because Solomon did not live by Bible teaching. Can we afford to risk whatever empires we have?

Some of us assign ourselves a certain number of chapters a day, and neglect whatever we have to neglect in order to read those chapters. But some chapters take longer than others, so some of us reserve a certain time each day. Many of us plan to read the entire Bible each year, and some eager ones read it two or three times in a year. Many of us could read it four times a year simply by giving up the worse half of the television programs we watch. If anyone is too busy for Bible study, that person is too busy.

Are you wise enough to find time to become wiser?

D. Prayer

Dear Father in Heaven, thank You for sharing Your wisdom and truth with us. Confessing that we have neither learned nor followed Your Word as well as possible, we beg You to forgive us and help us to do better. In Jesus' name, Amen.

E. Thought to Remember

Read the Bible!

Home Daily Bible Readings

Monday, Nov. 21—Solomon's Achievements (Ecclesiastes 2:4-9)
Tuesday, Nov. 22—God Sees Into the Heart (Proverbs 16:1-9)
Wednesday, Nov. 23—Solomon Disobeys God's Command (1 Kings 11:1-8)
Thursday, Nov. 24—Solomon's Kingdom Will End (1 Kings 11:9-13)
Friday, Nov. 25—Edomite Foes Organize Against Solomon (1 Kings 11:14-22)
Saturday, Nov. 26—Other Adversaries Take Action (1 Kings 11:23-27)
Sunday, Nov. 27—Ahijah's Prophecy About Jeroboam's Reign (1 Kings 11:28-40)

Learning by Doing

This page contains an alternate lesson plan emphasizing learning activities. Classes desiring such student involvement will find these suggestions helpful.

Learning Goals

Students in today's class should:

1. List the factors that contributed to Solomon's downfall.

2. Discuss six principles related to God and how Solomon's downfall illustrates the importance of each one.

3. Choose one of the principles to remember and apply in the following week.

Into the Lesson

Write the following scrambled sentences (with the punctuation and capitalization shown here) on notecards, one sentence per card. To begin this session, divide your class into pairs or groups of three or four and give a card to each group. Ask each group to unscramble its sentence to reveal an important truth. (The scrambled sentences are included in the student book.)

1. conventional we God. become wisdom wisdom, we world's may blindly blind to When accept the the from

(When we blindly accept the world's conventional wisdom, we may become blind to the wisdom from God.)

2. blessing wisdom, When wisdom. comes habit of God's lose lose the the that may from living studying by we we God's

(When we lose the habit of studying God's wisdom, we may lose the blessing that comes from living by God's wisdom.)

3. often disobedience. with failure minimal Monumental starts

(Monumental failure often starts with minimal disobedience.)

4. governed with God. God; with be by rules from otherwise, Relationships relationships relationship others others can with interfere must with our

(Relationships with others must be governed by rules from God; otherwise, relationships with others can interfere with our relationship with God.)

5. first straw the hearts last Our for is another god God. in our making

(Our making another god first in our hearts is the last straw for God.)

6. depending Those by God God. are blessed most susceptible on their most blessings failing to to and follow

(Those most blessed by God are most susceptible to depending on their blessings and failing to follow God.)

When the groups have finished their work, ask them to share the results with the class. (You may want to prepare a poster before class with the correct sentences on it. If so, display it after the groups report so all may see the unscrambled sentences.) Ask class members to comment briefly on them. Which sentence most "strikes a chord" with them? Which do they have the most trouble understanding? Is there a sentence with which they disagree? Is there a sentence that explains a principle that class members can illustrate with examples from their own lives?

After several minutes of discussion, tell the class that each of these sentences contains a truth that is illustrated by the story told in today's Scripture text.

Into the Word

Remind the class of last week's study of Solomon, the world's wealthiest and wisest man. Tell them that today's text describes the sad decline of Solomon. Ask a volunteer to read the Scripture text aloud while class members listen and decide why Solomon failed.

If students worked in pairs or groups for the first activity, ask them to return to the same groupings. Distribute paper and instruct the groups to examine today's text and list what it indicates Solomon did that was wrong. After about five or six minutes, ask volunteers to share as you make a list on the chalkboard. Ask, "What was so wrong with these things?"

Then have the class decide how the example of Solomon illustrates each of the principles stated in the unscrambled sentences. You may want to assign a different sentence to each group, or let each group choose a sentence.

Into Life

Ask students to decide which of these principles is the greatest challenge to them. Invite each student to choose one of the sentences and to write it on a notecard as a reminder of today's discussion.

Ask volunteers to share which sentence they chose, and why. Close the class session with sentence prayers, mentioning especially the concerns that your students have shared.

Let's Talk It Over

The questions on this page are designed to encourage review of the lesson Scriptures and to promote discussion of the lesson by the class. The answers provided are only discussion starters. Let your class talk it over from there.

1. Solomon was among the many rulers in history who fell prey to the corrupting effects of power. How can those who lead today avoid this corrupting influence?

Paul's reminder in Romans 13:1 is appropriate here: "There is no power but of God: the powers that be are ordained of God." This was written with particular reference to civil power, but it surely is true of power in the church, in business, and in other human organizations. Those Christians who gain access to power in any organization must remind themselves, "This power is not mine; it is God's, and I am responsible to God for the way I use it." Furthermore, it is one aspect of our function as salt of the earth (Matthew 5:13) to assist non-Christian leaders in recognizing the ultimate source of their authority and to challenge them when they exceed the proper bounds of their authority.

2. God forbade the Israelites to intermarry with people of heathen nations. Parallel to this is the warning that Christians should avoid marriage with non-Christians. Why does this warning need to be stressed today?

"Be ye not unequally yoked together with unbelievers" is a New Testament principle, which, in its application, clearly includes marriage, (2 Corinthians 6:14). But we are seeing many examples of this unequal yoking, as young men and young women from the church marry non-Christians and often drift away from the church afterward. Sometimes the believing partner expects that he or she will lead the unbelieving spouse to conversion, but the opposite often occurs. Once again we are reminded of how vital it is that the church provide solid teaching to its young people regarding courtship and marriage.

3. Those who are young or middle-aged adults may worry about whether or not they will turn away from the Lord in old age, as Solomon did. What can one do to keep this from happening?

Solomon's decisions in his younger days were largely responsible for his drifting away from the Lord later in life. Life's later years can be a time of temptation. On the one hand, retirement and the enjoyment of comforts gained over a lifetime may breed complacency. On the other hand, the diminishing of physical and mental prowess and the failure to fulfill certain lifelong dreams may create disillusionment. Either circumstance could be spiritually perilous. Younger adults who are careless regarding spiritual duties and moral decisions may be putting themselves in jeopardy of a later abandonment of the faith. If the habits of personal Bible study, prayer, and enthusiastic involvement in the church are developed early on, one will be more likely to remain faithful to the Lord, whatever old age may bring.

4. It is alarming to imagine the Lord's being angry with us. How is it helpful to us to consider the anger of the Lord?

While we are to seek the "perfect love [that] casteth out fear" (1 John 4:18), the New Testament indicates that there is a kind of fear the Christian should maintain. Jesus himself said that we should "fear him which is able to destroy both soul and body in hell" (Matthew 10:28). Twice in Peter's first epistle we are urged to fear God (1:17; 2:17). This fear is not the kind that is meant to leave us quaking with dread, but it should instead prod us to holiness. It is a good idea, therefore, for us to take note of those occasions in the Bible in which God is described as becoming angry. We should ask ourselves if we have been guilty of similar anger-provoking behavior. And then we should in reverent fear resolve to discontinue such behavior.

5. We speak of a person's being "worldly wise." Sometimes this type of wisdom is legitimate, but sometimes it can lead one astray. What are some means by which we can test it?

It is obvious that we need to have a thorough acquaintance with biblical wisdom if we are to recognize which aspects of worldly wisdom are out-of-bounds for us. We should master the great general principles the New Testament provides for testing moral and spiritual decisions. Some of these are found in Romans 14:19; 1 Corinthians 10:31; and Galatians 5:13. Through prayer we can look for guidance either by way of inward prompting or outward circumstances. Another means of testing is the counsel of Christian leaders and friends. They are not infallible, but their insights, when combined with Scripture and prayer, can be quite helpful.

Winter Quarter, 1994-95

Theme: Jesus the Fulfillment (Matthew)

Special Features

Lessons

Unit 1. Jesus and John: Setting the Scene

Unit 2. Immanuel: God With Us

Unit 3. Jesus: The Son of David

Unit 4. Jesus Christ: Victor Over Sin and Death

About these lessons

The focus of this quarter's study is on Jesus Christ as the fulfillment of the Old Testament promises. This emphasis is begun with two lessons on John the Baptist's ministry of preparation, prophesied by Isaiah. The theme is carried out in succeeding lessons on Jesus' birth, ministry, death, and resurrection.

Dec 4
Dec 11
Dec 18
Dec 25
Jan 1
Jan 8
Jan 15
Jan 22
Jan 29
Feb 5
Feb 12
Feb 19
Feb 26

Quarterly Quiz

The questions on this page may be used in several ways: as a pretest at the beginning of the quarter; as a review at the end of the quarter; or as a review after each lesson. The questions are based on the Scripture text of each lesson (King James Version). **The answers are on page 120.**

Lesson 1

1. When John the Baptist came preaching, what did he say was at hand? *Matthew 3:2*

2. What did John call the Pharisees and Sadducees who came to his baptism? *Matthew 3:7*

3. What happens to every tree that does not bring forth good fruit? *Matthew 3:10*

Lesson 2

1. Where was John the Baptist when he sent two of his disciples to ask Jesus if He was the One who was to come? *Matthew 11:2*

2. Jesus identified John the Baptist as being which Old Testament prophet who was to come? *Matthew 11:14*

Lesson 3

1. When Joseph discovered that Mary, his betrothed, was with child, he decided to divorce her privately, not wanting to make her a _____ _____ . *Matthew 1:19*

2. Who told Joseph that Mary's child was conceived of the Holy Ghost? *Matthew 1:20*

Lesson 4

1. The wise men who came to Jerusalem were from the _____ . *Matthew 2:1*

2. What had they seen there? *Matthew 2:2*

3. What did King Herod demand of the chief priests and scribes? *Matthew 2:4*

Lesson 5

1. Jesus met two possessed with devils in the land of the Gergasenes. Where did the devils go when Jesus cast them out? *Matthew 8:32*

2. By healing the palsied man, Jesus showed that He had authority to do what? *Matthew 9:6*

Lesson 6

1. After Jesus healed the man with a withered hand on the Sabbath, the Pharisees met to determine what? *Matthew 12:14*

2. Jesus fulfilled Isaiah's prophecy of God's servant, who would neither break a ____ ____ nor quench ____ ____ . *Matthew 12:20*

Lesson 7

1. The Canaanite woman who begged Jesus to heal her demon-possessed daughter was from the vicinity of what two cities? *Matthew 15:21*

2. How did Jesus first respond to the woman's request? *Matthew 15:23*

3. Jesus said her faith was _____ . *Matthew 15:28*

Lesson 8

1. Which disciples witnessed Jesus' transfiguration? *Matthew 17:1*

2. Who appeared and spoke with Jesus when He was transfigured? *Matthew 17:3*

3. Which disciple suggested that they build three tabernacles on the mount? *Matthew 17:4*

Lesson 9

1. Jesus sent two disciples to what village to get the animals He needed for His triumphal entry into Jerusalem? *Matthew 21:1, 2*

2. What did the multitudes of people place before Jesus as He rode down the Mount of Olives toward Jerusalem? *Matthew 21:8*

Lesson 10

1. How did Jesus identify the one who would betray Him? *Matthew 26:23*

2. At the last supper, Jesus gave His disciples a cup to drink, saying, "This is my ____ of the new ____ , which is shed for many for the _____ of sins." *Matthew 26:28*

Lesson 11

1. Who presided over Jesus' nighttime trial before the scribes and elders? *Matthew 26:57*

2. The council sought false witness against Jesus for what purpose? *Matthew 26:59*

3. The council accused Jesus of blasphemy for making what claim? *Matthew 26:63-65.*

Lesson 12

1. Who put a scarlet robe on Jesus, a crown of thorns on His head, and a reed in His hand and then mocked Him as king? *Matthew 27:27-29*

2. What does *Golgotha* mean? *Matthew 27:33*

3. What was written over Jesus' head when He was crucified? *Matthew 27:37*

Lesson 13

1. What two emotions did the women experience as they departed Jesus' tomb after seeing and hearing the angel? *Matthew 28:8*

2. Who met the women as they ran to tell the disciples of Jesus' resurrection? *Matthew 28:9*

Jesus, the Promised One

by Carl Bridges

THIS QUARTER'S LESSONS focus on Jesus as portrayed by Matthew. Even though the writers of all four Gospel accounts agreed on who Jesus was, what He did, and what He means to everyone, still each of them emphasized certain aspects of His character. Matthew, more than any other writer, highlighted Jesus' role as fulfiller of prophecy. He called attention to an Old Testament prophecy by means of an introductory statement such as this one in chapter 1, verse 22: "All this took place to fulfill what had been spoken by the Lord through the prophet."* Other similar statements are found in 2:15, 2:17, 2:23, 4:14, 8:17, 12:17, 13:35, 21:4, 27:9. These "formula quotations," as some scholars call them, serve as only the most noticeable mark of Matthew's concern with prophecy. All through his Gospel account we see him present Jesus as the promised One, the son of David, the divine Savior to whom all the prophets pointed.

A secondary theme of this quarter's lessons comes to the surface as we see how different people responded to Jesus. John the Baptist, the wise men, King Herod, and Jesus' own disciples, among others, could accept Him or reject Him, but they couldn't ignore him. We see in their varied responses to God's Son a pattern repeated in our day as people accept Jesus, turn Him away, or try to ignore Him.

In all four Gospels we find the *kerygma*, the proclamation, of Jesus as Messiah, Son of God, and Savior. As people have often said, the Gospels do not function simply as biographies of Jesus. In addition to telling us facts about His life, they provide a God-inspired interpretation of who He is. When Peter preached to the Pentecost crowd (Acts 2), when Philip talked to the Ethiopian (Acts 8), when Paul spoke in the synagogue at Antioch in Pisidia (Acts 13), or when any early proclaimer of Jesus told anyone else about Him, they gave the same message. The facts of Jesus' ministry, His teaching, His death and resurrection, together with the promise of His coming again to judge the world, provided the "pegs" on which the apostolic preachers hung what they had to say. These basic facts about Jesus, His nature and work, we find highlighted in all the Gospels, including the one we study this quarter. Matthew's Gospel, like the other three, serves not just as fact but also as interpretation, not only as biography but as proclamation as well.

Jesus and John: Setting the Scene
(Unit 1)

The lessons in this study don't go in strict chronological order. The first unit has to do with John the Baptist, who served as Jesus' forerunner, and Jesus' reaction to John. In **lesson 1** we hear John's stern message of repentance to the Israelites of his time, as he called them to turn away from evil and turn to the God of Abraham in order to get ready for the judgment to come. We also hear his promise of the coming Messiah, and we see that promise begin to find fulfillment in Jesus' baptism and the descent of the Holy Spirit upon Him.

The Scripture text for **lesson 2** comes from later in Jesus' ministry, when John the Baptist sent a message from prison to ask Jesus if He really was the promised One. After telling John's messengers to go back to John with a report of the messianic signs they saw Jesus performing, Jesus addressed the crowds, evaluating John's character and ministry. John was not a weakling, Jesus said, nor did he desire a life of luxury. Instead this rugged man, who lived an austere life in the desert, was strong and immovable. He was a dedicated servant of God, who had been privileged to announce the coming kingdom.

Immanuel: God With Us
(Unit 2)

The second unit of the Winter quarter focuses on Jesus as Immanuel, "God with us." In **lesson 3** we consider Mary's miraculous pregnancy and the reaction to it of her fiance, Joseph. We learn of the angel's appearance to Joseph, the divine name the new child was to bear, and a seven-hundred-year-old prophecy, which promised that He would be born of a virgin. This lesson reveals Jesus' birth to be both a historical event, something that happened to real people in a real time and place, and as a cosmic event, something that affects all people of all times and places.

In **lesson 4** we meet some of the most mysterious characters in the Bible, the "wise men from the East" (2:1). Profound students of nature, they came to greet the infant King after seeing a special star rise when He was born. In this lesson we also meet Herod the Great, the king who sat uneasy on his throne and saw the baby Jesus as a dangerous rival.

Jesus: The Son of David
(Unit 3)

In the third unit, we see how Matthew presented Jesus as the son of David, the royal descendant of the ideal king, the One who would sit on His ancestor's throne and rule God's people with justice. In the Scripture passages contained in this unit, we find the record of some of Jesus' marvelous deeds, the messianic signs that proved who He was.

Lesson 5 deals with two notable miracles, the healing of two demon-possessed men in the region of Gadara, and the restoration of a paralyzed man whom some friends carried to Jesus for help. In these miracles we see Jesus' power over the forces of disease and evil that darken people's minds and twist their bodies.

As time went by, Jesus' enemies began to press Him, and in **lesson 6** we see how He dealt with them. Jesus entered a synagogue, where He met a man with a withered hand. Jesus' antagonists, less concerned with the man's wholeness than with the question of whether Jesus would "break" the Sabbath by healing him, made the man's situation a test case. After Jesus healed many more persons among the crowds who followed Him, the amazed people wondered aloud, "Can this be the Son of David?" (12:23).

Lesson 7 tells of Jesus meeting a Canaanite woman, a Gentile, and how He dealt with one who was not a member of God's chosen people. It shouldn't surprise us to find Him meeting her deep need by healing her daughter. From this incident in Jesus' life, we learn one of the truths Matthew points to again and again: God loves people of all kinds and doesn't play favorites.

Lesson 8 deals with the dramatic event in Jesus' ministry known as His transfiguration. While on a mountain with three of His disciples, Jesus was visibly changed before them and then joined by Moses and Elijah. Thus those disciples were given a glimpse of Jesus' true nature. At the same time, God the Father spoke out of Heaven with words of approbation similar to those spoken at Jesus' baptism.

Lesson 9 covers Jesus' triumphal entry into the city of Jerusalem. At this time many people, including children, proclaimed Him as the son of David, the messianic king. By riding on a donkey in fulfillment of prophecy, Jesus deliberately declared himself as the promised deliverer of Israel.

Jesus Christ: Victor Over Sin and Death (Unit 4)

The fourth and final unit of this quarter's study deals with Jesus' death and resurrection, and events associated with them. **Lesson 10** tells of the Passover meal Jesus ate with His disciples shortly before His arrest. During the meal He designated the bread as a memorial of His body, about to be broken on the cross, and the cup as a memorial of His blood, about to be shed to atone for the sins of the world.

Lesson 11 presents us with one of the ugliest events recorded in Scripture, the trial of Jesus. Confronted with faked evidence and facing a hostile court, Jesus maintained His integrity as the Son of man and bore without flinching the rage of His enemies. We can hardly fail to be moved by such a graphic picture of what our Lord went through for the people He loved so much.

Jesus' crucifixion serves as the subject of **lesson 12.** Although we may be shocked by the brutality and injustice of what people did to Him, we cannot help being grateful for His suffering on our behalf. When the soldiers mockingly said, "Hail, King of the Jews!" (27:29), they spoke more truth than they knew.

Lesson 13 presents Matthew's account of the resurrection, the event that showed Jesus to be the Son of God and Savior of mankind. Some women who followed Jesus came intending "to see the tomb" (28:1), but found instead an angel who told them that their Friend and Master was not there, that He had been raised from the dead. Leaving the tomb "with fear and great joy" (28:8), they hurried to tell Jesus' disciples. By Jesus' appointment, these men met Jesus again on a mountain in their native Galilee and received a commission from Him that is still in force today, the command to "go . . . and make disciples of all nations, baptizing them in the name of the Father and of the Son and of the Holy Spirit, and teaching them to obey everything that I have commanded you" (28:19, 20). They also received from Jesus a promise that His followers claim even today: "And remember, I am with you always, to the end of the age" (28:20).

At the very end of John's Gospel we find these words: "But there are also many other things that Jesus did; if every one of them were written down, I suppose that the world itself could not contain the books that would be written" (John 21:25). We too are aware of the abundance of material from which to draw in considering the life of Christ, since the study we are now beginning can deal with only a few passages taken from Matthew's long Gospel. Still, the record of Jesus' sayings and doings is precious, and we gain much even if we study but a limited part of it. The good news of Jesus, if we will let it, will change our lives forever.

---

*Scripture quotations are taken from the *New Revised Standard Version* of the Bible.

Responding to Jesus

by Knofel Staton

GOD CREATED HUMANS to have a positive, dynamic relationship with Him and with each other. Sin, however, brought a shattering to that ideal and disrupted those relationships. Christianity is God's strategy for restoring broken relationships.

Christianity is *the* relational religion. That should not surprise us, for God is love (1 John 4:16). Haven't you at times thought that too many Christians place more emphasis on "head" than on "heart," more on legalism than on love-ism?

Jesus came into a world dominated by the legalistic dimension of religion, but He came demonstrating and teaching its relational aspects. When He was tested with the question, "Which is the greatest commandment in the Law?" He answered that it was to love God first and foremost, and then to love others as you love yourself. In other words, He stressed *relationships* of love. Then He dropped the bombshell: "All the Law and the Prophets hang on these two commandments" (Matthew 22:35-40, *New International Version*).

Even in the Sermon on the Mount, Jesus stressed relationships: "For I tell you that unless your righteousness surpasses that of the Pharisees and the teachers of the law, you will certainly not enter the kingdom of heaven" (Matthew 5:20, *New International Version*). *Righteousness always has to do with the right kind of relationships*. We demonstrate the righteousness God desires when our inner character results in outer behavior showing that God and others are important to us.

Responding to Relationships

Whatever we are and however we think is in large part a product of our various relationships—whether that response is positive or negative, good or bad. We are all developing as the result not only of what is within us but also the people who are around us.

All of us are changing daily. The question is, into what are we changing and developing? A Christian's development should be governed by his or her relationship with Jesus. Just how are you responding to Jesus?

In this quarter of lessons, we will see how different people responded to the presence, the fellowship, the friendship of Jesus. We will see how those various responses can be applied to our lives today.

From a Potential Big Head
to a Big Heart

John the Baptist had the people in the palm of his hands. They flocked from all avenues of Judaism to hear him preach. If he were living today, he doubtless would be a "top draw" on religious programs; he would be invited to the nationally televised talk shows.

Jesus said that the person had not been born who was greater than John the Baptist (see Matthew 11:11). Many thought that John the Baptist was the Messiah (Luke 3:15)

But instead of getting a big head, John was humbled in the presence of Jesus and chose to continue to be only a servant. John was satisfied to be the preparer of people to become disciples of Jesus.

John's greatness was seen in his attitude, not just in his activities. His attitude was summed up when he said, referring to Jesus, "He must increase, but I must decrease" (John 3:30). As we study these lessons, walk along with Jesus and ask, "What specific situations did He face that are similar to what we face today?" Then do what John the Baptist did and say to your attitudes, to your reactions, "I must decrease, and He must increase."

In this day when self-evaluation rotates around possessions and position, and we tend to feed the ego in us rather than Immanuel who is in us through His Spirit, we can learn from John the Baptist. If our material wealth should increase, shouldn't our thought be, "I now have more to manage for God"? If we rise to a higher position in any worthy endeavor, should not we feel a greater responsibility to mirror God's character for others to see Him living in us?

From a Tornado to a Soothing Breeze

James and John were brothers, and one wonders if they might not have been quite spoiled in their younger days. In the course of their traveling with Jesus, He nicknamed them "The sons of thunder" (Mark 3:17), perhaps because they blew up at the smallest disappointments. Can any of us relate to that?

They wanted to destroy an entire village because Jesus was denied lodging there (Luke 9:51-56). They must have petitioned their mother to lobby that they would be given the number one and number two positions in Jesus' new kingdom, a request that certainly upset the other disciples (Matthew 20:20-24).

James and John changed, however. James was the first apostle to be executed because he was a disciple of Jesus (Acts 12:1, 2). As saddened as John undoubtedly was, there is no indication that he reacted in a violent manner to his brother's death. In fact, John became known as the apostle of love. He wrote, "Whoever loves God must also love his brother" (1 John 4:21, *New International Version*).

Do you have a problem with your temper? Do you want to take revenge when someone "does you in"? You don't have to stay that way. Spending time with Immanuel—God with us—as seen in this study of Matthew can help turn you from being a tornado to a soothing breeze, from being negative to being positive.

From Taking Advantage of People to Serving People

Matthew was a man people loved to hate. He was a tax collector (Matthew 9:9). In that day, tax collectors made their profit by intentionally (and legally) cheating and taking advantage of people. Tax collectors were locals who were employed by the Roman authorities. Anything above what Rome required from their tax collection was theirs to keep. Rome didn't care how they assessed the taxes.

Some scholars estimate that some tax collectors made tens of thousands of dollars a year, while the average day laborer made less than one hundred dollars a year. And those tax collectors felt no guilt about cheating these hard-working people.

Jesus said to Matthew, "Follow me." That meant to go with Jesus and spend time with Him. It also meant to observe Jesus' life-style and emulate it. Matthew got up and left everything—his prestigious position and source of extremely high revenue—and went with Jesus (Luke 5:28). The first lesson he learned from Jesus was, "I desire mercy" (Matthew 9:13, *New International Version*).

Matthew lived out a life of mercy, one in which relationships, not resources, had priority. Throughout his Gospel account, Matthew shows that all kinds of people are acceptable to God: rich and poor, Jew and Gentile, healthy and sick. No longer viewing people as objects to be used to increase his wealth, Matthew came to see that people are objects of God's love and are to be served in His name.

Doesn't Matthew teach us something today? Isn't it easy to focus on our possessions instead of people? Matthew came to understand that things don't last—but people do. He learned that in business money is the profit, and people are often just tools; but with Christ, people are the profit, while money and possessions become tools in the service of people.

From Ugliness in Life-style to the Beautiful

The woman had lived a sin-filled life (Luke 7:37), but she came into the Pharisee's house where Jesus was dining and did an unbelievable thing. She brought a jar full of very expensive perfume, broke the jar, and poured the perfume over Jesus.

The Pharisee knew the woman's reputation, and thought less of Jesus because He let the woman touch Him. But Jesus made it clear that the woman was expressing her sincere love and appreciation; she loved much because she had been forgiven of much (Luke 7:39-47). She had come to realize that in the forgiveness of Jesus, her future was going to be different. She was so grateful for her new and beautiful future that she gave generously to Him.

What does her action teach us today? It teaches us that none of us have to be cemented to our past mistakes. When Jesus forgives, the slate is made clean. We do not have to let the ugly things we do determine our self-worth. Do not allow your past reputation to make you feel ugly and determine your future, your relationship with God and Christ, and the church. See the beauty that Jesus brings into your life!

From Mocking to Mimicking

The soldiers who were in charge of Jesus' crucifixion mocked Jesus (Matthew 27:27-31). Before the day had ended those same soldiers along with their military leader proclaimed, "Truly this was the Son of God" (Matthew 27:54). There are a couple of lessons we can learn from that: (1) Our past negative attitudes about Jesus can change and become positive attitudes. This study in Matthew can help with that. (2) As disciples of Jesus, we should live in such a way that people can catch on to what Jesus is like by their relationship with us. Thus they, too, can move from being negative to being positive.

Who Was He Anyway?

Who was this One who made such an impact among people? He was Immanuel—which means "God with us" (Matthew 1:23). Do you want to know what God is really like? Then look at Jesus. God is like Jesus. Do you want to know what we can and should be like? Look at Jesus. For we have been created and recreated in the image of God (Genesis 1:26) in order to be like God (Ephesians 4:24) in all our relationships.

God's Royal Son

by Dennis C. Gaertner

JUSTIN SIMON REMEMBERS a "brush with history" few of us would be able to keep to ourselves. In the summer of 1949 he sat in a Chicago airport with forty-six students ready to fly to war-damaged Europe as youthful ambassadors of goodwill. Discovering in Alaska Airlines a fare that would allow each student to fly at a cost of only two hundred dollars, Justin rounded up his group and waited for departure time.

A few hours before departure, Justin discovered that a snag had developed. The Alaska Airline flight did not have permission from the Civil Aeronautics Authority to land. Justin frantically began phoning every official he could think of in order to get help, but to no avail.

When he ran out of names, he decided to act on a truly desperate idea. He called person-to-person to the White House in Washington, D. C. It was 4:30 in the morning, but on the third ring he heard a man answer with "a slow, deliberate voice that twanged with a Midwestern accent." It was President Harry Truman. Justin apologized profusely for bothering the president at that hour. Truman responded by saying, "Well, I don't much mind that you've called me. I was up anyway." After Justin explained the situation with the college students, the president gave him instructions—a name and a phone number to contact— and the problem was on its way to solution.

Few Americans expect this kind of access to their president. In the ancient world the distance between the king and his subjects was even more pronounced. Ordinary people had no expectation of gaining access to the king. This fact of life provides the element of surprise in Jesus' parable about the king who ordered his servants to "go to the street corners and invite to the banquet anyone you find" (Matthew 22:9).*

Jesus as Royalty

Passages in the Old Testament speak of One who was to come at some time in the future and rule in the Spirit and power of Jehovah. His rule would be characterized by righteousness and faithfulness. His coming is pictured as one for which the Jews should prepare. "In the desert prepare the way for the Lord; make straight in the wilderness a highway for our God," says Isaiah (40:3). His arrival would inspire celebration and hope because "the Sovereign Lord comes with power, and his arm rules for him" (Isaiah 40:10).

This coming Ruler is portrayed as one who would be established in the line of David, the royal line of Israel. Isaiah calls Him "the Root of Jesse" and describes His influence as reaching far beyond Israel (11:10). As the kings of ancient Israel were consecrated to their office by being anointed with oil (see 1 Samuel 10:1; 16:13; 1 Kings 1:39), this Ruler would be anointed to His office. He was known as the "Messiah," a Hebrew term that means "anointed one." The Greek equivalent is "Christ." In the case of the Messiah, the anointing would come from God.

By the time of the birth of Jesus, expectations about the Messiah, the coming King, were being heard from several sources within Judaism. Today scholars can read Jewish literary works such as the Apocalypse of Ezra, the Apocalypse of Baruch, 4 Ezra, and the Dead Sea Scrolls to see what the Jews thought the Messiah would be like.

When the wise men came from the East inquiring about the One who was born King of the Jews, the chief priests and scribes furnished the information that the King would be born in Bethlehem (Matthew 2:5, 6). The New Testament describes Simeon's waiting in Jerusalem "for the consolation of Israel" (Luke 2:25). When he saw the baby Jesus he recognized the One designated as "the Lord's Christ" (vv. 26-32). Samaritans also were anticipating the coming of the Messiah (John 4:25, 29).

Evidence of Jesus' Royalty

Much of what Jesus did during His ministry raised in His audience the anticipation of His position as King. His miracle of feeding the multitudes caused some of the Jews to plan to force Jesus to be their king (John 6:15). Jesus' miracles were proof to them that He was the Prophet who was "to come into the world" (v. 14). However, these nationalistic Jews misunderstood the nature of the divine rule spoken of by the prophets. When Jesus declared its spiritual nature, many of these people lost interest in Him (vv. 25-66).

By riding on a donkey into Jerusalem at His triumphal entry, Jesus was declaring that He was the King of David's line spoken of by the prophets (Zechariah 9:9). Those who lined the way into the city understood this and shouted, "Hosanna to the Son of David! Blessed is he who comes in the name of the Lord!" (Matthew 21:9).

Nevertheless, Jesus made clear that His reign was to be spiritual, not political. The tension between these concepts surfaced on several occasions during Jesus' final hours. At Jesus' hearing before Pontius Pilate, the accusers of Jesus charged Him with claiming "to be Christ, a king" (Luke 23:2). Their accusations were built on the notion of a reign in which taxes would be raised and armies formed for the defeat of Rome. Though Jesus freely admitted that He was "king of the Jews" (Matthew 27:11), He was not the worldly, political king His accusers were trying to make Him out to be (see John 19:12). To Pilate he said, "My kingdom is not of this world. If it were, my servants would fight to prevent my arrest by the Jews. But now my kingdom is from another place" (John 18:36).

The misunderstanding of this point explains some of the treatment of Jesus during the hours of the crucifixion. The soldiers placed on Him a scarlet robe, a crown of thorns, and then put a reed in His hand, and mockingly bowed before Him as if showing respect to a monarch (Matthew 27:27-30). At the cross some ridiculed Him by jeering, "Let this Christ, this King of Israel, come down now from the cross, that we may see and believe" (Mark 15:32). Meanwhile the inscription over His head announced: "JESUS OF NAZARETH, THE KING OF THE JEWS" (John 19:19).

Jesus' Spiritual Reign

Soon after the resurrection of Jesus, the apostles understood the spiritual nature of Jesus' reign. On the Day of Pentecost the residents of Jerusalem heard Peter proclaim that God had raised Jesus from the dead. For this reason Peter could confidently announce that "God has made this Jesus, whom you crucified, both Lord and Christ" (Acts 2:36). At God's right hand Jesus could exercise authority to grant forgiveness of sins, and Peter insisted that the audience must, therefore, turn to Jesus through repentance and baptism in His name in order to receive salvation from sin (v. 38).

Whenever a repentant sinner responds to the gospel invitation, the reign of Jesus is advanced. Whenever we confess that we believe that Jesus is the Christ, the Son of the living God, we pledge our loyalty to the spiritual King of our lives.

Beginning at the Day of Pentecost the apostles consistently declared Jesus to be the Son of God with power. Paul affirms that Jesus descended from the royal line of David (Romans 1:3). John wrote His Gospel account in order that readers might believe "that Jesus is the Christ" (20:31). Descriptive terms such as "Lord," "Christ," and "Son of David" demonstrate how exalted is Jesus' status in God's eyes. Paul further states that "God exalted him to the highest place and gave him the name that is above every name."

Honor is to be given Him, for "at the name of Jesus every knee should bow, in heaven and on earth and under the earth, and every tongue confess that Jesus Christ is Lord, to the glory of God the Father" (Philippians 2:9-11).

The decision we make about whom we acknowledge as king and ruler of our lives brings eternal consequences. The New Testament assures us that we are making no mistake by extending our worship to Jesus as King. John records the scene in Heaven, in which the four living creatures give "glory, honor and thanks" to God, who sits on the throne, and the twenty-four elders fall down before Him and worship Him (Revelation 4:1-11). In the next chapter (5:11-14) John records another scene. He heard multiplied thousands of angels praising the Lamb who had been slain, singing that He is worthy of "honor and glory and praise." As if in echo, "every creature in heaven and on earth and under the earth and on the sea, and all that is in them, " could be heard singing, "To him who sits on the throne and to the Lamb be praise and honor and glory and power, for ever and ever!" To that the four living creatures said, "Amen," and "the elders fell down and worshiped." As the royal Son of God, Jesus deserves our worship.

---

*Scripture quotations in this article are taken from the *New International Version*.

John Heralds Jesus' Coming

December 4
Lesson 1

DEVOTIONAL READING: Isaiah 40:3-11.

LESSON SCRIPTURE: Matthew 3.

PRINTED TEXT: Matthew 3:1-15.

Matthew 3:1-15

1 In those days came John the Baptist, preaching in the wilderness of Judea,

2 And saying, Repent ye: for the kingdom of heaven is at hand.

3 For this is he that was spoken of by the prophet Isaiah, saying, The voice of one crying in the wilderness, Prepare ye the way of the Lord, make his paths straight.

4 And the same John had his raiment of camel's hair, and a leathern girdle about his loins; and his meat was locusts and wild honey.

5 Then went out to him Jerusalem, and all Judea, and all the region round about Jordan,

6 And were baptized of him in Jordan, confessing their sins.

7 But when he saw many of the Pharisees and Sadducees come to his baptism, he said unto them, O generation of vipers, who hath warned you to flee from the wrath to come?

8 Bring forth therefore fruits meet for repentance:

9 And think not to say within yourselves, We have Abraham to our father: for I say unto you, that God is able of these stones to raise up children unto Abraham.

10 And now also the axe is laid unto the root of the trees: therefore every tree which bringeth not forth good fruit is hewn down, and cast into the fire.

11 I indeed baptize you with water unto repentance: but he that cometh after me is mightier than I, whose shoes I am not worthy to bear: he shall baptize you with the Holy Ghost, and with fire:

12 Whose fan is in his hand, and he will thoroughly purge his floor, and gather his wheat into the garner; but he will burn up the chaff with unquenchable fire.

13 Then cometh Jesus from Galilee to Jordan unto John, to be baptized of him.

14 But John forbade him, saying, I have need to be baptized of thee, and comest thou to me?

15 And Jesus answering said unto him, Suffer it to be so now: for thus it becometh us to fulfill all righteousness. Then he suffered him.

GOLDEN TEXT: I indeed baptize you with water unto repentance: but he that cometh after me is mightier than I, whose shoes I am not worthy to bear: he shall baptize you with the Holy Ghost, and with fire.—Matthew 3:11.

Jesus the Fulfillment
(Matthew)
Unit 1. Jesus and John: Setting the Scene (Lessons 1, 2)

Lesson Aims

At the completion of this lesson the students should:

1. Be able to describe briefly the message of John the Baptist.

2. Be able to define repentance.

3. Believe that Jesus is the Christ prophesied in Scripture and make Him Lord of their lives.

Lesson Outline

INTRODUCTION
    A. "I'll Preach Until You Repent!"
    B. Lesson Background
I. JOHN'S MINISTRY (Matthew 3:1-6)
    A. Forceful Preaching (vv. 1, 2)
    B. Fulfillment of Prophecy (v. 3)
    C. Personal Characteristics (v. 4)
    D. The People's Response (vv. 5, 6)
       Credibility
II. JOHN'S MESSAGE (Matthew 3:7-12)
    A. Challenge to Leaders (vv. 7-10)
    B. Coming of the Messiah (vv. 11, 12)
       Whom Shall We Fear?
III. JOHN'S MASTER (Matthew 3:13-15)
    A. Objection to Jesus' Request (vv. 13, 14)
    B. Acquiescence to Jesus (v. 15)
CONCLUSION
    A. Turning to God
    B. Let Us Pray
    C. Thought to Remember

Visual 1 of the visuals packet summarizes the lessons for this quarter in chronological order. The visual is shown on page 125. Visual 14 illustrates the theme of the quarter. It will be helpful if both visuals are displayed for several weeks.

Introduction

A. I'll Preach Until You Repent!"

A preacher preached on repentance every Sunday until his congregation got tired of it. It wasn't always the same sermon—he would use different texts, different illustrations, and different words—but it was always about repentance.

Finally a delegation of the church's leaders went to the preacher and asked him to change his theme. "Why do you always talk about re-

pentance?" they asked. "Don't you have anything else to say?"

The preacher replied, "I'll stop preaching about repentance when you repent. Then I'll go on to something else."

John the Baptist was a preacher whose theme was repentance. He urged Israel to turn from sin and get ready for the Messiah, God's chosen Deliverer, who was soon to make His appearance. Today's text contains a sample of John's preaching and the record of Jesus' coming to John for baptism in order to comply with God's will.

B. Lesson Background

The text for this lesson tells of John the Baptist's great work of announcing the coming of the Messiah. Luke indicates that the word of God came to John in the fifteenth year of the Roman Emperor Tiberius, that is, A.D. 26 or 27 (Luke 3:1). John then began his ministry of calling God's people to prepare to receive the Christ.

In chapter 1 of his Gospel account, Matthew tells of Jesus' human family line and His virgin birth. Chapter 2 contains the record of the visit of the wise men and Joseph and Mary's flight to Egypt with the young child Jesus to escape King Herod's attempt to kill Him. Nearly thirty years of Jesus' life are passed over in silence from the end of chapter 2 and the beginning of chapter 3. There Matthew records John the Baptist's entrance upon the scene and his startling announcement.

I. John's Ministry
(Matthew 3:1-6)

A. Forceful Preaching (vv. 1, 2)

1. In those days came John the Baptist, preaching in the wilderness of Judea.

In those days. This evidently points back to the last verse of chapter 2, and refers to the days when Jesus was still living in Nazareth. *John the Baptist.* In the Synoptic Gospels—Matthew, Mark and Luke—John is identified as the "baptizer" or the "baptist." This description refers to John's most noticeable activity, the practice of immersing people in water as a sign of their change of heart toward God and His moral requirements.

The wilderness of Judea was the desert area by the Dead Sea. Verse 6 tells us that John was baptizing in the Jordan, so we conclude that he was preaching by the Jordan where it flows through the wilderness just before entering the Dead Sea.

2. And saying, Repent ye: for the kingdom of heaven is at hand.

John called for people to turn from sin and to dedicate themselves to obeying God; that's what repentance is. They needed to repent because

God was about to do something marvelous in their time. That which had been predicted in both the law and by the prophets—the coming of the Messiah and the establishment of His heavenly rule—would soon occur. If they were indifferent regarding obedience to the law that they had already been given, they would not be prepared to receive the revelation the King would bring.

John preached, *The kingdom of heaven is at hand,* or near. The idea is that the kingdom was poised on the edge of the stage of history, "waiting in the wings" to appear. With the beginning of Jesus' ministry, the kingdom would break in upon God's creation in all its majestic power.

Today, as well as in John's time, people need to repent to get ready for God's kingdom. Only when our hearts and minds are turned toward God and we are ready to do wholeheartedly what He wants us to can Jesus enter our hearts to rule our lives.

B. Fulfillment of Prophecy (v. 3)

3. For this is he that was spoken of by the prophet Isaiah, saying, The voice of one crying in the wilderness, Prepare ye the way of the Lord, make his paths straight.

Matthew refers to the prophecy in Isaiah 40:3. There the prophet called on God's people to prepare the way for God to come and rescue them from captivity in Babylon. Just as God delivered Israel from physical captivity in the sixth century B.C., He would now rescue from the power of sin and death all who would accept the Deliverer He was sending.

John the Baptist's mission was to get people ready for the Messiah. He called on them to *prepare . . . the way* and to *make his paths straight.* By preaching repentance and administering a preparatory baptism, John prepared people to hear and receive Jesus, God's own Son. We have a similar task today as believers in Jesus; part of our job is to prepare the way for people to come to faith in Him, a process one writer has called "pre-evangelism." By pointing people to God's moral requirements and gently helping them to see their need for a Savior, we can get them ready to meet Jesus and put their lives in His hands.

VISUALS FOR THESE LESSONS

The *Adult Visuals/Learning Resources* packet contains classroom-size visuals designed for use with the lessons in the Winter quarter. The packet is available from your supplier. Order no. 292.

C. Personal Characteristics (v. 4)

4. And the same John had his raiment of camel's hair, and a leathern girdle about his loins; and his meat was locusts and wild honey.

John's clothing was a coarse fabric woven from camel's hair, held around him by a *leathern girdle,* that is, a belt of animal hide. This unusual clothing, similar to the "rough garment" worn by the prophet in the days of Zechariah, marked John as a prophet (Zechariah 13:4). *Locusts,* declared edible by the law (Leviticus 11:22), were easily captured; and honey, stored in caves by wild bees, was available for John's eating. His total life-style was characterized by austere self-denial, most appropriate for one who was calling a nation to repentance.

John's dress and diet marked him as different from the people of his time and place. Most of us who are followers of Christ today don't stand out from our contemporaries in the same manner as John did. But people should be able to tell that we are different from those who are controlled by the world's system of values. Can others tell by our attitudes and actions and speech that we have committed our lives to Christ?

D. The People's Response (vv. 5, 6)

5. Then went out to him Jerusalem, and all Judea, and all the region round about Jordan.

A road that was much traveled forded the Jordan River near Jericho. Perhaps it was here where John began his preaching. His first hearers were so impressed that they told others. Soon people were coming in multitudes from the whole surrounding area to hear John.

6. And were baptized of him in Jordan, confessing their sins.

Perhaps curiosity for this unusual-appearing preacher drew the people to him in the wilderness region by the Jordan, but something more kept them there. Verse 2 indicates that the theme of John's preaching was repentance, and it is obvious from the people's response that his preaching carried great conviction. The people were confronted with their sins, they admitted their guilt, and were baptized by John in the river. Thus they committed themselves anew to God in preparation for the coming of His kingdom.

CREDIBILITY

On October 28, 1992, the announcement appeared in at least one newspaper in Oregon and one prestigious newspaper on the East coast. The head of a world mission church based in Korea had proclaimed that the world would end on October 31 of that year. There appeared to be very few believers. Perhaps it was because the head of the mission had been accused of fraud by the government of Korea and had purchased long-term bonds that would mature after the advertised date of the end of the world!

John the Baptist came preaching that people should repent because the kingdom of Heaven was at hand. Multitudes went out to hear him, and they believed and obeyed his message. His announcement was based in the prophecy of Isaiah, which his hearers knew and believed. Furthermore, John's life-style was consistent with his message. Everything about John spoke of self-denial and surrender to God. Nothing in his manner or message gave even the least hint of a desire for personal gain.

Few will believe an announcement if they doubt the credibility of the proclaimer. Let's be sure that our motives, our methods, and our manner of life are in line with the gospel we preach and teach.   —W. P.

II. John's Message
(Matthew 3:7-12)

A. Challenge to Leaders (vv. 7-10)

7. But when he saw many of the Pharisees and Sadducees come to his baptism, he said unto them, O generation of vipers, who hath warned you to flee from the wrath to come?

Among the multitudes who came to hear John's preaching were members of the two principal groups of religious leaders in Israel—*the Pharisees and Sadducees*. The name *Pharisees* came from a Hebrew word that meant *separated*. Members of this party were very careful to keep themselves separated from anything and anyone regarded as legally unclean. They had elevated the traditions of the elders to such an extent that they were regarded as being equal in authority to the written law of God. The Pharisees made a great show of keeping the outward forms of the law, but they had little regard for the spirit of it. Late in His ministry Jesus exposed this group for the hypocrites that they were (see Matthew 23:1-36).

The Sadducees held views that were directly opposite of those held by the Pharisees. The Sadducees openly cooperated with the pagan Romans who ruled Palestine at this time. They rejected the authority of oral tradition, and instead of making a great show of piety they lived in a luxurious manner. Whereas the Pharisees believed in the resurrection of the dead and the existence of angels and spirits, the Sadducees denied both (Acts 23:8).

John was aware of the true character of these leaders, so he knew that they did not *come to his baptism* with good motives. Rather than coming to accept it in humble penitence, it seems that they came to reject and ridicule it. John's calling them a *generation* (or "offspring") *of vipers* here and his comments in verse 9 suggest this.

8. Bring forth therefore fruits meet for repentance.

Here John represents human beings as fruit trees. He called on all persons, even these religious leaders, to repent of their sins and to produce *fruits*, that is, to live in a manner that would indicate their change of heart. Pretense of piety would not obtain God's mercy; only genuine repentance followed by godly living is acceptable to Him.

9. And think not to say within yourselves, We have Abraham to our father: for I say unto you, that God is able of these stones to raise up children unto Abraham.

Many of John's hearers, and certainly the Pharisees and Sadducees, were intensely proud of their Jewish heritage. The mere fact that they were Abraham's descendants, the chosen people of God, led them to believe that they had nothing to fear from the wrath of God. It was a general feeling among those in John's audience that when the Messiah came and established His kingdom, all the Jews would be a part of it. In contrast to this way of thinking, John made it plain that no one is born into God's favor, that behavior counts more than birthright in His sight. We can easily picture John pointing to the *stones* on the ground to illustrate that God could take any material He desired and by His power make *children unto Abraham*, if that generation despised Him and refused to live as He required.

We too need to be careful that we don't depend on others to put us in good standing with God. The faith of one's parents, spouse, or children cannot, by itself, bring one into God's favor. Each individual must establish and maintain a relationship with God through sincere faith and the wholehearted commitment of his or her life to the Lord.

10. And now also the axe is laid unto the root of the trees: therefore every tree which bringeth not forth good fruit is hewn down, and cast into the fire.

John introduced the metaphor of fruit trees (v. 8) and here he returned to it. He compared

---

How to Say It

ISAIAH.   Eye-*zay*-uh.
PHARISEES.   *Fair*-ih-seez.
SADDUCEES.   *Sad*-you-seez.
TIBERIUS.   Tie-*beer*-ee-us.
ZECHARIAH.   Zek-uh-*rye*-uh.

his hearers to trees in an orchard, which were being carefully observed by the fruit grower. Each tree, of course, occupied valuable space in the orchard and was expected to bear fruit for its owner. If it did not, the tree would be cut down and *cast into the fire.*

John was announcing the coming of the Messiah, who would establish His kingdom and bring salvation to mankind. But the Messiah was to be judge as well as Savior. Those among His chosen people who were corrupt, who refused to produce the *good fruit* of righteousness in their lives, would be removed, just like a fruitless tree in an orchard. The *fire* is a reference to Hell.

This passage shouldn't terrify us, but it should remind us that God put us on earth for a reason. He expects our lives to count for something, to "bear fruit" in the biblical sense. The fruit we bear should include the "fruit of the Spirit" that the apostle Paul identifies in Galatians 5:22, 23. It should also include acts of service to God and to other people. It is appropriate to ask ourselves from time to time what our lives have counted for in the past, and what they count for now. Is the way of someone in need being made easier by what we do? Is someone who is outside of Christ being drawn closer to Him by the attitudes we manifest, by our speech, and by our conduct?

B. Coming of the Messiah (vv. 11, 12)

11. I indeed baptize you with water unto repentance: but he that cometh after me is mightier than I, whose shoes I am not worthy to bear: he shall baptize you with the Holy Ghost, and with fire.

Here John drew a contrast between his baptism and that of the mighty One who would come after him. John's baptism was *with water*, which may also be translated "in water." Water was the substance in which the person was plunged, the physical medium by which the baptism was accomplished. More than that, John's baptism was a baptism *unto repentance*, a ceremony that publicly marked a person's turning away from sin and toward God and His ways.

Speaking of the One who was coming, John said, *he shall baptize you with the Holy Ghost, and with fire.* When Jesus was about to ascend into Heaven, He repeated the first part of the promise to His chosen apostles: "Ye shall be baptized with the Holy Ghost not many days hence" (Acts 1:5). This was fulfilled about ten days later on Pentecost (Acts 2:1-4). Some suggest that the baptism with the Holy Ghost and fire were the same event, noting that "tongues like as of fire" sat on those who received the Holy Spirit on Pentecost. Jesus, however, made no mention of a

visual 1

baptism with fire in His statement in Acts 1:5. John's statement recorded here by Matthew is set in a context of fiery destruction, first of fruitless trees (v. 10) and then of useless chaff (v. 12). It seems more likely, therefore, that John was speaking of two different events: the baptism of the Holy Spirit on Pentecost and the baptism of fire for the wicked at the last day (Matthew 25:41; Revelation 21:8).

The One who was coming after John was the Messiah, and John confessed to being unworthy even to carry His shoes. At this point the other Gospels quote John as saying, that he was not worthy to untie the straps of his sandals (Mark 1:7; Luke 3:16, John 1:27). Either way John meant that the Messiah was so much greater than he that John felt himself unworthy even of the most menial service to this great figure.

12. Whose fan is in his hand, and he will thoroughly purge his floor, and gather his wheat into the garner; but he will burn up the chaff with unquenchable fire.

Once again John referred to the separation of the wicked and the pretenders from God's people. In this verse he presents another picture of the separation of the useless from the valuable.

The *fan* was a winnowing shovel. After the heads of wheat were trampled, farmers threw the broken heads of grain into the air. The wind blew away the useless chaff, while the heavy grain fell to the threshing floor. The grain was stored for use, but the chaff was burned up. Thus, the winnowing shovel in the Messiah's hands would serve as an instrument of judgment, like the axe of verse 10.

WHOM SHALL WE FEAR?

Jim and John walked slowly home from school, deep in conversation about what had happened on the school grounds that day. They had seen and heard it all. One of their classmates had been beaten up by the gang of toughs who dominated the students. Jim was in favor of telling their father about it and asking him what to do. John felt differently. He said, "Dad will make us tell the principal, and then we'll be the next ones in trouble with the gang."

As it turned out, the boys did tell their Father, and he went with them to bolster their courage in telling what they had witnessed.

John the Baptist spoke of the Messiah's blessing and judgment. Pride, prejudice, worldly desires—perhaps these or other motives kept many of the religious leaders from responding to John's prophetic message. Others, heard and obeyed John's call to reformation of life. They chose to do right rather than keep silent and find favor with those who rejected God's call for change.

Don't let fear of any person determine your response to Jesus. Wiser is it to fear Him who "is able to destroy both soul and body in hell" (Matthew 10:28).　　　　　　　　　—W. P.

III. John's Master
(Matthew 3:13-15)
A. Objection to Jesus' Request
(vv. 13, 14)

13. Then cometh Jesus from Galilee to Jordan unto John, to be baptized of him.

Jesus grew up in Nazareth and then, when ready to begin His ministry, came south to where John was baptizing. He came for the particular purpose of receiving baptism at John's hands.

14. But John forbade him, saying, I have need to be baptized of thee, and comest thou to me?

At this point, John had not received the divinely promised sign that would identify the Messiah. That came *after* Jesus was baptized (see John 1:33, 34). Yet John now recognized Jesus' greatness, and in proper humility, confessed that it was more appropriate for Jesus to baptize him. Since the mothers of John and Jesus were related (Luke 1:36), quite possibly the families were together often in Jerusalem for the annual feasts. Surely John knew of Jesus' miraculous birth and His superior sanctity. It may be that when Jesus came to him, John was virtually certain of Jesus' true nature; but he would not know positively until the Holy Spirit descended upon Jesus after His baptism.

B. Acquiescence to Jesus (v. 15)

15. And Jesus answering said unto him, Suffer it to be so now: for thus it becometh us to fulfil all righteousness. Then he suffered him.

Suffer means "allow." The *Good News Bible* has this translation: "Let it be so for now. For in this way we shall do all that God requires." John then baptized Jesus, and, as the following verses state, God's Holy Spirit descended like a dove and lit on Jesus. God's voice from Heaven confirmed the sign and showed His approval of this act of obedience by His Son.

Conclusion
A. Turning to God

Repentance is more than sorrow for sin; it is more than the decision to stop following the devil and to begin following God. Repentance is complete when one actually stops pursuing the ways of the world and begins to do the will of God.

John called the people of his time to repentance, to reject sin and to turn toward God in their hearts and minds and to express that change in the way they lived. The exciting reason for John's demand was that "the kingdom of heaven is at hand." The Messiah was in their midst and would soon make himself known. Only by turning their hearts and lives back to God would they be prepared to receive the long-awaited Redeemer.

For nearly two thousand years now the message has rung out: "The Messiah has come, and He has made a way of escape from our sins!" Turn to God through Him and receive forgiveness and eternal life.

B. Let Us Pray

Lord, deliver us from a shallow "repentance" that fails to touch our hearts or our behavior. May we turn from the ways of evil and walk wholeheartedly in the paths of righteousness through the strength that Christ provides. In His name, amen.

C. Thought to Remember

May we show by the way we live that Christ rules our lives.

Home Daily Bible Readings

Monday, Nov. 28—The Lord's Messenger (Malachi 3:1-7)
Tuesday, Nov. 29—John the Baptist Preaches Repentance (Matthew 3:1-6)
Wednesday, Nov. 30—One Greater Than John Is Coming (Matthew 3:7-12)
Thursday, Dec. 1—Jesus Convinces John to Baptize Him (Matthew 3:13—4:1)
Friday, Dec. 2—Jesus Preaches Repentance (Matthew 4:12-17)
Saturday, Dec. 3—Jesus Calls Disciples and Begins Ministering (Matthew 4:18-25)
Sunday, Dec. 4—God's Promise Fulfilled in Jesus (Acts 13:16-26)

Learning by Doing

This page contains an alternate lesson plan emphasizing learning activities. Classes desiring such student involvement will find these suggestions helpful.

Learning Goals

After this session, the class members will:

1. Know and be able to describe the person and ministry of John the Baptist.

2. Be able to define repentance.

3. Choose one area of their lives in which they need to make a change and commit themselves to making that change.

Into the Lesson

Before the class session begins, write the following questions on the chalkboard or overhead projector: "What preacher would you most prefer to hear preach? Why?"

As your students arrive, encourage them to think about the questions and to be prepared to give their answers in a few minutes.

Begin the session by asking for your students' responses to the questions. List on the chalkboard what the class finds appealing in a preacher. Allow four to five minutes for this opening discussion.

Make transition to the lesson text by pointing out that John the Baptist was a popular preacher in his day, but perhaps not for the reasons the class listed. Encourage them to watch for comparisons.

Into the Word

Begin the Bible study by sharing the information from Lesson Background. Then have a class member read the text aloud (Matthew 3:1-15). Malachi 4:5, 6 may also prove helpful to the class as you teach about John's role in fulfilling prophecy and preparing people for the beginning of Jesus' ministry.

By means of the following questions, encourage the students to examine and discuss the Scripture text:

1. What does this passage say about the lifestyle of John the Baptist?

2. What one word best describes John's message? (Divide the students into groups of two or three to discuss this and compile a list. Have them consider also Luke 3:1-18 for a more detailed account. Allow four or five minutes for discussion, and then let the groups share their conclusions. (John was stern and bold in his preaching. Luke emphasizes that he was also very practical in teaching about changes the people needed to make in their lives.)

3. How did John's message and manner compare with the qualities we listed earlier as being desirable in a preacher? Would his life-style and message draw you to him or push you away? Why?

4. People came with different motives to hear John. What were some of those motives? (Some came out of curiosity and some out of a sincere desire to hear a message from God. The Pharisees and Sadducees came to hear John, perhaps out of curiosity, or fear of his success, or the desire to catch him in error to discredit him.

5. Why was the message of John to the Pharisees and Sadducees so negative? (See comments under verse 7.)

6. The core of John's message was repentance. In the Biblical sense, what does it mean to repent? (It means to turn one's heart and mind from sin and to dedicate oneself to obeying God in all of life.)

7. John encouraged the people, "Produce fruit in keeping with repentance" (verse 8, *New International Version*). What does this mean? (It means that our conduct will give evidence of our changed heart and mind. For specifics, see Galatians 5:22, 23.)

8. On what basis did John at first refuse to baptize Jesus? (John's baptism was a baptism of repentance. He refused on the basis of Jesus' holiness and his own sinfulness.) What thoughts do you think were going through John's mind?

Into Life

Ask these questions to apply the lesson:

1. John came to prepare the hearts of the people for Jesus' ministry. People today need to receive Christ for the forgiveness of sins and the spiritual life He offers. Mention some specific ways in which each of us can be a "John the Baptist" for someone who does not know Jesus.

2. John preached repentance to the citizens of Jerusalem and the surrounding region. What sins might there have been in that society from which the people needed to repent? How different are the sins in our society?

Conclude this session by having each student privately examine his or her own life. Each should ask himself or herself, "Do my words and my actions show that I genuinely love Jesus and that I have committed myself to following in His ways?"

Let's Talk It Over

The questions on this page are designed to encourage review of the lesson Scriptures and to promote discussion of the lesson by the class. The answers provided are only discussion starters. Let your class talk it over from there.

1. Describe the life-style and ministry of John the Baptist.

John's life-style was different from that of most people, to say the least. He lived in the wilderness, a desolate, forbidding area that most people avoided. His clothing was rough. He wore a camel's pelt for a garment, bound to him by a leather strap around his waist. This was hardly the choice of clothing even by the average person in that day. His diet consisted of wild honey and locusts, not exactly gourmet fare! He arrived on the scene pronouncing judgment and calling for repentance, an activity not likely to win friends and influence people.

John did not adopt this life-style; he was *called* to it by God. John was the one spoken of centuries before by God's prophet Isaiah, when he foretold of a person who would come crying "in the wilderness, Prepare ye the way of the Lord" (Isaiah 40:3; Matthew 3:3). Before John's birth, an angel foretold that he would "be great in the sight of the Lord," and would drink "neither wine nor strong drink." Also, he would "be filled with the Holy Ghost, even from his mother's womb" (Luke 1:15). It seems safe to say that the citizenry of Judea and the area round about the Jordan valley had never before seen or heard anyone like John. Fearlessly he proclaimed a message as swift and straight as lightning. Like the blazing and shadowless intensity of the desert noonday sun, that message scorched the hearts of the self-righteous, exposed the sins of the rich and powerful, and lighted the way to new standards of ethical conduct. Most important, John the Baptist prepared the way for the Messiah. He came in the spirit and power of Elijah. He lived and carried out his God-given prophetic ministry as did Elijah.

2. What is repentance?

Popular thinking often confuses sorrow for sin with repentance. Judas felt remorse for his betrayal of Jesus, but he did not repent (Matthew 27:3, *New International Version*). Sorrow for sin *leads* to repentance (2 Corinthians 7:9, 10); it is not to be equated with repentance. The Greek word in the New Testament literally means "to have another mind." Thus, repentance is "a change of mind that reveals itself in a changed life." This change of mind includes a change of will. A person who repents has a change of mind about his or her sinful life-style and determines to seek God's forgiveness and to live in a manner consistent with His Word.

3. Jesus came to John to be baptized. What does this teach us?

When Jesus presented himself to John for baptism in the Jordan, John remonstrated with Him. John confessed that it was more appropriate for him to be baptized by Jesus. Jesus insisted on being baptized, however, to "do all that God requires" (Matthew 3:15). *Today's English Version*). Baptism was important to Him personally, and its importance was indicated by His command. Before returning to His Father in Heaven, Jesus instructed His disciples to: "Go ye therefore, and teach all nations, baptizing them in the name of the Father, and of the Son, and of the Holy Ghost" (Matthew 28:19). By His example Jesus showed the importance of man's obedience to the Father in Heaven.

4. For whom is God's message of judgment intended today?

God's message of judgment is *always* for those who do not obey the gospel of Jesus Christ. Lest Christians become complacent in their faith, however, let it be remembered that judgment begins with the church! Peter writes "For it is time for judgment to begin with the family of God" (1 Peter 4:17, *New International Version*). What a sobering reality!

5. Why are some Christians reticent to "speak out" for their faith?

At least four reasons may be given. (1) They fear they will lose popularity. What "others" think about them dominates their decisions and behavior. (2) They fear that the unpopular stand may cost them financially. One who is in business may lose customers. (3) They wish to minimize pain. Normal people don't want to suffer. If one is in the minority, one could become a martyr. (4) They fear that they will not be able to answer adequately the challenges of unbelievers. The greater the discrepancy between the demands made upon a person and that person's perceived ability to respond, the greater the level of stress and fear.

Jesus Affirms John's Message

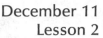
DEVOTIONAL READING: John 1:1-14.

LESSON SCRIPTURE: Matthew 11:2-15.

PRINTED TEXT: Matthew 11:2-15.

Matthew 11:2-15

2 Now when John had heard in the prison the works of Christ, he sent two of his disciples,

3 And said unto him, Art thou he that should come, or do we look for another?

4 Jesus answered and said unto them, Go and show John again those things which ye do hear and see:

5 The blind receive their sight, and the lame walk, the lepers are cleansed, and the deaf hear, the dead are raised up, and the poor have the gospel preached to them.

6 And blessed is he, whosoever shall not be offended in me.

7 And as they departed, Jesus began to say unto the multitudes concerning John, What went ye out into the wilderness to see? A reed shaken with the wind?

8 But what went ye out for to see? A man clothed in soft raiment? behold, they that wear soft clothing are in kings' houses.

9 But what went ye out for to see? A prophet? yea, I say unto you, and more than a prophet.

10 For this is he, of whom it is written, Behold, I send my messenger before thy face, which shall prepare thy way before thee.

11 Verily I say unto you, Among them that are born of women there hath not risen a greater than John the Baptist: notwithstanding, he that is least in the kingdom of heaven is greater than he.

12 And from the days of John the Baptist until now the kingdom of heaven suffereth violence, and the violent take it by force.

13 For all the prophets and the law prophesied until John.

14 And if ye will receive it, this is Elijah, which was for to come.

15 He that hath ears to hear, let him hear.

GOLDEN TEXT: Behold, I send my messenger before thy face, which shall prepare thy way before thee.—Matthew 11:10.

Jesus the Fulfillment (Matthew)

Unit 1. Jesus and John: Setting the Scene (Lessons 1, 2)

Lesson Aims

After participation in this lesson a student should:

1. Know the circumstances of John's arrest and imprisonment.

2. Understand why John began to have doubts about Jesus.

3. Recognize the signs that proved Jesus to be God's Messiah.

4. Know how to resolve doubts.

Lesson Outline

INTRODUCTION
  A. The Anatomy of Doubt
  B. Lesson Background
  I. JOHN'S DOUBTS (Matthew 11:2-6)
  A. He Questioned Jesus (vv. 2, 3)
  B. He Received an Answer (vv. 4-6)
      Going to the Source
 II. JOHN'S CHARACTER (Matthew 11:7-11)
  A. He Was Strong (vv. 7, 8)
  B. He Was a Prophet (v. 9)
  C. He Was a Messenger (v. 10)
      My Messenger
  D. He Was Great (v. 11)
III. JOHN'S MISSION (Matthew 11:12-15)
  A. He Proclaimed the Kingdom (v. 12)
  B. He Began a New Era (v. 13)
  C. He Fulfilled Prophecy (vv. 14, 15)
CONCLUSION
  A. Learning From John
  B. Lessons for Life
  C. Let Us Pray
  D. Thought to Remember

Visual 2 of the visuals packet draws attention to John the Baptist, "My Messenger" of Matthew 11:7-10. The visual is shown on page 132.

Introduction

A. The Anatomy of Doubt

There are two kinds of faith. The first is the acceptance of facts as being true when they are presented to us. We might call this *intellectual* belief. The other kind of faith involves confidence in a person. It is the assurance we feel regarding a person that he or she is reliable and will never let us down. This is a matter of trust, which we might call *interpersonal* belief.

For example, a woman who meets a man and dates him for a while may have faith in the first sense but not in the second regarding him. She may be convinced that every fact he has told her about himself is true, that he has the job he says he has, that his family background is what he claims, and so on. But she may not trust him enough as a person to marry him. Even so, we may believe the facts of the Christian faith—that God exists, that He sent His Son to die on the cross, and that He raised Him from the dead—and yet be unwilling to trust God personally, unwilling to put our lives in His hands.

The faith that leads to salvation is comprised of both intellectual and interpersonal belief. It is, first of all, acceptance of the facts of the good news of Jesus. But more than that, it is complete trust in Jesus, a trust that leads us to base our whole lives on Him. We need to believe *that* certain things are true regarding Jesus, and we also need to believe *in* Jesus Christ as one who is a trustworthy person.

The opposite of faith is doubt. We can believe facts intellectually, or we can doubt those facts. Likewise, we can trust in a person, or we can doubt that person. Our Christian faith can come under attack at either of these points, the intellectual or the interpersonal. The devil may try to persuade us that what we have believed simply isn't true, that we have been factually deceived. If this strategy doesn't work, he may try to lead us to mistrust God, to refuse to put our lives in His hands. Most people who doubt God don't doubt the facts of who He is or what He has done so much as they doubt His ability or willingness to take care of them; they are unwilling to trust Him with their lives. Either kind of doubt, the intellectual or the interpersonal, can be fatal to our faith if it becomes a way of life.

B. Lesson Background

Our quarter's study began last week with the introduction of John the Baptist. He preached of One who was coming to establish "the kingdom of heaven." Boldly he called for all persons, even the arrogant and self-righteous religious leaders, to repent and prepare to receive the Lord. In response to his forceful preaching, many of his hearers confessed their sins and were baptized. Jesus also came and was baptized by John.

Immediately Jesus was led into the wilderness, where He faced a period of temptation by the devil. Afterward Jesus embarked on His ministry.

The event that is recorded in our lesson text occurred more than a year later. John had continued preaching, but his ministry declined as Jesus' popularity grew, and John accepted that fact without jealousy (John 3:25-30). At some point John was arrested and imprisoned for reproving Herod the tetrarch for the evils he had done, notably for taking the wife of his brother Philip (Luke 3:19, 20). This Herod, known as Herod Antipas, ruled the territories of Galilee and Perea, the areas where the ministries of both Jesus and John were, for the most part, conducted.

While Jesus was in the midst of His Galilean ministry, messengers came to Him from John with an important question.

I. John's Doubts
(Matthew 11:2-6)

A. He Questioned Jesus (vv. 2, 3)

2. Now when John had heard in the prison the works of Christ, he sent two of his disciples.

The Jewish historian Josephus tells us that John was imprisoned in the fortress of Machaerus, near the eastern shore of the Dead Sea. Herod had a winter palace there. Even though John was in prison, he was not isolated from the outside world. Apparently he was allowed visitors, from whom he heard about Christ's ministry. He was permitted also to send messages by them, as we see in this verse.

3. And said unto him, Art thou he that should come, or do we look for another?

John had been certain enough of who Jesus was, as we saw in last week's lesson. When Jesus came to John for baptism, John didn't want to baptize Him at first, because he knew Jesus was so much greater than he (Matthew 3:14). Furthermore, John had publicly identified Jesus (John 1:29). Why, then, did John seem to be expressing doubt concerning Jesus now?

The Bible doesn't give us a direct answer to this question, but several thoughts come to mind. First, John was a rugged person who had spent his entire life in the outdoors. For months, some say for six months or more, he had been cooped up in prison. His confinement and enforced inactivity may have had a debilitating effect on his spirit. Contributing to this, perhaps, was the fact that Jesus had made no move to free

---

How to Say It

ANTIPAS. *An*-tuh-pas.
JOSEPHUS. Joe-*see*-fus.
MACHAERUS. Muh-*key*-rus or Muh-*kye*-rus.
PEREA. Peh-*ree*-uh.
ZECHARIAH. Zek-uh-*rye*-uh.

---

him. Second, it seems certain that John did not understand the program that would be developed by the Messiah, whom he had announced. He knew that the Messiah was going to establish a kingdom of godly rule. He may have wondered, therefore, why Jesus had not announced himself as the Messiah and begun to seize the government from the hands of godless rulers. From the reports John had received, Jesus was conducting a simple ministry of preaching and healing. John's resulting disappointment and perplexity, therefore, may have prompted his question.

B. He Received an Answer (vv. 4-6)

4. Jesus answered and said unto them, Go and show John again those things which ye do hear and see.

The best cure for doubt is fact. Jesus didn't rebuke John, nor did He ask, "Why don't you trust Me?" Instead, He gently urged John to weigh again the facts that he already knew. He had heard of Jesus' miracles, and now Jesus instructed John's disciples to report to their teacher about the miracles they themselves were witnessing (see Luke 7:20-22). These were supernatural works and provided undeniable evidence that He whom John had announced was indeed "the Son of God" (John 1:34).

5. The blind receive their sight, and the lame walk, the lepers are cleansed, and the deaf hear, the dead are raised up, and the poor have the gospel preached to them.

The prophet Isaiah spoke of a time when God would open blind people's eyes and unstop deaf ears, when a lame person would "leap like a deer, and the mute tongue shout for joy" (Isaiah 35:5, 6, *New International Version*).

In another place Isaiah spoke of the Messiah, who would be "anointed . . . to preach good tidings unto the meek . . . to bind up the brokenhearted, to proclaim liberty to the captives, and the opening of the prison to them that are bound" (Isaiah 61:1, 2). Through His preaching and miraculous healing, Jesus was doing what Isaiah said the Messiah would do. If John would simply believe the evidence his representatives brought back to him, he would have no doubt at all that Jesus really was "he that should come."

6. And blessed is he, whosoever shall not be offended in me.

Here Jesus came as close as He ever did to correcting John, but notice the Master's gentleness and the positive nature of His words. Instead of scolding, He pronounced a blessing on John or anyone else who would not *be offended* in Him.

To *be offended* in Jesus means to find an occasion of stumbling in Him. Some were offended in

Jesus because He saw through their hypocrisy and condemned their sins. Others, who desired a worldly Messiah, were offended in Jesus because He did not raise an army to overthrow the Gentile oppressors. The Messianic kingdom was spiritual in nature, and Jesus' ministry was being conducted according to the will of His heavenly Father. Blessing would come to all who trusted Jesus, even through what they regarded as delay and disappointment. The same promise of blessing comes to all today who hold on to faith in Jesus regardless of what others say about Him.

GOING TO THE SOURCE

The Sacramento River irrigates the Central Valley of California. Beginning just below Mount Shasta in northern California, it winds its way 382 miles to the delta, where it joins with the San Joaquin River, and both then flow into the north arm of San Francisco Bay. Along the way it supplies water to the tremendous farm lands that produce food for millions of people all across America.

One of the river's amazing features is the huge, flowing spring from which it arises. Almost immediately the river is born, and animal and bird life are instant users of its life-sustaining water. Until a person goes and sees that spring, it is hard to believe that a river could begin so suddenly and in just a few feet start to fulfill the function of feeding and blessing so many.

So it is with Jesus. John wondered if He was truly the source of life come into the world. When John sent His disciples to ask, Jesus made no claims; He simply told them to tell John of His works of healing and of His preaching of the "good news."

Here is the test of reality. One may doubt, but the results of blessing and truth reveal the power of the source. Jesus, who is the water of life, had God's power from the moment He began His ministry. He was able to do the works of God because He was God in human form. He was the Source.   —W. P.

visual 2

II. John's Character
(Matthew 11:7-11)
A. He Was Strong (vv. 7, 8)

7. And as they departed, Jesus began to say unto the multitudes concerning John, What went ye out into the wilderness to see? A reed shaken with the wind?

As the disciples of John left Jesus to return to their imprisoned teacher, Jesus began to speak to the crowds surrounding Him. Among His hearers were some who had been disciples of John the Baptist. Perhaps they were inclined to think the less of John because of the question John sent.

By means of three questions directed to these in the crowd, Jesus issued a stirring tribute to John. First, when they went out to hear John speak, did they expect to see a weakling, like a *reed shaken with the wind?* Of course not! John was a strong, bold proclaimer of God's word. Then let them not interpret any doubt in John's question as an indication of weakness.

8. But what went ye out for to see? A man clothed in soft raiment? behold, they that wear soft clothing are in kings' houses.

More than that, John did not seek luxury or comfort. Nor did he wear *soft raiment*, that is, fine clothing, such as was worn by royalty. He lived in the outdoors, and the rough clothing he wore indicated it. He was a plain-speaking man of God, whose only concern was to tell people what God wanted them to know, regardless of his own comfort or even his own safety.

B. He Was a Prophet (v. 9)

9. But what went ye out for to see? A prophet? yea, I say unto you, and more than a prophet.

Having heard of John's bold preaching by the Jordan River, the people had thronged to see and hear him. Was it because they suspected he was a prophet? Whatever their expectations that drew the people to him, all came to conclude that he *was indeed* a prophet (see Matthew 21:26). With this opinion Jesus concurred, but added that John was even more.

C. He Was a Messenger (v. 10)

10. For this is he, of whom it is written, Behold, I send my messenger before thy face, which shall prepare thy way before thee.

This explains what Jesus meant by "more than a prophet." He referred to Malachi 3:1, and identified John as the one foretold there, the special *messenger* who would prepare the way for God's chosen One. John did this by calling the nation to repentance and urging all to make the Messiah's paths straight so He could enter their hearts and lives.

MY MESSENGER

In one of her poems, Amy Carson Phillips describes God working in creation with the names "Hack" and "Hew." Hack carved out the mountains, scooped out the seas, and dug the great valleys. These were the frames for the creative artistry of Hew. Hew gave song to the birds and the colors to dawn and sunset. He caused the rose to bloom, and made all creation beautiful. The poet called Hack and Hew the "Sons of God." By them God made the world ready for the creation of man.

In the Gospels, John the Baptist was God's messenger to prepare the way for Messiah's coming. John was "Hack," the rugged instrument of God who made the road straight and the call for repentance clear. Our Lord honored John for his tough message and his faithfulness as the preparer for Jesus' own ministry that brought healing to those needing His touch of love and grace.

The world today still needs to hear the clarion call of those who will turn people's hearts to the Lord, for He alone can restore the wholeness that all were created to have. God used John to begin the restoration that Christ would complete. He can use us also to bring people to the cross, where they can find forgiveness and eternal life.   —W. P.

D. He Was Great (v. 11)

11. Verily I say unto you, Among them that are born of women there hath not risen a greater than John the Baptist: notwithstanding, he that is least in the kingdom of heaven is greater than he.

Because of John's courage and faithfulness in fulfilling his mission, Jesus gave high praise to him. Up to this time, Jesus said, no human

Home Daily Bible Readings

Monday, Dec. 5—Jesus and His Disciples at Work (Matthew 9:35—10:4).

Tuesday, Dec. 6—Jesus Sends Out Twelve Disciples (Matthew 10:5-15)

Wednesday, Dec. 7—Conditions of Discipleship (Matthew 10:37—11:1)

Thursday, Dec. 8—Jesus' Deeds Answer John's Inquiry (Matthew 11:2-6)

Friday, Dec. 9—Jesus' Affirmation of John (Matthew 11:7-15)

Saturday, Dec. 10—Jesus' Rebuke of the Unrepentant (Matthew 11:16-24)

Sunday, Dec. 11—Jesus' Invitation to Follow Him (Matthew 11:25-30)

being, no one *among them that are born of women,* was greater than John. This tribute gave reassurance to any who might be inclined to think ill of John for his doubt. From there, Jesus moved on to an important truth regarding the *kingdom of heaven* that John could only announce, and that is that the lowliest citizen of that kingdom has higher standing than John. By saying this, Jesus wasn't putting John down. Instead, Jesus emphasized as strongly as He could what wonderful blessings would be bestowed on those in God's kingdom that was being established.

III. John's Mission (Matthew 11:12-15)

A. He Proclaimed the Kingdom (v. 12)

12. And from the days of John the Baptist until now the kingdom of heaven suffereth violence, and the violent take it by force.

Bible translators and commentators have proposed differing views of the meaning of this verse. Where our version says that *the kingdom of heaven suffereth violence,* the *New International Version* regards that violence as a good thing by saying, "The kingdom of heaven has been forcefully advancing." That same version has "forceful men" in place of *the violent* (people). This reading leads us to understand Jesus to be saying that God's kingdom is a powerful, world-changing force, whose coming shakes things up. More than an academic philosophy or a gentle appeal to people to live better, the gospel causes drastic changes in the way people think, talk, and behave. Furthermore, halfhearted, fainthearted people aren't quickly drawn to it. Only the brave, the ones who seek God with their whole hearts, will have the courage to embrace the kingdom message. It takes "forceful" people to follow Jesus.

Other recent translations, however, agree with the reading given in the *King James Version.* Thus, in saying that *the kingdom of heaven suffereth violence,* Jesus meant that as soon as John the Baptist appeared with his dramatic announcement concerning the coming kingdom, and right on up to the time Jesus spoke, people attacked what God was trying to do in the world. Examples may be seen in Herod's seizure and imprisonment of John, the opposition of the Jewish religious establishment to Jesus, and the attempts of the Zealots, who advocated the violent overthrow of Rome, to turn Jesus' power and popularity to the accomplishment of their purposes (see John 6:15).

Would these violent people succeed? Can anyone take God's kingdom by brute force? Of course not. *The violent take it by force* doesn't necessarily mean that anyone can seize God's kingdom. Perhaps the *Good News Bible* has captured the meaning in its translation, "violent men try to seize it." The idea is that people who try to pervert God's plan, to hammer God's kingdom into a movement that will serve their own ends, will not succeed.

It is difficult to choose between these two ways of understanding the verse, because both of them have merit.

B. He Began a New Era (v. 13)

13. For all the prophets and the law prophesied until John.

All the prophets and the law prophesied. The whole Old Testament, even the parts that we call law or history or poetry, as well as the portion that we identify as prophecy, looked forward to the coming of God's glorious kingdom.

Until John. John the Baptist's ministry marked a turning point in God's plan for the world. As the forerunner of Christ and the one who announced that "the kingdom of heaven is at hand" (Matthew 3:2), John marked the change from the old agreement between God and His people, the covenant with Israel, to the new agreement sealed with Jesus' blood (Matthew 26:28). John's ministry was the hinge point upon which the new era turned.

C. He Fulfilled Prophecy (vv. 14, 15)

14. And if ye will receive it, this is Elijah, which was for to come.

More than four hundred years earlier, the prophet Malachi promised that God would send the prophet Elijah "before the coming of the great and dreadful day of the Lord" (Malachi 4:5). This is not to say that God would reincarnate Elijah. The meaning is clarified by the words of the angel Gabriel spoken to Zechariah, the father of John the Baptist, when the angel told Zechariah that he and his barren wife would have a son. The son to be born would go before the Lord "in the spirit and power of Elijah" (Luke 1:17). Here Jesus corroborates the angel's message, while affirming that the prophecy of Malachi was fulfilled in John the Baptist. If Jesus' hearers would *receive it*, that is, if they had spiritual eyes to see what God was doing at this point, they would realize that John fulfilled Malachi's prophecy.

15. He that hath ears to hear, let him hear.

The coming of John's disciples with their teacher's question for Jesus led Jesus into a discussion concerning this great man and his place in God's overall plan. John's mission, prophesied centuries earlier, was to announce the coming of the One who would bring redemption to the world. Jesus pronounced that John had done his job well, thus indicating that He, Jesus, who stood in their midst, was the one of whom John spoke. With the statement in this verse Jesus implied that God had given all the ability to understand these things, and that the wise would act on their understanding.

Conclusion

A. Learning From John

We have seen in this lesson that John the Baptist, great man though he was, came to a period in his life when questions were raised in his mind concerning Jesus. And from John we learn a valuable lesson; namely, when questions or doubts trouble us, we must work at resolving them. If one begins to doubt God, it is too easy not to do anything to settle those doubts, simply to go along in an indifferent manner until doubt solidifies into a permanent viewpoint. Equally, if not more important, is what we do to resolve our questions. Notice: John had questions about Jesus, so he went directly to Jesus for answers. So must we. If we have questions about the Christian life or about God's care for His people, let us go to Him in prayer and study His Word anew. It may be that our doubts are the result of faulty understanding of God's promises.

Another valuable lesson we learn from John's experience is that we who belong to God's kingdom rate highly with Him. Even though we stand in awe before a man like John, when we hear Jesus' words, "He that is least in the kingdom of heaven is greater than he," (v. 11) we can't help but be overwhelmed by the magnitude of what God has done for us through His Son.

B. Lessons for Life

Where does John's story leave us, then? It should move us to gratitude toward God for what He has done for us. It should also help us with the doubts that may come to us from time to time, making us determined to resolve them before they poison our relationship with Christ.

C. Let Us Pray

Father in Heaven, we confess that we haven't always trusted You as we should. Grant us assurance of Your love and concern for us, and enable us to trust you enough to base our whole lives on Your promises. We want to be people of faith, not doubters. Through Christ our Lord we pray, Amen.

D. Thought to Remember

Jesus' words and works verify that He is the Christ.

Learning by Doing

This page contains an alternate lesson plan emphasizing learning activities. Classes desiring such student involvement will find these suggestions helpful.

Learning Goals

After studying this lesson from Matthew 11:2-15, the pupils will:

1. Understand how trust plays a role in many things we do in life.

2. Be able to identify circumstances that cause doubt in their lives.

3. Commit to do one act of encouragement for a church leader this week.

Into the Lesson

As the class time begins, ask class members to assemble themselves in groups of four or five. To half of the groups assign the first activity below; assign the second activity to the rest of the groups. For the first activity, bring several newspapers for the students' use.

1. Those doing this activity are to scan the newspapers to find articles about situations in which people showed trust or faith. A member from each group should prepare to share one or two of the best illustrations of trust, and the role trust played in the situation.

2. Have groups work to compile a list of everyday actions or events that require trust or faith. You may need to help get their thinking started by sharing one or two examples (such as, when driving a car, we trust that the car will work and that the other drivers will stay on their side of the road).

Give the groups five to seven minutes to work, and then ask for a report from each group.

Make transition to the Bible study part of this session by sharing insight from the lesson introduction ("The Anatomy of Doubt"). Point out that today's lesson focuses on John the Baptist. We will consider the question he raised about Jesus, and how Jesus reassured John and affirmed John's message and role as the forerunner of Christ.

Into the Word

Begin the Bible study by having a class member read the Scripture text aloud to the class. Then use the following questions to develop class discussion:

1. Verse 2 indicates that John the Baptist was in prison. Why was he there? (See the lesson background; see also Mark 6:17-20.)

2. At Jesus' baptism, John was certain that Jesus was the Messiah (John 1:29-34). Why, then, did John ask the question recorded in verse 3? (See lesson notes on verse 3. John had been in prison for months, and Jesus had not made any attempt to rescue him. Perhaps this had something to do with John's question. Also, John, like many others, may have been expecting the Messiah to be the strong leader of a political kingdom, not a meek, mild, servant King.)

3. Have class members read aloud the following passages: Isaiah 29:18-21; 35:4-6; 61:1-3. Based on these prophecies, what might have been some of John's expectations of Jesus as the Messiah? What expectations was he meeting? What expectations was he not meeting?

4. What six proofs of His messiahship did Jesus give John's disciples? (See verses 4-6. Luke 7:20, 21 indicates that Jesus performed these miracles *after* John's disciples had posed the question to Him; therefore, they would have witnessed these miracles of Jesus.) Why do you think Jesus answered John's question with evidence, rather than specifically with a "yes"?

5. While Jesus affirmed that John was indeed a great man, He also indicated that the "least" in the kingdom of Heaven is greater than John. How are we "greater" than John?

6. What are some examples of how Jesus and His followers "suffered violence"? (See the comments for verse 12.) Encourage your students to think also about how their efforts to share the good news of God's kingdom have encountered opposition.

Into Life

Have your class members return to the same small groups in which they worked at the beginning of the class. Give each group a copy of the following assignments. Plan your lesson to allow about ten minutes for discussion.

1. The Scripture text does not indicate that Jesus criticized John for asking his question. What circumstances in life may cause a person today to question God?

2. In those times of questioning, how can a person find renewal of faith and hope?

3. The event we have studied shows us that even leaders need encouragement. List ways you can be of encouragement to the church leaders.

Challenge each class member to select one way he or she can encourage a church leader and then offer that encouragement in the next week.

Let's Talk It Over

The questions on this page are designed to encourage review of the lesson Scriptures and to promote discussion of the lesson by the class. The answers provided are only discussion starters. Let your class talk it over from there.

1. What is "faith"?

The answer most commonly given may be *belief*, but there's more to faith than that. Belief implies the giving of intellectual assent to truth or reality. Regarding faith in God, James 2:19 states that "the devils also believe, and tremble." We can see, therefore, that the faith we are exhorted to possess is not identical with belief. The devils believe in God, but they tremble with fear at the thought of Him. One who has faith in God does not respond to Him in that manner. Faith moves beyond belief that remains simply an intellectual assent. Faith is belief coupled with, and energized by, *trust*. Consider Abraham, noted for his "faith." He believed God and did as God commanded, for he trusted Him to lead, to provide, and to enable. In the faith that God requires of us, belief must be based on valid witness and testimony, then coupled with our trust. We believe the reliable witness and testimony of Scripture that Jesus Christ is the Son of God, and we entrust ourselves to Him as Savior and Lord.

2. What is doubt, and what effects can it have on a person?

Doubt is uncertainty of belief. Remember that doubt is not the opposite of faith; unbelief or disbelief is. Doubt *can* lead to disbelief if it is allowed to "go to seed," if one makes no attempt to find the answers to troubling uncertainties. If, however, doubt causes one to search for verification of truth, faith can be strengthened as a result.

3. How should a person respond to doubt?

John the Baptist experienced "the dark night of the soul" while he was in prison. Questions (some would say doubt) arose in his mind as to whether Jesus was the Messiah. Regardless, he did the right thing: he sent trusted followers to Jesus to get straight, reliable answers to his questions. He sought trustworthy witness and testimony to the truth he already held. John was blessed in not giving in to his questions and doubts. We will be too, if we follow a similar course. Our response to doubt should be to seek to affirm the truth we have embraced. Healthy doubt does not reside in attacks seeking to destroy or undermine truth, but rather in testing what we have been taught and have believed as we search for a more mature faith. There is *no* mature faith that has not gone through the crucible of doubt. One should not respond to doubtings in fear or with guilt, but in a vigorous search for truth to affirm. That's what John did!

4. What "credentials" did Jesus provide for His messiahship?

Jesus' words and deeds were the credentials He offered for John's disciples to take back to their teacher: what they heard and what they saw. They heard "good news" of forgiveness and eternal life in Him. They saw Him perform miracles of healing. His message and His miracles authenticated who Jesus was—the long-awaited Messiah.

5. What high compliment did Jesus pay John?

Jesus affirmed that John had faithfully fulfilled his mission of preparing the people to receive Him. He paid John the highest tribute possible: "Verily I say unto you, Among them that are born of women there hath not risen a greater than John the Baptist" (Matthew 11:11). Of significance to Christians today is this "tag line" Jesus added to the compliment of John: "notwithstanding, he that is least in the kingdom of heaven is greater than he." Jesus gave the highest praise for the one who prepared the way for the kingdom. He gave the greatest reassurance for those who would be citizens of His kingdom.

6. What barriers tend to keep persons from making healthy, appropriate changes in their lives?

Several may be noted. (1) Pride. The need to change implies deficiency. Too many feel, "I'm OK as I am." (2) Fear of the unknown. Change requires one to walk on a road that he or she has never traveled before. Fear can paralyze a person. (3) The comfort of the known. Here's a barrier that has always existed! We have our "comfort zones" and most persons prefer to stay in them. (4) The effort (and pain) that may be involved. John the Baptist preached repentance as a prerequisite to entrance into the kingdom of Heaven, and repentance is verified by change. One who comes to Jesus will find in Him the strength to overcome these and all barriers to discipleship.

Jesus Is Born

December 18
Lesson 3

Dec
18

DEVOTIONAL READING: Isaiah 9:2-7.

LESSON SCRIPTURE: Matthew 1.

PRINTED TEXT: Matthew 1:18-25.

Matthew 1:18-25

18 Now the birth of Jesus Christ was on this wise: When as his mother Mary was espoused to Joseph, before they came together, she was found with child of the Holy Ghost.

19 Then Joseph her husband, being a just man, and not willing to make her a public example, was minded to put her away privily.

20 But while he thought on these things, behold, the angel of the Lord appeared unto him in a dream, saying, Joseph, thou son of David, fear not to take unto thee Mary thy wife: for that which is conceived in her is of the Holy Ghost.

21 And she shall bring forth a son, and thou shalt call his name JESUS: for he shall save his people from their sins.

22 Now all this was done, that it might be fulfilled which was spoken of the Lord by the prophet, saying,

23 Behold, a virgin shall be with child, and shall bring forth a son, and they shall call his name Immanuel, which being interpreted is, God with us.

24 Then Joseph being raised from sleep did as the angel of the Lord had bidden him, and took unto him his wife:

25 And knew her not till she had brought forth her firstborn son: and he called his name JESUS.

GOLDEN TEXT: Behold, a virgin shall conceive, and bear a son,
and shall call his name Immanuel.—Isaiah 7:14.

Jesus the Fulfillment
(Matthew)
Unit 2. Immanuel: God With Us
(Lessons 3, 4)

Lesson Aims

After this lesson a student should:

1. Be able to tell why belief in the virgin birth of Christ is vital to the Christian faith.

2. Recognize the importance of predictive prophecy.

3. Believe that Jesus is the Son of God and our Savior.

4. Commit his or her life to Jesus as Lord.

Lesson Outline

INTRODUCTION
    A. The Miracle of Life
    B. Lesson Background
  I. THE SITUATION (Matthew 1:18, 19)
    A. Mary's Pregnancy (v. 18)
    B. Joseph's Response (v. 19)
 II. THE VISION (Matthew 1:20, 21)
    A. God's Intervention (v. 20)
    B. God's Promise (v. 21)
III. THE PROPHECY (Matthew 1:22, 23)
    A. Matthew's Comment (v. 22)
    B. Isaiah's Prediction (v. 23)
      Child of Promise
IV. THE BIRTH (Matthew 1:24, 25)
    A. Joseph's Obedience (v. 24)
    B. Jesus' Birth (v. 25)
      Following Orders
CONCLUSION
    A. He Will Save His People
    B. God Is With Us
    C. Let Us Pray
    D. Thought to Remember

Visual 3 of the visuals packet illustrates Joseph's dream (Matthew 1:20, 21). It also previews events to be studied in future lessons of this quarter. The visual is shown on page 140.

Introduction

A. The Miracle of Life

"I believe in miracles," Barry said. "Every time I see a sunset, or hear a newborn baby cry, every time I look into the night sky and see the stars, I realize that all of life is a miracle." Do you agree that we see miracles all around us in nature and in human life? Or is a miracle something else?

Of course, in one sense we have to agree with Barry. All the things God has created are wonders, things that cause us to marvel. One of the Hebrew words translated "miracle" in the Old Testament emphasizes this thought. But the miracles of the Bible are to be understood in a more restricted sense. It is obvious that they are God's special actions that lie outside the normal course of events.

C. S. Lewis, the well-known Christian writer of this century, describes a miracle in this narrower meaning of the word. He defines it as a new event that God puts into the normal chain of cause and effect that makes up our world. Regular patterns of events, involving both the inanimate and animate, may be observed in our world: the sun rises and sets daily, the seasons change in an unvarying manner, the crops go through their appointed growing cycle, and all living creatures go through their life cycles too. One event causes another, which causes the next, which causes the next, and so on. It is only right for us to see God's hand in these events and to thank Him for the beauties and bounties of nature, as well as the joys of human life, because all these flow out of God's original creative act. Because He set these events in motion, they display His glory. But now and again, for a special purpose at a special time, God has "slipped in" an event that we can't account for by the natural laws of cause and effect: a sea that parted, someone who walked on water, someone who rose from the dead. These events are signs, evidence, of a power that is able to control, indeed override, the forces we observe in nature. These meanings also are found in words translated "miracle" in the Bible.

What do you think of Barry's statement? Is he wrong, then, to call all of life a miracle? Of course not, because everything God has provided produces wonder in our hearts. But in a more technical sense, only certain events properly may be called miracles because they supersede the normal course of events as a result of God's direct intervention in His world.

This lesson deals with Jesus' birth. The Bible plainly states that Jesus was born of a virgin, an event that qualifies as a miracle by any standard. Though one may call the birth of a baby in 1994 a miracle in the larger sense, Jesus' birth was a miracle in a special sense, because God's own Son came into the world without the involvement of a human father.

The virgin birth of Jesus plays an essential role in our understanding of who He is. It marks Him as a human being, yet one who is more than human; it identifies Him as God's own Son, one who is qualified to be our Savior.

B. Lesson Background

In beginning his account of the life of Jesus, Matthew traces Jesus' human ancestry starting with Abraham, from whom sprang the Jewish race. The first seventeen verses of chapter 1 deal with this genealogy.

Matthew presents Jesus' ancestors in three groups, corresponding to three periods of Israel's history. The first group includes those from Abraham to David, the second group those from David to the Babylonian captivity, and the third group those from the captivity to Jesus. Those named in the first group were patriarchs, those of the second were kings, and those of the third were citizens. By identifying Jesus as a descendant of Abraham, Matthew shows that Jesus was a member of God's covenant people. As a descendant of David, Jesus was in the royal line and was qualified to rule over God's people. Mention of the Babylonian captivity calls to mind the fact that Jesus' purpose in coming was to release His people—all people who would accept Him—from eternal captivity to sin.

Without further introduction, Matthew begins to relate the miraculous birth of Jesus, the one whose coming would change the whole world forever.

I. The Situation
(Matthew 1:18, 19)

A. Mary's Pregnancy (v. 18)

18. Now the birth of Jesus Christ was on this wise: When as his mother Mary was espoused to Joseph, before they came together, she was found with child of the Holy Ghost.

Matthew begins the account of Jesus' birth without any preliminary remarks. We learn that Jesus' mother, Mary, was *espoused* to a man named Joseph. Espoused in that day meant more than an engagement means today. It was a publicly recognized commitment to marry, a solemn contract that could be set aside only by an explicit, written statement such as was used in the divorce of a married person. This explains why Matthew refers to Joseph and Mary as husband and wife as he relates this narrative (see verses 19 and 20). *Before they came together.* Although this couple could be called husband and wife, Matthew is very clear in stating that they were not living together, they had not yet experienced the intimacies reserved for those who are living in matrimony. It was while Joseph and Mary were betrothed to one another that Mary was *found with child of the Holy Ghost.* Writing many years after this event, Matthew could give the identification given here. But, at the time,

---

How to Say It

ALMAH (Hebrew). al-*mah.*
BABYLONIAN. Bab-uh-*low*-nee-un.
JEHOSHUA. Je-*hosh*-u-a.
JESHUA. *Jesh*-yoo-uh.
PARTHENOS (Greek). par-*then*-ahss (*th* as in *thin*).

Joseph knew only that his betrothed was carrying a child that was not his. Luke 1:26-38 records the angel's announcement of this miraculous conception.

B. Joseph's Response (v. 19)

19. Then Joseph her husband, being a just man, and not willing to make her a public example, was minded to put her away privily.

Did Mary tell Joseph of the angel's visit and announcement? If so, how did he react to it? We are not told. Judging from the verse before us, Joseph believed what was most natural to believe: that Mary had been unfaithful to him and was about to bear a child by another man.

Joseph was *a just man,* that is, one who obeyed the law of Moses. If it could be proved that Mary had willingly engaged in fornication, punishment called for by the law might be administered. This would require a court trial and would involve an investigation into Mary's conduct. Joseph, however, did not want *to make her a public example.* These, then, were the options before Joseph. He could be vindictive and push for the law to take its course, or he could let the matter drop as quietly as possible and simply dissolve the marriage before it even began. Joseph *was minded to put her away privily.* Being a *just man,* Joseph wanted to do what was right; but his justice was not the type that considers only the letter of the law. It was tempered with mercy and compassion. He loved Mary, and he could not expose her to shame and punishment. But neither could he proceed with the marriage. He decided, therefore, to terminate their relationship quietly.

II. The Vision
(Matthew 1:20, 21)

A. God's Intervention (v. 20)

20. But while he thought on these things, behold, the angel of the Lord appeared unto him in a dream, saying, Joseph, thou son of David, fear not to take unto thee Mary thy wife: for that which is conceived in her is of the Holy Ghost.

While he thought on these things. How many heartbreaking, sleepless nights of reflection both Joseph and Mary experienced is not indicated. Finally Joseph came to the decision mentioned in verse 19, and even now he must have dreaded the thought of informing his beloved of it. Perhaps he was in the throes of deciding how to do that when God brought an end to his anguish. *The angel of the Lord.* It was the angel Gabriel who had come to Mary some months before with the announcement that she would give birth to a son, but the angel who spoke to Joseph is not named.

Thou son of David. Though an obscure carpenter in a Galilean town, Joseph was a descendant of David, a member of the royal line. Predictions in the Old Testament were clear that the Christ would be of the seed of David. Did the angel's form of address cause Joseph to think that his wife's son could possibly be the Christ? If not, what the angel said next certainly could have. Joseph was not to be afraid of marrying his betrothed wife. She had done nothing wrong. The power of God had overshadowed her (Luke 1:35), so that that which was conceived in her was of the Holy Ghost. Mary's pregnancy did not come about in the normal manner. The conception was miraculous.

B. God's Promise (v. 21)

21. And she shall bring forth a son, and thou shalt call his name JESUS: for he shall save his people from their sins.

As the legal father, Joseph would name Mary's Son; but he would not be free to choose the name. The angel told him that he was to name the child *Jesus.* This name is the Greek equivalent of the Hebrew name *Joshua,* which also appears in the Bible as *Jehoshua* or *Jeshua.* This name contains the Hebrew name for the God of Israel, and the whole name means "Jehovah is salvation."

Mary's child would bear a name that described His role as Savior: *he shall save his people from their sins.* In the full light of New Testament revelation, it is clear that God didn't intend to restrict this promise to any one people. *His peo-*

visual 3

ple are all the people of the world who will accept Jesus. Whosoever comes to Him will be saved from the eternal consequences of the wrongs they have done.

III. The Prophecy
(Matthew 1:22, 23)
A. Matthew's Comment (v. 22)

22. Now all this was done, that it might be fulfilled which was spoken of the Lord by the prophet, saying.

Jesus' divine conception wasn't a last-minute decision on God's part. He had planned it long ago and had revealed it through one of His ancient spokesmen, *the prophet* Isaiah.

This is the first of ten times in his Gospel that Matthew called attention to the fact that an event he was reporting was the fulfillment of prophecy. (The other places are 2:15, 17, 23; 4:14; 8:17; 12:17; 13:35; 21:4, and 27:9). In each of these ten instances he said, "Now all this happened in order that the word of the prophet might be fulfilled," or words to that effect. This suggests that the people to whom this Gospel account was written were Jewish Christians, who would have been very familiar with the Old Testament and the prophecies it contained.

Several values of predictive prophecy may be noted. First, such prophesies underscore the importance of the events that came to pass in time, showing that those events were part of a plan; second, they enabled God's people to be prepared for those events when they occurred; and third, they give assurance that the events predicted were of God, for the passing of many centuries between prophecy and fulfillment rules out the possibility of human origin for them.

B. Isaiah's Prediction (v. 23)

23. Behold, a virgin shall be with child, and shall bring forth a son, and they shall call his name Immanuel, which being interpreted is, God with us.

This statement quoted by Matthew was part of a prediction spoken by the prophet Isaiah in the eighth century B. C., at a time when the land of Judah was in danger of invasion by Israel and Syria. The prophecy was fulfilled within a few years, except the part that Matthew quotes.

A virgin shall be with child. There is no doubt that Matthew, here, and Luke in his Gospel, make it very clear that Mary was a virgin before and after Jesus was conceived. He was the result of God's visitation of Mary through the Holy Spirit.

The passage in Isaiah, in the original Hebrew, contains the word *almah,* which, according to many capable scholars, may be translated "young woman." Thus it does not necessarily mean "virgin," but may properly be so used, depending upon the circumstances. However, the Greek translation of the Old Testament, known as the Septuagint, was the "Bible" most in use in the time before Jesus' birth, and in this translation the word *almah* is translated as *parthenos*, which means "virgin." Thus, from as early as the middle of the third century B. C., the date generally accepted for the translation of the Septuagint, the prophecy had been understood to say that a *virgin* would conceive. Matthew, who wrote under the inspiration of the Holy Spirit, also uses the term *parthenos* where the prophecy in Isaiah has *almah*. Thus we are led to understand the meaning of Isaiah's prophecy of this miraculous event centuries earlier. The Bible must be allowed to interpret itself. The same Holy Spirit who moved Isaiah to speak also spoke through Matthew, and the message was the same: this special child was conceived of a virgin.

They shall call his name Immanuel. This does not seem to have been literally applied to Jesus as a name by which He is called in the Gospels. However, the whole emphasis of the New Testament is focused on the fact that God did become man and came to be "with us" in Jesus. In His teaching and ministry Jesus would reveal His true nature. It would be very clear that in Him God was indeed with mankind.

CHILD OF PROMISE

Look through a Bible dictionary and you will see that the names given to persons mentioned in the Bible had significance. They were not just letters put together to form a word (name) that was pleasant-sounding. The names were a word, or a combination of words, that had a meaning. Some of the name choices are explained for us in the Biblical text. For example, Abram's name was changed to *Abraham* ("father of a multitude") because of God's promise that he would have great progeny. One Joses was given the name *Barnabas* ("son of consolation") because of encouragement he gave the church in Jerusalem.

The angel who told Joseph in a dream that the child conceived in Mary was of the Holy Spirit also instructed him what to name the child. *Immanuel* means "God with us," and *Jesus* means "Savior." This holy child's person and work were indicated by His names. He was the promised Messiah sent from God. His names revealed His mission among us.

We might do well to give our children names indicating value and virtue, in hopes that they might try to live up to them. Regardless, in Jesus, all believers wear the name *Christian.* Are you living up to the meaning of that name?   —W. P.

Jesus is identified in Scripture as the Son of God and the Son of man, titles that He alone deserves. The fact that He was born without a human father shows Him to be Son of God in a unique sense. The fact that He was born of a woman shows Him to be Son of man, a human being like the rest of us. It is difficult for us to understand how one person could be fully God and fully human. But this was a miracle, and we are not called upon to understand it, only to believe. Only thus can we receive the eternal blessing Immanuel came to bestow.

IV. The Birth
(Matthew 1:24, 25)
A. Joseph's Obedience (v. 24)

24. Then Joseph being raised from sleep did as the angel of the Lord had bidden him, and took unto him his wife.

We can only imagine Joseph's thoughts when he awoke: to know that Mary's character was vindicated. Though we are not told what he thought, we know what he did—he obeyed the angel's order and brought Mary into his home. Thus he gave Mary the protection and social standing that was necessary for God's Son to be brought into the world. Joseph's quiet obedience serves as a model for many of us, whose roles in the church and in the world may not be very noticeable but are still important to the accomplishing of God's purposes.

B. Jesus' Birth (v. 25)

25. And knew her not till she had brought forth her firstborn son: and he called his name JESUS.

Knew her not. With similar words Mary had indicated to the angel Gabriel that she had never had sexual relations with a man (Luke 1:34). So, here, Matthew indicates that Mary remained a virgin *till* she gave birth to *her firstborn son.* The natural understanding of this expression is that after the birth of Jesus, the relationship of Joseph and Mary was that of a normal married couple.

In Luke 1:31 we read that Mary was to call her Son's name "Jesus." In the verse before us we are told that Joseph did as the angel commanded (v. 21) and bestowed that name on her Son. So they acted in harmony in giving the child the specified name, which indicated that in Him the salvation of Jehovah would be brought to mankind.

FOLLOWING ORDERS

The mountain gorge looked deep and foreboding, the rushing stream, far below, frightening. All the exhilaration of climbing the mountain trail evaporated as the group of boys came to the narrow path that hugged the mountainside above the roaring river.

Clifton, the trail leader, walked slowly ahead in the sight of the boys until he reached a wider, safer part of the path. Then he invited the boys to do as he had done, one by one. Soon all but Gene had made it across. Gene couldn't move—he hugged the cliff wall and, in fright, stared down at the stream. Clifton walked carefully back to him, took his hand, and said, "Gene, I'll hold on to you. Don't look down at the river. We'll move just one step at a time. Hang on! Do exactly what I tell you to do."

The fearful boy inched along the path, leaning into the cliff wall, and, with Clifton's help, safely negotiated the dangerous part of the trail.

Clifton let go of his hand, patted his shoulder, and said, "I knew you could do it!"

Gene's reply was, "I couldn't do it alone, but I knew you wouldn't ask me to do it if you thought I would fall."

Joseph faced a problem he did not know how to solve. The victory came when he abandoned his fears and did exactly what he was told to do. The Lord will guide us through life by His Word if we will let Him.   —W. P.

Conclusion

A. He Will Save His People

We sometimes sing a song that goes like this: "Jesus, Jesus, Jesus—there's just something about that name." There certainly is "something about that name." It means "Savior," and it means He has come to rescue us from the penalty of the wrongs we have done and the power of those wrongs to corrupt our lives.

"Thou shalt call his name Jesus," the angel instructed Joseph, "for he shall save his people

Home Daily Bible Readings

Monday, Dec. 12—The Darkness Becomes Light (Isaiah 9:2-7)

Tuesday, Dec. 13—The Salvation of God Is Coming (Isaiah 52:1-10)

Wednesday, Dec. 14—The Angels' Message About Jesus (Matthew 1:18-25)

Thursday, Dec. 15—The Birth of Jesus (Luke 2:1-7)

Friday, Dec. 16—Praise From Angels and Shepherds (Luke 2:8-20)

Saturday, Dec. 17—Jesus' Presentation in the Temple (Luke 2:21-35)

Sunday, Dec. 18—Anna Gives Thanks for Jesus (Luke 2:36-40)

from their sins." We who have put our trust in Jesus, who obey Him with our whole hearts and look for nothing better in life than to be like Him, know that this is true. We have experienced in our own lives God's saving power through Jesus Christ His Son. Did the angel say, "He shall save His people"? We can say, "He *has* saved His people, and *we* are those people!"

This is a message worth proclaiming. The message of Jesus isn't primarily one of judgment, though judgment has a part in it. First and foremost it is the good news that God has come to the aid of the people He made, that He hasn't left them to suffer the consequences of the evil in their lives. He offers them full and free pardon and life eternal with Him. Can we believe these truths and not find our lives changed? Can we know these things and not tell others who need to hear them?

B. God Is With Us

Years ago a preacher preached an unforgettable sermon on Jesus as Immanuel, God with us. In the development of his message, the preacher gave the word *with* several different meanings. "God is 'with' us in Jesus," he said, "in the sense that He became one of us and lived right here among us. More than that, God is 'with' us in Jesus in that He is on our side, standing shoulder to shoulder beside us in the troubles of life."

Many people throughout history have believed in gods who are far removed from them and care little about them. The essence of the Christian faith, and the heart of the Christmas message, is that the high and holy God, who "dwells in unapproachable light" (1 Timothy 6:16, *New Revised Standard Version*), has come to earth to be one of us and will take us to Heaven to be with Him. Our God is not remote, nor is He unconcerned about our needs. To the contrary, He cared so much for us that He became one of us, so we might eventually become like Him. That's something to celebrate, at Christmastime or anytime!

C. Let Us Pray

O Lord our God, for Your faithfulness in fulfilling Your promise of old to come and dwell among us, we praise You. For Christ Jesus, who relinquished His heavenly glory and became one with us that He might bring us to You, we are truly grateful. May our gratitude be seen in our obedience to all He has commanded us. Amen.

D. Thought to Remember

"Thou shalt call his name Jesus: for he shall save his people from their sins" (Matthew 1:21).

Learning by Doing

*This page contains an alternate lesson plan emphasizing learning activities. Classes
desiring such student involvement will find these suggestions helpful.*

Learning Goals

After this lesson, class members will:

1. Know the importance the genealogy in Matthew has in establishing Jesus as the Messiah.

2. Understand the problems Mary's pregnancy may have created for Mary and Joseph.

3. Understand the importance of Jesus' being born of a virgin.

Into the Lesson

Invite a class member or guest who has an interest in genealogies to talk to your class briefly about them. Encourage the speaker to share some of the challenges faced by his or her ancestors.

Following this introduction, make your transition to the Bible study portion of this session by saying, "The genealogies recorded in the Bible are often overlooked. In addition to studying Matthew's record of the events leading up to the miraculous birth of Jesus, we will examine Jesus' family history to consider its importance."

Into the Word

Divide the class into groups of five or six students each. Assign to the groups different sections of the genealogy for study according to these verse divisions: verses 2-6a: 6b-11; and 12-16. Give each group a copy of the following questions and allow ten minutes for discussion.

• What names do you recognize in this genealogy?

• What facts can you remember about these persons?

• Which persons in the list are most significant in establishing who Jesus is?

• What word would you use to summarize the generations in this section of the genealogy?

Ask for a brief summary from each group. Then guide the class in discussing these questions:

Why would Matthew begin his Gospel with a genealogy? (He was writing primarily to Christians with a Jewish background, and family heritage was very important to them.)

How does this genealogy answer the question, "Is Jesus really the Messiah?" (See Lesson Background.)

Matthew uses two titles for Jesus (vv. 1, 16). What are they? (Son of David and Christ, or Messiah.) What significance would each of these names have to Matthew's readers?

What reason does Scripture give for the choice of Mary to be the mother of Jesus? What commendable qualities are revealed about her character? (See Luke 1:30-38.)

What was Joseph's initial reaction to Mary's news? How did his plans change following his dream? What does this tell you about Joseph?

Read aloud Isaiah 7:14. Share with the class a summary of the lesson notes on verses 21-23, and emphasize the significance of Jesus' virgin birth. Apart from fulfilling prophecy, why do you think it was necessary for Jesus to be born of a virgin?

Into Life

The impact of Mary's pregnancy on the lives of Mary and Joseph is sometimes overlooked. To help the class gain insight, and increased appreciation for this couple, do the following:

Divide the class into four groups and give each group one set of the following questions. Group members are to imagine that they are the person or persons identified in their set of questions and answer the questions on that basis.

Group 1—*Joseph.* You are Joseph, and Mary has just explained the cause of her pregnancy. What is your reaction? How do you feel? What questions do you ask? What reactions do you expect from your family? From your friends?

Group 2—*Mary.* An angel has announced to you that you will give birth to the Son of God as a result of God's power through the Holy Spirit. What are your thoughts? What will you say to Joseph? How will you explain this to your family? To your friends?

Group 3—*Parents of Mary and Joseph.* If you are Mary's parents, how do you react to her revelation that she is pregnant? If you are Joseph's parents, what advice do you give to Him? How does Joseph's dream affect your advice?

Group 4—*Friends in Nazareth.* What kind of gossip do you hear about Mary and Joseph? As a friend of Mary, what are your thoughts regarding her pregnancy? As a friend of Joseph? What *will* you do? What *should* you do?

After ten minutes let the groups report their conclusions to the class. Discuss as necessary. Then make application by discussing these questions: What does this lesson teach us about submission to God? Obedience to God? Commitment to others?

Let's Talk It Over

The questions on this page are designed to encourage review of the lesson Scriptures and to promote discussion of the lesson by the class. The answers provided are only discussion starters. Let your class talk it over from there.

1. What feelings and thoughts may Joseph have experienced when he learned of Mary's pregnancy?

No doubt Joseph had mixed feelings. Because unfaithfulness carried a severe social stigma, Joseph certainly would have felt humiliated by Mary's apparent misconduct. At first he probably would have felt resentment and anger—he knew he was not the father of the child to be born. Surely he would have been disappointed with Mary. Yet, even with these feelings, he did not feel vindictive or vengeful. He cared for her and cared about what would happen to her. In his sensitivity to her, he determined "to have the marriage contract quietly set aside" (Matthew 1:19, *The Revised English Bible*). However, Joseph's thoughts and feelings were interrupted by the angel's appearance and the message brought to him. The divine intervention and revelation changed everything.

2. What are some of the dominant feelings experienced by parents at the birth of their child?

These feelings can be classified as positive and negative. Some of the positive feelings are these: (1) Happiness. The birth of a child is a time of beginning, a time for rejoicing, a time for celebration. (2) Gratitude. Thanksgiving wells up within the hearts of parents when they reflect on the gift of a child, the answer to prayer. (3) Awe. Sharing with God in the creation of new life is an awe-inspiring experience. (4) Relief. The birth of a child is a long-awaited event. Especially if mother and child are both in good health, relief is felt. (5) Dedication. A strong feeling of commitment to rearing a child "in the nurture and admonition of the Lord" (Ephesians 6:4) marks the experience of conscientious new parents. Some of the negative feelings are as follows: (1) Resentment. Sometimes a baby is viewed as an "intruder," as a nuisance. Resentment may be felt because of the immediate and potential demands the baby makes on the new parents. (2) Depression. When a baby finally arrives, a sense of "letdown" tends to follow. Modern obstetrics acknowledges that most, if not all, new mothers experience some degree of postpartum depression. (3) Anxiety. Some parents may feel overwhelmed by all of the new responsibilities of parenthood. They feel very inadequate and unprepared.

Obviously, a wide range of complex and diverse feelings can accompany the birth of a child.

3. Mary's child was to be named Jesus. What is the meaning of that name?

This significant name given to the child born of Mary was bestowed by God himself. The name *Jesus* is the Greek equivalent of the Hebrew *Joshua*, which means "Jehovah is salvation." The child would also be called Immanuel, meaning "God with us." Joseph was directed to call his name *Jesus*, for He came to "save his people from their sins."

4. What lessons may we learn from the example of Joseph?

Joseph is worthy of emulation. He was a man of principle, expressed in his initial intention to divorce Mary. Yet, the fact that he would do it quietly shows that he was a person of discretion and sensitivity. He was unwilling to disgrace Mary. When God revealed to Joseph that that which was conceived in Mary was of the Holy Ghost, Joseph neither questioned nor doubted the word of the Lord. He obeyed God and took Mary into his home. Joseph was also disciplined, for the Scripture notes that he did not have sexual relations with Mary before the birth of Jesus. From his admirable qualities, Joseph teaches us valuable lessons.

5. If an unmarried woman of a congregation becomes pregnant, how should the members of the congregation respond and relate to her?

The first mandate of Christians is to love one another with a love that is identified by the Greek *agape*. It may be defined as *"unconditional self-giving that seeks the highest good of another."* This mature love embodies acceptance, which is not the same as approval. The church can be supportive of the woman, providing her with counsel and resources, rather than being judgmental and ostracizing her. The church's purpose should always be to attempt to save or restore sinners, and not to condemn in such a way as to discourage repentance by anyone who is guilty of wrongdoing.

The Wise Men Worship Jesus

December 25
Lesson 4

DEVOTIONAL READING: Isaiah 11:1-9.

LESSON SCRIPTURE: Matthew 2.

PRINTED TEXT: Matthew 2:1-12.

Matthew 2:1-12

1 Now when Jesus was born in Bethlehem of Judea in the days of Herod the king, behold, there came wise men from the east to Jerusalem,

2 Saying, Where is he that is born King of the Jews? for we have seen his star in the east, and are come to worship him.

3 When Herod the king had heard these things, he was troubled, and all Jerusalem with him.

4 And when he had gathered all the chief priests and scribes of the people together, he demanded of them where Christ should be born.

5 And they said unto him, In Bethlehem of Judea: for thus it is written by the prophet,

6 And thou Bethlehem, in the land of Judah, art not the least among the princes of Judah: for out of thee shall come a Governor, that shall rule my people Israel.

7 Then Herod, when he had privily called the wise men, inquired of them diligently what time the star appeared.

8 And he sent them to Bethlehem, and said, Go and search diligently for the young child; and when ye have found him, bring me word again, that I may come and worship him also.

9 When they had heard the king, they departed; and, lo, the star, which they saw in the east, went before them, till it came and stood over where the young child was.

10 When they saw the star, they rejoiced with exceeding great joy.

11 And when they were come into the house, they saw the young child with Mary his mother, and fell down, and worshipped him: and when they had opened their treasures, they presented unto him gifts; gold, and frankincense, and myrrh.

12 And being warned of God in a dream that they should not return to Herod, they departed into their own country another way.

GOLDEN TEXT: When they were come into the house, they saw the young child with Mary his mother, and fell down, and worshipped him: and when they had opened their treasures, they presented unto him gifts; gold, and frankincense, and myrrh.—Matthew 2:11.

Jesus the Fulfillment
(Matthew)
Unit 2. Immanuel: God With Us
(Lessons 3, 4)

Lesson Aims

This lesson should lead students to:

1. Understand that the revelation granted to the wise men and their coming to worship the King indicated that the salvation Jesus brought was for all people.

2. Join the wise men in their adoration of the King.

3. Select one way they will express their love and devotion to Christ.

Lesson Outline

INTRODUCTION
  A. Written in the Stars
  B. Lesson Background
 I. THE NEW KING'S STAR (Matthew 2:1, 2)
  A. Journey of the Wise Men (v. 1)
  B. Quest of the Wise Men (v. 2)
    A Sign From Above
 II. THE OLD KING'S PLOT (Matthew 2:3-8)
  A. Demand of the King (vv. 3, 4)
  B. Report of the Priests and Scribes (vv. 5, 6)
  C. Instructions for the Wise Men (vv. 7, 8)
III. THE WISE MEN'S SUCCESS (Matthew 2:9-12)
  A. Appearance of the Star (vv. 9, 10)
    Locating the King
  B. Gifts for the Child (v. 11)
  C. Departure of the Wise Men (v. 12)
CONCLUSION
  A. Gifts Fit for a King
  B. For All People
  C. Let Us Pray
  D. Thought to Remember

Visual 4 of the visual packet pictures the wise men presenting their gifts to the Christ child. The visual is shown on page 149.

Introduction

A. Written in the Stars

It's hard to tell if we are seeing a trend or not, but it seems that every year more and more people advertise themselves as palm readers, psychics, or astrologers. For a modest fee they will tell us what the future holds for us—whether we will get the job we want, find a loving mate, or enjoy good health, etc.

The astrologers make especially interesting claims, believing as they do that the stars, planets, and other heavenly bodies control or, at least influence, human life. The more we know about how the stars influence us, they say, the more we will know how to handle our lives, avoid disaster, and reach our personal goals.

Scripture teaches differently, however. There we learn that we have life as a gift of God and that to a large extent the things that happen to us in life are the result of the deliberate choices we make. The heavens don't determine our fate. Rather, as David affirmed in Psalm 19:1, "The heavens declare the glory of God." The stars don't map out the path that lies ahead of us. To the contrary, we choose the direction our lives will take. Each individual's personal choice of good or evil, and one's personal responsibility for the choices he or she makes, are clear teachings running through all of Scripture. (See Joshua 24:15.) For the safest and happiest future, let us not look to the stars, but to Him who created the heavens and the earth.

B. Lesson Background

In today's lesson we meet some men who might be called astrologers, who came to honor the child Jesus after they saw a star that signaled His birth. The fact that these men are spoken of in a favorable manner in Matthew's Gospel might surprise us, in view of the fact that the Bible speaks against astrology and similar arts. (See Isaiah 47:8-15, especially verses 13 and 14.) Daniel in his day overcame all the "magicians, and the astrologers, and the sorcerers" (Daniel 2:2) who competed with him as they served King Nebuchadnezzar of Babylon.

Perhaps it is not fully accurate to describe these men as astrologers. They were Magi, learned men, instructed in the wisdom of the East. From history we form a picture of them as the ancient equivalents of scientists, philosophers, and advisers, all rolled into one. Of particular interest to them was the study of astronomy. When the Son of God came into the world, He "made His mark" on the natural order of things, and His star arose. In some way the wise men recognized this mark when they saw it, and they came to honor Him. How much they understood of Jesus' divine nature, either at first or later on, the Scripture does not state, but at least they honored Him as no ordinary person.

In the first two lessons of this quarter's study we considered John the Baptist, whose divinely appointed task was to prepare God's people to receive the Messiah when He began His public ministry. Last week's lesson took us back thirty years before that time, to the occasion when

God's angel announced to Joseph that his promised wife, Mary, who was a virgin, would give birth to a child conceived in her of the Holy Spirit. The first chapter of Matthew ended with a matter-of-fact reference to the birth of her child, whom Joseph named *Jesus* according to the angel's instruction (1:21). The event recorded in this lesson took place some time after Jesus was born.

I. The New King's Star (Matthew 2:1, 2)

A. Journey of the Wise Men (v. 1)

1. Now when Jesus was born in Bethlehem of Judea in the days of Herod the king, behold, there came wise men from the east to Jerusalem.

Now when Jesus was born in Bethlehem of Judea. Matthew gives us but a brief account of the birth of Jesus, as noted above. We turn to the Gospel of Luke for the information that all this took place in Nazareth of Galilee. It is Luke who explains why Joseph and Mary were *in Bethlehem* when Jesus was born. Luke also tells of the crowded conditions there, the stable, the song of the angels, and the visit of the shepherds.

In the days of Herod the king. This Herod was the ruler known to history as Herod the Great, who ruled Judea under the Romans as a client king. In 40 B.C. the Roman senate appointed Herod king over the Judean territory, but it took him three years to conquer it and come into full power as its ruler.

Herod was a man of great natural abilities, physical strength, and intellectual powers. He was a shrewd military leader and a great builder. He rebuilt the old city of Samaria, built Caesarea as a port city, and started construction on the Jerusalem temple that was standing during Jesus' earthly ministry. Known for his ruthlessness, Herod would do nearly anything to keep his subjects under his control and thus retain the favor of the Romans. In the waning years of his life, Herod became insanely jealous of his power. Becoming suspicious of his favorite wife, Mariamne, and his two sons by her, Herod had the three of them executed. Another son met the same fate shortly before Herod's own death.

From the Jewish historian Josephus, other historians, and archaelogical data, we know that Herod the Great died in 4 B. C. The mistake in our calendar was made by a monk in the sixth century. By the time the mistake came to light, the calendar was too familiar to change. Allowing a year or two for the events of Jesus' early life before Herod died, and remembering that Jesus was about thirty in the fifteenth year of Tiberius Caesar, that is in A.D. 26 or 27 (Luke 3:1), we conclude that Jesus was born in 5 B.C., give or take about a year.

Wise men from the east. Where exactly in the East these wise men came from we are not told. The usual guess is Persia. The plural *men* indicates that there were more than one. The fact that they brought three types of gifts has led to the speculation that there were only three men.

To Jerusalem. The wise men were looking for one who was born "King of the Jews," as we see in verse 2. It was natural, therefore, that in their search they should come to the capital city of the Jews.

B. Quest of the Wise Men (v. 2)

2. Saying, Where is he that is born King of the Jews? for we have seen his star in the east, and are come to worship him.

Where is he that is born King of the Jews? Arriving in Jerusalem, the wise men must have immediately asked this question in the city streets. Wouldn't everyone know of such a great event and be able to give them the information they sought? We can see these men going from person to person, repeating their inquiry, but gaining no information.

For we have seen his star in the east. These men studied the heavens, and when a special star made its appearance it did not escape their notice. Attempts have been made to explain this star on the basis of natural occurrences, but these explanations are unsatisfactory. The biblical account leads us to conclude that the appearance of this star was miraculous. The next question is, How did these men know what this star signified? The most satisfactory explanation is that they received a direct revelation from God concerning it. The history of the events surrounding the birth of Jesus suggests this conclusion. The shepherds were informed of the birth in this way, as were Simeon and Anna. And by God's direct communication with them, the wise men were instructed not to return to Herod with word of the child's whereabouts, but to go home by another route.

The Greek word translated *to worship* means "to bow down to do homage." We do not know

---

How to Say It

BABYLONIANS.   Bab-uh-*low*-nee-unz.
CAESAREA.   Sess-uh-*ree*-uh.
JOSEPHUS.   Joe-*see*-fus.
NEBUCHADNEZZAR.   *Neb*-you-kad-*nezz*-er (strong accent on *nezz*).

how much the wise men understood of the divine nature of the King who was born. Surely, however, they knew that He was more than the heir to the throne of a tiny kingdom enslaved by Rome. Why else would they come from so far away with expensive gifts to do homage to Him?

A SIGN FROM ABOVE

On a clear night in Chile the stars in the southern hemisphere are bright and glistening. The wonder of God's creative power is fully displayed in the innumerable luminaries hung across the limitless reaches of space.

On such a starry night a few years ago, during the week of Christmas, several missionaries were having a retreat near the ocean. At a break time we all watched as two luminaries moving in opposite directions crossed overhead and disappeared in the horizon. Were they a sign from Heaven? Were they two comets speeding through the velvet black sky? No, they were two space satellites, one American and the other Russian, racing in their orbits around the earth. Eerie, beautiful, mysterious, silent in their journey, they held us entranced as we watched their passage.

Imagine the wonder and the excitement of the wise men when they observed in the the Eastern sky the star of the King of the Jews. This sign in the heavens brought them westward to Judea to worship. By contrast, that same sign greatly troubled King Herod.

It is Christmas once more. God's signs given through His Word still beckon us to come to Jesus and to worship Him as the King. How do you respond to God's call?   —W. P.

II. The Old King's Plot
(Matthew 2:3-8)

A. Demand of the King (vv. 3, 4)

3. When Herod the king had heard these things, he was troubled, and all Jerusalem with him.

Word of the wise men's inquiry soon was brought to the attention of *Herod the king.* The aged monarch knew nothing of the birth of One who was held to be a claimant to his throne. Learning of it, the king *was troubled.* Even though Herod was nearing the end of his own reign, he was consumed with jealousy and fear for his position. *All Jerusalem* was troubled as well, for the people knew the crimes an enraged Herod was capable of committing against anyone he imagined was a threat to him.

4. And when he had gathered all the chief priests and scribes of the people together, he demanded of them where Christ should be born.

Whatever the wise men understood concerning this One who was born "King of the Jews," Herod understood Him to be *Christ,* the Messiah, God's anointed one. Herod knew that the Scriptures of the Jews predicted the coming of the Messiah and that the people were looking for Him, so he assembled those persons who would be able to answer his question. *The chief priests* were the men in charge of the temple worship; *the scribes* were the experts in the law of Moses. *Demanded.* Rather, inquired. Herod could be courteous when it served his purposes.

B. Report of the Priests and Scribes
(vv. 5, 6)

5. And they said unto him, In Bethlehem of Judea: for thus it is written by the prophet.

The chief priests and scribes answered immediately that the Messiah was to be born in Bethlehem, King David's hometown, just five miles south of Jerusalem. God had said this through His prophet long ago.

The main role of the prophets of Old Testament times was to give God's message to His stubborn people and to call them to turn from their sins and come back to God. Although predicting future events wasn't the prophets' main task, they often did make predictions, and the predictions always came true.

6. And thou Bethlehem, in the land of Judah, art not the least among the princes of Judah: for out of thee shall come a Governor, that shall rule my people Israel.

The prophecy came from the writings of the prophet Micah (Micah 5:2), who lived more than seven hundred years earlier. In poetic utterance, Micah addressed Bethlehem, a small village in the land of Judah. Though insignificant when compared with the splendid capital of Jerusalem, Bethlehem would gain fame in all the world and for all time. From this village would come *a Governor,* the great Ruler of Israel.

C. Instructions for the Wise Men
(vv. 7, 8)

7. Then Herod, when he had privily called the wise men, inquired of them diligently what time the star appeared.

Having received the information he needed from the chief priests and scribes, Herod dismissed them. Then he summoned the wise men *privily,* or as we would say, "privately," for a conference. He now knew where the child was born, but he needed to know when the birth had taken place. Where the text says he *inquired of them diligently,* later translations say he inquired "accurately" or "exactly" regarding when the star had appeared. Apparently Herod felt that the child had been born at the very time the star had appeared. We learn from verse 16 that Herod ordered the killing of all the male children in and near Bethlehem who were two years old and under. This suggests that the star appeared perhaps as much as a year earlier. Herod probably would have increased or even doubled the time mentioned by the wise men in order to make sure he included the child he feared when the killings at Bethlehem took place.

8. And he sent them to Bethlehem, and said, Go and search diligently for the young child; and when ye have found him, bring me word again, that I may come and worship him also.

In his private interview with these men, Herod not only was successful in obtaining the information he sought, but he also was able to assess their character. It seems that he judged them to be honest men, for he sent them unaccompanied to Bethlehem and piously requested that they bring him word when they found the young child so that he might *come and worship him also.* Of course, Herod had no intention of paying any kind of homage to the child. His intention was to kill the child, and deceitfully he would use these innocent men to accomplish his malicious purpose.

III. The Wise Men's Success (Matthew 2:9-12)

A. Appearance of the Star (vv. 9, 10)

9. When they had heard the king, they departed; and, lo, the star, which they saw in the east, went before them, till it came and stood over where the young child was.

With the knowledge that the child whom they sought was in Bethlehem, the wise men departed the king's presence and started for the village, even though night was falling. *The star, which they saw in the east.* Some think this implies that they had seen the star when they were in the East, and that they had not seen it since then. *Went before them.* Because the star led them

directly to where Jesus was, others conclude that the star had given them similar guidance throughout their journey.

10. When they saw the star, they rejoiced with exceeding great joy.

Seeing the miraculous star again, they rejoiced greatly. The divine guidance given by the star clearly confirmed the prophecy of the Old Testament. The travelers knew that they were nearing the end of their search.

LOCATING THE KING

In the story, *The Prince and the Pauper,* the exchange of roles between the future king and another young man who looked like him was rather easily accomplished because of the fixed ideas surrounding royalty. Princes are found in castles; paupers in humble abodes. Princes wear royal garments; paupers wear peasant garb. Princes act with assurance of position; paupers go quietly about their everyday tasks.

To locate a child who is to become king, one would look in the king's palace. So the wise men came to Jerusalem, expecting to find Him who was born King of the Jews. Herod, however, knew nothing of the birth. But he learned that God's prophet had said the King would come out of Bethlehem of Judea, so he sent them there.

The star they had seen earlier led them from the palace in Jerusalem to the place where the young child was. Without God's direction by Scripture and star, they could not have found the King whom they sought. If they had not trusted the revelation given to them, they would have continued to inquire in the wrong place.

God says we must come to the manger, the cross, and the empty tomb to find the One who alone qualifies to be the King of our lives. The world says royalty is found elsewhere. To whom will you listen?   —W. P.

B. Gifts for the Child (v. 11)

11. And when they were come into the house, they saw the young child with Mary his mother, and fell down, and worshipped him: and when they had opened their treasures, they presented unto him gifts; gold, and frankincense, and myrrh.

We notice that Matthew refers to Jesus as a *young child,* and that the family was living in a *house,* not a stable. This indicates that some time had passed from the time of Jesus' birth until the arrival of the wise men in Bethlehem.

When they entered the house and saw Jesus, they *fell down* before Him and *worshipped* Him. They knew from the events in Jerusalem that this child was the Christ. How much beyond that they knew of His nature we do not know.

They knelt down and worshiped him.

visual 4

The valuable gifts they brought included *gold,* a fitting present for a king, *frankincense,* a kind of incense such as a priest might burn before God (see Exodus 30), and *myrrh,* a spice used in burial (see John 19:39). Taken together, these offerings were most suitable for One who would serve as king, priest, and sacrifice.

C. Departure of the Wise Men (v. 12)

12. And being warned of God in a dream that they should not return to Herod, they departed into their own country another way.

Herod had duped the wise men, but God intervened so that they would not unwittingly give Herod the information he sought. Just as God spoke to Joseph in a dream (Matthew 1:20) and would do so twice again (2:13, 19) to protect the Christ, He warned these visitors from the East not to return to Herod in Jerusalem. In obedience to God's word, they went to their homeland by a different route, and stepped off the stage of the gospel story.

Conclusion

A. Gifts Fit for a King

"The Little Drummer Boy" has been a popular Christmas song in America for many years. Of course, the song is fictional. Even so, it carries truth worthy of consideration. You probably remember how the song goes. A boy with a drum goes along with the shepherds to visit the infant Jesus. Troubled because he doesn't have a gift fit for a king, the boy finally plays on his drum to please the baby. "I'll play my drum for Him," the boy says. "I'll play my best for Him."

From the drummer boy's statements two thoughts emerge. The first is this: If we do not have possessions of great value to offer to Christ, let us recognize the value of what we do possess and of it make an offering to Him. The wise men presented to the Christ child gifts of gold, frankincense, and myrrh. These were wonderful gifts, and they enabled Joseph and Mary to flee to Egypt with Jesus and to provide for Him there. But one wonders if the lowly shepherds on the day following Jesus' birth did not return to the stable with warm, wholesome food and other necessities—simple gifts that they had in their power to bring.

Some persons today can and do give to the Lord plots of land, buildings, and large sums of money. These are wonderful gifts and they advance the Lord's cause. Most persons, however, do not possess resources of such magnitude. But what we do have can be offered to Christ, and He will not reject it. When we give what we have, our Lord is pleased.

The second thought is that we should give our best for Christ. No half-hearted effort would express the reverence the drummer boy felt in his heart for the Christ child at His birth. How, then, can we, who know not only of His wondrous birth but also of His life and sacrificial death in our behalf, give Him anything less than our best? We begin by giving Him ourselves without reservation. Once we have done that, can we ever entertain the thought of giving to Him of our resources only after we have satisfied our own selfish desires? God gave His Son, the most precious gift mankind has ever received. The wise men made great sacrifice of time and effort to present to Jesus gifts fit for a king. Let us do no less today.

B. For All People

Today's Scripture passage indicates that God's plan of salvation is intended for the whole world. God's Son came to earth as a child born of the Jewish nation, in keeping with God's plan announced as far back as the time of Abraham (Genesis 12:1-3). But God's promise revealed His intention to bless all nations through Abraham. By sharing the announcement of Jesus' birth with the wise men, who were Gentiles, God showed that this good news was meant for all persons—Jew and Gentile alike.

C. Let Us Pray

Father, we thank You for the marvelous gift of Your Son. May we show our heartfelt gratitude by giving Him the best gift we can, the gift of ourselves. Amen.

D. Thought to Remember

The best gift we can give at Christmas is the gift of ourselves, both to God and to other people.

Home Daily Bible Readings

Monday, Dec. 19—The Rule of the Messiah (Isaiah 11:1-9)

Tuesday, Dec. 20—The Day of Deliverance (Zechariah 9:9-13)

Wednesday, Dec. 21—The Deliverer to Come From Bethlehem (Micah 5:1-5a)

Thursday, Dec. 22—Wise Men Directed to Bethlehem (Matthew 2:1-6)

Friday, Dec. 23—The Wise Men Worship Jesus (Matthew 2:7-12)

Saturday, Dec. 24—The Escape to Egypt (Matthew 2:13-18)

Sunday, Dec. 25—Return From Egypt (Matthew 2:19-23)

Learning by Doing

This page contains an alternate lesson plan emphasizing learning activities. Classes desiring such student involvement will find these suggestions helpful.

Learning Goals

After this lesson, class members will be able to:

1. State in proper sequence the events included in the visit of the wise men to Jesus.

2. Explain who these men were.

3. Relate the search these wise men made for Jesus to their own search for Him.

Into the Lesson

As you begin, take some time to allow class members to share some of their childhood memories about Christmas Day.

After several members have shared, make transition to the lesson time. Though the visit of the wise men is often associated with the events of the night of Jesus' birth, we will see today that in fact it occurred some time later.

Into the Word

Prior to class time, write the following events from today's lesson text on sheets of paper, one event per sheet. (Write the words large enough so that your students will be able to read them from where they are seated.) The events in their proper order are as follows: Jesus is born; Wise men see the star; Wise men come to Jerusalem; Wise men talk with Herod; Herod consults Jewish priests and teachers; Herod secretly talks to wise men; Wise men are led by the star; Wise men go to Bethlehem; Wise men present gifts to Jesus; Wise men return home.

Ask for ten volunteers to come to the front of the room. Scramble the sheets and give each of the ten students a sheet. Ask them to hold up the sheets so all in the class may see the events written on them. Then have the class, without referring to the Scripture text, move the students around so as to arrange the events in order.

When the class is certain they have the events in the proper order, ask a volunteer to read aloud the lesson text, Matthew 2:1-12. Then, using the following questions, plus insights from the lesson commentary, lead the class in a discussion of the lesson.

Where was Bethlehem? What events and persons mentioned in the Old Testament were associated with this town?

(It was about five miles south of Jerusalem. Rachel was buried there (Genesis 35:19); the story of Ruth and Boaz took place there; Bethlehem was David's home.)

What was the significance of Jesus' being born in Bethlehem? (Micah prophesied that the Christ would come out of Bethlehem. See Micah 5:2.)

Who were the wise men who came searching for the King of the Jews?

What was King Herod's reaction to the news of the birth of a King? Why did he react in this manner? (See comments under verse 1.)

Why were the citizens of Jerusalem troubled? (See verse 3.)

When Herod spoke with the wise men, what specific information did he seek from them? (See verse 7.) What was his motive for wanting to know this? (See also Matthew 2:16.)

It has been estimated that the journey of these men from their home in the East to Jerusalem occupied a number of weeks, if not months. Why do you suppose they were willing to leave everything and make such a long trek after seeing that special star in the sky? What are some of the "stars" people today are willing to follow? (Focus your discussion on false gods people follow today. Some examples are money, job status, power over others, pleasure.) Where are these "stars" leading them?

What was the response of these men when they finally found Jesus (v. 11)? How was their response similar to the response of an unbeliever who finds Jesus for the first time?

Have the class brainstorm for a few minutes to compile a list of occasions on which people give gifts. Then ask them to share some of the reasons (both good and bad) why we give gifts. Why do you think the wise men gave gifts to the Christ child?

Using the comments under verse 11 as a resource, discuss with your class the symbolism that some have seen in the three gifts these men gave to Jesus.

Into Life

Take some time to have volunteers from your class share the story of their own search for Jesus. Limit each testimony to one or two minutes. If you know of class members whose testimonies are especially dramatic or moving, plan for them to share last. Otherwise, some might feel that their testimony is "boring" or of no value, and thus might be unwilling to share.

Close the class with prayer, thanking God for the incomparable gift of His Son Jesus.

Let's Talk It Over

The questions on this page are designed to encourage review of the lesson Scriptures and to promote discussion of the lesson by the class. The answers provided are only discussion starters. Let your class talk it over from there.

1. What can we learn about worship from the visit of the wise men?

Consider the expense of money, time, and effort required of these men to get them to the presence of the child. The implications in this regard are strong concerning our stewardship. Consider the focus of their attention. They were not worshiping the flowers, the music, the beauty, other valuable people, or things along the way. They sought only the Christ child. Consider the fact of their bowing before this baby born of humble parentage. They knew they were not in the presence of someone who was merely their peer. The circumstances surrounding their arrival in the presence of this child suggests that they regarded Him more than just an earthly king.

Our own times of worship are not for our pleasure, nor for the honoring of any human being. We are to bow before and in the presence of God and His Son, and honor them alone.

2. The wise men presented gifts of gold, frankincense, and myrrh to the Christ child. Discuss the significance of these gifts.

Some Bible students see in the three gifts symbols of Christ's identity and mission. Gold was the gift fit for a king. Frankincense was a gift for deity, appropriate for a priestly offering before God. Myrrh, used in the preparation of bodies for burial, suggested the fact that He was "born to die." Thus they see these as gifts for One who would serve as king, priest, and sacrifice! Others have suggested that Joseph and Mary were of limited financial means, and that the price these gifts brought assisted them in their stay in Egypt, which followed immediately upon the departure of the wise men.

We must note, however, that Scripture is silent regarding the gifts, other than stating that valuable gifts were given. Perhaps that is the greatest significance regarding them. Could it be that we are to understand from this that token gifts have no place in the genuine worship of Christ?

3. What motivates people to give gifts at Christmastime?

A variety of motives may be noted. Let's start with the highest and most valid motive: (1) *Love.*

People *do* give to others because they care, because they seek the good of the other. When we love family and friends, we want to give to them. Love also prompts us to give to needy people whom we do not know. (2) *Expectations.* Some give only because family, friends, and co-workers are perceived to be expecting gifts. (3) *Tradition.* This motivation is closely allied with *expectations.* Tradition dictates, "That's what we've always done." This is what we're supposed to do at Christmas. (4) *Reciprocity.* You give to me, and I give to you. No one suffers too much, and we all fulfill our obligation. (5) *To impress others.* Distressing as it is, some give so that others will take note of their generosity, liberality, and thoughtfulness. They want others to be impressed! (6) *To obligate others.* Sadly, there are those who give to put people in their debt. These are givers who want to feel powerful and in control. They give to others so that at some future time they can "call in those debts." (7) *To feel good about oneself.* Some give, not because they care about others, but because they care about themselves. Such a person wants to feel that he or she is a noble and generous person.

May our giving at Christmas, and at all other times, emulate the divine motivation: "God so loved . . . that He gave. . . ."

4. List some Christmas traditions that focus appropriately on Christ's birth.

Giving gifts. Jesus was God's gift to the world. The wise men brought gifts.

Caroling. The beautiful music of the season tells of Jesus Christ, pointing all to Him.

Christmas Eve services. Through music and message, Scripture and symbols, our thoughts are focused on Jesus and the meaning of His birth.

Nativity scenes. Visually, we are told the first Christmas story with figurines or life-size reality, as in "living" Nativity scenes sponsored by many churches.

Reading the Christmas story within the family. Many Christian families do this annually. Before any gifts are opened, the true meaning of Christmas is reverently shared with the reading of Luke 2:1-20.

In these ways and more we are reminded of "the true reason for the season"!

Deliverance and Forgiveness

DEVOTIONAL READING: Luke 4:16-21.

LESSON SCRIPTURE: Matthew 8:1—9:8.

PRINTED TEXT: Matthew 8:28—9:8.

Matthew 8:28-34

28 And when he was come to the other side into the country of the Gergesenes, there met him two possessed with devils, coming out of the tombs, exceeding fierce, so that no man might pass by that way.

29 And, behold, they cried out, saying, What have we to do with thee, Jesus, thou Son of God? art thou come hither to torment us before the time?

30 And there was a good way off from them a herd of many swine feeding.

31 So the devils besought him, saying, If thou cast us out, suffer us to go away into the herd of swine.

32 And he said unto them, Go. And when they were come out, they went into the herd of swine: and, behold, the whole herd of swine ran violently down a steep place into the sea, and perished in the waters.

33 And they that kept them fled, and went their ways into the city, and told every thing, and what was befallen to the possessed of the devils.

34 And, behold, the whole city came out to meet Jesus: and when they saw him, they besought him that he would depart out of their coasts.

Matthew 9:1-8

1 And he entered into a ship, and passed over, and came into his own city.

2 And, behold, they brought to him a man sick of the palsy, lying on a bed: and Jesus seeing their faith said unto the sick of the palsy; Son, be of good cheer; thy sins be forgiven thee.

3 And, behold, certain of the scribes said within themselves, This man blasphemeth.

4 And Jesus knowing their thoughts said, Wherefore think ye evil in your hearts?

5 For whether is easier, to say, Thy sins be forgiven thee; or to say, Arise, and walk?

6 But that ye may know that the Son of man hath power on earth to forgive sins, (then saith he to the sick of the palsy,) Arise, take up thy bed, and go unto thine house.

7 And he arose, and departed to his house.

8 But when the multitude saw it, they marveled, and glorified God, which had given such power unto men.

GOLDEN TEXT: Jesus seeing their faith said unto the sick of the palsy; Son, be of good cheer; thy sins be forgiven thee.—Matthew 9:2.

> *Jesus the Fulfillment*
> *(Matthew)*
> Unit 3. Jesus: The Son of David
> (Lessons 5-9)

Lesson Aims

As a result of studying this lesson the students should understand that Jesus, the Son of David:

1. Has power to overcome all the evil forces that seek to destroy man.

2. Has power and authority to forgive and heal the effects of sin in man's heart, life, and body.

3. Is concerned and willing to help each person who comes to Him.

Lesson Outline

INTRODUCTION

    A. Everyone Needs Deliverance

    B. Lesson Background

  I. DELIVERANCE FROM THE FORCES OF EVIL (Matthew 8:28—9:1)

    A. Confrontation With Evil (vv. 28-31)

    B. Deliverance (v. 32)

    C. Rejection (vv. 33—9:1)

 II. DELIVERANCE FROM THE EFFECTS OF EVIL (Matthew 9:2-8)

    A. Forgiveness (v. 2)

       True Wholeness

    B. The Question of Authority (vv. 3-6)

    C. Healing (vv. 7, 8)

       Proving His Word

CONCLUSION

    A. Jesus, Our Deliverer

    B. Let Us Pray

    C. Thought to Remember

Display visual 5 of the visuals packet throughout the class session. Based on the account of the man suffering with palsy, it illustrates the concept of forgiveness. The visual is shown on page 157.

Introduction

A. Everyone Needs Deliverance

Everyone needs deliverance. We need deliverance from the snares of Satan, from the evil that holds us captive and helpless in its power. We need deliverance from our guilt. We need deliverance from the burdens, the disappointments, the problems of life. We must have deliverance, because we cannot deliver ourselves.

The ancient Israelites needed deliverance from the Philistines and other enemy nations, and God raised up David to lead in their deliverance. God sent Jesus to be our Deliverer. Jesus deals with us as individuals, not just as a mass. In the lesson for today we will see three persons whom Jesus delivered. Two He freed from the shackles of Satan, and one He freed from guilt and disease.

B. Lesson Background

In the lessons of Units 1 and 2 of this quarter's study, we have seen that Old Testament prophecies were fulfilled in the ministry of John the Baptist, who heralded Jesus' coming, and in the events surrounding our Savior's birth. Unit 3 further emphasizes Jesus' connection with persons and prophecies of the Old Testament.

As we begin our study of Unit 3 it is important to remember that this is a topical, rather than a chronological, study of the life of Christ. The title of this unit is, "Jesus: The Son of David." The lessons in this unit focus on events that illustrate how Jesus fulfilled the title, "Son of David."

David was the most heroic and beloved of Israel's kings. Under his leadership the nation prevailed over her neighboring enemies and was free and prosperous. David was a good king, not a tyrant. He was concerned for the welfare of his people. His great sin notwithstanding, David was a religious leader who led the people to remain faithful to the Lord. The Lord promised David that in time to come He would set one of his descendants on the throne of an everlasting kingdom. (See 2 Samuel 7:12-16.) This promised descendant came to be known as "the Son of David." The Jews looked for him to be a second David, one who was like David but was even greater than the ancient king.

This lesson shows that Jesus was a deliverer just as David was. Jesus, however, performed the greater work of delivering the people from spiritual enemies and bondage. Furthermore, His work was not limited to the people of the nation of Israel. Jesus brought deliverance for all of mankind.

The first event recorded in our lesson text, the healing of the two demoniacs, took place as Jesus and His disciples reached the eastern shore of the Sea of Galilee after Jesus calmed the storm. The second event, the forgiveness and healing of the paralytic, though it immediately follows in the text, probably took place some time earlier. Both Mark and Luke record it as taking place earlier in Jesus' ministry. This is not a contradiction between the accounts, because Matthew evidently wrote a topical account of Jesus' life rather than a strictly chronological one.

I. Deliverance From the Forces of Evil (Matthew 8:28—9:1)

A. Confrontation With Evil (vv. 28-31)

28. And when he was come to the other side into the country of the Gergesenes, there met him two possessed with devils, coming out of the tombs, exceeding fierce, so that no man might pass by that way.

Jesus and the disciples landed on the eastern shore of Galilee in the region of the *Gergesenes.* A town named Gergesa, or Gerasa, was located near the lake shore. Gadara, a larger town, was located a few miles to the southeast. The people of the area were known by each of these names (see Mark 5:1; Luke 8:26).

Two possessed with devils. Mark and Luke also record this event, but they mention only one man. Probably one was much more prominent in the scene, and so they focused on him. Mark 5:9 indicates that many demons were living in one man, making him exceedingly strong at times. The demons who possessed these men reduced them to a pitiful existence. The men were without rational control. Violent and raving, they wore no clothes and lived in caves that were used as tombs.

The demons actually took over the minds and bodies of these men, producing the extreme effects noted. The same effects to a lesser degree are seen in all who are under the influence of Satan. Such persons often are violent and behave irrationally. The more evil takes over their lives, the more they are cut off from others.

29. And, behold, they cried out, saying, What have we to do with thee, Jesus, thou Son of God? art thou come hither to torment us before the time?

The demons spoke these words. As spirit beings they recognized Jesus to be the Son of God, and they feared Him. They knew that eternal torment was their ultimate destiny and that Jesus had the power to bring that about. They were afraid their torment might begin immediately.

How to Say It

CAPERNAUM. Kuh-*per*-nay-um.
GADARA. *Gad*-uh-ruh.
GERASA. *Gur*-uh-sah.
GERGESA. *Gur*-guh-sah.
GERGESENES. *Gur*-guh-seenz.
PHARISEES. *Fair*-ih-seez.
PHILISTINES. *Fil*-iss-teens or Fi-*liss*-teens.

30, 31. And there was a good way off from them a herd of many swine feeding. So the devils besought him, saying, If thou cast us out, suffer us to go away into the herd of swine.

Many Gentiles lived in this area, so it seems most likely that the hogs were raised by some of them. The request of the demons leads us to conclude that evil spirits will go to extremes to keep from being disembodied. Living in a hog doesn't seem like much of an existence, even for demons, but apparently they considered the alternative to be worse. With our present level of understanding, of course, we cannot explain this.

B. Deliverance (v. 32)

32. And he said unto them, Go. And when they were come out, they went into the herd of swine: and, behold, the whole herd of swine ran violently down a steep place into the sea, and perished in the waters.

Mark 5:13 tells us that about two thousand swine were in the herd. Apparently the demons couldn't control the swine as they could the two men, for in their terror and madness the hogs stampeded down the hill. In the locale where this event took place, the hill slopes steeply down to within about forty feet of the shore. The herd rushed on, plunged into the lake, and were drowned.

Jesus, who knows all things, surely knew that this would happen, and this raises the question of why He allowed the destruction of this property. It seems likely that He permitted it in order to provide a very dramatic demonstration of the forces that were at work. These events showed Jesus to be a deliverer and the demons to be destroyers. The deliverance of the demoniacs drew attention, but coupled with the destruction of the herd the impact on the people of the area was much stronger. Intended or not, this was the evident result, because, as verse 34 mentions, everyone from the city came out to see what had happened.

It has become common in modern times to discount the existence of demons as superstition. And many Christians believe that demons existed on earth in Jesus' day only. It is true that in the New Testament period there was a concentration of demon possession. It is evident that when God was bringing to fulfillment His plan of redemption through His Son, Satan did all in his power to oppose Him. However, there is no indication in Scripture that all demon activity has ended. Our knowledge of the spirit world is extremely limited. From Hebrews 1:13, 14 we learn that God's angels are "ministering spirits, sent forth to minister for them who shall be heirs of salvation." Since this is so, is it too much to believe that demonic spirits exist to achieve Satan's purposes? Exactly what form this spiritual activity takes is difficult to say.

The apostle Peter warns that "the devil, as a roaring lion, walketh about, seeking whom he may devour" (1 Peter 5:8). We are urged to resist him by standing firm in the faith (v. 9). Those who disregard the Bible's warnings of danger from Satan and engage in witchcraft, spiritualism, and the like are seeking a communion with a spiritual power that can only lead to the most horrible kind of enslavement.

Most persons, however, are not possessed by demons in the way the two men in our text were. But this does not mean that people today are not bound by Satan's power. All sin and come under the curse of death. And all sinners are bound by the chains of sin, being unable to resist it and unable to escape its grim curse. Jesus came to deliver all from this bondage, to rescue us from Satan's dark kingdom and power and bring us into His glorious kingdom of light (Colossians 1:13). Jesus is willing and able to be deliverer for all who call upon Him today.

C. Rejection (vv. 33—9:1)

33, 34. And they that kept them fled, and went their ways into the city, and told every thing, and what was befallen to the possessed of the devils. And, behold, the whole city came out to meet Jesus: and when they saw him, they besought him that he would depart out of their coasts.

The swineherds, filled with consternation, fear, and amazement, quickly carried the news to the nearby city. Almost everyone in town hurried out to the scene, and when they saw Jesus they asked Him to leave.

Why did these people react this way? Were they afraid that Jesus would cause further economic losses? Were they angry? Perhaps they realized that they were in the presence of deity and they feared Him. It is impossible to say what their reasons were, but we can say with certainty that they were very foolish in asking Jesus to leave.

Jesus had performed a wonderful, miraculous work of deliverance on the two demoniacs. Surely many sick people and perhaps even other demoniacs lived in the region. These townspeople would have been wise to beg Jesus to stay and heal others. He did as much elsewhere. The miracle established that Jesus was sent from God; and so they would have been wise to ask Him to stay and teach them God's will. He did elsewhere. If Jesus had stayed, He would have enriched people's lives many times more than the cost of the dead hogs. As it was, only the

two men, and perhaps their families, profited from Jesus' visit on this occasion.

The continuing tragedy is that many people today refuse to allow Jesus to come into their lives. They reject the deliverance, freedom, and healing that He can give and wants to give. They forfeit so much by making the same foolish decision that these people made.

Could it be that all of us keep Jesus out of some areas of our lives? Are there sins that we won't let Him help us overcome? Are there hurts that we won't let Him heal?

9:1. And he entered into a ship, and passed over, and came into his own city.

Jesus did as the people requested and returned to Capernaum on the western side of the lake.

II. Deliverance From the Effects of Evil (Matthew 9:2-8)

In chapter 8 Matthew has given a collection of Jesus' miracles, showing the different kinds of miracles Jesus performed in this early period of His Galilean ministry. To this list he now adds the healing of the paralytic in Capernaum, although this miracle probably occurred at an earlier time in that city.

A. Forgiveness (v. 2)

2. And, behold, they brought to him a man sick of the palsy, lying on a bed: and Jesus seeing their faith said unto the sick of the palsy; Son, be of good cheer; thy sins be forgiven thee.

From the parallel accounts of this event (Mark 2 and Luke 5), we learn that Jesus was teaching in a house that was filled to overflowing. Scribes and Pharisees from many cities of Galilee and Judea, and even from Jerusalem, were among the great crowd that filled the house in Capernaum. *They brought to him a man sick of the palsy.* Mark 2:3 says there were four men carrying the stricken man. *Palsy* is a general term, but evidently the man was paralyzed to the extent that he could not move about on his own. The *bed* on which he was lying was simply a mat.

Jesus seeing their faith. The faith of all five of these men was demonstrated in the unusual steps taken to get the paralytic into Jesus' presence. Unable to enter the crowded room, the four carried their friend up to the roof of the house, broke loose some of the tiling, and lowered him to the feet of Jesus.

Son, be of good cheer; thy sins be forgiven thee. The Jews commonly believed that disease was the direct result of some personal sin (compare John 9:2). Perhaps this man felt a great burden of guilt and condemned himself for his pitiable condition. Perhaps he feared that Jesus would not heal him because of his sins. If that was the case, then Jesus' words certainly were reason for him to *be of good cheer*. Jesus' statement was not a prayer that the man be forgiven; it was a statement of fact, a direct pardon. The paralytic came to Jesus seeking healing, but he received much more.

TRUE WHOLENESS

Wholeness is the longed-for vision of man. We want to be free from disease, injury, disability—any and all infirmities of the body. Andy Cole wanted wholeness, too. However, his dissolute life, including addiction to alcohol and drugs, prevented him from coming even close to it. Dissipation had disturbed his emotional stability and diminished his work skills. In his thirties, he was already an old man, shunned by most and an alien to his own family. Those who had tried to help Andy had long before given up in their attempts.

Then Andy heard the gospel—the message of God's love and forgiveness—and he let Jesus come into his life. What nothing else could do, Andy's genuine conversion to Christ accomplished. The scars of abuse remained, but Andy, new in spirit and forgiven of sin, found freedom from its chains by believing and following Jesus. He became a man of integrity and a Christian example to all. Andy Cole's changed life was little short of miraculous.

We make a mistake if we treat symptoms only and neglect their cause. Jesus knew that sin is the cause of all of our problems, and He provided its cure. Only in Him can we be made truly whole.   —W. P.

B. The Question of Authority
(vv. 3-6)

3. And, behold, certain of the scribes said within themselves, This man blasphemeth.

The *scribes*, experts in the law, immediately seized on Jesus' words. Their reasoning *within themselves* went like this; No one can forgive sin except God, and any man who claims the prerogatives of God is guilty of blasphemy (so far, they were correct). But their conclusion that Jesus was only a man, hence guilty of blasphemy, was false.

4. And Jesus knowing their thoughts said, Wherefore think ye evil in your hearts?

Hearts are an open book to Jesus, and He knew *their thoughts*. These scribes probably were rather startled when Jesus looked them in the eyes and revealed their evil, accusing thoughts for all to hear.

5. For whether is easier, to say, Thy sins be forgiven thee; or to say, Arise, and walk?

visual 5

Both of these statements are easy *to say*, but both require God's power to perform. In effect, Jesus asked which was easier to demonstrate. Anyone could claim to forgive sins, because it would be impossible to know whether the sins were actually forgiven. But if someone said, *Arise, and walk*, immediate, visible, miraculous results would be required to show that that one possessed supernatural power.

6. But that ye may know that the Son of man hath power on earth to forgive sins, (then saith he to the sick of the palsy,) Arise, take up thy bed, and go unto thine house.

Jesus proposed to demonstrate His invisible power and authority *to forgive sins* by visibly demonstrating His power to heal. If Jesus could heal the man, which could be done only by God's power, then it would prove that He also could forgive sins. This is based on the premise that God would not give anyone the miraculous power to heal the most hopeless physical ailments if that person was at the same time blaspheming. If Jesus could heal the man, then He could not be blaspheming.

Without hesitation Jesus ordered the paralyzed man to get up, pick up his bed, and walk home. The truth would soon be known.

C. Healing (vv. 7, 8)

7. And he arose, and departed to his house.

Instantaneously the man was healed and able to do what Jesus commanded (see Mark 2:12). One can imagine that he raced home in order to be the first to tell the joyous news to his family.

PROVING HIS WORD

Millie Phillips, the wife of a Canadian preacher, is an excellent fisher. One day, however, she made a claim that seemed too bold. Her husband and his brother just returned from a morning of fishing on Buffalo Lake in Alberta, each with his limit of ten pike. Millie said, "Let me fish for just one hour, with Jim running the boat and taking off the hook the fish I catch, and I'll catch as many as you did. And mine will be bigger!" Jim agreed, and in a few minutes they were out on the lake.

In one hour they were back at the shore. Millie had her limit of ten fish, and they were as big as, and perhaps bigger than, the fish the men had taken all morning to catch. It really was no contest. Millie had proved her word.

To make a claim is one thing; to prove one's words is another. The scribes thought, "Blasphemy," when Jesus said, to the paralytic, "Thy sins be forgiven thee." His claim to possess divine authority to forgive sins was proved, however, when He demonstrated divine power by healing the paralytic. The greater healing was the forgiveness of sins. The proof that Jesus could offer such a gift silenced His accusers.

In Christ we have the promise of the forgiveness of our sins. Must we wait to see proof that He can do all he has promised, or will we walk by faith in His Word?   —W. P.

8. But when the multitudes saw it, they marveled, and glorified God, which had given such power unto men.

Jesus was vindicated. His power and authority were demonstrated beyond reasonable refutation. *The multitudes*, seeing what happened, *marveled.* They were astounded. They knew of Jesus' power and believed He could heal, else they would not have come to Him in the first place. Beyond this, Jesus had challenged them to think more deeply about the source and extent of His power. He claimed power that God did not delegate—the power to forgive. The discerning among the people must have realized the implications, Jesus claimed to be equal with God, and He had given sufficient proof to establish His claim.

The reaction of the scribes is not mentioned. While they may have marveled, it is unlikely that they *glorified God.* Sadly, most of the Pharisees and scribes chose to remain blind to the truth and to oppose Jesus throughout His ministry.

Jesus has furnished sufficient evidence for belief in Him today. He does not ignore the educated and sophisticated and appeal only to the masses. Sadly, however, the more worldly wisdom one has the harder it seems for that person to see the simple, obvious truth that Jesus is indeed the Son of God.

Again, the Son of David was greater than His noble ancestor. David could not deliver his people from guilt; nor could he heal. But He who descended from him could do both.

Conclusion

A. Jesus, Our Deliverer

Today's lesson shows that Jesus can deliver us in two important ways.

First, He is able to deliver us from the power of Satan. Many, on their own, have tried to break sin's dreadful hold on their lives, only to fail. Jesus delivers today just as surely as He delivered the two possessed of demons. He takes the liar, the drunkard, the thief, the adulterer, the abuser, the addict, and delivers them from the bondage of their sins. He has changed countless lives. He can change the lives of the people in your class, of their families, of their friends and neighbors.

Second, Jesus delivers us from the dreadful effects of sin, namely guilt and death. We all need forgiveness, and He extends it. We all need fresh starts, and He gives them. And those He forgives He also heals. It is true that we still suffer disease and death, but Jesus has conquered death so that He might deliver us from it once and for all when He returns to gather His own.

David was a great deliverer, but a greater Deliverer has come. Jesus delivers people of all nations from the worst of enemies. May all claim His deliverance, and not make the foolish error of those who asked Jesus to depart from their midst. To reject Jesus is to reject the only possible hope of deliverance.

B. Let Us Pray

Lord of all, thank You for sending our Deliverer. He has overcome Your enemy and ours, Satan. Through Him You have freed us from the bonds of evil so that we might serve You in righteousness. We are proud yet humbled, overjoyed even overwhelmed, to acknowledge Him as the Son of David, our eternal King. Help us, Lord, to be faithful to Him. Amen.

C. Thought to Remember

David was a great deliverer, but a greater deliverer has come—Jesus Christ, the Son of God.

Home Daily Bible Readings

Monday, Dec. 26—Teaching on the Mountain (Matthew 5:1-13)

Tuesday, Dec. 27—Do Not Judge Others (Matthew 7:1-5)

Wednesday, Dec. 28—Hearers and Doers of Jesus' Words (Matthew 7:24-29)

Thursday, Dec. 29—Healing a Leper and a Centurion's Servant (Matthew 8:1-13)

Friday, Dec. 30—Healing and Fulfillment of Prophecy (Matthew 8:14-22)

Saturday, Dec. 31—Restoring Two Demoniacs (Matthew 8:23-34)

Sunday, Jan. 1—Forgiving and Healing a Paralytic (Matthew 9:1-8)

Learning by Doing

This page contains an alternate lesson plan emphasizing learning activities. Classes
desiring such student involvement will find these suggestions helpful.

Learning Goals

As a result of participating in today's lesson, a student will be able to:

1. Understand that Jesus has the power to overcome all the evil forces that seek to destroy man.

2. Explain how evil comes in many different forms.

3. Respond personally to Jesus' deliverance and forgiveness.

Into the Lesson

Begin by posing this question for consideration and discussion:

Is it worse (a) to be totally under Satan's control and hopelessly lost without any knowledge of Jesus; or (b) to be blinded by the arrogance of self-righteousness when you really don't understand Jesus at all?

Allow a brief time for the students to discuss the question, and affirm the thinking that is expressed. The purpose of the question is to get people involved and thinking, so don't worry about trying to reach a "right" answer.

Explain that today's lesson deals with the spiritual warfare that is recorded in Matthew 8:28—9:8. A variety of persons were involved, and each responded differently to Jesus' deliverance and forgiveness.

Into the Word

Divide the class into two groups. Assign one group the first narrative (Matthew 8:28—9:1) and the second group the other narrative (9:2-8). Ask each group to develop a five-minute TV newscast of the event assigned to it, with one or two reporters and others playing the various roles (the first group has demoniacs, swineherds, and townspeople; the second group has a paralytic, those who carried him, the scribes, and the observing crowd). The students are to work together within their groups to create the dialogue for interviews concerning what events happened, how they happened, what the results were, why the persons thought the events happened, and how they felt about them. For example, questions might be: *How long had you been demon-possessed? Why did you want Jesus to leave? What did you think when Jesus said you were forgiven? Why were you scribes so upset when Jesus said the man was forgiven?* Encourage creativity within the facts presented in the Scripture. The point is to probe the realities of the spiritual warfare that took place and the reactions of the various people in both of these incidents.

After each group has had adequate time to prepare, each is to present its newscast. Lead directly into a discussion with this question: *When people realized that Jesus had the power and authority to overcome evil and forgive sin, why were their reactions to Him so different?* Wrap up the discussion with conclusions regarding how evil appears in different ways in these events (the demoniacs, the paralytic, and the scribes) and how the reactions of the Gergesene townspeople and the Capernaum crowd were so different. The important thing is for each of us to respond in faith to Jesus' deliverance and forgiveness.

Into Life

Brainstorm with the class how evil presents itself in our world today. Some possible answers include: demon possession (see comments under verse 32), cults, the New Age Movement, gangs, rising crime rates, and drug abuse. Write the responses on a chalkboard in one column. Now ask how evil can show up in *our* lives, and list the responses in a second column on the chalkboard. Possible responses include: angry outbursts, materialism, gossip, pursuit of pleasure.

Have the class divide into groups of four or five persons each to discuss in what ways they could relate to each of the persons who were involved in the events of today's text.

1. The two demoniacs (out of control, straining relationships).

2. The Gergesene townspeople (concerned with possessions, uneasy about power encounters, unsure about Jesus' impact on life-style).

3. The paralytic (weak, a victim, needing forgiveness).

4. The scribes (self-righteous, critical, overly skeptical).

5. The Capernaum crowd (filled with awe because of Jesus' power, praising God).

Let those who are willing share their responses with the class. Then have the class separate into pairs. Ask each person to share a response to these two questions and then pray for one another: How do I need Jesus' deliverance and forgiveness right now? How will I respond?

Let's Talk It Over

The questions on this page are designed to encourage review of the lesson Scriptures and to promote discussion of the lesson by the class. The answers provided are only discussion starters. Let your class talk it over from there.

1. Why did the Gergesenes beg Jesus to leave their territory after He had cast the demons out of two persons who were demon-possessed

The Scriptures do not indicate the people's motivation. Two suggestions have been made by Bible students, however. The first is that the residents may have feared additional economic loss. They had suffered financially already—when the demoniacs were healed, two thousand hogs were drowned in the sea. Perhaps the citizens of the area were more concerned about protecting their possessions than they were about the relief of human suffering that Jesus could bring.

Others suggest that the people feared Jesus' supernatural power. The people may have feared that the power that freed the demon-possessed and commanded demons might be turned on them for their sins.

2. Why do people today reject Jesus?

Several significant reasons may be noted.

(1) People are reluctant to abandon pride and pleasure. When they hear Jesus' demands of discipleship, they balk. Who wants to "deny oneself" and "die to self"? At the root of all sin lies pride: self-will, self-exaltation. Accepting Jesus as Savior and Lord strikes the axe-blow to the taproot of sin. And much of what the world regards as "pleasure" centers around sinful behavior. It is the perception of many that to accept Jesus is to forego all that is enjoyable.

(2) Some persons fear that the demands may be greater than they can handle. They fear that "they are not good enough" to live up to the standards expected of Jesus' disciples.

(3) There are those who fear that accepting Christ will cost them dearly. They will lose popularity. What "others" think dominates their decision-making. They fear that relationships will be affected—they will lose friends. Or they fear that discipleship will cost them financially, in one way or another.

(4) Some wish to minimize pain—they do not want to suffer, nor do they want their comfort zone disturbed. Thinking that they will be in the minority, they fear that they may become a martyr.

(5) Many persons feel no need of Jesus Christ. After all, they are getting along very well, thank you. They have everything they need—good job, nice family, comfortable home, excellent health, and the prospects of a great retirement—in short, the "good life," according to Madison Avenue. What do they need with Jesus?

3. What is the connection between sin and human sickness and suffering?

It was commonly believed among the Jews in the first century that there was a direct and an immediate relationship between sin and a person's sickness and suffering. In response to the disciples' question regarding the man born blind, Jesus declared that that conclusion was not valid in every instance (John 9:2, 3).

It is true of course, that sin is the underlying cause of all sickness, suffering, and death. These resulted from the disobedience of the first human pair (Genesis 3:3, 14-19), and it is easily seen that some sickness and suffering *is* the direct result of a person's sinful behavior (for example, sexually transmitted diseases and suffering that arises from drugs and alcohol abuse). However, such a close connection between sin and suffering cannot be established for every human disorder.

Not every person suffers from a serious physical disorder such as that of the paralytic in our lesson text. But we all need spiritual healing, because we all have sinned. By making the paralytic's body whole, Jesus gave proof that He has the power to forgive sins and thus provide the spiritual healing we need.

4. What can be said about the friends who carried the paralytic to Jesus, and what lessons can we draw from this incident?

The friends of the paralytic had exceptional character traits. First, they were faithful to their friend; they did not abandon him in his stricken condition. Physically they carried him to Jesus—not an easy task. Second, they would let nothing hinder them from getting their friend to Jesus—not the overflowing crowd in the house where Jesus was, nor the roof over His head! Third, when they lowered the man into Jesus' presence, *their* faith was noted by Jesus. Their faith in Jesus' ability to bring healing opened the door to the power of the Lord for their friend.

If we are truly concerned for the lost, we will do all in our power to bring them to Jesus, where they can find healing for their souls.

Jesus, the Son of David

DEVOTIONAL READING: Isaiah 42:1-9.

LESSON SCRIPTURE: Matthew 12.

PRINTED TEXT: Matthew 12:9-23.

Matthew 12:9-23

9 And when he was departed thence, he went into their synagogue:

10 And, behold, there was a man which had his hand withered. And they asked him, saying, Is it lawful to heal on the sabbath days? that they might accuse him.

11 And he said unto them, What man shall there be among you, that shall have one sheep, and if it fall into a pit on the sabbath day, will he not lay hold on it, and lift it out?

12 How much then is a man better than a sheep? Wherefore it is lawful to do well on the sabbath days.

13 Then saith he to the man, Stretch forth thine hand. And he stretched it forth; and it was restored whole, like as the other.

14 Then the Pharisees went out, and held a council against him, how they might destroy him.

15 But when Jesus knew it, he withdrew himself from thence: and great multitudes followed him, and he healed them all;

16 And charged them that they should not make him known:

17 That it might be fulfilled which was spoken by Isaiah the prophet, saying,

18 Behold my servant, whom I have chosen; my beloved, in whom my soul is well pleased: I will put my Spirit upon him, and he shall show judgment to the Gentiles.

19 He shall not strive, nor cry; neither shall any man hear his voice in the streets.

20 A bruised reed shall he not break, and smoking flax shall he not quench, till he send forth judgment unto victory.

21 And in his name shall the Gentiles trust.

22 Then was brought unto him one possessed with a devil, blind, and dumb: and he healed him, insomuch that the blind and dumb both spake and saw.

23 And all the people were amazed, and said, Is not this the Son of David?

GOLDEN TEXT: It is lawful to do well on the sabbath days.—Matthew 12:12.

Lesson Aims

After this lesson the students should:

1. Be convinced that doing God's will is more important than keeping man-made traditions.

2. Be able to state at least two facets of Jesus' servanthood.

3. See clearly that Jesus is the true Son of David.

Lesson Outline

INTRODUCTION
  A. Eyes That Will Not See
  B. Lesson Background
 I. LORD OF THE SABBATH (Matthew 12:9-14)
  A. A Double-Edged Question (vv. 9, 10)
  B. Do Good on the Sabbath! (vv. 11-13)
  C. Mindless Tradition Kills Truth (v. 14)
    Conflicting Values
II. GOD'S SERVANT (Matthew 12:15-21)
  A. Many Are Healed (vv. 15, 16)
  B. The Chosen Servant (vv. 17-21)
III. THE SON OF DAVID (Matthew 12:22, 23)
  A. Sight and Speech (v. 22)
  B. Seeing Jesus Clearly (v. 23)
    Why?
CONCLUSION
  A. What Do We Give the Lord?
  B. Let Us Pray
  C. Thought to Remember

Visual 6 of the visuals packet is a helpful chart contrasting Jesus' view of people with the view held by the Pharisees. The visual is shown on page 164.

Introduction

A. Eyes That Will Not See

No one is so blind as the one who closes his or her eyes to the truth and refuses to see. To some extent, we all close our eyes to things we don't want to see. We refuse to see a loved one's failing health. We refuse to see problems in relationships. We refuse to see the need to make hard choices and hard changes. We refuse to see our own faults.

Hatred also causes deliberate blindness. Hatred can be so strong that it causes one to see truth or fairness or innocence. The Pharisees had such hatred for Jesus. They refused to hear the truth of His words. They refused to acknowledge the power of His miracles. They were blind to the obvious.

Others, however, looked at Jesus with open eyes. They saw His miraculous deeds and understood that these words verified His message. They accepted what He said, and Jesus was able to show them many things.

We must ask ourselves whether or not we have open eyes.

B. Lesson Background

The Pharisees, who were offended by Jesus, continually sought ways to criticize and attack Him. One charge they pursued vigorously was that Jesus and His disciples violated the Sabbath. The first part of Matthew 12 introduces this controversy, as the Pharisees criticized the disciples for supposedly violating the Sabbath by plucking heads of grain and eating them. Jesus said they were innocent (see verse 7) and appealed to Hosea 6:6, to prove His point. He also appealed to the case of David, who on one occasion ate bread of the tabernacle, which was intended for the priests only. This is interesting in the context of this lesson, which proclaims Jesus as the Son of David. The Son appealed to the example of the father (Matthew 12:1-7).

Jesus concluded that confrontation by stating, "For the Son of man is Lord even of the sabbath day" (v. 8). In other words, Jesus, as the lawgiver himself, had the authority to interpret the law of the Sabbath and pronounce whether or not it had been violated. The Pharisees caught the implications of this statement, and at the earliest opportunity sought to trap Him regarding appropriate conduct on the Sabbath.

I. Lord of the Sabbath
(Matthew 12:9-14)

A. A Double-Edged Question (vv. 9, 10)

9. And when he was departed thence, he went into their synagogue.

Matthew's transitional statement *when he was departed thence*, is intended only to convey that he is moving from one event to another. Luke makes it clear that this confrontation in the synagogue took place on another Sabbath than the one just mentioned, perhaps the next one. However, it did occur in *their synagogue*. Therefore, the same Pharisees who questioned Jesus about the grain now put another question before Him.

10. And, behold, there was a man which had his hand withered. And they asked him, saying, Is it lawful to heal on the sabbath days? that they might accuse him.

Whether by accident or by prearrangement, a man with a *withered* hand was in the synagogue on this day. The Pharisees asked Jesus, *Is it lawful to heal on the sabbath days?* According to their tradition, certain treatments might be given on the Sabbath to keep a patient from becoming worse; but efforts to bring healing were not to be made until the following day. It seems clear that these legalists expected Jesus to heal this impaired man, for they posed this question *that they might accuse him,* that is, that they might publicly declare Him to be a Sabbath breaker.

This incident reveals the perversity of the hearts of these men. They had seen Jesus heal many who were diseased, disabled, and demon-possessed, and they knew that His healings were genuine miracles. Going on the logical presumption that only God can work miracles, (and take note that all of Jesus' miracles brought only healing, and not hurt, to mankind), they should have realized that Jesus was from God. As Nicodemus said, "No man can do these miracles that thou doest, except God be with him" (John 3:2). At the very least they should have regarded Him as a prophet. In fact, Jesus worked so many miracles and such great miracles that He eclipsed any of the Old Testament prophets. And if Jesus was a prophet, then they should have come to Him humbly seeking God's message and God's will. But they were not seekers of truth. Closing their eyes to it, they approached Jesus with the intention of overcoming Him and obscuring the truth.

B. Do Good on the Sabbath! (vv. 11-13)

11. And he said unto them, What man shall there be among you, that shall have one sheep, and if it fall into a pit on the sabbath day, will he not lay hold on it, and lift it out?

As He did on many occasions, Jesus answered His questioners with questions of His own. In so doing He exposed their hypocrisy and wickedness. So here He posed a situation that would have been familiar to all. He asked what one of them would do if one of his sheep fell *into a pit on the sabbath day.* Would he say, "Hold on little sheep; I'll rescue you tomorrow"? Everyone in the synagogue knew the answer to this. Anyone would naturally rescue the sheep immediately, even on the Sabbath, and no one would accuse him of breaking the Sabbath for doing so.

12. How much then is a man better than a sheep? Wherefore it is lawful to do well on the sabbath days.

If it is permissible to help a sheep on the Sabbath, then obviously *it is lawful to do well* to one's fellowman *on the sabbath days.* This conclusion is so clear and powerful that it exposes the foolish-

---

How to Say It

ISAIAH. Eye-*zay*-uh.
NICODEMUS. Nick-uh-*dee*-mus (strong accent on *dee*).
PHARISEES. *Fair*-ih-seez.

---

ness of the original question. Why would anyone even ask if healing on the Sabbath is right? On the face of it, it is always right to heal and help.

One might even ask how it would be possible to heal on the Sabbath if God did not approve it. Who could heal but by God's power? If a miracle of healing were done on the Sabbath, it must be done with God's permission and active cooperation.

God's Commandment regarding the Sabbath was, "Six days shalt thou labor, and do all thy work: but the seventh day is the sabbath of the Lord thy God: in it thou shalt not do any work" (Exodus 20:9, 10). "Labor" means all the work involved in earning a living and running a household, be it plowing, building fences, making pots, cooking, cleaning, or any such thing. God allotted six days for these activities, but prohibited them on the seventh. The idea was for the people to have rest from their daily toils. These were the kinds of activities that were prohibited. The Jewish scholars' interpretations of this Commandment over the course of time became hardened into traditions, which transformed the Sabbath law into something that God never intended it to be.

13. Then saith he to the man, Stretch forth thine hand. And he stretched it forth; and it was restored whole, like as the other.

Jesus did not do any visible work of any kind. He simply told the man to *stretch forth* his hand. Jesus did not even say that He intended to heal it. Yet when the man stretched out his hand *it was restored whole.* That which had been useless to the man became strong and functional. It was obvious to all that Jesus used His power to heal the man's hand, but what work did He do? He did not prepare an ointment or massage the hand or even touch it. How could the Pharisees object to this? Yet they did.

C. Mindless Tradition Kills Truth (v. 14)

14. Then the Pharisees went out, and held a council against him, how they might destroy him.

The Pharisees left the synagogue in such a rage that they immediately began to make plans to *destroy him.* Their actions make obvious that they really had no interest in learning whether healing on the Sabbath was legal. They wanted one thing only: to discredit and eliminate Jesus. How twisted and perverted and hardened their consciences were! They could not approve an act of mercy on the Sabbath, but they saw nothing wrong with plotting murder on the sacred day.

We see from this that the Pharisees' mindless devotion to their traditions blinded them to the truth revealed by Jesus. He gave sufficient proof that He spoke with God's authority, but the Pharisees rejected this proof and Jesus along with it.

Let us take care not to harden our hearts against Jesus, as the Pharisees did. Rather, whatever Jesus has said in explaining God's will, let us accept, no matter how it may contradict what we have believed or done, or want to do or don't want to do. May our attitude be that we will do whatever Jesus has said we must do in order to be pleasing and acceptable to God, even if it means changing our lives, our beliefs, or our traditions.

CONFLICTING VALUES

Hundreds of thousands of people died of starvation in 1992. The news of the drought and the desperate need for food to sustain life touched the world. From many nations, and especially from the United States, millions of tons of wheat and other food staples, along with medical supplies, poured into ships and transport planes to relieve the hunger and to fight illness and disease.

Volunteer workers from many relief organizations came to Somalia to see that the food was properly distributed and that medical aid was offered. These volunteers were committed to relieving the suffering of the Somali people; but factional warlords, bent on gaining control of the land, hindered them from their humanitarian efforts. The warlords' greed for power was more important in their eyes than the lives of their suffering countrymen.

As one relief worker put it, "The old and young get the least aid, but I have not seen an unfed soldier on either side." Such always seems to be the result when self-interest and concern for the needy meet head-on.

visual 6

When Jesus healed the sick and infirm, there should have been universal rejoicing among all of His countrymen. Instead, the Pharisees plotted Jesus' destruction. They rejected Heaven's values and replaced them with their own. Let us not be guilty of the same.   —W. P.

II. God's Servant
(Matthew 12:15-21)

A. Many Are Healed (vv. 15, 16)

15. But when Jesus knew it, he withdrew himself from thence: and great multitudes followed him, and he healed them all.

Aware of the Pharisees' intention to kill Him, Jesus *withdrew* from the area. He would not use force or miraculous power to resist His enemies. Instead, He fulfilled His own injunction to His apostles: "When they persecute you in this city, flee ye into another" (Matthew 10:23).

Great multitudes followed him. The leaders may have been angered by Jesus' action, but not the common people. Many persons afflicted with all sorts of diseases and disabilities thronged after Him, hoping that He would heal them. Mark indicates that the crowds came from Galilee, Judea, Jerusalem, and from areas inhabited by Gentiles (Mark 3:7, 8). This throws light on Matthew's statement in verse 21 below. *He healed them all.* Jesus may have been angered by the hardhearted, hypocritical leaders, but He had unbounded compassion for those who suffered.

16. And charged them that they should not make him known.

It is easy to see how the people's excitement resulting from Jesus' miracles could have gotten out of control. Among His hearers were many militaristic Zealots, who desired to throw off forcibly the rule of Rome. If the knowledge of Jesus' miraculous power spread, the people might be encouraged to rebel, expecting Him to use His power to overcome the enemy. But such a program had no part in Jesus' ministry. He came to reveal God's will to man, and the miracles were signs to show that the revelation came from God. Overemphasis on the miracles could cause the people to ignore the revelation.

B. The Chosen Servant (vv. 17-21)

17. That it might be fulfilled which was spoken by Isaiah the prophet, saying.

The following four verses are a quotation from Isaiah 42:1-4. Matthew says that the prophecy of these verses was fulfilled in Jesus.

18. Behold my servant, whom I have chosen; my beloved, in whom my soul is well pleased: I will put my Spirit upon him, and he shall show judgment to the Gentiles.

Isaiah spoke of the Christ as God's servant, who was loved by God and who pleased God by doing His will. It is obvious that Jesus was He. See Matthew 3:17. God's Spirit came to Jesus when He was baptized, and remained with Him (Matthew 3:16; John 1:32, 33). Jesus' miracles gave further demonstration that God was pleased with Him.

He shall show judgment to the Gentiles. To show judgment is to bring justice, to rule justly. The prophecy stated that Christ's kingdom was for all nations. As noted in the comment under verse 15, Gentiles were among the multitudes who followed Jesus, even at this time. Before returning to His Father in Heaven, Jesus commanded that the gospel message be proclaimed to all nations so that the Gentiles as well as the Jews might be included in God's kingdom (Matthew 28:19).

19. He shall not strive, nor cry; neither shall any man hear his voice in the streets.

This verse and the next give a general description of the manner in which Jesus conducted His ministry. This verse does not mean that the Christ would not teach in public. To the contrary, He preached and taught continually. And repeatedly He was engaged in controversy with the religious leaders, but He always moved to keep such controversies from becoming more intense. In His teaching He usually did not raise His voice in strife; instead, He spoke quietly and logically. A rabble-rouser might take to *the streets* to stir up a mob and create an uprising against the authorities, and this is exactly what many wanted Jesus to do. Stirring up a violent mob, however, was just what He was trying to avoid.

20. A bruised reed shall he not break, and smoking flax shall he not quench, till he send forth judgment unto victory.

A bruised reed is hardly strong enough to stand erect, or perhaps it is bent with its head toward the earth. In this weakened condition it is easily broken off entirely. *Flax* was used for lamp wicks. A wick that is smoking is one that has been left untended, and it will soon die out. That God's chosen servant would not break the weak reed or extinguish the flickering wick was an emphatic way of declaring that His mission was to heal and restore, not to destroy. His manner would be to show tenderness and compassion, not harshness.

This is exactly the kind of ministry that Jesus conducted. When He walked among His people during His earthly ministry, there were brought to Him those who were diseased, disabled, and possessed of demons, and He healed them. Tenderly He cared for those who were hurt, not only physically but spiritually also, those under stress, caught up in sin, oppressed, depressed, and downtrodden. These too He restored to wholeness. Jesus' compassion extends to us today. To those who respond to Him and accept Him, He shows himself to be tender and loving. Christ knows the weakness of His people and will not lean on them too much or give them a load heavy enough to break them. See 1 Corinthians 10:13. His people are the light of the world (Matthew 5:14). Often their light is smoky and dim, but Christ preserves them instead of putting them out. How long will He continue to do this? *Till he send forth judgment unto victory.* Though in His ministry Jesus showed tenderness and compassion, He will be the conqueror of all. In the end the gospel will prevail; Christ will bring His just and righteous kingdom to complete victory.

21. And in his name shall the Gentiles trust.

Isaiah's prophecy indicated that Christ's kingdom would be opened to the Gentiles (v. 18). In this verse that thought is completed; the Gentiles would respond to the invitation and receive the gospel. They would place their hope in Jesus Christ and trust Him to be their Savior and king.

Verse 21 of our text is different from our version of Isaiah, but it follows the Greek version that was used in Matthew's time.

III. The Son of David
(Matthew 12:22, 23)
A. Sight and Speech (v. 22)

22. Then was brought unto him one possessed with a devil, blind, and dumb: and he healed him, insomuch that the blind and dumb both spake and saw.

Demons evidently had differing effects on those whom they possessed. The man afflicted here was made *blind* and *dumb.* Jesus cast the demon out of the man and *healed him,* so that he could both see and speak.

This miraculous healing gave sight to the man who had been possessed by a demon, and it also caused the people who witnessed it to take a close look at Jesus, perhaps really seeing Him for the first time. They saw one who was much more than an ordinary man.

B. Seeing Jesus clearly (v. 23)

23. And all the people were amazed, and said, Is not this the Son of David?

From our perspective, some two thousand years removed, we may be inclined to become casual when reading about another healing; but on the day it occurred, *all the people were amazed.* They were so impressed that they asked each other whether Jesus could be *the Son of David.* This was equivalent to wondering whether He was the Messiah. How this reaction contrasts to that of the Pharisees! Those leaders of the people were blinded by their jealousy, hatred, and traditions. These common people, however, had the honesty to consider Jesus and His works objectively. Doing so led them to ask the right question.

Matthew included this question not only as a record of the thoughts of the people on that day long ago, but as a question for all of his readers to consider and answer for themselves. Indeed, the purpose of his book is to record enough of Jesus' deeds and words to convince people from that day forward that Jesus is in fact the Son of David, the Messiah.

WHY?

"We prayed for both newborn twins. We believe God hears our prayers. One baby lived, and the other died. Why did God make a choice? Why weren't both healed?" The young parents' inquiry to their minister came from faith, not from doubt. The loss of their child brought them seeking an answer to a great mystery. When we pray, why do some become well and others die? Why, under the skilled hands of a gifted surgeon, does one heart patient survive to live a full life and another perish during the procedure?

Perhaps we view healing from the wrong perspective. Death will come to us all. Even Lazarus, who was raised from the grave by Jesus, died again. The main purpose of Jesus' miracles of healing must be kept in mind. First and foremost they attested to His deity. The crowds who saw Jesus heal the demon-possessed man who was blind and mute asked the right question. They did not challenge the miracle. They had seen it occur. They knew the Messiah was to come, and their question was not, "Why this healing and not another?" Their question was, "Could this be the Son of David," the promised one?

Healing does occur. It is a mystery in its distribution, but an evidence of God's power in our Lord Jesus Christ. Accept the gift and honor the Giver, no matter who is the recipient. Perhaps at a later time the mystery will be explained.

—W. P.

Conclusion

A. What Do We Give the Lord?

People often give what they want to give rather than what the recipient needs or wants. Parents may give their children money or things rather than the time and attention they crave and need. Friends sometimes give advice rather than a listening ear.

God's people sometimes do the same thing with Him. The ancient Jews developed a great number of traditions regarding their religious life. They were very zealous in observing these traditions, and in doing so they felt that they were serving God. But their traditions often became more important to them than God's revealed law. In fact, Jesus charged the scribes and Pharisees with setting aside God's laws in order to keep their traditions. See Matthew 15:1-9. They gave God what they wanted to give instead of what He asked for.

One who loves Christ and is devoted to Him will give to Him what He requires. Basically, He requires us to follow His example in attitude, in holiness of life, and in serving others. He calls us to be peaceful and meek, to tenderly heal broken hearts and lives and bodies. He asks us to carry the message of salvation to all peoples of the world. As members of Christ's church, it is appropriate for us to be concerned about maintaining attractive and functional church buildings, providing programming that we feel is appealing and uplifting, and the like. These are good, but let us not allow them to become substitutes for giving to Jesus what He has asked of us—lives that proclaim His glory and saving power.

B. Let Us Pray

Gracious Lord, help us see clearly the service that You would have us render for You. Keep us from becoming so attached to familiar practices that we become blind to Your commands. Give us hearts full of gratitude for the healing You have brought to our lives. May all that we do bring glory to Your holy name. Amen.

C. Thought to Remember

None is so blind as a person who will not see.

Home Daily Bible Readings

Monday, Jan. 2—The Lord's Servant Will Establish Justice (Isaiah 42:1-9)

Tuesday, Jan. 3—Lord of the Sabbath (Matthew 12:1-8)

Wednesday, Jan. 4—Healing on the Sabbath (Matthew 12:9-14)

Thursday, Jan. 5—The Mission of God's Chosen Servant (Matthew 12:15-21)

Friday, Jan. 6—Jesus' Power Comes From God (Matthew 12:22-37)

Saturday, Jan. 7—Request for a Sign (Matthew 12:38-42)

Sunday, Jan. 8—Jesus' True Family (Matthew 12:46-50)

Learning by Doing

*This page contains an alternate lesson plan emphasizing learning activities. Classes
desiring such student involvement will find these suggestions helpful.*

Learning Goals

As a result of participating in today's lesson, a student will be able to:

1. State how Jesus, as the Son of David, ministered with compassion and power.

2. Respond to Jesus' example by putting ministry ahead of tradition.

Into the Lesson

Ask the class to define the following: *tradition* and *status quo*. Allow individuals to briefly clarify the meaning of each term. If no one brings it up, point out that: (a) *Tradition* is a man-made belief or custom that achieves a high degree of importance; and (b) *Status quo* comes from Latin, and the literal translation is, "the state in which." It means "the existing condition." Next, probe why so many people insist on maintaining traditions and the *status quo*. Some answers could be: (1) That's all some people have ever known. (2) They provide security and safety. (3) Some don't like risks at all. (4) Some confuse them with God's will.

Make the transition to the study of today's Bible text by saying that Jesus was confronted by the Pharisees more than once regarding His apparent disregard for their traditions.

Into the Word

Divide the class into three groups for study. Give each group one of the following assignments:

1. Research these Old Testament passages to discover what God intended when He instituted the Sabbath: Exodus 20:8-11; 31:14-17; 35:2, 3; Leviticus 23:3; and Deuteronomy 5:12-15.

2. Summarize Jesus' teachings in Matthew 12:1-8.

3. Analyze Matthew 12:15-21 and clarify how Jesus fulfilled each point in Isaiah 42:1-4. For assistance, see the comments under these verses in this manual.

Allot approximately ten minutes for the groups to complete their study. When the groups have finished, ask a spokesperson from each group to present their conclusions in the same order as the above assignments.

Summarize and explain that the issue in Matthew 12:9-23 is tradition *versus* a ministry of love and kindness. The Pharisees were blinded by their allegiance to their traditions and battled to maintain the *status quo*. In doing that, they were missing what the crowds were beginning to see—that Jesus was fulfilling His messianic role as the Son of David by acts of compassion and power. If we are to be faithful to Him, we must avoid the attitude of the Pharisees and place above all else God's will for us to evangelize and minister to others above.

Into Life

Direct the students to the activity in the student book called "Six Familiar Sayings." (If they don't have student books, make and distribute copies of the six statements below, omitting the italicized words. Mention that these are statements that are sometimes used by people who want to keep things the way they are. Allow some time for each one to complete the sentences by filling in the blanks. Approach this as a light-hearted and fun activity.

1. We've never *done it* that *way before*.
2. This is not the *time*.
3. We *tried* it before and it didn't *work*.
4. That's not our *responsibility*.
5. It *costs* too much.
6. We are doing *okay* without it.

Ask the class to suggest some traditions or customs in your church that are highly valued, though not really Scripturally based, which, if changed, in all likelihood would cause quite a stir. Some possibilities might be: only the minister or an elder can give a Communion meditation; we stand to sing certain songs; and the choir wears robes.

Discuss how holding onto a tradition could possibly keep the church from ministering with love and compassion. For example, "To be welcome in our church, a person must wear a coat and tie, not jeans and a sweatshirt."

Ask if anyone is aware of a tradition in *this* church that has hindered the church's ability to minister effectively to members or to the unchurched community. Keep the discussion focused on the need for us to follow Jesus' priorities, emphasizing ministry over man-made traditions.

Conclude by asking the class to work in pairs to share answers to these questions: What can we as a church do to make sure that we do not allow man-made traditions to take precedence over doing Christ's will? How can I minister to others with compassion and kindness?

Let's Talk It Over

The questions on this page are designed to encourage review of the lesson Scriptures and to promote discussion of the lesson by the class. The answers provided are only discussion starters. Let your class talk it over from there.

1. List some causes of the Pharisee's "blindness" to Jesus.

(1) Power and control. The Pharisees were among the most powerful religious leaders in Israel. They saw Jesus as a threat to both their power and their control over the religious establishment of the day.

(2) Obsession with law. "Rules" mattered most to the Pharisees. Observance of the letter of the law and scrupulous outward obedience occupied the Pharisaic mind. In their intense concern and efforts to keep even minutest rules, they overlooked matters of the spirit. Jesus called these "the more important matters of the law—justice, mercy and faithfulness" (Matthew 23:23, *New International Version*).

(3) Tradition. Their traditions, built on their interpretations of the law, were equated with the law itself. When Jesus rejected their traditions, they rejected Him.

(4) Hatred. The three factors just cited combined into seething hatred of Jesus. Their hatred completely blinded them to truth, beauty, righteousness, and light. They were blinded to the very presence of God in their midst.

2. Is it possible for Christians to become "blind" to Jesus? If so, how?

As noted in the last sentence of the answer above, God came and dwelt in the midst of His people in His Son, Jesus. Daily the common people saw Jesus, heard His marvelous teaching, and witnessed the awe-inspiring miracles He performed. Even so, however, many of the people fell away from Him (see John 6:66). Did their familiarity with Him, their nearness to Him, cause them to regard that which was divine as commonplace?

We are part of the church, the Lord's body. We worship regularly, we speak and sing the Lord's praises, we hear His Word proclaimed. The question each must ask himself or herself is, "Do I really listen to Jesus as He speaks through His Word, and do I put His teachings into practice in my daily life?" The people of Jesus' time referred to in the paragraph above came to Jesus with their own agenda and tried to impose it on Him. They were looking for physical things, but He offered that which was spiritual. We must continually keep our eyes open to the true nature of Jesus' teaching, lest we become blind to how He would have us think and act.

3. What is tradition, and what is its function?

A tradition is a handed-down pattern of thought or action. Families and communities may have traditions of various kinds, and these provide continuity from generation to generation. Traditions may be good or bad, depending on their validity. Churches may have tradition too. If a tradition is of human origin, a problem may arise if that tradition is elevated to the place where it is regarded as having a genuine sacred character, as though it came from God himself.

In some circles the very thought of tradition causes a negative reaction, because it is equated with something extra- or anti-scriptural. However, Paul calls for Christians to hold to the traditions taught by the apostles (2 Thessalonians 2:15). These traditions are valid and necessary. It is the role of tradition to preserve that which is important, and it is vitally important for the tradition of Christ to be handed down from generation to generation. That tradition preserves not just what is important, but that which is essential to life.

4. At the time of the events recorded in our lesson text, why did Jesus instruct those He healed *not* to tell others?

Jesus did not want people coming to Him for the wrong reasons. He was not interested in gaining fame or in wielding political power. He had come to fulfill God's purpose, which was to provide redemption from sin for mankind. Spreading the word of His miracles of healing at this point would have taken the emphasis of His ministry from the spiritual and placed it on the physical.

5. On the basis of our lesson text, how might Jesus' style of ministry be described?

It was tender, caring, gentle, kind, and compassionate. In a word, His ministry was *loving*. He did good deeds and worked wondrous miracles in a spirit of true concern for others. Jesus' ministry epitomized the perfect union of act and appropriate attitude

A Foreigner's Faith

DEVOTIONAL READING: Isaiah 35:5-10.

LESSON SCRIPTURE: Matthew 15:1-31.

PRINTED TEXT: Matthew 15:21-31.

Matthew 15: 21-31

21 Then Jesus went thence, and departed into the coasts of Tyre and Sidon.

22 And, behold, a woman of Canaan came out of the same coasts, and cried unto him, saying, Have mercy on me, O Lord, thou Son of David; my daughter is grievously vexed with a devil.

23 But he answered her not a word. And his disciples came and besought him, saying, Send her away; for she crieth after us.

24 But he answered and said, I am not sent but unto the lost sheep of the house of Israel.

25 Then came she and worshipped him, saying, Lord, help me.

26 But he answered and said, It is not meet to take the children's bread, and to cast it to dogs.

27 And she said, Truth, Lord: yet the dogs eat of the crumbs which fall from their masters' table.

28 Then Jesus answered and said unto her, O woman, great is thy faith: be it unto thee even as thou wilt. And her daughter was made whole from that very hour.

29 And Jesus departed from thence, and came nigh unto the sea of Galilee; and went up into a mountain, and sat down there.

30 And great multitudes came unto him, having with them those that were lame, blind, dumb, maimed, and many others, and cast them down at Jesus' feet; and he healed them:

31 Insomuch that the multitude wondered, when they saw the dumb to speak, the maimed to be whole, the lame to walk, and the blind to see: and they glorified the God of Israel.

GOLDEN TEXT: Woman, great is thy faith.—Matthew 15:28.

Lesson Aims

This lesson should help students:

1. Recall with gratitude that Jesus broke through barriers to reach people.

2. Identify boundaries that need to be crossed today so that all people may have an opportunity to respond to God's reconciling love.

3. Examine their actions, attitudes, and prejudices in light of the example of Jesus.

Lesson Outline

INTRODUCTION
   A. Boundaries
   B. Lesson Background
I. JESUS RESPONDS TO A WOMAN OF FAITH (Matthew 15:21-28)
   A. Leaving Galilee (v. 21)
   B. An Urgent Plea (v. 22)
   C. The Disciples' Response (v. 23)
   D. Persistent Pleading (vv. 24-27)
   E. Request Granted (v. 28)
     Tenacious Faith
II. JESUS PERFORMS MANY MIRACLES (Matthew 15:29-31)
   A. Return to the Sea of Galilee (v. 29)
   B. Return of the Crowds (v. 30)
   C. Amazement and Praise (v. 31)
CONCLUSION
   A. Persistent and Faithful
   B. Prayer
   C. Thought to Remember

Four factors essential to faithful living, which are drawn from the Canaanite woman's faith and action, are highlighted on visual 7 of the visuals packet. The visual is shown on page 174.

Introduction

A. Boundaries

Who can forget the day the television cameras brought into our homes images of people dancing with glee atop the Berlin Wall? Half the population of Berlin, it seemed, chipped away at this monument to the Cold War. Once this wall had been patrolled by border guards armed with machine guns. And from time to time the guards used their lethal power to stop those who sought to flee. But suddenly this broken and disappearing wall symbolized freedom. Friends and relatives shut off from one another for so long were free to visit again. And, after a time, a city and a nation were reunited. A repressive regime had crumbled. The hated wall had become irrelevant, something to be carted away in slabs to museums or to be broken into bits by souvenir hunters. Soon little chunks of the wall began showing up on desks and coffee tables.

Walls, whether literal or figurative, play important parts in our lives. Some walls are indeed hated. But in other instances walls or boundaries are, in fact, appropriate and helpful. The owners of a vacation home in the mountains of North Carolina have named their cabin simply, "Four Stone Walls." Walls can help to provide a place of comfort, a place protected from the elements. Walls also provide protection from various threats to the welfare of a family. When we are responsible for the care of children, for example, we spend a considerable amount of our time calling attention to "walls," or boundaries. Responsible parents of young children must often draw distinctions between those things that are good for them and those things that are not. And so they tell their children, "Do this, but don't do that." The point is that safety is to be found in certain circumstances, within certain parameters, and threats lurk beyond.

The problem, of course, is that some boundaries have been drawn improperly. The surveyor was in a hurry. The person who drew the map was careless. And sometimes the parent was filled with animosities, was unreasonably fearful, or was poorly informed.

Sometimes the boundaries that have been drawn improperly have been in place for longer than anyone can remember. And if tradition prescribes inappropriate lines, it can be extraordinarily difficult for the heirs of that tradition to sense that anything is wrong, much less to feel free to cross the boundary.

Jesus often encountered people who were stubbornly committed to maintaining improperly drawn boundaries, inappropriate barriers, walls that divided people from people, walls that kept people from doing the will of God, walls that had "always" been there. Jesus frequently encountered people who were confused about such questions as the lines between pleasing and displeasing God, between respectable and disreputable people, between righteousness and sin, and between what was possible and impossible. We often find Jesus confronting people whose world was topsy-turvy. Not only were lines improperly drawn, but the wrong labels were used. "Up" was "down"; "down" was "up."

In the first century, as in every century since then, what Jesus had to say was not what many wanted to hear. It was not, and is not, easy to listen to the Master. Discipleship is rewarding, but it is also costly. As followers of Jesus, we are often called upon to struggle against opposition, against barriers to faithfulness. Even though Christians draw strength from the grace and mercy of God and have the support of fellow believers, the struggles are real. Through the centuries, listening to Jesus has sometimes cost believers their lives. At the very least, listening to Him will often inconvenience us and sometimes set us at odds with family and friends. Squaring our lives with our faith is the work of a lifetime. Listening to the Master requires us as honestly as possible to examine our actions, our attitudes, and, yes, our prejudices. What is more frustrating than to recognize that a wall that has provided us with a certain sense of security is not God's wall? What is more frustrating than to recognize that we have sometimes been on the wrong side of a wall?

B. Lesson Background

The fifteenth chapter of Matthew begins with Jesus in Galilee responding to Pharisees and teachers of the law who had come all the way from Jerusalem. They were concerned. They had come a long way to ask why the disciples of Jesus were "crossing over the line." Why were they violating tradition? The disciples, after all, did not wash their hands before they ate a meal. How offensive!

Of course, we are inclined to think that people ought to learn to wash their hands before they eat. It is traditional for us too. Besides, we know something about bacteria and personal hygiene. But for a group of grown men to undertake an arduous journey to tell another adult that He and His disciples should wash their hands in the prescribed fashion—and as a matter of religious obligation—is a bit much! As is often the case as we consider the questions put to Jesus by the religious leaders of the day, we wonder if there is not more than meets the eye here. Is there a hidden agenda?

Jesus then turned the tables on His critics. Why did they nullify the clear command of God? Why did they use the tradition of the elders as a means of evading their responsibilities to their mothers and fathers? These defenders of orthodoxy, these "border guards" from Jerusalem, were, in a word, hypocrites! They never neglected to wash their hands, but thought nothing of neglecting the needs of their parents. Ignoring weighty matters, these men from Jerusalem specialized in the trivial (vv. 1-9).

How to Say It

CAESAREA PHILIPPI.   Sess-uh-*ree*-uh Fih-*lip*-pie or *Fil*-ih-pie.
CANAANITE.   *Kay*-nan-ite.
DECAPOLIS.   Dee-*kap*-uh-lis.
PHARISEES.   *Fair*-ih-seez.
PHOENICIA.   Fih-*nish*-uh.

Jesus went on to explain that cleanness and uncleanness were ultimately matters of the heart. From an unclean heart came such sinful behavior as evil thinking, murder, adultery, other sexual immorality, stealing, lying, and slander. His critics would do well to give more attention to real uncleanness. Sinful actions issuing from the heart mattered infinitely more than eating with unwashed hands. Real defilement mattered infinitely more than ritual defilement. In comparison to obeying God out of a sense of gratitude, merely going through a routine prescribed by the tradition of the Pharisees mattered not at all (vv. 10-20).

Then Jesus and His inner circle crossed a geographical, ethnic, and religious border. They left Galilee for a time. They made their way toward the coastal region of Phoenicia, where Galileans were outsiders.

I. Jesus Responds to a Woman of Faith (Matthew 15:21-28)

A. Leaving Galilee (v. 21)

21. Then Jesus went thence, and departed into the coasts of Tyre and Sidon.

As was often the case, Jesus went from one place to another, not just for a change of scenery, but also hoping for a change of activity. Jesus often sought solitude, especially after attending to the needs of the multitudes. We recall, for example, Jesus' crossing the Sea of Galilee searching for solitude, a time for prayer and rest, but finding a crowd that grew to more than five thousand. After healing the sick who were among them, and then miraculously feeding that vast throng, He sent the multitudes home for the night. Then He walked alone up the mountainside to pray (Matthew 14:13-23).

Jesus rarely ventured into Gentile areas. (We read of His going to Samaria, to Caesarea Philippi, and to the Decapolis, the region southeast of the Sea of Galilee.) Another occasion is described in this text, when He and His disciples made their way into Phoenicia, and particularly into *the coasts* (or areas around) *Tyre and Sidon*, the principal cities of the region. We cannot be certain how long this visit lasted or how many miles it covered. It is about thirty-five miles from the northern edge of the Sea of Galilee to the ancient port of Tyre. The coastal city of Sidon was more than twenty miles north of Tyre. The borders of these regions were, of course, somewhat closer to the point where the journey began. Thus Jesus and His disciples did not undertake a trip of hundreds of miles, but any of us would consider their journey a very ambitious walk. This region offered Jesus and the disciples the prospect of a retreat, the prospect of relief from the stress of the crowds and the controversies with Israel's religious leaders. Here thousands would not be seeking His healing touch. Here, in fact, Jesus and His disciples might be more or less anonymous.

B. An Urgent Plea (v. 22)

22. And, behold, a woman of Canaan came out of the same coasts, and cried unto him, saying, Have mercy on me, O Lord, thou Son of David; my daughter is grievously vexed with a devil.

Even in the region of Tyre and Sidon, however, Jesus' coming was known by at least one person. A certain Gentile woman (called here *a woman of Canaan*) learned somehow that Jesus had come into the area, and she came out to meet Him. Furthermore, she doubtless knew that Jesus had cast out demons from many persons in Galilee. This woman was not timid. She was determined to get help for her daughter. With her insistent cries for mercy for herself and for her daughter, this devoted mother disturbed whatever peace and quiet Jesus and His party may have been enjoying. Convinced that Jesus had it within His power to end the suffering of her demon-possessed daughter, the distressed woman cried out, explaining her plight and begging Jesus to help. We cannot know how much this woman knew about Jesus or precisely what the words she used to address Him meant to her. *Lord* was used commonly in that day as a term of respect. It was often used in a way equivalent to our word *sir.* *Son of David* is recognized by Christians as a Messianic title, but we cannot know that she used it in this manner. At the very least, however, she honored Jesus greatly and had the highest confidence in Him. and she clearly believed that He had the power to work miracles.

C. The Disciples' Response (v. 23)

23. But he answered her not a word. And his disciples came and besought him, saying, Send her away; for she crieth after us.

Usually Jesus helped all who came to Him. In this instance, however, *he answered her not a word.* The silence of Jesus constituted a barrier for the woman. But she kept crying out. The disciples appear to have been annoyed with the woman, and they urged Jesus to send her on her way. They may have meant that He should grant her request promptly so that peace and quiet could be restored. Or they may have been urging Him to send her away without granting her request. We can't be sure which. As on other occasions, so here, they were quick to give Jesus advice. And they seem quite self-centered in this instance. They were insistent: "Do something!" they said in effect. "We've heard enough from this noisy Gentile woman!"

D. Persistent Pleading (vv. 24-27)

24. But he answered and said, I am not sent but unto the lost sheep of the house of Israel.

First, the woman encountered the barrier of silence, and then came these discouraging words that served as yet another barrier. He was sent to *the lost sheep of the house of Israel,* and this woman was not a part of that flock. Jesus' words remind us that His mission during His earthly ministry was not to right every wrong throughout the world all at once. His mission was limited by the restrictions related to His humanity. He had only so much energy. He could travel only so far. But His mission was also limited by an intentional design. While Jesus made rare exceptions to this general rule of devoting His attention to the house of Israel, later He would commission His disciples to take His gospel throughout the world.

25. Then came she and worshipped him, saying, Lord, help me.

The woman may have heard Jesus' response to the urging of His disciples. But, regardless, she had no intention of slipping away in defeat. Instead, she continued to seek Jesus' mercy relentlessly. Kneeling before Him, she continued to beg for His help.

26. But he answered and said, It is not meet to take the children's bread, and to cast it to dogs.

Now another barrier is noted, and words are expressed that constituted a further test of the woman's faith. On the face of it, Jesus' statement appears to be an insensitive response to the heartbroken woman's cries. *It is not meet,* or "it is not fitting," Jesus observed, as He used what was perhaps a common saying about the inappropriateness of giving the food intended for children to dogs. The contempt of the Jews for Gentiles was deeply rooted. *Dogs* was a term used among Jews of that day to express their contempt for Gentiles. The epithet called to mind undesirable, unclean animals, not cuddly household pets. Jesus was indicating that He was sent to the Jews, and that the woman was a Gentile. By employing a term that was in common use, He meant merely that it was not in keeping with the design of His personal ministry to grant to Gentiles the benefits that were intended for the Jews. In our day of heightened sensitivity to language that is "politically correct," this remark likely will strike many as awkward. It is evident, in light of His teaching in general as well as His ultimate response to this woman, that Jesus did not regard her as an inferior person. Nor was He giving His approval to the abusive term. Once again, the statement may have been as strong as it was because it was intended as another test of the woman's spirit. It was a recognition of the barrier that existed between the two peoples. Would she allow that barrier to keep her from receiving a favor from a Jew?

27. And she said, Truth, Lord: yet the dogs eat of the crumbs which fall from their masters' table.

Regardless of precisely how Jesus delivered His words, the essential point was that at this time His mission had limits. But the humble, persistent woman protested. Granting that the main course was for Israel, did the Gentiles not have a right to the scraps? She was convinced that all would be well if Jesus would grant her just a little attention. She had encountered several barriers, but she would not give up her hope that Jesus would help.

E. Request Granted (v. 28)

28. Then Jesus answered and said unto her, O woman, great is thy faith: be it unto thee even as thou wilt. And her daughter was made whole from that very hour.

Jesus paid the woman a high compliment. Her faith was great! Perhaps the Canaanite woman did not fully comprehend what she was saying. Perhaps she could not have presented a carefully reasoned discourse on God's boundless love for the whole world. But the persistent cries that the disciples found so bothersome were an eloquent testimony to her faith as far as Jesus was concerned. He paid this Gentile woman a compliment that any of His Jewish disciples would have been grateful to receive. Great was her faith! Her faith was tough. Her faith struggled against obstacles. (We are reminded of the account in Mark 2:1-12 of the faith and the struggle of those who tore a hole in the roof so that they could lower their paralytic friend into the house where Jesus was. (See lesson 5.) Thus Jesus granted her request.

It may be of interest to note similarities between this passage and Matthew 8:5-13. When Jesus paid tribute to the Roman centurion who successfully pleaded with Jesus to heal his servant, He declared that this Gentile had faith greater than He had found in Israel. And in response to the urgent requests of both the centurion and the Canaanite woman, Jesus worked the miracles at a distance.

TENACIOUS FAITH

Roy Gault's light plane ride had turned into a tragic nightmare. Just a few minutes out of the airport near Anchorage, Alaska, the pilot had run into trouble. The plane was too close to the mountain. As the pilot tried to turn to avoid a crash, Roy knew they were not going to make it. The plane plowed into the mountainside, and both pilot and passenger were thrown clear. They were too injured to call, signal, or do anything to attract attention.

Night fell, and Roy awoke to hear the sound of animals nearby. "How horrible," he thought, "to live through the crash only to be mauled or eaten by bears!" Morning light showed the animals to be goats, but no rescue plane cheered their hopeless situation. Finally, however, the two were found.

Roy had broken bones throughout his body. The doctors said he would live but never walk again. In time he was dismissed from the hospital, but he was in a special bed and unable to care for himself. His mother and father took care of him, and they refused to give up hope. Slowly the impossible began to happen. Bathed in his parents' faith and prayers, Roy was nursed back to health. Their faith would not be deterred from seeking wholeness for their son. Roy now captains a large fishing vessel in Alaskan waters.

Jesus healed the Canaanite woman's daughter for the same great, overcoming faith. Listen to

Home Daily Bible Readings

Monday, Jan. 9—Help Promised for God's People (Isaiah 35:3-7)

Tuesday, Jan. 10—Gentiles Are God's People (1 Peter 2:4-10)

Wednesday, Jan. 11—Traditions: Good or Bad? (Matthew 15:1-9)

Thursday, Jan. 12—Living From the Heart (Matthew 15:10-20)

Friday, Jan. 13—Jesus Responds to a Gentile's Faith (Matthew 15:21-28)

Saturday, Jan. 14—A Man's Hearing and Speech Restored (Mark 7:31-37)

Sunday, Jan. 15—We Are One in Christ (Galatians 3:23-29)

His words: "O woman, your faith is great; be it done for you as you wish" (*New American Standard Bible*). Christ will reward those who refuse to relinquish their faith in Him.   —W. P.

II. Jesus Performs Many Miracles (Matthew 15:29-31)

A. Return to the Sea of Galilee (v. 29)

29. And Jesus departed from thence, and came nigh unto the sea of Galilee; and went up into a mountain, and sat down there.

After His visit to the region of Tyre and Sidon, Jesus returned to the vicinity of the Sea of Galilee. Perhaps wishing to avoid the excitable multitudes and the hostile Pharisees, Jesus did not return to Galilee itself. Instead, He went to the region of the Decapolis southeast of the Sea of Galilee (Mark 7:31).

B. Return of the Crowds (v. 30)

30. And great multitudes came unto him, having with them those that were lame, blind, dumb, maimed, and many others, and cast them down at Jesus' feet; and he healed them.

Earlier, Jesus had cast the demons out of two men in this area, and the citizens had asked Jesus to leave (see lesson 5). Now *great multitudes* came to Him gladly. People from Decapolis had followed Jesus on His first tour through Galilee (Matthew 4:25). It would seem that their testimony and that of the healed demoniac (see Mark 5:18-20) brought about the people's marked change of attitude toward Jesus.

In great numbers they came seeking healing. They brought with them *those that were lame, blind, dumb, maimed, and many others.* And Jesus healed them.

C. Amazement and Praise (v. 31)

31. Insomuch that the multitude wondered, when they saw the dumb to speak, the maimed to be whole, the lame to walk, and the blind to see: and they glorified the God of Israel.

visual 7

Jesus broke through the barriers of what could ordinarily be expected. Those who saw Him heal the sick were amazed, for most of them probably had never seen such mighty acts performed before. The phrase *the God of Israel* strongly suggests that the crowd was drawn largely from the Gentile population in the Decapolis area. One wonders if any of these were led to a faith as invincible as that of the Canaanite woman of Phoenicia.

Conclusion

A. Persistent and Faithful

In the eyes of some, the Canaanite woman was not worthy of attention for many reasons. She was "from the wrong side of the tracks." She was a Gentile. She did not worship in Jerusalem. And, besides, she was a woman.

Like those who thronged around Jesus when He was on the shore of the Sea of Galilee, she sought Him eagerly, expectantly.

But Jesus singled out this woman for praise. Great was her faith! There were all sorts of boundaries that could have deterred her. She could have given up, retreating in sullen silence. But she was as relentless as an army with a battering ram at the gate to a besieged city. For her persistence, for her great faith, Jesus praised her; and even though we don't know her name, we remember her. We, like Jesus, pay tribute to her for her persistent faith.

If all we do is admire this woman, however, our response to these verses in Matthew is incomplete. What boundaries do we need to cross for the sake of our relationship to Jesus Christ? What prejudices limit our effectiveness as His servants? Just how great is our faith?

B. Prayer

You were in Christ reconciling us, O God. You loved us while we were content to live in sin, while we were separated from You by our own waywardness. You saw the barriers and broke through them. You came seeking us. You came in Jesus Christ, who refused to observe artificial boundaries of man's making. You came in Jesus Christ, crucified, risen, victorious! Because we are grateful, help us to seek others for You with the same compassion and persistence. Help us to break through the walls that separate us from those You are seeking today. Amen.

C. Thought to Remember

Jesus said to the Canaanite woman, "Great is your faith!" How do we respond to the challenges, the barriers, we confront as believers? What would Jesus say of our faith?

Learning by Doing

This page contains an alternate lesson plan emphasizing learning activities. Classes desiring such student involvement will find these suggestions helpful.

Learning Goals

At the conclusion of this examination of Matthew 15:21-31, the students will be able to:

1. Explain how Jesus used this event to break through barriers to reach people.

2. Identify those boundaries that must be crossed today if people are to have an opportunity to respond to God's reconciling love.

3. Examine personal actions, attitudes, and prejudices in light of Jesus' example.

Into the Lesson

Put the word *wall* on the chalkboard or a sheet of newsprint before the class members arrive. As they arrive, have them form groups of three or four students each. Call attention to the word *wall*. Ask each group to brainstorm to see what images come to their minds when they think of this word. Allot three to five minutes for this. Have a person from each group write their responses on the chalkboard or newsprint. Then lead a brief discussion as the groups share their responses.

Make the transition into the Bible study section by stating that today's passage of Scripture looks at invisible walls that sometimes divide people, and that Jesus will show us how to deal with those barriers.

Into the Word

Use the material from the Lesson Background section to establish the context of the event in today's Scripture text. Then have a class member read Matthew 15:21-31 aloud as class members follow along.

Assign the class members to work in pairs to find the answers to the following questions from the text:

1. What specific barriers are present in this passage that could have prevented the woman from asking Jesus for what she needed? (The woman was not a Jew; her daughter was possessed by a demon; what she asked defied natural law.)

2. After the woman pled for mercy, why did Jesus state that He was sent only to "the lost sheep of the house of Israel"? (v. 24). (Perhaps He wanted to test the extent of her faith.)

3. Jesus responded to the woman's second plea by saying, "It is not meet to take the children's bread, and to cast it to dogs" (v. 26). His answer seems abrupt and uncaring. How would you explain this? (This saying pointed up the barrier that separated Jew from Gentile. It seems that Jesus was probing to see if the woman's faith would overcome that barrier.)

4. What do you conclude about the woman by her response recorded in verse 27? (She was humble and persistent. She was convinced Jesus could help her daughter.)

5. Why do you think Jesus eventually granted the woman's request? (v. 28). (It was surely because of the depth of her faith.)

6. What was the response of the multitudes who witnessed Jesus' miracles? (They glorified the God of Israel.)

Allot ten to twelve minutes for the pairs to work together to find the answers. Then at the designated time, call the groups together and proceed with a discussion of the text, using the students' answers as the basis for the discussion. Be sure to fill in any details that were missed by the groups. Summarize the teaching of this passage.

Into Life

To apply this lesson, quote the lesson writer's statement in the Conclusion section: "If all we do is admire this woman, however, our response to these verses in Matthew is incomplete." Use his questions to guide a discussion:

1. What barriers exist today that inhibit the proclamation of Jesus Christ to those who need to hear? (The answers may include ethnic and cultural barriers; concern for health and personal welfare, such as when working with AIDS victims; indifference to the needs of those who are different from us.)

2. What boundaries do we in this congregation need to cross for the sake of our relationship to Jesus Christ? (Keep probing until specific barriers are mentioned.)

3. What prejudices limit our effectiveness as His servants? (Seek specific answers.)

Conclude by asking, "How great is your faith? Could you overcome barriers to take Christ to another? How persistent are you?" Distribute small index cards to the class and ask each student to complete this sentence: "I want to overcome barriers to faith by. . . ." If time allows, let them share their answers with two others. Then close with prayer.

Let's Talk It Over

The questions on this page are designed to encourage review of the lesson Scriptures and to promote discussion of the lesson by the class. The answers provided are only discussion starters. Let your class talk it over from there.

1. Describe and evaluate the response of Jesus' disciples to the Canaanite woman's urgent plea for help for her daughter.

In essence, the disciples said to Jesus, "Get rid of her! She's bothering us with her begging." First, it should be noted that they presumed to tell their Master what to do. That was hardly appropriate behavior for a disciple. Second, by their response, the disciples certainly gave the appearance of being self-centered on this occasion. There is no evidence of their having any sensitivity to this woman's desperate need, no compassion such as was shown by Jesus in His ministry. It may well be that because of their inappropriate response, Jesus engaged in the "repartee" with the woman for His disciples' benefit as well as for hers!

2. List some of the characteristics of the faith of the woman in our lesson text, a faith that Jesus described as "great." What does this woman's example say to us?

Jesus praised the great faith of the Canaanite woman, and justifiably so. Her faith was tough, it was persistent, and it transcended obstacles that were put in its way. A lesser faith would have retreated and quit. But not hers! This woman believed in Jesus; she was fully convinced that He could heal her daughter. Tenaciously, therefore, she persisted to entreat Jesus for the help she *knew* He could give.

Each of us would do well to examine his or her faith in Jesus in light of this woman's faith. Do we approach Him boldly, seeking His grace to help us in time of need? (Hebrews 4:16). Do we believe He *will* help? If sickness, financial difficulty, or any other kind of reversal strikes, how do we respond? Let us be like the Canaanite woman and never stop believing that He can help us. Let us never stop trusting Him.

3. What attitude do many persons have regarding others who are different from them in some way? Give some examples of this. How does the gospel of Christ speak to this attitude?

Many persons have the attitude that others are inferior or wrong, solely because others are different from them. This is seen in matters regarding national origin, race, economic status, or educational attainment.

This ungodly attitude has been manifested even in the church. A person may be quite convinced that others are wrong, simply because they hold views that differ from his. It is one thing to regard another person's belief as invalid if it does not square with God's Word; it is another to do so because it differs from one's own view.

The gospel shows that all of us are wrong in God's eyes, for all have sinned (Romans 3:23). But He loves each of us in spite of it, and sent Jesus to be the Savior for all people. Since we all stand on the same plane before God, as undeserving, lost sinners, how can anyone view another person as inferior, or reject that person, on the basis of some outward or superficial characteristic?

4. "Salvation is personal, but it is never private." What is meant by this?

Salvation involves each one very personally in the conversion of his or her life. It is a matter that takes place within a person and involves only that person and the Lord. But the Lord does not single out persons or groups of persons for special treatment in this regard. We are all born the same way. This fact enhances our sense of community with all believers.

5. From the account of the Canaanite woman, what are some conclusions we may draw concerning prayer?

We learn that Jesus is approachable by anyone. Regardless of the disciples' impatience with this Gentile woman, Jesus heard her request. He made time for her, even though she was not one of the covenant people. He would help her with her need. We also learn that Jesus works in His time. He did not immediately answer her request. By delaying, He challenged her faith in Him and taught the disciples (and us) an important lesson about persistence and patience when approaching God with our requests. We also learn that we can approach the Lord openly, honestly, and without fear of rejection. Finally, we learn to accept whatever the Lord may give in answer to our prayers. The woman would accept even "crumbs." Jesus cares for us and seeks to give only good gifts. Will we accept His answers?

Jesus Is Transfigured

DEVOTIONAL READING: 2 Peter 1:16-21.

LESSON SCRIPTURE: Matthew 17:1-23.

PRINTED TEXT: Matthew 17:1-13.

Matthew 17:1-13

1 And after six days Jesus taketh Peter, James, and John his brother, and bringeth them up into a high mountain apart,

2 And was transfigured before them: and his face did shine as the sun, and his raiment was white as the light.

3 And, behold, there appeared unto them Moses and Elijah talking with him.

4 Then answered Peter, and said unto Jesus, Lord, it is good for us to be here: if thou wilt, let us make here three tabernacles; one for thee, and one for Moses, and one for Elijah.

5 While he yet spake, behold, a bright cloud overshadowed them: and behold a voice out of the cloud, which said, This is my beloved Son, in whom I am well pleased; hear ye him.

6 And when the disciples heard it, they fell on their face, and were sore afraid.

7 And Jesus came and touched them, and said, Arise, and be not afraid.

8 And when they had lifted up their eyes, they saw no man, save Jesus only.

9 And as they came down from the mountain, Jesus charged them, saying, Tell the vision to no man, until the Son of man be risen again from the dead.

10 And his disciples asked him, saying, Why then say the scribes that Elijah must first come?

11 And Jesus answered and said unto them, Elijah truly shall first come, and restore all things.

12 But I say unto you, That Elijah is come already, and they knew him not, but have done unto him whatsoever they listed. Likewise shall also the Son of man suffer of them.

13 Then the disciples understood that he spake unto them of John the Baptist.

Jan 22

GOLDEN TEXT: This is my beloved Son, in whom I am well pleased; hear ye him.
—Matthew 17:5.

Jesus the Fulfillment (Matthew)
Unit 3. Jesus: The Son of David
(Lessons 5-9)

Lesson Aims

The study of this lesson is designed to help the student:

1. Understand what the transfiguration meant to Jesus and the disciples and what it means to us.

2. Appreciate who Jesus is and what He did for us on the cross.

3. Seek to be a witness to God's grace and Christ's glory.

Lesson Outline

INTRODUCTION
  A. Christ, Our Focal Point
  B. Lesson Background
I. THE SON CHANGED (Matthew 17:1-4)
  A. A Place Apart (v. 1)
  B. A Change in Christ's Appearance (v. 2)
  C. A Comforting Conversation (v. 3)
  D. A Challenging Response (v. 4)
II. THE SON CONFIRMED (Matthew 17:5)
  A. The Father's Testimony (v. 5a, b)
  B. The Disciples' Responsibility (v. 5c)
    Hear Him!
III. THE SON COMFORTS AND COMMANDS (Matthew 17:6-13)
  A. Comfort for Christ's Disciples (vv. 6, 7)
  B. Focal Point for the Disciples (v. 8)
    Who Is Left?
  C. Command for the Disciples (v. 9)
  D. Question and Answer (vv. 10-12)
  E. Understanding (v. 13)
CONCLUSION
  A. Reassurance
  B. Prayer
  C. Thought to Remember

Visual 8 is a photograph of Mount Tabor, which some think was the site of Jesus' transfiguration. The visual is shown on page 181.

Introduction

A. Christ, Our Focal Point

Being the father of two teenagers who love amusement parks, I have learned how to survive roller coaster rides. My method is simple: I find something inside the coaster to focus my eyes on while the ride is in progress. That object becomes my focal point: my eyes never deviate from it. By being able to do this I have found that the heights and depths of the rides no longer frighten me.

The disciples were in their third year of close association with Jesus. During this time they had heard His marvelous teaching, had seen Him confound the religious leaders and the teachers of the law in debate, and had been eye-witnesses of His tremendous miracles of healing wherever He went. Varied and exciting were the many high points they shared in ministry with their Master.

At the time of the event recorded in our lesson text, however, the bottom had dropped out of everything for the disciples—grief and dismay had overtaken them. Jesus knew the cause of their spiritual "low" and He had a remedy for it. They needed a positive, spiritual focal point. Our lesson shows how Jesus provided for the disciples' need.

B. Lesson Background

Last week's lesson ended with Jesus in the region known as Decapolis, southeast of the Sea of Galilee. He spent three days there healing those who were lame, blind, mute, and those suffering from various other physical disorders. At the end of that time He miraculously fed the multitude, which numbered four thousand. After dismissing the multitude, He entered a boat with the disciples and crossed over to the western shore of the Sea of Galilee to the town of Magdala (Matthew 15:32-39).

In Magdala Pharisees and Sadducees demanded that He show them a sign from Heaven. Exposing their hypocrisy, Jesus rebuffed them briskly and departed. Returning by boat with the disciples to the eastern shore of the lake, Jesus warned them to beware of the leaven (the teachings) of these corrupt leaders (Matthew 16:1-12).

Next the little band moved northward to the vicinity of Caesarea Philippi. There Peter answered Jesus' inquiry with words that are among the most sublime in all of Matthew's Gospel. Speaking for himself and all of the disciples, he declared their conviction that Jesus was the Christ, the Son of the living God. In response, Jesus spoke a blessing upon Peter.

Soon, however, the mood changed. Jesus' ministry was turning toward its climax, and the disciples needed to know it. And so He revealed to them clearly for the first time that He must go to Jerusalem and suffer at the hands of the nation's religious leaders and be killed. Peter expressed the horror of the whole group at this suggestion, but he was silenced by the stern rebuke of Jesus. The Lord continued speaking to them on the theme of taking up one's cross and following Him. This turn of events left the disciples in the darkness of despair (vv. 13-28).

I. The Son Changed (Matthew 17:1-4)

A. A Place Apart (v. 1)

1. And after six days Jesus taketh Peter, James, and John his brother, and bringeth them up into a high mountain apart.

After six days. Nearly a week had passed since Jesus announced to the disciples that He was to suffer and die. They must have found this week the heaviest of their lives. Surely much earnest discussion had taken place among them, and they probably had gotten little sleep. They needed help in dealing with their despair. Understanding this, Jesus took the three leaders of the group into a *high mountain apart*, where they could be given private instruction and encouragement to help them conquer their doubt and dismay. The spiritual uplift these three were to receive would soon be radiated to the rest of the disciples. Peter had made the good confession in the vicinity of Caesarea Philippi, and it seems that Jesus and the disciples were still in this same general area. The mountain that Jesus and the three disciples ascended most likely was Mount Hermon, the highest in the region.

B. A Change in Christ's Appearance (v. 2)

2. And was transfigured before them: and his face did shine as the sun, and his raiment was white as the light.

The word *transfigured* means "transformed" or "changed." From Luke's account, we learn that Jesus' appearance changed while He was praying (Luke 9:29). His face and His garments began to shine brilliantly. The disciples were given a glimpse of Jesus' majesty; His glory was shown before their very eyes. The darkness of sadness, confusion, and despair that had filled their hearts regarding their beloved Master was dispelled by the radiance that issued forth from Him. Years later Peter wrote of this scene and its message: "For we . . . were eyewitnesses of his majesty. For he received from God the Father honor and glory . . . when we were with him in the holy mount" (2 Peter 1:16-18).

C. A Comforting Conversation (v. 3)

3. And, behold, there appeared unto them Moses and Elijah talking with him.

Apparently the three disciples were asleep when the transfiguration occurred and Moses and Elijah appeared and began talking with Jesus. Awaking from their slumber, the disciples saw the three and overheard their conversation: they were talking about Jesus' death, which was to occur in Jerusalem (Luke 9:30-32). Moses and Elijah may be considered key representatives of the law and the prophets. Did the disciples at this time understand the significance of Moses and Elijah's appearing with Jesus and discussing His death? If not, they would in time come to realize that Jesus' death was completely in harmony with God's will as revealed in the Old Testament (see Luke 24:44).

D. A Challenging Response (v. 4)

4. Then answered Peter, and said unto Jesus, Lord, it is good for us to be here: if thou wilt, let us make here three tabernacles; one for thee, and one for Moses, and one for Elijah.

Luke indicates that Peter uttered these words as Moses and Elijah started to leave (Luke 9:33). Not knowing what to say, Peter suggested that they make *three tabernacles*, one for each of these great teachers (see Mark 9:6). The word *tabernacles* here probably means shelters made from tree branches, such as the Jews dwelt in during the Feast of Tabernacles (Leviticus 23:39-43). Perhaps Peter thought that by providing shelter for the three they would stay awhile longer so the disciples could hear them all. Did he also think that by having them all stay on the mountain Jesus' death could be forestalled?

In the Christian life there are occasions we call "mountaintop experiences." These may be quiet times of retreat from the world's influences, when we can reflect privately on things spiritual. Or they may be times when we gather with other Christians to share our hope and joy in the Lord and thus encourage one another. Peter wanted his mountaintop experience to continue. We can understand that. But we also know that in order for God's will to be fully accomplished, one must come down from the mountaintop and, with Jesus, walk in the paths of service, even the way of the cross.

II. The Son Confirmed (Matthew 17:5)

A. The Father's Testimony (v. 5a, b)

5a, b. While he yet spake, behold, a bright cloud overshadowed them: and behold a voice out of the cloud, which said, This is my beloved Son, in whom I am well pleased.

While Peter was speaking, God interrupted. A brilliant cloud appeared, and a voice came out of the cloud—both indications of the presence of God. Only days before, Peter had proclaimed

How to Say It

DECAPOLIS.   Dee-*kap*-uh-lis.
MAGDALA.   *Mag*-duh-luh.
PHARISEES.   *Fair*-ih-seez.
SADDUCEES.   *Sad*-you-seez.

that Jesus was God's Son. Now God confirmed what Peter had spoken. Jesus was indeed the Son of God. And because Jesus had chosen to follow the path to Calvary, fulfilling God's purpose, the Father expressed His pleasure in the Son.

We note the similarities between Jesus' baptism and His transfiguration. By means of His baptism, Jesus publicly affirmed His purpose to shed His blood for a world lost in sin. At that time God spoke from Heaven, indicating His approval of His Son. Only a week before the transfiguration, Jesus rejected Satan's attempt to get Him to avoid the cross (Matthew 16:23); and, while on the mount, Jesus calmly spoke with Moses and Elijah about His coming death in Jerusalem. Both incidents were reaffirmations of Jesus' desire and determination to fulfill God's will, to make possible the redemption of a lost world, by sacrificing himself. And, as at Jesus' baptism, God clearly identified Jesus as His Son and spoke His approval of Him.

B. The Disciples' Responsibility (v. 5c)

5c. Hear ye him.

To Peter and the other two disciples, God said, "Listen to My Son. Because of who He is you are to accept His teachings. You must accept His words that He is to suffer and die."

Do you remember "Follow the leader," the game you played as a child? No matter what the leader did, you imitated him. So the Christian life, from beginning to end, is a life of following our leader—Jesus. We are to understand who Jesus is and what His life was all about. It was about service to others, about self-denial, about bearing the cross. We are to listen to Him and follow in His steps.

HEAR HIM!

The Mall, stretching westward from the U. S. Capitol in Washington D. C., is lined with important buildings. Among them are the White House, the Smithsonian Institute, and the National Art Gallery. Millions of people have come to the nation's capitol to visit these structures and to view their historic contents.

The Washington Monument, the Lincoln Memorial, and the Jefferson Memorial occupy places of prominence here also. These are not tombs. The men whose names they bear are buried in other places. These structures are memorials to these great presidents who led in the founding and the preserving of the United States of America. These memorials help us remember that this country was established on the principles of liberty and justice for all.

Peter may have felt the need to build monuments at the site of the transfiguration of Jesus. Here Jesus talked with Moses, the great leader and legislator of Israel, and with Elijah, one of the nation's great prophets. They were men to remember!

Peter's suggestion was made in haste. God used the proposal as a means of elevating Jesus as His beloved Son, whom everyone should hear and honor. He would create a new people out of all who would come to Him. The church, the body of Christ, is His living memorial. We remember and honor Him best as we live by His teachings and share Him with all the world.

—W. P.

III. The Son Comforts and Commands (Matthew 17:6-13)
A. Comfort for Christ's Disciples (vv. 6, 7)

6. And when the disciples heard it, they fell on their face, and were sore afraid.

When they first saw Jesus transfigured before them, the three disciples were frightened. Now, having seen this brilliant cloud and heard God speak, Peter, James, and John were "terrified" and fell down with their faces to the ground (*New International Version*). Indeed, they made the only appropriate response that weak and sinful man could make in the presence of the Almighty.

7. And Jesus came and touched them, and said, Arise, and be not afraid.

With tenderness and compassion Jesus came to the terrified disciples to banish their fear. What can be more comforting to one who is frightened than the reassuring voice and touch of a trusted loved one? Even so, nothing could have stilled the minds and hearts of these three disciples more than the touch and the voice of the Master they knew so well.

B. Focal Point for the Disciples (v. 8)

8. And when they had lifted up their eyes, they saw no man, save Jesus only.

In the Greek text the word *only* appears last in this sentence for emphasis. Moses the lawgiver and Elijah the prophet were gone; only Jesus remained. Thus was signified that the

Old Covenant had done its work and must make way for the new dispensation. God's purpose centered on Jesus, and on Him alone, and He was soon to complete the great work He had come to earth to do.

As disciples we must focus on Jesus alone. He will prove sufficient for our needs. When all else leaves or fails, Jesus remains to comfort and to guide.

WHO IS LEFT?

When men began to climb Mount Everest, in attempts to reach the pinnacle of earth's highest mountain, expedition after expedition ended in failure. Avalanches, crevasses, and extreme steepness combined with strong winds and thin air to keep most climbers from even getting close to the mountain's summit.

Finally, in 1953, the news flashed around the globe that Edmund Hillary of New Zealand and Tenzing Norway, a Nepalese Sherpa tribesman, had scaled the mountain, stood at the highest point on earth, and safely returned to their advance camp. Their feat was acclaimed by the whole world. Since then others have made the rugged climb to Everest's peak, but none have had the instant fame that Hillary and Norway attained by their historic climb.

Perhaps Peter, James, and John felt that what they had witnessed on the mount of transfiguration was the highest spiritual experience one could have. They had seen and heard Moses and Elijah, giants in the Old Testament galaxy of heroes, talking with Jesus. But God wanted them to climb higher, to the mountaintop of all spiritual reality. They must understand that Jesus stands alone as the pinnacle of man's return to God. Men would come to know in Him life on its highest plane. Don't settle for anything or anyone as a substitute for Jesus.   —W. P.

C. Command for the Disciples (v. 9)

9. And as they came down from the mountain, Jesus charged them, saying, Tell the vision to no man, until the Son of man be risen again from the dead.

As recently as a week before the transfiguration, Jesus had instructed the disciples not to tell the people at large that He was the Christ (see Matthew 16:20). The disciples themselves didn't understand what was involved in His messiahship, namely that He must die for the sins of the people and be raised again. If the disciples didn't understand that, the crowds certainly did not. The people were bent on having an earthly Messiah, one who would be their political savior. To announce publicly Jesus' deity and messiahship would only stir up national excitement and lead to reckless actions by the zealous militarists.

As Jesus and the three disciples came down from the mount of transfiguration, He cautioned them not to tell anyone at that time of the vision they had been given on the mountain. To do so would only increase the excitement of the multitudes and cause them to interfere with the course His ministry must take. The time would come when they would be able to speak of the vision, and that would be after He was raised from the dead. Then the disciples themselves would better understand the nature of His kingdom, and the people would be better prepared to receive their teaching concerning it.

The months that lay ahead in Jesus' ministry were going to be difficult ones for the disciples, and the vision of the transfigured, glorified Christ would sustain them during that time. Knowing that death could not hold Jesus, should sustain every disciple today through the hard times of life.

D. Question and Answer (vv. 10-12)

10. And his disciples asked him, saying, Why then say the scribes that Elijah must first come?

The word *then* indicates that the disciples' question related to something in the immediate past, and that seems to have been Elijah's appearance with Jesus when Jesus was transfigured. Explaining the prophecy in Malachi 4:5, 6, the scribes taught that Elijah would come and fulfill the work assigned to him before the Messiah arrived. The disciples acknowledged Jesus as the Messiah, but Elijah had only now shown himself. Furthermore, Elijah appeared to the three of them only, and they couldn't see how, in his brief appearance, he could accomplish the work spoken of by the prophet. The disciples were confused.

11. And Jesus answered and said unto them, Elijah truly shall first come, and restore all things.

In His reply, Jesus harked back to the prophecy in Malachi, which explains His use of

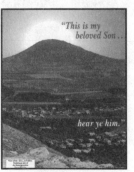

"This is my beloved Son . . . hear ye him."

visual 8

the future tense, "shall first come." Jesus confirmed that the scribes were correct in their teaching in this instance. Elijah was to come before the Messiah and *restore all things*. Some have interpreted Malachi's prophecy to mean that Elijah will appear in person before the second coming of Jesus and effect some great work of restoration. The following verses, however, seem to indicate that the restoration spoken of by Malachi was the repentance preached by John the Baptist to prepare the way for Jesus' ministry.

12. But I say unto you, That Elijah is come already, and they knew him not, but have done unto him whatsoever they listed. Likewise shall also the Son of man suffer of them.

Jesus said that Malachi's prophecy had been fulfilled: Elijah had already come. *They knew him not, but have done . . . listed.* By saying this, Jesus made it clear that He was not referring to Elijah's appearance on the mountain, but to John the Baptist (v. 13). See also Luke 1:17.

The ruling powers in Palestine did not acknowledge John as a messenger sent by God. Instead, they did to him *whatsoever they listed*, whatever they pleased. John sought to see people restored to God, but he was rejected and killed. Even so would Jesus suffer at the hands of the rulers and be slain.

We are reminded that we must be sensitive to God's work and God's will. We must not be like the religious leaders of Jesus' day who resisted God's actions and desires because He was not acting the way they thought He should.

E. Understanding (v. 13)

13. Then the disciples understood that he spake unto them of John the Baptist.

As the disciples came to this understanding, did they begin to understand also what the cost of their discipleship might be? Jesus had begun to speak of His death at the hands of the nation's rulers, a fate already suffered by John. Surely they would recall Jesus' teaching just six days before: "If any man will come after me, let him deny himself, and take up his cross, and follow me. For whosoever will save his life shall lose it: and whosoever will lose his life for my sake shall find it" (Matthew 16:24, 25). Though the cost of discipleship is great, the reward is infinitely greater. These disciples remained faithful to Christ—may we do likewise.

Conclusion

A. Reassurance

The transfiguration of Jesus was an event filled with reassurance not only for Him, but for the disciples. It had been more than two years since Jesus' baptism, and the beginning of His ministry. He had been received by the common people, but vehemently opposed by the leaders of the nation. When for a brief time Christ's essential glory shined through the body of Jesus, and He heard the Father's words of approval, surely God's chosen Servant was encouraged in the way He was going and was strengthened to continue in it to the end.

The disciples had been facing despair over Jesus' announcement of His death. But seeing the glory of God shining in and through Jesus gave them reassurance that their Master would ultimately be victorious. There was much they did not understand, but certainly they descended the mount with an understanding and a hope that they did not have before.

We too are blessed by this event. The testimony of these eyewitnesses strengthens our faith in Jesus (see John 1:14; 2 Peter 1:16-18). Further, we are assured that one day we will be like Him (1 John 3:2). O glorious day! Until then, may we heed the Father's words spoken of His Son and "hear . . . Him."

B. Prayer

O God, who before the passion of Your only Son did reveal His glory upon the mountain, grant to us a vision of His coming glory so that we may be strengthened to obey Your command to carry the cross and carry the gospel to the people around us, and throughout the entire world. Until we are changed into His likeness from glory to glory, may we live for and pray in Jesus' name, Amen.

C. Thought to Remember

Let us keep our eyes focused on Jesus and our ears attuned to His words.

Home Daily Bible Readings

Monday, Jan. 16—Elijah to Appear Before the Messiah (Malachi 4:1-5)

Tuesday, Jan. 17—Witnesses to Christ's Glory (2 Peter 1:16-21)

Wednesday, Jan. 18—Peter Says Jesus Is the Messiah (Matthew 16:13-20)

Thursday, Jan. 19—Conditions of Discipleship (Matthew 16:21-28)

Friday, Jan. 20—The Transfiguration of Jesus (Matthew 17:1-8)

Saturday, Jan. 21—Jesus Will Suffer (Matthew 17:9-13)

Sunday, Jan. 22—Jesus Heals an Afflicted Child (Matthew 17:14-23)

Learning by Doing

This page contains an alternate lesson plan emphasizing learning activities. Classes desiring such student involvement will find these suggestions helpful.

Learning Goals

This lesson should enable the students to:

1. Explain what the transfiguration meant to the disciples in Jesus' day and to us today.

2. Acknowledge a desire to "hear" Jesus and obey His teachings.

Into the Lesson

As the class members arrive, have them form groups of four to six. Give each group a copy of the following situation:

You are among a privileged few who have been permitted to catch a glimpse of Heaven. You take the trip and discover that Heaven is as it is described in Revelation 21. It is a beautiful place, perfectly formed with all kinds of precious jewels. A river runs through the middle of the city. On each side of the river are fruit-bearing trees. No light is needed there, for God and His Son Jesus are in the very middle of the city. You receive one message from Jesus while you are there: "Behold, I am coming soon! Blessed is he who keeps the words of the prophecy in this book" (Revelation 22:7, *New International Version*). When you and your group return, what will you tell those waiting to hear your report?

Let the groups work together for five to seven minutes to determine the message they would give. Then let the groups share their responses.

After the group sharing, make the transition to the study of today's Scripture text. Point out that in a special moment, three of Jesus' disciples were given a brief glimpse of His essential glory as it shone through the human form that He wore. At that time they were given a most important word from God. This event is known as the transfiguration.

Into the Word

Present the thoughts in the Lesson Background section to connect last week's lesson to the event we are studying in this lesson. Then read the Scripture text aloud in its entirety. After that is completed, lead the class in a Bible discussion, using the questions below as a guide.

1. Who went with Jesus to the mount of transfiguration? (v. 1). (Peter, James, and John—the three disciples who were closest to Jesus.)

2. What did Peter, James, and John see during the transfiguration? (vv. 2, 3). (Jesus' face shone like the sun, and His clothes were white as the light. Moses and Elijah were speaking with Him.)

3. What proposal did Peter make in response to what he saw? (v. 4). (He suggested that they build three shelters there—one each for Jesus, Moses, and Elijah.)

4. How were Peter's plans aborted? (vv. 5, 6). (A brilliant cloud appeared, and God spoke from the cloud, announcing that Jesus was His Son and that He was to be listened to.)

5. Why would Jesus ask the disciples not to tell anyone what they had seen until after His resurrection? (v. 9). (Not long before this, the crowds had thoughts of forcing Jesus to be their political leader (John 6:15). Word of His transfiguration would only intensify these misguided efforts. After His resurrection the true nature of His kingdom would be understood.)

6. What prompted the disciples' question recorded in verse 10? (see the lesson comments on this verse.)

7. What was the gist of Jesus' answer to the disciples' question? (vv. 11, 12). (The prophet Malachi spoke figuratively when he said Elijah would precede Messiah's coming. The prophecy was fulfilled in John the Baptist.)

8. What was the significance of this event for Jesus' disciples? (They were given convincing evidence that Jesus truly was the Son of God, and that He alone was worthy of their praise and obedience. They were also given divine testimony to help them understand that Jesus' impending death in Jerusalem was in accordance with God's will.)

Into Life

We have considered Jesus' transfiguration from the disciples' viewpoint, but what does it mean to us? Have a student read 2 Peter 1:16-18 aloud to the class at this time; then lead a discussion of this passage. Consider the blessing that it gives us (the certainty that the disciples were not duped regarding Jesus, the fact that they were eyewitnesses of His divine majesty, the solid basis we have for our faith in Jesus).

Ask, "What do we learn from Jesus' transfiguration that we are to do?" (Let the students express the need to listen to Jesus, obey Him, and proclaim Him to all.) Close with prayer.

Let's Talk It Over

The questions on this page are designed to encourage review of the lesson Scriptures and to promote discussion of the lesson by the class. The answers provided are only discussion starters. Let your class talk it over from there.

1. Jesus was transfigured before three of His disciples. What was this transfiguration, and what were the implications of it?

Jesus' transfiguration was a transformation, or change, in His appearance. Luke says, "The appearance of his face changed, and his clothes became as bright as a flash of lightning" (Luke 9:29, *New International Version*). Matthew records that "his face did shine as the sun, and his raiment was white as the light" (Matthew 17:2). Apparently, then, Jesus' bodily nature remained in its entirety when this change occurred. Permeating His body was a radiant splendor that indicated the Godhead.

Jesus' transfiguration was the divine seal upon His ministry. All He had done up to that time, and what He was going to do (specifically, His death on the cross) had the Father's approval. The transfiguration implied the fulfillment of the Old Covenant, as Moses, representing the law and Elijah representing the prophets, first appear and then depart, leaving only Jesus. The transfiguration carried with it the profound implication of the enthronement of Jesus Christ as prophet, priest, and king.

2. How are followers of Christ to be "transformed" or "changed"?

We may consider this question as both command and promise. In Romans 12:2 Christians are commanded not to be conformed to this world but to be "transformed" by the renewing of their minds, that they may prove what is the good, and acceptable, and perfect will of God. We are to be transformed into the likeness of Christ. We do this by the renewing of our minds, specifically by having the mind of Christ. We adopt His attitude as the controlling force in our daily lives (Philippians 2:5). As we follow His example of self-denial, service to others, and obedience to God (vv. 6-8), we become more and more like Him.

In 2 Corinthians 3:18, Paul states, "But we all, with open face beholding as in a glass the glory of the Lord, are changed into the same image from glory to glory, even as by the Spirit of the Lord." Paul's use of the present tense implies that a gradual transformation occurs in us as we center our thoughts, and thus our lives, on Jesus. This transformation into the likeness of Christ is mystical and spiritual, but it occurs in the present life as we separate ourselves from worldly thinking and behavior and draw ever closer to Christ.

Our transformation will be complete at the resurrection, when the trumpet of God shall sound. Then "the dead shall be raised incorruptible, and we shall be changed" (1 Corinthians 15:52). First John 3:2 contains God's promise: "Dear friends, now we are children of God, and what we will be has not yet been made known. But we know that when he appears, we shall be like him, for we shall see him as he is" (*New International Version*).

3. When we truly understand who Jesus is, how should we respond to Him?

The first and most natural response is to worship and adore Him. Peter's suggestion to erect three tents on the mount suggests that he saw Moses and Elijah as being on the same plane as Christ, and clearly that was a mistaken notion. God's spoken words on that occasion showed that Christ stands alone above every person. Later, when the risen Jesus appeared to Thomas and the other disciples Thomas responded, "My Lord and my God" (John 20:28). That is the response each person should make.

Recognizing Christ's deity leads one also to do what He asks. Jesus appeared to Saul on the road to Damascus. When Saul understood who He was, the persecutor responded, "Lord, what wilt thou have me to do?" (Acts 9:6). Worship and service are man's appropriate responses to Jesus.

4. The danger exists for us to give to a human leader the allegiance that Christ alone deserves. How can we keep this from happening?

The 1993 tragedy in Waco, Texas, was a grim reminder of the danger of a person's being drawn away from Christ by the influence of an outwardly impressive human leader. It is absolutely essential that our faith be centered in Christ, and not in a minister, an elder, a building, a form of service, or a doctrine. Obviously, the better we are grounded in the Scriptures the less likely we are to be swayed by the notions of a false teacher.

The People Proclaim Jesus the Son of David

DEVOTIONAL READING: Matthew 20:17-28.

LESSON SCRIPTURE: Matthew 20:17—21:17.

PRINTED TEXT: Matthew 21:1-11, 14-16.

Matthew 21:1-11, 14-16

1 And when they drew nigh unto Jerusalem, and were come to Bethphage, unto the mount of Olives, then sent Jesus two disciples,

2 Saying unto them, Go into the village over against you, and straightway ye shall find an ass tied, and a colt with her: loose them, and bring them unto me.

3 And if any man say aught unto you, ye shall say, The Lord hath need of them; and straightway he will send them.

4 All this was done, that it might be fulfilled which was spoken by the prophet, saying,

5 Tell ye the daughter of Zion, Behold, thy King cometh unto thee, meek, and sitting upon an ass, and a colt the foal of an ass.

6 And the disciples went, and did as Jesus commanded them,

7 And brought the ass, and the colt, and put on them their clothes, and they set him thereon.

8 And a very great multitude spread their garments in the way; others cut down branches from the trees, and strewed them in the way.

9 And the multitudes that went before, and that followed, cried, saying, Hosanna to the Son of David: Blessed is he that cometh in the name of the Lord; Hosanna in the highest.

10 And when he was come into Jerusalem, all the city was moved, saying, Who is this?

11 And the multitude said, This is Jesus the prophet of Nazareth of Galilee.

. . . .

14 And the blind and the lame came to him in the temple; and he healed them.

15 And when the chief priests and scribes saw the wonderful things that he did, and the children crying in the temple, and saying, Hosanna to the Son of David; they were sore displeased,

16 And said unto him, Hearest thou what these say? And Jesus saith unto them, Yea; have ye never read, Out of the mouth of babes and sucklings thou hast perfected praise?

GOLDEN TEXT: Hosanna to the Son of David: Blessed is he that cometh in the name of the Lord; Hosanna in the highest.—Matthew 21:9.

Jesus the Fulfillment
(Matthew)
Unit 3. Jesus: The Son of David
(Lessons 5-9)

Lesson Aims

This lesson is designed to help the students:

1. Affirm that Jesus is the Messiah, who came as the fulfillment of biblical prophecy.

2. Recognize that Jesus is the King of kings, whose kingdom is not of this world.

3. To allow Jesus to reign in their lives, governing their attitudes and actions.

Lesson Outline

INTRODUCTION
   A. Speaking a Different Language
   B. Lesson Background
I. PREPARATIONS FOR THE KING (Matthew 21:1-7)
   A. Arrival at the Mount of Olives (v. 1)
   B. Instructions From Jesus (vv. 2, 3)
   C. Fulfillment of Prophecy (vv. 4, 5)
   D. Obedient Disciples (vv. 6, 7)
II. PRESENTATION OF THE KING (Matthew 21:8-11)
   A. The Triumphal Entry (v. 8)
   B. The King Acclaimed (v. 9)
   C. Curious Crowds (v. 10)
   D. Reserved Reply (v. 11)
III. PRAISE FOR THE KING (Matthew 21:14-16)
   A. Healing in the Temple (v. 14)
   B. Contrasting Reactions to Jesus (v. 15)
   C. Scriptural Defense (v. 16)
     Unashamed Praise
CONCLUSION
   A. Proclaim Jesus King
   B. Prayer
   C. Thought to Remember

Visual 9 of the visuals packet summarizes the multitudes' acclamation of Jesus at the triumphal entry. The visual is shown on page 189.

Introduction

A. Speaking a Different Language

Many years ago, a man from Greece committed a minor crime while visiting in an American city. The police were unable to communicate with the man in his native language, so they placed him in a mental hospital, intending to deal with his case in a short time.

Unfortunately, the records of this incident were misplaced, and this Greek-speaking gentle-man was left for years in the mental hospital. There he learned to speak English, but he learned it from *English-speaking mental patients.* As a result, he learned only the dysfunctional language of the mental patients. This led his doctors, who spoke with him only in English, to diagnose him as mentally ill. In fact, the man could have demonstrated himself healthy if he had been given the opportunity to communicate with his doctors *in his own language.* Before the mistake was corrected, the man had spent half his life in a mental hospital.

Jesus Christ was God's Son who came to earth as God's Messiah. He came speaking *the language of the kingdom of God,* but many people were unprepared to understand that language.

In Jesus' miracles the people saw the power of God; in His teaching they recognized an authority greater than man's. These combined to create in the people's hearts the hope that Jesus would become their deliverer. The hopes and expectations they had placed in Jesus were given full expression in His triumphal entry, when they acclaimed Him as the King who came in the name of the Lord. The events of the week that followed, however, revealed that they really didn't understand the deliverance He brought, nor the nature of the kingdom He came to establish.

B. Lesson Background

Jesus' disciples were slowly learning the nature of His divine purpose on earth. At Caesarea Philippi, Peter had demonstrated his growing awareness of the identity and mission of Jesus when he testified, "Thou art the Christ, the Son of the living God" (Matthew 16:16). On the mount of transfiguration, Peter, James, and John had heard the voice of God proclaim, "This is my beloved Son, in whom I am well pleased" (Matthew 17:5).

Jesus spent the next six months preparing His disciples for His coming death. In His third passion prediction (Matthew 20:17-19), Jesus forewarned His disciples that catastrophic events were on the horizon: (1) The chief priests and scribes would deliver Him to the Gentiles to be mocked and scourged; (2) He would be condemned to death by crucifixion; (3) He would rise again from the dead.

In today's lesson, the time of the fulfillment of the ancient prophecies is at hand. Jesus said to His disciples, "Behold, we go up to Jerusalem" (Matthew 20:18). Thousands of Jews from Galilee, Perea, and the Decapolis were also journeying there to celebrate the Passover.

On their way to Jerusalem, Jesus and His disciples passed through Jericho, where Jesus bestowed sight on two blind men, one of whom was named Bartimeus (Matthew 20:29-34; Mark 10:46-52). In this city Jesus also visited in the home of Zaccheus (Luke 19:1-10). From Jericho, the Lord and His disciples traveled to Bethany, a small village on the southeastern slope of the Mount of Olives, and spent the Sabbath in the home of Mary, Martha, and Lazarus (John 12:1-8). On the next morning, Jesus made His descent from the Mount of Olives into Jerusalem, the event known as "the triumphal entry."

I. Preparations for the King (Matthew 21:1-7)

A. Arrival at the Mount of Olives (v. 1)

1. And when they drew nigh unto Jerusalem, and were come to Bethphage, unto the mount of Olives, then sent Jesus two disciples.

On the day following the Sabbath, Jesus and His disciples left Bethany and came to the small village of *Bethphage*, located on the eastern slope of *the mount of Olives*, between Bethany and Jerusalem. The Mount of Olives, just east of Jerusalem, was separated from the city by the Kidron Valley. The summit of the mount, about a mile east of the city, rose about three hundred feet above the temple hill and provided a panoramic view of the city. In Jesus' day, this mount must have been thickly wooded with olive groves, palm trees, and other vegetation.

B. Instructions From Jesus (vv. 2, 3)

2, 3. Saying unto them, Go into the village over against you, and straightway ye shall find an ass tied, and a colt with her: loose them, and bring them unto me. And if any man say aught unto you, ye shall say, The Lord hath need of them; and straightway he will send them.

The two disciples, who are not named, were sent to Bethphage to secure an ass and her colt. It is unclear as to whether Jesus had made arrangements for these animals to be available, or if He foreknew supernaturally that they would be there and that the owner would gladly let the disciples bring them to Him.

The Lord hath need would imply that the owner of the animals was a disciple of Jesus. The same is indicated by the fact that, when the disciples gave explanation, the man would immediately comply with the request.

Only Matthew says there were two animals; Mark mentions only one (Mark 11:2) and describes it as a *colt*, that is, a young ass. Mark also tells us that the animal was unbroken—it had never been ridden. Having the colt's mother alongside would perhaps make the animal easier to handle. In any case, the unbroken animal remained calm under the hands of Jesus.

C. Fulfillment of Prophecy (vv. 4, 5)

4. All this was done, that it might be fulfilled which was spoken by the prophet, saying.

While Jesus was deliberately fulfilling messianic prophecies, there was no attempt on His part at manipulation. That is to say, He did not look into the Old Testament to find out what the Messiah would do, and then set out to fulfill those prophecies. Rather, God had directed the prophet to make this prediction, and Jesus, being the Messiah spoken of, now fulfilled those prophecies. This was for Him an act of self-disclosure. In the past, Jesus maintained a cloak of limited secrecy over His messianic intentions; that cloak was now lifted.

5. Tell ye the daughter of Zion, Behold, thy King cometh unto thee, meek, and sitting upon an ass, and a colt the foal of an ass.

Tell ye the daughter of Zion. These opening words are quoted from Isaiah 62:11. *The daughter of Zion* is a reference to Jerusalem herself. Zion was the principal hill on which the city was built. Of course, the inhabitants of the city were included in this term.

Behold, thy King cometh unto thee. These and the remaining words of this verse are quoted from the prophecy in Zechariah 9:9. The context in Zechariah shows that this was spoken concerning the Messiah. The nature of the Messiah's reign was indicated also by the prophet. He would be *meek*, a fact that would be emphasized by His riding into Jerusalem on *the foal of an ass.*

In Western societies the ass is often a despised animal. This was not necessarily true in Eastern lands. In Israel of old, judges and chieftains often came riding them. To do so was a sign that these dignitaries came in peace (Judges 5:10; 10:4). The horse, on the other hand, was often a mount of war.

In the manner of Jesus' coming to Jerusalem, therefore, Matthew indicates that Jesus fulfilled all that Zechariah had prophesied. He came in

---

How to Say It

BARTIMEUS.   *Bar*-tih-*me*-us (strong accent on *me*).

BETHPHAGE.   *Beth*-fuh-gee.

CAESAREA PHILIPPI.   Sess-uh-*ree*-uh Fih-*lip*-pie or *Fil*-ih-pie.

DECAPOLIS.   Dee-*kap*-uh-lis.

JEHU.   *Jee*-hew.

ZACCHEUS.   Zak-*kee*-us.

ZECHARIAH.   Zek-uh-*rye*-uh.

meekness as the Prince of peace, the ruler of a spiritual, not a material, kingdom.

Jesus came to Jerusalem as Israel's King, yet He was not the kind of king they were prepared to receive. They did not want a king who was *meek*, but one who was warlike, one who would reflect the power of Israel's past kings and reaffirm Israel's splendor among the nations.

D. Obedient Disciples (vv. 6, 7)

6. And the disciples went, and did as Jesus commanded them.

These disciples were, no doubt, filled with confusion, curiosity, and apprehension about coming events. Only a few months earlier in Jerusalem, during the Feast of Dedication, the religious authorities had attempted to kill Jesus (see John 10:31, 39). The disciples were certain that danger still awaited their Master in the capital city (compare John 11:14-16). Yet, there was no hesitation or questioning when Jesus gave them instructions.

We have to be impressed at this point with the unquestioning obedience of the disciples. And what of us, Jesus' disciples today? In the New Testament, we have His commands for His followers in every generation. Do we obey without hesitation, or do we find reasons for not doing as He wishes us to do?

7. And brought the ass, and the colt, and put on them their clothes, and they set him thereon.

The disciples brought the animals to Jesus, realizing that He was going to ride on one of them. Since they did not know which animal He planned to ride, they spread *their clothes*, their heavy outer garments, on both animals. To surrender one's garment in such a manner was to extend great homage to Jesus.

Matthew writes, *they set him thereon.* The better attested reading is "he sat thereon." Notice that (1) Jesus rode with no saddle, though He was seated on borrowed garments; (2) No one had ever ridden on this animal before. Only animals that had never been used were considered fit for sacred use. According to the law, the red heifer that was used for the ceremonial cleansing of sin must be an animal "upon which never came yoke" (Numbers 19:2-9).

In God's design, Jesus was born to a woman who had never known a man (Luke 1:34; Matthew 1:20, 23). After His death on the cross, Jesus was buried in a tomb that had never been used (Matthew 27:60). It is appropriate that, at His triumphal entry, Jesus rode an animal that had never before been ridden.

On all previous occasions, Jesus had walked into Jerusalem; now He came like David or one of the judges—riding an ass.

II. Presentation of the King (Matthew 21:8-11)

A. The Triumphal Entry (v. 8)

8. And a very great multitude spread their garments in the way; others cut down branches from the trees, and strewed them in the way.

Many worshipers were coming to Jerusalem to observe the Passover, and as they came nearer to the capital city they merged into *a very great multitude.* Many of these people were from Galilee, and no doubt had either witnessed Jesus' ministry and miracles firsthand or knew others who had. Many believed Him to be a prophet, or even the Messiah. As the people came to the realization that Jesus was in their midst, excitement began to rise. And when they saw Him mount the animal, their enthusiasm increased. Would He at this time reveal His plan and use His great power to establish His kingdom?

Seeing the disciples remove their cloaks and put them on the animals for Jesus to sit on, some of the people in the crowd began to remove their outer garments, perhaps their very best for the Passover (?), and to *spread their garments in the way* for Jesus to ride on. Others in the crowd *cut down branches from the trees* for the same purpose. John, in his Gospel account, mentions specifically that the branches of palm trees were used (John 12:13). However, olive and other trees grew there, so branches and leaves of those trees also may have been cut or plucked to lay in Jesus' path.

We read in the Old Testament that after Jehu was anointed king of the northern kingdom, "they hasted, and took every man his garment, and put it under him on the top of the stairs, and blew with trumpets, saying, Jehu is king" (2 Kings 9:13). So, by spreading their garments and small branches in the way over which Jesus rode, the people were expressing their feeling that Jesus was royalty.

B. The King Acclaimed (v. 9)

9. And the multitudes that went before, and that followed, cried, saying, Hosanna to the Son of David: Blessed is he that cometh in the name of the Lord; Hosanna in the highest.

The multitudes that went before, and that followed. This indicates two different groups. Some of the pilgrims to the Passover feast were already in Jerusalem. John mentions that when they heard Jesus was coming, many took palm branches and went out to meet and honor Him (John 12:12, 13). At some point on the Mount of Olives this multitude met the one in the midst of which Jesus was riding. The former then turned back toward the city, so that they then were going before Him.

The title *Son of David* must be understood against the backdrop of Jewish history. King David was among the most esteemed of Israel's rulers. During His reign, the united kingdom of Israel was a powerful, sovereign nation, one to be reckoned with. Israel's days as an international power were short-lived, however, and in time they lost their independence. For centuries they were ruled by other nations, a condition that continued in the days of Jesus by the domination of the Romans. Historically, Jewish hopes were centered on a future King who would come from the line of David—a son of David. This leader would be the Anointed One, or Messiah, who they believed would lead Israel back to her position of splendor and power. Jesus clearly left the impression that He was this King.

Hosanna means literally, "save now." Originally a prayer of supplication, this term had come to be an expression of joy and congratulation.

Blessed . . . in the name of the Lord. The crowds invoked God's blessing on Him who had come "as the Lord's representative, God's Messiah."

Hosanna in the highest is somewhat equivalent to "Glory to God in the highest" (Luke 2:14). The people were thanking God in the highest heavens for sending the Messiah.

Whereas earlier in His ministry Jesus discouraged His disciples from spreading the word that He was the Christ, now He openly asserted His claims to that title. He accepted the homage of the multitudes, making no attempt to quiet them. His acquiescence encouraged the people to increase their shouts of acclamation, with the result that the excitement of throngs intensified as Jesus made His way down the Mount of Olives to the gate of the city.

Although the people were rightfully acclaiming Jesus as the Messiah, their concept of the Messiah was decidedly incorrect. They believed God's Anointed would lead a political-military movement that would deliver them from the yoke of bondage to Rome. Jesus, however, came in meekness, for His was a mission of peace and salvation.

C. Curious Crowds (v. 10)

10. And when he was come into Jerusalem, all the city was moved, saying, Who is this?

As Jesus and the great crowd descended the Mount of Olives, they were in full view of the throngs of people assembled in the city of Jerusalem for the Passover. Matthew tells us that the vast crowds were *moved* at this unusual procession as it made its way into the city. No doubt among the general populace many entertained hope that the moment of victory over Roman oppression had come. The religious au-

thorities, on the other hand, were aroused to greater envy and hatred (see John 12:19).

Among the crowds in the city were Jews from all parts of the world who had come to celebrate the Passover. Perhaps they were the ones who asked, *Who is this?*

D. Reserved Reply (v. 11)

11. And the multitude said, This is Jesus the prophet of Nazareth of Galilee.

The multitude, that is, the people who were in the procession, kept repeating to the inquiries, *This is Jesus the prophet of Nazareth of Galilee.* It was a modest reply, one that could not be denied. Nor would it stir up controversy. Had the crowds continued calling Jesus their "King" (Luke 19:38; John 12:13), the Roman authorities might have taken swift and strong measures to break up the procession.

III. Praise for the King
(Matthew 21:14-16)

A. Healing in the Temple (v. 14)

14. And the blind and the lame came to him in the temple; and he healed them.

Early in His ministry, Jesus cleansed the temple, driving out the money changers and those who sold animals there (John 2:13-15). He cleansed the temple once again following His triumphal entry. Mark, giving careful notations of time in His account, indicates that this cleansing took place on the day following the triumphal entry (Mark 11:11-15). The healings recorded in this verse in our text took place after this cleansing of the temple.

The authority Jesus assumed in cleansing the temple was supported by His miracles of healing. Both actions were steps in His revealing himself to be the Messiah.

B. Contrasting Reactions to Jesus (v. 15)

15. And when the chief priests and scribes saw the wonderful things that he did, and the children crying in the temple, and saying, Hosanna to the Son of David; they were sore displeased.

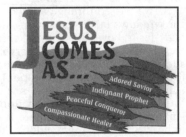

visual 9

The crowds were overjoyed as they saw miracle after miracle of healing, and the children took up the chant of the multitudes the day before (v. 9). Already furious because Jesus had expelled their crooked market from the temple, the religious leaders were filled with envy at the honor and acclaim being given Jesus.

C. Scriptural Defense (v. 16)

16. And said unto him, Hearest thou what these say? And Jesus saith unto them, Yea; have ye never read, Out of the mouth of babes and sucklings thou hast perfected praise?

Hearest thou what these say? The praises implied high homage. Professing to be zealous for God's honor, the chief priests and Pharisees appealed to Jesus to put a stop to this behavior. A paraphrase of their words might be, "Jesus, why are you allowing the people to treat you like God? Stop immediately these blasphemous words from being spoken!"

In response, Jesus stated that the children's praise fulfilled the word of Psalm 8:2, a psalm acknowledged as messianic. Jesus affirmed that He was indeed God's Messiah and, therefore, worthy of the praise being given Him.

It is noteworthy that little children hailed Jesus as the Messiah, whereas sophisticated religious leaders rejected Him. Even today, the humble often perceive spiritual truth more readily than the sophisticated (1 Corinthians 1:26-28).

UNASHAMED PRAISE

Jamaican believers love to sing praises to Jesus. Across the hills and valleys of that lovely land one can hear the people singing hymns and choruses on Sunday, and at street corners during the week. Their natural desire to praise Jesus causes them to share their faith in song.

Our family served as missionaries in Jamaica in the 1950s. Our four children began singing from early childhood, and they felt at ease singing hymns and choruses in the car while we were in that land. While we were on furlough in the United States, the children entertained themselves by singing as we traveled the highways from appointment to appointment. Even Mom and Dad would join in.

As we passed through a town or city with the car windows open, the singing would continue, and "Jesus Loves Me" would resound from the car for all to hear. Dad got nervous, and on one such occasion he made an unfortunate remark to Mother. "Couldn't you just quiet them down? I might not hear an ambulance or police car!" Mother's reply was, "You don't mind their singing the gospel when there is no one around to hear. Sing with them. I don't think we'll be ar-

rested for praising the Lord with such joy!" Dad was properly rebuked.

The religious leaders in Jerusalem didn't want to hear the praise of Jesus either. Our Lord replied to their objection to the children's expressions of praise, "Have you never read, 'From the lips of children and infants you have ordained praise'" (*New International Version*). Children have no fear in singing what they believe. Do you?   —W. P.

Conclusion

A. Proclaim Jesus King

Jesus rode into Jerusalem amid the plaudits of crowds who hailed Him as the One who came in the name of the Lord. His divine mission and authority had been revealed throughout His ministry among the people in the obscure towns and desert places of Galilee and elsewhere. That revelation continued right in the nation's capital following His triumphal entry, as He cleansed the temple and performed miracles of healing.

The religious authorities rejected Him. It seems that even those who hailed Him as King at His triumphal entry turned from Him by week's end.

Is Jesus our King? Do we allow Him to rule our hearts?

B. Prayer

Father, this day we declare with the angels in heaven: "To him who sits on the throne and to the Lamb be praise and honor and glory and power, for ever and ever!" (Revelation 5:13, *New International Version*).

C. Thought to Remember

Today and forever, Jesus is King!

Home Daily Bible Readings

Monday, Jan. 23—Thanksgiving for God's Salvation (Psalm 118:19-29)

Tuesday, Jan. 24—Followers of Jesus Must Serve Others (Matthew 20:17-28)

Wednesday, Jan. 25—Jesus Heals Two Blind Men (Matthew 20:29-34)

Thursday, Jan. 26—Jesus Approaches Jerusalem (Matthew 21:1-5)

Friday, Jan. 27—The Crowds Welcome Jesus (Matthew 21:6-11)

Saturday, Jan. 28—Jesus Cleanses the Temple and Heals (Matthew 21:12-17)

Sunday, Jan. 29—Jesus' Authority Questioned (Matthew 21:23-32)

Learning by Doing

This page contains an alternate lesson plan emphasizing learning activities. Classes desiring such student involvement will find these suggestions helpful.

Learning Goals

After this lesson the students will:

1. Understand the significance of the events in this passage of Scripture.

2. Yield more fully to the lordship of Christ.

3. Determine a way to express Jesus' lordship to those who do not know Him.

Into the Lesson

During the week before class, prepare several sets of words as follows: On a sheet of paper write, "Hosanna to the Son of David: Blessed is he that cometh in the name of the Lord; Hosanna in the highest." Cut the words apart, scramble them, and put them in an envelope.

As the class members arrive, play a tape of songs that emphasize the majesty of Christ. Divide class members into groups of three or four. Give each group an envelope containing a set of the words, and ask them to put the words in the correct order. If they have difficulty doing this, tell them they can refer to Matthew 21:9 for help. Allot five to seven minutes for this, then have the class members read aloud the verse they unscrambled.

Make the transition into the Bible study by stating that this verse is central to today's lesson.

Into the Word

The Lesson Background section mentions some of the events that occurred between Jesus' transfiguration (last week's lesson) and the triumphal entry, which we will examine today. Present these thoughts now to establish the background for today's study.

Ask several class members ahead of time to read the Scripture text. Have one be the narrator, who reads all of the connecting materials; another to read the words spoken by Jesus; a third to read the words of the prophet; and a fourth to read the words of the crowd. Have them read the text to the class at this time.

Now divide the class into five groups, and give each group one of the following tasks to complete.

Group 1. Read Matthew 21:1-11, 14-16. Describe these events from the point of view of Jesus' disciples.

Group 2. Read Matthew 21:1-11, 14-16. Describe these events from the point of view of a person in the crowd in whose midst Jesus rode into Jerusalem.

Group 3. Read Matthew 21:1-11, 14-16. Describe these events from the point of view of a resident of Jerusalem who witnessed them, but who was not a participant.

Group 4. Read Matthew 21:1-11, 14-16. Describe these events from the point of view of the enemies of Jesus.

Group 5. Read Matthew 21:1-11, 14-16. Describe these events from Jesus' point of view.

Allow the groups six to eight minutes to complete their work. Then briefly explain today's Bible text. After you have completed the explanation, ask the groups to report their conclusions in the numerical order shown above.

Into Life

Develop a discussion to apply the lesson to life. Use the following questions as a guide.

1. What is the central teaching of today's text, and what are its implications for us? (Jesus is the Messiah, who fulfilled Old Testament prophecy. He came as a King, sent and approved by the Lord. Possessing the authority of God, Jesus deserves our obedient service.)

2. The triumphal entry was a spontaneous event, in which the multitudes suddenly began praising Jesus. What reasons do we have to praise Jesus? (Let the pupils brainstorm reasons for praising Jesus. Be sure the list includes His redemptive work for us.).

3. How can we proclaim the lordship of Jesus so that those who don't know Him will be drawn to Him? (We should begin by making Him the Lord of our lives. If we love others and serve them as Jesus has shown and taught us, people will be attracted to our Lord. As opportunity arises, we will then be able to share the message of Christ with them.)

4. When we share the good news of Jesus with those who don't know Him, what should we tell them? (Let the class give suggestions. Among the cardinal facts that we would share about Jesus are these: Who He is, why He came to earth, His death on the cross, His resurrection, and what His redemptive work accomplished for us.)

Conclude the session with these activities:

1. Ask class members to reconsider their personal commitment to Jesus Christ.

2. Ask them to share their responses to Jesus, and then pray together.

Let's Talk It Over

The questions on this page are designed to encourage review of the lesson Scriptures and to promote discussion of the lesson by the class. The answers provided are only discussion starters. Let your class talk it over from there.

1. What guidelines should a Christian consider in responding to requests for material assistance?

It is good to be generous with our possessions as well as our time and talents, but generosity often is loaded with problems. We may turn down a plea for help because we do not realize that Jesus is asking, and so we come face to face with the warning, "Inasmuch as ye did it not to one of the least of these, ye did it not to me" (Matthew 25:45). Jesus said, "Give to him that asketh thee" (Matthew 5:42), but 2 Thessalonians 3:10 makes it plain that there is a time to refuse to give. It is quite common for a Christian to receive so many pleas for help that he cannot possibly answer all of them; but we cannot escape the problem by refusing to answer any. Thoughtfully and prayerfully each person must decide what response or responses would be acceptable to Jesus.

2. What is the significance of Jesus' entering Jerusalem riding on a donkey instead of on a horse?

Military conquerors rode on horses. Had Jesus chosen to ride a horse or steed, He would have projected the image of a warrior. Jesus, however, came in peace, and He came bringing peace. His riding on a donkey signified this.

Of key importance is the fact that this action was the fulfillment of Zechariah 9:9. This Old Testament prophecy indicated that the Messiah, who would bring salvation to the people, would come to Jerusalem in this manner. Thus we see that this was an act of self-disclosure. Jesus was declaring himself to be the Messiah and at the same time accentuating His humility and the nature of His kingdom and His kingship.

3. The crowds were excited and acclaimed Jesus King as He rode in their midst to the city of Jerusalem. How can we recreate a measure of this excitement and enthusiasm in our worship today?

Perhaps the first step is to be certain that we are more concerned about praising our heavenly Father and magnifying Christ than we are about our own convenience and satisfaction in our worship assemblies. If we come together with selfish thoughts, the spirit of worship will be crushed. Perhaps too it would be helpful to put more emphasis on Jesus' promises recorded in Matthew 18:20 and 28:20. These assure us of Jesus' presence as we are involved in sharing and serving in His name. Thus we may be certain that He will be as much with us as He was with the multitudes on the day of His triumphal entry into Jerusalem.

4. It is Luke who includes the notation that as Jesus neared Jerusalem, He wept over the city. What response do you think Jesus would make in observing our cities today?

We hear a great deal about the plight of our modern cities. They are ravaged by poverty, pollution, crime, and violence. Many persons who live in them suffer from loneliness, emptiness, and despair. Viewing the pervasive effects of sin and irreligion on one hand, and indifference on the other, Jesus surely would weep over the cities of today, too.

5. The people of Israel in Jesus' day held differing views regarding Him. What were some of them?

(1) Prophet. Matthew 21:11 records that the multitude acclaimed Him as "the prophet of Nazareth of Galilee." Many in the crowd regarded Jesus as a prophet who had come to foretell the reign of God.

(2) Liberator. The most nationalistic among the people felt that Jesus would be, or should be, a military leader. They looked for Him to use His great power to lead them in throwing off the yoke of Roman tyranny.

(3) Earthly king. Many in the triumphal entry crowds expected Jesus to establish His kingdom and rule in the tradition of David.

(4) Impostor. The religious leaders in Israel knew that Jesus claimed to be equal with God, and for this they regarded Him as a blasphemer and an impostor—one who was worthy of death.

(5) Troublemaker. The greedy and the powerful saw Him as their enemy, for He exposed their selfish motives and was a threat to their influential position among the people.

(6) The Son of God. Those who were closest to Jesus, who received His teachings and observed His miracles with an open mind, came to this conviction.

Jesus Institutes the Lord's Supper

DEVOTIONAL READING: John 6:30-40.

LESSON SCRIPTURE: Matthew 26:17-35.

PRINTED TEXT: Matthew 26:20-30.

Matthew 26:20-30

20 Now when the even was come, he sat down with the twelve.

21 And as they did eat, he said, Verily I say unto you, that one of you shall betray me.

22 And they were exceeding sorrowful, and began every one of them to say unto him, Lord, is it I?

23 And he answered and said, He that dippeth his hand with me in the dish, the same shall betray me.

24 The Son of man goeth as it is written of him: but woe unto that man by whom the Son of man is betrayed! it had been good for that man if he had not been born.

25 Then Judas, which betrayed him, answered and said, Master, is it I? He said unto him, Thou hast said.

26 And as they were eating, Jesus took bread, and blessed it, and brake it, and gave it to the disciples, and said, Take, eat; this is my body.

27 And he took the cup, and gave thanks, and gave it to them, saying, Drink ye all of it;

28 For this is my blood of the new testament, which is shed for many for the remission of sins.

29 But I say unto you, I will not drink henceforth of this fruit of the vine, until that day when I drink it new with you in my Father's kingdom.

30 And when they had sung a hymn, they went out into the mount of Olives.

Feb
5

GOLDEN TEXT: This is my blood of the new testament, which is shed for many for the remission of sins.—Matthew 26:28.

Jesus the Fulfillment
(Matthew)
Unit 4. Jesus Christ: Victor Over Sin and Death (Lessons 10-13)

Lesson Aims

This lesson should enable students to:

1. Understand the significance of the last supper.

2. Have a deeper love for Jesus, who gave His life for our redemption.

3. Participate in the Lord's Supper with renewed meaning.

Lesson Outline

INTRODUCTION
　A. Meals and Memory
　B. Lesson Background
I. THE MEAL BEGINS (Matthew 26:20)
II. THE BETRAYAL ANNOUNCED (Matthew 26:21-25)
　A. Self-Examination (vv. 21, 22)
　B. It Is He! (vv. 23, 24)
　C. Is It I? (v. 25)
III. THE MEAL WITHIN THE MEAL (Matthew 26:26-29)
　A. The Bread and the Body (v. 26)
　　Symbol of Life
　B. The Cup and the Covenant (vv. 27-29)
　　Cup of Sacrifice
IV. THE MEAL CONCLUDES (Matthew 26:30)
CONCLUSION
　A. A Matter of Life and Death
　B. Prayer
　C. Thought to Remember

Visual 10 of the visual packet is a comparison of the new covenant with the old covenant based on Matthew 26:28. The visual is shown on page 196.

Introduction

A. Meals and Memory

Many of the most memorable moments in my life have one thing in common—they were associated with meals. Perhaps the same is true for many others as well.

The disciples of Jesus shared a memorable meal with Him after His resurrection (see John 21). The first Christians experienced happiness and unity in meals taken together (Acts 2:46). And the consummation of the ages will take place at the marriage supper of the Lamb (Reve-

lation 19:6-9). We are not surprised, therefore, that Jesus chose the occasion of the Passover meal, to impart to His disciples the significance of His death, and to establish a memorial to it.

No doubt Jesus and His disciples had celebrated the Passover meal together on other occasions. But this celebration would be different. A new and deeper meaning would be given to this ancient memorial, a significance that would even have implications for eternity.

B. Lesson Background

For centuries Jews had commemorated the Passover. The Passover meal was a memorial to Israel's exodus from Egypt.

Beginning on Passover and continuing for one week, the Jews ate their bread without leaven. This recalled that their forefathers left Egypt in such haste that they had no time to leaven the dough (Exodus 12:30-34, 37-39; 13:3-7). Also on the night preceding the exodus, at God's instruction the Israelites daubed the blood of the Passover lamb on the lintel and door posts of their homes. Thus Israel was spared when the Lord brought death to all the firstborn of Egypt (Exodus 12:21-28). In this lesson we will see the new significance Jesus gave to the unleavened bread, and the eternal rescue that would be gained by the shedding of His blood.

The last supper occurred on Thursday evening of the "last week" of Jesus' earthly ministry. He entered the city to great acclaim on Sunday. On Monday He indicated the spiritual nature of His mission by cleansing the temple. Back in the temple on Tuesday, He engaged in discussion and debate for the final time with the religious leaders. It seems that He rested with friends in Bethany on Wednesday. Then on Thursday He instructed His disciples to prepare for the Passover meal.

I. The Meal Begins
(Matthew 26:20)

20. Now when the even was come, he sat down with the twelve.

In the upper room on the evening before His death, Jesus would deal with the disciples' desire for greatness, wash the feet of His disciples, command them to love one another as He had loved them, and reassure them of the presence of God's Spirit. Now He must turn to the matter at hand—His ensuing death.

The twelve were Jesus' closest followers and comprised His family for the Passover celebration. They were more, however; they were His best hope for comprehending and carrying on His work.

II. The Betrayal Announced (Matthew 26:21-25)

A. Self-Examination (vv. 21, 22)

21. And as they did eat, he said, Verily I say unto you, that one of you shall betray me.

The Passover meal was well under way when Jesus interjected a sobering thought—He would be betrayed by one of the disciples seated at the table! We should not become so quickly absorbed in the shocked reaction of the disciples that we fail to gauge Jesus' own feelings of sadness. Imagine the sense of betrayal He felt. One of those whom He had chosen and taught and loved was rejecting Him, His teachings, and His care. An enemy might oppose, but only a friend can betray.

We who follow Jesus may also be betrayed by someone we love. If a family member or a fellow Christian lets us down, we have the assurance that Jesus understands our feelings. He experienced a similar hurt.

22. And they were exceeding sorrowful, and began every one of them to say unto him, Lord, is it I?

Jesus' shocking words brought deep sadness to the disciples. Each of them except Judas knew he had no intention of betraying Jesus, but each feared the possibility that he might be the agent of betrayal. At different times some of the disciples had displayed attitudes and actions that were in conflict with Him whom they called their Lord. James and John had suggested destroying a Samaritan village with fire from Heaven (Luke 9:54), and Peter had had the effrontery to rebuke Jesus and try to keep Him from going to Jerusalem. (Matthew 16:22). As it turned out, each one of them ran and hid at the moment of their Master's greatest need, and Peter even denied he knew Him. Not only did each disciple recognize at this moment his potential for betrayal, but each acted it out in one way or another before this night ended. It is to their credit, therefore, that *every one of them* began to search his own heart instead of trying to determine which of the others was guilty.

We who are Jesus' disciples must realize that whenever our selfish agendas override our loyalty to Jesus, we are at risk of betraying Him.

B. It Is He! (vv. 23, 24)

23. And he answered and said, He that dippeth his hand with me in the dish, the same shall betray me.

During the Passover meal, herbs, bread, and meat were dipped into a vessel of sauce, which was served to the participants in common. Thus Jesus would dip with all of the disciples, in a sense, since all at one time or other would dip his food into the common bowl. Some, however, feel that the expression *dippeth his hand with me in the dish* suggests that the traitor was seated near Jesus. From the Gospel of John we conclude that John, the beloved disciple, was reclining to the right of Jesus (see John 13:23-25). Thus some feel that Judas was reclining immediately on Jesus' left. If this is correct, then the exchange that took place between Jesus and Judas (see verse 25) may have been in an undertone that the others did not catch.

The seats on either side of Jesus were places of honor. Had Jesus invited His own betrayer to this position of intimacy and honor? Had He done so as one last appeal to Judas to alter his intentions?

How ironic that the sign of the betrayal came in and through an act of fellowship and shared life! This fact reemphasizes the perfidy of the traitor.

24. The Son of man goeth as it is written of him: but woe unto that man by whom the Son of man is betrayed! it had been good for that man if he had not been born.

Avoiding titles of power such as "Messiah" and "Son of God," Jesus usually called himself the *Son of man,* a phrase rich in personal meaning and prophetic significance. The phrase sometimes served as a simple substitute for the pronoun "I." It also would have reminded Jews of its use in Ezekiel, where it described the faithful prophet of God. Daniel used the phrase to prophesy the coming of one who would receive an everlasting kingdom, which would never pass away nor be destroyed (Daniel 7:13, 14). In other words, this title suggested appropriately enough Jesus' humanity, His humility, His suffering, His prophetic role, and His victorious rule.

The prophecy referred to here—*the Son of man goeth*—refers to the whole cluster of events surrounding His death. Psalm 22 and Isaiah 53 are two of the Old Testament passages that clearly foreshadow those events and indicate that Jesus died *as it is written of him.*

Jesus turned from the prophesied fact of His death to the personal facilitator of it—Judas. Some people think Judas was personally predestined by God to betray Jesus. Indeed, the book of Acts implies that the need to replace one of the twelve had been prophesied (Acts 1:20; Psalms

---

How to Say It

CAIAPHAS.   *Kay*-uh-fus or *Kye*-uh-fus.

69:25; 109:8). However, because God knew in advance what would happen and inspired His prophets to write of it hundreds of years earlier does not mean that He caused it to happen. Speaking of Judas's betrayal of Jesus, the fourth-century church father Chrysostom said, "The prescience of God is not the cause of men's wickedness, nor does it involve any necessity of it; Judas was not a traitor because God foresaw it, but he foresaw it because Judas would be so." Jesus' words in this verse strongly suggest that the responsibility for the decision lay with Judas himself.

C. Is It I? (v. 25)

25. Then Judas, which betrayed him, answered and said, Master, is it I? He said unto him, Thou hast said.

Like the others, Judas asked the same question. But why? Was it to hide his intentions from Jesus? But surely He knew of Jesus' ability to discern the heart of a man (see Matthew 9:4). Was it to conceal his plans from his fellow disciples? Perhaps. Or was it a desperate act of self-delusion, denying to himself the deed he had decided to do?

Perhaps the most enlightening facet of Judas's question is the title he used in addressing Jesus. The other disciples had called Jesus "Lord," even as they contemplated their own potential for betrayal. But Judas called Jesus *Master* (Rabbi), not "Lord." That title—Rabbi, honored Teacher—may indicate the deficiency in Judas's loyalty that led to the betrayal. To the rest, Jesus had become their Lord; but Judas's understanding of Jesus may have progressed little since the early days in Galilee. Jesus responded to Judas with the same words He would use when Caiaphas would ask Him if He were the Christ—*Thou hast said.* Judas's own words condemned himself as the betrayer.

An important question for us remains: Is Jesus our Rabbi, or our Lord? For many people Jesus is little more than a great moral teacher, whose insights can be followed on the path to a good life. But Jesus is Lord. He calls for absolute loyalty, and that loyalty is the path to eternal life.

III. The Meal Within the Meal (Matthew 26:26-29)

A. The Bread and the Body (v. 26)

26. And as they were eating, Jesus took bread, and blessed it, and brake it, and gave it to the disciples, and said, Take, eat; this is my body.

Jesus took bread. This was the unleavened bread of the Passover feast. The practice of tak-

visual 10

ing the flat loaf of bread, giving thanks to God, tearing it into pieces, and distributing it was part of the ceremonies observed at the Passover. Jesus had given the disciples instructions regarding preparations for the meal (see Luke 22:7-13), and He presided over it as the father of any Jewish family would do.

The words Jesus spoke at this point in the Passover meal, however, were a departure from every Passover the disciples had ever observed. Distributing the bread, Jesus said, *This is my body.* These new and shocking words shifted the focus from the past to the present, from history to Him. Eating this bread is the means for disciples to maintain a spiritual communion with Jesus, whose body is given for them (Luke 22:19).

Every time we lift the loaf at the Communion table, we are participating in the history of God's deliverance then and now. But we are also participating in the mystery of "Christ in you, the hope of glory" (Colossians 1:27).

SYMBOL OF LIFE

The vast wheat fields of Kansas, stretching across the high plains, are green in winter until snow covers them. The warming sun of spring and summer mature the crop until the fields are a beautiful light tan, ready for harvest. Food for the hungry world can be seen in those fields of waving wheat. Marjorie was a city girl reading a book as the car sped eastward across Kansas. After a while she put the book down and looked up, eyed the acres of wheat, and remarked, "Isn't that the most desolate sight you have ever seen?"

Her husband was offended and speechless. That bountiful harvest would provide bread for multitudes of people and income for the farmers who planted and reaped their crops. How could anyone use the word *desolate* to describe the graceful undulation of ripe wheat gently swaying in the Kansas wind? His wife's statement seemed incomprehensible. He knew wheat and its worth; his wife did not.

Jesus is the bread of life. In the Lord's Supper, He offers himself in bread, the symbol for His body given as a sacrifice acceptable to God for our sins. Many do not know this truth. If one comes to the Lord's Supper unaware of its meaning, its spiritual value will be neither recognized nor received. Let us first remember our Lord's death, and give thanks for the life it makes possible. —W. P.

B. The Cup and the Covenant
(vv. 27-29)

27. And he took the cup, and gave thanks, and gave it to them, saying, Drink ye all of it.

In recording the institution of the Lord's Supper, the Gospel writers state that Jesus "blessed" the elements as well as *gave thanks* for them. This has led to the notion that Jesus did something to the loaf and to the cup, effecting a transformation of the bread and wine into His actual body and blood. The two terms, however, are virtually identical. In thanking God for the loaf and the cup, Jesus was asking the Father to consecrate them for their intended purpose. Thus, in partaking of these elements we remember Jesus' sacrifice of His life to effect our salvation and at the same time we give thanks for it. When we hear the "blessing of the loaf and cup," we should direct our thoughts in thanksgiving to the source of salvation, to God himself.

After taking a cup, giving thanks, and giving it to the disciples, Jesus gave a special invitation: *Drink ye all of it*. The word *all* refers to the disciples, not to the contents of the cup—"All of you must drink of it." It is difficult to tell exactly at what point Judas left the upper room. If he was still there at this time the word *all* takes on added poignancy in view of the traitorous act he was contemplating.

The invitation in this verse is still a timely one. Drink of it, all of you. I have known Christians who have deliberately declined to partake of Communion, usually because on that day they felt especially unworthy of God's saving grace and were repentant for a week of thoughts and actions that disregarded God. But there is no better time to partake of Communion than when we feel overwhelmed by our sin. The Lord's Supper is spread for none other than sinners. No one is ever worthy of God's grace. This cup is for all of us, all of us who in some way have betrayed, denied, doubted, or disobeyed our Lord. This cup is always for us all.

28. For this is my blood of the new testament, which is shed for many for the remission of sins.

At this point Jesus gave new significance to the cup, even as He had to the bread. The cup stood for His *blood of the new testament*.

The word translated *testament* means covenant, a word that was rich in meaning for the Jewish people. God had made a personal covenant with Abraham, and had formalized it with his descendants by the law of Moses.

Blood was an important feature of that covenant. When Israel was encamped at Mount Sinai, they entered into the covenant with God, promising to do all He commanded. That covenant was ratified by blood, as Moses sprinkled the blood of the sacrificed animals on God's altar and on the people themselves (Exodus 24:6-8). According to the law, burnt offerings were offered daily in which the blood of the sacrificed animal was sprinkled on the altar. And once each year, on the Day of Atonement, the high priest sprinkled the blood of animals on the mercy seat of the ark of the covenant to make atonement for the priesthood and the people.

Jesus declared that a new covenant between God and man was being established, and it was based on the sacrifice of himself on the cross. Remission of sins would come through the shedding of His blood, and the cup He now offered to the disciples was emblematic of it.

We see, therefore, that Communion is more than a ritual, or a remembrance. It is the renewal of a covenant initiated by the grace of God and entered into by all those who accept Jesus Christ as Savior and Lord. In partaking of the loaf and the cup of the Lord's Supper, we remember Him who died to save us from our sins, and we recommit ourselves to Him as His loyal servants.

CUP OF SACRIFICE

It was Memorial Day, 1988. At the Golden Gate National Cemetery, lying in the hills just south of San Francisco, the flags of all fifty states were displayed with the United States flag, which was at half-mast to commemorate the sacrifice of the men buried there. Rows of uniform white grave markers stood out against the green grass on the hills.

A gentle breeze ruffled the flags. Relatives of those who were buried there brought flowers to remember and to honor their dead. After some time, here and there a group would turn away after one final touching of a grave marker bearing the name of one dear to them.

There were no Memorial Day parades here—this was not the right location. This is a resting place to honor those who gave their life's blood to keep America free, and to thank others, now buried here, who survived their years of honorable service to be carried to this place and laid to rest with comrades lost in battle.

There is no place where the body of Jesus Christ lies buried. But there is a memorial to His blood, which was shed at Calvary in mortal conflict with sin. Come quietly, reverently; keep the memorial He gave us. It is not a tomb, but a cup.

"Drink from it, all of you," He said. "For this is My blood of the new covenant, which is shed for many for the remission of sins" (Matthew 26:27, 28, *The New King James Version*). Jesus won the battle; let us remember the sacrifice.   —W. P.

29. But I say unto you, I will not drink henceforth of this fruit of the vine, until that day when I drink it new with you in my Father's kingdom.

This was the last supper: Jesus would not again drink with His disciples before He shed His blood for them. Some believe *drink it new with you in my Father's kingdom* refers to Jesus' fellowship with His disciples in the kingdom that was ushered in by His glorious resurrection a few days later. At that time Jesus did have meals with His disciples, as He communed with them, confirmed the reality of His resurrection to them, and commissioned them to preach the good news of salvation (Luke 24:30; Acts 10:41). Others think Jesus meant His fellowship with His people in the Lord's Supper in the church. Still others think this refers to Christ's fellowship with His people in the world to come at the marriage supper of the Lamb (Revelation 19:6-9).

In any case, we live with the assurance that when we partake of the Lord's Supper we share in the ever-present victory won by Christ's death and resurrection, and we share a foretaste of eternity with God.

IV. The Meal Concludes
(Matthew 26:30)

30. And when they had sung a hymn, they went out into the mount of Olives.

Jews customarily closed their Passover celebration by singing from Psalms 115-118. If cus-

---

Home Daily Bible Readings

Monday, Jan. 30—Jesus Is the Bread of Life (John 6:30-40)
Tuesday, Jan. 31—The Great Commandment (Matthew 22:34-40)
Wednesday, Feb. 1—A Woman Anoints Jesus (Matthew 26:6-13)
Thursday, Feb. 2—Judas Will Betray Jesus (Matthew 26:14-25)
Friday, Feb. 3—Jesus' Last Supper With His Disciples (Matthew 26:26-30)
Saturday, Feb. 4—The Disciples Promise to Remain Loyal (Matthew 26:31-35)
Sunday, Feb. 5—In Remembrance of Jesus (1 Corinthians 11:23-29)

---

tom was followed, Jesus and the disciples concluded this somber meal by singing songs of trust and love and praise and thanks to God. In them, however, were expressions such as the "sorrows of death" and the "cup of salvation" and the "sacrifice of thanksgiving" (116:3, 13, 17)—words suggestive not only of the meaning of the Passover, but also of the saving, sacrificial death of Jesus.

The Mount of Olives, just east of the city of Jerusalem, was the place where the events that Jesus had just symbolized and prophesied would be set in motion. There, in an olive grove, He would pray that some other way might be found to fulfill God's plan—some way other than His death. But it was there also that Jesus would choose to conform His human will with the Father's will. This night He would be met by His betrayer and the temple police, and He would be arrested for claiming to be the Messiah.

Conclusion
A. A Matter of Life and Death

The last supper was one of the most serious moments in the life of Jesus. It was a matter of life and death, and as such was a paradox. On the one hand it demonstrated the certainty of Jesus' death and of the sad complicity of one of Jesus' own disciples in it. On the other hand it intimated that there was something beyond that death, something to be remembered. The last supper was a matter of death and life.

The Lord's Supper, Communion, is one of the most serious moments of our lives. It too is a paradox, because in partaking of it we clearly are involved in a matter of life and death. On the one hand it reminds us of our sin, which demanded Jesus' death, and of our potential for betrayal, which dishonors His death. On the other hand it celebrates His death, which made the hope of eternal life a reality for all who accept Him as Savior and Lord. The Lord's Supper is a matter of death and life.

B. Prayer

Our Father, we thank You for the Lord's Supper, which reminds us of Jesus' great love for us. As we partake may we remember His sacrifice and find strength to rid our lives of sin. In Jesus' name we pray, amen.

C. Thought to Remember

The Lord's Supper is our link to the past—Jesus' saving death; to the present—His spiritual presence; and to the future—His victorious return.

Learning by Doing

*This page contains an alternate lesson plan emphasizing learning activities. Classes
desiring such student involvement will find these suggestions helpful.*

Learning Goals

After today's lesson, each student will:

1. Be able to relate the details of the last supper story.

2. Partake of the Lord's Supper with renewed appreciation.

3. Identify an area in which his or her actions betray the Lord, and resolve to stop that activity.

Into the Lesson

Before the class enters the room, write the following dates on the board:

March 6, 1836

February 15, 1898

December 7, 1941

Begin the class period by asking the class if these dates remind them of an event. Most will associate the last with the Japanese attack on Pearl Harbor. Perhaps a few will recognize the first as the date of the fall of the Alamo, and the second as the date of the sinking of the U. S. battleship *Maine* in Havana Harbor. Point out that after each of these events, the nation was galvanized into action by a call to remembrance: "Remember the Alamo!" "Remember the *Maine!*" "Remember Pearl Harbor!"

Now have someone read 1 Corinthians 11:23-25. Ask the class what Jesus intended the purpose of His Supper to be, based on His words here. (See also Luke 22:19.) The Lord's Supper is a call to "Remember the cross!"

Into the Word

Prepare a script from the text of Matthew, to be used by class members acting out the story of the last supper. Include dialogue from Luke's account (Luke 22:14-23) and from Paul's discussion in 1 Corinthians 11:24, 25. It may be helpful to use a contemporary translation of the text. Speaking parts include Jesus, Judas, and other disciples (see Matthew 26:22).

When the skit has concluded, point out that there are really two stories here: the prediction of the betrayal and the institution of the Lord's Supper.

Lead a discussion of the betrayal prediction with questions such as the following:

What does "betray" mean?

How did Judas betray Jesus?

Is there any significance in the fact that the eleven disciples addressed Jesus by using the word *Lord* whereas Judas addressed Him as *Master* or *Rabbi* (v. 25)? Does it show a defect in Judas's understanding of who Jesus was?

Next, ask the class members to think of a time when they betrayed (that is, failed) Jesus by their action or lack of action. Let them have a minute or two to identify the incident and to decide what they should have done differently.

Moving to a discussion of the Lord's Supper, write these two words as column headings on the board or overhead: *Bible* and *Tradition.* Point out that there are a number of things we do in our church (we are referring specifically to your local church here) when the Communion is served. Ask them to name as many of them as they can, then determine together whether each practice comes from the Bible or is part of our tradition. Write each item under the appropriate heading. Encourage the class to compare the items with the text in Matthew, Luke 22:14-23, and 1 Corinthians 11:23-34.

You may need to prompt them with such items as these: an elder always gives a meditation and a prayer, we sit with bowed heads and closed eyes, we consider the death of Christ and our sinfulness, we use unleavened wafers and fruit of the vine, etc.

Note that few details are given in Scripture regarding how the Communion service is to be conducted. Emphasis is given rather on what we are to focus our thoughts on and the manner in which we are to do that.

Into Life

Divide the class into three groups. Assign each a different one of these passages: Matthew 26:20-25; Matthew 26:26-29; 1 Corinthians 11:28, 29.

Ask the members of each group to take a few minutes to reflect on the passage assigned to them and to suggest several ideas that could be used in a Communion meditation. Have each group choose one or two of the ideas and compose a brief meditation.

To conclude the class session, have a volunteer from each group present the group's meditation as though for a Communion service. Before they do this, ask the students to recall the incident of betrayal they identified earlier in the lesson. Encourage them to lay it at Jesus' feet and resolve not to repeat the betrayal.

Let's Talk It Over

The questions on this page are designed to encourage review of the lesson Scriptures and to promote discussion of the lesson by the class. The answers provided are only discussion starters. Let your class talk it over from there.

1. What should be the primary focus of a shared meal?

The common assumption persists that we eat primarily for nourishment in order that we might survive physically. Of course we must eat to live, but a *shared* meal takes on a different perspective. In a shared meal the focus belongs on feeding the relationship of those eating together, rather than simply feeding physical bodies. Eating together fosters bonding, it builds relationships. Enemies do not eat together. Hence the term "peace meal." When people were no longer enemies (they were at peace), and they signified this by sharing a meal.

The same principle applies today. As families eat together, their focus should be more on the family relationship than the food. Mealtime should be an occasion for enriching family ties. Recent research shows that one of the traits of a healthy family is the focus on family "table time," with conversation around the table.

How significant that Jesus shared "the last supper" with His apostles, His closest friends! How appropriate that He instituted the Lord's Supper for communion with His followers in the divine family!

2. As we partake of the Lord's Supper, with whom do we commune?

First and foremost, of course, we commune with the Lord Jesus. We gather around His table at His invitation, and our principal purpose in doing so is to remember His body, which was broken for us, and His blood, which was shed for the remission of our sins. There is another element regarding Communion, however, that should be kept in mind. Participation in the Lord's Supper is not an isolated act of worship involving "just Jesus and me." It is a *corporate* act involving all the members of the family of God. Paul affirms, "Because there is one loaf, we, who are many, are one body, for we all partake of the one loaf" (1 Corinthians 10:17, *New International Version*). Then in 1 Corinthians 11:29 he reminds us that "anyone who eats and drinks without recognizing the body of the Lord eats and drinks judgment on himself." Some see in this statement not only a reference to the physical body of Jesus on the cross, but also the body of Christ, the church. As we remember the Lord's death, we are to consider also His church, which He purchased with His blood, and how we can make that body stronger, healthier, and more unified.

3. What purposes may be noted in our observing the Lord's Supper?

There are at least four crucial purposes for our observing the Lord's Supper. The first is *commemorative*. The Lord's Supper is a memorial to Jesus' death, so as we partake we remember His sacrifice for us. The second purpose is *covenantal*. By His death Jesus established a new covenant between God and man. We who are Christians have entered this covenant, and each time we partake of the Lord's Supper we renew our commitment to that covenant. The third purpose is *communion*. As indicated in question 2 above, we affirm our oneness with the Lord and His body, the church. The fourth purpose is *anticipatory*. We "proclaim the Lord's death until he comes" (1 Corinthians 11:26, *New International Version*). We look forward to the second coming of Christ. How rich in meaning and purpose is the Communion!

4. What feelings are appropriate during the Lord's Supper?

Many varied and valid feelings come together at the Lord's Supper. We approach this time in a serious, thoughtful manner. After all, we are remembering the death of the Lord Jesus. Quiet, solemn feelings naturally accompany the time of Communion.

We also experience the feeling of gratitude. As we contemplate the great sacrifice Jesus made for us at Calvary, we cannot but be overwhelmed with this emotion. Upon reflection, we must acknowledge that without Him we are sinners, lost, and without hope. "All we like sheep have gone astray; we have turned every one to his own way; and the Lord hath laid on him the iniquity of us all" (Isaiah 53:6). We are grateful that by the shedding of His blood we can have forgiveness of our sins.

Another appropriate feeling is joy. We commune with a living Lord and a living body. We celebrate these relationships. We celebrate *life*. As we do so in anticipation of the Lord's return, should we not do so in a spirit of joy?

Jesus Is Rejected

DEVOTIONAL READING: Isaiah 53:1-12.

LESSON SCRIPTURE: Matthew 26:36-68.

PRINTED TEXT: Matthew 26:57-68.

Matthew 26:57-68

57 And they that had laid hold on Jesus led him away to Caiaphas the high priest, where the scribes and the elders were assembled.

58 But Peter followed him afar off unto the high priest's palace, and went in, and sat with the servants, to see the end.

59 Now the chief priests, and elders, and all the council, sought false witness against Jesus, to put him to death;

60 But found none: yea, though many false witnesses came, yet found they none. At the last came two false witnesses,

61 And said, This fellow said, I am able to destroy the temple of God, and to build it in three days.

62 And the high priest arose, and said unto him, Answerest thou nothing? what is it which these witness against thee?

63 But Jesus held his peace. And the high priest answered and said unto him, I adjure thee by the living God, that thou tell us whether thou be the Christ, the Son of God.

64 Jesus saith unto him, Thou hast said: nevertheless I say unto you, Hereafter shall ye see the Son of man sitting on the right hand of power, and coming in the clouds of heaven.

65 Then the high priest rent his clothes, saying, He hath spoken blasphemy; what further need have we of witnesses? behold, now ye have heard his blasphemy.

66 What think ye? They answered and said, He is guilty of death.

67 Then did they spit in his face, and buffeted him; and others smote him with the palms of their hands,

68 Saying, Prophesy unto us, thou Christ, Who is he that smote thee?

Feb
12

GOLDEN TEXT: Then the high priest rent his clothes, saying, He hath spoken blasphemy; what further need have we of witnesses? behold, now ye have heard his blasphemy. What think ye? They answered and said, He is guilty of death.—Matthew 26:65, 66.

Jesus the Fulfillment (Matthew)

Unit 4. Jesus Christ: Victor Over
Sin and Death (Lessons 10-13)

Lesson Aims

As a result of this study, students should:

1. Know some key facts about the arrest and trials of Jesus.

2. Share the sense of rejection that Jesus experienced.

3. Resolve to respond to physical and verbal abuse without violence.

Lesson Outline

INTRODUCTION
    A. Pleading the Fifth
    B. Lesson Background
  I. THE ARREST (Matthew 26:57, 58)
      To See the End
  II. THE TRIAL (Matthew 26:59-62)
    A. The Court Convened (v. 59)
    B. The Prosecution in Disarray (v. 60)
    C. The Charge That Might Stick (vv. 61, 62)
      True or False?
 III. THE SURPRISE WITNESS (Matthew 26:63-65)
    A. Direct Question (v. 63)
    B. Direct Answer (v. 64)
    C. Desired Result (v. 65)
 IV. THE VERDICT (Matthew 26:66-68)
    A. Voice Vote (v. 66)
    B. Violent Reaction (vv. 67, 68)
CONCLUSION
    A. The Sanhedrin and the Savior
    B. Prayer
    C. Thought to Remember

Visual 11 of the visuals packet summarizes the rejection of Jesus and holds a challenge for us. The visual is shown on page 204.

Introduction

A. Pleading the Fifth

"I refuse to answer on the grounds that it may tend to incriminate me." Some of us may remember hearing these words in a radio broadcast of a real-life Senate hearing. Others have heard them only in a fictional television courtroom drama. We call it "pleading the Fifth Amendment." Under our system of justice, people are not required to give testimony that would indicate their own guilt.

At His trial before the Jewish authorities, Jesus was asked a question, which, if answered truthfully, would incriminate Him in the thinking of His accusers. The question was, "Are you the Christ the Son of God?" Jesus did not "plead the Fifth." Without hesitation He openly admitted that He was. To the religious leaders that confession was blasphemy. To us, however, it is the truth, the whole truth, and nothing but the truth—the foundation of our faith and the basis of our hope of life in the world to come.

B. Lesson Background

Last week's lesson ended with Jesus and His disciples going to the Mount of Olives following their observance of the Passover meal, during which Jesus instituted His memorial feast, the Lord's Supper. On the slopes of the mount, in a garden called Gethsemane, Jesus agonized over His impending death. Throughout the intense struggle, however, His prayer was, "Father . . . not as I will, but as thou wilt." With the struggle came unfazed resolve: He was ready to fulfill His purpose in coming to earth. (See Matthew 26:36-46.)

Very soon thereafter came Judas leading a great multitude of armed persons from the chief priests and elders of the people. With a kiss Judas betrayed his Master, and at that signal the guards stepped forward and arrested Jesus (vv. 26:47-56).

After his late-night betrayal and arrest, Jesus endured a series of exhausting trials. First, He was taken before Annas, the former high priest who had been removed from that position by the Roman authorities but who was still highly respected among the Jews. Eventually Annas's son-in-law, Caiaphas, the current high priest, convened a representative group of the Council to try Jesus. This is the hearing mentioned in our printed text.

The Council, or Sanhedrin, was the supreme judicial authority of the Jewish people, operating under the authority of Rome and by its own rules of conduct. One of those rules stated that court proceedings were to be conducted only in daylight. Because the trial recorded in today's lesson was held in the pre-dawn darkness, another hearing (see Matthew 27:1; Luke 22:66-71) had to be convened to make the guilty verdict official. Only then was Jesus escorted to the

---

How to Say It

CAIAPHAS.   *Kay*-uh-fus or *Kye*-uh-fus.
SANHEDRIN.   *San*-huh-drun or San-*heed*-run.

Roman governor Pontius Pilate, then to Herod, then back to Pilate for the final disposition of His case. But it was this trial before Caiaphas, which we study in our lesson today, that gave the Sanhedrin the grounds they sought for insisting on Jesus' crucifixion.

I. The Arrest
(Matthew 26:57, 58)

57. And they that had laid hold on Jesus led him away to Caiaphas the high priest, where the scribes and the elders were assembled.

The soldiers who seized Jesus were not Roman soldiers but the temple police, a Jewish militia under the authority of the priests who controlled the temple. Jesus' cleansing of the temple and His recent authoritative teachings there had angered and threatened these priests who now took the initiative to eliminate Him.

Caiaphas was not especially religious, but he was wealthy and powerful. It was he who determined that it was expedient for one man to die for the sake of the people; that is, that Jesus must be killed (see John 11:49, 50).

Caiaphas's motives appear to have been purely political: Jesus had become a threat to priestly authority. Along with the priests were gathered scribes, that is, teachers of the law, and elders, spiritual leaders from around Judea.

It is a sobering thought that those who opposed Jesus so intensely were the very persons who should have recognized and welcomed His coming. Those who lead the church today must remain vigilant against allowing a desire for authority to undermine their loyalty to Jesus.

58. But Peter followed him afar off unto the high priest's palace, and went in, and sat with the servants, to see the end.

The disciples of Jesus ran for their lives when Jesus was arrested (Matthew 26:56). Peter, however, and another disciple, probably John (see John 18:15) circled back to the city. Staying back and out of sight, Peter followed the crowd as Jesus was taken to the high priest's palatial mansion, where the Council had been hastily summoned. The word translated *palace* also means a courtyard. It seems most likely that it was the courtyard that Peter entered.

In a sad footnote to the arrest and trials of Jesus, Peter showed both boldness and cowardice. He brashly entered the courtyard of the palace where Jesus was being examined, but later he refused the opportunity to speak in Jesus' defense. Notice the hopelessness of Peter. He followed his Master, but only *to see the end,* that is, the outcome. In spite of Jesus' repeated predictions of His death and subsequent resur-

rection, the disciples appear not to have expected either.

We who follow Jesus today must have the courage to stand up and speak up for the Savior.

TO SEE THE END

Queen Mary I of England, daughter of Henry VIII and Catherine of Aragon, attempted to revoke the Protestant Reformation achieved in England under the reign of her half brother, Edward VI. A sizable segment of the English clergy refused to accept the return to the Roman Church theology, which Mary demanded. Most Protestant clergy fled to the Continent to escape the persecution Mary instituted, but three hundred ministers in England were martyred for their faith. The best known of these men were Latimer, Ridley, and Cranmer.

Imprisoned by the authorities, Cranmer was forced to witness the martyrdom of Latimer and Ridley who were burned at the stake. It was Latimer who, while in the flames, encouraged Ridley with the words, ". . . we shall this day light such a candle, by God's grace, in England as I trust shall never be put out." In his weakened condition Cranmer recanted the position he had taken favoring the Protestant Reform movement. In spite of that, his political enemies condemned him to be burned at the stake also.

Latimer's courage, which he had witnessed earlier, helped Cranmer retract his recantation. When he was burned, he put his right hand, with which he had signed away his religious conviction, in the flames so that it burned before his body was destroyed. Cranmer's courage was reborn by the example of Latimer.

Peter followed to see the outcome of the proceedings against Jesus. The courageous example of Jesus eventually brought Peter out of his denial and into a dynamic faith and witness.

How would we act under such harrowing testings? (Pray that your faith would overcome your fears.) Cranmer, as Peter, learned that "faith is the victory that overcomes the world."   —W. P.

II. The Trial
(Matthew 26:59-62)

A. The Court Convened (v. 59)

59. Now the chief priests, and elders, and all the council, sought false witness against Jesus, to put him to death.

It is clear that from the outset the religious authorities had only one thing in mind, and that was to kill Jesus. Having no interest in truth or justice where Jesus was concerned, they *sought false witness* against Him, hoping to find testimony plausible enough to justify His execution.

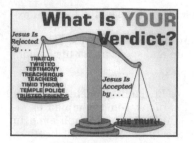

visual 11

Not only were these authorities acting illegally in conducting this hearing at night, but they also hypocritically ignored their laws regarding fair testimony, most of which were meant to protect the rights of the accused.

B. The Prosecution in Disarray (v. 60)

60. But found none: yea, though many false witnesses came, yet found they none. At the last came two false witnesses.

The authorities bribed or pressured people to fabricate charges against Jesus. Because the hearing had been called so hastily however, there was no time to coach these false witnesses in the giving of their testimony. As might be expected of those who deal in lies, their reports were inconsistent. Not one of the charges brought against Jesus met the Sanhedrin's own requirements for valid testimony—charges substantiated by two or three witnesses. The testimony of these false witnesses was so contradictory (Mark 14:56) that it was of no value.

C. The Charge That Might Stick
(vv. 61, 62)

61. And said, This fellow said, I am able to destroy the temple of God, and to build it in three days.

Finally two false witnesses brought a charge in which they appeared to be in agreement enough to satisfy the Sanhedrin's requirements that a charge be confirmed by at least two witnesses. Perhaps Matthew reported it because it was the most weighty of all the false testimony brought against Jesus.

Three years earlier, Jesus had cleansed the temple in Jerusalem by driving out the money changers and those who sold animals. The testimony of these two false witnesses was a twisted report of what Jesus said on that occasion (see John 2:18-22). They not only misinterpreted Jesus' words, they misquoted Him. Jesus had said, "[You, not I] destroy this temple, and in three days I will raise it up" (John 2:19). Second, He was referring to His own body, prophesying His death and resurrection, and was not speaking of the temple building in Jerusalem (v. 21).

The false witnesses twisted Jesus' words to make it look as though He threatened destruction of the sacred temple, a charge of sufficient severity to warrant the death sentence. It is interesting to note that even these two witnesses had disagreement in their accusation (see Mark 14:57-59).

It ought to be clear that we who are friends of Jesus must be careful to present His statements accurately when we teach and share His message. Consideration must be given to the context of His words, as well as to whether He is speaking literally or figuratively in each instance, so as not to misrepresent Him.

TRUE OR FALSE?

Jeremy became a youthful "truthful deceiver." His dad paid him five dollars a week to mow their lawn with their riding mower. At first Jeremy enjoyed the task, but after a while his enthusiasm for mowing waned.

Having recently read Mark Twain's tales of Tom Sawyer, Jeremy made a quick application of one of the stories. He always cut the lawn on Saturday, when his dad played golf and his mother visited the beauty shop. Many of his young friends wanted to run the riding mower. At twenty-five cents for fifteen minutes he let them do his work. Eight working rides in two hours added two dollars to the five he was paid by his dad. His scheme went well for several weeks, and his dad always complimented him on his faithfulness in mowing the yard.

Jeremy's enterprise came to a halt one Saturday when his dad came home early from his golf game. His words were stern. "Jeremy, it's your job. I warned you never to let anyone else ride the mower. An injury to a friend would be a disaster for us." Jeremy protested. "But, Dad, I did mow the lawn!" In his eyes the completed job was more important than his dad's rules.

Truth can be twisted, but it cannot be destroyed. Do we deceive ourselves and others by interpreting truth to suit our own ends? The false witnesses at Jesus' trial attempted that, but failed. Ultimately, truth will triumph.   —W. P.

62. And the high priest arose, and said unto him, Answerest thou nothing? what is it which these witness against thee?

With a pretense of fairness, the high priest gave Jesus the opportunity to respond to the charge brought by the two men. It was obvious that their twisted testimony was a deliberate attempt to discredit Him before all the Jews who respected the temple as the place where God was worshiped. In all likelihood the high priest hoped Jesus would say something that could be used against Him.

Self-defense does not seem to have been the high priority for Jesus that it is for so many others. On the other hand, when Jesus was asked a legitimate question, even when it was asked with an accusatory purpose, He answered openly.

How should the people of God respond to false charges? First, let us be certain to live our lives so as to insure that such charges are in fact false. Second, we must learn not to retaliate when slandered, so that we may avoid adding a real offense to the false one. When we are attacked, silence may be the best defense. When we are questioned as to our allegiance to Christ, we must speak the truth in love.

III. The Surprise Witness (Matthew 26:63-65)

A. Direct Question (v. 63)

63. But Jesus held his peace. And the high priest answered and said unto him, I adjure thee by the living God, that thou tell us whether thou be the Christ, the Son of God.

Jesus refused to dignify the false and malicious charges with even a reply. In response to Jesus' silence, Caiaphas made a strategic move. The false and fumbling testimony of the witnesses having failed, the high priest called the defendant to testify against himself, on an even more incriminating charge. He demanded that Jesus state under solemn oath whether or not He was *the Christ, the Son of God.*

For a person to claim to be *the Son of God* was to claim to be a divine person, one who was equal with God (see John 5:18). Caiaphas had heard reports that Jesus had stated that God was His Father. Caiaphas hoped, therefore, to force Jesus into a confession that would settle the matter once and for all. If Jesus said no, He would be discredited as an impostor; but if He said yes, he would be denounced as a blasphemer.

B. Direct Answer (v. 64)

64. Jesus saith unto him, Thou hast said: nevertheless I say unto you, Hereafter shall ye see the Son of man sitting on the right hand of power, and coming in the clouds of heaven.

When Jesus responded to the interrogation with the words, *Thou hast said* (that is, "You said it"), He acknowledged His true nature. But Jesus forced the actual testimony to come from the high priest's own lips—*You* said it! Jesus' answer turned the condemnatory question of Caiaphas into a proclamation of His person—the Christ, the Son of the living God—from Caiaphas's own lips.

Hereafter shall ye see the Son of man sitting on the right hand of power. Jesus proceeded to announce His glorious exaltation to God's right hand.

These judges, who now were sitting in judgment of Him and plotting to kill Him, would one day stand before Him to be judged. *Coming in the clouds of heaven.* The imagery comes from Daniel 7:13, 14. There the prophet described the glorification of the Son of man and announced the eternal kingdom that would be His. This was a forthright declaration by Jesus of His nature and power, one that would not be misunderstood by the men before whom He stood and which, He knew, would seal His condemnation.

C. Desired Result (v. 65)

65. Then the high priest rent his clothes, saying, He hath spoken blasphemy; what further need have we of witnesses? behold, now ye have heard his blasphemy.

The high priest rent his clothes. This was done by slitting the garment at the throat and then tearing it downward for several inches. Among the Jews the tearing of the clothing indicated a deep grief, horror, or dismay. Normally this was done as an expression of one's genuine feeling in this regard. In the case of Caiaphas, however, the tearing of his garments was a hypocritical display. This illegal nighttime hearing was conducted for the sole purpose of fabricating a charge against Jesus so these authorities could put Jesus to death (v. 59). For all his histrionics, for all his feigned horror, Caiaphas was quite satisfied at the turn of events.

He hath spoken blasphemy. The false witnesses that the Council had either bribed or blackmailed into testifying against Jesus had failed to produce credible testimony against Him. Now, however, the high priest was convinced that Jesus had incriminated himself. Blasphemy is the act of showing contempt or lack of reverence for God. Caiaphas declared Jesus guilty of this for elevating himself, a mere man (in Caiaphas's view), to the position of God. Leviticus 24:16 makes the seriousness of the offense very clear: "And he that blasphemeth the name of the Lord, he shall surely be put to death, and all the congregation shall certainly stone him." Blasphemy against God was the ultimate offense a person could commit. Caiaphas knew well that Jesus' self-incrimination was enough for a conviction by the Sanhedrin.

What further need have we of witnesses? One can well imagine how relieved Caiaphas must have been not to have to seek any more witnesses and induce them to commit perjury in order to obtain the judgment he sought against Jesus.

Now ye have heard his blasphemy. Everyone in the room had heard what Jesus said. Caiaphas pressed his advantage and declared that Jesus had convicted himself in their presence.

IV. The Verdict
(Matthew 26:66-68)

A. Voice Vote (v. 66)

66. What think ye? They answered and said, He is guilty of death.

Caiaphas asked not for formal deliberation concerning Christ's guilt. He sought an immediate vote by acclamation, and he received it. All declared Christ *guilty of death.*

By conducting this hearing the way they did, these religious authorities violated almost every rule they had created to assure justice for the individual. They had met in the dark, although their rules specified that hearings were to be held only in daylight. They had gathered at the high priest's house instead of the appointed chamber where trials were to take place. And they knowingly had received the testimony of false witnesses, which, of course, was forbidden. Because this was not a regular session of the Sanhedrin, a meeting of the full body had to be convened in the morning to consider how this informal sentence should be carried out (Matthew 27:1). Capital punishment was in the hands of Rome. All that remained was to convince the Romans that Jesus was worthy of death.

There is a great irony in the death sentence that the priests (the leaders of worship), the scribes (the teachers of the law), and the elders (the spiritual guides of the people) handed down upon Jesus. He died because of the guilt of the very ones who declared Him guilty of death.

B. Violent Reaction (vv. 67, 68)

67. Then did they spit in his face, and buffeted him; and others smote him with the palms of their hands.

With the pronouncement of the guilty verdict, all semblance of order in the room disappeared, and Jesus was subjected to brutal cruelty and mockery. Was it the rough temple guards, the servants, or the sophisticated priests and elders themselves who did the despicable things mentioned in this verse and the following verse? The text allows for the horrible possibility that the religious leaders, who condemned the Son of God by means of this miscarriage of justice, stooped even lower to the vicious, demeaning treatment described. If they did not actually spit with their own mouths and slap with their own hands, it is obvious that they permitted the others present to do it.

They spit in his face. This is an indignity that all people of all times have regarded as extraordinarily vicious. *They buffeted him,* that is, they struck Him with their fists. Others insultingly slapped Jesus *with the palms of their hands.*

68. Saying, Prophesy unto us, thou Christ, Who is he that smote thee?

Luke 22:64 says that at some point after the physical abuse began, Jesus was blindfolded. Then one after another they hit Him in the face, challenging Him to tell them which person had hit Him. But through it all—the verbal and physical abuse and the blasphemies spoken against Him (see Luke 22:65)—Jesus refused to retaliate. What an example He has given us of self-restraint in the face of persecution by our enemies!

Conclusion

A. The Sanhedrin and the Savior

The world has known judges and juries who have convicted innocent persons. But never was there a greater miscarriage of justice than when the Sanhedrin in Jerusalem declared Jesus Christ, the Son of God, guilty of blasphemy and worthy of death.

Ironically, He whom these judges condemned would ultimately be their judge. His resurrection from the dead vindicated the quiet claim they had condemned as blasphemous, and His exaltation to the right hand of God confirmed His claim to divine power and authority. Ultimately, all of us must stand before Him in judgment.

B. Prayer

Forgive us, O God, when any of our actions bring disgrace upon Your Son and our Savior. Help us to follow Him all the way to His cross, and ours. In His name we pray. Amen.

C. Thought to Remember

The confession that led to Jesus' death is the very confession of faith that leads us to life.

Home Daily Bible Readings

Monday, Feb. 6—Rejection of the Lord's Servant (Isaiah 53:1-5)
Tuesday, Feb. 7—Jesus' Prayer in Gethsemane (Matthew 26:36-41)
Wednesday, Feb. 8—Jesus Accepts God's Will (Matthew 26:42-46)
Thursday, Feb. 9—Refuge in God (Psalm 118:5-9)
Friday, Feb. 10—Judas Betrays Jesus (Matthew 26:47-56)
Saturday, Feb. 11—Jesus Before Caiaphas (Matthew 26:57-68)
Sunday, Feb. 12—Peter's Denial of Jesus (Matthew 26:69-75)

Learning by Doing

*This page contains an alternate lesson plan emphasizing learning activities. Classes
desiring such student involvement will find these suggestions helpful.*

Learning Goals

Participation in this lesson will help the students:

1. Know the details of the account of Jesus' trial before the Sanhedrin.

2. Understand Jesus' experience of being rejected.

3. Resolve to stand up for Jesus, no matter the cost.

Into the Lesson

Prior to class time, have three or four class members selected and prepared for what you will do when class begins. Then when it is time to begin, speak to each in a conversational way, as if you were still just visiting, but loud enough so others can hear. Make comments such as these: "I see you are having a bad hair day today." "Did you select your clothes in the dark this morning?" Have one of your people sit on the front row, then tell him or her that you would prefer that they move to the back of the room. "It may drive our visitors away if they see your type sitting in the front."

Before you proceed with the lesson, make sure *everyone* realizes that the whole thing was set up in advance to make a point. Then have someone read James 2:1-4 aloud. Point out that the exercise was intended to be a visual demonstration of this passage, showing how people sometimes treat others. Perhaps we are not so blatantly rude, but we can still hurt others greatly by rejection. Today we are considering the rejection of Jesus.

Into the Word

Begin this part of the lesson by having a class member read Matthew 26:57-68 aloud from a contemporary translation. Use the text as the springboard for a discussion of the various persons or groups present at Jesus' trial. Write the following phrases across the board or overhead:

Why there?

Desired result?

Outcome?

Discuss these questions for each person or group in the scene. Encourage speculation, but be sure that what is actually in the text is included. Write the responses under the appropriate headings. Some possible answers are included here.

1. *Peter. Why was he there?* The text says he was there "to see the outcome" (v. 58, *New International Version*), indicating curiosity. Perhaps he also wanted to be there in case Jesus needed him to effect an escape. *What was Peter's desired result?* No doubt he was hoping for Jesus' release, so things could get back to normal for Jesus and His disciples. *What was the outcome?* Jesus was condemned (v. 66), and Peter decided it would be safer for him to disavow any knowledge of Him (vv. 69-75).

2. *The witnesses. Why were they there?* Were they subpoenaed? Bribed? Blackmailed? *What was the witnesses' desired result?* Was it to please the rulers? To make money? To bring about Jesus' death? *What was the outcome?* Their testimony was discredited (v. 60). They distorted the truth (compare verse 61 with John 2:19). They became accomplices in the greatest crime in history.

3. *The Sanhedrin. Why were they there?* Verse 59 gets to the heart of the matter: they were holding this illegal trial so that they could "put [Jesus] to death." They had such animosity for Him that they resorted to lies to convict Him. *What was their desired result?* Again, they wanted to kill Him, no matter what it meant to their integrity. *What was the outcome?* The Sanhedrin, led by Caiaphas, will be remembered through all history as conniving, irrational, ungodly men. They succeeded in having Jesus executed, but in rejecting Him they brought upon themselves their own rejection by God (see Luke 20:9-19).

Into Life

Divide the class into three groups. Assign each group one of the three persons or groups discussed in this lesson: Peter, the witnesses, the Sanhedrin. Give them about five minutes to identify ways that people today imitate their assigned characters in rejecting Jesus. Then bring the class together and have the groups report the results of their discussions.

Have each student think about the times he or she has rejected Jesus, whether by silence or embarrassment (like Peter), or by putting material success ahead of integrity (like the witnesses). Then form a prayer circle and have them pray silently, asking God for strength to stand up for Jesus. As a conclusion to the prayer, lead the class in singing the first stanza of "Have Thine Own Way, Lord!"

Let's Talk It Over

The questions on this page are designed to encourage review of the lesson Scriptures and to promote discussion of the lesson by the class. The answers provided are only discussion starters. Let your class talk it over from there.

1. What was the Sanhedrin and what was its function in Jewish society?

The Romans controlled Israel, but the Jews were given some authority over religious and minor civil disputes. The Jewish ruling body was called the Council (or Sanhedrin), made up of seventy-one of Israel's religious leaders. In a way, this Council was the Jewish supreme court, the most powerful religious and political body of the Hebrew people. The Sanhedrin was allowed by Rome to make many of the local decisions affecting daily life. However, a death sentence had to be approved by the Romans. The Sanhedrin might try Jesus and decide that He deserved to die, but only Pilate, the Roman governor, could sentence Him to be crucified.

2. Why did Peter follow Jesus at a distance after Jesus was arrested?

It is most likely that two dynamics were operative here. Peter followed Jesus to see how it all would end. He was not a disinterested spectator. He wanted to know what was going to happen to Jesus. Peter followed at a distance, however, because he did not want to suffer with Jesus. He did not want to assume any risk at this point in time. Thus, when he was accused of being a follower of Jesus, he vehemently denied any relationship to his Lord.

3. How do people today attempt to follow Jesus on their own terms?

For one thing, people are often inclined to make up their own minds about what is involved in becoming a Christian. Ignoring the Scriptural plan of salvation, they lay hold of an indefinable faith or pronounce themselves Christians on the basis of their adherence to the Ten Commandments or some other moral code. Some who follow the New Testament pattern for becoming a Christian will then proceed to use their own standard for determining how much Bible study, prayer, worship attendance, Christian service, etc., is adequate for maintaining their discipleship.

4. How do adults respond when they are threatened or abused?

When adults suffer verbal and/or physical abuse, they essentially have three options.

1. *Retaliate.* When Jesus was arrested, Peter responded to the threat with violence. He cut off the ear of a servant of the high priest. In an increasingly violent culture, Americans are responding to abuse of threat with retaliation. Some justify this response by citing the Jewish mandate of "an eye for an eye." But Jesus refused to retaliate in the face of all physical and verbal abuse. He warned Peter that those who live by the sword will perish by the sword.

2. *Be passive.* Some suggest that when you are abused, you should take the abuse without complaint. You are the better person to suffer rather than to respond in kind.

3. *Return good for evil.* This third option takes attitude and action to the highest possible level. When you are abused, do not retaliate or simply suffer passively. Respond to a negative with a positive. Return good for evil. Jesus exemplified this option on the cross when He prayed that His Father would forgive those who were crucifying Him. Romans 12:14-21 records some specific ways in which Christians can overcome evil with good.

5. The apostle Paul states that "all that will live godly in Christ Jesus shall suffer persecution" (2 Timothy 3:12). If we are not facing any persecution for our faith, what may be wrong with our Christianity?

Persecution can range from simple mockery, insults, and false gossip circulated about us, to physical abuse and financial loss. The lack of it may indicate that we are too silent about our faith, that we are not vigorous enough in opposing evil, or that our lives are falling short of the holiness God expects of us.

6. What can we do to develop a boldness similar to that displayed by Jesus?

Jesus' boldness arose in part from His knowledge of who He was. We will be bolder as we increase in our awareness that we are His and that His Spirit dwells within us. Also, Jesus was bold because He knew to "fear not them which kill the body, but are not able to kill the soul: but rather fear him which is able to destroy both soul and body in hell" (Matthew 10:28). He urges us and challenges us to master that same lesson.

Jesus Is Mocked and Crucified

DEVOTIONAL READING: John 3:14-21.

LESSON SCRIPTURE: Matthew 27:1-61.

PRINTED TEXT: Matthew 27:27-44.

Matthew 27:27-44

27 Then the soldiers of the governor took Jesus into the common hall, and gathered unto him the whole band of soldiers.

28 And they stripped him, and put on him a scarlet robe.

29 And when they had platted a crown of thorns, they put it upon his head, and a reed in his right hand: and they bowed the knee before him, and mocked him, saying, Hail, King of the Jews!

30 And they spit upon him, and took the reed, and smote him on the head.

31 And after that they had mocked him, they took the robe off from him, and put his own raiment on him, and led him away to crucify him.

32 And as they came out, they found a man of Cyrene, Simon by name: him they compelled to bear his cross.

33 And when they were come unto a place called Golgotha, that is to say, a place of a skull,

34 They gave him vinegar to drink mingled with gall: and when he had tasted thereof, he would not drink.

35 And they crucified him, and parted his garments, casting lots: that it might be fulfilled which was spoken by the prophet, They parted my garments among them, and upon my vesture did they cast lots.

36 And sitting down they watched him there;

37 And set up over his head his accusation written, THIS IS JESUS THE KING OF THE JEWS.

38 Then were there two thieves crucified with him; one on the right hand, and another on the left.

39 And they that passed by reviled him, wagging their heads,

40 And saying, Thou that destroyest the temple, and buildest it in three days, save thyself. If thou be the Son of God, come down from the cross.

41 Likewise also the chief priests mocking him, with the scribes and elders, said,

42 He saved others; himself he cannot save. If he be the King of Israel, let him now come down from the cross, and we will believe him.

43 He trusted in God; let him deliver him now, if he will have him: for he said, I am the Son of God.

44 The thieves also, which were crucified with him, cast the same in his teeth.

GOLDEN TEXT: They that passed by reviled him, wagging their heads, and saying, Thou that destroyest the temple, and buildest it in three days, save thyself. If thou be the Son of God, come down from the cross.—Matthew 27:39, 40.

Jesus the Fulfillment
(Matthew)
Unit 4. Jesus Christ: Victor Over Sin
and Death (Lessons 10-13)

Lesson Aims

The study of this lesson is meant to help students to:

1. Feel the sense of rejection that Jesus experienced when He was mocked and crucified.

2. Resolve to face scorn and mockery as Jesus did.

Lesson Outline

INTRODUCTION
  A. Faces in the Crowd
  B. Lesson Background
 I. JESUS MOCKED (Matthew 27:27-31)
  A. The Praetorium (v. 27)
  B. Perverse Pleasure (vv. 28-30)
  C. Enough (v. 31)
    The Road to Calvary
 II. JESUS CRUCIFIED (Matthew 27:32-38)
  A. The Approach (v. 32)
  B. The Place (v. 33)
  C. The Preparation (v. 34)
  D. The Crucifixion (v. 35)
  E. The Wait (vv. 36-38)
III. JESUS REVILED (Matthew 27:39-44)
  A. The Passersby (vv. 39, 40)
  B. The Authorities (vv. 41-43)
  C. The Criminals (v. 44)
CONCLUSION
  A. Voices at the Cross
  B. Prayer
  C. Thought to Remember

The truth that Jesus alone paid the price for our forgiveness is forcefully conveyed by visual 12, which is an illustration of the crucifixion. The visual is shown on page 213.

Introduction

A. Faces in the Crowd

Have you ever turned your gaze from the center of attention at a gathering of people—the basketball game, the parade, the bride and groom—and looked at the onlookers? In their faces you can see anguish and elation, excitement and disappointment, the twinge of loss and the joy of gain. In fact, you can almost follow the action just by watching the faces in the crowd.

The Gospel accounts record the details of Jesus' crucifixion. But they also focus on those who observed it. By looking at the onlookers—disciples, soldiers, religious leaders, bystanders, thieves—we see their varied reactions to Jesus' suffering and death. As we do, we experience the feeling of being there, of witnessing the crucifixion itself.

The crucifixion of Jesus occupies a central place in God's plan of redemption, thus, in all of Scripture. It is an event that is ever before us, confronting us with its horror and its power. It is filled with horror, because the sins of mankind, our sins, made the death of the innocent One necessary. In that same death, however, is "the power of God" that brings salvation to man (1 Corinthians 1:18). When we view the cross, what can be seen in our faces?

B. Lesson Background

As we saw in last week's lesson, in a nighttime trial the Jewish authorities condemned Jesus to death for what they considered His blasphemous claim to be the Christ, the Son of God. They could not carry out the death sentence, however; only the Roman authorities could do that. Therefore, they had to convince the Roman governor, Pontius Pilate, that Jesus should be put to death.

Early in the morning, following the official meeting of the Sanhedrin in which Jesus was formally declared to be worthy of death, the authorities took Him to Pilate (Matthew 27:1, 2; Mark 15:1; Luke 22:66—23:1). The Jewish leaders had difficulty convincing Pilate that Jesus was a rival king and thus a threat to Caesar's authority. But when they suggested that to release Jesus would be interpreted as a sign of disloyalty to Caesar, Pilate ordered the execution (see John 19:12-16).

The Romans were not the inventors of crucifixion as a means of capital punishment, but by the first century A.D. it had become their favorite method of execution. The Jews were no strangers to crucifixion, for thousands of their countrymen had been crucified since Rome took control of Palestine. In Jesus' day it may not have been an uncommon sight to see the body of a rebellious Jew hanging on a Roman cross alongside a road in Palestine. For the Romans, and in a sense for the Jews, Jesus' death was business as usual.

By the time of the event in the opening verses of today's text, Jesus had been without sleep for at least twenty-four hours. During that time He had spent the evening instructing His disciples. Afterward, in the garden of Gethsemane, He experienced a period of intense, anguished prayer.

Following His arrest He endured the night trial, which ended with the abuse and physical beating administered by those who were in attendance. Then came the morning trials before Pilate, then Herod, then last before Pilate once again.

Attempting to gain the crowd's assent that Jesus should be released, Pilate ordered Jesus to be scourged. This failed to satisfy them, however; they wanted Jesus put to death. Pilate then gave Jesus up to be crucified.

I. Jesus Mocked
(Matthew 27:27-31)

A. The Praetorium (v. 27)

27. Then the soldiers of the governor took Jesus into the common hall, and gathered unto him the whole band of soldiers.

The Roman soldiers led Jesus from Pilate's judgment seat into *the common hall* (literally, the Praetorium), where He would be held while preparations were made for the crucifixion.

The quarters of the Roman governor were called the Praetorium. The soldiers were a special contingent of imperial troops numbering in the hundreds, whose duty was to guard and carry out tasks for the governor. The governor may have been occupying the Tower of Antonia, a fortress built just north of and overlooking the temple. From here the Romans could keep an eye on the Jews in the temple, where revolts were likely to start.

Some think the governor may have been residing in Herod's palace in the northwestern part of Jerusalem. In either case, the guard assigned to Jesus summoned their bored comrades for some entertainment at the expense of their prisoner.

B. Perverse Pleasure (vv. 28-30)

28. And they stripped him, and put on him a scarlet robe.

The verse probably does not mean stripped naked. The soldiers removed Jesus' long outer robe, the one commonly worn by Jewish men, and draped around His shoulders the bright red or purple cloak of a Roman officer. Some think that the *robe* was a cast-off garment from the wardrobe of Herod, which the soldiers found. In either case, they deemed the garment a fitting costume for this Jewish peasant who had been sentenced as a pretender to royalty.

29. And when they had platted a crown of thorns, they put it upon his head, and a reed in his right hand: and they bowed the knee before him, and mocked him, saying, Hail, King of the Jews!

To continue the royal motif and the ridicule, the Roman soldiers took branches from a thorn-bush and fashioned them into a "victor's crown," similar in design to the laurels given to conquering generals or athletes. This one, however, had sharp thorns. Thorn bushes grew throughout Palestine, and their only practical use was as firewood or for the making of fences to contain grazing animals.

The soldiers' mockery continued as they placed a reed in Jesus' hand for a scepter, a token of His "royal" authority. This must have been a rather thick and solid cane for the soldiers to use it as described in verse 30.

Once Jesus looked the part, the callous soldiers knelt before Him, doing mock obeisance to Him as King. The irony, of course, is that the soldiers pretended that Jesus was what He in truth is, and they did in derision what they and all other persons one day shall do in all earnestness (see Philippians 2:9-11).

30. And they spit upon him, and took the reed, and smote him on the head.

In that hall, hundreds of soldiers passed before Jesus, each kneeling and hailing Him as "King of the Jews." Eventually, however, they tired of the charade, and mockery gave way to violence. Contemptuously they spit on Him, and each in turn took the reed from His trembling hands and hit Him on the head with it, doubtless driving the thorns deeper into His flesh.

As we consider the horror of this scene, let us remember two things. First, we can add to Jesus' indignities by betraying Him with our thoughts, denying Him with our words, or rejecting Him by our actions. Will we? Second, Jesus kept His dignity by refusing to retaliate against those who abused Him. When we are treated with contempt, can we react as He did?

Apparently at this point Pilate had Jesus brought out before the people, and made one more futile attempt to save Him from death (see John 19:4-16).

C. Enough (v. 31)

31. And after that they had mocked him, they took the robe off from him, and put his own raiment on him, and led him away to crucify him.

The mockery finally ended. The scarlet robe they had put on Jesus (v. 28) was removed, and

How to Say It

CYRENE. Sye-*ree*-nee.
GOLGOTHA. *Gahl*-guh-thuh.
SANHEDRIN. *San*-heh-drun or San-*heed*-run.

His own garment returned to Him. All preparations having been made for the execution, the soldiers *led him away to crucify him.*

THE ROAD TO CALVARY

The pilgrims come year by year. They are the modern counterpart of those who have come throughout the centuries to remember the suffering Savior. They are believers who, in the week each year when Jesus' sufferings and death are commemorated, want to walk the road to Calvary. It is called Via Dolorosa, the Way of Sorrow.

Every follower of Jesus needs to walk with Him to Calvary. We cannot, like Simon of Cyrene, carry Jesus' cross; but we can, at Jesus' invitation, take up our cross and follow Him. We can look around us and see the pain, suffering, shame, and hopelessness of those without Jesus and begin to share the burden of their anguish. In so doing we can be the bearers of the message of God's love, forgiveness, and reconciliation that came together at Calvary. We are not without modern examples. In Calcutta's morass of sin, idolatry, poverty, and death, Mother Teresa carries her cross. It is the caring ministry of love that comforts the dying and consoles the bereaved.

We cannot die to offer salvation to anyone. However, we can live as Jesus lived among us. We can feed the hungry, heal the wounded, encourage the stumbling, and thus reduce Satan's power and hold on mankind. We can carry our cross by fulfilling Jesus' ministry in the world, wherever we are. We can proclaim life, eternal life, by walking with humility and gratitude the road to Calvary and witnessing to the spiritual wholeness we were given there.   —W. P.

II. Jesus Crucified (Matthew 27:32-38)

A. The Approach (v. 32)

32. And as they came out, they found a man of Cyrene, Simon by name: him they compelled to bear his cross.

John 19:17 indicates that Jesus began the journey to the crucifixion site carrying His cross. No doubt weakened by the ordeal He had undergone, it must have been literally impossible for Jesus to bear the weight of the cross and walk along as fast as the soldiers wanted to go.

A man from Cyrene happened to be passing by. The soldiers seized him and compelled him to carry the heavy cross the rest of the way. *Cyrene* was a city of Libya on the north coast of Africa. *Simon* was probably a Jew who had come to Jerusalem for the Passover celebration. We have no idea if this Simon became a follower of Jesus, but his children were well known to

many when Mark wrote his Gospel account (see Mark 15:21).

As we consider the fact that one was compelled to carry Jesus' cross, the real question is not who was Simon, but where were the disciples? Those whom Jesus had challenged to take up their cross and follow Him had not followed Him to help bear His. The disciples, who promised to follow Jesus to Jerusalem even if it meant dying with Him (John 11:16), were not with Him now because they were afraid they might really have to die.

And what of us? Will we abandon Him when He needs us most?

B. The Place (v. 33)

33. And when they were come unto a place called Golgotha, that is to say, a place of a skull.

The place of crucifixion was called *Golgotha,* a Hebrew word meaning "skull." The Latin word *Calvary* has the same meaning. The location of this place is unknown. Why the place was given its name is unknown also. Some feel that the present Church of the Holy Sepulchre stands on the site. Others feel that it was a hill, which is located north of the present city. Of greatest importance is not the location of Golgotha, but the death of God's Son that occurred there. The Person, and not the place, is to be revered.

C. The Preparation (v. 34)

34. They gave him vinegar to drink mingled with gall: and when he had tasted thereof, he would not drink.

Preparations for the crucifixion began. *They gave him vinegar.* The drink the soldiers offered Jesus before they affixed Him to the cross was a mild painkiller, a drop of kindness in the flood of contempt. When Jesus tasted it, however, He refused to drink it. He chose to endure all of the agony of the cross, and to do so with a clear mind. Some months earlier He had set His face to go to Jerusalem. Several times He had told His disciples of the violent death that awaited Him there. He had wrestled in the garden with the agony of His impending death. He had faced the fear; He could face the fact. Jesus was no victim; His was a voluntary death.

D. The Crucifixion (v. 35)

35. And they crucified him, and parted his garments, casting lots: that it might be fulfilled which was spoken by the prophet, They parted my garments among them, and upon my vesture did they cast lots.

To be *crucified* is to be put to death by having one's hands and feet nailed or bound to a cross.

When Jesus was crucified large nails were driven through His hands and feet to hold Him to the cross. It has well been said that one who was crucified "died a thousand deaths."

It was customary for the soldiers assigned to execution duty to divide the victim's clothing among themselves. *Casting lots* refers to some method whereby a chance decision could be reached, whether by throwing dice, flipping a coin, drawing straws or some other way. When the soldiers did this, the prophecy of Psalm 22:18 was fulfilled.

E. The Wait (vv. 36-38)

36. And sitting down they watched him there.

The soldiers were responsible to see that no one came near, so they sat down to keep watch. Death on a cross could take days. Even when victims were nailed to the cross, death usually came by exhaustion or exposure, not from loss of blood.

37. And set up over his head his accusation written, THIS IS JESUS THE KING OF THE JEWS.

In the case of prominent prisoners, a sign was affixed to the cross, indicating the crime for which the person was being crucified. It was to be a warning to passersby not to contemplate such criminal behavior. John 19:20 tells us that the message was written in three languages: Hebrew (probably actually Aramaic, the language of the Jews), Latin (the official language of the Roman government), and Greek (the world language of commerce and culture). Ironically, the sign above Jesus' head proclaimed not a heinous crime but a wondrous truth about Him.

38. Then were there two thieves crucified with him; one on the right hand, and another on the left.

The *thieves* who were crucified with Jesus probably were not petty thieves. The word describing them means "robbers," those who stole with force and violence. The priests would not have been unhappy with this arrangement, be-

"Must Jesus Bear the Cross Alone?"

"For by grace are ye saved" (Ephesians 2:8)

visual 12

cause it suggested that Jesus was a common criminal like these robbers. Thus was the prophecy of Isaiah 53:12 fulfilled (see Mark 15:28).

III. Jesus Reviled
(Matthew 27:39-44)

A. The Passersby (vv. 39, 40)

39. And they that passed by reviled him, wagging their heads.

The crucifixion occurred out in the open for all to see. Some of those who passed by were the enemies of Jesus, and they *reviled* Him as He hung on the cross. *Reviled* means blasphemed. They were guilty of doing to the Son of God, however ignorantly, what He had been accused of doing to God.

40. And saying, Thou that destroyest the temple, and buildest it in three days, save thyself. If thou be the Son of God, come down from the cross.

They threw back in Jesus' face a completely twisted version of the statement He had made three years earlier. He had actually said, "[You] destroy this temple, and in three days I will raise it up" (John 2:19). He was speaking, of course, of His crucifixion and resurrection. Even though these enemies may not have understood what Jesus meant by His cryptic statement, it clearly implied that He possessed miraculous power. Coupling that with His own claim when He stood before Caiaphas (Matthew 26:64), these revilers challenged Jesus to give proof of His deity and *come down from the cross.*

B. The Authorities (vv. 41-43)

41. Likewise also the chief priests mocking him, with the scribes and the elders, said.

Some of the members of the Sanhedrin that had convicted Jesus were present. The *priests,* who had pressed the prosecution, seem to have taken the initiative once more. The *scribes* and *elders* also lowered themselves to the level of the crude populace by joining in the mockery.

42. He saved others; himself he cannot save. If he be the King of Israel, let him now come down from the cross, and we will believe him.

The rulers could hardly deny that Jesus had healed people of grievous diseases and had raised people from the dead. Now, however, they seized their opportunity to undermine Jesus' credibility by pointing out His inability to rescue himself from suffering and death. Before Pilate He had asserted that He was the King of the Jews. The rulers now sneered that if that were true, He should now display His power and authority by freeing himself from the cross.

A great irony appears here. The religious leaders of Jesus' day claimed that they would believe in Him if He came down from the cross; we believe in Him precisely because He did not. The fact that He stayed on the cross is not a sign to us that He was a deceiver, but, rather, proof that His claims were authentic. We take it not as a sign of His weakness, but as the surest token of His strength of will to carry out the plan of God.

Sometimes we may forget just how strange it must be to the world when we Christians claim to believe that One who was executed as a criminal was the powerful Son of God. There was so much about Jesus—in His life and in His death—that the world counts for weakness. But the glory of the Son of God was in His suffering, His power was in His sacrifice, and His strength was in the voluntary nature of His death.

43. He trusted in God; let him deliver him now, if he will have him: for he said, I am the Son of God.

The gist of the rulers' argument was that Jesus had lied in claiming to be *the Son of God.* If Jesus really was the Son of God, they implied, God would save His Son from death. These rulers took the death of Jesus as proof that Jesus was not the Son of God; we know that it was the clearest evidence that He was. The Jews took the death of Jesus as a sign that God had rejected Him; we know that by His death Jesus was accomplishing the will of God.

C. The Criminals (v. 44)

44. The thieves also, which were crucified with him, cast the same in his teeth.

The robbers who were crucified with Jesus would have liked nothing better than for Jesus to demonstrate divine power and show that He was the King of Israel. The overthrow of the Roman government might mean rescue for them also. Jesus' kingdom, however, was not a political/military one, and His victory was not of this type. When the robbers realized that there would be no miracle or display of divine power, they joined in the jeers. The phrase *cast the same in his teeth* vividly describes the force of their reviling. Luke 23:39-43 records that one of the two robbers repented, sought Jesus' favor, and was promised a place in paradise.

Conclusion

A. Voices at the Cross

The death of Jesus is a mirror in which we see our own reflections to His death. How do we respond to the death of Jesus? With whose voice do we speak?

Are we like the soldiers, oblivious to the spiritual revolution occurring around us, focused only on mockery, on the moment, on the material? Some who profess to follow Jesus mock Him by their life-styles; they devalue eternal life, which He has won for them, by living only for the moment; and they reject the spiritual salvation He offers by living lives focused on the material.

Are we like the passersby, unwilling to consider seriously who Jesus is? As believers, do we just go through the motions, refusing to examine the implications of the death of Jesus lest we be challenged to change our priorities or our life principles?

Are we like the religious leaders, who sought to protect their own power by rejecting His? Do we also fail to see that the salvation God offers is founded not on spectacular display but on self-sacrifice?

Or are we like the thieves, who would minimize the fact of their sin and the extent of their guilt?

With our hearts and voices let us confess our sins before God and thank the Lord Jesus for His sacrifice that makes forgiveness of sin possible. Then by our lives let us honor Him who suffered the greatest dishonor and shame that we might live eternally.

B. Prayer

O God, be merciful to us, who are sinners. We thank You for Your inexpressible gift of forgiveness through Your Son, Jesus. In His name we pray. Amen.

C. Thought to Remember

The scoffers said they would have believed in Jesus if He had come down from the cross. We believe precisely because He did not.

Home Daily Bible Readings

Monday, Feb. 13—Jesus Is Taken to Pilate; Judas' Death (Matthew 27:1-10)

Tuesday, Feb. 14—Jesus Is Silent Before Pilate (Matthew 27:11-20)

Wednesday, Feb. 15—Barabbas Released and Jesus Condemned (Matthew 27:21-26)

Thursday, Feb. 16—Jesus Is Mocked and Led Away (Matthew 27:27-31)

Friday, Feb. 17—The Crucifixion (Matthew 27:32-44)

Saturday, Feb. 18—The Death of Jesus (Matthew 27:45-54)

Sunday, Feb. 19—The Burial of Jesus (Matthew 27:55-61)

Learning by Doing

This page contains an alternate lesson plan emphasizing learning activities. Classes desiring such student involvement will find these suggestions helpful.

Learning Goals

This session will help the learners;

1. Understand the horror and the glory of Jesus' crucifixion.

2. Offer praise and thanks to God for the victory Jesus won on the cross.

3. Commit themselves to follow Jesus in taking up their crosses.

Into the Lesson

Demonstrate the horror of crucifixion by comparing it with other methods of capital punishment. Prepare six large strips of paper and write one of the following methods on each:

Gas Chamber
Lethal Injection
Hanging
Firing Squad
Electric Chair
Crucifixion

Display them across the front of the room. (Or write them on the board, if you prefer.)

Lead the class in discussing these forms of execution one at a time. Consider such questions as, What physical suffering is involved? What humiliation is involved? Discuss crucifixion last. Point out the excruciating pain of having spikes driven through hands and feet (or wrists and ankles); the labor and agony of each breath, as a result of hanging in an unnatural position; the humiliation of hanging nearly naked (if not completely naked) before a crowd; the incredible thirst brought on by the dehydration of blood loss and hanging in the hot sun.

Note: the point of this introduction is to show the horrible death our Lord died, *not* to debate the pros and cons of capital punishment. The discussion here is physical, not ethical.

Into the Word

Write on slips of paper the text of the following verses of today's passage, one verse per slip: 27, 28, 29, 30, 35, 37, 38, 39, 40, 41, 42, 43, 44. Pass these out to thirteen class members. Have the verses read one at a time in the order given. As each verse is read, ask the class to define the insult or mockery contained in it. (For instance, in verse 27 the humiliation is seen in the fact that the soldiers on duty woke up all the other soldiers, very early in the morning, to gather around and ridicule Jesus.

Also, have the class note the irony in such statements as verse 29 (their mocking statement was true!); verse 37 (again, Pilate's ridicule was absolutely true, see John 19:19-22); verse 42 (again, the insult was true: had He saved himself, all of us would be lost). Announce to the class, in your best Paul Harvey inpersonation, "You know the news. Now, you're going to hear—the rest of the story!"

Point out that the other Gospel writers give additional details regarding the crucifixion, and that, most important, the story of Jesus does not end at the cross.

1. *The robbers.* Have someone read Matthew 27:38, 44. Ask the class what they would assume the final destination of these men would be if we had only Matthew's Gospel. Then have someone read Luke 23:39-43. The "rest of the story" for one of the robbers is given here. What *two* promises made to him by Jesus are recorded in verse 43? (In addition to the promise of paradise, Jesus told him that he would be there *today*; he would not have to hang on the cross for several days, as was often the case.)

2. *Jesus.* Have someone read Matthew 27:50. What were the results of Jesus' death? (See, for example, Romans 4:25; Hebrews 2:14, 15.) Point out, however, that Jesus would have been just a statistic in a Roman archive, if not for the "rest of the story," seen in Matthew 28:5-7; 1 Corinthians 15:3-8.

Into Life

Have four students read to the class the stanzas of John Bowring's hymn, "In the Cross of Christ." As each student reads, have the class discuss briefly the reason given in that stanza for glorying in the cross.

Next, have someone read aloud Matthew 16:24, 25. Ask the class what it means to take up our cross. Remind the class that a cross was a means of execution, and that verse 24 is explained by verse 25. Lead the class to see that taking up our cross is to endure reproach or dishonor in the eyes of the world, even the loss of life, in serving Christ.

Urge the class members to commit themselves anew to a life of cross-bearing, putting their lives on the line for Jesus. Then close with a prayer of praise and thanks for Jesus' sacrifice on the cross.

Let's Talk It Over

The questions on this page are designed to encourage review of the lesson Scriptures and to promote discussion of the lesson by the class. The answers provided are only discussion starters. Let your class talk it over from there.

1. In what ways may some Christians today be guilty of mocking Jesus?

Some may protest that Christians do not mock Jesus. They may argue that only unbelievers, the enemies of Jesus, do that. Not so! All too often the most damaging mockery of Jesus today comes from Christians who do not live what they profess. Usually, Christians mock Him in their life-styles. No, they will not say one word against Him. But actions *do* speak louder than words. By living a life focused on, or obsessed with, the material, they mock Him and what He reveals as being of the greatest value and importance. By living for the moment, they mock Him and deny the ultimacy of eternity. Numerous respected Christian leaders have observed in recent years that they cannot see any difference in the life-style of non-Christians and that of many professing Christians. If that doesn't mock Jesus, what does?

2. In Psalm 22 there are at least six specific statements that relate to the crucifixion of Jesus. How many can you name?

Psalm 22 is an important psalm, for it contains predictions of specific details relating to Jesus' crucifixion. In the first verse of the psalm may be found the very words of Jesus on the cross, "My God, my God, why hast thou forsaken me?" (Matthew 27:46). In the Jewish faith this was called "the cry of the ancient sufferer," and it has obvious messianic implications. Verse 7 refers to the mocking and the scornful "wagging of heads" of those who observed Him during His agony (Matthew 27:39). Verse 8 records the taunt of the priests: "He trusted on the Lord that he would deliver him: let him deliver him" (Matthew 27:43). Verse 15 refers to the thirst He experienced on the cross (see John 19:28). Verse 18 of the psalm prophesies the gambling for Jesus' clothing: "They part my garments among them, and cast lots upon my vesture" (Matthew 27:35). Finally, verse 22 speaks of the sufferer's relationship with the Father (see Hebrews 2:10-12). Psalm 22 remarkably foreshadows the crucifixion of Jesus Christ!

3. What can we learn from the way in which Jesus accepted criticism that may help us when we must face it?

Fighting back is of no help against the determined critic. When we are criticized without justification, our quiet endurance and patience is a much better testimony than any kind of argument or countercriticism. Because Jesus endured the criticism of the sharpest of all critics, we can take courage and not be weary when we must face this.

4. How do people usually respond to the experience of dying?

Modern research shows that most people respond with fear to the experience of dying. They do not state that they fear death itself; the experience of dying is what they fear. Their fear focuses on these questions: How will I respond to pain, particularly if it continues for a long period of time? Will I lose control? What will it be like if I am terminally ill for an extended time? If the terminal experience leaves me debilitated, how will I feel being completely dependent upon others? Will my loved ones be able to handle my dying—how will it impact them emotionally and psychologically?

Jesus was not eager to face the experience of dying. As He prayed in Gethsemane in the shadow of the cross, He wondered if there were any other way for the Father to achieve the redemption of the world. At one level, He desired that the cup of suffering and dying would pass from Him; at the deeper level, however, He submitted himself in obedience to the Father. So He prayed, "Not my will, but thine, be done." (Luke 22:42).

5. How does a Christian "take up his cross" and follow after Jesus?

In His demands of discipleship, Jesus said to His disciples, "If any man will come after me, let him deny himself, and take up his cross, and follow me" (Matthew 16:24). What is one's cross? The responsibility of caring for one's infirm parent or handicapped child is not the cross of which Jesus spoke. Nor is being stricken with a debilitating illness this cross. Those responsibilities and experiences come to persons whether or not they are followers of Christ. One's cross is what one uniquely suffers and bears because, and only because, of his or her allegiance to Jesus Christ.

The Risen Christ Commissions Disciples

DEVOTIONAL READING: Acts 10:34-48.

LESSON SCRIPTURE: Matthew 27:62—28:20.

PRINTED TEXT: Matthew 28:1-10, 16-20.

Matthew 28:1-10, 16-20

1 In the end of the sabbath, as it began to dawn toward the first day of the week, came Mary Magdalene and the other Mary to see the sepulchre.

2 And, behold, there was a great earthquake: for the angel of the Lord descended from heaven, and came and rolled back the stone from the door, and sat upon it.

3 His countenance was like lightning, and his raiment white as snow:

4 And for fear of him the keepers did shake, and became as dead men.

5 And the angel answered and said unto the women, Fear not ye: for I know that ye seek Jesus, which was crucified.

6 He is not here: for he is risen, as he said. Come, see the place where the Lord lay.

7 And go quickly, and tell his disciples that he is risen from the dead; and, behold, he goeth before you into Galilee; there shall ye see him: lo, I have told you.

8 And they departed quickly from the sepulchre with fear and great joy; and did run to bring his disciples word.

9 And as they went to tell his disciples, behold, Jesus met them, saying, All hail. And they came and held him by the feet, and worshipped him.

10 Then said Jesus unto them, Be not afraid: go tell my brethren that they go into Galilee, and there shall they see me.

· · · · · · · · · · · · · ·

16 Then the eleven disciples went away into Galilee, into a mountain where Jesus had appointed them.

17 And when they saw him, they worshipped him: but some doubted.

18 And Jesus came and spake unto them, saying, All power is given unto me in heaven and in earth.

19 Go ye therefore, and teach all nations, baptizing them in the name of the Father, and of the Son, and of the Holy Ghost:

20 Teaching them to observe all things whatsoever I have commanded you: and, lo, I am with you alway, even unto the end of the world. Amen.

GOLDEN TEXT: Go ye therefore, and teach all nations, baptizing them in the name of the Father, and of the Son, and of the Holy Ghost: teaching them to observe all things whatsoever I have commanded you: and, lo, I am with you alway, even unto the end of the world. Amen.—Matthew 28:19, 20.

Feb
26

Jesus the Fulfillment
(Matthew)
Unit 4. Jesus Christ: Victor Over Sin and Death (Lessons 10-13)

Lesson Aims

As a result of studying this week's lesson, the students should:

1. Have a greater knowledge of the facts regarding Jesus' resurrection.

2. Rejoice in Jesus' victory over death.

3. Resolve to tell at least one person this week of what Jesus' resurrection means to mankind.

Lesson Outline

INTRODUCTION
    A. Aftermath of the Resurrection
    B. Lesson Background
  I. THE EMPTY TOMB (Matthew 28:1-8)
    A. The Women Approach (v. 1)
    B. The Angel Appears (vv. 2-4)
    C. The Angel Announces (vv. 5, 6)
    D. The Angel Instructs (vv. 7, 8)
        He's Alive!
  II. THE RISEN LORD (Matthew 28:9, 10)
    A. Meeting Along the Way (v. 9)
    B. Message Repeated (v. 10)
 III. THE GREAT COMMISSION (Matthew 28:16-20)
    A. The Authority of the Lord (vv. 16-18)
    B. The Commission to the Disciples (vv. 19, 20a)
    C. The Promise of His Presence (v. 20b)
CONCLUSION
    A. Evidence of Things Unseen
    B. Prayer
    C. Thought to Remember

Visual 13 illustrates the relevance of Jesus' resurrection and the Great Commission for every generation. The visual is shown on page 221.

Introduction

A. Aftermath of the Resurrection

In the appearances of the risen Christ, there was at first the urgent necessity to make sure that Jesus was actually risen from the dead. This surety was given.

The women who were on their way to tell His disciples of the empty tomb and angel's message met Jesus on the way. Coming to Him, they fell down before Him and clasped His nail-pierced feet (Matthew 28:9). They knew it was Jesus.

When Jesus appeared to the eleven and those who were with them later in the day of the resurrection, He showed them His hands and His feet and urged them to touch Him so they would know He was not an apparition. Then He ate food before them (Luke 24:36-43). They were convinced Jesus was standing before them.

A week later Thomas, who was not present at the earlier meeting and who protested that he would not believe unless He saw the scarred body of His Lord, was given the same evidence, and he too confessed his belief in the risen Christ (John 20:26-29).

Once these witnesses were certain that Jesus was risen from the dead, they faced these questions: "What are we to do about this? May we tell others? When? How shall we proceed?" So, the great commission was the natural outcome of the resurrection.

We today still face the question as to what we will do about the resurrected Christ. It is not enough for us to strengthen our personal faith and hope, to treasure our redemption in Christ. We must share it with others or we will lose it ourselves.

B. Lesson Background

Although Jesus had been on the cross for only six miserably long, mercifully short hours, the Roman soldiers confirmed that Jesus was dead. To remove any possibility of doubt of this fact, one of the soldiers thrust his spear through the side of Jesus' body, causing blood and water to issue from it. Jesus' death occurred at 3:00 P.M. (Luke 23:44-46), so there was just enough time for His followers hurriedly to place His body in a borrowed tomb before the Sabbath began at sunset on that Friday evening. Attention to the corpse would have to wait until after the Sabbath, when the darkness of Saturday night gave way to Sunday morning's dawn. Only then could Jesus' faithful followers come to the tomb to complete the burial customs.

It is important to remember that the women who came to the tomb as the first day of the week was dawning came to minister to a dead Master, not a risen Lord. They could have expected His resurrection, perhaps they even should have. On three separate occasions Jesus had foretold that He would be handed over to the authorities, put to death, and raised on the third day (Matthew 16:21; 17:22, 23; 20:17-19). These women were among those disciples who had heard Jesus' dire predictions (see Luke 24:6-8), but they must have dismissed them as being incredible, just as Peter had done (Matthew 16:22).

Sadly, therefore, they came to Jesus' tomb that morning to attend to His permanent burial.

What caused the transformation in their lives—and the lives of the eleven disciples—from defeat and disappointment to firm faith and courageous testimony? The resurrection of Jesus.

I. The Empty Tomb
(Matthew 28:1-8)

A. The Women Approach (v. 1)

1. In the end of the sabbath, as it began to dawn toward the first day of the week, came Mary Magdalene and the other Mary to see the sepulchre.

These two women had been followers of Jesus since the days of His ministry in Galilee. They had traveled with Him, ministering to Him and giving financial support to His ministry (Matthew 27:55, 56; Luke 8:1-3). These two followed when Jesus' body was taken down from the cross and watched when it was placed in the tomb (Matthew 27:61; Mark 15:47).

The Sabbath had ended at sundown on what we call Saturday evening, but Sunday morning was the women's first opportunity to attend to Jesus. Elsewhere we learn that they came to the tomb bringing their prepared spices to complete the preparations for the burial of their dead Master, and that other women were in their company (Luke 23:55—24:1, 10; Mark 16:1). John tells us that the dark of the night had not yet completely disappeared when they arrived.

B. The Angel Appears (vv. 2-4)

2. And, behold, there was a great earthquake: for the angel of the Lord descended from heaven, and came and rolled back the stone from the door, and sat upon it.

No mortal eye observed as Jesus came forth from the closed tomb, so we do not know the precise time when the resurrection occurred. It is implied, however, that the descent of the angel, the earthquake, and resurrection were nearly simultaneous in occurrence and that this all happened while the women were making their journey to the tomb. (Compare Luke 24:1, 2.) Clearly, it was not necessary for the angel to roll back the stone from the door to permit Jesus to come forth from the tomb. The angel's appearance struck terror in the hearts of the guards, and his opening of the tomb permitted the women and others to enter it.

3. His countenance was like lightning, and his raiment white as snow.

The angel's appearance confirmed his identity as a being who had come from the presence of God. Jesus had revealed His divine identity to His disciples by a similar glorious appearance at the transfiguration.

4. And for fear of him the keepers did shake, and became as dead men.

The keepers were Roman guards assigned by Pontius Pilate at the request of the Jewish religious leaders to keep watch over the sealed tomb. The angel seemingly had a countenance that was severe and fearsome, for as the guards looked at him they began to shake uncontrollably and fainted dead away. Although the soldiers did not see Jesus as He came forth from the tomb, when they regained consciousness and went into Jerusalem they were able to testify to the presence and power of this divine being and to the empty tomb.

C. The Angel Announces (vv. 5, 6)

5. And the angel answered and said unto the women, Fear not ye: for I know that ye seek Jesus, which was crucified.

When the women arrived at the tomb and saw that the stone was rolled away from it, they entered and discovered that the body of Jesus was missing (Mark 16:4-6; Luke 24:2-5). It was after this that the angel spoke to them.

The angel answered all the unspoken questions swirling in the minds of the women: "What had happened? How did it happen? Why did it happen? What might happen next?" *Fear not ye.* The women naturally were afraid at the sight of a being who obviously was divine. Theirs was an appropriate fear, a fitting response in the presence of one who has come from the presence of God.

The angel knew, however, that their fear also centered about their thoughts of Jesus who had been crucified. He acknowledged this before leading them on to the undreamed-of truth of the resurrection.

Fear—reverential awe—is a proper response to almighty God as we realize that we live in His presence daily. But that fear does not terrorize us. By all He has done, especially in the death and resurrection of His Son, He has shown His love for us. The fear we have for God leads us to greater faith, and greater love for Him.

6. He is not here: for he is risen, as he said. Come, see the place where the Lord lay.

He is not here. The first part of the angel's statement spoke only of absence and might have provoked further confusion and consternation in the women's minds. But the second part of it spoke of life, of resurrection. This is the great

---

How to Say It

MAGDALENE.   *Mag*-duh-leen or Mag-duh-*lee*-nee.

good news! Jesus is not held in the grip of the grave. He is freed from death and is able to free from death all those whose sins He bore. *As he said.* To give force to his assertion, the angel reminded the women that Jesus had promised to rise (see Luke 24:6, 7).

The women hesitated, still fearful, so the angel invited them to come close and examine the place where Jesus' body had lain. This at least confirmed His absence and for the time being suggested His resurrection. Before long, Peter and John would study that empty tomb and its contents—the linen bandages that had been wound around Jesus' body, limb by limb, and the neatly folded head scarf. The empty tomb, however, was not the ultimate basis for their faith, any more than it was the ultimate proof of the resurrection. The risen Lord himself would be the evidence and object of their faith.

"Come, see" is an invitation that is extended to every person in every age. We cannot with certainty examine the empty tomb of Jesus, but we can carefully consider all the evidence that shows that Jesus rose from the dead. The resurrection invites personal involvement as the basis for personal testimony.

D. The Angel Instructs (vv. 7, 8)

7. And go quickly, and tell his disciples that he is risen from the dead; and, behold, he goeth before you into Galilee; there shall ye see him: lo, I have told you.

The women were not allowed to linger at the empty tomb for long. They were commissioned to *go quickly, and tell* the greatest good news the world has ever heard—Jesus *is risen from the dead!* The gospel has had many messengers, and these women were the first. Mary Magdalene apparently was the first of the women to reach the tomb. Without waiting to see or hear more than that the tomb was empty, she had run to tell Peter and John (see John 20:1, 2). The other women, who had remained at the tomb were now commissioned by the angel to carry to the disciples the news of Jesus' resurrection.

He goeth before you into Galilee. The band of disciples had been shaken by the events of the past several days, and it had been temporarily disintegrated. This group, upon whom so much depended, needed to be formed again, and the peace, seclusion, and safety of Galilee was well suited for this. Many of these men were from Galilee, and it was there that they were called to be His followers. Now it would be the site of their recommissioning to an even greater ministry, service in the light of the resurrection. The foundation of their recommissioning would be their reunion with their living Lord himself.

Our lives, our ministries, must also be based on the person of Jesus Christ. Though we do not see Him in the flesh, we meet Him and come to know Him as we read His Word. Thus "seeing" Him, we too are led to serve Him.

HE'S ALIVE!

"Missing in Action" has been an emotional, political, and personal tragedy for Americans ever since Vietnam. The pain of not knowing if one you love is dead or alive is devastating. The records of MIAs in Vietnam are still incomplete.

The long, black marble Memorial Wall in Washington D. C. testifies to the sacrifice of America's known dead in the war in Vietnam, and it honors their memory. MIAs are those whose bodies were not recovered or those who may have died as prisoners of war and their deaths not reported by North Vietnamese officials. Some speculate that there may be a few still alive somewhere in southeast Asia. It is a festering wound in the heart of our nation.

Jesus died on the cross and was buried in the tomb; but when the women came with their burial spices, He was not there. The greatest mystery and tragedy of all earth's history would have been the empty tomb with no certainty of where Jesus' body had been taken. Thank God, Jesus' death on the cross was true—it was an acknowledged and verified fact. He was buried, and the tomb's location was known. And the tomb was well guarded by Roman soldiers.

The angel did not say, "Jesus' body is missing." The angel's message from Heaven was an announcement that makes the gospel message the hope of mankind: "He is not here: for he is risen . . . he goeth before you into Galilee; there shall ye see him" (Matthew 28:6, 7). No MIA. No mystery. History certifies that He is alive!

—W. P.

8. And they departed quickly from the sepulchre with fear and great joy; and did run to bring his disciples word.

The women did as they were instructed by the angel, and they ran from the tomb *with fear and great joy.* It may seem strange that these two emotions burned within the hearts of the women as they hurried to the disciples, but we can surely understand it. They had seen a heavenly visitor in blinding appearance who had spoken to them. They had been in the presence of the supernatural. Any response other than *fear* would have been most unnatural. No sooner than thinking of this divine visitation, however, their minds turned to the message that was given them—Jesus is risen! and they were filled with *great joy.*

Convinced of the truth of Jesus' resurrection and all its meaning for a lost world, we too should hasten to *go* and *tell* those who have not heard.

II. The Risen Lord
(Matthew 28:9, 10)

A. Meeting Along the Way (v. 9)

9. And as they went to tell his disciples, behold, Jesus met them, saying, All hail. And they came and held him by the feet, and worshipped him.

Even before the women reached the disciples to share their wonderful news, they were confronted with an even more wonderful reality. Jesus himself met them. He spoke the simple, quiet words of salutation common in their day: "Greetings." Thus their testimony would not just be word of an empty tomb, but the good news of, "We have seen the Lord."

Their reactions were wholly fitting: they knelt before Jesus in awe *and worshipped him.* As they did so they clasped His feet in their great desire to be fully assured that His presence was real. This passage shows that the sense of touch also attested to the resurrection.

B. Message Repeated (v. 10)

10. Then said Jesus unto them, Be not afraid: go tell my brethren that they go into Galilee, and there shall they see me.

Once again the women received the instruction to let awe give way to action. An important message was to be given to the disciples. Neither in the angel's instructions to the women nor in Jesus' words here was mention made that the disciples would see Jesus that very day. The faith of the disciples, already sorely tested, would be tested further by the events of this day.

III. The Great Commission
(Matthew 28:16-20)

A. The Authority of the Lord (vv. 16-18)

16. Then the eleven disciples went away into Galilee, into a mountain where Jesus had appointed them.

Matthew does not mention the exact time or location of this meeting with Jesus. More than a week had passed since the resurrection, however. Jesus appeared to the group on the evening of resurrection day when Thomas was absent, and again eight days later when Thomas was with the rest of the group (John 20:19-29).

On the eve of His crucifixion Jesus had spoken to the eleven disciples of this meeting (Matthew 26:32). The angel at the tomb gave the women instructions for the disciples regarding this meeting (28:7), as did Jesus when He met them in the way (28:10).

So *the eleven disciples* (Judas having hanged himself) went to a mountain in Galilee as Jesus had instructed them, doubtless in one of His earlier appearances to them. Galilee was the place where they were called to service, trained for service, and sent out in service. They surely knew that being summoned to Galilee meant that they were being summoned to service. The reality of the resurrection and our believing response to it are not ends in themselves. They anticipate a call to service. We too must move from our Jerusalems, our weekly worship services celebrating the resurrection, into our Galilees, to our own mountains of opportunity for witness and service to which we have been called.

17. And when they saw him, they worshipped him: but some doubted.

The worship of God is the highest duty of human beings. Besides the Father himself none is worthy of worship other than the One who was God and had fully and finally manifested God to the human race. And there could be no greater moment to worship than in the presence of the risen Lord, who had nullified the unnatural domination of sin and death and had begun the process of restoring us to our natural relationship with God through the resurrection of the dead.

Matthew mentions that at the appearance of Jesus *some doubted.* This certainly cannot refer to any of the eleven disciples, for they had seen Him more than once at Jerusalem and had been given indubitable proofs that He had risen from the dead. Perhaps this was the occasion when Jesus was seen by more than five hundred persons at once (1 Corinthians 15:6). The eleven were slow to believe that Jesus had risen (Mark 16:9-14), and Thomas's hesitance is well known (John 20:24-29). It is not surprising, therefore, that other followers of Jesus were hesitant to believe the resurrection reports. But consider this: if those who doubted had accepted the wonder of the resurrection too readily, too thoughtlessly, they would not be credible witnesses. Those on

visual 13

whose testimony our faith is based were not gullible. And their testimony was not based on wishful thinking or secondhand reports or mass hallucinations, but on what they themselves witnessed. We can be grateful for the faith of these first followers. But we can also be grateful for the doubt that assured that their eventual faith was founded in fact.

18. And Jesus came and spake unto them, saying, All power is given unto me in heaven and in earth.

The word translated *power* actually means authority. There is a significant difference. Jesus did have power, power that He demonstrated on many occasions by His miracles. But He possesses something far greater even than supernatural power; it is the authority of God.

Neither the church today nor anyone in the church possesses inherent authority. Like the apostles themselves, as we do the Master's bidding we do so in the confidence that we are carrying out the Commission of the One to whom all authority is given and in whom all authority resides, our risen Lord.

B. The Commission to the Disciples (vv. 19, 20a)

19. Go ye therefore, and teach all nations, baptizing them in the name of the Father, and of the Son, and of the Holy Ghost.

All Christians of every age are bound by this command of our Lord. *Teach all nations.* Teaching is more than passing on information about Jesus, more than creating learners. This teaching involves calling others to commitment to Jesus. It is the process of making disciples. There are no national or ethnic or racial prerequisites to becoming a disciple, only wholehearted commitment to Christ. Baptism is not only the way in which our Lord commanded us to express our commitment to Him, but it is an eminently appropriate way. Thus we are incorporated into Christ by symbolic but real identification of ourselves with His saving death on the cross and His victorious resurrection.

20a. Teaching them to observe all things whatsoever I have commanded you.

Teaching precedes baptism, and teaching must follow baptism. Just as newborn infants must be fed to sustain life and promote growth, so those born again in Christ must receive teaching so they can mature in Christian thought, speech, and conduct.

C. The Promise of His Presence (v. 20b)

20b. And, lo, I am with you alway, even unto the end of the world. Amen.

When God commissioned Moses, He said He would be with him. When God called Joshua, He gave the same promise. Here Jesus gives the promise of His presence to His disciples. It is the greatest promise we have—that He will continue to be with us until we are able to be with Him.

Conclusion

A. Evidence of Things Unseen

As wonderful as the discovery of the empty tomb was, it was not enough. It was necessary for the women and the disciples to see and communicate with the risen Lord. If it was essential for them to see not only the empty tomb but also the risen Lord, is it not essential for us also? No. We have the testimony of eyewitnesses, many eyewitnesses, who saw what they never expected to see, whose fear became faith, whose lives and attitudes were transformed, and who gave their lives—in more ways than one—for the One whom they had seen after He was risen from the dead. The resurrection of Jesus cannot be explained, but their testimony to the reality of the resurrection cannot be explained away. Their testimony is the evidence of things we cannot see, and on that we base our faith. There will come a time when we will see Jesus face to face. Until then let us continue to tell the good news to all—He is risen from the dead!

B. Prayer

O God of life, we thank You for the witness You provided to Your Son's resurrection, and for the hope of eternal life that is ours in His victory over death. In the name of the risen Lord we pray. Amen.

C. Thought to Remember

Our risen Lord commissions us to go and tell others He is risen. Let's not fail Him.

Home Daily Bible Readings

Monday, Feb. 20—Witness to Jesus' Resurrection (Acts 10:34-43)

Tuesday, Feb. 21—A Guarded Tomb (Matthew 27:62-66)

Wednesday, Feb. 22—The Empty Tomb (Matthew 28:1-7)

Thursday, Feb. 23—Jesus' Resurrection Discounted (Matthew 28:8-15)

Friday, Feb. 24—He Has Risen (Mark 16:1-8)

Saturday, Feb. 25—Jesus Appears to Mary and His Disciples (John 20:1, 11-23)

Sunday, Feb. 26—Jesus' Commission to His Disciples (Matthew 28:16-20)

Learning by Doing

This page contains an alternate lesson plan emphasizing learning activities. Classes desiring such student involvement will find these suggestions helpful.

Learning Goals

After participating in this lesson, the students will:

1. Experience the joy of the resurrection.
2. Understand the message of the Great Commission.
3. Resolve to be involved in the work of making disciples.

Into the Lesson

Give each class member a sheet of paper. Provide a pen or pencil for each person who needs one. Have your class members write the following three questions on their papers as you read them aloud. Give them two or three minutes to write their answers.

1. What is the most joyful memory from your childhood (before you were eighteen years old)?
2. What factors made this a particularly joyful event?
3. What do you have to aid your memory of the event? (For example, photographs, letters, home movies, etc.)

Have your class members divide into pairs (married students pairing off with those who are not their spouses) and ask them to share their answers to the questions. Allow about two minutes for each question.

Now, ask the class, "What do you think is the most joyful event in all of human history?" The answer you are looking for, of course, is the resurrection of Jesus. If other answers are given, acknowledge them as good answers!

Second, ask what it is about the resurrection that makes it particularly joyful.

Finally, ask the class what we have to remind us of Jesus' resurrection. Possible answers may include the Bible, the Holy Spirit, or Easter. But it is the Lord's Day, the first day of the week, that the church has set apart from earliest days as a time to celebrate the resurrection of the Son of God on the first day of the week nearly two thousand years ago.

Into the Word

Have four students read aloud to the class the Scriptures in parentheses at the end of this paragraph. Before the readings, ask the class to be listening to discover something the verses have in common. (Luke 1:13; Luke 1:30; Luke 2:10; Matthew 28:5)

(The common element is the angel's command not to be afraid.) The women in our text obviously were terrified. Have the class examine the text to see what other emotion the women felt. (Joy, verse 8.)

Now lead into a discussion as follows: State, "We are convinced of the resurrection of Jesus by the testimony in the Word. We have identified with His death and resurrection through baptism, and we have the promise of His unfailing presence in our lives." Then ask, "Do we experience a great sense of joy as the women at the tomb did in thinking of His resurrection? If not, what can we do to rekindle the spark of sheer amazement and joy?"

Give two good readers the following short script, and have them read it now.

Doctor (*excitedly*): I've done it! I've just discovered the cure for cancer! It's been right under our noses all the time!

Assistant: That's great news, Doctor! Shall I call the media, the Centers for Disease Control, the president?

Doctor (*more subdued*): No, I don't really want all the publicity. I'm just a quiet kind of guy. Let's just forget about this and get back to the cure for the common cold we've been working on.

Assistant: OK. You're the boss.

Ask, "What is wrong here?" After a brief discussion, point out that we often are just like the doctor. We have the greatest news in history—Jesus is risen!—and we remain quiet about it!

Write on the board or overhead the words, *"Great Commission."* Have someone read Matthew 28:18-20. Now write on the board or overhead these questions one at a time, or have a transparency prepared that will allow you to uncover them one at a time. Write each answer beside the question as the class gives it.

Whose authority? (Jesus')

When? (As you go)

What? (Make disciples)

How? (1. Baptizing them, 2. teaching them)

How long? (Until the very end of the age)

Into Life

Ask each class member to think of one person they know who does not know the Lord. Just *one!* Then have them pray for the person, and for an opportunity to share Jesus with that person.

Let's Talk It Over

The questions on this page are designed to encourage review of the lesson Scriptures and to promote discussion of the lesson by the class. The answers provided are only discussion starters. Let your class talk it over from there.

1. What implications does Jesus' resurrection have for Christians?

Jesus' resurrection is *the* key for the Christian life. Note these fundamental aspects of it:

(1) *Promise.* Jesus said He would rise from the dead, and He did! We can be confident, therefore, that He will do as He promises. One of His most precious promises is this: "I am the resurrection, and the life: he that believeth in me, though he were dead, yet shall he live: and whosoever liveth and believeth in me shall never die" (John 11:25, 26).

(2) *Reality.* His resurrection was a *bodily* resurrection. It was not the resurrection of His influence nor the raising of His popularity. This was a *real*, lasting resurrection. The living Lord is ruler of God's eternal kingdom.

(3) *Future.* Life beyond the grave is confirmed. We *too* will be raised on that Great Day (see John 5:28, 29). As the apostle Paul affirms, Christ is "the firstfruits of them that slept" (1 Corinthians 15:20). This statement indicates sequence. Christ was the first to come out of the grave, never to die again, and we shall follow!

(4) *Basis.* His resurrection is the foundation of our witness to the world. We sing, "I serve a risen Savior, He's in the world today!" We do not follow a dead hero, but a living Lord!

2. What is the basis for our believing that Jesus rose from the dead?

Our faith is solidly grounded in credible witness and testimony. Those who knew Him well saw Him alive after His death and burial. They talked with Him. They touched Him. They ate with Him. They met Him in many different places and circumstances. Those who at first disbelieved were moved to new faith and reverently acknowledged, "My Lord and my God!" There were no mass hallucinations, nor was there any hocus-pocus. Listen to the testimony of Paul recorded in 1 Corinthians 15:5-7: the risen Lord appeared to Peter, to the apostles, to more than five hundred disciples at one time (and Paul notes that most of them were still alive when he wrote this—they could be questioned), to James (Jesus' brother who had not believed in Him at first), and finally to Paul himself.

Credulity may find ample reason for belief in mere speculation, but faith is rooted in reliable witness and testimony. The resurrection of Jesus Christ is a fact of history, attested to by reliable witnesses. *That's* the basis of our faith!

3. How does the command to "disciple the nations" challenge us today?

The "nations" literally translated from the Greek text means "people (or ethnic) groups." There are hundreds upon hundreds of "people groups" all around the globe, and many have not yet heard of Jesus. Obviously, Jesus' Commission remains unfulfilled while this condition exists. Christians must go to these peoples with the spoken word of the gospel. The written Word must be made available to them, also. This can be done through groups who disseminate Bibles in foreign languages. There are many people groups, however, who do not have written languages. Some Christians are at present working among these peoples to reduce their spoken languages to writing, and in the process are translating the Bible into those languages. These Christians, and those who support their work, are fulfilling Jesus' Great commission.

4. How may the "Go ye" of the Great Commission be misunderstood by Christians regarding their personal witness for Jesus?

Obviously, great emphasis must be placed on Christian missions, so that all persons everywhere may learn of Jesus. But let us not overlook the fact that Jesus' Commission was for all of His followers, not for a relatively small group of workers who are willing to travel to far-off places with the gospel. We must understand that Jesus' "Go ye" can be fulfilled by each of us as we go to our place of employment, or to school, or any other place we visit.

5. How can we restore the quality of urgency in evangelism that characterized the apostolic church?

The key is in impressing Christians with the Biblical concept that persons are lost without Christ. When we see friends and neighbors outwardly successful and content, we may tend to think all is well with them. If we saturate our minds with the Bible's many warnings regarding man's lost condition, we will be less likely to fall into such complacency.

Spring Quarter, 1995

Theme: Christians Living in Community (1 and 2 Corinthians)

Special Features

Lessons

Unit 1. Responding to Challenges of Life in Community

Unit 2. Nurturing the Life of the Community

Unit 3. Ministering as a Christian Community

About these lessons

The lessons of the Spring Quarter are based on the apostle Paul's letters of 1 and 2 Corinthians. In them Paul addressed a variety of problems and issues involving the first-century Christians in Corinth. The principles he enunciated provide guidance for Christians today as well. This study emphasizes that the church is a community, and that all Christians are to promote the health and growth of that community.

Mar 5

Mar 12

Mar 19

Mar 26

Apr 2

Apr 9

Apr 16

Apr 23

Apr 30

May 7

May 14

May 21

May 28

Quarterly Quiz

The questions on this page may be used in several ways: as a pretest at the beginning of the quarter; as a review at the end of the quarter; or as a review after each lesson. The questions are based on the Scripture text of each lesson (King James Version). **The answers are on page 232.**

Lesson 1

1. What was the main subject of Paul's preaching in Corinth? *1 Corinthians 2:2*
2. What did Paul choose rather than enticing words? *1 Corinthians 2:4, 5*
3. What kind of things has God revealed by His Spirit? *1 Corinthians 2:9, 10*

Lesson 2

1. What important thing is required of stewards? *1 Corinthians 4:2*
2. Who were regarded as fools for Christ's sake? *1 Corinthians 4:9, 10*
3. Why was Paul writing these things to the Corinthians? *1 Corinthians 4:14*

Lesson 3

1. Israel's wilderness experience warns of what five things? *1 Corinthians 10:6-10.*
2. What should one do when he thinks he is standing firm? *1 Corinthians 10:12*
3. What will God make with every temptation we face? *1 Corinthians 10:13*

Lesson 4

1. Whom should Christians examine to see if they are in the faith? *2 Corinthians 13:5*
2. How did Paul feel when he was weak and the Christians in Corinth were strong? *2 Corinthians 13:9*

Lesson 5

1. How many spirits take part in giving different spiritual gifts? *1 Corinthians 12:11*
2. When one member of the church is honored, what do the other members do about it? *1 Corinthians 12:26*

Lesson 6

1. In what should we be children, and in what should we be mature? *1 Corinthians 14:20*
2. If many are speaking in tongues, what will a visitor say? *1 Corinthians 14:23*
3. God is not the author of confusion, but of what? *1 Corinthians 14:33*

Lesson 7

1. How did the apostles respond when some women told them angels said Jesus had risen from the dead? *Luke 24:11*

2. As we thank God for giving us victory through our Lord Jesus Christ, what else should we do? *1 Corinthians 15:58*

Lesson 8

1. What dangerous thing may a Christian's liberty be to a weak brother? *1 Corinthians 8:9*
2. If we sin against weak brethren, against whom else do we sin? *1 Corinthians 8:12*
3. If eating meat would cause a brother to sin, what would Paul do? *1 Corinthians 8:13*

Lesson 9

1. What makes us able to comfort those who are in trouble? *2 Corinthians 1:3, 4*
2. How did the Corinthians help to rescue Paul? *2 Corinthians 1:10, 11*
3. Who will make Paul happy in the day of the Lord? *2 Corinthians 1:14*

Lesson 10

1. What was the seal that proved Paul was an apostle? *1 Corinthians 9:1, 2*
2. Why did Paul become "all things to all men"? *1 Corinthians 9:22*
3. What kind of a crown do faithful Christians win? *1 Corinthians 9:25*

Lesson 11

1. Who is a new creature? *2 Corinthians 5:17*
2. What ministry has God given to those reconciled to Him? *2 Corinthians 5:18, 19*
3. What plea does a reconciled person extend to others? *2 Corinthians 5:20*

Lesson 12

1. If we sow our gifts bountifully, what kind of harvest results? *2 Corinthians 9:6*
2. What kind of a giver does Paul say God loves? *2 Corinthians 9:7*
3. What does generous giving produce besides help for the poor? *2 Corinthians 9:12*

Lesson 13

1. What is needed to give value to spiritual gifts and abilities? *1 Corinthians 13:1-3*
2. What never fails? *1 Corinthians 13:8*
3. What things abide? *1 Corinthians 13:13*
4. What is the greatest of the three abiding things? *1 Corinthians 13:13*

The Church as a Community

by Johnny Pressley

THERE IS NOTHING QUITE LIKE sitting in the grandstand and watching a baseball game. Of course, watching a game on TV has its advantages. The television camera allows you to witness a crucial play up close, and from a variety of angles, and even in slow motion replay. You are not affected by adverse weather or an inconsiderate crowd. You have the convenience of having your refreshments only a few steps away in the kitchen. And best of all, you get to watch the game in the comfort of your favorite chair.

What more could you want from a baseball game? Well, how about the feel of the crowd as their reactions to the game echo throughout the stadium? How about the sense of being there, of being able to say, "I was there when it happened"? For all the comfort and convenience of watching a game at home, it cannot match the excitement of actually being at the game.

The same can be said about our participation in the activities of the church. Many people prefer to watch from a distance. Some get their fill from religious programming on TV. Others attend worship services, but draw back from other activities of the church, such as Sunday school, Bible studies, and fellowship gatherings.

We cannot say these people are not receiving any spiritual benefits. Religious programs on TV can be edifying, and even a restricted diet of church worship provides some spiritual nourishment.

But interaction with people also is an integral part of the nature of the church.

From the beginning, the church has been associated with the Greek word *koinonia* (Acts 2:42). Our English Bibles translate *koinonia* with such words as *fellowship, sharing, participation,* and *communion.* All of these terms indicate that the members of the church are interacting with one another, providing mutual support, guidance, and encouragement. Those who worship from a distance never fully appreciate the idea that the church is a *community.*

The theme for this quarter's lessons is "Christians Living in Community." Each lesson spotlights a different aspect of what it means to participate in the church as an active member. The Scripture texts are appropriately taken from Paul's two letters to the church in Corinth, for no other New Testament epistles provide as much information regarding church life and community.

Paul knew the church at Corinth in a very personal way. On one of his missionary journeys, he stayed and preached in Corinth for eighteen months (Acts 18:11). When he moved on to minister in other places, he continued to hear about activities in Corinth from friends in the church (1 Corinthians 1:11), and from fellow workers such as Titus (2 Corinthians 7:6, 7). With full knowledge Paul wrote about matters related to the community life of the church.

A Place for Challenges

Much of 1 and 2 Corinthians deals with difficulties in the church at Corinth. In like manner, our studies for March focus on some of the problems that can arise in a church community today. The purpose of these lessons is not to bemoan the fact that churches often have problems. This would create a negative attitude regarding the church. The group of studies for March is entitled "Responding to Challenges of Life in Community." The idea is to view difficult situations as challenges that can be dealt with in positive and effective ways, resulting in the further growth of the church.

Lesson 1, March 5. To respond effectively to a difficulty in a church, one must present his resolution of the matter with clear reasoning that is grounded in the Word of God. Paul shunned the use of fancy words and fancy ideas, which are often a cover for worldly counsel (1 Corinthians 2:1-5). As Lesson 1 explains, Paul exemplifies a better approach to resolving issues: "Speaking the Truth Plainly."

Lesson 2, March 12. In a lesson entitled "Being Faithful Under Stress," we gain insights into how a Christian should deal with stressful situations. In 1 Corinthians 4, Paul describes the type of difficulties he and the other apostles had to confront often as they ministered to the churches. Paul's advice in verse 16 is that his readers imitate him, and so this lesson concentrates on Paul's approach to dealing with tough situations.

Lesson 3, March 19. First Corinthians 10 draws upon Old Testament history to teach a lesson to New Testament Christians. The Israelites who left Egypt and wandered in the wilderness for forty years were often punished because they continued to find occasion for sin and rebellion against God. Their story shows the folly of repeatedly giving in to temptation. As Paul declares, "God is faithful, who will not suffer you to be tempted above that ye are able; but will with the temptation also make a way to escape, that ye may be able to bear it" (v. 13). Lesson 3 gives practical guidance for "Resisting Temptation."

Lesson 4, March 26. This study reminds us that some difficulties in the church can escalate till firm disciplinary measures must be applied in order to resolve a situation and maintain the integrity of the church. In 2 Corinthians 13 Paul anticipates this possibility, and gives us some ideas for our disciplinary actions when we are "Dealing With Conflict."

A Place for Growth

One of the benefits of dealing responsibly with challenges is that we learn lessons that aid us in the future. But this is only one way that participation in the church fellowship helps us to grow in spiritual maturity and wisdom. In the Corinthian epistles Paul expresses a concern that individual Christians take advantage of the opportunities for growth afforded by the church. This will be evident in the five lessons for April. This group of studies is entitled "Nurturing the Life of the Community."

Lesson 5, April 2. This lesson is entitled "Building Up the Body." Attention is given to 1 Corinthians 12 and the matter of spiritual gifts. We may consider whether or not the Holy Spirit is still distributing miraculous gifts such as speaking in tongues, but the emphasis of the lesson will be the same as that of chapter 12. Whatever gifts and abilities an individual has should be put to use for the growth and enrichment of the church.

Lesson 6, April 9. The study entitled "Growing Through Worship" focuses on 1 Corinthians 14, where Paul discusses tongues-speaking and prophesying in a worship service. For that large segment of the present-day church that does not practice the first-century miraculous gifts, it may seem that a study of this chapter would have little relevance. However, Paul's guidelines for the proper manner of participation in a worship service will speak to us as clearly today as they originally did to the church in Corinth.

Lesson 7, April 16. On Easter Sunday it is appropriate that the lesson centers on the resurrection of Christ. The account of the resurrection day is retold through a study of Luke 24, and the lesson also examines the way Paul links Christ's resurrection to our present life and future hope. The emphasis upon growing in the church will be evident in this lesson's suggestions for "Being a Resurrection People."

Lesson 8, April 23. Some of the difficulties that arise within a church community are related to the fact that the individual members are at different levels of spiritual growth. Often

there is tension when we have to work with fellow believers who do things we think are inappropriate for Christians, and when our own practices are challenged by others. The study of 1 Corinthians 8 in Lesson 8 shows the challenge we each face in "Exercising Liberty Wisely."

Lesson 9, April 30. One of the sure signs of growth is that Christians begin to direct their attention away from their own needs and desires and give more thought to "Caring for One Another." Lesson 9 develops Paul's theme in 2 Corinthians 1: those who work through times of trial and tribulation without faltering in their faith prepare themselves to be a source of comfort for others when it is their turn to suffer.

A Place for Service

Christians who actively participate in church fellowship experience spiritual growth as they interact with other members in the various activities of the church (April lessons), and as they deal with difficulties and conflicts in a biblical manner (March lessons). But the church also offers another means for Christian growth that is equally important: "Ministering as a Christian Community." Our lessons for May deal with this.

Lesson 10, May 7. "Living in Christian Freedom" is the title of a lesson that focuses on the ways in which Paul was willing to give up his rights as an apostle in order to serve the needs of the Corinthians and facilitate their growth (1 Corinthians 9). Since our present age is marked by the pursuit of individual rights by all kinds of special interest groups, this lesson should provide some much-needed balance between personal rights and ministry to others.

Lesson 11, May 14. Paul's desire to serve the needs of others reached its finest expression in his devotion to the ministry of preaching the gospel of Jesus Christ. In Lesson 11, "Working for Reconciliation," the text of 2 Corinthians 5 is used to remind us of our top priority as servants of Christ: to share the message of Calvary with those in need of reconciliation to God.

Lesson 12, May 21. An obvious way of carrying out this month's theme of serving others is by contributions of money and supplies to fellow Christians who are in need. The study of 2 Corinthians 9 in Lesson 12 will present the rationale and benefits of "Sharing Blessings With Others."

Lesson 13, May 28. There could be no grander conclusion to a study of the Corinthian epistles than to focus upon 1 Corinthians 13: the famous "Love Chapter." Lesson 13 encourages us to be active in "Expressing Love to All." Thus it reminds us of the key ingredient that makes the church more than just a gathering of people, but also a *community*.

Don't Forget the Family

by Edwin V. Hayden

REMEMBER ROBINSON CRUSOE? The lone survivor of a shipwreck on an uninhabited island, he built his dwelling, clothed and fed himself, all with tools salvaged from the ship. He also found, read, and believed the captain's Bible, and he worshiped God.

Some say that *Robinson Crusoe's* author, Daniel Defoe, set out to examine whether a person thus alone can be a whole man and a Christian, and that he found it to be impossible. God's man simply must have other persons with whom he can interact and live his faith. So Robinson Crusoe had to rescue and teach his man Friday before Crusoe himself could be a whole man in Christ.

Not Good to Be Alone

Defoe echoed the teaching of Genesis, that God found it not good for a man to be alone, even in Eden, and so established the family. Defoe echoed also the teaching of Acts, which tells of God's establishing the church, so each child of God can live in community with fellow Christians, for the sake of all concerned.

The Bible does, in fact, speak of the church in terms of the family, with God as the Father of such as come to Him in Christ, and with His believing children living as brothers and sisters to one another. Biblical teaching for the natural family at home and for the spiritual family, the church, is sometimes so closely interwoven that it is hard to distinguish one from the other. See Ephesians 5:23—6:4, for example. Biblical teaching about the natural family, therefore, is instructive to the church, and scriptural teaching about the church is instructive to the family. For the present, we shall think about the family.

Togetherness, Not Sameness

First of all, God saw and met Adam's need for companionship by creating Eve, not like Adam, but different, physically, emotionally, and intellectually. She was designed to supply what he lacked, and to have him supply what she lacked, being strong where he was weak and depending on his strength where she needed it.

That bonding plan for the family has been denied and resisted, with vast injury to society in general, as men and women have tried to look alike, to act alike, and to live together in twisted pairings, thus forfeiting and reversing God's intended blessings.

God's plan for marriage and family provided for the strongest possible bonds in love and commitment for a permanent relationship.

Romantic love between the man and the woman was established and blessed, with a strong basis in compatible friendship in idyllic surroundings. Unselfish devotion grew naturally out of shared responsibilities and response to each other's innate strengths and weaknesses. There is nothing unreasonable in the expectation that a husband love his wife as a vital part of himself, following the example of Christ in giving himself up for His bride, the church (Ephesians 5:23-33). The kind of love that considers the loved one's interests ahead of the interests of the loving one is, in fact, the active attitude most fervently insisted upon in all Christian teaching and example.

Lesson 13 applies that instruction to the life of the church.

The love between partners in marriage leads to a *commitment* of highest priority and permanence. At the outset, before Adam and Eve became parents, God said that a man should leave his father and mother as he was joined to his wife; "and they shall be one flesh" (Genesis 2:24). Jesus used the same words in His teaching about marriage (Matthew 19:5; Mark 10:7, 8), and Paul quoted them in his writing to the Corinthians (1 Corinthians 6:16) and the Ephesians (5:31). That is strong language when compared with the repeated command for children of all ages to honor, obey, and support their parents (Exodus 20:12; Matthew 19:19; Ephesians 6:1, 2). The family one establishes with his marriage still takes precedence over the one in which he was brought up.

Even in the growing-up family, togetherness, rather than likeness, is the key to family life. Differences among children of the same parents can lead either to strength or to strains in the family, depending on the outcome of the contest between natural affection and human selfishness.

Selfishness brought tragedy between Cain, Adam's firstborn farmer, and Abel, the younger herdsman (Genesis 4:1-10). But what about Seth, a third son, and his uncounted brothers and sisters? (Genesis 5:4, 5). Then as now, one tragedy occupied the headlines.

Happier events resulted from the differences among Moses, his brother Aaron, and their sister Miriam—lawgiver, orator, and musician in the service of God and Israel. In spite of one notable falling out (Numbers 12), they may even have provided an early example for all those happy families who blend their different voices in singing at the close of day: "Daddy sang bass, and mamma sang tenor," and young folk grew up, each lending his or her own special voice to the harmonious whole.

When the larger family of Israel needed to build God's tabernacle in the wilderness of Sinai, God found among them a wide variety of necessary skills for provision and construction. Prominently mentioned were Bezaleel and Aholiab, whose craftsmanship covered a multitude of skills, including the ability to instruct others in their work (Exodus 35:30-35). Thank God they were not exactly alike!

Romans 12:4-8 and 1 Corinthians 12—14 develop this principle as applied to the church (lessons 5 and 6).

Instruction in Truth

The family is the first and most effective teaching agent on earth. That is true for good in God's provision. It is true, for good or evil, wherever children are born and grow.

If respect for truth is not present, family members will gain false impressions from falsehood, and learn from what they see rather than from what they hear.

A case in point is the sad story of Rebekah and Jacob's deception of aged Isaac (Genesis 27). Rebekah and Jacob were not habitual liars, or Jacob would not have believed them rather than the testimony of his senses. Yet that one elaborate deception scarred their experience for the rest of their lives, and it mars our memory of Rebekah forever. It made headlines.

Yet when God would make His works and His words known to future generations, He committed the teaching to the parents in Israel—the sons of Jacob and the daughters of Rebekah. They were to tell their children what God did in bringing them out of Egypt (Exodus 13:11-16).

They were to impress upon their children that the Lord God is one, and they must love Him with all their being (Deuteronomy 6:1-9). These truths came from God, not from human wisdom.

The New Testament takes up the theme where the Old Testament leaves it, urging that parental instruction be done gently and patiently (Ephesians 6:4; Colossians 3:21). It insists also that before a man accepts a position as teaching elder in the Lord's church he establish himself as a teacher of his own children at home (1 Timothy 3:4, 5).

In Lesson 1 the principle is further applied to the church.

A Strong Rope

Ecclesiastes 4:9-12 does not mention the family as such, but it sets forth family values. Family caring, family sharing, and family supportiveness provide strength not available from any other source. The one who falls has someone to lift him up. The sleeper has warmth in cold weather. The traveler has protection against brigands. In brief, the family is like a rope of several strands, resistant to the strains that would break any one strand alone.

In faith, the member of a strong family has assurance to face the shifting winds of popular opinion. In morals, the young member of a strong family knows that not everybody "is doing it." Several very important people at home are not! So he has a shield against temptation. (Compare Lesson 3.)

Then there are those times when everything goes wrong, bringing storms of discouragement and depression. That's when home and family offer a haven for an outpouring of anguished tears, without fear of rejection or violation of confidence. And if the problem involves loss of job, or health, or financial standing, it is family that assures, "You won't sink as long as I can swim."

Some of the strongest, happiest families I have known have grown up in houses with wheelchairs as part of the furniture. The care for a loved one crippled by age or illness has done much to give the family members a sense of purpose and to rid them of debilitating selfishness! King David was never more royal than when He made Jonathan's crippled and orphaned son a member of his own family (2 Samuel 9). Compare Lessons 8, 9, 12.

Healing the Wounds

Not all families live up to God's perfect plan for them. Among God's people Jacob and Esau, Joseph and his brothers, David and Bathsheba all made headlines for their failures, but that was not the end of the story. God's plan provides also for repentance, forgiveness, and reconciliation. Jacob and Esau embraced in generous forgiveness and finally joined in burying their father (Genesis 33:4-11; 35:29). Joseph fully forgave his penitent brothers and brought them to Egypt under his protection (Genesis 45:4-15). David sought and found forgiveness for his sin, and with Bathsheba he became the father of Solomon.

Yet not the families of men, but the family of God, His church, must be the center of ultimate forgiveness and reconciliation for all mankind. May your family and mine have some part in serving that eternal purpose.

Help One Another

by James B. North

WHEN THOMAS CAMPBELL began the movement that grew into the Restoration Movement, one of his primary emphases was for the unity of the church. "The Church of Christ upon earth is essentially, intentionally, and constitutionally one," he wrote in the *Declaration and Address*. The unity of God's people on earth remained a firm commitment for him through his entire life.

Campbell could easily have taken much of his cue for this emphasis from Paul's letters to the Corinthians. Throughout these letters, Paul also emphasized the unity of God's people. Alternately cajoling and upbraiding, he urged the Corinthians to demonstrate that unity.

One of the applications of that theme is that the unified Corinthians were to help one another. This helping has both negative and positive aspects.

Avoid Division

One of the negative applications of Paul's concern was to warn the Corinthians against division (1 Corinthians 3). Some Corinthians had formed a Petrine party; others were Paulites, Apollosites, and even Christites. Such sectarian splits created stress in the body and worked against the healthy, wholesome attitudes necessary for mutual cooperation within the church.

Division is a corrosive factor wherever it is found. Division pits members of the same body against each other. This is counterproductive. The health of the body depends upon its wholeness, and that means the healthy acceptance of each member by all the other members. One of the major emphases of the Restoration Movement has been to work for the unity of God's body on earth. This is to be done not through creedal consensus, but by agreement of our common commitment to Christ. Whether we are thinking of a local congregation, or relationships between congregations, or even developments between different fellowships of believers, the commonness of Christians is found in their mutual commitment to Christ. If this is not present, there is no unity, and mutual help is strictly limited.

Paul was certainly aware of the frailties of human nature. He said we have the treasure of the gospel in jars of clay (2 Corinthians 4:7). Because we are weak clay we need to make every effort to avoid problems within the body.

Yield to a Brother

Another negative application came out in Paul's discussion of meat offered to idols (1 Corinthians 8 and 10). We are to refrain from any activity that might offend another member of the body. The principles of this passage lead us to sacrifice our *rights* so we can serve each other's *needs*.

One of the marks of a mature Christian is the willingness to yield to a weaker member of the body over issues that are not essential to salvation. In essential matters there can be no yielding. But in matters of discretionary activity, the mature Christian yields to keep from offending a weaker member.

The original context of this concern was in the matter of meat offered to idols. Paul said the meat itself was not the problem. The real problem lay with the implications and value judgments brought in by people who had just recently come out of paganism.

As Paul explains in 1 Corinthians 10:23-33, many things that are permissible may not be expedient. Christians help one another by foregoing what is *allowed* in order to do what is *advisable.* We can do all things to the glory of God, but we can do them in ways that keep others from stumbling. This is self-sacrifice for the good of the larger body.

There are numerous applications of these principles in the present. Christians today can demand the right to wear certain clothes, watch certain movies, have a certain hairstyle, purchase certain products, read certain books, patronize certain stores, listen to certain music. The list could go on and on. The real question, however, is not their *right,* but the effect it may have on someone else who is offended by such activities. Christians today can help one another by giving up their right to certain activities out of sensitivity to the conscience of others.

This yielding is not a matter of weakness, but of strength. It is done not out of cowardice or fear, but out of love and concern for one another. This is maturity in conscientious, discretionary behavior.

The Body Is a Unit

We have mentioned some negative applications of Paul's teaching on unity. One of the positive aspects is his illustration of Christians as members of the same body (1 Corinthians 12).

Paul mentions that some members of the body are ears while some are eyes; some are hands while others are feet. It is not that these members are in competition with each other. It is simply that they have different abilities. All these abilities are used for the common good. By serving the common good the members help each other. When the eye sends messages to the brain so the body does not walk into a wall, the eye helps itself at the same time it is helping all other members of the body. When the hand puts food in the mouth, the hand ultimately gets the nourishment; but of course the rest of the body does too. Think what a mess it would be if the hand tried to get the nourishment directly without sharing it with the rest of the body. Members of the body help each other because they are a *body*. The whole idea of being a member means that each unit is part of a larger whole. A member of the body has life, usefulness, and purpose only if it is attached to the rest of the body. Various members best serve themselves when they help one another.

In Ephesians 4:16 Paul describes the whole body joined together, with each part doing its work. Some parts of the body are bone; others are muscle; others are the ligaments that tie the whole thing together. A body that is all bone without muscle is dead. A body that is all muscle without bone has no structure and can do nothing but flop around. Some Christians are like bones—hard, sometimes brittle. Some Christians are like muscle—they are active without a purpose. Bone-Christians provide the direction for the church, but muscle-Christians provide the action. Ligament-Christians are the ones who succeed in tying the whole thing together. Each fulfills its role, but it takes all together to get the job accomplished.

Contributions

Paul also taught the Corinthians to help one another by sharing their financial resources (1 Corinthians 16; 2 Corinthians 8). Members of the church in Corinth could help members of the church in Jerusalem. Both the Galatian and the Macedonian churches were involved in this. The imagery is much the same as in the previous idea. The hand shares resources for the common good. The digestive tract and cardiovascular system share these same resources for the common good. Even so Christians in the body of Christ share their resources for the common good.

When a member of the body is wounded, white corpuscles rush to that spot to bring healing. Other members of the body do not respond by saying, "Serves him right. That's his misfortune; I'm only glad it didn't happen to me!" The body would soon die if its members acted in this way.

Sharing Concerns

A further positive application of Paul's emphasis on unity is seen in 2 Corinthians 1:7. Paul says the Corinthians have shared his sufferings as well as his comfort. When Paul wrote to the Galatians he said, "Bear ye one another's burdens" (6:2). The same idea is here.

When a physical body bears a burden, the entire body becomes involved. Muscles in the shoulders, the arms, the back, the abdomen, and the legs all strain under the load. Whatever the body undertakes, the entire body supports. Christians can help one another by doing likewise. We can share grief as well as joy, suffering as well as enjoyment, frustration as well as excitement.

The body is fitted together for the good of the whole. Members help one another as naturally as breathing. The body does not concentrate on breathing—it happens automatically. If the body had to think about breathing to get the job done, life could be very tenuous. Breathing happens almost all by itself, yet the entire body benefits. In the same way, members of the church help one another automatically. It does not take a good deal of concentration or thoughtful contemplation. It just happens. That is the body at work. Helping one another.

Answers to Quarterly Quiz on page 226

Lesson 1—1. Christ and Him crucified. 2. demonstration of the Spirit and power. 3. things unseen, unheard, unimagined. **Lesson 2**—1. faithfulness. 2. the apostles. 3. to warn them. **Lesson 3**—1. lust, idolatry, fornication, tempting God, murmuring. 2. take heed lest he fall. 3. a way to escape. **Lesson 4**—1. themselves. 2. glad. **Lesson 5**—1. one. 2. rejoice. **Lesson 6**—1. malice, understanding. 2. ye are mad. 3. peace. **Lesson 7**—1. believed them not. 2. be steadfast and abundant in the Lord's work. **Lesson 8**—1. a stumblingblock. 2. Christ. 3. eat no meat. **Lesson 9**—1. God's comfort to us. 2. by praying. 3. those whom he won to Christ. **Lesson 10**—1. Corinthians he led to Christ. 2. to save some. 3. incorruptible. **Lesson 11**—1. one who is in Christ. 2. ministry of reconciliation. 3. be ye reconciled to God. **Lesson 12**—1. bountiful. 2. cheerful. 3. thanksgiving to God. **Lesson 13**—1. charity. 2. charity. 3. faith, hope, charity. 4. charity.

Speaking the Truth Plainly

March 5
Lesson 1

DEVOTIONAL READING: 1 Corinthians 1:18-25.

LESSON SCRIPTURE: 1 Corinthians 1:18—2:16.

PRINTED TEXT: 1 Corinthians 2:1-13.

1 Corinthians 2:1-13

1 And I, brethren, when I came to you, came not with excellency of speech or of wisdom, declaring unto you the testimony of God.

2 For I determined not to know any thing among you, save Jesus Christ, and him crucified.

3 And I was with you in weakness, and in fear, and in much trembling.

4 And my speech and my preaching was not with enticing words of man's wisdom, but in demonstration of the Spirit and of power:

5 That your faith should not stand in the wisdom of men, but in the power of God.

6 Howbeit we speak wisdom among them that are perfect: yet not the wisdom of this world, nor of the princes of this world, that come to nought:

7 But we speak the wisdom of God in a mystery, even the hidden wisdom, which God ordained before the world unto our glory;

8 Which none of the princes of this world knew: for had they known it, they would not have crucified the Lord of glory.

9 But as it is written, Eye hath not seen, nor ear heard, neither have entered into the heart of man, the things which God hath prepared for them that love him.

10 But God hath revealed them unto us by his Spirit: for the Spirit searcheth all things, yea, the deep things of God.

11 For what man knoweth the things of a man, save the spirit of man which is in him? even so the things of God knoweth no man, but the Spirit of God.

12 Now we have received, not the spirit of the world, but the Spirit which is of God; that we might know the things that are freely given to us of God.

13 Which things also we speak, not in the words which man's wisdom teacheth, but which the Holy Ghost teacheth; comparing spiritual things with spiritual.

GOLDEN TEXT: I determined not to know any thing among you, save Jesus Christ, and him crucified.—1 Corinthians 2:2.

Christians Living in Community
Unit 1: Responding to Challenges of Life in Community
(Lessons 1-4)

Lesson Aims

After this lesson, each student should:

1. Evaluate claims to Christian maturity according to the norm of a wise and holy life-style.

2. Defeat the world's attempts to undermine his or her confidence in the Word of God.

Lesson Outline

INTRODUCTION

    A. "Deeper Wisdom From *Before* the Dawn of Time"

    B. Lesson Background

 I. CHRIST CRUCIFIED IS THE CENTRAL TRUTH (1 Corinthians 2:1, 2)

    A. Focusing on Leaders Is Wrong (v. 1)

    B. The Cross Is the Central Truth (v. 2)

 II. GOD'S POWER KEEPS FAITH STRONG (1 Corinthians 2:3-5)

    A. Arrogance in Leaders Is Wrong (vv. 3, 4)

    B. Humility Keeps on Depending on God (v. 5)
      The Smooth Divine

III. GOD'S WISDOM REWARDS TRUE MATURITY (1 Corinthians 2:6-9)

    A. True Versus False Maturity (vv. 6-8)
      Crucified, Yet Conqueror

    B. True Wisdom and Maturity Rewarded (v. 9)
      Things Prepared

IV. GOD'S REVELATION GIVES CONFIDENCE (1 Corinthians 2:10-13)

    A. Guarantee of Truth (vv. 10, 11)

    B. Speaking the Truth (vv. 12, 13)

CONCLUSION

    A. "We Have the Mind of Christ!"

    B. Let Us Pray

    C. Thought to Remember

Display visual 1 of the visuals packet before the class. It is shown on page 237.

Introduction

A. "Deeper Wisdom From *Before* the Dawn of Time"

In C. S. Lewis's story of *The Lion, the Witch, and the Wardrobe*, four children of one family find themselves in a magical country where a wicked white witch claims to be queen and wants to keep humans out of her territory.

Tension develops between Edmond and the other children, and Edmond plots to help the witch capture the others. Instead of rewarding Edmond, the witch prepares to kill him. According to deep magic from the dawn of time, she says, she is entitled to the blood of traitors.

The lion offers to be killed in Edmond's place. The witch agrees, intending to kill him first and Edmond afterward. But her knowledge reaches only to the dawn of time. Unknown to her, there is a deeper magic from *before* the dawn of time. According to that, she forfeited her right to Edmond's blood when she killed a willing but innocent victim in his place. So Edmond goes free and is reconciled to his brothers and sisters.

Here fiction touches reality. There was tension in the Christian community in Corinth, and Paul sought to overcome it by talking plainly about the foundation and center of the Christian faith, a deeper wisdom from before the dawn of time.

B. Lesson Background

This lesson is taken from the letter we know as 1 Corinthians. About A.D. 55, perhaps 56 or 57, Paul wrote it from Ephesus to the church he had established in Corinth about five years earlier. Corinth was famous as the capital of the province of Achaia and the most important commercial city of the region, but it was also infamous for its gross immorality.

Most of the Christians in Corinth were converted Gentiles. They were still struggling to overcome their former pagan life-style (1 Corinthians 6:9-11; 8:7). Paul had written them once before, in a letter we no longer have, telling them that they needed to clean up their living (1 Corinthians 5:9, 10). They in turn had sent him a letter with some questions that he answers in this letter we are studying (1 Corinthians 7:1, 2).

But first Paul had to deal with a very urgent matter. He had heard that the Christians were dividing into cliques, each promoting its favorite teacher (1 Corinthians 1:10-12). In doing this they were losing sight of God's deeper wisdom and the very center of their faith.

I. Christ Crucified Is the Central Truth (1 Corinthians 2:1, 2)

A. Focusing on Leaders Is Wrong (v. 1)

1. And I, brethren, when I came to you, came not with excellency of speech or of wisdom, declaring unto you the testimony of God.

Before coming to Corinth, Paul was in Athens. There he preached to the most intelligent and the best educated people of that day (Acts 17:15-34). He saw the limitations of even the best of human *excellency of speech or of wisdom*. So Paul came to Corinth determined to bring glory to Christ, not to the human messenger.

The focus of his ministry was on *the testimony of God:* he preached the word of the cross (literal translation of 1 Corinthians 1:18); he told what God had done in Christ. He would not let the cross be emptied of its power by emphasis on the wisdom of merely human words (1 Corinthians 1:17).

After those founding days, Apollos had ministered in the Corinthian church. He was an educated, eloquent man, having great boldness, vigor, and knowledge of the Scriptures (Acts 18:24-28). The apostle Paul valued Apollos greatly as a fellow Christian leader (1 Corinthians 3:4-9; 16:12).

Unfortunately, some of the Corinthians became enamored with Apollos's rhetorical abilities. Comparing the two leaders, they perceived that Paul was less eloquent, less polished in speech. Worse than that, they went on to conclude that his message was inferior. Perhaps they complained that he gave only elementary teaching, feeding them with milk rather than meat (1 Corinthians 3:2).

As a result, the church in Corinth was plagued by strife and tension (1 Corinthians 1:10-13; 3:3, 4; 11:18; 2 Corinthians 12:20). Underlying these were their perceptions of their leaders! How much tension and strife can be avoided in our churches today if people will think of their leaders as no more than servants and stewards! (1 Corinthians 3:5; 4:1).

B. The Cross Is the Central Truth
(v. 2)

2. For I determined not to know any thing among you, save Jesus Christ, and him crucified.

Paul regarded the Christians in the Corinthian church as brothers (1 Corinthians 1:10, 26; 2:1; 3:1). There should be no divisions among Christian brothers. All serve one Master, *our* Lord Jesus Christ (1 Corinthians 1:2, 10) and all experience one baptism in one name (1 Corinthians 1:13-15). All Christians stand on common and level ground before the cross! Wherever there is arguing and bickering in the church, almost cer-

---

VISUALS FOR THESE LESSONS

The *Adult Visuals/Learning Resources* packet contains classroom-size visuals designed for use with the lessons in the Spring Quarter. The packet is available from your supplier. Order no. 392.

---

tainly Christians have forgotten what life in sin was like before Calvary.

> "Mercy there was great, and grace was free;
> Pardon there was multiplied to me;
> There my burdened soul found liberty,
> At Calvary"!
> —WILLIAM R. NEWELL

II. God's Power Keeps Faith Strong (1 Corinthians 2:3-5)

A. Arrogance in Leaders Is Wrong (vv. 3, 4)

3, 4. And I was with you in weakness, and in fear, and in much trembling. And my speech and my preaching was not with enticing words of man's wisdom, but in demonstration of the Spirit and of power.

Paul would not detract from God's glory in the gospel message or the church's life. When he first came to Corinth, he did not seek to impress the hearers with his powerful personality, but with his suffering Lord.

The power of the gospel lies in God (Romans 1:16), but the Corinthian Christians were boasting as if the faith were an achievement of human thought or wisdom (1 Corinthians 1:29, 31; 3:21; 4:6, 7). Paul would not boast of anything but his own *weakness* and what God's might had done through his weakness (2 Corinthians 11:30; 12:5-9) *in demonstration of the Spirit and of power.*

What is this *demonstration of the Spirit and of power?* It may be that Paul is referring to the special miraculous signs and wonders that he worked in Corinth as evidence of his authority as an apostle of Jesus Christ (2 Corinthians 12:12). But we can see from the rest of the letter that Paul thinks the Corinthians are already putting too much emphasis on the sensational and ecstatic signs of the Spirit (1 Corinthians 12—14). Or it may be that he is referring to the moral change in the Corinthians' converted lives. This was very strong proof that the Spirit of God was at work in the message Paul preached.

There is no room for arrogant boasting and self-reliance among Christians. The cross must be kept central. At the foot of the cross, even leaders in the church can only acknowledge their unending and humble dependence on God. Many of the hymns that we sing today speak of giving God alone the glory for the cross: "My richest gain I count but loss, and pour contempt on all my pride." "Forbid it, Lord, that I should boast, save in the death of Christ, my God." "There to my heart was the blood applied; glory to His name." "King of my life, I crown Thee now, Thine shall the glory be." "In the cross of Christ I glory, tow'ring o'er the wrecks of time." "In the cross, in the cross, be my glory ever"! Do our preaching and our living match our singing?

B. Humility Keeps on Depending on God (v. 5)

5. That your faith should not stand in the wisdom of men, but in the power of God.

There was a very good reason why Paul did not want the human presentation of the gospel to distract from the divine content of the gospel: he wanted the Christians' *faith* to depend on the supernatural reality of God, not on the persuasive power of human salesmanship.

Paul wanted the Corinthians to realize that once the power of God is lost in a Christian's life, that Christian's faith has lost the only foundation that can keep it plausible and credible in a naturalistic world (1 Corinthians 3:10-13).

This verse then cautions us to examine how we today present the gospel to outsiders. For instance, some professors in Bible colleges are concerned about how much we use sports and entertainment to recruit students. The reason for concern is expressed in the principle, "What you win them with is what you win them to." Are we confronting prospective converts with the demands of the gospel for repentance and holiness, or are we winning them by telling of our convenient location, winsome preacher's family, and wonderful programs? "What you win them with is what you win them to."

THE SMOOTH DIVINE

Above is the title of a section in a long poem called *The Triumph of Infidelity*. It was written by Timothy Dwight and printed in 1788. This section is an attack on those who seek to preach or teach "with enticing words of man's wisdom" instead of stressing "Jesus Christ, and him crucified." Dwight says of this clergyman:

> No terrors on his gentle tongue attend;
> No grating truths the nicest ear offend.
>
> . . . .
>
> Plato's fine tales he clumsily retold,
> Trite, fireside, moral seesaws, dull as old;
> His Christ and Bible placed at good remove,
> Guilt hell-deserving, and forgiving love.

Paul is pointing out a danger faced by those who speak about Christian truth in any age. It is the danger of losing the heart of their message.

It is true that we ought to be concerned about juvenile delinquency, about homeless people, and about the care of the elderly. These and many more legitimate matters may well be subjects for our consideration and action as *citizens*.

But they are not the heart and power of the Christian message to our world.

As Paul says so vigorously, we bring something else to the people of our era. That is the reality of Jesus as God's promised Messiah who has died on the cross to make possible the forgiveness of our sin. We do not aim to flatter our hearers, or to impress them with our eloquence, or to make them more civilized or "socialized." We aim to bring them to the cross of Jesus, where they can find a suffering Savior and forgiven sin.

—J. G. V. B.

III. God's Wisdom Rewards True Maturity (1 Corinthians 2:6-9)

A. True Versus False Maturity (vv. 6-8)

6, 7. Howbeit we speak wisdom among them that are perfect: yet not the wisdom of this world, nor of the princes of this world, that come to nought: but we speak the wisdom of God in a mystery, even the hidden wisdom, which God ordained before the world unto our glory.

Sometimes Christians fail to discern between what the world counts as *wisdom* and what God says *wisdom* is. Then they often act foolishly and inconsistently (1 Corinthians 3:1-8). That was happening in the Corinthian church with its immorality, boasting, and envying. When a Christian community has these kinds of activity, it looks foolish not only to God but also to the nonbelievers around it.

Paul invited all Christians in Corinth to close ranks and to stand firmly with him in rejecting worldly ideas of what wisdom, power, and nobility are all about (1 Corinthians 1:20-29).

Surely it is clear today that what the world counts as "grown-up" and "adult" is often more adolescent and childish than really mature and responsible (1 Corinthians 3:1). Paul is appealing to every Christian who is truly adult and mature (this is the meaning of the word translated *perfect*) to take careful note of how shallow the world's wisdom really is in comparison to the deeper *mystery* of God's wisdom.

8. Which none of the princes of this world knew: for had they known it, they would not have crucified the Lord of glory.

Worldly knowledge is great, and modern science and technology astound us with what human reason can know about our universe —but it cannot know God (1 Corinthians 1:21; 2:14; 3:19; 8:2, 3). Paul speaks the truth plainly on this matter: the cross of the crucified Messiah is the irrefutable historical proof of the inability of human wisdom to find God and to make peace with Him. In fact, in their relentless pursuit of something to "glory" in (1 Corinthians 1:29, 31), the world and its leaders, both political and religious, wound up crucifying *the Lord of glory*! (Acts 4:23-30).

Unless God reveals His will to mankind, and unless humans accept His revelation, humanity's wisdom, power, and vaunted nobility will prove ultimately to be foolish, weak, and worthless. But once God's revelation of himself in the crucified Christ is accepted, God's alleged foolishness and weakness prove to be very wise, most powerful, and filled with the promise of glory! (2 Corinthians 4:16-18).

CRUCIFIED, YET CONQUEROR

Julian was a Roman leader in the fourth century A.D. He had been educated by Christians and had been a Christian teacher for a time, but then he abandoned Christianity. Known as "Julian the Apostate," he restored the pagan temples and showed extreme hostility to Christians. He was killed in a battle with Persian forces after reigning as a Caesar only two years. While he was not actually fighting Christians at the time of his death, it is reported that his dying words were "Galilean, thou hast conquered."

"The princes of this world" not only were responsible for Jesus' death on the cross, but through centuries they have often been opposed to His way and His people. A vivid modern example of this has been the oppression of Christians and the obvious attempt to eliminate the Christian religion from the atheistic, Marxist Union of Soviet Socialist Republics.

Just as Julian failed in his attack on the reality of Jesus and the church, so the Russian experiment came to nought. The "princes of this world" in education, philosophy, science, art, and entertainment may be willing to ignore, demean, or destroy Him, but they falter and are defeated. The "wisdom" of Paul's world scorned and scoffed at the crucified "Lord" of Christians, but He was ultimately victor. He will conquer the wisdom and power of our scornful world. "For it is written, I will destroy the wisdom of the wise, and will bring to nothing the understanding of the prudent" (1 Corinthians 1:19; Isaiah 29:14)   —J. G. V. B.

B. True Wisdom and Maturity Rewarded (v. 9)

9. But as it is written, Eye hath not seen, nor ear heard, neither have entered into the heart of man, the things which God hath prepared for them that love him.

Truly wise and truly mature people are people who *love* God. Paul cited Isaiah 64:4 to show that

visual 1

God has *prepared* wonderful things to reward those who show their love by living in accordance with His revealed divine wisdom. Already in this life these people are receiving many blessings: they are chosen by God (1 Corinthians 1:27, 28), called by God (1:2, 9, 24, 26), and being saved by God (1:18).

But the blessings of God's grace and providence in this life, with all the love, peace, and joy they bring, are not all there is. More than the human *heart* can even think or imagine lies in store in the future for those who choose to live by divine wisdom. And all these present blessings and all our hope for future bliss are stored in Jesus Christ our risen Lord! (1 Corinthians 1:30; Ephesians 1:3).

THINGS PREPARED

I had learned to read and loved to do so, but as a child I was allowed to draw books from only the juvenile section of our city's public library. I've never forgotten the thrill of presenting proof of my admittance into high school and of being allowed to utilize the books of the adult department. Here were thousands and thousands of books, arranged, shelved, and made available. Things prepared!

I was thrilled again with the first art gallery I was able to visit. What gorgeous paintings, what colors, what portraits, what beautiful scenes! They all had been painted, purchased, and were now exhibited. Things prepared!

So it is with laboratories available for the use of microscopes, chemicals, Bunsen burners—all the equipment one can use to unlock physical conundrums and to explore our created world. So it is with autos to drive, planes to fly, and buildings to utilize. Things prepared.

Spiritually we learn of things we never could have conceived of by our human wisdom and observation. We are told in the Spirit-revealed Word about a city of God gleaming with eternal light, about a spiritual body that will be powerful, glorious, and incorruptible. We are informed about an everlasting fellowship of rejoicing, purified beings similar to the happy fellowship of a wedding feast. Things prepared!   —J.G.V.B.

IV. God's Revelation Gives Confidence (1 Corinthians 2:10-13)

A. Guarantee of Truth (vv. 10, 11)

10, 11. But God hath revealed them unto us by his Spirit: for the Spirit searcheth all things, yea, the deep things of God. For what man knoweth the things of a man, save the spirit of man which is in him? even so the things of God knoweth no man, but the Spirit of God.

Some Corinthian may have been wondering, as a Christian today may wonder: how do we know that what we teach is really God's wisdom and not just another form of human wisdom? How can we be sure that the Scriptures really express God's will for our lives? After all, other religions also claim to have revelations and sacred scriptures.

From the Garden of Eden on, Satan has always sought to use the world and the flesh (our human nature) to tempt us to distrust the Word of God. In today's world, entertainment, the media, education, and advertisement all seem united in attacking Christian beliefs and values.

Paul used a helpful analogy to bolster the Corinthians' confidence in the truth of God's Word. In each human being is a *spirit* that examines each thought, feeling, decision, and action of that person; God also—in whose image we are made—has a *Spirit* that knows even *the deep things of God.* This is the Spirit that Jesus sent to guide Bible writers into all truth (John 16:13).

B. Speaking the Truth (vv. 12, 13)

12, 13. Now we have received, not the spirit of the world, but the Spirit which is of God; that we might know the things that are freely given to us of God. Which things also we speak, not in the words which man's wisdom teacheth, but which the Holy Ghost teacheth; comparing spiritual things with spiritual.

How this strengthens our confidence in the authority of the Scriptures! Paul and other apostles were guided by God's all-knowing Spirit. They passed on His revelation, not in the language of human wisdom, but "in words taught by the Spirit, expressing spiritual truths in spiritual words," as the *New International Version* translates the last phrase of verse 13.

This does not mean that we may use only the very words that we find in the Scriptures. To do this, we would have to speak in Greek and Hebrew. But it is important for all of us to express as closely as we possibly can those meanings intended by the original authors of the Scriptures.

This verse calls for a responsible and intentional mode of Christian thinking and speaking that is in harmony with the original revelation of God's wisdom as given to us by the Spirit.

Two important benefits result if Christians speak of spiritual matters in appropriate spiritual ways. First, the Christian community remains "perfectly joined together in the same mind and in the same judgment" (1 Corinthians 1:10). Second, the church maintains its confidence that the Scriptures reflect the mind of God.

Conclusion

A. "We Have the Mind of Christ!"

Whose mind then should a community of believers unite on? That of the preacher? Of a leading elder? Of a knowledgeable church member of long standing? Of Paul? Of Peter? Of Apollos?

The apostle Paul says our rallying point should be the mind of Jesus Christ (1 Corinthians 2:16). And we can know His mind from the Scriptures as we carefully study and reflect, and as the Holy Spirit conforms our minds more and more to that of Christ (Galatians 5:22, 23). Therefore, "be not conformed to this world: but be ye transformed by the renewing of your mind" (Romans 12:2).

B. Let Us Pray

Dear Lord and Father of mankind,
    Forgive our foolish ways!
Reclothe us in our rightful mind;
    In purer lives Thy service find,
In deeper rev'rence, praise.
              —JOHN G. WHITTIER

C. Thought to Remember

Bind us together, Lord; bind us together with cords that cannot be broken. Bind us together with love.

Home Daily Bible Readings

Monday, Feb. 27—The Power of Christ's Cross (1 Corinthians 1:18-25)

Tuesday, Feb. 28—God's Wisdom Revealed in Christ (1 Corinthians 1:26-31)

Wednesday, Mar. 1—God's Power Is Faith's Foundation (1 Corinthians 2:1-9)

Thursday, Mar. 2—God's Spirit Gives Understanding (1 Corinthians 2:10-16)

Friday, Mar. 3—Honor Christ as Lord (1 Peter 3:8-18)

Saturday, Mar. 4—Live as Children of God (Romans 8:12-25)

Sunday, Mar. 5—Firm Counsel for Christian Living (Colossians 3: 1-7)

Learning by Doing

This page contains an alternate lesson plan emphasizing learning activities. Classes desiring such student involvement will find these suggestions helpful.

Learning Goals

Each pupil will be able to:

1. Contrast the preaching of Paul with the wisdom of the world.

2. Understand that the way of receiving spiritual wisdom differs radically from the ways in which people gain the world's wisdom.

3. Prepare a personal testimony.

Into the Lesson

Distribute paper and pencil and ask each student to write as many wise sayings as he can remember—not biblical sayings, but things the secular world deems wise. For example, "A penny saved is a penny earned." "Take care of number one." After about three to five minutes, ask people to share their sayings. Award a candy sucker to the person who has the most.

Make the transition into the Bible study by stating that catchy maxims often have more appeal to people than do the deeper teachings of the Bible. The apostle Paul found his preaching being judged to be not as powerful as that of some other preachers. Consequently he defended his kind of preaching and contrasted it with the wisdom of the world. (Share insights from the lesson background as they apply.)

Into the Word

Stimulate some practical insights by asking the class, "What are some qualities that a powerful, convincing speaker has?" Make two columns on a sheet of newsprint. List the responses about a powerful speaker in the left column. Then ask students to read 1 Corinthians 2:1-13 and find out what kind of a communicator the apostle Paul was. Put their description of Paul's style in the other column. Lead the class to contrast the two columns. Point out that although Paul may have lacked some of the qualities that contemporary society applauds, he had one essential ingredient that made his communication powerful—content.

Let students find answers to the following questions by pairing off and searching the Scriptures. Write these questions on the board before the class arrives, or have them on handouts. They are also in the student quarterly.

1. What one central truth had Paul tried to proclaim, according to 1 Corinthians 2:2? How was this different from what others had done?

2. What was the source of the wisdom Paul sought to share with the believers in the church at Corinth, as seen in 1 Corinthians 2:4, 10-13? How does this source differ from the world's source of wisdom?

3. How could the unity of the church at Corinth be disrupted because of the differing sources of wisdom?

4. What is meant by the phrase "princes of this world" in 1 Corinthians 2:6, 8?

5. Why can't the wisdom of God be understood by the princes of this world?

6. What historical incident proves that people having only secular wisdom do not understand God's secret wisdom? (1 Corinthians 2:8). In your opinion, what is the primary content of God's secret wisdom?

After the pairs have worked on these questions for a few minutes, allow them to share their answers as you use them to develop the lesson for the class. Elaborate upon each question as you teach.

Into Life

Help your students apply the lesson by teaching them to write their personal testimony about Jesus. Type and photocopy the following directives. These are also in the student quarterly.

1. Choose a theme. Write about one area of your life that Christ has changed: for example, victory over a bad habit, peace of mind, etc.

2. Divide your testimony into three parts:

Your life before meeting Christ (tell about a specific lack or problem).

How you came to believe and commit your life to Christ.

How your life has changed since becoming a Christian (be specific).

3. Helpful Insights:

Don't use religious jargon or cliches.

Accentuate interesting aspects, but avoid boring details.

If time allows, or if someone is prepared in advance, have a personal testimony shared by a member of the class. Close the session by reminding the class of Paul's example of a simple, straightforward witness to the person of Jesus Christ. Point out that personal testimonies should focus upon the Savior. If time allows, discuss some obstacles that must be overcome in sharing one's personal testimony.

Let's Talk It Over

The questions on this page are designed to encourage review of the lesson Scriptures and to promote discussion of the lesson by the class. The answers provided are only discussion starters. Let your class talk it over from there.

1. Why must we be careful about using complex theological terms or scholarly discussions in our communication of the gospel?

We do not want to give the impression that the gospel is only for those who are highly educated or intellectually superior. Biblical truth can, of course, provide a challenging level of study for the keenest minds and the best-trained scholars. But the basic truths of God's Word are readily grasped by people from all levels of educational attainment. It was said of Jesus that "the common people heard him gladly" (Mark 12:37), and those who speak for Him today must make it their aim that common people will be able to hear, understand, and apply the message delivered to them. Jesus, of course, tried to raise His hearers' level of understanding so that they could grasp loftier truths. We also can lead our hearers into more complex discussions once we are sure they have mastered basic truths.

2. How can we make sure that we put enough emphasis in the church on "Jesus Christ, and him crucified"?

One way is to make certain our observance of the Lord's Supper is cross-centered and not merely "upper-room centered." It is appropriate to speak at Communion time of the instituting of the Lord's Supper in the upper room, but Jesus' "Communion meditation" pointed ahead to the cross, and so should ours.

Another answer to this question lies in making sure that we do not neglect cross-centered hymns and gospel songs. Many "me-centered" songs can be used too, but we must not neglect the theme of Jesus and His cross.

Finally, preachers should remember that "Jesus Christ, and him crucified" is an inexhaustible theme for sermons—a theme that should be used constantly.

3. What are some examples of the shallowness of the world's wisdom?

The humanistic notion that man can fend for himself quite well without God's help is manifestly shallow. How quick we are to ignore the mess we have made here on earth with our wars, our crimes, our greed, and our selfishness! It is obvious that we need all the help we can get from God.

A related aspect of worldly wisdom is the persistent idea that material prosperity is man's highest goal. Yet we see evidence in the news every day that Jesus' assertion is true: "a man's life consisteth not in the abundance of the things which he possesseth" (Luke 12:15).

Worldly wisdom also teaches that human beings ought not to deny themselves any sexual pleasure. The dire results of this shallow viewpoint are constantly visible in AIDS, abortion, and shattered families.

4. Why is the principle of using "Bible names for Bible things" still a sound one, if employed carefully?

It is a principle that honors the Word of God. If we are to be "a people of the Book," we will want to use the terms the Book uses to describe the gospel, the church, and aspects of Christian worship and Christian living. For example, we do well to call the Lord's Supper or Communion by these names, because to call it by other names draws us away from the Bible. This principle, if generally practiced, could also reduce a great deal of confusion in the religious world. Non-biblical terms used by a particular religious group may sound like a kind of foreign language to those outside the group. We need not confine ourselves to words used in the Bible, but when clear biblical names are available, we should use them.

5. How can we develop in ourselves "the mind of Christ"?

To think as Jesus thinks, to have His attitudes and motives—that is a worthy aim. We are exposed to His thoughts and attitudes in the four Gospels, so a continuing study of these surely is a help in developing the mind of Christ. Such a study involves some prayerful meditation on statements of Jesus that provide insight into His character. No less attention should be given to actions that reveal His way of thinking.

Another way to cultivate the mind of Christ is to put ourselves into situations similar to those Jesus faced. For example, Jesus ministered to the poor and infirm. We can visit hospitals, nursing homes, needy families, and try to see the people as Jesus would. We cannot heal them by miracles, but we can have compassion and help them in other ways.

Being Faithful Under Stress

DEVOTIONAL READING: Romans 12:1-10.

LESSON SCRIPTURE: 1 Corinthians 4.

PRINTED TEXT: 1 Corinthians 4:1, 2, 6-16.

1 Corinthians 4:1, 2, 6-16

1 Let a man so account of us, as of the ministers of Christ, and stewards of the mysteries of God.

2 Moreover it is required in stewards, that a man be found faithful.

. . . .

6 And these things, brethren, I have in a figure transferred to myself and to Apollos for your sakes; that ye might learn in us not to think of men above that which is written, that no one of you be puffed up for one against another.

7 For who maketh thee to differ from another? and what hast thou that thou didst not receive? now if thou didst receive it, why dost thou glory, as if thou hadst not received it?

8 Now ye are full, now ye are rich, ye have reigned as kings without us: and I would to God ye did reign, that we also might reign with you.

9 For I think that God hath set forth us the apostles last, as it were appointed to death: for we are made a spectacle unto the world, and to angels, and to men.

10 We are fools for Christ's sake, but ye are wise in Christ; we are weak, but ye are strong; ye are honorable, but we are despised.

11 Even unto this present hour we both hunger, and thirst, and are naked, and are buffeted, and have no certain dwelling place;

12 And labor, working with our own hands: being reviled, we bless; being persecuted, we suffer it:

13 Being defamed, we entreat: we are made as the filth of the world, and are the offscouring of all things unto this day.

14 I write not these things to shame you, but as my beloved sons I warn you.

15 For though ye have ten thousand instructors in Christ, yet have ye not many fathers: for in Christ Jesus I have begotten you through the gospel.

16 Wherefore I beseech you, be ye followers of me.

GOLDEN TEXT: It is required in stewards, that a man be found faithful.—1 Corinthians 4:2.

Lesson Aims

After the completion of this lesson, each student should:

1. Understand that servanthood is an essential part of being a Christian leader.

2. Know the value of faithful leadership in the church.

3. Be able to imitate the faithfulness of good leaders.

Lesson Outline

Visual 2 of the visuals packet highlights the ministry of the apostles as described by Paul in the Scripture text. The visual is shown on page 245.

Introduction

A. "Your Obedient Servant, A. Lincoln"

Near Springfield, Illinois, lies a little place called New Salem. Here Abraham Lincoln lived for a few years in the early 1830s. The little village has been carefully restored to look as it did in those days long ago.

Every year a play is performed on the grounds, dramatizing the events of Lincoln's life. For years the most famous play has been one entitled "Your Obedient Servant, A. Lincoln."

This title is taken from one of Lincoln's distinctive ways of signing his letters. It tells us much about the man as well as about his concept of leadership. Though mocked by the press, ridiculed by opponents, and often treated disrespectfully by people working closely with him, Lincoln shepherded the nation through very painful years on the strength of his character as leader. He understood that leadership demands faithfulness and service.

This is what Paul wanted the Corinthian church to understand, as we see in our lesson.

B. Lesson Background

In the first two chapters of 1 Corinthians, Paul has spoken the truth plainly about what should be central to all Christian thinking and preaching: the cross of Jesus Christ. In chapters 3 and 4 he shifts his focus away from the message to the relationship between the messengers and the recipients of the message.

Just as Jesus the Christ is central to the message preached, so Jesus as Lord should be central to the relationship between leaders and followers in the church.

However, there were some people in the Corinthian church who were beginning to view the church as just another human organization in which the leaders exist primarily to meet the felt needs of the followers, and in which the followers derive their self-worth primarily from their leaders' power and importance. Paul saw how very lethal this wrong perspective could be to the spiritual life of a church, and therefore he spoke of it with great urgency and also great love.

I. A Proper Perspective on Leadership (1 Corinthians 4:1, 2)

A. Leaders Are Servants of Christ (v. 1)

1. Let a man so account of us, as of the ministers of Christ, and stewards of the mysteries of God.

Paul wanted the Corinthian Christians to see more clearly just what it means to be leaders and followers in Christ's church. They would not need to boast so much about their leaders if they would fully realize how important they themselves were to God.

It seems quite clear that some of the Christians in Corinth were trying to bolster their feeling of self-worth by *belonging* to some important human leader and his group (1 Corinthians 1:12; 3:4-9). Paul wanted them to understand that first they belonged to the most important leader of all: the Lord Jesus Christ. Because they belonged to Christ, all things that belonged to Christ also belonged to them, including Apollos, Cephas, and Paul himself (1 Corinthians 3:21-23).

If the Corinthian Christians would understand this, there would be no reason for one Christian to become "puffed up" against another Christian on account of one leader or another (1 Corinthians 4:6). Why not? Because all leaders would then be seen for what they really were: "ministers by whom ye believed" (1 Corinthians 3:5). The Greek word translated *ministers* can as properly be translated *servants*, but in the first verse of our text Paul uses a different word. This Greek word emphasizes the inferior and subservient position of the servant in relationship to his master. This is the proper view for Christian followers to have of their spiritual leaders. Every Christian leader is under Christ.

In our day of megachurches and multimillion-dollar television "ministries," Paul's words serve as an urgently needed reminder to both preachers and their supporters: leaders serve their followers because above all they are serving and following Christ (2 Corinthians 4:5).

In pagan Corinth, mysteries were secrets of various heathen religious groups. An outsider could not know the mysteries of a group until someone in the group revealed them to him. Christian *mysteries* do not focus on human leaders or imaginary deities, but on the real God: they are *the mysteries of God*. And God's great mystery, which was previously hidden, has now in the gospel been revealed: He wants Jews and Gentiles together to be saved as one new people in Jesus Christ (1 Corinthians 2:7; Ephesians 3:3-10).

B. Leaders Are Stewards of God (v. 2)

2. Moreover it is required in stewards, that a man be found faithful.

Verse 1 says Paul and other Christian leaders are humble servants of Christ and stewards of God's mysteries. As *stewards* accountable to God, they must be *faithful* in delivering the gospel entrusted to them, and faithful in managing their lives as directed by Christ the Lord.

Obviously Paul cared about what the Christians thought of him. But he was much more concerned about how God would judge him (1 Corinthians 4:3-5). Why is that? Because the apostles, and all leaders in the church, are accountable first and foremost to their Master, the Lord Jesus Christ.

In another place Paul asks, "Who art thou that judgest another man's servant? to his own master he standeth or falleth. Yea, he shall be holden up: for God is able to make him stand" (Romans 14:4).

God does sustain His faithful stewards; but we can be sure that neither God nor Paul would approve of a preacher today who lives immorally while warning potential critics not to speak against God's man.

Paul refused to let his followers be his ultimate judge, but that was not to lower the standards for his faithfulness. It was to raise them even higher! God was his judge.

BEING TRUSTWORTHY

Verse 2 in our lesson text speaks of "stewards"; today we would call them "managers" or "people in charge." We are familiar with situations in which some person is trusted to take care of something that belongs to others. We have grounds keepers on golf courses, baseball, football, and soccer fields. We have those who are responsible for the upkeep of swimming pools, and some who are gardeners on large estates or in public parks. Dietitians are responsible for supervising the food eaten by large numbers of people. There are administrators of hospitals, schools, and retirement homes. All of these people that are mentioned and large numbers of other people have responsibilities that are similar to what New Testament writers and characters call "stewardship."

It is required that such stewards "be found faithful." They must honestly and carefully manage the property or oversee the group or agency of which they have charge. Such trustworthiness is essential. Stewards are praised and rewarded if efficient, and penalized or criticized if they are careless or negligent.

The apostle Paul tells us he and his co-workers had been entrusted with "the mysteries of God." To them had been given the revelation that Jesus is Savior and Lord, and that the church is His body, purchased with His blood on the cross of Calvary. They must conserve and proclaim that revelation.

Is it not so with us? As Christians we are in responsible positions for God today. It is required of us that we be found faithful. If we do not love Jesus, seek to bring others to Him, and make His church a living power in our world —who will?   —J. G. V. B.

II. A Proper Perspective on Following (1 Corinthians 4:6-8)

A. Followers Should Not Misplace Loyalty (v. 6)

6. And these things, brethren, I have in a figure transferred to myself and to Apollos for your sakes; that ye might learn in us not to think of men above that which is written, that no one of you be puffed up for one against another.

Respect for worthy spiritual leaders in the churches is taught throughout the New Testament. But in the Corinthian church, the devotion of some to their leaders was threatening to become such loyalty as is due to the Lord only. Paul wondered whether they were forgetting who had been crucified for them and in whose name they had been baptized (1 Corinthians 1:13).

In this letter Paul has *in a figure transferred* things to Apollos and himself. In other words, he has been using Apollos and himself as examples to show how Christian leaders ought to relate to the Lord, to each other, and to their followers. Paul and Apollos were among the foolish, weak, and base things that God had chosen to use to reveal to the world His wisdom, power, and righteousness (1 Corinthians 1:26-31). They were fellow laborers in God's field, fellow builders in God's building (1 Corinthians 3:5-11), and fellow stewards accountable to the Lord (1 Corinthians 4:1, 2). Therefore it was wrong to champion one faithful preacher or teacher against another.

The phrase *above that which is written* is puzzling. Paul does not say what writings he has in mind, and so we cannot say. But it is clear that Christians should not overlook those writings and *be puffed up for one against another.* There was no quarrel between Paul and Apollos; there should be none between their followers.

B. Followers Should Not Forget Their Origins (v. 7)

7. For who maketh thee to differ from another? and what hast thou that thou didst not receive? now if thou didst receive it, why dost thou glory, as if thou hadst not received it?

By use of three painfully honest questions Paul gets to the core of the mistake he is seeking to correct in 1 Corinthians 1:10—4:21. Some people seemed to think they were worth more in God's eyes because they were won and taught by a superior leader, or because they had notable spiritual gifts (1 Corinthians 12). A Christian has much that is good and valuable; but it is nothing for him to brag about, because he has not gotten it by any merit or power or goodness of his own. He has *received* it as a gracious gift from God.

It appears that some of the Corinthians had been Christians long enough to forget what life was like before God's grace in Jesus Christ called them, forgave them, and empowered them through the Holy Spirit to live new lives (1 Corinthians 6:9-11). Losing sight of their origins in grace, they began to idolize their favorite leaders, and to boast as if they had already reached perfection.

C. Followers Should Not Become Arrogant (v. 8)

8. Now ye are full, now ye are rich, ye have reigned as kings without us: and I would to God ye did reign, that we also might reign with you.

Whether some Corinthians were saying these things in words or just showing them by their attitude, Paul directly confronts their arrogant pride. In the competition among factions (1 Corinthians 1:12), members of each faction fancied that they were *full* of truth and sound doctrine, *rich* in Christian character and goodness. They thought they already *reigned* as kings with Christ in His kingdom. And all this was *without us:* Paul, Apollos, and other teachers claimed no such exalted state.

Paul was not opposing any of their spiritual progress or victories. He wished they *did reign* so he could share in their triumph. But the facts of their spiritual life belied their grandiose claims.To those who think they are perfect, Paul says perfection has not yet arrived (1 Corinthians 13:9-12)

It is true that Christians here on earth already are tasting some of the blessings of the age to come (Hebrews 6:5). But some of the Corinthian Christians seemed to think they had finished the whole banquet. They were *full!*

We Christians today are in danger of a similar error if we suppose that here and now our faith gives us total freedom from all kinds of problems, weaknesses, and illnesses.

III. A Model of Faithfulness Under Stress (1 Corinthians 4:9-13)

A. Apostles Model Life Under a Cross (v. 9)

9. For I think that God hath set forth us the apostles last, as it were appointed to death: for we are made a spectacle unto the world, and to angels, and to men.

In stark contrast to the life some of the Corinthian Christians were boasting about, the life of Paul and the rest of the apostles was life under a cross. There was nothing in it to elevate their social status or give them something to boast about. The apostles were like those prisoners who came *last* in an emperor's triumphal parade. Those prisoners were *appointed unto death* in the arena, usually by lions, as the final *spectacle* of the evening.

B. Apostles and Corinthians Contrasted (v. 10)

10. We are fools for Christ's sake, but ye are wise in Christ; we are weak, but ye are strong; ye are honorable, but we are despised.

So Paul continues the contrast between the claims of some Corinthian Christians and the lives of the apostles. We can almost hear Paul ask, "Isn't it a little strange that *for Christ's sake* we apostles are treated like *fools*, made to feel *weak* and *despised*, while you who are our converts are accepted in the world as *wise, strong,* and *honorable?*"

Paul's point is not that Christians should intentionally act in foolish ways in order to invite ridicule, or try to justify foolish behavior because the Bible says we are to be fools for Christ. Rather, the point is that if we *for Christ's sake* are faithfully living under a cross, the world will almost inevitably think we are foolish, weak, and "not really with it."

We who are Christians living in developed countries need to ask ourselves this painful question: Is it possible that we are respectable in the eyes of our world to the degree that we are *not* following the apostles' model of daily faithful living under a cross?

C. Apostles Are Faithful Under Stress (vv. 11-13)

11-13. Even unto this present hour we both hunger, and thirst, and are naked, and are buffeted, and have no certain dwelling place; and labor, working with our own hands: being reviled, we bless; being persecuted, we suffer it: being defamed, we entreat: we are made as the filth of the world, and are the offscouring of all things unto this day.

No doubt Paul was deeply hurt because some of the Corinthian Christians were looking down on him. They interpreted his gentleness and meekness as signs of weakness and inferiority (2 Corinthians 10:10, 11; 11:7-9). But Paul's meekness was really that of Christ (10:1-3). Paul warned that he too could be hard on them if he had to (1 Corinthians 4:18-21).

Paul's sorrow over their attitude expresses itself with great passion here. Certainly he endured *hunger, thirst, persecution,* and manual *labor,* as well as other discomforts. Couldn't the

visual 2

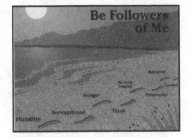

Corinthians see that he did it for their sake and for the sake of the advancement of the gospel? (1 Corinthians 9:1-23).

Paul did not deny that his biography was full of what society would look down upon as "unfortunate" incidents, and even some ugly episodes (2 Corinthians 11:23-30). But he wanted the Corinthians to see also the grace with which God enabled the apostles to respond in all those problems: *we bless* (as Jesus commanded in Luke 6:28), *we suffer* (endure) persecution, and we *entreat* (appeal humbly) even when slandered.

The true wisdom, power, and glory of the Christian life is not to deny, ignore, or, avoid suffering, but like Jesus to endure it faithfully under whatever stress the world may cause (Hebrews 5:7, 8; 12:2). Thus Christians can overcome evil with good (Romans 12:17, 21), even when they are called "the scum of the earth" (a phrase similar to the filth of the world).

SOME SCUM

The *New International Version* translates part of verse 13 as "we have become the scum of the earth." Paul is telling about the opposition and adverse attitudes he had encountered, along with the other apostles (v. 9). We now regard the apostles as Christian heroes, as the specially empowered, inspired, and blessed agents of God; but many of their contemporaries thought of them as weak and dishonored. They were cursed, slandered, and brutally treated.

Such mistreatment has been seen often in the history of our faith. Those who have sought to translate the Bible into the language of the people have often been scorned and made scapegoats. John Wycliffe oversaw the rendering of our Bible into English, but he was hated and harassed. Upon his death in 1400, some of the opponents said in the English of that time that he was "The Devells Instrument, Churches Enemy, Peoples Confusion, Hereticks Idoll . . . Hatreds Sower, Lyes Forger, Flatteries Sinke: who at his death . . . breathed forth his wicked soule to the dark mansion of the black Devell."

We may look at our missionaries as admirable and even heroic servants of our Lord, but they are not so regarded in all sections of our earth. In Muslim lands they often are scorned and opposed. This is also true in many areas of India and China.

It is true that in our day some have been murdered. But though regarded by misguided persons as "scum," they are indeed "fools for Christ's sake" (v. 10). They are yet God's heralds and Jesus' shining servants.   —J. G. V. B.

IV. An Appeal to Imitate Faithfulness (1 Corinthians 4:14-16)

A. An Appeal From Love (vv. 14, 15)

14, 15. I write not these things to shame you, but as my beloved sons I warn you. For though ye have ten thousand instructors in Christ, yet have ye not many fathers: for in Christ Jesus I have begotten you through the gospel.

Paul knew his straightforward language would bring shame to some of the Corinthian Christians. That was not his purpose here, though it was in some parts of the letter (1 Corinthians 6:5; 15:34). Here Paul's primary purpose was to *warn* the Corinthians to change their views of leadership in the church. After all, was he not their spiritual father? It was he who had brought the *gospel* by which they were begotten to be born again.

B. An Appeal to Action (v. 16)

16. Wherefore I beseech you, be ye followers of me.

Our lesson ends with Paul's plea for the Corinthians to be followers of him, not because he wanted his party to win after all (1 Corinthians 1:12; 3:5, 6), but because he himself was faithfully imitating Christ's faithfulness to the Father (1 Corinthians 11:1). Imitation means a changed behavior: Paul wanted the Corinthians not merely to admire faithfulness under stress, but also to practice it in their own lives.

IMITATORS

Paul said, "Wherefore I beseech you, be ye followers of me." The *New International Version* translates this, "Therefore I urge you to imitate me." In his reaction to scorn and insults, in his fortitude and faithfulness, Paul felt that he presented a worthy model.

We are constantly imitating others all of our lives. We learn our native language by making the same sounds we hear our parents and other adults making.

We tend to imitate the dress and deportment of people whom we admire. In many of life's activities we are not ashamed to be "copycats." Often one will ask how he serves a tennis ball, or how he baits hooks so he can catch fish. We buy cookbooks so we can utilize the recipes of others.

How important it is for us to be devoted to our Lord! We need to exhibit in our lives that humility, purity, compassion, and integrity we find in Him. We may be much less comfortable than Paul seems to have been in urging others to imitate us. Is this because we doubt that our words, attitudes, and actions are really so much like those of Jesus that we dare to ask others to follow our example? Others, however, may be imitating us even when we don't know it. What a challenge this is to us every day!   —J. G. V. B.

Conclusion

A. "A Diploma and a Towel"

It is a beautiful and meaningful tradition at Lincoln Christian Seminary that each graduate during the graduation ceremony receives a diploma in the right hand and a new towel over the left arm. This ritual expressed the firm expectation that each graduate will prove to be a faithful servant of the Lord, His Word, and His people. Only by faithful service should success in ministry ultimately be evaluated.

B. Let Us Pray

Father, help us to be faithful servants of Jesus, in spite of any and all persecutions. Amen.

C. Thought to Remember

"His lord said unto him, Well done, thou good and faithful servant: thou hast been faithful over a few things, I will make thee ruler over many things: enter thou into the joy of thy lord" (Matthew 25:21).

Home Daily Bible Readings

Monday, Mar. 6—Warning Against Relying on Human Wisdom (1 Corinthians 3:18-23)

Tuesday, Mar. 7—Servants of Christ (1 Corinthians 4:1-7)

Wednesday, Mar. 8—Faithfulness in Hard Times (1 Corinthians 4:8-13)

Thursday, Mar. 9—Fatherly Admonition (1 Corinthians 4:14-21)

Friday, Mar. 10—Christian Conduct in Adversity (Romans 12:9-21)

Saturday, Mar. 11—Meet Trials With Steadfast Faith (James 1:1-8)

Sunday, Mar. 12—Encouragement for Christians (1 Thessalonians 5:1-11)

Learning by Doing

This page contains an alternate lesson plan emphasizing learning activities. Classes desiring such student involvement will find these suggestions helpful.

Learning Goals

As a result of studying this lesson, a student will be able to:

1. Delineate specific characteristics of the ideal Christian leader as depicted by Paul.

2. Describe the negative attitudes of poor followers of Christ and determine to avoid them in his or her Christian walk.

3. Understand the difference between admonishing and shaming; resolve never to damage the personality of one who needs correcting.

Into the Lesson

Put this sentence on the board or flip chart: *List as many stressful experiences in the life of Paul as you can recall.* (This is in the student book as well.) Give each class member a blank sheet of paper for this purpose, or refer the class to the student book. After a few moments, write the remembrances of the class on the board as they are shared. Then ask what Paul's usual reaction was in stressful times. (Answers should include faithfulness, rejoicing, contentment, and endurance.)

Into the Word

Direct the students to read 1 Corinthians 4:11-13 and note Paul's struggles and stresses. Have them compare those with the list that the class compiled.

Go on to 1 Corinthians 4:14. Note Paul's purpose in sharing these things about himself: not to shame the readers, but to warn them, or to admonish them, as the *American Standard Version* has it. Have the class discuss the difference between the two. After hearing several answers, suggest that shaming is putting someone down, while admonishing is lifting him up. Shaming discredits and humiliates; admonishing corrects and encourages. Paul was sensitive to the need of the Corinthians to be corrected rather than put down.

Ask the class what tone of voice Paul would use if he were speaking the words of 1 Corinthians 4:8-10. One commentator suggests that the words were "sanctified sarcasm." Ask a capable person to read these verses in a sarcastic tone. Point out that there is no place for selfish pride in Christian service. The pride and self-satisfaction of some in the church at Corinth needed correcting. To correct it, Paul told some of his troubles and how he reacted to them. Then what did he tell the readers to do? Let students answer from verse 16. Did this show that Paul himself had the kind of pride he was warning against? Let students answer, telling why or why not. Point out that Paul was not presenting himself alone as a model, but all the apostles (v. 9). Their reaction was the normal one for Christians.

Turn the students' attention back to verses 1 and 2. Have them find two words that were used to describe leaders (servants, stewards). Point out that the Corinthians were dividing the church by their prideful loyalty to different leaders. Explain that a steward has important responsibilities, but still he is a servant answerable to his master.

Divide the class into groups of four to six to discuss these problems: Why did Paul have so much trouble when he was a devoted follower of Christ? Why do some of today's followers of Christ have an easy life while others have hard work, suffering, and pain? After five or ten minutes, have one person from each group share his group's conclusions. Close the discussion by saying that there are no pat answers to the latter question. The verses one clings to in times of adversity are answer enough. Read Romans 8:17, 18.

Into Life

Let students remain in their small groups to do this activity. Note again the mistake of some Christians in Corinth (v. 6). List some ways in which church members in our day make the same mistake. These thoughts may be included: choose a church because the preacher is eloquent, idolize a television evangelist while criticizing the minister of your home church, act smug and self-satisfied about your spiritual growth.

Bring the class session to a close by putting the word *stewards* on the flip chart and asking the class to make an acrostic to delineate the characteristics of a Christian leader. See the example below:

S erving rather than "bossing"
T aking time for others
E ncouraging others in good works
W orking diligently for the Lord
A llowing God to work through them
R elying upon God's direction
D esiring the best for God's people
S taying in touch with the Master in prayer

Let's Talk It Over

The questions on this page are designed to encourage review of the lesson Scriptures and to promote discussion of the lesson by the class. The answers provided are only discussion starters. Let your class talk it over from there.

1. Why do we need to keep before our minds the importance of faithfulness to God in performing our ministry or service for Him?

Because of our fallible human nature we may face the temptation to be satisfied "with eyeservice, as menpleasers" (Colossians 3:22). We must beware of that.

We must not let numerical or material successes become substitutes for genuine faithfulness. There are enough cults and extremist groups attracting large numbers to make it clear that numerical success is no sure sign of faithfulness to God.

The temptation to give up, to coast for a while, to "let someone else do it," is another reason why we need to be constantly urged to faithfulness in our Christian work. Listen to the exhortation given to the church at Smyrna: "Be thou faithful unto death, and I will give thee a crown of life" (Revelation 2:10).

2. "For who makes you different from anyone else? What do you have that you did not receive? And if you did receive it, why do you boast as though you did not?" (1 Corinthians 4:7, *New International Version*). Why does the church need to consider these questions today?

Pride in our Christian connections or our spiritual attainments can still be a source of disharmony. We sing, "To God Be the Glory." That should express our attitude toward all aspects of our Christian experience: the person who baptized us, the teachers who taught us, our talents, the offices we have held, the financial gifts we have given, the souls we have won, etc. To boast of these is to lose sight of the fact that God has given them to us.

3. What might be involved today in being regarded as "fools for Christ's sake"? Are we willing to be so regarded?

To take the Bible as literal truth and to take seriously the Bible's call to an obedient and holy life is enough today to make us fools in the eyes of many of our fellow human beings. They may not call us fools, but they do label us with titles like "Bible thumpers" or "religious nuts." We also run the risk of being regarded as fools when we oppose what is "politically correct" in our society, even if it is "biblically incorrect." There is little doubt that certain "enlightened" individuals in political office, in the news media, in the entertainment industry, and elsewhere view us as benighted fools because we do not acknowledge the legitimacy of abortion, homosexuality, and similar sins. When we remember that even Jesus' friends said of Him, "He is beside himself" (Mark 3:21), we should be willing to endure any insult in taking our stand for Him.

4. How might it be helpful if Christian leaders viewed their responsibilities in the church in terms of a father/children relationship?

We may tend to shy away from this because Jesus said, "Call no man your father upon the earth" (Matthew 23:9). But Paul did not violate that command when he pointed out that in a way he was father of the Christians in Corinth, and the duties of a Christian leader or teacher are in some ways like those of a father. A father cares for and protects his children, and a spiritual leader is to do the same for his people. A father wants to prepare his children for the time when they must "stand on their own two feet," and a spiritual leader should aim to bring his people to personal maturity in Christ. A father corrects his children when he sees them moving in the direction of danger, and a spiritual leader must make use of the word of reproof or correction when he sees his people straying from Christ.

5. Paul told the Corinthians, "Be ye followers of me." Is it proper for leaders in our church to offer that same exhortation? Why, or why not?

Paul expanded on that exhortation in 1 Corinthians 11:1: "Be ye followers of me, even as I also am of Christ." We are first of all to be faithful followers of Jesus Christ. However, there are men and women in the church who, like Paul, model the character of Christ in such a way that we can benefit from their example. If such persons were to urge us to follow *them*, we might regard them as vain and presumptuous. But if they were to say, "Follow me to the extent that you see me following Christ," that would be a legitimate exhortation. Paul's words constitute quite a challenge for the church's leaders today. Every leader should aim to model Jesus Christ in the way Paul did.

Resisting Temptation

DEVOTIONAL READING: Ephesians 6:10-18.

LESSON SCRIPTURE: 1 Corinthians 10:1-17.

PRINTED TEXT: 1 Corinthians 10:1-17.

1 Corinthians 10:1-17

1 Moreover, brethren, I would not that ye should be ignorant, how that all our fathers were under the cloud, and all passed through the sea;

2 And were all baptized unto Moses in the cloud and in the sea;

3 And did all eat the same spiritual meat;

4 And did all drink the same spiritual drink; for they drank of that spiritual Rock that followed them: and that Rock was Christ.

5 But with many of them God was not well pleased: for they were overthrown in the wilderness.

6 Now these things were our examples, to the intent we should not lust after evil things, as they also lusted.

7 Neither be ye idolaters, as were some of them; as it is written, The people sat down to eat and drink, and rose up to play.

8 Neither let us commit fornication, as some of them committed, and fell in one day three and twenty thousand.

9 Neither let us tempt Christ, as some of them also tempted, and were destroyed of serpents.

10 Neither murmur ye, as some of them also murmured, and were destroyed of the destroyer.

11 Now all these things happened unto them for ensamples: and they are written for our admonition, upon whom the ends of the world are come.

12 Wherefore let him that thinketh he standeth take heed lest he fall.

13 There hath no temptation taken you but such as is common to man: but God is faithful, who will not suffer you to be tempted above that ye are able; but will with the temptation also make a way to escape, that ye may be able to bear it.

14 Wherefore, my dearly beloved, flee from idolatry.

15 I speak as to wise men; judge ye what I say.

16 The cup of blessing which we bless, is it not the communion of the blood of Christ? The bread which we break, is it not the communion of the body of Christ?

17 For we being many are one bread, and one body: for we are all partakers of that one bread.

GOLDEN TEXT: There hath no temptation taken you but such as is common to man: but God is faithful, who will not suffer you to be tempted above that ye are able; but will with the temptation also make a way to escape, that ye may be able to bear it.—1 Corinthians 10:13.

Christians Living in Community

Unit 1: Responding to Challenges
of Life in Community (Lessons 1-4)

Lesson Aims

Today's lesson study is designed to help the student:

1. Recognize the danger and nature of the temptations faced in daily life.

2. Utilize the resources provided by the Lord to overcome temptation.

Lesson Outline

INTRODUCTION
    A. The Master of Deceit
    B. Lesson Background
  I. RECOGNIZING THE DANGER (1 Corinthians 10:1-5)
    A. Blessed of God (vv. 1-4)
        Examples
    B. Displeasing to God (v. 5)
 II. HEEDING THE WARNINGS (1 Corinthians 10:6-11)
    A. Examples From the Past (v. 6a)
    B. Perils of the Present (vv. 6b-10)
    C. Lessons for the Future (v. 11)
III. SEEING THE ALTERNATIVE (1 Corinthians 10:12, 13)
    A. Human Weakness (vv. 12, 13a)
    B. Divine Faithfulness (v. 13b)
        Load Limits
 IV. DECIDING TO RESIST (1 Corinthians 10:14-17)
    A. Avoiding the Sin (vv. 14, 15)
    B. Seeking the Lord (vv. 16, 17)
        Fellowship
CONCLUSION
    A. Never Say, "Impossible"!
    B. Prayer
    C. Thought to Remember

Visual 3 of the visuals packet calls attention to several main points of the Scripture text. The visual is shown on page 252.

Introduction

A. The Master of Deceit

Several artists were asked to illustrate their ideas of temptation. Most of them depicted scenes of decadence and evil. One drew a city scene with night clubs, bars, X-rated theaters, and sleazy characters lurking in the shadows. Another pictured the bright lights of Las Vegas.

The prize-winning canvas was different. Lovely wooded hillsides filled the frame. The picture radiated peace and serenity. A lone figure walked down a quiet lane in the woods. Branches arched overhead in a protective canopy. None of this seemed to suggest temptation—but ahead of the traveler was a fork in the road.

Most of the temptations that face us do not come with bright lights and warning signs. Satan, the great tempter, is a master of deceit. Often the key to resisting temptations is to recognize the importance of our simple, daily decisions.

B. Lesson Background

Faithfully following Christ in an immoral city like Corinth was not easy. The believers faced many temptations. There were divisions in the church and hostility without. Moral questions of every sort abounded.

In 1 Corinthians 8-10, Paul addresses the question of idolatry, the worship of various pagan gods and goddesses. This was no small issue, since much of Corinthian social life centered around religious ceremonies and festivities associated with pagan shrines. Many real-life questions faced these Christians. Apparently different believers at Corinth answered these questions in different ways. Some argued that anything associated with the pagan shrines was untouchable. Others contended that a true believer knew the idols were false, and therefore he could eat the sacrificial meat without joining in worship of the god.

Paul cautions both sides about the dangers of arguing their case at the expense of others. True, he insists, the pagan gods are really nothing, therefore one need not hesitate to eat the meat. However, not everyone can treat such matters so lightly. In deference to the weaknesses of other believers, every Christian needs to be very careful how he uses his freedom. Chapter 10 is a call to take seriously the dangers of idolatry and a call to follow the Lord without compromise.

I. Recognizing the Danger (1 Corinthians 10:1-5)

A. Blessed of God (vv. 1-4)

1. Moreover, brethren, I would not that ye should be ignorant, how that all our fathers were under the cloud, and all passed through the sea.

Moreover signals the close link between this chapter and the preceding one. Paul has spoken of his own commitment to personal holiness. He has recalled the danger of failing in his own spiritual life while teachings others. Having voiced his own concern as a model for the concern that every believer should have, he now turns to an illustration from the Old Testament.

All is a key word in this section. It is repeated five times in verses 1-4. All of the Hebrews followed the same cloud out of Egypt (Exodus 13:21, 22). Everyone passed supernaturally through the Red Sea (Exodus 14:15-22). Whatever differences developed later could not be explained by different starts.

2. And were all baptized unto Moses in the cloud and in the sea.

The cloud and sea through which they passed initiated them as followers of Moses. They all shared in this experience, and therefore all stood in the same relationship to Moses. Paul says *baptized* to make his readers think of their own lives. He is writing of Old Testament Jews, but he is thinking about the Corinthians. They had been baptized into Christ (1:10-17; Acts 18:8) and into blessings shared with all other believers because of their relationship with Christ.

Christian baptism is a beautiful bond that unites believers. It is a common event with a common meaning that each individual can look back upon and remember how he or she started in the walk of faith. Though we have come from different backgrounds, lived different kinds of lives, and belonged to different social circles, we all began our Christian lives in the same way. All of our differences fade when compared to the one great fact that we all have in common—our relationship with Jesus.

3. And did all eat the same spiritual meat.

Spiritual probably means supernatural. *Meat* means food. Paul refers to the heavenly nourishment provided for Israel, the manna that sustained the Hebrews during their wilderness wanderings (Exodus 16:1-18).

4. And did all drink the same spiritual drink; for they drank of that spiritual Rock that followed them: and that Rock was Christ.

Another blessing of Israel was the miraculous supply of water in the wilderness (Exodus 17:1-7; Numbers 20:1-13). It was spiritual in the same sense that the manna was spiritual. God provided it in a supernatural way.

Paul presses the analogy a bit further in order to make the application obvious. It is not necessary to suppose Paul thought a literal rock actually followed the Hebrew encampment through the desert. He is using the Rock as symbol of the divine provision that was never far from them.

That Rock was Christ emphasizes the truth that Christ is indeed the ultimate supply of all that every believer receives. Jesus claimed to give the living water that forever quenches the thirst of all who come to Him (John 4:10-14; 7:37, 38). Paul

here uses an Old Testament event as a symbol of what Christ does for those who place their trust in Him. Just as all who followed Moses drank of the water that (flowed from the *spiritual rock,*) all who come to Christ drink of the "living water."

EXAMPLES

Paul mentions several Old Testament events in our lesson text. In verse 6 he says they are "examples" (*New International Version*), or "symbols" (*The New English Bible*), or "types" (Greek text: *tupos*). One of the principal examples was the Red Sea crossing as the Hebrews fled from Egypt. There they were "baptized unto Moses in the cloud and in the sea" (v. 2).

This is a remarkable illustration of Christian baptism. They were covered by the cloud, which was overhead, and the sea water was a wall on each side. They thus passed across the sea as we, in baptism, are completely covered with water in our immersion into Jesus.

Further, they did this because of Moses' order, just as we are baptized at Jesus' command. They passed from an old life of slavery to a new life of freedom. So Paul, in Romans 6:16-18, says we have left sin's servitude to become the slaves of righteousness in Christ. Once they had been Egyptian slaves with no real identity, but now they had become a new people of God on the other side of the sea.

In the Exodus account we read that "Israel saw the Egyptians lying dead on the shore" (Exodus 14:30, *New International Version*). The brutal taskmasters, the arrogant soldiers, the vicious chariot drivers, the proud archers, the mighty nobles and princes now were all pale, stiff, inert, in the final ignominy of death. So we think of our baptism as the time when we look at our former sins, follies, and misdeeds as dead. We are forgiven and cleansed and united with Jesus, our Lord. Israel's baptism "unto Moses" testifies to us symbolically of our baptismal union with our Lord.   —J. G. V. B.

B. Displeasing to God (v. 5)

5. But with many of them God was not well pleased: for they were overthrown in the wilderness.

But introduces a strong contrast. One might mistakenly conclude that a people so blessed would all be destined for success. Starting together, however, does not necessarily guarantee finishing together. They were all blessed, but not all would see the promised land.

Many of them is an understatement. In fact, only Joshua and Caleb actually completed the journey and entered the promised land. Early in the journey, Joshua and Caleb were no more blessed than the rest of Israel, but they were the only ones to receive the full blessing that all started out to obtain.

Overthrown literally describes something strewn over the desert, scattered like the debris left in the path of a hurricane. It is a graphic description of the thousands of dead Hebrews left in the wake of God's judgment.

The ultimate verdict of Heaven and earth is found here. *God was not well pleased.* A person can please almost everyone and be thought a success. But if he fails to please God, that person's life is an eternal failure. What a glorious blessing it will be to hear those wonderful words, "Well done, thou good and faithful servant" (Matthew 25:21).

The Corinthians had been blessed by God in many ways. They knew it. The danger was that they might begin to take their privileges and blessings for granted and assume that they were somehow made immune from spiritual failure. Nothing could be farther from the truth.

If those in ancient Israel could fail when they had so much going for them, so can any of us fail if we do not take our calling seriously. This is why facing and resisting temptation is so important. Spiritual and moral success or failure hangs in balance.

II. Heeding the Warnings (1 Corinthians 10:6-11)

A. Examples From the Past (v. 6a)

6a. Now these things were our examples.

Paul comes to his point. He has cited Old Testament examples because they have lessons for his readers. Many things in the Old Testament provide examples for believers. In this case, they are negative examples, things to be avoided.

B. Perils of the Present (vv. 6b-10)

6b. To the intent we should not lust after evil things, as they also lusted.

To the intent indicates the purpose of the example previously cited. Paul begins a list of five sins of ancient Israel. All five are still very much alive in the world of his readers—in our world.

The first sin is *lust.* The original word means a strong desire of any sort, good or bad. In the New Testament, it usually refers to an evil desire. It often refers to sexual desire, but more probably it here means the Hebrews' dissatisfaction with God's provision, and their preference for the security of Egypt (Numbers 11:4-6).

7. Neither be ye idolaters, as were some of them; as it is written, The people sat down to eat and drink, and rose up to play.

visual 3

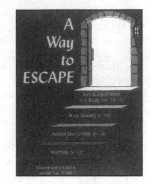

The worship of man-made gods or physical representations of the living God was a common vice of Israel. It came to prominence at the foot of Sinai when Aaron made a golden calf (Exodus 32:1-6). It plagued Israel till the nation again went into captivity.

8. Neither let us commit fornication, as some of them committed, and fell in one day three and twenty thousand.

Fornication is a general term for various kinds of sexual immorality. Paul refers to an incident involving men of Israel and women of Moab (Numbers 25:1-9). Sexual immorality was a real problem in Corinth. Often sexual activity was a part of the pagan religious ceremonies. Pagans thought intimate relations in sacred places or with sacred people, priests or priestesses, guaranteed the fertility of one's land or flocks.

Sin is a powerful force in human life, and sexual temptation is a very real problem today. Abandonment of moral absolutes has undermined our society and has caused many to view fornication as natural. The spread of obscenity and near-pornographic television has served as aggressive advertisement for sexual sin. The temptation has always been present, but recently it has virtually saturated our society.

Jesus raised the standard of sexual conduct when He placed lustful looking on the same plane as sexual misconduct (Matthew 5:27-30). No honest believer dare ignore his or her own vulnerability at this point. The failure of some well-known Christians and national leaders serves as a strong warning to us, just as does the example of the blessed but failing Israelites of old.

9. Neither let us tempt Christ, as some of them also tempted, and were destroyed of serpents.

Some of the most valued ancient manuscripts read *tempt the Lord* instead of *tempt Christ.* To tempt is to test. The Israelites tested the Lord by complaining about His provision and challenging Him to do better (Numbers 21:4-9).

10. Neither murmur ye, as some of them also murmured, and were destroyed of the destroyer.

Murmur means to grumble or voice an inner dissatisfaction. People of Israel complained about Moses and Aaron, saying they had killed some people who had been swallowed by the earth (Numbers 16:41-50). The complaint was actually against the Lord. He chose and directed the human leaders, and He caused the earth to swallow the rebels (Numbers 16:1-35).

Note that two vices of ancient Israel were sins of the tongue: tempting the Lord and murmuring. In the great catalogue of sins that soil and smear the believer's life, sins of the tongue stand near the top. No wonder James gives the powerful warning that he does (James 3:1-12).

C. Lessons for the Future (v. 11)

11. Now all these things happened unto them for ensamples: and they are written for our admonition, upon whom the ends of the world are come.

The Bible is largely history, but it is history with a purpose. The record is purposefully selective. Not everything that happened was written down. What was written serves to show readers the ways of God.

Those *upon whom the ends of the world are come* are those who live in the last period of world history. The term for *world* does not refer to the physical earth or universe, but to the ages or periods of the world's time. *Ends* means the goal or aim of history. That goal is the person and work of the Messiah. The Messiah has come, therefore the end has come upon those who are following Him. The grand finale awaits His return.

III. Seeing the Alternative (1 Corinthians 10:12, 13)

A. Human Weakness (vv. 12, 13a)

12. Wherefore let him that thinketh he standeth take heed lest he fall.

This is a word to those who may think they are immune to temptation, that they have risen above the plane of mere mortals who are vulnerable to the behaviors just listed. Arrogance and pride can be among the deadliest of sins. This warning is especially important to those who know they have been blessed of God.

13a. There hath no temptation taken you but such as is common to man.

Temptation is universal. All have faced it in the past and all will in the future. Our particular temptations have been here before. It is pointless to excuse ourselves by claiming to be different or in circumstances that are more difficult.

B. Divine Faithfulness (v. 13b)

13b. But God is faithful, who will not suffer you to be tempted above that ye are able; but will with the temptation also make a way to escape, that ye may be able to bear it.

Here is the great hope: not our ability, but God's. The God who saved us and who is with us promises to protect us. This protection does not mean freedom from temptation, but freedom from irresistible temptation. He pledges always to provide a way of escape. Temptation is inevitable, but giving in to it is not. Temptation can be overcome!

LOAD LIMITS

Paul assures us that God "will not suffer you to be tempted above that ye are able." Or as Phillips renders the last part of this passage, "beyond your powers of endurance." Frequently as we drive along secondary roads in our country we come to bridges crossing small rivers or streams. Often a sign is posted just before one comes to the bridge. It says "Load Limit," then "Five," "Ten," or "Twenty Tons." The bridge can support only a certain weight, and so a truck driver is warned that he may wreck his truck and the bridge if his load is heavy.

In a similar manner God knows the load limit of each of us. Others might easily surmount troubles that vex us terribly. On the other hand, we may feel little stress in a situation someone else would quickly find intolerable. God, our Father, is well acquainted with each one of us. While we are all similar in general construction and organization, our fingerprints are different, our hair texture is different, and our whole convoluted mix of psychical and emotional makeup is distinctive. Bloodhounds can sniff out the unique odor of each person, though we do not perceive it.

God knows all of us completely, and He tempers our trials to our individual "breaking points." True, we sometimes falter, mistrust, complain, or despair. But we must cling to this assurance: our Father cares and knows and oversees. Stormy seas may rear angry surges, but our ship of life is buoyant as we trust His promises.

—J. G. V. B.

IV. Deciding to Resist (1 Corinthians 10:14-17)

A. Avoiding the Sin (vv. 14, 15)

14. Wherefore, my dearly beloved, flee from idolatry.

Here is the conclusion. Idolatry is dangerous. Even the strongest believer must not trifle with it. Note the logical connection with the previous verse. God provides a way of escape. Use it!

15. I speak as to wise men; judge ye what I say.

Paul's readers claimed to be wise. He exhorts them to act like it when they face temptation. Only the foolish toy with temptation. The wise flee like Joseph from the bedroom of Potiphar's wife (Genesis 39:11, 12). There may be times to think and times to talk; but when confronted with temptation, it is time to flee.

B. Seeking the Lord (vv. 16, 17)

16. The cup of blessing which we bless, is it not the communion of the blood of Christ? The bread which we break, is it not the communion of the body of Christ?

To keep the readers far from idolatry, Paul calls them to remember their commitment to Christ. When a believer partakes of the cup and the bread of the Lord's table, he is renewing his pledge of allegiance to Christ. It is a participation (a communion) with Christ. To take such a pledge seriously should be enough to cause us to take sin and temptation seriously. We would never want to do anything to dishonor Christ, His message, or His people.

This verse provides a good incentive for keeping the Lord's Supper central to the regular weekly gathering of the church. It is more than just a reminder of what Christ did; it is also a renewal of our loyalty to Him.

17. For we being many are one bread, and one body: for we are all partakers of that one bread.

The common experience of the Lord's Supper is a symbol of the common faith that joins believers together. This solidarity should cause us to honor and protect each other. We ought never harm another believer any more than we would harm ourselves.

FELLOWSHIP

The term *communion*, which occurs twice in verse 16 of our lesson, in the Greek text is *koinonia*. This is sometimes rendered "participation" (*Revised Standard Version* and *New International Version*), or "sharing" (*New American Standard Bible*). Very often it is rendered "fellowship" in various contexts and various versions. The word *fellowship* is especially meaningful if we take it to mean "fellows on the same ship."

Anyone who has made an ocean crossing on a freighter has a keen realization of what such a condition is. One is out on a vast expanse of water in a relatively small ship. Perhaps there are about fifty-six persons on board—sixteen passengers and forty crew members. Some of these are mechanics. Others do the steering and map plotting. Others cook and serve meals, some make up beds and clean cabins. Passengers only enjoy the trip, but are taught the use of life jackets and the locations of life-boats. There are many different tasks and life-styles, but all are on the same ship. They are going where it goes and are dependent on its safety and well-being.

So we are divergent in life's tasks and interests, but we are all united in being on that ship of destiny, the church Jesus purchased with His blood and sustains with His living Spirit. Our communion at the Lord's table shows us we are together on the ship of salvation.   —J. G. V. B.

Conclusion

A. Never Say, "Impossible"!

A comic once declared, "I can resist anything except temptation." For many of us that is too true to be funny. But it need not be true. Resisting temptation is not "mission impossible."

Temptation can be resisted, but not because I am too strong to fall. It can be overcome because the God I serve is absolutely faithful. He promises to provide a way out. And He will!

B. Prayer

Lord, I am no stranger to temptation. I have faced it and failed more times than I can count. I know I will face temptation again, even today. I ask You to give me eyes to see the path of escape that You have faithfully provided. Please give me the will to walk that path.

C. Thought to Remember

Temptation is inevitable, but giving in to it is not. The secret of victory is God's faithfulness. Temptation can be overcome!

Home Daily Bible Readings

Monday, Mar. 13—God's Armor for Protection From Evil (Ephesians 6:10-18)

Tuesday, Mar. 14—Warning Against Overconfidence (1 Corinthians 10:1-13)

Wednesday, Mar. 15—Do Not Worship Idols (1 Timothy 6:9-19)

Thursday, Mar. 16—Pursue Righteousness (1 Timothy 6:9-19)

Friday, Mar. 17—Be Watchful and Firm in Faith (1 Peter 5:6-11)

Saturday, Mar. 18—God Helps Those Who Resist Evil (James 1:1-8)

Sunday, Mar. 19—Purity of Heart Is Blessed (Psalm 24:1-6)

Learning by Doing

This page contains an alternate lesson plan emphasizing learning activities. Classes desiring such student involvement will find these suggestions helpful.

Learning Goals

After this lesson the student will be able to:

1. Recite 1 Corinthians 10:13 from memory and be aware of the valuable resource that God makes available in times of temptation.

2. Identify the similarity in the idols in Old Testament times, New Testament times, and modern times.

3. Discover and list some positive steps that can be taken when temptations arise.

4. Understand the role temptations play in our spiritual development.

Into the Lesson

As students arrive, put them in pairs and give each pair a sealed envelope. Inside each envelope put 1 Corinthians 10:13. Have the verse typed in large print and then cut it apart so that it is in pieces that will be mixed up and need to be rearranged like a puzzle. Challenge the pairs to unscramble the verse and write it on the outside of the envelope. (To make it more fun, do not include the book, chapter, and verse reference.) Use the same version for all envelopes, so the students can recite the verse together when they have finished. Suggest that memorizing Scripture can be a strengthening force in their spiritual growth. Give a small prize to the couple who deciphers the verse first and can recite it by memory.

Continue the session by asking people to share the answer to this non-threatening question: What was one of your biggest temptations when you were a grade-school child? (Share your own answer first.) Answers may be something like this: "I was tempted to lie to my mother to escape punishment for things I did wrong." Allow as many to share as are comfortable doing so.

Into the Word

Lead into the Scripture by noting that people of all ages and from all stages in history faced temptations of a similar nature. In today's lesson we'll discover some of the basic temptations common to people down through the centuries. As Paul addresses the Christians at Corinth, he calls them to remember the history of the Israelites. Ask someone to read verses 1-5 aloud. Draw the students' attention to verses 6-11 and ask them to find the sins that Paul specifically cites. Write them on the board as members call them out (lust, idolatry, fornication, tempting God, murmuring or grumbling). Ask: Why should the behavior of the Israelites be of any importance to a New Testament church such as the one at Corinth? (Verse 11 answers this well.) Point out that all of these sins existed in the church at Corinth. Ask: Which of the sins seems to be of the most universal and timeless nature? (Grumbling is the best answer.) Elaborate upon what a strong temptation it is.

Put this statement on the board or flip chart and ask the class to agree or disagree: A Christian can be sure he will not give in to temptation. After allowing discussion, have someone read verse 12. Point out that pride is dangerous. Proverbs 16:18 said it! Christians at Corinth seemed to think they could handle any temptation, but Paul warns that they need to be on the alert.

Have the class repeat 1 Corinthians 10:13 from memory. Ask: What is the greatest assurance you get from this verse? (Answers may vary, but point out that the phrase "God is faithful" is the source of our greatest confidence.)

After having someone read verses 14-17 aloud, ask: What connection is there between the observance of the Lord's Supper and the rejection of idolatry? (One commits himself to Christ, by participating in the Lord's Supper. It would be dishonorable to dabble in the worship of idols.)

Into Life

Point out that Paul gives several positive actions to take in resisting temptation. Give each person an index card and ask that everyone write down the steps he or she discovered in this lesson. After a few moments, display the following steps on a piece of poster board or flip chart that you have prepared in advance:

1. Study the Old Testament and the New Testament. (Explain that this keeps us sensitized to possible temptations.)

2. Stay alert to the possibility of your own mistakes.

3. Look for God's alternatives in tempting situations and rely on Him to show you the way out.

4. Flee temptations. Being in the wrong place at the wrong time is best remedied by grabbing your hat and running.

Let's Talk It Over

The questions on this page are designed to encourage review of the lesson Scriptures and to promote discussion of the lesson by the class. The answers provided are only discussion starters. Let your class talk it over from there.

1. Is sexual temptation stronger today than it generally has been in the past? Why, or why not?

There are many factors that tend to make it stronger. The widespread rejection of biblical standards of morality is one. The highly publicized sexual escapades of various prominent people, tempting others to follow their example, is a second factor. The influence of television definitely contributes to immoral sexual behavior. We may also mention the provocative dress frequently seen in public places.

On the other hand, we have more compelling reasons to avoid sexual misbehavior. Those highly publicized sexual escapades mentioned above have often ended in scandal and disgrace. Also, we are probably aware of people whose marriage and home have been shattered by adultery. And then there is the haunting realization of the threat of AIDS and other such diseases.

2. Why do we need regular reminders that we are not immune to temptation?

Certain temptations arise rarely in life. We may handle with ease the day-by-day temptations we face in our work or recreation or family life. And the ease with which we say no to these minor allurements may lull us into a sense of overconfidence. Then suddenly we encounter one of those rare moments when a powerful temptation strikes—perhaps related to sex, money, or power—and we find ourselves shocked by how difficult it is to resist. Jesus' exhortation to His disciples serves as a reminder to us: "Watch and pray, that ye enter not into temptation" (Matthew 26:41).

Another aspect to consider here is our tendency to exclaim, when we hear of another believer's stumbling into sin: "Oh, I could never do that!" How much wiser and safer we are if we respond with the humble confession, "There but for the grace of God go I!"

3. How is it helpful to know that the temptations we face are not unique, but have been experienced and overcome by others?

Temptation can be a lonely thing. We wrestle with it in our innermost thoughts, our fleshly nature suggesting ways to justify sinful actions, and our spirits, prompted by God's Spirit, responding with biblical principles. Even if we share our struggle with a Christian friend, it is still up to us to make the decision. How good it is to realize that other believers, past and present, have grappled with very similar temptations! They also have dealt with the devil's tactics of furnishing us with clever arguments to justify immoral choices; they, like us, have been strengthened by the unchanging teachings of the Word. Jesus himself mastered temptations of all kinds, as Hebrews 4:15 declares. When we think about these things, we understand that temptation is not so lonely after all.

4. What are some examples of helps God gives to His people to enable them to escape temptation?

In verse 14 of our lesson text we are urged to "flee from idolatry." That can be taken quite literally. We can walk away from people who tempt us to use recreational drugs or to join them in criminal acts. Our feet are handy tools God has given us for escaping. We may also think of our eyelids as instruments for escaping. Job may have employed his eyelids to help him avoid lust. See Job 31:1, and compare Matthew 5:28). Some Christians bring up alternative activities when friends or companions suggest a questionable pastime. For example, if friends recommend going to an X-rated movie, Christians can graciously suggest attending a ball game or a concert featuring wholesome music.

5. The lesson writer says the Lord's Supper "is more than just a reminder of what Christ did; it is also a renewal of our loyalty to Him." How can we best use it to accomplish this purpose?

An obvious first step is to be at the Lord's table regularly. How can we speak of loyalty to the Lord if we allow trivial matters to keep us away from His table? Once we meet at the table, we need to use well the time provided for personal meditation. We can look back over the previous week, recall moments when our deeds or words have represented disloyalty to Christ, and ask for forgiveness. We can make the Lord's Supper an occasion of pledging ourselves to faithful Christian discipleship and call it to mind during the week whenever we are tempted to disloyalty.

Dealing With Conflict

DEVOTIONAL READING: Colossians 3:8-17.

LESSON SCRIPTURE: 2 Corinthians 12, 13.

PRINTED TEXT: 2 Corinthians 12:19-21; 13:5-13.

2 Corinthians 12:19-21

19 Again, think ye that we excuse ourselves unto you? we speak before God in Christ: but we do all things, dearly beloved, for your edifying.

20 For I fear, lest, when I come, I shall not find you such as I would, and that I shall be found unto you such as ye would not: lest there be debates, envyings, wraths, strifes, backbitings, whisperings, swellings, tumults:

21 And lest, when I come again, my God will humble me among you, and that I shall bewail many which have sinned already, and have not repented of the uncleanness and fornication and lasciviousness which they have committed.

2 Corinthians 13:5-13

5 Examine yourselves, whether ye be in the faith; prove your own selves. Know ye not your own selves, how that Jesus Christ is in you, except ye be reprobates?

6 But I trust that ye shall know that we are not reprobates.

7 Now I pray to God that ye do no evil; not that we should appear approved, but that ye should do that which is honest, though we be as reprobates.

8 For we can do nothing against the truth, but for the truth.

9 For we are glad, when we are weak, and ye are strong: and this also we wish, even your perfection.

10 Therefore I write these things being absent, lest being present I should use sharpness, according to the power which the Lord hath given me to edification, and not to destruction.

11 Finally, brethren, farewell. Be perfect, be of good comfort, be of one mind, live in peace; and the God of love and peace shall be with you.

12 Greet one another with a holy kiss.

13 All the saints salute you.

GOLDEN TEXT: Be perfect, be of good comfort, be of one mind, live in peace; and the God of love and peace shall be with you.—2 Corinthians 13:11.

Lesson Aims

This lesson is designed to help the student:

1. Learn to approach conflict positively.

2. Develop good conflict management skills.

3. Desire to become a peacemaker rather than simply one who avoids conflict.

Lesson Outline

INTRODUCTION
   A. Great Church Fights
   B. Lesson Background
 I. CAUSES OF CONFLICTS (2 Corinthians 12:19-21)
   A. Defending Ourselves (v. 19)
   B. Fighting Dirty (vv. 20, 21)
     Ruinous Reactions
II. HOW TO HANDLE CONFLICTS (2 Corinthians 13:5-10)
   A. Examining Ourselves (vv. 5, 6)
     Self-Examination
   B. Praying for Others (v. 7)
   C. Telling the Truth (v. 8)
     For the Truth
   D. Seeking the Best (v. 9)
   E. Caring to Confront (v. 10)
III. HOW TO PREVENT CONFLICTS (2 Corinthians 13:11-13)
   A. Striving for Peace (v. 11)
   B. Loving the Family (vv. 12, 13)
CONCLUSION
   A. Our Peace and His Prayer
   B. Prayer
   C. Thought to Remember

Visual 4 of the visuals packet shows some of the virtues Christians should aim for in life, and some evils that should be avoided. The visual is shown on page 260.

Introduction

A. Great Church Fights

Conflict! Nobody likes it, so they say, but everyone faces it. It comes in all sizes and shapes. Like or not, we deal with it in the family, at work, and, sad to say, even in the church.

A deacon was giving a friend a tour of the church building. As he pointed out the organ and the stained glass windows, his friend always seemed to recall something nicer or more expensive in his church. Finally the deacon called attention to an old Bible displayed on the Communion table.

"That Bible is nearly two hundred years old," he noted with some pride.

Not to be outdone, his friend quickly responded, "Two hundred years old! That *is* something. But in our congregation, we have church fights older than that!"

I think I know that church. In fact, I have known congregations that have fought over everything from the translation of the Bible that should be used, to the color of the carpet. I have heard of churches where members actually came to blows, and one where a deacon pulled a gun on another man in the midst of an argument over church matters. To be honest, church conflicts generally involve only a small number of people. But even that small number can exact an awful toll on the rest.

Nobody likes conflict, perhaps with the exception of a few depraved and disturbed individuals. Because of that, most of us are much better at ignoring it than dealing with it. Learning to deal constructively with conflict can be one of the most important lessons we ever learn in life.

B. Lesson Background

Paul was no stranger to conflict. His faith was born in the midst of it. He was battling Christians when he was confronted by the Lord on the Damascus road and converted from a foe to a friend. Throughout his ministry for Christ, Paul seemed to attract opposition like a lightning rod in a thunderstorm. He was shouted at by mobs, stoned and left for dead, imprisoned, insulted, and attacked in countless ways.

No other conflict seemed to disturb Paul as much as the one he faced in Corinth. This one was in the church, and his opponents were fellow believers. The entire book of 2 Corinthians is Paul's defense and response to his critics.

Why the conflict? It was undoubtedly tied to the divisions in the congregation. The attacks on Paul were in part "turf battles" for control of the church. It was also partly theological or doctrinal, but it became very personal. Opponents said Paul wrote great letters, but was puny in appearance and contemptible in speech (10:10). Some thought it was degrading for him to work and support himself with his own hands (11:7-11).

Second Corinthians is loaded with tension and emotion as Paul seeks to deal with these problems from afar. He opens his heart, exposes his most personal motives, and calls upon those in conflict with one another and with himself to resolve the problems so the church can move on to its real business. In the process he provides some valuable lessons for anyone facing conflict.

I. Causes of Conflicts (2 Corinthians 12:19-21)

A. Defending Ourselves (v. 19)

19. Again, think ye that we excuse ourselves unto you? we speak before God in Christ: but we do all things, dearly beloved, for your edifying.

Paul's response to the critics at Corinth reveals both positive and negative factors involved in conflict. Often a major factor in unhealthy conflict is defensiveness. Paul insists that while he may have appeared to be defending himself, that was not his real interest. It was the Lord who would indict or acquit him.

Excuse was a term used in law courts, meaning to defend oneself. *Unto you* implies that the readers were in the position of a judge or jury. But they were not the jury with which Paul was concerned. Any testimony he needed to give would be offered to *God in Christ.*

His motive was to *edify* the readers. *Edify* means to build, as in constructing a house. Here it refers to strengthening or promoting the spiritual growth of others.

There is a connection between the two thoughts. When one recognizes the Lord as his judge, he can be free to serve people honestly without concern about what others think.

B. Fighting Dirty (vv. 20, 21)

20. For I fear, lest, when I come, I shall not find you such as I would, and that I shall be found unto you such as ye would not: lest there be debates, envyings, wraths, strifes, backbitings, whisperings, swellings, tumults.

What a vivid description of the alternatives to selfless edification! This is exactly what happens when conflict and differences are not handled with loving care. Minor differences become major battles. Disappointments become disagreements. Disagreements escalate into division.

Paul acknowledges the potential for such. He knows it is possible that face to face he and some of his readers may discover differences. They may not be what he expects, and he may be something less than what they desire. In itself that need not be a problem. But where that leads can become a big problem!

Paul lists eight different (count them, eight!) evils that lead to wrongful conflict.

Debates is the word for strife or quarreling. It describes expressions of conflict that lead to factions and divisions. Such strife is one of the "works of the flesh" (Galatians 5:19-21).

Envyings is akin to jealousy, the desire to have what another has rather than finding satisfaction and contentment with one's present condition.

Wraths refers to anger that suddenly flares up and boils over. It is akin to losing one's temper.

Strifes describes the kind of conflict that results in parties or competing groups.

The Greek term for *backbitings* means speaking against someone. *Whisperings* is more like what we usually mean by the word backbiting. It means denouncing someone behind his back rather than to his face.

Swellings describes the condition of one who is puffed up with pride. Such arrogance can be a cause of the attacks described in the previous terms, or it can result from believing that one has won a conflict. It is the opposite of love (1 Corinthians 13:4).

Tumults is the consequence of the previous behaviors. It is a state of disorder and confusion, or even anarchy. It is used in 1 Corinthians 14:33: "God is not the author of *confusion,* but of peace."

These eight terms describe bad conflict. While Paul doesn't say it here, the obvious solution to conflict is simply to do the opposite of the things listed here. Coming together rather than staying apart and talking to one another rather than about one another can work wonders in promoting healing and reconciliation.

RUINOUS REACTIONS

Jesus said, "Every kingdom divided against itself will be ruined" (Matthew 12:25, *New International Version*). How true this is! Francisco Pizarro, the Spanish conquistador, landed on the coast of Peru in 1531 or 1532. His whole expeditionary force consisted of only 180 men. He was faced with an empire that was well organized. For hundreds of miles across the Andes this cohesive organization held sway with a remarkable system of roads and fortifications and many warriors. Pizarro faced a daunting task.

The secret of his military conquest was that this kingdom was in the throes of an internal conflict. The reigning monarch was fighting against powerful rivals. Pizarro allied himself with these forces and utilized their familiarity with roads and mountain passes to become victorious. Then he suppressed his native helpers and became master of the nation.

What a gruesome and graphic picture of spiritual "civil war" our printed text presents! Paul lists the internal difficulties he fears he may find among his Christian brothers in Corinth. He speaks of "debates, envyings, wraths, strifes, backbitings, whisperings, swellings, tumults"

(v. 20). Alas, such disturbances are a great impediment to Christian growth and victory. We must try to replace all such disruptions with love, kindness, and works of compassion.

Suspicions, accusations, peevishness, self-pity, and snarling quarrels bring the grace and glory of Jesus' church to ruin in any place where they are numerous and long continued.

—J. G. V. B.

21. And lest, when I come again, my God will humble me among you, and that I shall bewail many which have sinned already, and have not repented of the uncleanness and fornication and lasciviousness which they have committed.

Paul is concerned that when he returns to Corinth he will find the problems of the past still unresolved. That would be humiliating to him and to those he would be forced to confront at that time. But confront he will if those guilty of known sins do not repent.

Uncleanness refers to the kinds of thinking, speech, and action that were called dirty or indecent before our society became tolerant of moral filth. *Fornication* is sexual activity between persons who ought not to indulge in such intimate behavior. *Lasciviousness* is unbridled passion or unrestrained lust. It is the vice of a person who shows no more shame than an animal in the satisfaction of its physical appetites.

A secret cause of conflict in the church is sometimes hidden guilt. Behind divisive behavior and quarreling is often an individual who wants to keep attention away from his vices. Unfortunately, a divided church can seldom bring constructive discipline to those who need it most.

II. How to Handle Conflicts (2 Corinthians 13:5-10)

In this section, Paul models five constructive attitudes and activities that can bring reconciliation out of what might otherwise be devastating conflict. Note the order in which they are presented.

A. Examining Ourselves (vv. 5, 6)

5. Examine yourselves, whether ye be in the faith; prove your own selves. Know ye not your own selves, how that Jesus Christ is in you, except ye be reprobates?

Paul is addressing his critics in the conflicts at Corinth, but one can be assured that he has addressed the same instructions to himself. Self-examination is the first step in rightly handling any conflict. What have I done to contribute to the problem? Are my motives what they ought to be? Have I been guilty of the very things I am accusing or suspecting another of doing?

visual 4

Prove also means test or examine—or it means approve after testing. *Reprobates* literally means people unproven, people who have been tested and found wanting.

SELF-EXAMINATION

We all examine ourselves in many ways, and some of us submit to special regimens of self-testing. We all look at ourselves in mirrors to see if our hair is combed, and unusual irregularities of our complexion modified. Some undergo special self-inspection, as when women check their breasts for lumps and diabetics utilize machines to detect the glucose content of their blood. These are kinds of *physical* self-examination.

Mentally we read and reflect to check our knowledge of materials we need for communication and functioning in our crafts and occupations. The farmer checks his plans for crop sequences. The businessman, the physician, the architect, the engineer, the teacher often check their recollection of what they have learned.

Paul urges us to examine ourselves spiritually to renew our awareness of Jesus' presence with us and in us. Is prayer a matter of weights or wings? Is the worship of God exciting and enthralling? Do we find challenge and change as we share with our fellow Christians? We know where we have been, but where are we *now*? Our spiritual weight and blood pressure are the true vital signs of our lives.   —J. G. V. B.

6. But I trust that ye shall know that we are not reprobates.

Paul is willing to stand on his own record. He has tested himself and is willing for his readers, including his critics, to test him. Integrity is of prime importance in dealing rightly with conflict. Double standards will not work.

B. Praying for Others (v. 7)

7. Now I pray to God that ye do no evil; not that we should appear approved, but that ye should do that which is honest, though we be as reprobates.

In the midst of conflict, it is easy to pray for "our side" to win. It is better to pray that all sides find and do God's will. Then good can come out of the battle. Samuel's farewell pledge needs affirming in every church conflict: "God forbid that I should sin against the Lord in ceasing to pray for you" (1 Samuel 12:23).

C. Telling the Truth (v. 8)

8. For we can do nothing against the truth, but for the truth.

Paul declares his devotion to the truth. He will, indeed can, do nothing but stand for the truth. If that creates a problem, then there will be a problem. But he will cling to truth.

How people conduct themselves in the face of conflict reveals much about their character. The temptation is to "fight fire with fire." Such a practice may double the damage.

FOR THE TRUTH

Paul asserts, "We can do nothing against the truth, but for the truth." Weymouth translates this, "For we have no power against the truth, but only for the truth."

In 1843, in Lexington, Kentucky, Alexander Campbell and Nathan L. Rice engaged in several days of debate. They considered the action, subjects, and purpose of Christian baptism, the function of creeds in the church, and the nature and activity of the Holy Spirit. In the course of this discussion, Mr. Campbell said some things about truth that are beautiful and powerful and very pertinent to the apostle Paul's words in our text today.

"Truth, my friends, holy truth, stands upon the Rock of Ages. It lifts its head above the clouds—above the stars. . . . Its days are the years of God. Embodied in the Word of God, it came down from heaven and became incarnate. It is, therefore, immortal, and cannot be killed. It will survive all its foes, and stand erect when every idol falls. . . . It needs no fleshly wisdom, nor worldly policy, to give it power or gain it victory. It is itself redeeming, soul-redeeming, and disenthralling. . . . Light and fire, earth's purest elements, are but the shadows of its glory. The tongues of lambent flame that sat upon the heads of the apostles, were but indicative of its irradiating and consuming potency. But its language is that of love, of purity, and of peace."

In his poem "The Battle-Field," William Cullen Bryant has a stanza that is expressive of the attitude toward truth that Paul exhibits and that Campbell's words exemplify:

> Truth, crushed to earth, shall rise again;
>   The eternal years of God are hers;
> But Error, wounded, writhes in pain,
>   And dies among his worshippers.

—J. G. V. B.

D. Seeking the Best (v. 9)

9. For we are glad, when we are weak, and ye are strong: and this also we wish, even your perfection.

Wishing the best for our adversaries is never easy. But it is right. And it is Christian. Jesus taught us to "do good to them that hate you, and pray for them which despitefully use you, and persecute you" (Matthew 5:44). Paul recommends the advice found in Proverbs: "Therefore if thine enemy hunger, feed him; if he thirst, give him drink: for in so doing thou shalt heap coals of fire on his head. Be not overcome of evil, but overcome evil with good" (Romans 12:20, 21; Proverbs 25:21, 22).

Perfection is from a word that means to make fit or complete. It was used in the sense of setting bones or reconciling parties. A form of the same word was used of the fishermen "mending" their nets (Matthew 4:21). Paul used the same word to speak of "restoring" a brother in difficulty (Galatians 6:1). Paul was wishing for the Corinthians to repair the damage done by their quarreling and to become completely fitted for Christian living and service.

E. Caring to Confront (v. 10)

10. Therefore I write these things being absent, lest being present I should use sharpness, according to the power which the Lord hath given me to edification, and not to destruction.

Paul was writing these things in the hope that the Corinthians would correct what was wrong and would resolve their conflicts so he would not have to speak sharply later, when he would be *present* in Corinth. He preferred to avoid confrontation, but confrontation was better than letting the conflicts continue and grow.

As an apostle, Paul had been given special power; but it was intended for *edification*, building up, not *destruction*, tearing down. He was writing to build faith and right living and harmony in the church. Later he would be in Corinth and would speak with the same purpose. For that purpose he would speak a sharp rebuke if necessary, but he hoped he could speak praise instead.

Most of us will go out of our way to avoid confrontation. Lacking Paul's gift of special inspiration, we have the more reason to avoid sharpness if we can, to speak with Christian humility and respect for our brethren. But talking about opponents behind their backs adds fuel to a smoldering fire. If we really want reconciliation and peace, we may find that nothing works better than talking face to face with those who differ with us.

No one has ever proposed a better method for dealing with conflict than that outlined by Jesus in Matthew 18:15-20. It is amazing to see how rarely Christians follow these directives.

III. How to Prevent Conflicts (2 Corinthians 13:11-13)

A. Striving for Peace (v. 11)

11. Finally, brethren, farewell. Be perfect, be of good comfort, be of one mind, live in peace; and the God of love and peace shall be with you.

Paul's final appeal is for his readers to develop in their lives the qualities that contribute to peace and harmony. He issues five commands and then concludes with a promise.

Farewell is the rendering in the *King James Version,* but the Greek word is literally the imperative of a verb meaning *rejoice.* While it may be used as a simple parting salutation, it may also be understood as a command like the four that follow. If Paul meant it in that way, it is a call to turn attention to the positive, the joyous, and the blessed. The more we dwell on problems, the bigger they appear.

The second command, *be perfect,* is easily misunderstood. The term is not the usual word meaning complete or free of defect. Rather, the word is the same as in verse 9. It means to be fitted, mended, or restored.

Be of good comfort means to be encouraged or consoled. Forms of this word are used several times in 2 Corinthians (1:3, 4, 5, 6, 7; 7:4, 7, 13).

Be of one mind literally means to think the same thing. It calls for being harmonious and unified in word and deed as well as thought.

The fifth command, *live in peace,* calls for an end of quarreling. That does not mean there may be no differences of opinion; it means that Christians with minor differences work together harmoniously and happily.

B. Loving the Family (vv. 12, 13)

12. Greet one another with a holy kiss.

The kiss of greeting was a part of Mediterranean culture, akin to a hearty handshake or a warm hug in American society. But the Christian kiss was not just a social formality. It was *holy,* different, set apart. It was an expression of Christian oneness and solidarity.

13. All the saints salute you.

Paul reminds his readers that they are part of a larger Christian community. Who they are and how they behave matters to others beyond their own borders. People we will never meet and never know by name have a stake in the peace and harmony of our fellowship.

Conclusion

A. Our Peace and His Prayer

Conflict is a natural part of human experience, even in the church. In fact, conflict can be a sign of health. It shows that people are close enough and care enough to take a stand. Sometimes what appears to be harmony is really apathy. It results because people are too far apart to come into contact, much less conflict. But conflict can destroy health unless it is well managed. It is important for all of us to deal with conflict in a way that will glorify the Lord and edify His people.

Dealing with conflict matters, because our relationships in the church matter. Jesus said, "By this shall all men know that ye are my disciples, if ye have love one to another" (John 13:35). He prayed that believers in Him will all be one, one in Him and the Father, so the world will believe that the Father sent Him (John 17:21).

Restoring peace out of the midst of conflict is an answer to the Master's prayer!

B. Prayer

Lord, there is so much conflict in the world, too much! I pray that I may be part of Your solution and not one of the causes of conflict. Give me the grace to work for peace with those with whom I come into conflict. Lord, make me a peacemaker. In Jesus' name, amen.

C. Thought to Remember

Peacemaking is hard work. It is dangerous work. It forces us to become involved in other people's problems. But most of all it makes us deal with our own shortcomings.

Home Daily Bible Readings

Monday, Mar. 20—Confronting Opponents in the Church (2 Corinthians 10:1-12)

Tuesday, Mar. 21—Boast Only of the Lord (2 Corinthians 10:13-18)

Wednesday, Mar. 22—Refuting False Charges With the Truth (2 Corinthians 11:7-15)

Thursday, Mar. 23—Strength in Weakness (2 Corinthians 12:1-10)

Friday, Mar. 24—Paul Justifies His Actions (2 Corinthians 12:11-18)

Saturday, Mar. 25—Admonition to End the Dissension (2 Corinthians 12:19—13:4)

Sunday, Mar. 26—Live in Peace With One Another (2 Corinthians 13:5-13)

Learning by Doing

*This page contains an alternate lesson plan emphasizing learning activities. Classes
desiring such student involvement will find these suggestions helpful.*

Learning Goals

As a result of this lesson, students will:

1. Learn positive ways of dealing with conflict.

2. Be able to identify some of the underlying causes for conflict in the church.

3. Be able to become peacemakers in times of conflict within the church and family.

Into the Lesson

Call the attention of the class to the incomplete statements below. (They are in the student book, or you can put them on a flip chart or board.) Ask each student to complete the sentences and to share responses with two or three people seated near by.

1. I usually deal with conflict by—
2. People get in conflict because—
3. The best way to deal with conflict is—

Into the Word

Make the transition into the Bible study by pointing out that conflict is inevitable even in the church. Paul sent the church at Corinth a letter that had conflict as its main point. (Share further background information as you think best.) On the board make two columns. Label one *Conflict* and the other *Alternative*. (The exercise is in the student book as well.) Direct attention to 2 Corinthians 12:20. Ask the class to find eight expressions of conflicting behavior or attitudes that Paul mentions and list them in the first column. For each of these, ask students to think of a behavior or attitude that would be less conflicting. List those in the column labeled *Alternative*. (Some possible answers: debates-discussion; envyings-rejoicing; wraths-calm disagreement; strifes-unity; backbitings-complimenting; whisperings-silence; swellings-humility; tumults-stability.) Use the lesson commentary to explain the meaning of words that are unfamiliar to the class; for example, swellings.

Looking at verses 20 and 21, ask the class what Paul was concerned about and why he delineated the shortcomings in such detail. (Paul was afraid he would come to Corinth and find the problems unresolved. Then he would be forced to confront those who were doing wrong. By writing the letter he gave them opportunity to correct their attitude and behavior before his arrival. If he would come and find that no correction had been made, he would feel humiliated and grieved.) For an interesting discussion ask this question: How far do you think Paul would go to avoid direct confrontation? (Opinions may vary, but it is wise to point out that Paul did not back away from correcting Christian brothers face to face if they did not heed his letters.) Call attention to the fact that the sins mentioned in verse 21 all involve inappropriate sexual behavior or attitudes. In pagan Corinth, sexual immorality was considered normal and even had a part in some religious observances. Many of the Christians had been pagans, and some were slow to give up their immoral ways. Probably some church members tried to turn attention away from their own wrongdoing by being unduly critical of others. This contributed to the conflict in the church, the conflict that was so distressing to Paul.

On the board or a flip chart draw five steps. Tell the class that 2 Corinthians 13:5-10 suggests five constructive attitudes and activities that can bring about reconciliation instead of conflict. Write a descriptive phrase on each step as the class calls out suggestions based on these verses. (Suggestions: examine yourself, 13:5; pray for others, 13:7; be truthful, 13:8; wish your adversary well, 13:9; become mature, 13:9.)

Show that Paul was aware of the possibility of hurting people. Have someone read verse 10 aloud. Ask how Paul might be hurtful. Observe that God wants us to edify one another and not destroy one another when we have conflict. Explain that we need to be a construction crew and not a wrecking gang.

Into Life

Divide the class into two parts. Make a copy of the case history below for each group. Assign one group to deal with the situation negatively, as the church at Corinth was doing. Have the other group deal with it as Paul advocated. Allow five or ten minutes, then let the groups share their responses.

John, Henry, and several other elders believed that the minister should resign for the good of the church. They began talking to other influential people, and soon the church was buzzing and quarreling. Some concerned friends talked to the minister personally, but he adamantly refused to resign. How could the case have been handled?

Let's Talk It Over

The questions on this page are designed to encourage review of the lesson Scriptures and to promote discussion of the lesson by the class. The answers provided are only discussion starters. Let your class talk it over from there.

1. Why should we find it comforting to read in the New Testament about a church torn by conflicts as the Corinthian church was?

Here was a church to which Paul and Apollos had ministered, a church in which Peter also had wielded some influence (1 Corinthians 1:12). And yet it experienced an array of problems that went far beyond many of our church squabbles today. We are embarrassed and distressed when a major conflict arises in our church, but what happened at Corinth reminds us that even with spiritually mature, well-qualified leaders, even with a membership that has received excellent teaching, conflict can still take place. It is also comforting to note that, in spite of all its problems, Paul was not about to give up on the church at Corinth. We can conclude from this that our church also, whatever its failings, faults, and friction, is still precious to God and worthy of our continued faithfulness.

2. Without doubt, some of the conflicts within any church result from jealousy over different offices and roles within the church. How can we deal with this problem of jealousy?

We can teach that in the church everyone should be working for the glory of God, and that no member should perform his or her tasks for the purpose of receiving human praise. And yet we know that Christians are fallible human beings who can be hurt or offended if their efforts are not recognized. Jealousy and conflict result when one member sees others being applauded while his contributions are seemingly taken for granted. All of this should serve as a reminder of how important it is that members of the church make it a habit to thank one another for the singing of a solo, the teaching of a lesson, the preparation of Communion, service in the nursery, distribution of bulletins, and the countless other tasks that someone must do.

3. The terms "backbitings" and "whisperings" call to mind the tendency of some church members to engage in uncharitable criticism of the labors of other members. How can we deal with this tendency?

It is easy to criticize, and it makes us feel we are contributing something when we decry the inadequate efforts of others. But critics seldom offer any positive alternatives for the people whose labor they criticize. We must strongly urge church members to refrain from criticism that is not constructive, and from criticism that is not offered in love. Here is one aspect of the Christian life in which the diligent practice of the Golden Rule (Matthew 7:12) would bring about some very positive changes.

4. Why is the habit of self-examination one that Christians should cultivate carefully?

We all are acquainted with people who are too introspective. They fret over their words and deeds and the impressions they make on others. Some of them paralyze themselves into inaction. This certainly is not the healthy kind of self-examination Paul urged in 2 Corinthians 13:5. We do need to monitor our motives to keep track of our growth in the habit of doing everything in love (1 Corinthians 16:14, *New International Version*). It is also important to review our words and deeds, not to stop them if they are inadequate, but to improve them—and to seek forgiveness for any that have been sinful. As for the impressions we make on others, we must learn to be less concerned about the impression they have of us, and more concerned about the impression they have of Christ.

5. What are some ways in which prayer can help us overcome or resolve conflict?

In connection with the previous question, we can note that prayer is closely related to healthy self-examination. When we perceive that our motives or attitudes or habits are leading us into unnecessary conflict with a fellow church member, we can pray for God's help in correcting our shortcoming. If we are in the habit of praying for our brothers and sisters in Christ, we may also see attitudes and practices they exhibit which contribute to conflict in the church. We should prepare ourselves thoroughly with prayer before humbly approaching them in regard to these sensitive matters (see Galatians 6:1). It may also be noted that when we are investing prayer time and effort in a fellow believer's life, we are less likely to be inclined toward conflict with him or her. So the biblical exhortation to "pray one for another" (James 5:16) should be taken quite seriously.

Building Up the Body

DEVOTIONAL READING: Ephesians 4:4-16.

LESSON SCRIPTURE: 1 Corinthians 12.

PRINTED TEXT: 1 Corinthians 12:4-20, 26.

1 Corinthians 12:4-20, 26

4 Now there are diversities of gifts, but the same Spirit.

5 And there are differences of administrations, but the same Lord.

6 And there are diversities of operations, but it is the same God which worketh all in all.

7 But the manifestation of the Spirit is given to every man to profit withal.

8 For to one is given by the Spirit the word of wisdom; to another the word of knowledge by the same Spirit;

9 To another faith by the same Spirit; to another the gifts of healing by the same Spirit;

10 To another the working of miracles; to another prophecy; to another discerning of spirits; to another divers kinds of tongues; to another the interpretation of tongues:

11 But all these worketh that one and the selfsame Spirit, dividing to every man severally as he will.

12 For as the body is one, and hath many members and all the members of that one body, being many, are one body: so also is Christ.

13 For by one Spirit are we all baptized into one body, whether we be Jews or Gentiles, whether we be bond or free; and have been all made to drink into one Spirit.

14 For the body is not one member, but many.

15 If the foot shall say, Because I am not the hand, I am not of the body; is it therefore not of the body?

16 And if the ear shall say, Because I am not the eye, I am not of the body; is it therefore not of the body?

17 If the whole body were an eye, where were the hearing? If the whole were hearing, where were the smelling?

18 But now hath God set the members every one of them in the body, as it hath pleased him.

19 And if they were all one member, where were the body?

20 But now are they many members, yet but one body.

· · · · · · · · · · · · ·

26 And whether one member suffer, all the members suffer with it; or one member be honored, all the members rejoice with it.

GOLDEN TEXT: The manifestation of the Spirit is given to every man to profit withal.
—1 Corinthians 12:7.

Christians Living in Community
Unit 2. Nurturing the Life of the Community (Lessons 5-9)

Lesson Aims

After this lesson, the students should:

1. Be able to explain why we Christians do not all have the same gifts and abilities.

2. Have some understanding of the special spiritual gifts used in the early church.

3. See the value in their own gifts and abilities without envying those of others.

Lesson Outline

INTRODUCTION
  A. To Be a Star
  B. Lesson Background
 I. OUR DIVERSITY OF GIFTS (1 Corinthians 12:4-11)
  A. God's Manner of Distribution (vv. 4-7)
      Ants and the Church
  B. Examples of Spiritual Gifts (vv. 8-10)
      Life Manifested
  C. The Master Plan (v. 11)
 II. OUR UNITY AS A BODY (1 Corinthians 12:12, 13)
  A. Through Our Common Faith in Christ (v. 12)
  B. Through Our Common Experience With God's Spirit (v. 13)
III. OUR NEED FOR DIVERSITY AND UNITY (1 Corinthians 12:14-20, 26)
  A. For the Benefit of the Church (vv. 14-17)
  B. For the Glory of God (vv. 18-20)
  C. For the Encouragement of Each Member (v. 26)
CONCLUSION
  A. You Can Have It Both Ways
  B. Prayer
  C. Thought to Remember

Visual 5 of the visuals packet helps us to see why the participation of every member is important to the life of the church. The visual is shown on page 268.

Introduction

A. To Be a Star

My young cousin is a fan of Michael Jordan, the star basketball player. The walls of his bedroom are covered with Michael Jordan posters. He quotes statistics of Jordan's performance.

My cousin is not alone. Michael Jordan has become a worldwide, multimillion-dollar phenomenon. The response of our youth is more than just appreciation for a good performance. There is also a burning desire to play as well as Jordan.

It is not bad to want to improve your performance in any endeavor. But it is unhealthy to despise your own abilities because they do not match the abilities of someone else. In the church, each one should be able to appreciate the value of his or her own distinctive contribution to the life and ministry of the congregation.

B. Lesson Background

The church in Corinth apparently was beset with a problem of jealousy. If we read between the lines in 1 Corinthians 14, it seems evident that there was a widespread feeling within the congregation that speaking in tongues was the best spiritual gift a person could have. This idea resulted in a common desire for this gift, a feeling of superiority in tongues-speakers, and jealousy in others.

The apostle Paul responds to this problem with three lines of reasoning. In chapter 13 he argues that the attitude of love is more to be desired than any spiritual gift. In chapter 14 he argues that prophesying is more beneficial to the church than speaking in tongues. But laying the groundwork for these two arguments is chapter 12. Here Paul explains that a Christian should treasure and use whatever spiritual gift he or she has received from God, even if it is not speaking in tongues.

I. Our Diversity of Gifts
(1 Corinthians 12:4-11)

"Variety is the spice of life," we often say. Paul contends that a variety of spiritual gifts within a congregation is good for the church.

A. God's Manner of Distribution
(vv. 4-7)

4. Now there are diversities of gifts, but the same Spirit.

The Corinthians did not need to be told that Christians do not all have the same spiritual gifts. They knew this, and some did not like it. Paul is emphasizing that variety in spiritual gifts is right and proper. The Holy Spirit is not only the source of spiritual gifts, but also the source of the diversity of gifts.

5. And there are differences of administrations, but the same Lord.

A common literary device of Jewish literature is parallelism, in which a statement is immediately repeated in different words. Paul uses parallelism when he repeats the idea of "diversities of gifts" (v. 4) by using the phrase *differences of administrations.*

Parallelism gives emphasis to an idea. Paul uses a third parallel sentence in the next verse, and this suggests that the Corinthian problem required an exceptionally strong emphasis upon the validity of diversity in spiritual gifts.

6. And there are diversities of operations, but it is the same God which worketh all in all.

The triple parallel begun in verse 4 is completed with the phrase *diversities of operations.* The source of spiritual gifts is identified in verse 4 as the Holy Spirit, in verse 5 as the Lord (Jesus Christ), and in verse 6 as God (the Father). Similar linking of the Father, Son, and Spirit is seen in other New Testament passages such as Matthew 28:19 and 2 Corinthians 13:14. This supports the idea that there are three divine persons who live and work in perfect harmony as one God.

ANTS AND THE CHURCH

Some of the most unusual creatures in our world are those we call ants. Entomologists tell us some forty-five hundred species of ants have been identified. Ants always live in groups or colonies, so they are designated as social insects. Most species have groups called workers. These gather food, care for the young, and defend the colony. All eggs are laid by the queen, who makes this her sole occupation. Some species collect seeds of grain, which specialized ants with enlarged jaws crack for the other ants to eat.

Ants are mentioned twice in the Bible—in Proverbs 6:6-8 and 30:25. They are commended for their activity and for their provision for the future. One phrase in Proverbs 6:6 is apropos: "Consider her ways, and be wise."

Christians are social creatures too. As soon as the terms of pardon through Jesus' death and resurrection were proclaimed and people responded, they were gathered in a church. Our Christian faith expresses itself in the various functions that Jesus' disciples perform as members of this "colony of Heaven." So Paul says in verse 6 of our printed text, "There are different kinds of working, but the same God works all of them in all men" (*New International Version*). Just as ants are created by God to function in specific ways in the colony, so His Spirit enables Christians to function variously to accomplish His will through the church.   —J. G. V. B.

7. But the manifestation of the Spirit is given to every man to profit withal.

Paul's emphasis here is that spiritual gifts are intended to be used in ways that benefit others (*to profit withal*). This is a theme that is more fully developed in chapter 14.

Several spiritual gifts are named in the following verses. Many of us believe that these fulfilled their purpose in the infancy of the church, and therefore they are not needed by the church today. The following commentary will not only describe the nature of these gifts, but also point out why they are no longer necessary.

B. Examples of Spiritual Gifts
(vv. 8-10)

8. For to one is given by the Spirit the word of wisdom; to another the word of knowledge by the same Spirit.

This verse illustrates one of the difficulties we have in trying to understand Paul's teaching regarding spiritual gifts. Paul does not explain what each one of these gifts enabled a person to do. For those gifts that are not explained elsewhere in the New Testament, the best we can do is use the names themselves and devise a reasonable *guess* regarding the nature of each gift.

The *word of wisdom* may be an increase in one's ability to make wise and reasonable judgments. Many students connect this passage to James 1:5, which says, "If any of you lack wisdom, let him ask of God, that giveth to all men liberally." However, James seems to be referring to a blessing that is available to anyone who asks, while the spiritual gifts of 1 Corinthians 12 are distributed at the Spirit's will (v. 11)

It seems more likely that *word of wisdom* refers to an ability to receive some type of revelation from God. Revelation gifts were not uncommon in the early years of the church before the writing of the New Testament (Acts 2:17, 18; 11:27, 28; 13:1; 15:32; 21:8-10). Select individuals in the churches were used by the Holy Spirit to relay to their congregations whatever information God chose to give (1 Corinthians 14:29-31). It is reasonable to conclude that this method of divine guidance was used until the writings of the New Testament became available to the churches. Since that time, those writings provide all the inspired direction that mankind needs (2 Timothy 3:16, 17).

The *word of knowledge* sounds similar to the *word of wisdom.* It is grouped together with "revelation" and "prophesying" in 1 Corinthians 14:6 and with "prophecy" in 1 Corinthians 13:2. Without identifying the difference between the gifts of *wisdom* and *knowledge,* we conclude that both had to do with revelation.

9. To another faith by the same Spirit; to another the gifts of healing by the same Spirit.

visual 5

All Christians have faith in Christ. Apparently *faith* here means something else, a special gift given to some Christians, not all of them. The clue to identifying this gift of faith may be in 1 Corinthians 13:2: "Though I have all faith, so that I could remove mountains." The gift of faith may be the ability to perform miracles with nature, such as Jesus did when He changed water to wine, walked on the sea, and destroyed a fruitless tree. The disciples may have given this name to nature miracles because Jesus said anyone with a little faith would be able to move a mountain (Matthew 17:20).

Gifts of healing obviously refers to the ability to heal sickness, disease, or injury, and do it instantly. This divine power was often shown by Jesus and His apostles, as recorded in the four Gospels and the book of Acts. Apparently it was made available to select members of the early church. The plural *gifts* may be used because many kinds of sickness were healed.

Both nature miracles and healing miracles were used to show that the miracle workers were spokesmen for God, and thus to confirm the message they gave (Mark 16:20; Acts 8:6; Hebrews 2:3, 4). Such confirmation was needed in the early days of the church. Christians were presenting a new revelation from God, the New Covenant of Jesus Christ; but they did not yet have the written documentation. Miracles established the credibility of the Christian message. Soon that message was recorded in the New Testament. It seems reasonable to conclude that there was no need either of further revelation or of miracles in confirmation.

10. To another the working of miracles; to another prophecy; to another discerning of spirits; to another divers kinds of tongues; to another the interpretation of tongues.

Working of miracles obviously means an ability to perform some type of supernatural action, but it does not indicate what activity in particular.

In the Greek text the phrase *working of miracles* uses the word *dunamis* (power). Since this phrase immediately follows the references to nature miracles (*faith*) and healing miracles, it is likely that *working of miracles* refers to something

similar, a miraculous feat that impresses observers with its power. It was probably another gift for confirmation of the Christian message.

The gift of *prophecy* is the ability and privilege of receiving direct revelation from God, with the duty of passing on the message received. Obviously it is similar to the word of wisdom and the word of knowledge; how it differs from them is not readily apparent.

Discerning of spirits probably is an ability to perceive something in the spiritual realm that is not usually observable. This could be an ability to recognize a false prophet or false teacher. Falsehood usually was exposed by comparing new ideas to the established teaching of the Old Testament and the apostles (2 Timothy 3:14-17; 1 John 4:1-3), but possibly this gift enabled a person to detect error immediately.

Another possibility is that *discerning of spirits* means an ability to know of a demon's presence. Without this gift a person could identify a demon-possessed individual by observing his behavior over a period of time, but with the gift he could instantly recognize a demon and drive him away (Mark 16:17, 20).

The gift of *divers kinds of tongues* is what we commonly refer to as "speaking in tongues." It is clear that this sometimes means an ability to speak in languages unknown to the speaker. Acts 2:4-11 lists fifteen languages spoken by the apostles when they spoke in tongues. It is possible that there was also a second category of the gift of *tongues*, that involved strange nonhuman sounds, but this has not been clearly demonstrated with a New Testament reference. The tongue that "no man understandeth" (1 Corinthians 14:2) could be a real human language unknown to anyone who was there. The reference in 1 Corinthians 13:1 to "the tongues of men and of angels" indicates that angels speak, but it does not indicate what kind of language they speak. Neither does it say that Paul actually did speak in their language. For our study it will be more profitable to focus on the gift of tongues that we know existed in the beginning of the church, rather than to deal with that about which we can only guess.

The ability to speak a foreign language instantaneously, without a period of study, probably was used by some other evangelists as it was used by the apostles. The apostles used their fifteen tongues on Pentecost to get the attention of the temple crowd and show that something unusual was going on. Peter explained that the Holy Spirit brought this gift of tongues (Acts 2:14-18). Then the preaching of the gospel message was done by a single voice in a common language (Acts 2:22-40).

The gift of *interpretation of tongues* probably is the ability to instantaneously translate something spoken in an unfamiliar language. Obviously this could be used along with speaking in tongues to convey the message to people who did not understand the languages being spoken. Both these gifts could be useful in a coastal city like Corinth, where people of many nations mingled—commercial travelers, sailors, pleasure seekers on vacation, worshipers at pagan shrines.

LIFE MANIFESTED

A principle of life is characteristic of much that we observe in our world. We hold in our hand an acorn. It does not seem much different from a brown marble. Yet within the acorn is a reality that the marble does not possess. If the hard acorn is placed in moist, warm soil, it gradually will soften, then break open. A tiny plant will emerge. Given sufficient time it will, on one end, climb through the dark soil up to light and air and sunshine. The other end will plunge deeper as roots, groping for the chemicals and nutrients it needs to sustain its life. Eventually there will be a little tree, and finally a great, stalwart oak. The life force will be made manifest.

When we become new creations in Jesus, the Spirit of life is placed within us. If we nurture our existence in Him, this Spirit will be made manifest. It will be expressed as the life in the acorn is expressed in the oak. The various gifts of the Spirit will appear as words of wisdom, words of knowledge, or faith (vv. 8, 9). This is the manifestation or outward evidence of the inner Spirit.   —J. G. V. B.

C. The Master Plan (v. 11)

11. But all these worketh that one and the selfsame Spirit, dividing to every man severally as he will.

Paul brings his emphasis on the diversity of spiritual gifts to a grand conclusion. The selective distribution of spiritual gifts among the members of a congregation is not an unfortunate accident. It is a vital part of God's design. The Holy Spirit uses His wise judgment to spread the gifts throughout the church as He deems appropriate. We should not crave someone else's gift and let our own be unused. That would upset the balance intended by God.

This lesson can be readily applied to our modern-day church. We have little need for the gifts of revelation and confirmation that abounded in the first century, but we still profit from a host of nonmiraculous gifts. Some of them are named in Romans 12:6-8. These enable us to carry on the church's mission of evangelism and spiritual growth. Paul's principle of diversity in distribution is still applicable.

II. Our Unity as a Body (1 Corinthians 12:12, 13)

"Let not thy left hand know what thy right hand doeth" (Matthew 6:3). That is a hyperbole advising secret generosity; it is not literal advice for all the movements of a person. Neither does it state God's design for the church. Paul presents the concept of a body with all the parts working together in harmony for the good of the whole.

A. Through Our Common Faith in Christ (v. 12)

12. For as the body is one, and hath many members and all the members of that one body, being many, are one body: so also is Christ.

In faith we commit ourselves to Jesus Christ. This establishes a relationship not only with Him, but also with others who have made a similar commitment. Just as the brain in a human body is the common point of reference for all the parts of that body, Christ is a significant point of contact for all believers.

B. Through Our Common Experience With God's Spirit (v. 13)

13. For by one Spirit are we all baptized into one body, whether we be Jews or Gentiles, whether we be bond or free; and have been all made to drink into one Spirit.

The unity of Christians is evident not only in our commitment to the same Lord, but also in our common relationship with the Holy Spirit. All of us enjoy the Spirit's presence within our

Home Daily Bible Readings

Monday, Mar. 27—Spiritual Gifts Given by God (1 Corinthians 12:1-6)

Tuesday, Mar. 28—Gifts Are for the Common Good (1 Corinthians 12:7-11)

Wednesday, Mar. 29—Many Members, One Body (1 Corinthians 12:12-20)

Thursday, Mar. 30—Members Need One Another (1 Corinthians 12:21-26)

Friday, Mar. 31—The Church Is Christ's Body (1 Corinthians 12:27-31)

Saturday, Apr. 1—Live in Unity of Faith (Ephesians 4:1-7)

Sunday, Apr. 2—Build Up the Body of Christ (Ephesians 4:11-16)

hearts as He gives us new life and helps us to fight off temptation, lust, and sinfulness (Romans 8:11-13; 1 Thessalonians 4:3-8). An awareness of this shared blessing attracts us to each other.

This verse also reminds us of the significance of baptism. Not only does it provide the occasion for the Holy Spirit to begin His sanctifying work in our lives (Acts 2:38); it also is a means by which the Holy Spirit incorporates the individual into the fellowship of the saints. Our shared experience of baptism should break down all barriers and foster a spirit of unity.

III. Our Need for Diversity and Unity (1 Corinthians 12:14-20, 26)

"Opposites attract," we often say regarding romantic relationships. Whether that is true or not, we can see that Paul is leading us to the conclusion that it is good for the church to have diversity in the midst of its unity.

A. For the Benefit of the Church (vv. 14-17)

14. For the body is not one member, but many.

Paul returns to his earlier emphasis on variety in a human body and in the church.

15, 16. If the foot shall say, Because I am not the hand, I am not of the body; is it therefore not of the body? And if the ear shall say, Because I am not the eye, I am not of the body; is it therefore not of the body?

Of course body parts do not have the intellectual capacity to be jealous of one another. But this humorous picture well illustrates the jealousy that sometimes arises in the church over other people's gifts and abilities.

17. If the whole body were an eye, where were the hearing? If the whole were hearing, where were the smelling?

What an apt illustration of the way a church can become unbalanced if everyone seeks the same gifts! No one in his right mind wishes that all the parts of his physical body would perform the same function. If every body part were designed for vision, we would miss out on sounds, smells, tastes, and touch, not to mention the threat to continued existence when the internal organs would cease their normal functions and switch to vision. A healthy body requires diversity of functions.

B. For the Glory of God (vv. 18-20)

18. But now hath God set the members every one of them in the body, as it hath pleased him.

Dissatisfaction with the distribution of gifts is in effect a criticism of God's judgment, whether it is intended or not. We will do well to gladly accept whatever gifts and abilities God has graciously given us, and to use them for His service and glory.

19, 20. And if they were all one member, where were the body? But now are they many members, yet but one body.

Paul repeats his argument from verses 14-17, concluding with praise for diversity *and* unity.

C. For the Encouragement of Each Member (v. 26)

26. And whether one member suffer, all the members suffer with it; or one member be honored, all the members rejoice with it.

Try this experiment: smash your thumb with a hammer and see if only the thumb experiences feelings of pain and discomfort. Actually, none of us needs to perform this silly experiment, because we know from experience that a hurt in one part of the body is felt throughout the body.

This is the way it should be within the church. There should be such a union of purpose and love that we feel bonded to one another, that we care for one another, even to the point of sharing one another's sorrow and gladness. When this type of sympathy begins to occur naturally in a church, that is an indication that those Christians are beginning to achieve the balance between diversity and unity that Paul commended.

Conclusion

A. You Can Have It Both Ways

Some things in life are so different that you have to choose between the options. As we often say, "You can't have it both ways." But unity and diversity are not opposites of which one must exclude the other. As a musical quartet illustrates, diversity does not preclude harmony. Likewise, unity does not require an equal distribution of gifts and a strict conformity in activity. For a healthy church, diversity and unity are not opposites but complements of each other.

B. Prayer

Father, help us to properly value and use our own gifts and abilities while allowing others to do the same without any jealousy or interference from us.

C. Thought to Remember

As we learn to appreciate the beauty and worth of the variety of gifts and abilities within the church, we enable ourselves to enjoy more fully the unity that is possible among co-laborers for the Lord.

Learning by Doing

This page contains an alternate lesson plan emphasizing learning activities. Classes desiring such student involvement will find these suggestions helpful.

Learning Goals

Through today's lesson, the pupils will:

1. Understand the significance of spiritual gifts in the church.

2. Be able to contrast healthy and unhealthy views of the gifts others possess.

3. Desire to know their spiritual gifts.

Into the Lesson

Write these questions on the board before the class arrives: What was the best gift you ever received? What made it so very special to you? When the class arrives use the neighbor nudge. Have each student share the answers to the questions with a nearby neighbor. Bring the class together again by saying that it is often the giver of the gift that makes it so special to the recipient. (Be sure to share your own gift and why it was special to you.) Explain that the church at Corinth was experiencing disunity because members were focusing on the gifts instead of the Giver.

Into the Word

The apostle Paul approached the situation by calling the church's attention to the source of the diversity of gifts. Direct the students to 1 Corinthians 12:4-11 and ask them to be looking for the answer to this question: Whose idea was it to give such a diversity of gifts to the church? Have someone read the verses aloud. After the class has responded, explain that Paul's intent was to help the church focus on the fact that it was God's plan to meet the needs of the church by gifting its members with things that would be encouraging and build up the Body.

However, God's intent was being frustrated by the people in the church who had wrong attitudes. Give each student a copy of the word search below. (It is also in the student quarterly.)

```
o  z  k  c  o  v  e  t  o  u  s
p  r  a  s  t  u  n  p  p  c  t
i  y  r  y  a  c  v  e  r  f  f
w  s  x  m  e  o  y  k  i  b  i
a  u  l  j  g  e  o  l  d  o  g
b  o  g  g  e  l  y  o  e  r  d
s  l  d  i  v  e  r  s  i  t  y
h  a  r  m  o  n  y  s  o  o  n
t  e  a  s  l  d  s  a  t  p  p
q  j  o  k  e  i  s  o  n  y  u
```

Instruct them to find four words that describe what Paul desired for the church (diversity, harmony, love, gifts) and four words that describe negative attitudes that can threaten unity (covetous, envy, jealousy, pride).

After allowing time for individuals to complete the word search, share the answers and then go into the lesson background about what was going on at Corinth.

Continue the Scripture development, using the questions below as you interact with the students. Give specific verses to help them find answers.

1. What spiritual gifts are listed in verses 8-10? (Elaborate on the meaning of each.)

2. Who decides which gift or gifts a Christian receives? (v. 11—the Holy Spirit.)

3. Do you see a need for these gifts in today's church? (Explain why the early church definitely needed them. See the lesson commentary, especially on verse 9.)

4. What action brings us into the body of the church and brings to us the Holy Spirit and His gifts? (v. 13).

5. How are the members of the church like the parts of a human body? (vv. 14-20. They have different abilities to be used to the good of all.)

Into Life

Pass out construction paper and crayons. Ask each student to picture the part of the body that he or she is. For example, explain that you might be represented by a mouth because you are the teacher—but a mouth can also represent someone who invites others to come to church. One who is a good listener may draw a huge ear; one who works in the kitchen may draw a hand; one who does much calling may draw a foot. Allow a few minutes for thinking and drawing, then ask students to hold up their papers and to look around the class at the papers of others. While they are doing this, draw a huge stick figure on the board. Check off the body parts that are illustrated by students' drawings.

Probably some cannot so quickly draw appropriate pictures. Tell them that does not mean they are any less important. Liver and spleen and sweat glands are not easily pictured, but the body needs every one of its parts. Each one of us can do something in the work of the church.

Close with a prayer of gratitude for the body of Christ as it is represented in your class.

Let's Talk It Over

The questions on this page are designed to encourage review of the lesson Scriptures and to promote discussion of the lesson by the class. The answers provided are only discussion starters. Let your class talk it over from there.

1. What nonmiraculous gifts do we have that can contribute to the healing of physical or emotional ills?

"A merry heart doeth good like a medicine" (Proverbs 17:22). Some Christians have a special talent for bringing cheer to the sick. Their smile is contagious; they chase away the tension that can aggravate an illness. Other Christians are quieter, but they listen with empathy for those who suffer. Some have the gift of communicating confidence. In their presence, we cannot help feeling that everything is going to turn out all right; and that feeling can be an aid to healing. Finally, some Christians have a gift for intercessory prayer. They embody the promise, "The prayer of faith shall save the sick, and the Lord shall raise him up" (James 5:15).

2. Without the miraculous gift of "discerning of spirits," how can we use the New Testament to identify false prophets?

Jesus gave us one important guideline in Matthew 7:15-20: "Beware of false prophets. . . . By their fruits ye shall know them." Galatians 5:22-26 describes the kind of fruit that characterizes real Christians. When we see a preacher dominated by the contrasting fruit of lust or greed or strife or selfish ambition, we know that he is a false prophet. The New Testament also points to doctrinal tests that can be used to identify a false prophet. If a preacher fails to acknowledge Jesus Christ as both Son of God and Son of man, he "is not of God" (1 John 4:3). If a preacher proclaims a gospel of salvation by works, contrary to Paul's gospel of salvation through grace, he is subject to a curse (Galatians 1:8). We need to know precisely what is in the New Testament, so we can quickly discern any teaching that is contrary to it.

3. We have a diversity of nonmiraculous gifts to use in building up the church. Why should we rejoice in this diversity?

It is exciting to see how we complement one another. To blend our talents with those of our fellow members gives us all a wonderful sense of belonging and sharing in an eternal enterprise. And we see God's wisdom and handiwork in fashioning our congregation. He has provided some with gifts of leadership, some who excel in teaching, some who contribute enthusiasm and cheer, others with musical talent, still others who work effectively with their hands. Every church is a testimony to God's divine skill in drawing separate parts together to form a functioning body. This diversity also contributes to a healthy humility on the part of all members, as we recognize how much we need one another. It also contributes to the habit of giving glory to God.

4. Why do we need to put frequent emphasis on what we have in common as Christians?

This lesson focuses on our diversity. We not only differ in regard to our talents or gifts, but in any church there are people who differ from the majority in economic status or educational accomplishments or family background. These differences can foster misunderstanding and jealousy. It is important, therefore, to make much of the tremendous blessings we hold in common. Malachi asks, "Have we not all one father? hath not one God created us?" (Malachi 2:10). These questions are even more meaningful to Christians than they were to the Jews to whom they were first addressed. We follow the same Lord; our faith in Him as Son of God and Savior is similar; we responded to the same plan of salvation by trusting Christ, repenting of our sins, confessing our faith, and submitting to baptism. These are truths we should constantly emphasize.

5. What are some practical ways in which Christians can share in each other's sorrows and gladness?

We dare not take for granted that a grieving brother or sister knows of our sympathy and care. A card, a telephone call, or a personal visit can provide a practical demonstration of our caring. When a church member suffers a death in his or her family, it seems only right that other members will call at the funeral home. Sending food to a family at a time of bereavement is another beautiful expression of loving sympathy. As for times of gladness, church members should make a special effort to be present at weddings, graduation receptions, retirement parties, and other special occasions involving fellow members. Cards and telephone calls are always helpful, but they can be especially good for those who are shut-ins.

Growing Through Worship

DEVOTIONAL READING: Psalm 95:1-7.

LESSON SCRIPTURE: 1 Corinthians 14:1-33a.

PRINTED TEXT: 1 Corinthians 14:20-33a.

1 Corinthians 14:20-33a

20 Brethren, be not children in understanding: howbeit in malice be ye children, but in understanding be men.

21 In the law it is written, With men of other tongues and other lips will I speak unto this people; and yet for all that will they not hear me, saith the Lord.

22 Wherefore tongues are for a sign, not to them that believe, but to them that believe not: but prophesying serveth not for them that believe not, but for them which believe.

23 If therefore the whole church be come together into one place, and all speak with tongues, and there come in those that are unlearned, or unbelievers, will they not say that ye are mad?

24 But if all prophesy, and there come in one that believeth not, or one unlearned, he is convinced of all, he is judged of all:

25 And thus are the secrets of his heart made manifest; and so falling down on his face he will worship God, and report that God is in you of a truth.

26 How is it then, brethren? when ye come together, every one of you hath a psalm, hath a doctrine, hath a tongue, hath a revelation, hath an interpretation. Let all things be done unto edifying.

27 If any man speak in an unknown tongue, let it be by two, or at the most by three, and that by course; and let one interpret.

28 But if there be no interpreter, let him keep silence in the church; and let him speak to himself, and to God.

29 Let the prophets speak two or three, and let the other judge.

30 If any thing be revealed to another that sitteth by, let the first hold his peace.

31 For ye may all prophesy one by one, that all may learn, and all may be comforted.

32 And the spirits of the prophets are subject to the prophets.

33a For God is not the author of confusion, but of peace.

GOLDEN TEXT: When ye come together, every one of you hath a psalm, hath a doctrine, hath a tongue, hath a revelation, hath an interpretation. Let all things be done unto edifying.—1 Corinthians 14:26.

Christians Living in Community

Unit 2. Nurturing the Life of the

Community (Lessons 5-9)

Lesson Aims

When this lesson has been completed, the students should:

1. Have a desire to see that their own worship services are conducted in an orderly fashion.

2. Have an interest in participating in public worship in a way that benefits others.

3. Pay special attention to those portions of a worship service that present messages from the Word of God.

Lesson Outline

INTRODUCTION
    A. Order in the Court!
    B. Lesson Background
I. MATURE WORSHIP (1 Corinthians 14:20-22)
    A. A Call for Mature Thinking (v. 20)
    B. A Mature View of Tongues-Speaking (vv. 21, 22)
       Tongues
II. EDIFYING WORSHIP (1 Corinthians 14:23-26)
    A. The Benefits of Prophesying (vv. 23-25)
    B. A Call for Edification (v. 26)
       Sidewalk Superintendents
III. ORDERLY WORSHIP (1 Corinthians 14:27-33a)
    A. Guidelines for Tongues-Speaking (vv. 27, 28)
    B. Guidelines for Prophesying (vv. 29-31)
    C. A Call for Order (vv. 32, 33a)
CONCLUSION
    A. My Way
    B. Prayer
    C. Thought to Remember

Visual 6 of the visuals packet emphasizes a very important truth regarding the church's worship assemblies. The visual is shown on page 276.

Introduction

A. Order in the Court!

You have seen this scene on TV many times, from Perry Mason to Ben Matlock. The evidence weighs heavily against the defendant. The defense attorney appears to be running out of ideas. And then without warning he drops the bombshell, a piece of information that shocks the courtroom, implicates the prosecution witness, and clears his client. We know what happens next. Confusion and murmuring erupt in the courtroom, the judge pounds his gavel and demands, "Order in the court!"

It is a basic rule: if you want to carry on a meeting effectively, the participants must act in an orderly fashion. This is no less true in the church than in the courtroom. Paul wrote the fourteenth chapter of 1 Corinthians to straighten out a disorderly worship service, and at the same time to provide us with some helpful guidelines for an effective worship service today.

B. Lesson Background

The previous lesson from 1 Corinthians 12 pointed out that the Christians at Corinth had been arguing about spiritual gifts. It seems there was a common desire to speak in tongues, and a spirit of superiority in those who did possess that ability. Chapter 14 implies that problems arose in the worship services. Apparently participants competed for opportunities to speak in tongues, often interrupting other tongues-speakers and even those who were delivering a message from God's Word. The result was a confusion that threatened to hinder the spiritual growth of the participants and drive away new prospects. Chapter 14 addresses this dangerous situation with concrete, practical rules for worship.

I. Mature Worship
(1 Corinthians 14:20-22)

"Grow up," we often say to someone who is speaking or acting in a manner that does not reflect mature thinking. This phrase well typifies Paul's message to the Corinthians.

A. A Call for Mature Thinking (v. 20)

20. Brethren, be not children in understanding: howbeit in malice be ye children, but in understanding be men.

Be not children in understanding. It is childish to compete in a worship service for the opportunity to speak, or to interrupt others when they are speaking. Boasting about your own spiritual gifts is immature. The apostle Paul challenges the Corinthians to act like mature adults in their church gatherings.

To reinforce his point, Paul says, *In malice be ye children.* Sometimes children are used in Scripture to illustrate characteristics that are appropriate for God's people. Jesus taught that the kingdom of Heaven belongs to those who approach God with a childlike spirit (Matthew 18:3). For example, they need the unconditional love and trust that children typically have for their parents. In a similar fashion, Paul says that when it comes to malicious and hurtful conduct toward others, childlike innocence and ignorance are appropriate. If the Christians of Corinth want to act like children, it should be in a positive manner, not in bickering and fighting.

B. A Mature View of Tongues-Speaking (vv. 21, 22)

21. In the law it is written, With men of other tongues and other lips will I speak unto this people; and yet for all that will they not hear me, saith the Lord.

This quote from Isaiah 28:11, 12 comes from a chapter that prophesies the conquest of the southern kingdom of Judah by the Babylonians. God's people had refused to listen to His Word as spoken by prophets like Isaiah, so God said He would one day get their attention by using foreign invaders. Listening to the foreign language of Babylon would not be a pleasant experience, for the occasion would represent humiliation and defeat.

Paul uses this Old Testament passage to lead up to the idea that it is inappropriate to speak to your own people in a manner that is foreign and unintelligible, for in biblical history that symbolizes distress and grief. One problem with tongues-speaking in a worship service is that it alienates those who do not understand.

22. Wherefore tongues are for a sign, not to them that believe, but to them that believe not: but prophesying serveth not for them that believe not, but for them which believe.

The mention of tongues as a *sign* relates to our previous lesson in 1 Corinthians 12. In the beginning years of the church, supernatural spiritual gifts such as speaking in tongues, healing, and casting out demons were used by Christian evangelists as signs from God to indicate that they were spokesmen of God (Mark 16:20; Acts 8:6; Hebrews 2:3, 4). These "confirmation gifts" were needed when Christians were claiming a new revelation from God (the gospel of Jesus Christ), but did not yet have the written documentation that would later be provided by the New Testament writings.

Paul now reminds the Corinthians that confirmation signs such as speaking in tongues were designed for persuading non-Christians to listen to the gospel. They were not intended to be used among Christians.

In this chapter Paul challenges the Corinthian fascination with tongues-speaking by promoting the spiritual gift of *prophesying*. As we noted in our study of 1 Corinthians 12, this gift is the ability to receive direct revelation from God, with the responsibility for funneling that information to God's people. Apparently this "revelation gift" was given to select individuals in order that the churches would have a means of receiving divine guidance until the New Testament writings became available to them.

Paul says *tongues* are a sign for unbelievers, while prophesying is a sign for believers. This illustrates one difference between confirmation gifts and revelation gifts. The former were designed for use in evangelism. In the beginning years of the church they persuaded people to listen to this new religious group. The latter were intended to be used in the church for people who needed to be instructed in the beliefs and practices of the New Covenant. Paul's call for mature thinking among the Corinthians implies that it is time for them to move on from flashy confirmation gifts like speaking in tongues, and to give attention to the instruction of God being presented through the revelation gifts.

TONGUES

Paul says quite a bit about "tongues" in 1 Corinthians 14. His use of the term is much like ours when we speak of the French, Italian, and Swedish "tongues," or languages. Tongues were given to some of the early Christians for a sign to non-Christians. Some students think this gift was a supernatural ability to speak in tongues they had not learned, as the apostles did at Pentecost (Acts 2:1-11). Others believe the tongues at Corinth were an ecstatic form of utterance not in any known language.

However that may be, Paul was afraid an emphasis on "tongues" would obscure the common realities of Christian associations in love. So he began 1 Corinthians 13 with the warning, "I may be able to speak the languages of men and even of *angels,* but if I have no love, my speech is no more than a noisy gong or a clanging bell" (*Today's English Version*).

Ella Wheeler Wilcox looked in this direction when she discussed the "tongue" Jesus used:

The wise men ask, "What language did Christ speak?"
   They cavil, argue, search, and little prove.
O Sages, leave your Syriac and your Greek!
   Christ spoke the universal language—LOVE.

—J. G. V. B.

II. Edifying Worship (1 Corinthians 14:23-26)

When a joke is not funny, it is appropriate to say, "I don't get it." However, that is an undesirable response to anything in a worship service. As Paul now argues, everything that is said and done should be meaningful to those who are present.

A. The Benefits of Prophesying
(vv. 23-25)

23. If therefore the whole church be come together into one place, and all speak with tongues, and there come in those that are unlearned, or unbelievers, will they not say that ye are mad?

Some in Corinth thought it was great to stand before a congregation and speak prayer and praise in an unfamiliar language. Paul challenges them to step back and look at themselves from a different angle. Consider the view of the *unlearned* (those unaccustomed to tongues-speaking) and the *unbelievers* (the non-Christians). The apostle suggests that this strange conduct will bring a negative reaction from visitors, and will handicap the evangelistic mission of the church.

The truth of this statement should be evident to most of us who are working through this lesson. Those people today who often speak in tongues feel quite at ease with that practice, but many visitors think they are crazy.

24. But if all prophesy, and there come in one that believeth not, or one unlearned, he is convinced of all, he is judged of all.

Here is the key advantage of *prophesying* over tongues-speaking in a meeting. Whatever message a prophet receives from God is presented to the assembly in their common language. Everyone, including the visitor, has a fair opportunity to understand the message and to respond appropriately. Unlike the incomprehensible sounds of tongues-speaking, prophesying presents God's message in a way that can persuade the hearer and convict him of his errors.

This passage reinforces an idea noted earlier in this lesson. Confirmation gifts such as tongues-speaking and healing served a worthy purpose for evangelism in the marketplace. They caught attention and persuaded people that they were in the presence of a spokesman from God. But in a worship service the need is

visual 6

for clear instruction from God's Word. This was provided by revelation gifts such as prophesying. Rather than contribute to the growth of the congregation and its guests, tongues-speaking gifts tended to befuddle. They belonged somewhere else.

25. And thus are the secrets of his heart made manifest; and so falling down on his face he will worship God, and report that God is in you of a truth.

This verse amplifies the idea in the previous verse. The heart of an unbeliever can be challenged if he is given a clear communication of God's Word, as was done in prophesying.

B. A Call for Edification (v. 26)

26. How is it then, brethren? when ye come together, every one of you hath a psalm, hath a doctrine, hath a tongue, hath a revelation, hath an interpretation. Let all things be done unto edifying.

Here is a key principle for evaluating everything that is done in a worship service: *Let all things be done unto edifying.* The English word *edify* is best understood when we recall that we sometimes refer to buildings as "edifices." To *edify* is to build up, to do something that helps a person grow and develop.

The primary purpose of worship is to praise and glorify God. Our English word *worship* conveys this idea, being a shortened form of *worth-ship*. In worship we recognize the great worth of the Almighty.

Edification is another goal of worship. Not only is God to be praised, but those who participate in the praising should be blessed by the experience. They should be built up in knowledge, in understanding, in faith, in devotion. Edification does not outweigh our primary purpose of giving glory to God, but it is so important that Paul uses it to measure the value of each activity in a worship service.

Paul names some activities that apparently were common in the worship services at Corinth. Our study of 1 Corinthians has already acquainted us with some of these items: a *tongue* (an unfamiliar language) a *revelation* (a prophecy), and *interpretation* (of an unfamiliar language). *Psalm* obviously refers to the use of music in worship. *Doctrine* (teaching) could refer to a prepared lesson or sermon, but perhaps it refers to another revelation gift. The same word is used in the list of revelation gifts in 1 Corinthians 14:6.

It is not Paul's purpose to make an exhaustive list of worship activities, as if anything left out of this list (such as the Lord's Supper or the offering) were somehow inappropriate. Nor is it

Paul's purpose to require all of these items in our worship services today. We have already noted that we do not have the same need for the confirmation and revelation gifts today, now that the church is firmly established and the New Testament is available to guide us. Likewise, it is becoming apparent in this study that Paul saw little use for confirmation gifts such as tongues-speaking in the worship services of his own day.

Paul's purpose in listing these activities is to illustrate his principle of edification. All activities used in worship, including tongues and the other items in this list, are proper only if they promote the spiritual growth of the assembly.

SIDEWALK SUPERINTENDENTS

In speaking about the worship activities of the church at Corinth, Paul sums up his ideal for all of them: "Let all things be done unto edifying." In the *New International Version* this is translated, "All of these must be done for the strengthening of the church"; but the word literally means "building up."

There is something fascinating about the erection of a building.

Many people stop while shopping or walking to and from work to see "how it is coming along." Those who are just onlookers at the construction site are often called "sidewalk superintendents."

Paul indicates that the work and worship of God's people are for the purpose of "edification." They are for building up a structure of life and thought through which people are turned "from darkness to light, and from the power of Satan to God, so that they may receive forgiveness of sins and a place among those who are sanctified" (Acts 26:18, *New International Version*).

It is our responsibility to help this structure of faith and obedience to take shape and to become a reality. Are we willing to be only "sidewalk superintendents," not helping, only observing?

—J. G. V. B.

III. Orderly Worship
(1 Corinthians 14:27-33a)

After devoting three chapters to the misuse of spiritual gifts at Corinth, Paul concludes his discussion with a few simple rules for the orderly use of spiritual gifts in worship.

A. Guidelines for Tongues-Speaking
(vv. 27, 28)

27. If any man speak in an unknown tongue, let it be by two, or at the most by three, and that by course; and let one interpret.

Here are three rules for tongues-speaking in a worship service. First, there should be a limit of

---

Home Daily Bible Readings

Monday, Apr. 3—Worship God With Praise and Thanksgiving (Psalm 95:1-7)
Tuesday, Apr. 4—Use Spiritual Gifts to Edify Others (1 Corinthians 14:1-5)
Wednesday, Apr. 5—Unintelligible Speech Does Not Edify Anyone (1 Corinthians 14:6-12)
Thursday, Apr. 6—Speaking in Tongues Requires Interpretation (1 Corinthians 14:13-19)
Friday, Apr. 7—Be Mature in Using Spiritual Gifts (1 Corinthians 14:20-25)
Saturday, Apr. 8—Worshipers' Sharing Should Be Orderly (1 Corinthians 14:26-33
Sunday, Apr. 9—Meeting Regularly for Worship (Acts 2:38-47)

---

no more than two or three expressions of tongues in a given service. Paul does not encourage everyone to participate.

Second, speaking in tongues should be done *by course:* that is, by taking turns with other speakers and activities. Paul does not allow interruptions and competition among speakers. Nor does he allow simultaneous tongues-speaking, a choir of tongues. This would not help to win the visitor (as noted earlier).

Third, no one should speak in tongues unless there is someone to give a reliable interpretation of what is being said in the unfamiliar language. This is a logical implication from the principle of edification.

28. But if there be no interpreter, let him keep silence in the church; and let him speak to himself, and to God.

Paul has an interesting approach to the problem of tongues-speaking in the church. He has said enough to indicate that he does not believe tongues belong in a worship service. This spiritual gift is designed for evangelism outside the church. Even so, Paul does not command the Corinthians to stop speaking in tongues during public worship. Instead, he chooses to allow the practice, but under conditions that will minimize both its use and its negative impact.

Can this spirit of gracious concession still work among Christians who disagree sharply about modern-day tongues? Perhaps so. Many of us believe the confirmation and revelation gifts no longer are needed or given, but we need not make this issue a test of fellowship. We can maintain our position and challenge the views of others in a manner that does not alienate those who differ with us on this issue. It may be necessary to restrict a tongues-speaker according to the rules Paul gives, but his does not necessarily rule out fellowship in worship and service.

Those individuals who believe they have the ability to speak in tongues should follow Paul's instructions in this text. In keeping with the emphasis upon the principles of edification and order in worship, no individual should speak out in a tongue when doing so will be upsetting to the assembly.

The best advice for tongues-speaking in our time may be to minimize its use in public settings and leave it to the individual to determine what is appropriate in private devotion. This seems to fit the balance Paul strikes in this chapter, as he gives reasons why a tongues-speaker needs to *keep silence in the church* and yet may *speak to himself, and to God.*

B. Guidelines for Prophesying (vv. 29-31)

29. Let the prophets speak two or three, and let the other judge.

The Word of God belongs in a worship service. In 1 Timothy 4:13 Paul commends three ways to present God's Word to a congregation: the reading aloud of Scripture (without comment), preaching ("exhortation"), and teaching. The gift of prophecy also served to bring the Word of God into a service, as those who received a message from God relayed that message to the assembly.

Nevertheless, Paul does not want too much of a good thing. He limits the use of the gift of prophesying with some of the rules given for the gift of tongues. This suggests a principle to be applied to all the activities we use in worship today. We should seek a reasonable balance between all of our worship activities and not let any one item take up so much time that it detracts from the edification of the assembly.

Let the other judge, seems to say prophecies are to be evaluated. There were false prophets (Matthew 7:15; 2 Peter 2:1). They should be exposed. This could be done by comparing their words with the words of the Old Testament and the established teaching of the apostles (2 Peter 1:16-21; 1 John 4:1-3; Jude 3-5). The *other* (better translated in the plural as "others" may refer to other prophets, or perhaps it refers to the elders of the church, who must guard against false teaching (Acts 20:28-31).

30. If any thing be revealed to another that sitteth by, let the first hold his peace.

It would not be good to interrupt rudely; but if a prophet receives a revelation from God, it is proper to ask the speaker to pause for a few moments when he gets to an appropriate breaking point. In such a case the speaker ought to yield.

31. For ye may all prophesy one by one, that all may learn, and all may be comforted.

The principles of orderly procedure and edification are the foundation for Paul's rules.

C. A Call for Order (vv. 32, 33a)

32. And the spirits of the prophets are subject to the prophets.

The gift of prophecy is not so compulsive that a prophet has no control of himself. One who is talking is able to stop and let another have a turn.

33a. For God is not the author of confusion, but of peace.

If two so-called prophets insist on talking at the same time, at least one of them is not really inspired by God. Perhaps neither one is. The source of prophecy and tongues and all spiritual gifts is One who always operates in a reasonable fashion. We should follow His lead. Whatever gifts and abilities He gives us we should use them in an orderly manner.

Conclusion

A. My Way

One of Frank Sinatra's hits is the song "My Way." Many people like the lyrics, especially the idea of not allowing others to intimidate you. "Through it all . . . I did it my way."

But take another look at the line "I did it my way." This well describes the way many people approach worship. We know some groups have replaced the simple elements of New Testament worship with rituals and traditions of their own devising. We avoid that error and insist upon using the worship practices from the New Testament pattern: praying, preaching, singing, and the Lord's Supper. But sometimes we fail to consider how best to blend those practices together to glorify God and edify the worshipers. Often we settle for poorly planned services and mediocrity. As we criticize the Corinthian church for bringing disorder and confusion into worship, let us also evaluate what we ourselves do.

B. Prayer

Father, help us to worship You "in spirit and in truth," considering not only the attitude we bring to worship, but also the manner in which we worship.

C. Thought to Remember

If we want our worship to please God, then we should do it according to His instructions.

Learning by Doing

This page contains an alternate lesson plan emphasizing learning activities. Classes desiring such student involvement will find these suggestions helpful.

Learning Goals

After this lesson the pupils will be able to:

1. Enumerate things to be avoided in participating in a worship service.

2. Design a worship service that is orderly and inspirational.

3. Examine their own church's worship service and note possible improvements.

Into the Lesson

Secure a worship tape of vocal music in some language other than English. Have it playing as students arrive. As the session begins tell the class there will be a five-minute worship time listening to the tape. After five minutes turn the tape off. Ask the members to tell how they felt when they couldn't understand the language, but were being urged to worship.

Lead into the lesson by saying that speaking in tongues had become a problem in the worship services at Corinth. First Corinthians 14 addresses this problem.

Into the Word

Divide the class into two groups. Assign these sets of questions, one to each group. Let groups share their conclusions after about ten minutes.

Group 1: For whom is speaking in tongues intended? (v. 22). How would an unbeliever feel if he came into a worship service where everyone was speaking in tongues? (v. 23). What conditions were put upon the use of tongues in a worship service? (vv. 27, 28).

Group 2: For whom is prophesying designed? (v. 22). How is the unbeliever affected by prophesying? (vv. 24, 25).

While the groups are at work, draw this chart on the board to record the answers found by each group. (The chart is in the student quarterly.) Record the findings of each group and discuss.

	Speaking In Tongues	Prophesying
For whom?		
What purpose?		
Effect on un-believers?		
Conditions?		
Edifying today?		

Give each person a copy of this word puzzle. It contains worship activities practiced at Corinth and mentioned in our text. (Answers: 1. psalm, 2. doctrine, 3. revelation, 4. tongue.)

1. Use of music   3. Gift of prophecy
2. Teaching, sermon   4. Unfamiliar speech

After the puzzle is solved, direct the class in enumerating all the things done in your church's worship service. As teacher, you record them on the board. (For example: singing, praying, preaching.) Next, have the class look at verses 26-33 and discuss: How does Paul say we should determine what is to be done in a worship service? (The answer is that each activity be edifying.)

Into Life

Have students pair off and discuss the activities in your church's worship service. Let them rate each activity on a scale of 1 to 10 (10 being highest). The rating should relate to how edifying each activity is.

Let each group record its ratings on a sheet of paper and tape it to the board. (No names need be attached.) Compare the opinions.

Ask the students if personal taste probably had a part in the ratings. Remind them of Paul's criterion: each activity should be edifying. Discuss with the class how you determine whether something is edifying or not.

Suggestions: It's an activity modeled by the early church. It is well prepared and tastefully executed. The needs of people are considered. The content is biblically sound. The congregation is encouraged and built up through the activity. The activity glorifies God and makes Him central. The activity is done in an orderly fashion.

Let's Talk It Over

The questions on this page are designed to encourage review of the lesson Scriptures and to promote discussion of the lesson by the class. The answers provided are only discussion starters. Let your class talk it over from there.

1. What are some ways in which Christians sometimes behave in a childish manner? How can childishness be overcome?

When Christians bicker over trivial matters or refuse to speak to one another or pout over what they consider unfair treatment, they are acting childishly.

Paul calls for mature understanding. Perhaps the best way to overcome childish behavior is simply to realize, and help others to realize how childish it is.

To follow up on Jesus' teachings in Matthew 18:1-4; 19:13-15, we need to emphasize being *childlike* rather than *childish*. To be free from malice as a little child is, and to be humble, open, trusting, quick to forget past offenses—that is the proper alternative to childishness.

2. Paul's description in 1 Corinthians 14:25 of the convicted worshiper is very appealing: "Falling down on his face he will worship God, and report that God is in you of a truth." How can we make a similar impression on visitors who attend our services of worship?

The worshiper above was so affected by the power of the prophetic message. Surely today the Word of God, preached clearly and persuasively, can produce a similar effect. But the preacher needs help. If the visitor sees around him church members with open Bibles in their hands, uttering an occasional "Amen" at appropriate moments, that will impress him still more with the importance and power of biblical truth. But if he observes worshipers sleeping, whispering, or obviously daydreaming, the response Paul describes is not so likely to be duplicated.

3. Is our church's worship as worshipful as it should be? If not, what can we do to make it more worshipful?

We need to be clear that the test of worship is not how good it makes us feel, but how well it expresses praise and devotion to God. This applies to our music. Matters of beauty, rhythm, harmony, low or high volume are important, but secondary to whether or not the congregational hymns and special music lift our hearts and minds to our Father. The same distinction applies to the sermon. Worshipers need to be mature enough to recognize that the effectiveness of a sermon cannot be gauged by how entertaining or interesting or well crafted it is, but by whether or not it leads them to deeper trust in God, love toward Him, and praise for Him. We need to keep this distinction in mind when we plan every aspect of our worship service.

4. Is our church's worship as edifying for the individual worshipers as it should be? If not, what can we do to make it more edifying?

Good worship is not measured by how good the worshipers feel, and neither is good edification. Indeed, worshipers may need to feel bad about sins of omission and commission they must overcome in order to be edified, or built up in Christian faith and living. A balanced use of the Word of God will contribute to well-rounded edification. There are what we may call "feel-good" biblical passages (for example, Matthew 11:28-30; John 14:1-3, 27; Revelation 21:4). Certainly we should employ them often in our worship. But biblical calls to repentance and holiness, challenges to sacrificial service, and exhortations to mental and physical discipline should also be used in abundance, even if they do not make worshipers quite so comfortable.

5. The lesson writer deals with the difficult matter of how to preserve fellowship and cooperation between those who practice tongues-speaking today and those who oppose such a practice. What are some keys to working this out?

It is vital that neither side view this matter as a test of fellowship. Those who speak in tongues must steer away from the idea that the Holy Spirit is not present with any who do not speak in tongues, for that idea contradicts the twelfth chapter of 1 Corinthians. Individuals who oppose tongues-speaking must beware of attributing all such activity to the working of Satan. If tongues-speakers set forth "revelations" that are contrary to biblical doctrine, it is obvious that the source of these is something other than the Holy Spirit, but that does not mean truth is never spoken in tongues. One benefit the Holy Spirit unquestionably gives is the fruit of love (Galatians 5:22). That love should be in evidence in the lives of Christians who stand on both sides of any controversial matter.

Being a Resurrection People

DEVOTIONAL READING: Philippians 2:1-11.

LESSON SCRIPTURE: Luke 24:1-11; 1 Corinthians 15.

PRINTED TEXT: Luke 24:1-11; 1 Corinthians 15:12-17, 56-58.

Luke 24:1-11

1 Now upon the first day of the week, very early in the morning, they came unto the sepulchre, bringing the spices which they had prepared, and certain others with them.

2 And they found the stone rolled away from the sepulchre.

3 And they entered in, and found not the body of the Lord Jesus.

4 And it came to pass, as they were much perplexed thereabout, behold, two men stood by them in shining garments:

5 And as they were afraid, and bowed down their faces to the earth, they said unto them, Why seek ye the living among the dead?

6 He is not here, but is risen: remember how he spake unto you when he was yet in Galilee,

7 Saying, The Son of man must be delivered into the hands of sinful men, and be crucified, and the third day rise again.

8 And they remembered his words,

9 And returned from the sepulchre, and told all these things unto the eleven, and to all the rest.

10 It was Mary Magdalene, and Joanna, and Mary the mother of James, and other women that were with them, which told these things unto the apostles.

11 And their words seemed to them as idle tales, and they believed them not.

1 Corinthians 15:12-17, 56-58

12 Now if Christ be preached that he rose from the dead, how say some among you that there is no resurrection of the dead?

13 But if there be no resurrection of the dead, then is Christ not risen:

14 And if Christ be not risen, then is our preaching vain, and your faith is also vain.

15 Yea, and we are found false witnesses of God; because we have testified of God that he raised up Christ: whom he raised not up, if so be that the dead rise not.

16 For if the dead rise not, then is not Christ raised:

17 And if Christ be not raised, your faith is vain; ye are yet in your sins.

. . . .

56 The sting of death is sin; and the strength of sin is the law.

57 But thanks be to God, which giveth us the victory through our Lord Jesus Christ.

58 Therefore, my beloved brethren, be ye stedfast, unmovable, always abounding in the work of the Lord, forasmuch as ye know that your labor is not in vain in the Lord.

GOLDEN TEXT: Be ye steadfast, unmovable, always abounding in the work of the Lord, forasmuch as ye know that your labor is not in vain in the Lord.—1 Corinthians 15:58.

Lesson Aims

When this lesson has been completed, the students should:

1. Experience a sense of excitement and joy in reflecting upon Christ's resurrection.

2. See the significance of Christ's resurrection to our religious faith and our eternal hope.

3. Have a spirit of confidence based on a knowledge of the victory Christ has already accomplished in our behalf.

Lesson Outline

The wonder and power of Christ's resurrection is brought to mind by visual 7 of the visuals packet. The visual is shown on page 284.

Introduction

A. Prove It

Missouri is well known as "the Show Me State." To some this suggests a stubborn spirit, unwilling to believe. But to others it seems like a sensible approach: if you want me to accept something as true, then give me a reason.

The Christian faith is grounded upon one astounding claim, that Jesus Christ rose from the dead after three days in a tomb. We are not asked to believe this without any evidence. On the contrary, the New Testament emphasizes the historical credibility of this event. From the disappearance of Jesus' body from a guarded tomb to the eyewitness testimony of people who saw Jesus alive, we are given good reasons to believe in the resurrection.

As we review the facts, let us reflect not only on the reasons why we believe in Jesus' resurrection, but also on what difference this belief makes in our lives.

B. Lesson Background

After his lengthy discussion of spiritual gifts in 1 Corinthians 12—14, Paul launches into a different subject. In 1 Corinthians 15 he addresses the false idea that Christians who have already died will remain dead and miss the future blessings of Heaven (1 Corinthians 15:12).

Paul begins chapter 15 by reminding the Corinthians of the gospel sermons they heard him preach in the past (vv. 1, 2). He then rehearses the three cardinal truths of the gospel: Christ's death, burial, and resurrection. The first two items receive only a brief mention (vv. 3, 4), but as a prelude to the theme of this chapter, the evidence of Christ's resurrection is summarized in several verses (5-8). At this point Paul is ready to take the fact of Christ's resurrection and demonstrate how it has relevance to our lives as Christians. He will not only clear up the doctrinal problem of the Corinthians regarding those who are dead, but he will also promote a sense of confidence and victory among those of us who are still alive.

But first, let us review the story of Christ's resurrection as presented in Luke 24.

I. Faith in Christ's Resurrection (Luke 24:1-11)

We who have been Christians for a long time may think it is easy for a person to believe in Jesus Christ. The Gospel of Luke reminds us that the beginning of faith can be a struggle.

A. The Empty Tomb (vv. 1-3)

1. Now upon the first day of the week, very early in the morning, they came unto the sepulchre, bringing the spices which they had prepared, and certain others with them.

Luke 23 describes the crucifixion of Jesus and tells of some women from Galilee who were loyal friends of Jesus. They followed Joseph of Arimathea to the tomb where he placed Jesus' body. They then returned to their lodgings and prepared spices and ointments to embalm the body of Jesus. They could not return to the tomb on the day after the crucifixion because it was a Sabbath Day, and Jewish law would not permit them to attend to a burial on that day. They had to wait until Sunday, *the first day of the week.*

2. And they found the stone rolled away from the sepulchre.

As they walked, the women were wondering whom they could find to move the heavy stone that Joseph of Arimathea had used to close the door of the tomb (Mark 16:3). The answer was provided by an angel who came with a great earthquake and moved the stone from its place (Matthew 28:2).

3. And they entered in, and found not the body of the Lord Jesus.

The tomb presented perplexing clues for the women to consider. The stone was rolled away. The body of Jesus was gone, and in its place were the linens that had been wrapped around it when it was placed in the tomb Friday evening (John 20:6, 7).

B. The Word of God (vv. 4-8)

4. And it came to pass, as they were much perplexed thereabout, behold, two men stood by them in shining garments.

Matthew 28:5 confirms what the description in this verse suggests: the *two men in shining garments* were angels. Apparently they were not visible at first, but then they appeared.

5. And as they were afraid, and bowed down their faces to the earth, they said unto them, Why seek ye the living among the dead?

The women apparently came to the conclusion that these two men were angels. They reacted with the fear and awe that is common when angels appear. So did the shepherds of Bethlehem (Luke 2:9) and John on the island of Patmos (Revelation 22:8).

6. He is not here, but is risen: remember how he spake unto you when he was yet in Galilee.

This is the first recorded announcement of Jesus' resurrection. As the angels pointed out, the news should come as no surprise to anyone who had been a disciple of Jesus in Galilee. On at least three occasions He had predicted His death and resurrection (Matthew 16:21; 17:22, 23; 20:17-19).

Now consider the gentle rebuke given in the previous verse: "Why seek ye the living among the dead?" Had these women understood Jesus' teaching, they would not have been coming to His tomb to complete His burial. They would have been eagerly anticipating His return from the grave. The same rebuke was appropriate also

for other disciples, and was delivered by Jesus himself in due time (Mark 16:14; Luke 24:25, 26).

7. Saying, The Son of man must be delivered into the hands of sinful men, and be crucified, and the third day rise again.

Jesus' predictions of His death and resurrection were precise. He said He would be crucified in Jerusalem at the instigation of the Jewish religious leaders, and would rise on the third day following His death (Matthew 16:21; 17:22, 23; 20:17-19).

Sometimes we marvel that Jesus' disciples did not anticipate His resurrection, as if to say we would have done better. But we should remember that Jesus often spoke in parables and figures of speech. The disciples could easily think this talk of death and resurrection was some type of parable. They had always thought the Messiah would conquer and rule; they could not believe He would be killed by enemies. The angels were gracious in their rebuke, and we should not be too hard on the disciples.

8. And they remembered his words.

Here we see illustrated a key step in the process of developing a faith in Jesus Christ. Faith begins with our focusing upon the Word of God. As Paul declares in Romans 10:17, "Faith cometh by hearing, and hearing by the word of God."

Jesus had spoken the Word of God when He had predicted His death and resurrection. When the angel directed the women back to those divine words, he was pointing them to the source of a true faith in the risen Savior. If we want to grow in our faith in Jesus Christ, we too need to focus upon the Word we have been given.

C. The Challenge of Faith (vv. 9-11)

9. And returned from the sepulchre, and told all these things unto the eleven, and to all the rest.

The women reported their experience to a number of disciples of Jesus, including the apostles, who are now called *the eleven* because Judas had hanged himself (Matthew 27:5).

10. It was Mary Magdalene, and Joanna, and Mary the mother of James, and other women that were with them, which told these things unto the apostles.

Luke 8:2, 3 says many women in Galilee provided financial support and hospitality for Jesus during His ministry in that region. They began this after He healed them with His divine powers. Some of these women faithfully attended to Him even after His death.

11. And their words seemed to them as idle tales, and they believed them not.

The men who had received the most training by Jesus were not prepared to accept the idea of

His resurrection. For most of the disciples and apostles, faith did not come until they personally saw the risen Lord. At that point He rebuked them for their disbelief (Mark 16:14).

Is this to say there is little hope for modern man to be brought to faith in Jesus Christ, since we are twenty centuries removed from His personal appearances? Not at all. In the New Testament we have testimony from reliable eyewitnesses (1 Corinthians 15:5-8). Jesus anticipated that this testimony would lead many to believe in His resurrection, and He even promised a special blessing for those of us who arrive at faith without seeing the risen Lord (John 20:29-31).

WHO WON?

One of the world's decisive battles was fought on June 18, 1815, in Belgium, near a place named Waterloo. At one time during this conflict between the French, Prussians, Dutch, and British, fifty-seven thousand men lay dead, dying, or wounded within an area of three square miles. As everyone knows, the force under the Duke of Wellington defeated the famous Napoleon.

It is said, though I have not corroborated it, that an interesting incident occurred after the battle. A semaphore was set up to flash the news across the English Channel to Britain. When the message came, just two words were read between patches of drifting fog: "Wellington defeated." Anguish was intense in England. But that was not the full communication. Two more words made it complete: "Wellington defeated the enemy."

So it was with Jesus' struggle with sin and death at Calvary. He was dead, and laid in a tomb that was shut and sealed. But that was not the complete message. On the first day of the week, faithful women saw an angel of life and heard the message completed: "He is risen!" Jesus was not defeated! Instead, He had defeated the enemy.   —J. G. V. B.

visual 7

II. Hope From Christ's Resurrection (1 Corinthians 15:12-17)

Whether you are a twentieth-century modern thinker or a first-century disciple of Jesus, you are challenged to put your full confidence in the gospel of Jesus Christ. For those of us who come to faith, there is a great hope for the future.

A. The Basis for Our Preaching (vv. 12-15)

12. Now if Christ be preached that he rose from the dead, how say some among you that there is no resurrection of the dead?

This verse provides the first clue to the false idea that Paul is correcting in this chapter. Some at Corinth believe that a Christian who dies will remain in a state of death and not participate in the future blessings of Christ at His return. Their hope for the future lies in their remaining alive until the second coming.

Paul notes the fallacy of their thinking. On the one hand, these Christians apparently believe the fundamental truth that Christ rose from the grave on the third day. Yet, on the other hand, they say there is no such thing as resurrection from the dead. This is a contradiction, plain and simple.

13. But if there be no resurrection of the dead, then is Christ not risen.

If there is no such thing as resurrection from the dead, then the logical conclusion is that Christ himself was not raised alive from the dead. This is in fact the view of many today who have adopted a "modern" approach to theology. They believe that the universe always operates by natural law without any breakthrough of supernatural activity. They discount the idea of creation, revelation, incarnation, miracles, and resurrection. In doing so they not only reject the concept of a future day of resurrection, but also the story of the resurrection of Christ from the grave.

14. And if Christ be not risen, then is our preaching vain, and your faith is also vain.

The basic message that we proclaim to the world is that Jesus Christ died for our sins on the cross of Calvary and then rose from the grave (vv. 3-8). If that is not true, then it is a waste of time for us to preach the gospel. It would be foolish to pretend to deliver a serious message that you believe is nothing more than a religious fairy tale. To deny Christ's resurrection undermines our evangelistic witness and the whole vocation of preaching.

15. Yea, and we are found false witnesses of God; because we have testified of God that he raised up Christ: whom he raised not up, if so be that the dead rise not.

Not only does a denial of Christ's resurrection make our preaching and witnessing a waste of time; it also calls into question our integrity. We are preaching a lie, if it is true that there are no resurrections from the dead. And we have spread this lie in the name of God and religion.

B. The Basis for Our Salvation
(vv. 16, 17)

16. For if the dead rise not, then is not Christ raised.

Paul repeats the logical implication he has drawn from the Corinthians' position; no resurrection of the dead, then no resurrection of Christ.

17. And if Christ be not raised, your faith is vain; ye are yet in your sins.

Ye are yet in your sins. This may be the most sobering statement Paul makes in his argument. If the resurrection of Christ is not a historical fact, then there was no forgiveness of sins accomplished at Calvary.

We understand that Christ died at Calvary as an atonement for our sins. That is to say He suffered on the cross in a way that was equivalent to the penalty we sinners deserved from God. So how does His resurrection relate to His work at Calvary? Some have reasoned that we would still be forgiven of our sins even if Christ had remained in the tomb, because forgiveness is based upon His death, not His resurrection. Our penalty has been paid and then some.

The problem with this idea is that the New Testament presents the resurrection of Christ as the crucial test of whether or not Christ accomplished what He set out to do at Calvary. Jesus claimed that His sacrificial death would be sufficient to appease God. He promised that God would raise Him on the third day after His death as a public declaration that God had accepted His work in our behalf. Thus Paul concludes that if there is no resurrection on the third day, then God has not accepted Christ's death for our atonement. *If Christ be not raised . . . ye are yet in your sins.*

But we celebrate the reality of our salvation because we believe in the reality of Christ's resurrection. As Paul proclaims in Romans 1:4, Jesus was "declared to be the Son of God with power . . . by the resurrection from the dead."

"IF . . . NOT"

"If Christ be not risen" has been called "the most potent negative supposition" that can be made about the Christian religion. The plan of redemption revolves around two great focuses —the coming of Jesus into the world from the virgin's womb, and the coming of Jesus back into the world from the guarded tomb.

If Christ had not come, there would have been no fulfillment of prophecy and no Savior to redeem us. Robert Browning speaks about Jesus' birth and resurrection together because they both are so vital. He does this in a major poem, "Christmas-Eve and Easter-Day":

> Earth breaks up, time drops away,
> In flows Heaven, with its new day
> Of endless life . . . .

Later Browning speaks of what Jesus' salvation means to us:

> What is left for us, save, in growth
> Of soul, to rise up, far past both,
> From the gift looking to the giver,
> And from the cistern to the river,
> And from the finite to infinity,
> And from man's dust to God's divinity?

In his poem he speaks of man's frustrations and failures, his doubts, denials, lapses, and losses. But beyond all these are God's great acts of redemption in His Son:

> But, Easter-Day breaks! But Christ rises! Mercy every way is infinite,—and who can say?

> —J. G. V. B.

III. Victory Through Christ's Resurrection (1 Corinthians 15:56-58)

A. The Promise of Victory (vv. 56, 57)

Paul has demonstrated the fallacy of the idea that there will not be a day of resurrection in the future by showing its negative implication upon the resurrection of Christ. Paul now concludes his argument by working in reverse. Our view regarding the resurrection of Christ likewise has an implication for the final resurrection. If Christ has been raised from the dead as He promised, then we have reason to believe that He will raise us from the dead as He promised.

56. The sting of death is sin; and the strength of sin is the law.

Why does man die? Death is part of the curse that God placed upon creation when Adam and Eve first sinned (Genesis 2:17; 3:22-24). When the time came for us to take our place in God's creation, we did no better than Adam, for "all have sinned, and come short of the glory of God" (Romans 3:23). Our death is not just Adam's fault; it is something we deserve because we have chosen to sin. *The sting of death is sin* is another way of saying "the wages of sin is death" (Romans 6:23).

Why does sin produce such a severe penalty as death? Because *the strength of sin is the law,* sin is a serious matter because it is a violation of the most serious law in the universe, the law of

God. To disobey the will of the Creator is to deserve a severe penalty.

57. But thanks be to God, which giveth us the victory through our Lord Jesus Christ.

No matter how depressing the reality of sin and death may seem, for the Christian there is great joy in our knowledge of the resurrection of Jesus Christ. Therein lies our hope for a deliverance from death in the future and an entrance into the eternal kingdom of God.

B. A Life of Victory (v. 58)

58. Therefore, my beloved brethren, be ye steadfast, unmovable, always abounding in the work of the Lord, forasmuch as ye know that your labor is not in vain in the Lord.

Our resurrection hope is not just a dream for the future, but also a source of inspiration for the present. It motivates us to serve the Lord faithfully now as we await His ultimate gift of eternal life. It prompts us to face the joys and sorrows of life with a spirit of confidence and determination. It keeps within our hearts each day a spirit of rejoicing in the victory we have attained through our Lord Jesus Christ.

FROM FEARS TO HOPE

It was in the late 1480s that a ship captained by Bartholomew Diaz De Novaes, blown by storm and a desire to explore strange seas, succeeded in sailing around the southern tip of South Africa. Diaz sailed north on the east side of Africa, and it became clear that he had found a way to sail from Europe to Arabia, India, and China. The fabled wealth, spices, and exotic woods and cloths of those lands were now open to the Portuguese. This cape, with its treacherous winds and currents, had been called *Cabo Tormentoso*—The Cape of Storms.

Home Daily Bible Readings

Monday, Apr. 10—The First Easter (Luke 24:1-11)

Tuesday, Apr. 11—Paul's Witness to the Resurrection (1 Corinthians 15:1-11)

Wednesday, Apr. 12—Faith Is Futile Without the Resurrection (1 Corinthians 15:12-19)

Thursday, Apr. 13—We Are Made Alive in Christ (1 Corinthians 15:20-28)

Friday, Apr. 14—Resurrection of the Imperishable Body (1 Corinthians 15:35-44)

Saturday, Apr. 15—A Spiritual Inheritance (1 Corinthians 15:45-50)

Sunday, Apr. 16—Victory Through the Risen Christ (1 Corinthians 15:51-58)

Certainly the resurrection of our Lord has many similarities to Diaz's heroic accomplishment. The Cape of Death threatened mankind for centuries upon centuries. As Shakespeare puts it in *Hamlet*, it was "the undiscovered country from whose bourn no traveller returns."

It was Jesus, by His return from death and the grave, who showed us that on the other side of this dread cape there are blessings, life, victory, and felicity. The Captain of our salvation voyaged around it for us. What was the passage of despair and doom became a voyage of hope. There still are storms to confront and shoals of doubt and disaster to navigate. But it has now become a "Cape of Good Hope."   —J. G. V. B.

Conclusion

A. I Know That My Redeemer Liveth

One of the most loved portions of Handel's *Messiah* is the song "I Know That My Redeemer Liveth."

The words are taken from Job 19:25, 26. "I know that my Redeemer liveth, and that he shall stand at the latter day upon the earth: and though after my skin worms destroy this body, yet in my flesh shall I see God." The most amazing thing here is not what Handel was able to do with these words. The marvel is that Job ever said these words.

It is remarkable that, in the midst of his great suffering, Job could express such a positive statement about his future prospects. But even more remarkable is that Job had such a clear understanding of resurrection at this early stage of biblical history. Centuries before Christ would rise from the tomb, Job already spoke of his Redeemer being eternally alive. Long before Paul penned the words that would explain the significance of Christ's resurrection to us personally, Job expressed the idea that the hope for his future resurrection into the presence of God rested upon the fact that his Redeemer lived. What an inspiration and challenge this amazing man presents to us! May we join him in declaring with hope and confidence, "We know that our Redeemer lives."

B. Prayer

Father, we thank You for the mighty work You displayed in raising up Your Son Jesus Christ, and for the strength and hope that His resurrection brings to our daily lives.

C. Thought to Remember

The resurrection of Christ is more than just an event in the past. It is the basis for our hope in the future.

Learning by Doing

This page contains an alternate lesson plan emphasizing learning activities. Classes desiring such student involvement will find these suggestions helpful.

Learning Goals

As a result of completing today's lesson, students will:

1. Be able to cite from the New Testament specific encounters that witness to the resurrection of Christ.

2. Be able to locate and refer others to biblical passages that declare the significance of Christ's resurrection to our Christian faith.

3. Express some of their questions about death and the resurrection.

Into the Lesson

Begin the session by asking, "What time do you normally have to get up in the morning?" Have people call out the times and jot them on the board. Call attention to who the early risers are. Then ask, "What time do you get up on your day off?" Comment that most of us enjoy sleeping a bit later on our day off, but that sometimes we have a special project that gets us out of bed even earlier on that day. Let students give examples of activities that may get them out of bed early on a holiday.

Into the Word

Note that after Jesus' death on the cross, some women arose quite early to go to the tomb. Who were they? (v. 10). What was their purpose in going so early? (v. 1). State that we all know a great surprise awaited them: the body was gone. Ask who was there in its place, and what message the women received (vv. 4-8). Close this question and answer time by asking one final thing: Why did the apostles not believe the women when they returned with the good news? Point out that the Jews expected their Messiah to live and rule forever (Isaiah 9:6, 7). When Jesus died, they must have decided that He was not the Messiah after all.

Distribute paper and pencils to the students. Tell them that many others had unusual experiences relating to the resurrection of Christ. Ask them to list as many of these people and experiences as they can. When they finish, share these Scriptures with them and see if they can add to their lists. You may want to use the matching game below. It is in the student book, or you can make photocopies for the students. Let each student draw a line from each witness to the Scripture reference that tells of his experience.

Simon Peter	Acts 7:55, 56
Disciples going into country	Revelation 1:12-20
Eleven disciples	1 Corinthians 15:6
Seven disciples by Sea	Acts 9-3-6
Five hundred	1 Corinthians 15:7
James	John 21:1-23
Eleven disciples in Galilee	Matthew 28:16-20
Witnesses of ascension	Mark 16:12
Stephen at his martyrdom	Acts 1:3-9
Paul on road to Damascus	Luke 24:34
Apostle John	Mark 16:14

Suggest that this information would be good to retain to share with skeptical friends who doubt the resurrection.

If you copy the matching game for the class, put the following exercise on the other side of the paper. Ask each student to complete each statement with information from 1 Corinthians 15:12-17 and 56-58.

1. Some in the church at Corinth were claiming that there is —

2. If it is true that no resurrection is possible, then —

3. If Christ was not raised from the dead, then Paul and the other apostles were —

4. If there is no resurrection of the dead, then people are still lost in .—

5. The thing that gives death its terrible sting is —

6. Because we know the truth about the resurrection, we ought to be—

Answers: 1—No resurrection of the dead. 2—Christ was not raised. 3—False witnesses. 4—Sin. 5—Sin. 6—Abounding in the work of the Lord.

Allow the students to share their answers.

Into Life

One week before presenting this lesson, appoint two people to work out a role play of this situation: Jack is a devout Christian who gives much of his money and time to the church. He is being attacked by his agnostic friend, Bill, for being overly committed and generous to a cause based on a dead hero and the myth of His resurrection. Have the two share the conversation that might transpire as Jack defends his faith. Two women instead of two men may do this.

Close by challenging each person to prepare his or her own defense of the resurrection.

Let's Talk It Over

The questions on this page are designed to encourage review of the lesson Scriptures and to promote discussion of the lesson by the class. The answers provided are only discussion starters. Let your class talk it over from there.

1. "He is not here, but is risen." How can we better appreciate the dramatic power in this angelic announcement to the women at the tomb?

It is a helpful exercise to put ourselves mentally into the place of Jesus' disciples. We need to feel their sense of expectancy, waiting for Him to reveal himself as the Messiah. We need to share their perplexity because He did not. We need to experience the desperation that must have gripped them when Jesus was arrested and condemned to die. We need to identify with the heartbreak and desolation they knew after the crucifixion. And we need to allow ourselves to be caught up in the growing excitement as the reality of His resurrection became clearer. This story is the most dramatic one ever told, and we should do all we can to keep a spine-tingling sense of its drama.

2. We Christians can say to any inquirer, "Examine with an open mind the evidence for the bodily resurrection of Jesus Christ, and you will come to believe." Why can we say this?

First, we have the wide array of eyewitnesses who have testified to the event. These include the skeptical Thomas and the scholarly Paul; the other apostles, who were all slow to believe; the several women who came to the tomb expecting it to be closed; and the remainder of the five hundred Paul mentioned in 1 Corinthians 15:6. Many of these witnesses endured suffering and death as a result of their testimony to a risen Christ. Second, the enemies of the gospel provide evidence because they cannot deny the resurrection or produce the body of Jesus. Third, the ingenious explanations advanced as alternatives to the actual resurrection do not take into account all the facts.

3. How is the career of the apostle Paul one of the most convincing evidences for the reality of Jesus' resurrection?

Few individuals in history have made the kind of dramatic turnaround Paul did. As Saul of Tarsus he was a vigorous and zealous persecutor of the church; as Paul the apostle he channeled that same vigor and zeal into advancing the cause of Christ. How can we account for such a transformation? The biblical record of his encounter with the risen Christ is the best answer. Furthermore, we see in Acts and his letters how Paul endured incredible persecutions and privations in connection with his service for Christ—see 2 Corinthians 11:23-29. How was he able to endure them? His answer is found in 2 Corinthians 1:9: "But we had the sentence of death in ourselves, that we should not trust in ourselves, but in God which raiseth the dead." To paraphrase a recent television commercial, "When Paul speaks, people should listen."

4. Why should Paul's declaration of victory through the resurrection (1 Corinthians 15:57) be especially appealing in our modern society?

With the nearly universal interest in sports in our society, victory is often on people's minds. However, the kind of victory an athlete wins is fleeting. The team that wins a championship one season often falls in the standings during the next season. The player who enjoys a banner season frequently finds his statistics at a much lower level one year later. In contrast to this, the victory we gain through the resurrection of Jesus Christ is irreversible. One year from now, ten years from now, a hundred years from now, and beyond, Christ's victory over death will be the same. This theme of victory should therefore be a valuable evangelistic tool for us.

5. How is it true that, because of the resurrection, our labor is not in vain?

As the familiar poem has it, we are "builders for eternity." The works of man are tremendous: spacecrafts to the moon and the planets, towering office buildings, military equipment, great dams controlling the might of rivers. But all of these will eventually crumble. On the other hand, the labor we invest in evangelism, teaching, youth work, Christian music, missions support, and other spiritual enterprises will be remembered into eternity. And it will take eternity for us to appreciate the fruitfulness of our present efforts. As we fulfill our duties as workers in the church or witnesses outside of it, sometimes we do not see any good that has come from our efforts. But when we look back on this earthly life from the perspective of eternity, surely we will understand how God has used every sincere effort for His glory.

Exercising Liberty Wisely

DEVOTIONAL READING: Romans 15:1-13.

LESSON SCRIPTURE: 1 Corinthians 8.

PRINTED TEXT: 1 Corinthians 8.

1 Corinthians 8

1 Now as touching things offered unto idols, we know that we all have knowledge. Knowledge puffeth up, but charity edifieth.

2 And if any man think that he knoweth any thing, he knoweth nothing yet as he ought to know.

3 But if any man love God, the same is known of him.

4 As concerning therefore the eating of those things that are offered in sacrifice unto idols, we know that an idol is nothing in the world, and that there is none other God but one.

5 For though there be that are called gods, whether in heaven or in earth, (as there be gods many, and lords many,)

6 But to us there is but one God, the Father, of whom are all things, and we in him; and one Lord Jesus Christ, by whom are all things, and we by him.

7 Howbeit there is not in every man that knowledge: for some with conscience of the idol unto this hour eat it as a thing offered unto an idol; and their conscience being weak is defiled.

8 But meat commendeth us not to God: for neither, if we eat, are we the better; neither, if we eat not, are we the worse.

9 But take heed lest by any means this liberty of yours become a stumblingblock to them that are weak.

10 For if any man see thee which hast knowledge sit at meat in the idol's temple, shall not the conscience of him which is weak be emboldened to eat those things which are offered to idols;

11 And through thy knowledge shall the weak brother perish, for whom Christ died?

12 But when ye sin so against the brethren, and wound their weak conscience, ye sin against Christ.

13 Wherefore, if meat make my brother to offend, I will eat no flesh while the world standeth, lest I make my brother to offend.

GOLDEN TEXT: Take heed lest by any means this liberty of yours become a stumblingblock to them that are weak.—1 Corinthians 8:9.

Lesson Aims

After this lesson the students should:

1. Evaluate their actions by New Testament teaching and make changes where appropriate.

2. Develop greater sensitivity to the impact of their actions upon other Christians.

3. Develop a spirit of conciliation that allows for differences among Christians who want to honor both God's Word and their conscience.

Lesson Outline

INTRODUCTION
   A. Responsible Freedom
   B. Lesson Background
 I. LIBERTY WITHOUT PRIDE (1 Corinthians 8:1-3)
   A. With a Humble Spirit (vv. 1, 2)
      Conceit
   B. With a Devotion to God (v. 3)
 II. LIBERTY WITHOUT GUILT (1 Corinthians 8:4-8)
   A. Through Knowing the Truth (vv. 4-6)
      Concepts
   B. By Heeding Our Conscience (vv. 7, 8)
III. LIBERTY WITHOUT OFFENSE (1 Corinthians 8:9-13)
   A. By Not Misleading Others (vv. 9, 10)
   B. By Considering Christ's Cause (vv. 11, 12)
   C. By Being Willing to Adapt (v. 13)
CONCLUSION
   A. A Gentle Spirit
   B. Prayer
   C. Thought to Remember

Visual 8 of the visuals packet suggests two ways of viewing a Christian's liberty. The visual is shown on page 292.

Introduction

A. Responsible Freedom

An old joke tells of a man just released from prison. He ran down the street, leaping for joy and yelling, "I'm free! I'm free!" A little boy replied, "That's nothing, mister; I'm four."

We hear about people released from imprisonment, slavery, or political tyranny; but most of us cannot identify with these situations. We can only imagine the excitement of being released from bondage. But when it comes to the freedom from sin and death that we enjoy through Jesus Christ, all of us Christians have personally experienced the excitement of being set free. Paul makes this freedom sound both exciting and challenging.

B. Lesson Background

Paul's first letter to the church at Corinth dealt with a number of problems. We have seen how Paul dealt with misunderstandings regarding spiritual gifts and the hope of our resurrection. Before his discussion of these issues is his treatment of an ethical issue involving meats sacrificed to idols.

Apparently there was much disagreement about the propriety of eating foods that had any association with the local idolatry. Some argued that it was simply a matter of conscience, while others contended that everyone should take the same position. In 1 Corinthians 8, Paul offers some insights on this subject.

But an even greater problem was the unloving way in which the Corinthians criticized those who reached ethical conclusions differing from their own. Corinth needed to learn the true nature of our liberty in Christ, to know it involves a certain amount of give-and-take with other sincere Christians.

I. Liberty Without Pride (1 Corinthians 8:1-3)

The spirit of pride and boasting was certainly a problem for the Corinthians in the area of spiritual gifts, as we noted in an earlier study. Now we discover that this attitude was present in other matters as well.

A. With a Humble Spirit (vv. 1, 2)

1. Now as touching things offered unto idols, we know that we all have knowledge. Knowledge puffeth up, but charity edifieth.

We all have knowledge. In 1 Corinthians, this is not a flattering statement. The first chapter contrasts the so-called wisdom of the world with the simple truths of Jesus Christ. Though the gospel message appears as foolishness in the eyes of the world, Paul concludes that "the foolishness of God is wiser than men" (1:25).

The second chapter contrasts Paul's simple preaching with the eloquence that many admire. Speaking of those who boast that they are wise and learned, chapter 3 calls them "babes in Christ," still limited to the "milk" of God's Word (3:1-3). Then Paul concludes by declaring, "If any man among you seemeth to be wise in this world, let him become a fool [that is, back away from the world's way of thinking], that he may be wise. For the wisdom of this world is foolishness with God (3:18, 19).

Then to say *we know that we all have knowledge* is a bit of satire against those who are proud of their knowledge. Such an attitude *puffeth up* a person, and makes him arrogant.

The antidote for this prideful spirit is a dose of love and concern for others. As Paul declares quite eloquently in chapter 13, a spirit of love displaces arrogance and motivates us to relate to others in a gracious and considerate manner. Indeed, *charity edifieth;* it acts in a way that is beneficial to others.

2. And if any man think that he knoweth any thing, he knoweth nothing yet as he ought to know.

Paul repeats the conclusion that he reached in the first three chapters regarding the folly of man's pursuit of knowledge without a solid foundation in the Word of God.

CONCEIT

We all have been aware of people who are very "wise in their own eyes." Just such a person is described by a character in Shakespeare's *Merchant of Venice:*

As who should say, "I am Sir Oracle,
And when I ope my lips let no dog bark!"

It appears that such were some of Paul's critics and opponents. Some questioned his apostolic authority, and some denied essential doctrines of Christian faith. Perhaps worst of all was the way they affirmed their doubts and denials. They claimed to be more spiritual, more informed, more aware of mystic realities, than the ordinary Christian or even Paul himself.

They were like a group of balloons at a party. Colorful they were, and bouncing around in a splash of brightness. But there was nothing solid or sustaining about them. They were very unsubstantial—"puffed up," but not built up.

—J. G. V. B.

B. With a Devotion to God (v. 3)

3. But if any man love God, the same is known of him.

A genuine relationship with God is a far greater achievement than the world's knowledge and skills. God does not focus His attention upon those who excel in the eyes of the world, but upon those devoted to knowing Him.

When dealing with bureaucracy and red tape, we sometimes say, "It's not what you know, but whom you know that counts." For a Christian who is seeking a real sense of satisfaction, the rule from this verse would be, "It's not whom you know, but who knows you."

II. Liberty Without Guilt (1 Corinthians 8:4-8)

Two critics on TV sometimes refer to certain movies as their "guilty pleasures." These are movies they like, but are embarrassed to admit it because of their poor quality or objectionable content. The phrase "guilty pleasures" could well describe some of the things we Christians do. We think they are not really sinful, and yet we feel a little guilty. Paul shows us how to attain the clear conscience that we desire.

A. Through Knowing the Truth (vv. 4-6)

4. As concerning therefore the eating of those things that are offered in sacrifice unto idols, we know that an idol is nothing in the world, and that there is none other God but one.

It was common practice to use only part of an animal sacrifice as a burnt offering, and then to sell the rest of the meat to the general public. In a pagan city like Corinth, virtually all of the meat sold in the marketplaces was first used in pagan sacrifices. Some in the church wondered if eating this "pagan meat" was proper.

Also troubling to Christians was the practice of blessing a meal with a prayer to a pagan deity. Though Christians would not say such a prayer in their own homes, they could not eat with non-Christian neighbors or participate in community meals without sitting through these pagan blessings. Was it better to withdraw further from the world and forfeit some opportunities for evangelism, or to sit through the prayers without an "amen" and appear to condone pagan activity?

The first thing the apostle Paul does to resolve this issue is to look for guidance in the basic truths of our faith. We know that our God is the only true deity. When dealing with difficult moral issues, the best place to begin is with the relevant truths we are given in God's Word. Not every ethical question is specifically answered in the Bible with clear rules to be followed, but when we have to make a judgment call, we can assume that the Bible will lay down some general principles that will point us in the right direction.

5. For though there be that are called gods, whether in heaven or in earth, (as there be gods many, and lords many).

In the Roman Empire at least one hundred pagan gods and goddesses were recognized—and this is mild compared to the claims of Hinduism, which speaks of millions of deities. Nevertheless, as verse 4 declares, none of these so-called gods have any reality.

6. But to us there is but one God, the Father, of whom are all things, and we in him; and one Lord Jesus Christ, by whom are all things, and we by him.

How do you know who is the real God in the midst of so many claimants? A key question is whether a particular "god" is created or uncreated. Certainly the statues of the pagan gods have been created by the hands of men. This implies that the gods themselves may also be nothing more than man's creation. With this thought in mind, we can understand why Paul said it was disastrous for mankind to worship and serve "the creature more than the Creator" (Romans 1:25).

This matter of identifying God is so significant that Paul often links God to the work of creation. In this verse he refers to *God, the Father, of whom are all things,* and His Son *Jesus Christ, by whom are all things.* This basic truth indicates that pagan deities are not real entities.

So how does this information relate to the issue of meats sacrificed to pagan idols? Since pagan deities are not real, it is reasonable to conclude that they cannot contaminate the meat and make it inedible for Christians. This is Paul's own conclusion in 1 Timothy 4:4, where he says, "Every creature [created thing] of God is good, and nothing to be refused, if it be received with thanksgiving." Those Christians in Corinth who felt free to eat meats purchased in the marketplace had made a proper judgment.

CONCEPTS

There were many so-called gods in the first century: Isis and Osiris of Egypt; the Persian deity, Mithra; and many local divinities such as Athena, patron goddess of Athens, and Aphrodite or Venus, worshiped in Corinth. Then there was the God of the Jews.

Paul went back to the absolute essentials when he said that, after all, there was but one *real* God and one *true* Lord. Devotion to our heavenly Father and dedication to Jesus, His Son, is the vital reality of our faith as Christians.

Often in athletic contests the great need is seen to "get back to the fundamentals." In football all depends on blocking, tackling, running with, throwing, catching and holding onto the ball. In baseball it lies in hitting, catching, running, and throwing. In basketball it is in shooting, dribbling, cutting, screening, and rebounding. These are the continually repeated actions on which all the patterns and developments of the games rest.

Whatever matters there are of meeting place, time of gathering, symbolic acts performed, and speakers heard, the real question is, "Who is the

visual 8

Stumbling Block ● Stepping Stone?

real, true, living God, the Creator and Sustainer of all things? Who is the One above all others who has the right to claim our loyalty and trust?" The answer: God the Father, and our Lord Jesus Christ.   —J. G. V. B.

B. By Heeding Our Conscience (vv. 7, 8)

7. Howbeit there is not in every man that knowledge: for some with conscience of the idol unto this hour eat it as a thing offered unto an idol; and their conscience being weak is defiled.

There was nothing wrong with the meat at Corinth, but not every Christian could eat it in good conscience. Some felt that they were doing wrong. Their feelings were wrong, their conscience was *weak;* nevertheless, that is how they felt. So Paul had to address the issue of what to do when your conscience is wrong.

God has given to every person a conscience that produces inner feelings when we make moral decisions. When we make bad decisions, our conscience should make us feel guilty. When we make good decisions, it should make us feel good. But reading the conscience is not always easy. When we play around with sin we can so harden our hearts that we cannot clearly hear the warning signals of the conscience. And then there is the problem illustrated by some in Corinth. Sometimes we interfere with the working of the conscience by bringing in ideas and rules devised by man's imagination rather than the Word of God. The idea that a pagan idol could somehow contaminate meat was wrong. Those who accepted this idea were causing their conscience to accuse them wrongfully.

There is reason to be concerned when someone's conscience is *weak* and not operating properly. But it is worse when a person with a weak conscience goes ahead and does the thing for which he feels guilty. That person becomes *defiled* or spiritually corrupted.

When dealing with the same issue in Romans 14, Paul advises his readers not to violate their conscience when it gives a warning, even if their conscience is wrong. "He that doubteth is damned if he eat, because he eateth not of faith: for whatsoever is not of faith is sin" (Romans 14:23).

8. But meat commendeth us not to God: for neither, if we eat, are we the better; neither, if we eat not, are we the worse.

The question of pagan meats turned out to be a false issue. It was commendable that the members of the church were concerned about doing right. It was unfortunate that not everyone was able to find the best answer, and that some violated their conscience.

How can we determine whether or not to proceed with an activity we are considering? There seems to be two key tests. First, is what we are about to do consistent with the Word of God? This does not mean an activity must be approved by name in the Bible (though when that happens it is quite helpful). Since much of what we do is not specifically mentioned in Scripture, we need to consider whether there is some biblical truth or principle that seems to contradict the activity in question. If there is not, then we can reasonably assume that the action is consistent with God's Word.

The second test is to consider whether or not our conscience is setting off any alarms. This is a good thing for us. The conscience can provide a ready safeguard if we miss something in our consideration of biblical principles. But this chapter has also shown that the conscience can unnecessarily restrict us when we have weakened it. Nevertheless, if our conscience says no, then we should proceed no further.

Of course you and I do not often have to determine whether or not to eat meat sacrificed to idols (and even if we did, we now know the correct answer). But consider some of the activities that we do have occasion to wonder about. Is it proper for a Christian to use tobacco or drink alcoholic beverages? Does it matter whether I choose caffeine or no caffeine, sugar or diet, salt or no salt, regular or low fat? Can a Christian listen to popular music (including rock and rap!) and enjoy modern dances? Can I watch movies and TV programs with all their wickedness as long as I do not consent to the immoral things that are said and done on the screen?

The apostle Paul's tests are just as valid with these issues as they were with pagan meats. We know that some of these activities look questionable in light of biblical principles, such as our responsibility to take good care of our bodies (1 Corinthians 6:12-20), and the challenge for us to devote our minds to things that are good and true (Philippians 4:8). The test of conscience also

snags some of these activities. We ought to be suspicious when we are doing something that we would not want the rest of the church members to know about.

III. Liberty Without Offense (1 Corinthians 8:9-13)

Those who reasoned through the meat issue correctly may be thinking at this point that they are in the clear with Paul. But it is not necessarily so. A person with a "strong" conscience must take care not to hurt his friend who has a "weak" conscience.

A. By Not Misleading Others (vv. 9, 10)

9. But take heed lest by any means this liberty of yours become a stumblingblock to them that are weak.

A *stumblingblock* is just what it sounds like, an object lying in someone's path that causes him to trip. Paul's fuller discussion of the idea of a stumbling block is found in Romans 14. The warning he gives there is similar to that given in this verse: "That no man put a stumblingblock or an occasion to fall in his brother's way" (Romans 14:13).

10. For if any man see thee which hast knowledge sit at meat in the idol's temple, shall not the conscience of him which is weak be emboldened to eat those things which are offered to idols?

To *sit at meat in the idol's temple* does not necessarily mean that some Christians were participating in pagan worship services. In Corinth and other pagan cities, civic and social functions often were held in rooms or porches of pagan temples. The temples served as public shelters for any community meeting.

Some of the Christians who mistakenly thought pagan meats are bad were eating those meats anyway because they saw the more mature Christians doing it. These weaker Christians were trying to rethink their position, but their conscience was still telling them they were doing wrong. Thus they ended up violating their conscience, contrary to Paul's teaching above—and the example of stronger Christians caused them to do it.

The stumbling block warning is usually given to strong Christians, not to those who are weak. A weaker Christian rarely becomes a stumbling block, because a mature Christian is not likely to follow the example of one who is less experienced. However, an immature Christian does often follow the lead of those he considers more advanced, and therefore the stronger needs to consider where he is leading his friend.

B. By Considering Christ's Cause (vv. 11, 12)

11. And through thy knowledge shall the weak brother perish, for whom Christ died?

If the weaker Christian is getting mixed-up signals from his conscience, one might be inclined to say, "Well, that is his problem." But Paul recommends a more considerate view. Considering how precious this individual is to Christ, we ought to seriously care about what he does to hurt himself, even if it is his fault.

12. But when ye sin so against the brethren, and wound their weak conscience, ye sin against Christ.

The weaker Christian sins when he disregards his conscience (Romans 14:22, 23). But likewise, the stronger Christian is wrong when he encourages his friend to violate his conscience (Romans 14:22, 23). One who is committed to Christ does not want to do anything that displeases his Lord.

C. By Being Willing to Adapt (v. 13)

13. Wherefore, if meat make my brother to offend, I will eat no flesh while the world standeth, lest I make my brother to offend.

Paul's personal resolution for dealing with the stumbling block issue is plain: stop doing whatever is leading a fellow Christian into sin.

It does not seem fair for a weaker Christian, who is thinking wrong on an issue, to dictate what mature Christians can do. But consider the following observations.

For one thing, weaker Christians do not have the right to require that other Christians make concessions to them. Weaker Christians are instructed in Romans 14:2-6 not to make an issue

---

Home Daily Bible Readings

Monday, Apr. 17—Avoid Disputes Over Opinions (Romans 14:1-9)
Tuesday, Apr. 18—Refrain From Passing Judgment (Romans 14:10-18)
Wednesday, Apr. 19—Seek Peace and Mutuality (Romans 14:19-23)
Thursday, Apr. 20—Bear With the Weak (Romans 15:1-6)
Friday, Apr. 21—Receive One Another in Christ (Romans 15:7-13)
Saturday, Apr. 22—Love, Not Knowledge, Aids Christian Growth (1 Corinthians 8:1-6)
Sunday, Apr. 23—Use One's Christian Liberty With Care (1 Corinthians 8:7-13)

---

out of differences of opinion and conscience. If the mature make any concessions, it should be done voluntarily, as Paul illustrates in this verse.

Furthermore, the stumbling block principle seems to refer only to those situations where the weaker Christian actually follows our example in opposition to his conscience. It does not encompass those who simply choose to criticize our actions. We do not lead them to violate their conscience, and so what we do is not a true stumbling block. Their criticism violates Paul's instructions to keep such judgment to yourself (Romans 14:3-6).

While a mature Christian need not concern himself about the unjustified sniping of others, he does want to do whatever he can within reason to keep from encouraging someone else to sin.

Conclusion

A. A Gentle Spirit

Numbers 12:3 says that "Moses was very meek, above all the men which were upon the face of the earth." In the western world we often think of meekness as a characteristic of someone who is weak and unwilling to stand up for himself and for his convictions. Not so with Moses.

Moses was indeed a man of power and determination. He stood before Pharaoh, and faced him down in a duel of wits and nerve. He stood before the people of Israel, and served as their leader and judge. He stood before the presence of God on Mount Sinai and received from God the law that he would later be responsible for enforcing in Israel. Moses was anything but weak and passive, and yet he was considered the meekest man on earth.

Moses had developed a style of conduct and leadership that allowed him to carry out his responsibilities and stand for his convictions in a way that impressed others favorably.

This is the impression we desire to leave with other Christians when we are discussing our differences of opinion. Our goal should be not only to be correct in our doctrinal and ethical thinking, but also to be considerate in the way we address our truth to others.

B. Prayer

Father, help us to be faithful to the teaching of Your Word and the guidance of our conscience, and to be gracious toward those with whom we disagree. In Jesus' name we pray. Amen.

C. Thought to Remember

It is hard to praise a person for being right on an issue when his manner of being right is all wrong.

Learning by Doing

This page contains an alternate lesson plan emphasizing learning activities. Classes desiring such student involvement will find these suggestions helpful.

Learning Goals

After studying 1 Corinthians 8, students will:

1. Be able to write a modern paraphrase of 1 Corinthians 8 to show how much liberty a person who is a Christian may exercise.

2. Discover that being loving and considerate of the weaker person is as important as being "right."

3. Examine issues that are potential stumbling blocks in the 1990s.

Into the Lesson

Write this sentence on the board: Love God and do as you please. Explain that these words were written by Augustine, one of the great early church fathers. Ask the students if they agree or disagree. After hearing their opinions, tell them that 1 Corinthians 8 deals with the issue of using liberty wisely, which is closely akin to the words on the board. Ask them to be watching for verses that apply to the above statement.

Into the Word

Tell about the issue of meat offered to idols and the problem it created at Corinth. (See the lesson background.) Give each class member a sheet of paper that has been divided into two columns with suggested Scriptures on each. Label one column "love" and the other "knowledge." Ask people to write phrases in each column to describe the actions and results pointed out in the suggested verses. (The student book has this in a different format.)

KNOWLEDGE

v. 1 Puffs up.
v. 2 Is incomplete at best.
v. 4 An idol is nothing.
v. 4 There is only one God.
v. 11 Weaker brother can be destroyed by it.

LOVE

v. 1 Builds up.
v. 3 God knows the one who loves.
v. 11 Refuses to ruin the weaker brother.
v. 12 Cares more about the weaker brother than about exercising his own freedom.

After the paper study is completed, share answers and then point out that the Corinthians had focused on knowledge and forgotten love.

Suggest that other passages reinforce the emphasis upon loving others. Let these verses be read aloud: Ephesians 4:15; John 13:35; Romans 13:10; Ephesians 4:1, 2; Matthew 22:39.

Return to the agree/disagree statement and ask what ideas students have now. Remember Matthew 22:37-39. If we love God we will keep His commandments, and that will be what pleases us (1 John 5:3). Chief among His commandments is that we love one another.

Use the word *conscience* to make an acrostic. Let students make short statements about the conscience. Some possible ideas are:

C alls out to us when we do wrong
O nly contains what it is taught
N ot always to be your guide
S eeks the good of the individual
C an be ineffective if wrongly taught
I t can be used by the Holy Spirit
E xhorts us to do right
N ot the same in all individuals
C an be silenced if ignored
E nergizes, encourages.

Remind the class that being right is not the only thing we have to think about. A Christian's love should control his behavior. Use this diagram to summarize the lesson:

Corinthians' Way	Paul's Insight
Knowledge	*Love*
↓	↓
prideful	God's way
↓	↓
painful	concern for others
↓	↓
stumbling block	self-denial

Discuss: Why must the stronger believer defer to the weaker? Is there ever a limit to this deferring? (The stronger defers to keep the weaker from falling and to help him grow and mature. The limit comes when the weaker demands pampering and makes unreasonable demands.)

Into Life

Draw several square blocks on the board and ask the class to suggest some issues in the 90s that might be considered stumbling blocks. Close with prayer focusing on growing in love.

Let's Talk It Over

The questions on this page are designed to encourage review of the lesson Scriptures and to promote discussion of the lesson by the class. The answers provided are only discussion starters. Let your class talk it over from there.

1. How should we respond to those who regard themselves as superior to us because of their knowledge or education?

It may be irritating to listen to a person who makes light of our convictions and appears smug in the assumption that he or she is intellectually superior. On such occasions we can take satisfaction from Paul's observation: "And if any man think that he knoweth any thing, he knoweth nothing yet as he ought to know" (1 Corinthians 8:2). On television a speaker may imply that if people were properly educated they would accept the legitimacy of abortion or homosexuality. We do not need to feel defensive or intimidated by such "intellectuals." With a simple knowledge of the Word of God we are in a better position than they to judge the issues confronting our society.

2. There is an increasing likelihood in our society that we are going to have contact with people who espouse a non-Christian religion. How shall we respond to such people?

Many people from Oriental and Middle Eastern countries live in our land. We need not be afraid to associate with them, nor should we make uncharitable attacks upon their religious views. Remember the apostle Paul's approach to the pagan worshipers in Athens. Graciously he said, "I see that in every way you are very religious" (Acts 17:22, *New International Version*). He of course went on to tell the people of Athens of the true and living God. In similar fashion we can be gracious to pagan neighbors without hesitating to point to Jesus Christ as the one Savior and Lord.

3. When deciding whether or not to participate in a certain activity, we may ask ourselves, "Is what I am about to do consistent with the Word of God?" What is involved in using this test?

First, we must become thoroughly familiar with the moral principles of the Word of God. If our knowledge is incomplete, we may not be equipped to answer the question above. The Ten Commandments (even though they are in the Old Testament), Jesus' Sermon on the Mount in Matthew 5-7, and Paul's listings of the lusts of the flesh and the fruit of the Spirit in Galatians 5:19-26 are some passages that can key us into biblical morality.

Second, realizing our human tendency to interpret the Bible according to our preconceptions, we need to consult mature fellow believers as a safeguard against error.

Third, we need to pray for the courage and boldness to follow what the Bible says, even when it goes against popular opinion.

4. When making a decision about participating in a certain activity, we may ask, "Does this in any way violate my conscience?" What is involved in using this test?

This test is similar to the one discussed in the question immediately above. We must work at programming our conscience according to the Word of God. Then if our conscience troubles us regarding any activity, we should be able to recall some biblical principle that lies behind the uncomfortable feeling. Our conscience, however, is not infallible; it can become oversensitized and disturb us over matters that are not in themselves sinful. An example of this is seen in persons who have been reared in an ultrastrict environment. Their conscience may give them difficulty over activities that most Christians consider unquestionably legitimate. This once again shows the importance of studying and discussing the Word of God with fellow believers, so that misinterpretations and misapplications can be seen for what they are.

5. Disagreements in the church may be inevitable. How can we learn to disagree with our fellow Christians in a gracious and tactful manner?

The Christian couple Priscilla and Aquila provide a good example in the way they dealt with the inadequately informed Apollos. Acts 18:24-28 describes how they heard him speak of Jesus in the synagogue at Ephesus and perceived that "he knew only the baptism of John" (v. 25, *New International Version*). They did not rudely take him to task on the spot, but "invited him to their home and explained to him the way of God more adequately" (v. 26, *New International Version*). Many of our disagreements can be resolved amicably if we discuss them in a relaxed setting, with a calm and reasonable approach.

Caring for One Another

DEVOTIONAL READING: Galatians 6:1-10.

LESSON SCRIPTURE: 2 Corinthians 1:1-14.

PRINTED TEXT: 2 Corinthians 1:3-14.

2 Corinthians 1:3-14

3 Blessed be God, even the Father of our Lord Jesus Christ, the Father of mercies, and the God of all comfort;

4 Who comforteth us in all our tribulation, that we may be able to comfort them which are in any trouble, by the comfort wherewith we ourselves are comforted of God.

5 For as the sufferings of Christ abound in us, so our consolation also aboundeth by Christ.

6 And whether we be afflicted, it is for your consolation and salvation, which is effectual in the enduring of the same sufferings which we also suffer: or whether we be comforted, it is for your consolation and salvation.

7 And our hope of you is stedfast, knowing, that as ye are partakers of the sufferings, so shall ye be also of the consolation.

8 For we would not, brethren, have you ignorant of our trouble which came to us in Asia, that we were pressed out of measure, above strength, insomuch that we despaired even of life:

9 But we had the sentence of death in ourselves, that we should not trust in ourselves, but in God which raiseth the dead:

10 Who delivered us from so great a death, and doth deliver: in whom we trust that he will yet deliver us;

11 Ye also helping together by prayer for us, that for the gift bestowed upon us by the means of many persons thanks may be given by many on our behalf.

12 For our rejoicing is this, the testimony of our conscience, that in simplicity and godly sincerity, not with fleshly wisdom, but by the grace of God, we have had our conversation in the world, and more abundantly to you-ward.

13 For we write none other things unto you, than what ye read or acknowledge; and I trust ye shall acknowledge even to the end;

14 As also ye have acknowledged us in part, that we are your rejoicing, even as ye also are ours in the day of the Lord Jesus.

Apr
30

GOLDEN TEXT: Blessed be God, even the Father of our Lord Jesus Christ, the Father of mercies, and the God of all comfort; who comforteth us in all our tribulation, that we may be able to comfort them which are in any trouble, by the comfort wherewith we ourselves are comforted of God.—2 Corinthians 1:3, 4.

Christians Living In Community

Unit 2. Nurturing the Life of

the Community (Lessons 5-9)

Lessons Aims

After this lesson the students should:

1. Have a better appreciation of why God allows good people to suffer.

2. See the need to be a care-provider for Christian friends when they are suffering.

3. Determine to pray when others ask prayer for their needs.

Lessons Outline

INTRODUCTION

    A. You Can't Hide

    B. Lesson Background

I. COMFORT FROM SUFFERING (2 Corinthians 1:3-7)

    A. As a Gift From God (vv. 3, 4)

        True Comfort

    B. As a Sharing With Christ (v. 5)

    C. As a Blessing for Others (vv. 6, 7)

II. DELIVERANCE BY PRAYER (2 Corinthians 1:8-11)

    A. Paul's Earlier Troubles (vv. 8, 9)

        Sentence of Death

    B. God's Gracious Response (v. 10)

    C. Corinth's Supportive Prayer (v. 11)

III. JOY IN FRIENDS (2 CORINTHIANS (1:12-14)

    A. An Honest Relationship (vv. 12, 13)

        Sincere Preaching

    B. A Mutual Respect (v. 14)

CONCLUSION

    A. Just Hold Me

    B. Prayer

    C. Thought to Remember

A positive aspect of personal suffering is carried by visual 9 of the visuals packet. The visual is shown on page 300.

Introduction

A. You Can't Hide

Remember the old comedy line: "Doctor, my arm hurts when I move it like this." "Then don't move it like that." If only the hurts of life could be dismissed so easily!

Suffering and sorrow are woven into the fabric of life. We can close our eyes to the news of disasters and famines, of criminal assault and unfortunate accidents. We can avoid those sections of town where we are likely to encounter poverty. Yet, suffering still finds us as it touches those we love and cherish, or takes its toll on our own physical health. We need to learn how to deal properly with suffering.

B. Lesson Background

Paul's first letter to Corinth must have been difficult for him to write. We often refer to it as "the sorrowful epistle" because the Corinthians were made sorrowful by its rebukes (2 Corinthians 7:8-11).

Paul's second letter to Corinth is more uplifting. According to Titus's first-hand report, things still are not perfect in the church, but they are improving. Especially encouraging to the apostle is the news that his friends in Corinth still love him despite his criticisms (2 Corinthians 7: 6, 7).

In light of all this, it is appropriate that 2 Corinthians deals with the theme of comfort. After agonizing within himself at having to write such a stern first letter, Paul enjoys the comfort of hearing good news from Titus. After being called to task in the first letter for their childish behavior, the Corinthians need a letter to comfort them with words of kindness and love. Chapter 1 not only describes the nature of comfort; it also brings comfort both to Paul and to his friends in Corinth.

I. Comfort From Suffering (2 Corinthians 1:3-7)

We readily echo the words of Hebrews 12:11: "No chastening [suffering] for the present seemeth to be joyous, but grievous." But the second half of the verse is harder to appreciate: "Afterward it yieldeth the peaceable fruit of righteousness unto them which are exercised thereby." The following verses likewise emphasize the benefits that derive from suffering.

A. As a Gift From God (vv. 3, 4)

3. Blessed be God, even the Father of our Lord Jesus Christ, the Father of mercies, and the God of all comfort.

There are many qualities of God that deserve our praise: His power, wisdom, holiness, faithfulness, justice, love, and so forth. Each one has relevance to our lives; each one contributes to our well-being. We especially enjoy celebrating God's mercy, comfort, and compassion.

Mercy is akin to compassion. It is to feel sad when others are grieving, to wish for relief. But there is more. As illustrated in the life of Jesus, compassion involves more than just feeling. Compassion leads one to do something to alleviate the hurt. Often the Gospels note that Jesus was "filled with compassion" as He looked at the people who surrounded Him, and then He would heal them or feed them with bread and fish. God does not simply watch us suffer, but He acts in our behalf because He is filled with mercy and compassion.

4. Who comforteth us in all our tribulation, that we may be able to comfort them which are in any trouble, by the comfort wherewith we ourselves are comforted of God.

The Greek word translated *comfort* literally means to be called to one's side to help and support him. This brings to mind those occasions when we visit a friend in the hospital or speak to a family at a funeral home. The important thing is not what we say, but the fact that we are there, that we care enough to be around, and wait, and listen. This picture does not exhaust the full meaning of how God *comforteth us*, but it is true that His caring presence is often felt by those who trust in Him.

Why do we have to go through all *our tribulation*? Why do God's people have to suffer? One answer is given in Hebrews 12. Tribulation is a tool used by God to discipline His children. The hardships of life toughen us and force us to grow in faith and perseverance. Discipline is never pleasant at the time, but as we mature we learn to appreciate the correction of our earthly parents and our heavenly Father.

Verse 4 of our text suggests another reason why God's people sometimes suffer. We learn how to deal with pain and grief through the aid of Christian friends and the ever-present peace of God. Then God expects us to take what we have learned and share it with others, that *we may be able to comfort . . . by the comfort wherewith we ourselves are comforted of God.*

TRUE COMFORT

We find the word *comfort*, in some form, five times in the third and fourth verses of 2 Corinthians. These verses are dear to us because we face many times of grief, anxiety, and loss. "The comfort wherewith we ourselves are comforted of God" is a reality blessed and beautiful. This is what the following poem expresses:

> The furrow on the brow of care,
> The mind near yielding to despair;
> The hollow gulf of lonely days
> The future holds, in all its ways;
> The sense of emptiness and grief,
> The constant weight, with scant relief—
>
> To these, what balm sweet comfort brings,
> To soothe our wounds, and give us wings
> With which to rise o'er darksome things;
> To change the bitter and the sour
> With sense of purpose and of power.

> The love of God, the grace of Christ
> Have blessed sad lives, and have sufficed
> To tinge with glory all the gloom,
> When His way and His Word have room.
> —J. G. VANBUREN
> —J. G. V. B.

B. As a Sharing With Christ (v. 5)

5. For as the sufferings of Christ abound in us, so our consolation also aboundeth by Christ.

In Philippians 3:10 Paul makes the strange statement that he wants to know Christ, "and the power of his resurrection, and the fellowship of his sufferings." This is not an irrational impulse to seek out harassment and persecution. Paul simply wants to be an active part of the Christian experience. Jesus had taught His disciples, "If they have persecuted me, they will also persecute you" (John 15:20). We are not to look for trouble; but we are to expect it, knowing that it is a common experience for us who are committed to Christ to have *the sufferings of Christ abound in us.*

The good news in all of this is that our sharing with Christ in suffering brings with it a sharing in the peace and comfort that He abundantly supplies to His friends. Restating his earlier emphasis upon God as the source of mercy and comfort, Paul declares that *our consolation also aboundeth by Christ.*

C. As a Blessing for Others (vv. 6, 7)

6. And whether we be afflicted, it is for your consolation and salvation, which is effectual in the enduring of the same sufferings which we also suffer: or whether we be comforted, it is for your consolation and salvation.

This is another way of expressing the idea from verse 4: Christians are expected to use their sufferings to help them help others who are suffering. Our insights can be *effectual* (effective) in helping our friends be strong and remain faithful to God as they are hurting.

Consider how Paul uses this concept to help himself in times of trouble. He says, *Whether we be afflicted, it is for your consolation and salvation.* Apparently he toughens his mind and emotions in the midst of suffering by telling himself that this is a part of his training for helping his friends. We can benefit by following Paul's example, by developing a positive attitude that will lessen the pain we are feeling.

7. And our hope of you is steadfast, knowing, that as ye are partakers of the sufferings, so shall ye be also of the consolation.

And our hope of you is steadfast. Paul is very serious about this mutual sharing of suffering and comfort. These are not simply nice-sounding words, but Paul is practicing what he is preaching by writing this letter of consolation as a follow-up to his "sorrowful epistle." He does care about the feelings of his friends in Corinth.

How serious are we about bringing comfort and relief to our Christian friends who are hurting? Are we listening as needs are expressed in our fellowship gatherings, and then remembering to pray? Are we taking the time to call our friends and check up on their progress, or to visit in their homes, in the hospital, and at the funeral home? Are we contributing funds and physical assistance when such things are in short supply? Many of us are doing these things. When we are, we are truly serving as agents of comfort for our brothers and sisters, just as "the Father of mercies and comfort" has done for us.

II. Deliverance by Prayer (2 Corinthians 1:8-11)

Paul has been through hurt, time and time again. He preached for the church at Corinth for a year and a half (Acts 18:11), and doubtless he had told about some of his difficulties. Now Paul gives a brief reminder of his own hardships, and of the relief that God always provided.

A. Paul's Earlier Troubles (vv. 8, 9)

8. For we would not, brethren, have you ignorant of our trouble which came to us in Asia, that we were pressed out of measure, above strength, insomuch that we despaired even of life.

Across the Aegean Sea from Corinth is the Roman province called Asia, where Paul recently was the focus of a city-wide riot (Acts 19:23-41). He may have faced other dangers (1 Corinthians 15:32). In 2 Corinthians 11:24-27 he lists some more of his troubles: "Of the Jews five times received I forty stripes save one. Thrice was I beaten with rods, once was I stoned, thrice I suffered shipwreck, a night and a day I have been in the deep [lost at sea]; in journeyings often, in perils of waters, in perils of robbers, in perils by mine own countrymen, in perils by the heathen, in perils in the city, in perils in the wilderness, in perils in the sea, in perils among false brethren; in weariness and painfulness, in watchings often, in hunger and thirst, in fastings often, in cold and nakedness." With a history like this, we understand why Paul says he sometimes felt tremendous pressure (*pressed out of measure*), or as we would say, beat all out of shape.

9. But we had the sentence of death in ourselves, that we should not trust in ourselves, but in God which raiseth the dead.

In our day Paul might say, "I felt like I was on death row." As he declares in the previous verse, there were times when things got so tough that he *despaired even of life*. He thought he actually was about to die.

Why did this great servant of God have to live through such anxiety that he feared for his life? So that he and his companions might learn not to trust in themselves, *but in God which raiseth the dead*. When you are pushed to the edge of a precipice, and you realize that there is nothing you can do to save yourself from plummeting to your death, you become keenly aware of your own limitations. We human beings are by nature self-reliant, thinking we can handle any situation that comes our way. God uses trials and tribulations to humble us and force us to look beyond ourselves and seek out His divine assistance. When we reach the end of our rope, we finally realize what we should have been doing all along: that is, looking to God for strength and guidance and deliverance.

SENTENCE OF DEATH

Paul is telling the Corinthians about his problems and perplexities. These were not just physical dangers, but also emotional and mental tensions. The *New International Version* renders part of verse 9, "In our hearts we felt the sentence of death."

How many times we find ourselves in similar situations! We go to a hospital for tests to determine if we have cancer or some other deadly disease. Often we become very despondent even before we learn the results. We feel in our hearts a "sentence of death." Sometimes this feeling comes when someone we love is wheeled into an operating room for major surgery. We are apprehensive and anxious. Sometimes we are concerned as friends or relatives are coming on a long highway through sleet, snow, fog, or heavy thunderstorms.

How exhilarating it is when all our dire forebodings are found to be in error. So it is with

visual 9

Paul. He has faced death, but God has delivered him (v. 10).

May our trust in God grow as we realize that whatever the "sentence of death" seems to be, there is one who can repeal the sentence and give us, as he gave Paul, new hope, new help, and new horizons of benefit and blessing.

—J. G. V. B.

B. God's Gracious Response (v. 10)

10. Who delivered us from so great a death, and doth deliver: in whom we trust that he will yet deliver us.

Past, present, and future. Paul has already experienced God's ability to help him through difficult times. He feels that he is enjoying a little bit of God's mercy in his current situation (of which we know little). And he believes there will yet be other occasions for the hand of God to assist him in times of trouble. What a well-rounded picture of the work of God!

The value of reflecting upon past mercies is well expressed by Johnson Oatman, Jr. in the words of his hymn "Count Your Blessings":

When upon life's billows you are tempest-tossed,
When you are discouraged, thinking all is lost,
Count your many blessings, name them one by one,
And it will surprise you what the Lord hath done.

When we proceed with this exercise, we do find a reason for encouragement, a reason for believing that God does care for us as individuals. We develop a confidence that God will continue to deliver us.

Of course, we know there came a day when life ended for Paul. Church tradition says that he was beheaded during the persecution of Nero. Does this mean Paul's hope in God's future deliverance finally played out? Not at all. Even in death there is deliverance for God's people: He takes us home to live with Him eternally. (See Psalm 23:6).

C. Corinth's Supportive Prayer (v. 11)

11. Ye also helping together by prayer for us, that for the gift bestowed upon us by the means of many persons thanks may be given by many on our behalf.

Why did God grant Paul the mercy, comfort, and deliverance that he experienced during his troubles? Partly because of the prayers of Paul's friends in Corinth. Paul tells the Corinthians of the report he had received from Titus regarding "your earnest desire, your mourning, your fervent mind toward me" (2 Corinthians 7:7). Paul credits the prayers of this church (along with the prayers of other friends) for bringing the relief he is now enjoying.

This serves as a reminder of how important prayer is in times of trouble, prayer not only for ourselves, but also for those we care about. We hear the needs of our friends as they are mentioned in public prayers in our church gatherings, and we give our silent assent. But do we remember to follow up with the same concerns in our private prayers throughout the week? When our assemblies are dismissed, we do well to take our prayer lists home and mention some of our church concerns throughout the week. If we do this, we will not only grow in a spirit of compassion and comfort, but will also be agents that bring relief from God for our friends.

III. Joy in Friends
(2 Corinthians 1:12-14)

"A friend in need is a friend indeed." In times of trouble we begin to see who our real friends are. We also see the great value in developing friendships, as we observe our friends ministering to our needs. It is fitting to close our study with a word of appreciation for friends.

A. An Honest Relationship (vv. 12, 13)

12. For our rejoicing is this, the testimony of our conscience, that in simplicity and godly sincerity, not with fleshly wisdom, but by the grace of God, we have had our conversation in the world, and more abundantly to you-ward.

The word *conversation* is an old word for one's behavior, conduct, or life-style. Paul describes his conduct, especially his behavior *to you-ward:* that is, the way he has behaved himself in regard to the Corinthians.

Paul has treated his friends at Corinth with *simplicity* and *godly sincerity.* Some ancient manuscripts and some modern versions have *holiness* instead of *simplicity.* Paul declares that he has been fair and played by the rules of God. He has never been deceitful, but has always spoken with *sincerity.* This statement is in harmony with *the testimony of our conscience:* that is, Paul can say this with a clear conscience.

Paul's behavior is in contrast to the way people of the world often treat their acquaintances, as they operate by the rules of *fleshly wisdom.* Such worldly aphorisms as "do unto others before they have a chance to stick it to you" are far removed from the way Paul treated his friends.

SINCERE PREACHING

Paul asserts he has conducted his Christian work among the Corinthians with "simplicity and godly sincerity." In the *New International Version* this is translated "in the holiness and sincerity that are from God."

Our English word *sincere* seems to be derived from two Latin words: *sin,* meaning *without,* and *cera,* meaning *wax.* The background of this term is explained in at least two ways. Some say it refers to honey on the Roman market. Sometimes a large amount of wax was mixed with the honey, so pure honey was labeled "without wax."

A second explanation is that sometimes pottery was cracked before sale. The cracks would be filled with wax and touched up so they would not show. Pottery "without wax" was undamaged.

Many times something is presented as "gospel preaching" when it is not "without wax." The Christian gospel is not a plea for democracy, or a more just social order, or the liberation of women, or kindness to children.

Such concerns have a valid place in Christian thinking, but the good news of God is that Christ died for our sins and rose again from the grave (1 Corinthians 15:3, 4), and that eternal life is for those who believe in Him (John 20:31). To proclaim this is to preach in *godly sincerity.*

—J. G. V. B.

13. For we write none other things unto you, than what ye read or acknowledge; and I trust ye shall acknowledge even to the end.

The Christians at Corinth know Paul so well that they themselves can testify to the truth of what he says in verse 12. They can recall what they observed during his ministry with them. Also they have his letters, by which they can judge what kind of attitude he has. So if asked whether or not Paul is telling the truth, the Corinthians should be able to *acknowledge* this *even to the end.*

B. A Mutual Respect (v. 14)

14. As also ye have acknowledged us in part, that we are your rejoicing, even as ye also are ours in the day of the Lord Jesus.

Some of the Corinthians do indeed acknowledge Paul; but some are devoted to other teachers (1 Corinthians 1:12). In their zeal for their favorites, they belittle or criticize Paul. He says he should not have to defend himself to them, for the fact that he led them to Christ is evidence that he is a good minister of the Master (2 Corinthians 3:1-3). Still he does defend himself. He defends his motives in chapter 6, his style of ministry in chapter 10, and his claim to apostleship in chapter 11. *In the day of the Lord Jesus,* the day when Christ comes to claim His own, Paul's *rejoicing* will be in those he has led to Christ. In anticipation of that day, he rejoices in them even now. Part of them likewise rejoice in him because he has led them to salvation and life. Paul

longs for all of them to rejoice in him in the same way. The mark of a good friendship is that each friend finds joy in the other and speaks well of him. The key is mutual respect.

Conclusion

A. Just Hold Me

There are times of sorrow in which words are meaningless. We are not of a mind to comprehend what is being said. Sometimes the best thing a friend can do for us is to give us a hug, and hold us tight while we deal with our emotions.

Knowing how much we benefit from the comfort of a friend, we should be quick to comfort our friends, especially those in our church fellowship. The church is an ideal setting for mutual care. It is composed of people who share with us a love for Christ and the doctrinal truths and moral values given in His Word. These are people that we value greatly. They deserve our concern when they are suffering, and we in turn can expect the same from them. To borrow a phrase from the translation of 2 Corinthians 1:5 in the *New International Version* the church should be a place where "comfort overflows."

B. Prayer

Father, continue to grant us Your comfort and peace when we are feeling the hurts that life brings our way, and then remind us to share that divine comfort with our friends when they are in need.

C. Thought to Remember

If it is truly "more blessed to give than to receive" (Acts 20:35), then we who have received comfort from the hand of God should be giving it away as much as we can.

Home Daily Bible Readings

Monday, Apr. 24—Sharing Both Suffering and Comfort (2 Corinthians 1:1-7)

Tuesday, Apr. 25—A Request for Prayer (2 Corinthians 1:8-14)

Wednesday, Apr. 26—Thankfulness for Faithful Christians (Romans 1:8-15)

Thursday, Apr. 27—Give Support to One Another (Galatians 6:1-5)

Friday, Apr. 28—Persevere in Doing Good (Galatians 6:6-10)

Saturday, Apr. 29—Be Kind to One Another (Ephesians 4:25-32)

Sunday, Apr. 30—Active Caring for a Friend (Mark 2:1-5)

Learning by Doing

This page contains an alternate lesson plan emphasizing learning activities. Classes desiring such student involvement will find these suggestions helpful.

Learning Goals

After studying today's lesson, students will be able to:

1. Cite specific Scripture that deals with the problem of why good people suffer.

2. Understand the apostle Paul better by putting themselves in his place—understanding his values, motives, and attitudes.

3. Commit themselves to intercessory prayer with the use of a prayer list.

Into the Lesson

Make copies of this exercise and give one to each class member. Introduce it by saying that it is helpful to be thoughtful when we are comforting people in their suffering.

Imagine that the sixteen-year-old son of a faithful Christian elder and his wife was killed in a head-on collision with a drunken driver. The drunken driver escaped unhurt. You are going to see the family at the funeral home and want to say something helpful to them. Which of these statements will be most appropriate? Check one and explain why you chose it.

___ The Lord gives and the Lord takes away.

___ What a senseless loss of life! Killed by a drunk!

___ Just remember Romans 8:28.

___ Your boy is with the Lord. Heaven is a much better place for him.

___ Give a hug and say, "You're in my prayers."

___ I know you'll be a good example to all of us through this time of pain.

Let the students form pairs and compare choices. Explain that the best way is to give a hug and offer the best help you can—intercessory prayer. The other statements are pat answers that give little consolation.

Among other things the text of this lesson helps us understand why good people suffer, and how a Christian's suffering can be relieved. (Share the lesson background in full with the class.)

Into the Word

Ask someone to read 2 Corinthians 1:1-9 aloud while the rest of the class listens for some reasons that Paul cites as an explanation of why there is suffering in the world, even the good person's world. (Verse 4 tells us that we are troubled and have suffering in order that we can comfort others with the same kind of comfort that God gives us. We can be more sympathetic. Verses 5 and 7 indicate that suffering brings us great comfort from the Lord. Times of suffering draw us closer to God. Verse 9 tells us that suffering causes us to rely more upon God and less upon ourselves. This same exercise is in the student book.) Note that James 1:2-4 says trials strengthen our Christian character. Add that 1 Peter 1:6, 7 indicates that suffering or persecution proves and refines our faith so it will bring us honor when Jesus comes again.

Paul illustrates what he is saying by citing several experiences from his own life. Ask the students to read verses 8 and 9 silently and then answer this question: "Why did Paul share so personally with the Corinthians?" (One answer is so they would know they were not alone, that even great men of faith were not spared the experience of suffering. Note that Paul's suffering brought growth: he learned to depend on God rather then himself. Verse 9 indicates this. Remind the class that some eager evangelists lead people to believe that wealth and health are blessings that always come with being a good Christian. Paul's life and the life of Jesus certainly show us that this is not always true. In John 16:33 we find Jesus explaining that His followers will have trouble and suffering in this world, but that He has overcome the world. If our Lord experienced suffering, how are we to ask to be excused from it? It brings many blessings.

Conclude the study by referring to verse 11 and asking, "What part could the Corinthians play in helping Paul and others through times of suffering?" (Their prayer support was vital.)

Into Life

Author Richard Foster tells us that intercessory prayer is a way of loving others and a sacred obligation. Ask the students to share some ways that they have found effective in helping them to be faithful in prayer for others. Prepare these suggestions on a flip chart: 1. Keep a prayer list. 2. Have a set time to pray for others. 3. Send up flash prayers all day. 4. Pray specifically. 5. Drop a note telling the person that he or she is in your prayers.

Let's Talk It Over

The questions on this page are designed to encourage review of the lesson Scriptures and to promote discussion of the lesson by the class. The answers provided are only discussion starters. Let your class talk it over from there.

1. The titles by which Paul describes God in 2 Corinthians 1:3—"the Father of mercies, and the God of all comfort"—are especially appealing. Why is this so?

The word "comfort" itself summons up some very appealing images. We may recall unhappy moments during childhood when we sustained some physical injury or emotional upset. The hug we received from our father or mother and the soothing words spoken were profoundly comforting. It is helpful to think of God as a heavenly Father who can comfort the hurts we receive as adults. Another image of childhood is the feeling of security that came when we were tucked into bed at night, knowing that our parents were not far away. In similar fashion we now take comfort in the fact that God is near and we are assured of His ongoing care.

2. One reason we encounter suffering is that it is a means by which God disciplines and trains us. How can we best use our sufferings to accomplish such a purpose in us?

"In what ways do I need to grow spiritually?" "How does God want me to become a more mature Christian?" These are questions we need to ask ourselves regularly. They are appropriate questions to have in mind when we are studying the Bible, when we are engaging in prayer, and when we are experiencing a season of personal suffering. The natural tendency during sufferings is to complain and to give in to an attitude of mourning. In his discussion of discipline in Hebrews 12, the writer urges us to approach our sufferings in a quite different manner: "Wherefore lift up the hands which hang down, and the feeble knees; and make straight paths for your feet" (Hebrews 12:12, 13).

3. One reason we encounter suffering is that it equips us to appreciate and minister to the sufferings of others. How can we best use our sufferings to accomplish this?

It is useful to examine our own sufferings in some detail. Some questions we may ask are these: "What was my initial reaction to the experience?" "What counsel received from my friends was genuinely helpful, and what was merely platitudes?" "How did the Bible and prayer provide guidance and strength?" "What eventual benefits did I gain from the experience?" It is easy to see how our answers to these questions will help us in ministering intelligently to others who are suffering. We will be better able to pray for them and to speak in a healing way to them. And similar suffering will make our words more significant to them.

4. Many churches publish a weekly prayer list. One wonders, however, just how much prayer is actually offered for the people listed. What can we do to make a prayer list a more effective tool for encouraging prayer?

It may be helpful to assign certain names from the list to different members, who will focus on praying for those over a week's or a month's time. Or we may urge members to select a few names from the list, pray for those people, and then send each of them a card or a note to tell of the prayers. Another method is to use directed prayer during a Sunday or midweek service. It may not be possible to cover the entire prayer list in one session, but over a period of time all those people who remain long on the list will receive special attention. One other practical approach would be to print the prayer list in the form of a checklist. Members could pray one time each week for every person listed and check off the name afterward.

5. Do we look for the best in and expect the best from our fellow Christians? How can we develop the habit of doing that?

Too often the attitudes Christians hold toward one another seem identical to the attitudes people outside the church exhibit: suspicion, contempt, jealousy, faultfinding. Instead of such a negative outlook, we should be looking for Christ to be formed within each brother or sister (see Galatians 4:19). In the world it may not be surprising to hear someone say of another, "He is of no account, and he never will be any different," or "I do not trust her, and I never will." But in the church the transforming power of Jesus Christ is present, so that we should expect our fellow Christians to grow in moral character, in effective discipleship, and in diligent service. We need to hold in our minds a vision of what each believer can be with Christ's power fully at work within him or her.

Living in Christian Freedom

DEVOTIONAL READING: Galatians 5:13-26.

LESSON SCRIPTURE: 1 Corinthians 9.

PRINTED TEXT: 1 Corinthians 9:1-7, 19-27.

1 Corinthians 9:1-7, 19-27

1 Am I not an apostle? am I not free? have I not seen Jesus Christ our Lord? are not ye my work in the Lord?

2 If I be not an apostle unto others, yet doubtless I am to you: for the seal of mine apostleship are ye in the Lord.

3 Mine answer to them that do examine me is this:

4 Have we not power to eat and to drink?

5 Have we not power to lead about a sister, a wife, as well as other apostles, and as the brethren of the Lord, and Cephas?

6 Or I only and Barnabas, have not we power to forbear working?

7 Who goeth a warfare any time at his own charges? who planteth a vineyard, and eateth not of the fruit thereof? or who feedeth a flock, and eateth not of the milk of the flock?

· · · · · · · · · · · · ·

19 For though I be free from all men, yet have I made myself servant unto all, that I might gain the more.

20 And unto the Jews I became as a Jew, that I might gain the Jews; to them that are under the law, as under the law, that I might gain them that are under the law;

21 To them that are without law, as without law, (being not without law to God, but under the law to Christ,) that I might gain them that are without law.

22 To the weak became I as weak, that I might gain the weak: I am made all things to all men, that I might by all means save some.

23 And this I do for the gospel's sake, that I might be partaker thereof with you.

24 Know ye not that they which run in a race run all, but one receiveth the prize? So run, that ye may obtain.

25 And every man that striveth for the mastery is temperate in all things. Now they do it to obtain a corruptible crown; but we an incorruptible.

26 I therefore so run, not as uncertainly; so fight I, not as one that beateth the air:

27 But I keep under my body, and bring it into subjection: lest that by any means, when I have preached to others, I myself should be a castaway.

GOLDEN TEXT: Though I be free from all men, yet have I made myself servant unto all, that I might gain the more.—1 Corinthians 9:19.

Lesson Aims

This study should equip the student to:

1. Name several ways in which the apostle
Paul voluntarily surrendered his own rights and
preferences in order to win others to Christ.

2. Name adjustments he or she can make in
order to present Christ more effectively to people who are different from himself or herself.

Lesson Outline

INTRODUCTION
    A. Tested by Freedom
    B. Lesson Background
I. THE RIGHTS OF AN APOSTLE (1 Corinthians 9:1-
    7)
    A. Paul Was an Apostle (vv. 1-3)
        Concerning Criticism
    B. Apostles Were Supported (vv. 4-7)
II. WINNING TO CHRIST AND WINNING IN CHRIST
    (1 Corinthians 9:19-27)
    A. Paul Adapted in Order to Win Others (vv.
        19-23)
        All Things to All Men
    B. Paul Contended for the Crown of Life (vv.
        24-27)
        Getting Serious
CONCLUSION
    A. Follow the Follower of Christ
    B. A Free Servant's Prayer
    C. Thought to Remember

*Paul's desire to bring all persons to the knowledge
of Christ is the message carried by visual 10. The visual is shown on page 308.*

Introduction

A. Tested by Freedom

"For seventy years we were tested by persecution. Now we are being tested by freedom."

That is the way a thoughtful Russian citizen
summarized the situation of Christians in the
former Soviet Union several months after the
collapse of Communism. It was great to be free
from heavy-handed control on every aspect of
living. But many persons were not prepared to
accept the continuing responsibility for their
own decisions and provisions. Becoming free

was one thing, but long-term living as free persons with others equally free was something
else, and much more demanding.

So it is also with the liberty we enjoy in
Christ Jesus. At immeasurable cost to himself He
offers freedom from sin and its slavery. As Christians we have chosen that freedom. Now we live
as responsible persons in that freedom.

Our springtime Bible lessons on "Christians
Living in Community" include two sessions
dealing with our experience as free Christians.
Lesson 8 urged the wise use of liberty so as to
help, rather than hurt, others in the church.
Now we are taught to use Christian freedom
helpfully toward folk who are not yet Christians.
This is geared to evangelism. Our Golden Text
says it: "Though I am free and belong to no man,
I make myself a slave to everyone, to win as
many as possible" (1 Corinthians 9:19, *New International Version*).

B. Lesson Background

Today's lesson from 1 Corinthians 9 is built
directly on the text studied two weeks ago from
the preceding chapter. In chapter 8 Paul dealt
with the relationship among Christians, asking,
"Should I eat meat that may have been dedicated to an idol?" Since an idol is nothing but a
figment of pagan imagination, Paul said, a Christian may normally regard such meat as any
other, to be accepted with thanks to God who
made all things. But some Christians still think
of idols as real beings and link the eating of
"their" meat with worshiping them. These brothers could be offended and misled by a believer's
eating the food in question. In such a case, Paul
said, he would do without such food entirely. He
would go hungry before he would influence another Christian to violate his conscience.

Some folk in Corinth were questioning Paul's
apostleship, thinking him weak and spineless (2
Corinthians 10-12). If he were really an apostle,
they said, he would know his rights and would
stand up for them. Chapter 9 answers that argument plainly. In it Paul shifts his viewpoint from
that of a brother yielding to the welfare of others
in the church, to that of an apostle surrendering
certain of his rights for the sake of winning unbelievers to Christ.

I. The Rights of an Apostle
(1 Corinthians 9:1-7)

Paul's respect for the conscience of the "weak"
brother did not include any surrender of his
apostleship or permanent cancellation of his
rights. He would remain free to make each decision on the merits of the issue at hand.

A. Paul Was an Apostle (vv. 1-3)

1, 2. Am I not an apostle? am I not free? have I not seen Jesus Christ our Lord? are not ye my work in the Lord? If I be not an apostle unto others, yet doubtless I am to you: for the seal of mine apostleship are ye in the Lord.

To be an apostle, one had to be an eyewitness of the risen Lord (Acts 1:21, 22). Jesus appeared to Saul on the road to Damascus and appointed him as apostle to the Gentiles (Acts 9:3-8; 22:6-11; 26:12-18). In pursuit of that apostleship Paul had come to Corinth, converting both Jews and Gentiles to Christ (Acts 18:1-11). Now they themselves were the *seal*—the mark of genuineness—in his apostleship. So by qualification, by appointment, and by accomplishment (see especially 2 Corinthians 12:11, 12), he was fully an apostle, entitled to all the rights and privileges, as well as the powers and responsibilities, of the office. So he was perfectly *free*, either to enjoy or to forgo the benefits that went with it. Likewise any mature Christian ought to be stable and confident, free and flexible, choosing the way of humble service in likeness to his Lord.

CONCERNING CRITICISM

It is helpful to know that even an inspired apostle, such as Paul, had many who were critical of him. We remember that many heroic servants of our Lord have been subjected to vilification and even to execution. John Wycliffe was treated severely, and his body was exhumed and burned after his death in 1384. In a letter to the Duke of Lancaster in 1381, he said, "I believe that in the end the truth will conquer."

William Lloyd Garrison led the abolition movement in New England. His newspaper office was wrecked and burned by his adversaries. He did not retreat or relent, but wrote in defiance, "I am in earnest—I will not equivocate—I will not excuse—I will not retreat a single inch; and I will be heard."

Jean Sibelius (1865-1957), the famous Finnish composer, once said, "Pay no attention to what the critics say; no statue has ever been put up to a critic." First we need to be sure our motives are honest and our efforts in line with the will of God and the truth and spirit of Jesus. Then we can be firm as Paul was, and unyielding in our continued work for our Lord, however severe the criticism against us may be.   —J.G.V. B.

3. Mine answer to them that do examine me is this.

What was Paul's defense, responding to his critics? (See 2 Corinthians 10:10 for the nature of their criticisms.) His answer could be the affirmation of his apostleship, just seen in verses 1 and 2. Or it could be his insistence that "they which preach the gospel should live of the gospel" (1 Corinthians 9:14)—an insistence expressed fully in verses 4-18 following. Either argument would be sufficient.

B. Apostles Were Supported (vv. 4-7)

4. Have we not power to eat and to drink?

The apostles' *power* (or right) *to eat and drink* included the thankful enjoyment of such food and beverage as were set before them, without asking questions "for conscience' sake," until and unless such enjoyment posed a problem for observers who still worried about spiritual pollution in the food (1 Corinthians 10:23-30).

Now Paul turned to the apostles' right to receive material support, including meals and lodging, from the people they served. Jesus had directed the twelve apostles to accept the hospitality of their hearers in the cities to which they went (Matthew 10:9-15). He said the laborer is worthy of his wages (Luke 10:7).

Paul had not exercised his right to "live of the gospel," however, when he labored in Corinth; and he still refused to claim it from the Corinthians, lest he "hinder the gospel" (v. 12). For a part of his time in their city he earned his living at tent making, and part of the time he accepted support from Christians elsewhere (Acts 18:1-7; 2 Corinthians 11:8).

5. Have we not power to lead about a sister, a wife, as well as other apostles, and as the brethren of the Lord, and Cephas?

It seems that other apostles were accompanied by their wives, as faithful helpers, when they traveled among the churches. Both husband and wife were supported. *Cephas* (Simon Peter) is named specifically.

Brethren of the Lord—sons of Joseph and Mary—are named in Mark 6:3 as James, Joses, Judas, and Simon. James became a leader in the church at Jerusalem (Galatians 1:19); he and Judas are known as the writers of New Testament letters, James and Jude. They seem to have been accompanied by their wives in evangelistic travels.

Evidently Paul was not married. If Barnabas had a wife, she did not travel with him.

6. Or I only and Barnabas, have not we power to forbear working?

Paul and Barnabas supported themselves by other labors while they preached, but that did not mean they did not have a right to be sustained by the people they taught. They simply chose not to exercise that right. No one could ever say they were using the gospel as a means of providing an easy life for themselves.

7. Who goeth a warfare any time at his own charges? who planteth a vineyard, and eateth not of the fruit thereof? or who feedeth a flock, and eateth not of the milk of the flock.

The basic right to receive one's living from his employment extends far beyond the work of an apostle. In a military campaign the soldier's expenses are paid by those who send him. The farmer lives on the products of his land and his labor. The herdsman makes his living from the animals he raises and feeds.

Verses 8-18 expand the argument. Quoted is Deuteronomy 25:4 with its provision that even an animal should be allowed to eat a little while he works. That is applied to God's concern for the persons who labor in His cause.

II. Winning to Christ and Winning in Christ (1 Corinthians 9:19-27)

A. Paul Adapted in Order to Win Others (vv. 19-23)

19. For though I be free from all men, yet have I made myself servant unto all, that I might gain the more.

Much more than daily upkeep was included in Paul's personal adjustments for the sake of winning others to Christ. It became an all-inclusive principle of his behavior.

As one born into Roman citizenship at Tarsus of Cilicia (Acts 21:39; 22:28), Paul enjoyed special privileges and protections, including the right to a hearing before being punished on any accusation (Acts 22:24-26). As a Christian, Paul cherished his freedom from the burdensome strictures of Jewish ceremonial law (Galatians 5:1). Especially he appreciated his liberation from the guilt and power of sin through the sacrifice of Christ. He knew, though, that liberty from outer controls could result in slavery to one's own passions and prejudices—an ever-present and all-inclusive servitude. "Ye have been called unto liberty," he wrote, "only use not liberty for an occasion to the flesh, but by love serve one another" (Galatians 5:13). The truest and most lasting freedom is the way of service to others, self-chosen and motivated by love. Martin Luther is quoted in a paraphrase of the verse before us: "A Christian man is the most free of all, and subject to none; a Christian man is the most dutiful servant of all, and subject to every one."

Paul's love-motivation reached in two directions—to Christ and to all people. Love of the Lord made him obedient to Jesus' Great Commission (Matthew 28:18-20; Acts 26:19, 20), and love of the people made him desire their salvation more than his own comfort or safety.

20. And unto the Jews I became as a Jew, that I might gain the Jews; to them that are under the law, as under the law, that I might gain them that are under the law.

Here is application of the principle just stated. Paul approached the Jewish people sympathetically, respecting their traditions. In each city, he addressed himself first to the Jews in their synagogues, using their Scriptures to establish the fact that Jesus was their promised Messiah. When he asked Timothy, the son of a Jewish mother and Gentile father, to be his helper, he made a concession to Jewish sensibilities by having Timothy circumcised (Acts 16:1-3). To avoid offending zealous Jews, Paul participated in the ceremonial vows of certain Jews in the temple at Jerusalem (Acts 21:17-26). Yet he made it clear that his salvation did not depend on his being a Jew and keeping the law.

21. To them that are without law, as without law, (being not without law to God, but under the law to Christ,) that I might gain them that are without law.

Gentiles would not be won by citing the law and the prophets. So Paul approached them in terms they understood. He showed the futility of their idols, and he spoke of God, who created the world they knew. He named Jesus, risen from the dead, as the revealer of God (Acts 17:16-34). He made it clear that the Gentiles' salvation did not depend on their following the law of the Jews. The way of salvation to Jew and Gentile alike lay in Jesus (Acts 15:11).

The *law to Christ* was not negotiable. It could not be compromised. How could one bring converts to Him if in the effort he condoned in Jew or Gentile the attitudes and actions that Jesus opposed? The law of Christ, seen in His life, His teaching, and His cleansing grace, provided the unchangeable core of Paul's commitment. All else was negotiable.

22. To the weak became I as weak, that I might gain the weak: I am made all things to all men, that I might by all means save some.

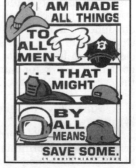

visual 10

The *weak* are described in 1 Corinthians 8:7-13 and Romans 14:16—15:3 as those Christians whose faith was not vigorous enough to disregard the dedication of meats to lifeless images. Paul was willing to follow the "weak" ones' scrupulous practices if in doing so he could win them to Christ—and then teach them not to demand the same compliance on the part of others.

That I might by all means save some. This was the uncompromising purpose for which Paul would compromise on most other matters. What, then, among *our* rights, privileges, and preferences is so important that it must be protected at the cost of hindering another in his approach to Christ?

ALL THINGS TO ALL MEN

We all know an actor or actress may play many roles. But all these various activities are aimed at one end—the entertainment and involvement of the hearers and viewers.

There is great variety in the activities of parents also. Sometimes the parent is a play partner with the child. Sometimes the parent is a provider—cooking food, supplying clothes and a sleeping place at night. Sometimes the parent is a healer, bandaging scrapes or giving medicine. Often the parent is a teacher. Sometimes the parent is an encourager as the child engages in some activity. But all this is aimed at one thing—the development and learning of the child.

Paul presented himself in various guises as Jew or Gentile, as weak or strong, as bound by law or as free from law—all so he might lead people to salvation in Jesus. There are many different ways to interest people in spiritual realities. Some may come by way of music, or art, or scientific pursuits, or civic concern, or athletic endeavors. Whether through drama or discussion, small groups or large assemblies, our purpose is the conversion, conservation, and character-building of our fellows.   —J. G. V. B.

23. And this I do for the gospel's sake, that I might be partaker thereof with you.

The gospel was the cause for which Paul would compromise almost anything else.

Partaker thereof with you. Partaking, or sharing, works in two directions. Paul would *give* to others, including the Corinthians, the gospel that had come to him. Paul would *receive*, along with others, the blessings available in the gospel. His motivation was two-directional. He would sacrifice his ease and self-interests both for the sake of others, to save them; and for his own sake, to fulfill his own salvation. Apostle though he was, he had his own salvation to "work out . . . with fear and trembling" (Philippians 2:12).

B. Paul Contended for the Crown of Life
(vv. 24-27)

24. Know ye not that they which run in a race run all, but one receiveth the prize? So run, that ye may obtain.

In several of his epistles Paul compared the Christian experience with an athletic contest, with its demand for discipline, observance of rules, strenuous participation, patient continuance, and rewards for successful completion (Philippians 3:13, 14; 2 Timothy 2:5; 4:7, 8; Hebrews 12:1, 2).

The famous Isthmian Games were held near Corinth every two years; Paul's readers knew them well. They would surely scoff at the silly suggestions of modern lottery and sweepstakes promoters—or evangelists and funeral orators—indicating that "all you have to do is enter" to win fabulous rewards. It is simply not so!

The *prize* Paul mentioned here has been called the "umpire's award," given to the contestant who was judged to have observed all the rules and finished first in any race. And there was only one winner in any race.

In Christ the winner's circle is not limited to one, but neither is it gained by all who enter the race. Consider Paul's vivid description of winning: "I have fought a good fight, I have finished my course, I have kept the faith: henceforth there is laid up for me a crown of righteousness, which the Lord, the righteous judge, shall give me at that day: and not to me only, but unto all them also that love his appearing" (2 Timothy 4:7, 8). The reward is for those who love Christ and finish the course.

25. And every man that striveth for the mastery is temperate in all things. Now they do it to obtain a corruptible crown; but we an incorruptible.

Rigid self-discipline in persistent training is the price of successful accomplishment on any meaningful level. It demands purposeful, total direction, not trading off one virtue for another self-indulgence, nor a general program of virtue for an occasional binge. But for the Christian the rewards are immeasurably greater than the efforts (2 Corinthians 4:17, 18).

A corruptible crown—a circlet, either of green herbs or of pine—was worn by a winner in the Isthmian Games. It didn't last long. For the Christian, by contrast, is the crown of righteousness unchanging (2 Timothy 4:8), the crown of life eternal (James 1:12; Revelation 2:10), the "crown of glory that fadeth not away" (1 Peter 5:4).

26. I therefore so run, not as uncertainly; so fight I, not as one that beateth the air.

The direction of verse 25 finds substance in Paul's example, cited here. The course of his life was not wavering and aimless; he looked straight ahead and pressed toward his chosen goal (Philippians 3:13, 14). Or if you change the figure from the racetrack to the boxing ring, his blows were directed, every one toward its mark to defeat the enemy, Satan. Or if you accept the Lord's figure of the workman putting his hand to the plow, Paul was not looking back (Luke 9:62).

27. But I keep under my body, and bring it into subjection: lest that by any means, when I have preached to others, I myself should be a castaway.

The human body can become a spoiled tyrant. Its appetite for food, for ease and comfort, for sexual satisfaction, or for pride in its own power and appearance, can become insatiable.

Paul would not have his body bossing him around. He treated it severely, he said, showing it who was boss and keeping it under subjection to his God-serving purposes. He refused to be a slave to his bodily demands. Instead, he made his body the obedient servant to his spiritual will.

There was necessity in this. As a preacher of the Word he had been like a herald at the Isthmian games, announcing the contests, summoning and instructing the competitors, and declaring the winners. What shame, then, if he himself should be disqualified and expelled for violating the rules he declared to others!

GETTING SERIOUS

Paul uses the athletic efforts of the Greeks and Romans to illustrate the intensity with which we should discipline ourselves for Christian activity. Athletes are "temperate in all things" or go, as the *New International Version* translates, "into strict training." This they do for a fast-fading laurel crown, whereas we are looking forward to an everlasting reward.

Home Daily Bible Readings

Monday, May 1—Live by the Spirit (Galatians 5:13-21)

Tuesday, May 2—Fruit of the Spirit (Galatians 5:22-26)

Wednesday, May 3—Rights of an Apostle (1 Corinthians 9:1-7)

Thursday, May 4—Refusing to Claim One's Rights (1 Corinthians 9:8-18)

Friday, May 5—Free to Adapt for Christ's Sake (1 Corinthians 9:19-27)

Saturday, May 6—The Lord's Spirit Gives Freedom (2 Corinthians 3:12-18)

Sunday, May 7—Christ Frees Us From Condemnation (Romans 8:1-11)

Often we use the expression "get serious." In basketball, baseball, or football, all kidding or "fooling around" is held down when the "big game" is near. The coach says, "Let's get serious."

We may live through a period when eating is a wild delight and a frenzy of calorie-disregarding adventure. But one day we look in astonishment at the numbers on a scale, and say, "I must get serious about losing weight."

The apostle is urging us to regard our Christian life with a sense of its supreme significance. We are living in a world in which there is real sin. People are hurt, humiliated, and harassed. There is a real death to be faced and an endless eternity to be entered. It is indeed important to get serious about our way and our work in Christ.

—J. G. V. B.

Conclusion

A. Follow the Follower of Christ

The apostle Paul was not original in his exercise of freedom to forfeit his own rights, comforts, and interests for the sake of those he had come to serve. Because he was following another who had gone the same way before him, he could recommend that others follow him. "Be ye followers of me," he said, "even as I also am of Christ" (1 Corinthians 11:1). Hear again his description of the one he had chosen to follow: "Your attitude should be the same as that of Christ Jesus: Who, being in very nature God, did not consider equality with God something to be grasped, but made himself nothing, taking the very nature of a servant, being made in human likeness. And being found in appearance as a man, he humbled himself and became obedient to death—even death on a cross!" (Philippians 2:5-8, *New International Version*).

In response to this kind of self-sacrifice to save others, God himself supplies the ultimate glory to Christ, to Paul, and to those who follow in the way of their leading.

B. A Free Servant's Prayer

Thank You, our God and Father, for Jesus, who willingly surrendered His glory and His life to save us. Thank You for Paul and others who freely gave of themselves to bring the saving gospel to us. Thank You for the freedom in which we live, to follow in their path for the sake of others. May we follow it well, for Jesus' sake. Amen.

C. Thought to Remember

"Ye have been called unto liberty; only use not liberty for an occasion to the flesh, but by love serve one another" (Galatians 5:13).

Learning by Doing

This page contains an alternate lesson plan emphasizing learning activities. Classes desiring such student involvement will find these suggestions helpful.

Learning Goals

As a result of studying 1 Corinthians 9:1-7, 19-27, students will:

1. Become aware of specific things that tend to limit Christian freedom.

2. Learn to practice some growth techniques that help Christians mature and be faithful.

3. Learn to limit their freedom because of their responsibility to others.

Into the Lesson

To open the session share this statement by a Russian citizen: "For seventy years we were tested by persecution. Now we are being tested by freedom." Divide the class in half and tell one half to give specific ways in which persecution tests people. Assign the other half to list specific ways in which people are tested by freedom. Make two columns on the board, labeling one PERSECUTION and the other FREEDOM. Record the answers of the class in the appropriate columns. Some possible responses are: Persecution tempts one to protect oneself by denying ones faith. Freedom tempts one to drift away and be distracted by all of the opportunities available. (A similar exercise is in the student book.)

Lead into the lesson background by saying that Paul seems to be declaring his freedom but not using it. (Use the material from the lesson background in the commentary.)

Into the Word

Type the following questions on index cards and distribute them to class members. Allow their answers to be the springboard for the lesson development. (They are also in the student book.)

1. Read 1 Corinthians 9:1-3. What were some things that Paul would not surrender in spite of all criticism? Where did the Corinthians fit into the picture? (Possible answers: His apostleship, his freedom to make personal choices. The Corinthians were the "seal" or living proof of his apostleship.)

2. What were things Paul was being examined and criticized about? Read 1 Corinthians 9:4-7. (Answers: his right of choosing what to eat and drink, his right to have a wife, his right to be paid for his preaching.) What is your opinion of the choices Paul made? For example, would he have been more effective if he had not taken time for his tent-making? Explain.

3. What was Paul's supreme motivation whenever he had to choose whether or not to exercise a particular freedom? Read 1 Corinthians 9:19-22. (Best answer: A love that made him care for the lost and want to convert them at whatever cost to his own personal freedoms.)

4. In what specific ways did Paul accommodate himself to Jews, to Gentiles, and to the weak? Read 1 Corinthians 9:20-22.

5. How did Paul regard the role of personal discipline and self-mastery? Read 1 Corinthians 9:24-27. (Possible answers: Personal discipline and self-mastery make a more effective servant, and that was what Paul was intent upon. His deepest desire was to convert others to Christ. In the illustration of the games, only one person wins the prize, but in Christ all are winners if they keep on doing their best.)

Into Life

Point out that our freedom in Christ does not excuse us from disciplining ourselves in order to be more effective in winning others. Put the following verses on the board or photocopy them. Ask the class to study the verses and find techniques that are effective in keeping Christians faithful for a lifetime as well as useful in reaching the lost. (They are also in the student book.) Matthew 16:24. (Self-denial, personal sacrifice, obedience to Christ.) Colossians 4:2, 3. (Devoted prayer and supplication for open doors for the gospel.) Colossians 4:6. (Grant grace to others and be ready with your Christian witness.) Philippians 2:5-15. (Have the mind of Christ, be willing to submit to others, don't complain, etc.) Ask the class for other suggestions.

Explain that curtailing one's freedom by voluntary self-discipline is different from accepting unreasonable limits. Paul would not accept the notion that all Christians must keep the Old Testament law (Galatians 5:1). See if class members can mention traditions or opinions that would limit our freedom unreasonably. We must not violate Bible teaching in order to be agreeable with those around us.

Close with prayer focusing upon reaching the lost with love. Encourage the students to be specific in asking God to use them in reaching those for whom they pray.

Let's Talk It Over

The questions on this page are designed to encourage review of the lesson Scriptures and to promote discussion of the lesson by the class. The answers provided are only discussion starters. Let your class talk it over from there.

1. We are free to enjoy or to forgo some privileges or benefits that are part of the Christian life. How may we apply this freedom to the matter of attending church services?

There is no New Testament command that requires us to be present at every service of worship or Bible study our church offers. Hebrews 10:25 cautions against neglecting our assembling, but it can hardly be taken as a command to attend every meeting.

What we must keep in mind is the responsible use of our freedom. If we fall into the habit of chronic inattendance, we can weaken our own faith and by our example the faith of fellow believers. On the other hand, using our freedom to practice faithful attendance can contribute to our personal growth in Christ and can also give encouragement to Christian brothers and sisters who look to us for an example.

2. Ministers and other church workers who are paid for their labors must be especially careful in their financial dealings. Why is this so?

Paul's decision not to accept financial support from the church at Corinth does not reflect unfavorably on those persons who receive pay for spiritual labors today. Paul did accept such support from other churches (Philippians 4:14-19). In our time some religious leaders have so abused their prerogative of soliciting financial support that it has caused many observers to be suspicious of all paid religious workers. That makes it essential that ministers, evangelists, music evangelists, and those with television or print ministries demonstrate unimpeachable integrity in their acceptance and use of money donated by fellow believers.

3. The word "compromise" is generally viewed in an unfavorable way in the church. How can we distinguish between legitimate and unacceptable compromise?

When it comes to the truth, we must imitate Paul's determination in connection with the "false brethren" mentioned in Galatians 2:4, 5: "to whom we gave place by subjection, no, not for an hour; that the truth of the gospel might continue with you." We dare not compromise on plain truths, nor can we compromise on clear standards of morality. Stealing, lying, adultery, homosexuality, and the like are sins, and we cannot regard them as anything less. But in contrast to these matters of truth and moral standards, there are countless areas of personal opinion and individual liberty in which we can work out a compromise with other people.

4. What are some valuable spiritual lessons that athletic events illustrate for us today?

Athletes have specific goals in view: victories, championships, record-setting performances. As individual Christians and as churches we need to have clear goals regarding accomplishments we want to achieve and victories we want to win in the Lord. Athletes undergo training in order to excel in their sport. We should submit ourselves to training in faith and holiness and godliness (1 Timothy 4:7, 8). In many athletic enterprises teamwork is essential to success. While the apostle Paul's athletic illustrations relate to individualistic events like running a race or boxing, there is much in the New Testament that ties in with the concept of teamwork. We Christians need encouragement and help from our spiritual "teammates." And in the church a consistent team effort is vital in order to maintain effective programs of worship, evangelism, and education.

5. Why do we need to practice physical discipline in order to maintain spiritual health?

Let us focus on a typical Sunday morning worship service. Who are the people least likely to be alert and responsive during singing, the Lord's Supper, and the sermon? The answer is, those who are overfed, under exercised, and lacking in proper rest. Dietary discipline and physical exercise are important, not only to those who place a high value on personal appearance, but also to us who want to be physically fit for our worship, our study of the Word, and our service. Physical discipline is also related to the biblical admonition to treat the body as the temple of the Holy Spirit (1 Corinthians 6:19, 20). Sexual sin, drug and alcohol abuse, and careless dietary and exercise habits can destroy the temple of the Holy Spirit. It is our spiritual duty to discipline, protect, and preserve our bodies.

Working for Reconciliation

DEVOTIONAL READING: 1 John 4:7-21.

LESSON SCRIPTURE: 2 Corinthians 5.

PRINTED TEXT: 2 Corinthians 5:11-21.

2 Corinthians 5:11-21

11 Knowing therefore the terror of the Lord, we persuade men; but we are made manifest unto God; and I trust also are made manifest in your consciences.

12 For we commend not ourselves again unto you, but give you occasion to glory on our behalf, that ye may have somewhat to answer them which glory in appearance, and not in heart.

13 For whether we be beside ourselves, it is to God: or whether we be sober, it is for your cause.

14 For the love of Christ constraineth us; because we thus judge, that if one died for all, then were all dead:

15 And that he died for all, that they which live should not henceforth live unto themselves, but unto him which died for them, and rose again.

16 Wherefore henceforth know we no man after the flesh: yea, though we have known Christ after the flesh, yet now henceforth know we him no more.

17 Therefore if any man be in Christ, he is a new creature: old things are passed away; behold, all things are become new.

18 And all things are of God, who hath reconciled us to himself by Jesus Christ, and hath given to us the ministry of reconciliation;

19 To wit, that God was in Christ, reconciling the world unto himself, not imputing their trespasses unto them; and hath committed unto us the word of reconciliation.

20 Now then we are ambassadors for Christ, as though God did beseech you by us: we pray you in Christ's stead, be ye reconciled to God.

21 For he hath made him to be sin for us, who knew no sin; that we might be made the righteousness of God in him.

GOLDEN TEXT: God . . . reconciled us to himself by Jesus Christ, and hath given to us the ministry of reconciliation.—2 Corinthians 5:18.

Christians Living in Community

Unit 3. Ministering as a Christian

Community (Lessons 10-13)

Lesson Aims

This lesson should equip the student to:

1. Show how Jesus has brought about the student's own reconciliation to God.

2. Indicate specific changes that have taken place with his being made new in Christ.

3. Accept some definite responsibility in the work of reconciling sinners to God.

Lesson Outline

INTRODUCTION
  A. The King's Business
  B. Lesson Background
I. RECONCILING CORINTHIANS TO PAUL (2 COR-inthians 5:11-15)
  A. Supplying an Answer (vv. 11, 12)
    Exteriorization
  B. "Thinking of You" (v. 13)
  C. Controlled by Christ's Love (vv. 14, 15)
    Love's Compulsion
II. RECONCILING MEN TO GOD (2 CORINTHIANS 5:16-21)
  A. New Viewpoint of a Newly Created One (vv. 16, 17)
  B. New Mission of Reconciliation (vv. 18-20)
    God's Initiatives
  C. The Means of Reconciliation (v. 21)
CONCLUSION
  A. Who? Me?
  B. A Prayer From the Embassy
  C. Thought to Remember

One's newness in Christ is the theme of visual 11 of the visuals packet. The visual is shown on page 317.

Introduction

A. The King's Business

This is the message that I bring,
A message angels fain would sing:
"O be ye reconciled,"
Thus saith my Lord and King,
"O be ye reconciled to God."

In his song, "The King's Business," Dr. E. T. Cassel has caught and expressed the center and spirit of our lesson text from 2 Corinthians 5. Reconciliation—especially the restoration of warring factions to harmony and cooperation—is kingly business. To serve under the king's direction, promoting the royal program of reconciliation, is truly to be on business for the king. How grandly that is true in the reconciling business of the King of kings and Lord of lords!

To accomplish reconciliation in its full and scriptural sense is, in fact, possible to none other than God himself. Let us consider.

The word Paul uses for *reconcile* means to change something or someone thoroughly, to make an adjustment that brings into agreement those who have been at odds, to restore to friendship or harmony those who have become enemies.

Since God is unchanging, He cannot be adjusted to bring Him into conformity to any other. The adjustment must come the other way. It's a little like the reconciliation that is frequently necessary between my bank's monthly statement of my checking account and the figures I keep for myself. Very seldom do I find the bank in error. A careful search finds, instead, some error of mine that needs to be corrected. Likewise, God is not in error. Reconciliation brings us into harmony with His truth, goodness, and mercy.

God is not our enemy. His love is constant. If we are uncomfortable with Him, it is because we, like Adam (Genesis 3:7-10), have sinned and so desire to run and hide, building a wall of resentment between God and us. The enmity is on our part. The initiative and the provision for reconciliation are from Him. He offers the hand of friendship and the encircling arm of support; it is ours to acknowledge and accept.

B. Lesson Background

First Corinthians, including last week's lesson text, was written from Ephesus during Paul's third missionary journey. It included plain words concerning serious problems; also plain answers to those who challenged Paul's apostleship. How would it be received? When should Paul go again to Corinth to face the issues in person? Titus went to Corinth to learn the answers to those questions.

Restless with waiting, Paul left Ephesus on his way toward Corinth. Titus met him in Macedonia. The news he brought from Corinth was generally good, though some problems with false teachers and opposers still remained. Still in Macedonia, approximately three months after he wrote 1 Corinthians, Paul wrote the second epistle and sent it to Corinth.

Appropriately for its mission to mend the relationship between Paul and the Corinthian church, this letter contains more autobiographical material than any other of Paul's writing. Its early chapters deal with his afflictions, his commitment, his commitment, his dangers and difficulties, including Corinthian challenges to his apostleship. Chapter 5 begins with a cheerful acceptance of his own mortality and the coming judgment. In this awareness he continued to minister, and he advised the church to continue its ministry. That ministry included an outreach to all the world with the message of God's reconciliation through His Son Jesus.

I. Reconciling Corinthians to Paul (2 Corinthians 5:11-15)

The apostle turned his attention to some "housekeeping chores," seeking to improve relationships between his readers and himself.

A. Supplying an Answer (vv. 11, 12)

11. Knowing therefore the terror of the Lord, we persuade men; but we are made manifest unto God; and I trust also are made manifest in your consciences.

Fully aware of God's power, holiness, and knowledge of all things, Paul was moved by reverence and awe for the Almighty. Having bowed humbly before God, he was not afraid of men. And the people in Corinth who questioned Paul's apostleship needed to learn some things they didn't know. The ones with whom he had worked most closely knew already, down deep in their *consciences*, what sort of ministry Paul was rendering.

Persuade. Paul's word indicates "bringing about a change of mind by the influence of reason or moral considerations" (W. E. Vine, *New Testament Words*). The use of political pressure to win compliance is not the apostle's way.

12. For we commend not ourselves again unto you, but give you occasion to glory on our behalf, that ye may have somewhat to answer them which glory in appearance, and not in heart.

Among those who would be reading his letter, Paul saw no need for a continuing campaign of self-justification. He hoped, however, to provide them with grounds for some legitimate pride in him. Thus they could answer false teachers who scoffed at them for taking seriously an apostle who was not imposing in physical appearance or show of human authority. Even in Corinth some might boast of having seen Jesus in the flesh, or having associated with the apostle Peter. They might boast a more imposing presence, or dress, or life-style. They might be proud of being "above" doing manual labor.

Among ourselves there is always a temptation to judge a preacher by the size of "his" church,

or to judge a stranger by his physical appearance, or to judge a church by the size of its budget or its building. It is less easy to find our satisfaction in the inner realities of faith, love, and character, as Jesus urged: "Judge not according to the appearance, but judge righteous judgment" (John 7:24).

EXTERIORIZATION

The Corinthians were in danger of being led astray by people who pretended to be pious. This is a pretense that is widespread.

Remember the small town in the old west, as recreated on movie sets? The stores on the dusty main street appear to be two or three stories high, but are only one story. The added stories are just false fronts. This is seen in an even more exaggerated form in the Indian city of Jaipur, where the rose-red buildings on the main street seem to be several stories high, but are just facades on top of one-story structures.

This is an example of *exteriorization,* attention to appearance instead of reality. Another example is the application of rouge to cheeks so they *appear* flushed with healthy blood when they're not. Sometimes people wear clothes that seem to have pockets, but do not. It is possible to talk about books one really has never read. People buy academic degrees from "mail order" colleges that offer no courses, but only sell empty titles.

We must not aim at looking good without being good. Jesus had nothing but scorn for the religious leaders who "for a pretense" made long prayers. They were like sepulchers, whitewashed on the outside, but inside they were full of dead men's bones (Matthew 23:14, 27, 28). We need a zeal that is real, a genuine devotion, not just a pumped-up emotion. —J. G. V. B.

B. "Thinking of You" (v. 13)

13. For whether we be beside ourselves, it is to God: or whether we be sober, it is for your cause.

Paul's extreme zeal for Christ, with his lack of ambition for himself, made some suspect him of being out of touch with reality. His trances, visions, and revelations caused critics to call him mad (Acts 26:24, 25). Paul was quite willing to be thought a fool for Christ's sake (Corinthians 4:10). In presenting the gospel, however, he spoke and wrote plainly with sober reasoning. He avoided flowery rhetoric or sensationalism, lest some should be won to Paul's artistry rather than to God's truth (1 Corinthians 2:1-5). For the sake of his hearers he kept his message simple. How wealthy Paul could have become if he had thought more of himself and less of those to whom God sent him!

C. Controlled by Christ's Love
(vv. 14, 15)

14. For the love of Christ constraineth us; because we thus judge, that if one died for all, then were all dead.

The love of Christ came to bear on Paul from several different directions. (1) Christ loved Paul and gave himself for Paul's redemption—as also for us all. (2) Paul loved Christ, and that love became within him the dominant motivation for all he was and all he did. (3) Christ supplied to Paul a capacity to love others in a way he could not have attained otherwise. (4) Christ supplied to the brethren a capacity to love one another (1 Corinthians 12:31—13:13)—including Paul—in a way that held the body of Christ together in spite of all difficulties.

The constraining or controlling power of Christ's love was like walls alongside a road, preventing the traveler from wandering off his course, or like a vise holding a piece of work from coming apart as it was being fashioned.

Christ's love was expressed most prominently in His self-sacrifice on the cross, where He died willingly for all mankind. As believers participate in that death—dramatized and realized in Christian baptism (Romans 6:1-11)—they become *dead*, not only to sin and its guilt, but also to the selfish ambition that would prevent their following Christ. Christianity is indeed a matter of death and life—first in Christ, who died and conquered death; then in the believer who dies to self that he may live to God in Christ. The natural person, self-centered and self-serving, is transformed into the selfless, self-sacrificing, and self-giving image of Jesus. This is indeed no less radical than death and resurrection. It was this death/resurrection experience that motivated Paul's behavior, which was beyond comprehension to those who had never outgrown the "first law of [earthly] nature"—self-protection and self-preservation.

LOVE'S COMPULSION

In relation to his work for God, Paul asserted that "the love of Christ constraineth us." The *New International Version* translates it, "for Christ's love compels us."

There are many kinds of love that compel people to act in certain ways. The love of golf causes people to arise at dawn and drive for miles to get on the course in good season. The love of money and gambling drives people to spend countless hours at slot machines in smoke-filled casinos. The love of gardening impels many to spend long periods of time on their knees cultivating the soil.

A mother's love for her children causes her to be available to bandage cuts, kiss bruises, wipe away tears, and help with playtimes. The love of learning about antiquity drives archaeologists to live for months in desert areas to discover ancient pottery, artifacts, and writings.

Should it then be considered strange if those who love Jesus and trust in Him feel obligated to go into all the world in an effort to lead others to know Him too?   —J. G. V. B.

15. And that he died for all, that they which live should not henceforth live unto themselves, but unto him which died for them, and rose again.

The central fact of the gospel, received as the basis of faith, is here repeated for emphasis: Christ *died for all.* The resurrection life has a new center and purpose—Christ rather than self. Christ's self-giving not only makes the new life possible; it establishes the standard and the energy for its development. The believer is able to serve others, not alone for their sakes, but especially for Christ's sake. So one result of Christ's death and resurrection is finally to remake believers into the kind of extreme—"mad" persons Paul was!

II. Reconciling Men to God
(2 Corinthians 5:16-21)

There was sober method, or purpose, in Paul's "madness." It was to convey to every living person the message of God's reconciliation of mankind to himself. Since it was manifestly impossible for Paul to do it by himself, he would enlist the entire church—including the reconciled brethren at Corinth—in the effort.

A. New Viewpoint of a Newly Created One
(vv. 16, 17)

16. Wherefore henceforth know we no man after the flesh: yea, though we have known Christ after the flesh, yet now henceforth know we him no more.

The worldly person evaluates all things—including all persons—by material standards. What does he look like? What does he wear? How wealthy is he? How influential? What abilities or accomplishments can he boast? That is the way Paul's critics were looking at him.

Such thinking belongs to the pre-Christian person. It is to be rejected because of Christ. In Him, all judgment is to be made from the spiritual or eternal viewpoint, and every person is to be known as one for whom Christ died.

Paul confessed that formerly he had judged Jesus himself by worldly standards, looking for a conquering Messiah/King. From that viewpoint he had resisted and opposed Jesus as a false pretender.

After his conversion, Paul recognized Jesus for His eternal qualities. His emphasis is on God's Son who surrendered Heaven's glory for earth's sorrows; who gave himself in death for our redemption, who broke the bonds of death for our resurrection, and who will come again in glory to claim His own.

17. Therefore if any man be in Christ, he is a new creature: old things are passed away; behold, all things are become new.

In Christ one is united with Him through faith in Him and commitment to Him. Thus one becomes *a new creature*, or creation. God, who created all things in the beginning, creates believers anew in Christ. They become different in every important way, including the way they look at and evaluate people; including themselves. As a new creation I am committed to new purposes. As new creations my Christian friends are endowed with new possibilities and prospects, to be evaluated for their eternal worth.

Among the *old things* that have *passed away* is the old habit of judging according to outward appearances, along with old sins and their guilt, old grudges, old self-centeredness, old isolation and alienation. Among the new things of the new creation are new affections growing from God's love; new purposes, seeking first the kingdom of God; new aspirations and hopes, leading to Heaven, and new Christ-centered activities suitable to the new nature.

B. New Mission of Reconciliation
(vv. 18-20)

18. And all things are of God, who hath reconciled us to himself by Jesus Christ, and hath given to us the ministry of reconciliation.

God is the supplier of the new creation, just as He first supplied the creation of the world. In the matter of reconciliation, He takes and maintains the lead in repairing broken relationships. Paul and his readers, like all other believers, had been estranged from God and had been brought back by God's ministry through Jesus. Now God

visual 11

was making them His agents, charged with carrying to others the reconciling gospel they had received. Here is the mission of the church as a ministering community. The saved are engaged in the salvation of others.

19. To wit, that God was in Christ, reconciling the world unto himself, not imputing their trespasses unto them; and hath committed unto us the word of reconciliation.

Let no reader fail to understand what Paul meant by "the ministry of reconciliation" (v. 18). Paul now specifies, repeats, and explains. It is indeed a staggering declaration, and it may not be accepted on the first presentation. The ministry of reconciliation began with the act of God in visiting earth in the person of Jesus of Nazareth, to attract and win rebellious mankind to himself by His self-sacrifice. In this, God removed from all mankind the penalty for their sins by paying it himself. He made redemption available to all who will accept it, and so become reconciled, or adjusted, to Him. Then God moved to win as many as possible to that salvation. He charged the reconciled ones to carry the message of reconciliation to the persons around them.

Committed is a serious word, describing a responsibility. It speaks of a commission, and it demands devotion in carrying it out. The *us* to whom the commission is committed are the ones who have received God's merciful ministry of reconciliation.

GOD'S INITIATIVES

Paul was very much aware of the fact that *God* had initiated the whole of what one Bible scholar called "The Scheme of Redemption." Paul tells us, "All things are of God (v. 18)," or, as the *New International Version* reads, "All this is from God." It was God who caused the babe of Bethlehem to be born, He who impelled His words and His ways, and who made clear His will in Gethsemane's garden. He it was who sustained Jesus on the cross and raised Him from the guarded tomb to everlasting life. God it was who initiated all the main acts in the drama of human salvation from sin.

When there is a labor-management dispute and a strike, unless someone is willing to present some ameliorating or softening proposal, both sides will remain aloof and alienated. Occasionally family members become disaffected because of something one or another has done or not done. When a mutual relative has died, one may say, "Aunt Rachel promised me I could have her cherry chest of drawers, and that Ida Mae just went in there and took it. I'll never forgive her for such a selfish action!" This may provoke a "family feud" that goes on for years.

In all such instances someone must take the initiative if there is to be a reconciliation. God took the initiative in an effort to woo man back to himself. Jesus' coming and His loving life, sacrificial death, mighty resurrection, and empowerment of His church show us the initiative God has taken. Now the opportunity and challenge to us is, "Be ye reconciled to God" (verse 20).   —J. G. V. B.

20. Now then we are ambassadors for Christ, as though God did beseech you by us: we pray you in Christ's stead, be ye reconciled to God.

An *ambassador* is literally a veteran, a mature person who has received and must convey the authorized message. He is one who has outgrown any temptation to prove or promote himself, and so can give his whole attention to fulfilling his assignment. He does not speak in his own name, act in his own way, or communicate his own ideas. God's original ambassadors—the apostles and their companions—were commissioned, directed, and empowered by the Holy Spirit. We do not stand in that same level of authorization; but as a faithful messenger of the embassy, any one of us can deliver the same reconciling word. It is God's appeal, coming through the mouth of any faithful messenger, and it ought to be respected for its divine source.

"We implore you on Christ's behalf: Be reconciled to God" (*New International Version*). Yield to God's plea for conformity to Him! Cease your resentment and resistance to the Almighty! Cease making gods, or any god, with your own hands or your own imagination. Adjust your fickle self to the reality of the unchanging Creator. Yield to the divine purpose for which Christ died.

That is the message and ministry of the Lord's church.

C. The Means of Reconciliation (v. 21)

How will earth-bound, sin-stained mortals ever become worthy to carry God's ministry of reconciliation to their fellowmen? Simply by becoming themselves reconciled to Him as He has provided.

21. For he hath made him to be sin for us, who knew no sin; that we might be made the righteousness of God in him.

A double transformation is involved in our salvation-cleansing. God's one and only Son became something that He was not, in order that we might become something that we were not! By nature He was the embodiment of righteousness. At the conclusion of His earthly life span, exposed to the same kinds of temptations that beset and upset all of us, He could not be rightly charged with any fault in word or deed (John 8:46; Hebrews 4:15). Yet for our sakes He went to a criminal's death as the very embodiment of sin.

Our sins were attributed to the sinless One in order that His righteousness might be attributed to us sinners. The ultimate result is even more than that. It is more than having good things made available to us or credited to our account; it is shaping us into the image and character of God. We become something we were not. We are born anew from above. And that is an experience abundantly worth sharing!

Conclusion
A. Who? Me?

All this about the old being gone and the new having come is a bit extreme, isn't it? What living person is a candidate for that kind of transformation? And where is the living demonstration that it actually takes place? Certainly not in me?

Yes, in you! As for demonstration, the text before us provides it in the apostle Paul! It can happen. It has happened. It does happen. It will happen. But not without the permission of the person involved. And that is where you come in. Yes, you!

B. A Prayer From the Embassy

How greatly You have blessed us, O God, in giving us a place in Your embassy to mankind! Give us grace, we pray, to be faithful in delivering Your message to those about us. May our lives never be such as to deny the truth of what we say. In Jesus' name, amen.

C. Thought to Remember

Be reconciled to God!

Home Daily Bible Readings

Monday, May 8—One Who Loves Knows God (1 John 4:1-7)

Tuesday, May 9—We Love Because God Loves Us (1 John 4:13-21)

Wednesday, May 10—God's Spirit Sustains Us (2 Corinthians 5:1-5)

Thursday, May 11—Aim to Please God (2 Corinthians 5:6-10)

Friday, May 12—Christ's Love Controls Us (2 Corinthians 5:11-15)

Saturday, May 13—The Ministry of Reconciliation (2 Corinthians 5:16-21)

Sunday, May 14—Seek Reconciliation Before Worshiping (Matthew 5:21-26)

Learning by Doing

This page contains an alternate lesson plan emphasizing learning activities. Classes desiring such student involvement will find these suggestions helpful.

Learning Goals

As a result of completing this lesson students will be able to:

1. Define, understand, and illustrate the meaning of reconciliation.

2. Describe the changes that occur when a person becomes reconciled to God.

3. Be purposeful and committed to reaching out to reconcile the lost to Christ.

Into the Lesson

Tape a length of butcher paper or shelf paper to the chalkboard and letter on it these words: "Reconciliation in everyday life is needed in the following situations: warring tribes, quarreling children—" Ask class members as they arrive to add other situations. (Provide magic markers for this purpose.) This is also in the student book.

Lead into the Scripture by saying that sinful mankind needs to be reconciled to a righteous and holy God. This is the greatest reconciliation of all, and it will lead to reconciliation in everyday life situations as well. Chapter 5 of 2 Corinthians concentrates on the importance and significance of being reconciled and leading others to be reconciled also.

Into the Word

Briefly present the information included in the Lesson Background section. Then have someone who has been assigned in advance read 2 Corinthians 5:11-21 to the class. Tell the students to be looking for answers to the following questions as the passage is read. Develop the lesson in response to the answers discovered by the class.

1. What was Paul's motivation for talking so much about himself in the second letter to the church at Corinth? (To give the Corinthians ammunition to counteract the statements of false teachers who laughed at Paul as a leader.)

2. Apparently some thought Paul to be overly zealous even to the point of madness. What was his explanation for his behavior? (In verse 13 Paul makes it clear that he had two motives—to serve God and to help the Corinthians.)

3. What in Paul's experiences might have led people to think he was out of touch with reality? (Have students read Acts 26:24, 25. Remind them of Paul's visions and trances (Acts 9:3-9; 22:17-21).

4. What one thing constrained or compelled all of Paul's life? (Verses 14-16 point out that it was the law of Christ who died for all.)

5. What does it mean to be in Christ? (Verse 17 declares that we become new creations and that old things are passed away.)

6. Whose responsibility is it to share the good news that God has reconciled sinful people to himself through Jesus Christ? (Verses 18-20 suggest that every reconciled person should be helping others to be reconciled.) This responsibility is not merely for missionaries, ministers, and other "hired help." See Acts 8:1, 4.

Into Life

Pass out blank sheets of paper (or refer to the student book) and ask the class members to make two columns. Label one OLD SELF and the other NEW SELF. Then direct students to list as many characteristics as they can of each to show the contrast between life without Christ and life in Christ. (Some typical examples might be: OLD SELF—self-giving, self-righteous, egotistical. NEW SELF; self-giving, declared righteous in Christ, humble.

After students share their ideas, ask, "Do all of these changes into a new creation occur instantly, or in a lifelong process?" (Point out that we become new creatures instantly when we are baptized into Christ (v. 17). However, we then are newborn babes in Christ. We need to grow and mature (1 Corinthians 3:1; 1 Peter 2:2). This growing involves changes in our attitudes and our actions that may continue as long as we live on earth. Have each person write this statement on the bottom of the sheet of paper and complete it as he wishes: "One attitude or action that I will ask God to help me change is _____." Allow five minutes of silence for meditation as people prepare their statements.

Go on to explain that sometimes Christians fail to grow because they do not realize that they need any change. All of us have blind spots about ourselves. Have the class assist you in listing some often overlooked attitudes and behaviors in the lives of Christians. Some ideas: bias or prejudice about races or ethnic groups, negativism that results in grumbling and complaining, hateful attitudes toward those with whom we disagree. Suggest that each one pray daily for needed change in his or her own life.

Let's Talk It Over

The questions on this page are designed to encourage review of the lesson Scriptures and to promote discussion of the lesson by the class. The answers provided are only discussion starters. Let your class talk it over from there.

1. Why do we need to know the terror or fear of the Lord, and how can we grow in such knowledge?

The word *terror* may not seem appropriate to describe a Christian's response to God's power and holiness. We have experienced the love and grace of God, and while we retain a sense of reverential fear toward Him, it is something other than terror. However, it should still be terrifying for us to contemplate the ultimate fate of the unsaved. That kind of terror can be an aid to us in developing an urgency in our efforts to win unsaved family members and friends. It is sadly true that Scriptures dealing with God's fiery judgment on those who reject His Son are absent from many sermons and lessons today. We need to be stirred by Jesus' pronouncement of the fate of the unfaithful in Matthew 25:41, by Paul's vivid description of Jesus' return in 2 Thessalonians 1:7-9, and by the account of the final judgment in Revelation 20:11-15.

2. What are some ways in which the love of Christ constrains or controls us?

Christ's love for us and our responding love for Him impel us to holy and righteous living. We may be motivated somewhat by our fear of God's judgment or our hope of rewards in Heaven, but love is the highest motivation. As we grow in our understanding of His love for us we will find increasing delight in demonstrating our love for Him by living in a way that will please Him. The same can be said for our service as Christians. The love of Christ controls us in our relationships within the church. Like other human beings we are prone to pride, jealousy, thoughtless remarks, uncharitable acts—the kinds of things that generate conflict and division. The shared love of Christ enables us to surmount such failings and preserve our fellowship.

3. What are some examples of the ways people judge Jesus Christ "after the flesh" today?

Many people see in Jesus of Nazareth nothing more than a carpenter/teacher of ancient times around whose personality and teachings a great religion eventually developed. They have no appreciation for the facts of Jesus' divine nature, of His miracles, and of His atoning death and resurrection. Others try to fit Jesus into a preconceived mold in order to give divine authority to their personal agenda. In this way Jesus can be made a symbol for pacifism or organized labor or an anti-establishment viewpoint or various other causes. However worthy any political or social movement may seem, its advocates cannot properly claim Jesus as their forerunner, because He simply will not fit into any humanly devised mold.

4. Since we have become new creatures in Christ, what are some ways in which our newness should be made evident?

The Christian should have a new set of goals. No longer can acquisition of wealth and enjoyment of unrestricted pleasure be one's major aims. Bringing glory to God, serving our fellow human beings in the name of Jesus Christ, growing in knowledge of the Word and in effectiveness in prayer must now receive priority. The Christian should develop a new set of attitudes. Greed, selfishness, hatred, jealousy, and a spirit of vengeance must give way to love, compassion, generosity, and a spirit of humility. Colossians 3:5-17 speaks of this as a matter of putting off the old attitudes and habits and putting on new ones. The Christian should demonstrate a new approach to the use of his money. Instead of seeing it as his, to be spent in any way that suits him, he now recognizes that he is simply a steward of what God owns.

5. Since the doctrine of reconciliation involves the idea that all non-Christians are enemies of God, some may protest, "I have nothing against God—how can I be His enemy?" How should we answer this?

We must start with the biblical teaching that God is our Creator. He therefore has the prerogative to make the rules as to how He wants us to live. If we deviate in any way from those rules, we in effect take a stand against our Creator. While many people appear to accept the fact that God is the Creator, they fail to grasp the full implications of that fact. They tend to think of themselves as autonomous, answerable only to themselves for the way they live. Such a viewpoint is characteristic of the world, and "whosoever therefore will be a friend of the world is the enemy of God" (James 4:4).

Sharing Blessings With Others

DEVOTIONAL READING: Matthew 25:31-46.

LESSON SCRIPTURE: 2 Corinthians 8, 9.

PRINTED TEXT: 2 Corinthians 9:1-15.

2 Corinthians 9:1-15

1 For as touching the ministering to the saints, it is superfluous for me to write to you:

2 For I know the forwardness of your mind, for which I boast of you to them of Macedonia, that Achaia was ready a year ago; and your zeal hath provoked very many.

3 Yet have I sent the brethren, lest our boasting of you should be in vain in this behalf; that, as I said, ye may be ready:

4 Lest haply if they of Macedonia come with me, and find you unprepared, we (that we say not, ye) should be ashamed in this same confident boasting.

5 Therefore I thought it necessary to exhort the brethren, that they would go before unto you, and make up beforehand your bounty, whereof ye had notice before, that the same might be ready, as a matter of bounty, and not as of covetousness.

6 But this I say, He which soweth sparingly shall reap also sparingly; and he which soweth bountifully shall reap also bountifully.

7 Every man according as he purposeth in his heart, so let him give; not grudgingly, or of necessity: for God loveth a cheerful giver.

8 And God is able to make all grace abound toward you; that ye, always having all sufficiency in all things, may abound to every good work:

9 (As it is written, He hath dispersed abroad; he hath given to the poor: his righteousness remaineth for ever.

10 Now he that ministereth seed to the sower both minister bread for your food, and multiply your seed sown, and increase the fruits of your righteousness:)

11 Being enriched in every thing to all bountifulness, which causeth through us thanksgiving to God.

12 For the administration of this service not only supplieth the want of the saints, but is abundant also by many thanksgivings unto God;

13 While by the experiment of this ministration they glorify God for your professed subjection unto the gospel of Christ, and for your liberal distribution unto them, and unto all men;

14 And by their prayer for you, which long after you for the exceeding grace of God in you.

15 Thanks be unto God for his unspeakable gift.

GOLDEN TEXT: He which soweth sparingly shall reap also sparingly; and he which soweth bountifully shall reap also bountifully.—2 Corinthians 9:6.

Lesson Aims

This study should enable the student to:

1. Name Paul's two main purposes in raising funds among Gentile Christians to help the "poor saints" in Judea.

2. Cite benefits to the contributor of such funds, as noted in Acts 20:35: "It is more blessed to give than to receive."

3. Review his own pattern of contributing financially to the cause of Christ.

Lesson Outline

INTRODUCTION
    A. Fund Raising by Mail
    B. In Debt to the Teacher
  I. PLANNED GENEROSITY (2 Corinthians 9:1-5)
    A. Good Beginning (vv. 1, 2)
    B. Help on the Way (vv. 3-5)
 II. JOYOUS GIVING (2 Corinthians 9:6-9)
    A. God's Pleasure (vv. 6, 7)
      Cheerful Giving
    B. God's Example (vv. 8, 9)
      About Abounding
III. PROVISION AND PRAISE (2 Corinthians 9:10-14)
    A. God Supplies (vv. 10, 11)
    B. God Is Praised (vv. 12-14)
IV. GOD'S MATCHLESS GIFT (2 Corinthians 9:15)
    God's Gift
CONCLUSION
    A. Who Was Blessed?
    B. Prayer for the Grace of Giving
    C. Thought to Remember

Visual 12 highlights some of the blessings that result from the offering of our gifts to God. The visual is shown on page 324.

Introduction

A. Fund Raising by Mail

As a sometime contributor to "good causes," I find my mailbox loaded with letters of appeal from all manner of agencies—Christian, social, moral, educational, and political. I have sought to reduce the volume by asking for financial statements from the fund raisers; then actively discouraging all but those in whom I have the greatest interest. Fewer than half responded to my request for financial reports. The reports showed an average of about eighty percent of income finding its way past the costs of fund raising and administration to program accomplishment.

That does not measure up to the level of Paul's fund raising among Gentile Christians in Europe and "Asia" for the relief of poverty among Jewish Christians in Judea. Paul differed from modern fund raisers in many ways. He never named an amount of money expected or called it "voluntary dues." Instead, the gift was to be as God had prospered the Christian being approached. The amount or the proportion was to be determined freely and deliberately by the donor. Paul was very careful that the moneys be handled by dependable persons chosen from among the givers. No breath of scandal must be allowed to dishonor Christ in this raising, handling, and delivering of funds. Would that the cause of Christ might always be so respected! The eighth and ninth chapters of 2 Corinthians provide a model for Christian fund-raising letters.

B. In Debt to the Teacher

Those who are taught worthwhile truths owe something to their teachers. So says the apostle in a passage dealing with Christians' responsibilities to one another: "Let him that is taught in the word communicate unto him that teacheth in all good things" (Galatians 6:6).

Paul applied that principle plainly to the Gentile Christians' obligation toward the Jewish pioneers from whom they had received the gospel of Christ. To the Romans Paul wrote, "I am on my way to Jerusalem in the service of the saints there. For Macedonia and Achaia were pleased to make a contribution for the poor among the saints in Jerusalem. They were pleased to do it, and indeed they owe it to them. For if the Gentiles have shared in the Jews' spiritual blessings, they owe it to the Jews to share with them their material blessings" (Romans 15:25-27, *New International Version*).

That clarifies one important reason Paul pushed the project. He was a Jew carrying the gospel to Gentiles. He was anxious to establish a strong bond of unity among Christians from the two diverse backgrounds. Nothing would serve that purpose better than for the Gentiles to express real appreciation and concern for their Jewish brethren. The second obvious reason was that the Christians in Jerusalem had exhausted their resources in seeing the church through its difficult infancy, and they were in real need.

Acts 2:41-47 and 4:32-37 reveal that the earliest Christians left homes and employment to receive daily teaching from the apostles. Many who had traveled from distant places to the city of Jerusalem for the great Feast of Pentecost remained there, supported by their brethren in Judea, who even sold their fields and houses to provide for those in need. The Judean Christians so drained their resources that when a general famine occurred some years later, the disciples at Antioch recognized the need at Jerusalem, and sent financial help, "every man according to his ability" (Acts 11:27-30).

A longer-term, more substantial collection for Jewish Christian relief became a major project of Paul's third missionary journey. He promoted it among the churches of Galatia, and while in Ephesus he sent directions for the gathering of gifts in Corinth and the surrounding country, Achaia (1 Corinthians 16:1-3). Titus became his emissary to develop the project in Macedonia, where it was eminently successful, and also in Achaia (2 Corinthians 8). The eighth and ninth chapters of 2 Corinthians are given over to it.

For us, the events offer a marvelous study in Christian generosity.

I. Planned Generosity (2 Corinthians 9:1-5)

A. Good Beginning (vv. 1, 2)

1. For as touching the ministering to the saints, it is superfluous for me to write to you.

The Gentiles' financial help to the poor saints in Judea is the subject for the previous chapter. It deals with an unselfish sharing of blessings with others—people different in cultural and ethnic background; people from whom no further benefit could be expected.

Chapter 8 describes the exemplary generosity with which the relatively poor churches in Macedonia had responded to Paul's appeal, and tells that he was now sending Titus and two other trustworthy messengers to help the churches in Achaia to gather their funds in preparation for Paul's arrival.

2. For I know the forwardness of your mind, for which I boast of you to them of Macedonia, that Achaia was ready a year ago; and your zeal hath provoked very many.

The people of Achaia seem to have been naturally excitable and enthusiastic. On Paul's first presentation of the need in Judea, made more than a year earlier, they had responded with immediate plans for generous participation. Paul had spoken of this to the folk in Macedonia, and they had been motivated to a surprisingly generous response. But in the meantime the churches in Achaia had lagged in fulfillment of their plan. Now they needed prodding. They needed to act as the Macedonians had acted. Plans and promises must be followed by performance.

B. Help on the Way (vv. 3-5)

3. Yet have I sent the brethren, lest our boasting of you should be in vain in this behalf; that, as I said, ye may be ready.

Paul was sending a blue ribbon committee to help the Achaian Christians complete their benevolent project. The three messengers are introduced in 2 Corinthians 8:16-23. Best known was Titus, Paul's partner in the project. The others, "messengers of the churches," are not named, but one had already "proved diligent in many things" associated with the apostle. The third was apparently known to Paul only by a generally excellent reputation "throughout all the churches." Paul was being careful to provide things honest in the sight of all men. It was almost as if he foresaw and shuddered at the damage done to the cause of Christ by fiscal irresponsibility on the part of some prominent evangelists in our day.

The Achaian brethren must be *ready* with their offering, as Paul had said they would be.

4. Lest haply if they of Macedonia come with me, and find you unprepared, we (that we say not, ye) should be ashamed in this same confident boasting.

Paul was in Macedonia at the time of this writing. Sopater of Berea, and Aristarchus and Secundus of Thessalonica, all in Macedonia, would be named to travel with the party delivering the collection to Jerusalem (Acts 20:4). They or other Macedonians might come with Paul to Corinth. They had heard Paul's glowing report of the good start made by the brethren there a year ago. If the visitors were to find the project stalled in Achaia, Paul would be humiliated. That humiliation would be shared by the churches at Corinth.

5. Therefore I thought it necessary to exhort the brethren, that they would go before unto you, and make up beforehand your bounty, whereof ye had notice before, that the same might be ready, as a matter of bounty, and not as of covetousness.

How to Say It

ACHAIA.   Uh-*kay*-yuh.
ACHAIAN.   Uh-*kay*-yun.
ARISTARCHUS.   Air-iss-*tar*-cuss.
BEREA.   Beh-*ree*-uh.
GALATIA.   Guh-*lay*-shuh.
MACEDONIA.   Mass-eh-*doe*-nee-uh.
SECUNDUS.   Se-*kun*-dus.
SOPATER.   *So*-pah-ter or *Sop*-a-ter.

Here the apostle spells out the assignment given to Titus and his two companions, to help the Achaian churches overcome their present stalemate. *Bounty* here is an unusual translation of a common word, usually rendered "blessing"—an expression of generous goodwill. Made up freely beforehand, the gift would be a happy expression of love to the Jewish brethren.

II. Joyous Giving
(2 Corinthians 9:6-9)

There follows a description of giving that brings pleasure to God and man because it reflects the nature of God himself.

A. God's Pleasure (vv. 6, 7)

6. But this I say, He which soweth sparingly shall reap also sparingly; and he which soweth bountifully shall reap also bountifully.

In Galatians 6:7 we are reminded that a person reaps *what* he sows; here we note that he reaps (continuously and habitually) *as* he sows, stingily or generously.

Bountifully repeats the "blessing" theme of the previous verse: "in a manner of blessing." One should dispense, and receive, liberally as he has been blessed and expects to receive blessing. Both in sowing seed and in bestowing gifts, one accepts the possibility of losing what he has distributed, but he acts in faith, expecting God to bring from it something far more valuable.

7. Every man according as he purposeth in his heart, so let him give; not grudgingly, or of necessity: for God loveth a cheerful giver.

Christian giving is voluntary. Each person must make up his own mind and act accordingly. Paul would not recommend schemes and gimmicks designed to act like novocaine injected into purses to reduce the pain of coin extraction.

Not grudgingly; literally, "not from grief." Not *of necessity*—either the giver's need to give or the recipients' need for the money. Either of these would provide sufficient reason to give, but would rob the act of its proper joy, "The cheerful giver God loves." The sentence is so arranged in the Greek for emphasis.

God's pleasure is in those who are enough like himself to give unsparingly because of love.

CHEERFUL GIVING

There are many types of giving about which we need to be gracious and glad. One is the matter of giving *in.* We may have some aim we feel determined to accomplish. We "hold on" even though circumstances make the outcome we desire most unlikely. Finally we have to give in to reality: our wishes are not going to be realized. It is important to do this without whining or complaining or blaming others, to be *cheerful* when giving *in.*

There is also the matter of giving *up.* There are times when we have to give up our wish to have certain pews chosen for a building, or a certain mission liberally supported, or a certain minister called. We need to be able to give *up* without bitterness or moodiness—to give up cheerfully.

We often come to the place where we must give *away* money, or effort, or valued earthly treasures. This we should do ungrudgingly; not in a morose manner, but with good cheer and goodwill.

As we become advanced in years we sometimes discover occasions when in our work for God we just give *out.* "The spirit is willing, but the flesh is weak." We must not let this discourage or defeat us. We must do what we can with joy, and with joy pass the baton in the relay race of life to fresher and younger runners, urging them on to stronger endeavors with glad hands and happy hearts.

Cheerful giving. It should characterize the life of every follower of Jesus.   —J. G. V. B.

B. God's Example (vv. 8, 9)

8. And God is able to make all grace abound toward you; that ye, always having all sufficiency in all things, may abound to every good work.

God's abundant, overflowing *grace*, providing all things good and necessary, acts in at least three ways to encourage Christian generosity. (1) It provides the perfect example. (2) It promises a more than adequate reward to the generous giver. (3) It assures a continual supply from which the generous one can draw for continued generosity. When the windows of Heaven are opened to provide overflowing supply (Malachi 3:10), it includes, but is definitely not limited to, things material. God's abundant grace is given to be shared in our ministry of doing good.

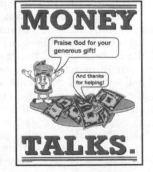

visual 12

ABOUT ABOUNDING

It is interesting to visit the Hershey chocolate factory in Hershey, Pennsylvania, where candy bars, cocoa, and other chocolate goodies are manufactured. As one tours the factory, one sees chocolate bars on conveyor belts as they go to be packaged for shipment to outlets everywhere. We all have seen a box or two of such bars in a candy counter. But here are thousands and thousands of such bars, a veritable river of chocolate bars flowing in an unceasing stream. This is *abundance* objectified.

Likewise God's grace or kindness and His empowering blessings flow to us in an avalanche of bounty. God is able to do all this when *our* surrender of heart and life enables Him to fulfill His will in and through us. —J. G. V. B.

9. (As it is written, He hath dispersed abroad; he hath given to the poor: his righteousness remaineth for ever.

The quotation is from Psalm 112:9. The entire psalm speaks of prosperity for the person who fears the Lord. Scripture everywhere indicates God's special care for those who cannot take care of themselves. In this psalm is particular reference to the *godly* poor; hence it is appropriate to Paul's present purpose. Because the recipients are God's people, they have a special claim to the Lord's good offices; and because the donors are God's people, they have a special motivation to serve as the channels of divine beneficence.

III. Provision and Praise
(2 Corinthians 9:10-14)

The apostle's appeal approaches its climax in describing the Gentiles' generosity as a means of bringing praise to God, the provider of all things to all mankind.

A. God Supplies (vv. 10, 11)

10. Now he that ministereth seed to the sower both minister bread for your food, and multiply your seed sown, and increase the fruits of your righteousness.)

Here is reference to the seedtime and harvest mentioned in verse 6. God *ministereth*, or provides abundantly, in the manner of a wealthy patron providing for a public program. The portion of grain that goes into the ground as seed, and that which is retained to make bread, and the sprouting and growing that bring a bountiful harvest, all come from God. In the *King James Version* this appears as a prayerful wish that generous giving may be answered with more generous supply. Most recent translations present it as

a prediction or promise. The divine Provider *will* multiply your goodness with blessings not limited to things material.

11. Being enriched in every thing to all bountifulness, which causeth through us thanksgiving to God.

The *New International Version* expresses it thus: "You will be made rich in every way so that you can be generous on every occasion, and through us your generosity will result in thanksgiving to God." The generous person will be made able to continue generously—perhaps in ways other than material.

B. God Is Praised (vv. 12-14)

12. For the administration of this service not only supplieth the want of the saints, but is abundant also by many thanksgivings unto God.

Where there was lack of material supply in Judea, the offering would serve to fill it. But the spiritual benefit would be even greater; it would overflow in thankful praises to God. Jesus' judgment scene of Matthew 25:31-46 comes to mind. Those who supply the hunger of the needy will discover that they have inherited an overflow forever with their Lord. The Christian's ultimate goal, not only in offerings but in all else, is brought into focus. "Seek ye first the kingdom of God"; His glory above all!

13. While by the experiment of this ministration they glorify God for your professed subjection unto the gospel of Christ, and for your liberal distribution unto them, and unto all men.

Like a successful laboratory *experiment*, the Achaian Christians' offering will convince their brethren in Judea that the Gentiles' obedience to *the gospel of Christ* is deeper and more meaningful than mere words. They will praise God again for the gospel's power to change lives. They will praise Him, too, for the benefit that has now come to themselves because of the gospel for which they have made so great sacrifices. And they will praise Him because such benefit is available not only to them but to all nations.

14. And by their prayer for you, which long after you for the exceeding grace of God in you.

The Judeans' prayer response will include not only thanks and praise, but also petitions on behalf of the Gentile Christians, who have now become objects of friendly affection. Paul has written of "the grace of our Lord Jesus Christ" in surrendering the riches of Heaven for the poverty of earth (2 Corinthians 8:9), and he has spoken of generous giving as a "grace" (8:6). It is indeed an attractive and lovable quality in any person—especially as it reflects the boundless self-giving of Christ. Something more than ordinary gratitude for material relief would be needed to break down the "wall of partition" between Jew and Gentile; but Paul was confident that in Christ that something was present (see Ephesians 2:14).

IV. God's Matchless Gift (2 Corinthians 9:15)

The final verse of our text concludes the message with a triumphant doxology.

15. Thanks be unto God for his unspeakable gift.

How shall one find words in spoken language to describe the gift of God's Son for the world's salvation? John comes close to it in John 3:16. But how shall one express appropriate gratitude? Material payment is impossible, and to suggest it is almost an insult to the Almighty. Thanksgiving becomes a lifelong project, and ceaseless hymns of thanks are both an obligation and a privilege. God's indescribable gift becomes the pattern and motivation for the kind of giving Paul urged upon the Corinthians. The exercise of generosity in Jesus' name becomes in itself an appropriate expression of thanks to God for His gift.

There is something fascinating about the singular *gift*—not gifts. Paul had spoken of God's supplying food continually in abundant measure (v. 10), but seed and food and every other material provision—even physical life itself—are but loans, to be called in at a time of final accounting. Only Jesus is totally and eternally God's *gift* to mankind, to be enjoyed by grateful recipients forever. In the light of that gift, what believer could refuse to share his blessings with others?

GOD'S GIFT

Accustomed as we are to giving and receiving gifts, we can think of none to compare with God's gift of His Son as our Example, Redeemer, Savior, and Master. His gift meets our greatest needs; it is absolutely vital to us. Such a gift is characteristic of the God of love and wisdom.

Paul is unable to express how significant God's gift of His Son is to us. Our text describes God's Gift as "unspeakable."

Have you seen a gift so great that it left the recipient speechless? A couple is leaving a local church where they have served selflessly for many years. They are given an expense-paid trip to Bible lands or a new car. Such a gift may well render the recipients voiceless.

Still, such a gift is worth less than the decades of loving service it recognizes. God's great gift was not given in recognition of our "good" service; it was given while we were yet sinners. Then how much more should God's wonderful gift of His Son overwhelm our comprehension and still our utterance!   —J. G. V. B.

Conclusion

A. Who Was Blessed?

Acts 21:17 and 24:17 make it clear that Paul and his companions were successful in bringing the Gentile Christians' gifts to Jerusalem, and that they were well received. So Paul was blessed in the fulfillment of that mission. The poor among the saints in Judea were benefited by the money, but how long did it last? Certainly not past the destruction of Jerusalem ten years later. The comfort that came from knowing the care of their brethren was longer lasting.

The choicest blessings were reserved, however, for those who gave—with greatest pleasure and liberality. Theirs was a special fellowship with God, the giver of all; with Christ, who gave of His very self; and with the grateful recipients of the benefit. They enjoyed especially the approval of their Lord (Matthew 25:34).

B. Prayer for the Grace of Giving

Thank You, our heavenly Father, for the undeserved gifts by which You have provided life and all that makes life meaningful—especially the gift of Your Son. In His name we plead for that grace which would make us most like yourself—the grace of a generous spirit, to share our blessings with others. Amen.

C. Thought to Remember

"It is more blessed to give than to receive" (Acts 20:35)

Home Daily Bible Readings

Monday, May 15—Works of Compassion Are Blessed (Matthew 25:31-41)

Tuesday, May 16—Give Freely to Help Others (2 Corinthians 8:1-7)

Wednesday, May 17—Give in Proportion to One's Means (2 Corinthians 8:8-15)

Thursday, May 18—Responsible Accounting in the Church (2 Corinthians 8:16-24)

Friday, May 19—Be Ready With One's Gifts (2 Corinthians 9:1-5)

Saturday, May 20—Share With Cheerfulness (2 Corinthians 9:6-10)

Sunday, May 21—Enriched by Generosity (2 Corinthians 9:11-15)

Learning by Doing

This page contains an alternate lesson plan emphasizing learning activities. Classes desiring such student involvement will find these suggestions helpful.

Learning Goals

As a result of completing this lesson, students will be able to:

1. Cite several different motives for giving generously to others, and choosing the best.

2. Examine their life-styles and determine what would have to change if they were to become more generous givers.

3. Write a thank-you note to God for all of His generous gifts and especially for His one indescribable gift, Jesus Christ.

Into the Lesson

One week prior to this lesson ask two people to prepare a skit in which one portrays the apostle Paul and the other a modern fund raiser. Have them develop a plot in which your church is trying to raise a large sum of money for the missionaries your church supports. In class let Paul tell how he would go about securing the needed funds, then let the modern fund raiser tell how he would do it. After the presentation, have the students vote on which fund raiser they would prefer. (Allow about five minutes for the skit and vote.)

Into the Word

Share the thoughts in the section entitled "In Debt to the Teacher," which is included in the introduction to this lesson. This explains why the Jerusalem church needed special gifts from other churches.

Ask the class why it is necessary to encourage Christians to give generously. Some possible answers: People are basically selfish; times are difficult and money is in short supply; some people have tunnel vision and need to have their vision expanded; some fail to see any connection between giving to others and what Christ has given to them. Show that Paul was not reticent about talking about generous gifts. Have everyone read 2 Corinthians 9:1-15 silently, looking for five special encouragements that Paul gave the Corinthians: 1. Their giving stirred the Macedonians to action. 2. Their giving would meet special needs. 3. Their giving would glorify God. 4. Their giving would bless them personally. 5. Their giving would unite God's people.

After these answers are found ask: Why did Paul send messengers to Corinth before the gift was to be ready? (Verses 3 and 9 indicate that Paul understood the inclination to procrastinate. The advance messengers would assure the readiness of the gift, assure its generosity, and keep all parties involved from being humiliated.) Have each person turn to a neighbor and discuss honestly: How do you feel when you are reminded that you need to give generously to the church? How much do you resent sermons and lessons about money? Point out that Paul was very tactful in his letter. He praised rather than harangued the readers about their promise to give. Go on to explain that giving is an integral part of being a Christian. Refer the class to 2 Corinthians 9:6-11 and ask people to enumerate the blessings that come to the generous giver. (Some answers are: a generous return, the love of God for his cheerfulness in giving, the continued blessing of God so that he can continue to give.)

Refer the class to the student book, or photocopy the following Scripture references, leaving a blank space after each reference so the student can write a brief summary similar to the one printed here. Romans 15:25-27: Paul praised the churches' contribution, but said they owed it to the church at Jerusalem. Proverbs 11:24, 25: Generosity is rewarding. Malachi 3:10: You can't outgive God. Matthew 25:31-46: As we give to others we are giving to Christ. Acts 4:34-37: Early disciples sold their property to meet the needs of others. Matthew 6:24: You must choose between serving God and materialism. Matthew 6:19, 20: Store up your treasures in Heaven, not on earth.

Summarize the Scripture study by saying that giving to others frees us from the tyranny of loving money and meets the needs of others as well.

Into Life

Divide the class into groups of four and assign the following sentences to be completed as agreed upon by the group:

1. If most Christians were to grow in their giving, these things would have to change:

2. Some wrong motives for generous giving are—

3. Some ways that we can teach our children or grandchildren to be generous are—

4. A generous one-time gift to a missionary from this Sunday school class should total—

Have one person from each group share the group's sentence completion with the class.

Conclude the class session with prayer.

Let's Talk It Over

The questions on this page are designed to encourage review of the lesson Scriptures and to promote discussion of the lesson by the class. The answers provided are only discussion starters. Let your class talk it over from there.

1. The lesson writer observes that Paul "was anxious to establish a strong bond of unity among Christians from . . . diverse backgrounds." This was one reason why he put so much emphasis on the collection for the Christians in Judea. How can our missionary giving foster similar unity between us and believers in other lands?

In answer to this we can draw a different application from Jesus' statement: "For where your treasure is, there will your heart be also" (Matthew 6:21). While Jesus was referring to our heart's being Heaven-directed, this statement can also describe what happens when we give sacrificially to a mission work in Africa, Asia, or elsewhere. Our heart will tend to be with the missionaries and the people among whom they are working. It is likely that our prayers and good wishes will follow our money, and we will become spiritually and emotionally involved with those fellow believers of another land.

2. In collecting funds for the Christians in Judea, those in Achaia started strong; but it seems that Paul was afraid they would lag before completing the task. That has a familiar ring. In our Christian work, how can we avoid the tendency to start with eagerness and then lag in completing it?

This seems to be a universal problem in churches. Some tasks are never completed because of this tendency. One approach to solving the problem is in setting deadlines for the completion of tasks. When plans are open-ended, and the attitude of "We'll get it done whenever we can" is adopted, this encourages the tendency to put off work indefinitely. Having a deadline is no guarantee of completing it on time, but it is a step in the right direction. It is also important to remind ourselves that talking about a matter, even extensively discussing it, is no substitute for action. We "talk to death" many vital projects, and they never get done.

3. What are some keys to developing cheerful giving rather than grudging giving?

The first key is in learning to acknowledge that all we own belongs to God. If what we give belongs to Him already, how can we begrudge it to Him? In connection with that we need to grow in our trust that "God shall supply all your need according to his riches in glory by Christ Jesus" (Philippians 4:19). We can give cheerfully if we have gained the confidence that God will respond to our sacrifice with His gracious bounty. Another key is in our realization of the good our gift can accomplish. We often waste money on leisure activities that bring no satisfaction, or on material things that we do not need. But when we consider how our gift to the church or to a missionary can contribute to the saving of eternal souls, to the teaching of eternal truths to children and adults, and to aiding people in need of food and clothing, it should make us cheerful indeed.

4. It is significant that Paul concludes his extensive discussion of Christian giving with the exclamation, "Thanks be unto God for his unspeakable gift." How should God's gift of His Son affect our giving?

From a negative standpoint, it should shame us if we give less than the best we can give. God gave the best, and we need to contemplate that biblical truth and pray over it until we appreciate the magnitude of the heavenly Father's sacrifice. From a positive standpoint, we should allow ourselves to be so awed by God's grace and love that our responsive thanksgiving and love will inspire us to give generously of all we have. In Revelation 5:9-14 we see the citizens of Heaven throwing all their energies into the worship of God and the Lamb. In our earthly worship, which includes our giving, we should similarly lose ourselves in such praise and adoration that it would not be possible for our gifts to be less than wholehearted.

5. God gave; Christ gave; many Christians in times past and in the present era have given sacrificially. How may we respond to their grand example?

We must beware of falling into the trap that caught Ananias and Sapphira as recorded in Acts 5. To take pride in the appearance of generosity; to covet the praise of others for our sacrifice. But what a privilege it is to join the universal fellowship of givers and to experience the joy of imitating the willing sacrifice of God and Jesus Christ and fellow believers!

Expressing Love to All

Devotional Reading: John 15:9-17.

Lesson Scripture: 1 Corinthians 13.

Printed Text: 1 Corinthians 13.

1 Corinthians 13

1 Though I speak with the tongues of men and of angels, and have not charity, I am become as sounding brass, or a tinkling cymbal.

2 And though I have the gift of prophecy, and understand all mysteries, and all knowledge; and though I have all faith, so that I could remove mountains, and have not charity, I am nothing.

3 And though I bestow all my goods to feed the poor, and though I give my body to be burned, and have not charity, it profiteth me nothing.

4 Charity suffereth long, and is kind; charity envieth not; charity vaunteth not itself, is not puffed up,

5 Doth not behave itself unseemly, seeketh not her own, is not easily provoked, thinketh no evil;

6 Rejoiceth not in iniquity, but rejoiceth in the truth;

7 Beareth all things, believeth all things, hopeth all things, endureth all things.

8 Charity never faileth: but whether there be prophecies, they shall fail; whether there be tongues, they shall cease; whether there be knowledge, it shall vanish away.

9 For we know in part, and we prophesy in part.

10 But when that which is perfect is come, then that which is in part shall be done away.

11 When I was a child, I spake as a child, I understood as a child, I thought as a child: but when I became a man, I put away childish things.

12 For now we see through a glass, darkly; but then face to face: now I know in part; but then shall I know even as also I am known.

13 And now abideth faith, hope, charity, these three; but the greatest of these is charity.

Golden Text: Now abideth faith, hope, charity, these three; but the greatest of these is charity.—1 Corinthians 13:13.

Christians Living in Community

Unit 3. Ministering as a Christian Community (Lessons 10-13)

Lesson Aims

This lesson should equip the student to:

1. Distinguish between "gifts of the Spirit" and the fruit of the Spirit that validates all gifts.

2. Report what Christian love does in terms of attitudes and actions.

3. Choose and activate a specific expression of love, as needed in his or her own life.

Lesson Outline

INTRODUCTION
  A. Getting the Idea
  B. Showing the Way
 I. LOVE IS ESSENTIAL (1 Corinthians 13:1-3)
  A. Noisy Talk (v. 1)
  B. Empty Accomplishments (v. 2)
    Love's Excellence
  C. Unprofitable Almsgiving (v. 3)
II. LOVE SERVES OTHERS (1 Corinthians 13:4-7)
  A. Love Opposes Selfishness (vv. 4-6)
    Love's Kindness
  B. Love "Hangs in There" (v. 7)
III. LOVE IS FOREVER (1 Corinthians 13:8-12)
  A. "Gifts" Will Vanish (vv. 8, 9)
    Love's Endurance
  B. What Is Complete Will Last (vv. 10-12)
IV. LOVE IS SUPREME (1 Corinthians 13:13)
CONCLUSION
  A. Follow Through With Love
  B. Lord, Teach Me to Love
  C. Thought to Remember

The excellence of Christian love is emphasized by visual 13 of the visuals packet. The visual is shown on page 333.

Introduction

A. Getting the Idea

He was a loving and lovable Christian gentleman, preaching and living faithfully what he found in Christ Jesus. Now he was fervently recommending that pattern to a friend who seemed more interested in establishing his own superiority over his neighbors. Finally the friend exploded in exasperation. "Love! Is that all you can talk about? The way you tell it, love is the be-all and end-all of Christianity!"

Here it was the preacher's turn to explode, but in delight he said, "Praise the Lord! You're beginning to get the idea!"

Readers of 1 Corinthians 13 might come to think of the apostle Paul as the impatient friend thought about our patient preacher—that he seemed to consider love as the be-all and end-all of Christianity. But Paul did not invent the idea. Jesus quoted two commandments as supremely important—to love God with your whole being, and to love your neighbor as yourself. He added, "On these two commandments hang all the law and the prophets" (Matthew 22:34-40). On the night before His crucifixion Jesus expounded the same idea to His apostles: "If ye keep my commandments, ye shall abide in my love"; and "These things I command you, that ye love one another" (John 15:9-17).

John, the "beloved apostle," wrote extensively on the same theme, saying, "He that loveth not, knoweth not God; for God is love" (1 John 4:7-21). Peter also wrote, "See that ye love one another with a pure heart fervently" (1 Peter 1:22). Paul summarized the subject in Romans 13:8-10: "Owe no man any thing, but to love one another. . . . Love is the fulfilling of the law."

Godly love—an unselfish seeking of another's good, without regard to the other's worthiness—is exemplified nowhere else so grandly as in God's gift of His only Son for our sins (John 3:16). It is not the kind of romantic passion into which one "falls," nor even the friendliness that graces society, or the warmth of family ties. Classical Greek literature had words for these, but those would not serve the Christian purpose. So the New Testament writers found in the Greek translation of the Old Testament another word—*agape*—into which they could pour the meaning of divine love and its human reflections. That is the word the apostles used and exemplified. Pagans in every age have found difficulty in understanding Christian love.

B. Showing the Way

Chapters 12—14 of 1 Corinthians deal with the subject of spiritual gifts, which seemed important to the church at Corinth. Paul and other apostles conveyed special powers of the Holy Spirit for special purposes with the laying on of their hands (compare Acts 8:14-20). Nine different special gifts are named in 1 Corinthians 12:8-10: wisdom, knowledge, faith (special measures and kinds of general abilities), healing, miracles, prophecy, discerning of prophecy (supernatural endowments), various kinds of tongues (vocal utterances), and interpretation of tongues. Verses 28 and 29 mention persons who employed some of these powers.

Chapter 14 picks up the same theme, as it deals especially with the gifts of prophecy (conveying messages by revelation from God) and tongues (speaking in words other than the languages normally learned). Paul preferred prophecy as more helpful to the church.

Bridging between chapters 12 and 14 is the biblical gem before us, dealing with love, not as a separate spiritual gift, but as a first fruit of the Spirit (Galatians 5:22). Hence it is the proper endowment of every believer and is necessary to validate every gift. It offers the "more excellent way" (12:31) to exercise whatever abilities one may possess, and it is to be "followed" in choosing and pursuing any course (14:1). Thus the bridge-chapter is anchored firmly at both ends in the discussion of spiritual gifts.

I. Love Is Essential
(1 Corinthians 13:1-3)

The first three verses of the chapter cite three extreme hypothetical circumstances to declare the futility of even the most remarkable accomplishments—in speech, in spiritual prowess, and in good works—without love.

Paul's argument is applied to himself personally; he was known to possess gifts of prophecy, tongues, and healing.

Agape, the word rendered *charity* in this passage, is translated *love* in other English versions, and elsewhere in the *King James Version. Charity* conveys a different meaning in modern English.

A. Noisy Talk (v. 1)

1. Though I speak with the tongues of men and of angels, and have not charity, I am become as sounding brass, or a tinkling cymbal.

The gift of speaking in "other" or "unknown" languages was prized in Corinth, so it is mentioned first. On the Day of Pentecost the apostles were heard in the native languages of at least fifteen different groups (Acts 2:4-12). But now Paul insists that even if he should become eloquent in every language employed by mankind or by heavenly messengers, but without love, his speech would be mere noise. *Brass* is known for its loud reverberation, even in band instruments, and cymbals are known for their clang. Together they are commonly used to create excitement without meaning. So is tongues-speaking for its own sake.

How to Say It

AGAPE.   Uh-*gah*-pay.

B. Empty Accomplishments (v. 2)

2. And though I have the gift of prophecy, and understand all mysteries, and all knowledge; and though I have all faith, so that I could remove mountains, and have not charity, I am nothing.

The gift of prophecy, to speak by inspiration, sometimes foretelling the future, was found in such first-century Christians as Agabus (Acts 11:27, 28; 21:10, 11). It was also claimed by other persons who were not at all pleasing to Christ (Matthew 7:15-23).

To know and understand secrets of God not yet revealed to others was a spiritual gift mentioned in 1 Corinthians 12:8. But to have such gifts even to the fullest extent (notice how the *alls* are piled up), in the absence of motivating love, would leave the possessor without value.

Mountain-removing *faith* is obviously not the same as saving faith or justifying faith in Christ. It is instead a power to work miracles. "Remover of mountains" was, we are told, an expression by which rabbis referred to a notably great teacher. Paul was evidently familiar with Jesus' similar expression (Matthew 17:20), but no such alteration of landscape is recorded among biblical miracles. In any case, the utmost of miraculous powers, exercised without love, would be *nothing*.

LOVE'S EXCELLENCE

The apostle Paul insists one may have *all* knowledge, but be nothing without love. A recent publication (1992) of *The Anchor Bible Dictionary* consists of six volumes written by nearly a thousand authors. It contains almost seven million words. All this Bible-related material might be understood, yet without love it would be meaningless.

Someone has said that love is like a digit placed before a series of zeros. It is possible to have nine zeros in a row, but this would add up to nothing. It is when the numeral 1 is placed before the first zero that it becomes a billion. Love is the one thing that, when placed first in our lives, transforms all our endeavors and makes significant what otherwise would be a string of nothingness.   —J. G. V. B.

C. Unprofitable Almsgiving (v. 3)

3. And though I bestow all my goods to feed the poor, and though I give my body to be burned, and have not charity, it profiteth me nothing.

Generosity in giving is elsewhere recommended to the Corinthians as a grace-gift to be cultivated along with their other accomplishments (2 Corinthians 8:6, 7).

Loveless speech is not hard to imagine. Loveless mastery of spiritual powers is a bit more difficult. But what about loveless giving—especially giving all a person has, or is? Yet if one were to indulge in the utmost generosity for the sake of displaying his piety or gaining merit for himself, his purpose would be defeated automatically. No matter how the recipient might benefit, the giver would gain nothing!

Scripture provides no clear example of one giving his body to be burned. We may think of young Isaac going to the altar (Genesis 22:7-9), and of Daniel's three companions yielding to the fiery furnace (Daniel 3:16-23), but we cannot improve on the idea that the ultimate giving is still of no benefit to the loveless giver. Experience shows that some apparently generous and helpful actions may result from pride, ambition, or vainglory. Without love, the user of impressive speech will produce nothing, the man of impressive performance will be nothing, and the giver of impressive donations will gain nothing. So says the Spirit!

II. Love Serves Others (1 Corinthians 13:4-7)

What is this love on which the apostle insists? A definition in descriptive and abstract terms may still not be helpful to the practical common mind. So Paul speaks again in personal terms, saying what love does and what love avoids. He seems to invite the reader to supply a name—Jesus, Paul, Mother, or my teacher—as the embodiment of love. Could you use your own name? The testing ground is at home and in the work place, and the testing time is every day.

A. Love Opposes Selfishness (vv. 4-6)

4. Charity suffereth long, and is kind; charity envieth not; charity vaunteth not itself, is not puffed up.

Immediately evident is the total contrast and conflict between Christian love and the self-indulgent, self-promoting pride of the pagan world, ancient or modern. What love does is what God has done, for God is love (1 John 4:8), and "the Lord is merciful and gracious, slow to anger, and plenteous in mercy" (Psalm 103:8).

To match the passive endurance of long-suffering with continuing active kindness is one of the notable achievements of our loving God and His loving children.

Add the mind-set of love, free from envy, even of another's fame as a tongues-speaker. That enables a person genuinely to rejoice with others in their good fortune as well as to grieve with them in their woe (Romans 12:15).

Consider the communication of love, totally free from boasting and inflated pride, the foolish puffery of "tooting one's own horn." Paul has already warned the Corinthians that knowledge puffs up, but love builds up (1 Corinthians 8:1).

LOVE'S KINDNESS

One of the characteristics of love is that it is kind. John Boyle O'Reilly wrote about kindness many years ago:

> "'What is the real good?'
> I asked in musing mood.
>
> Order, said the law court;
>   Knowledge, said the school;
> Truth, said the wise man;
>   Pleasure, said the fool;
> Love, said a maiden;
>   Beauty, said the page;
> Freedom, said the dreamer;
>   Home, said the sage;
> Fame, said the soldier;
>   Equity, the seer;—
>
> Spake my heart full sadly,
>   'The answer is not here.'
>
> Then, within my bosom
>   Softly this I heard:
> 'Each heart holds the secret;
>   Kindness is the word.' "
>
> —J. G. V. B.

5. Doth not behave itself unseemly, seeketh not her own, is not easily provoked, thinketh no evil.

Love does not indulge in boorish disregard for other people's feelings or preferences. It is courteous (1 Peter 3:8), and so can feed the spirit as well as the body of the recipient.

Love does not pursue selfish advantage, but considers the welfare of others as important as its own (Philippians 2:4). It will never make merchandise out of mountain-moving faith.

It does not respond in anger to neglect, wrong, insult, or abuse.

Love does not have a long memory to keep account of evils that are suffered, and does not dwell on the wickedness of the world around it. It thinks on what is good and godly (Philippians 4:8).

6. Rejoiceth not in iniquity, but rejoiceth in the truth.

Iniquity and *truth* are directly contrasted here, in deeds as well as in words. The apostle John rejoiced when he found his beloved "children" walking in truth (3 John 3, 4). In every respect love finds its pleasure in contemplating what is right and good, rather than what is wrong and wicked.

Reflected here is the biblical warning against enjoying in others the kind of behavior one would not indulge in himself (Romans 1:32). The dominant fare in popular entertainment invites one to enjoy iniquity! And the unloving spirit is sorely tempted to delight in the moral decline and fall of folk who excel us in wealth or prominence. Love chooses its sources of pleasure.

B. Love "Hangs in There" (v. 7)

7. Beareth all things, believeth all things, hopeth all things, endureth all things.

Love keeps on keeping on, never setting a limit beyond which it refuses to go, either in bearing its own burdens or helping another to bear his or hers (Galatians 6:2-5). In bearing, believing, enduring *all things*, love cannot set limits on the times, places, and persons of its involvement. It is available to all.

Love accepts the risk of giving another the benefit of the doubt. Love is not skeptical, cynical, fault-finding. It looks forward expectantly to the fulfillment of all God's promises. It protects both the lover and the loved ones from the erosion of spirit that plagues the doubter. Love is a survivor because it helps others to survive.

III. Love Is Forever
(1 Corinthians 13:8-12)

Love is an ingredient necessary to every spiritual gift before it can serve God's purposes, and love works. Moreover, it will keep on working after all the spectacular gifts have served their purposes and have vanished.

A. "Gifts" Will Vanish (vv. 8, 9)

8. Charity never faileth: but whether there be prophecies, they shall fail; whether there be tongues, they shall cease; whether there be knowledge, it shall vanish away.

Never faileth. Literally, it never falls away, like the petals of a withered flower. Love is constantly renewed and always fresh.

And now abideth
Faith,
Hope,
Charity,
these three,
but the greatest
of these is
CHARITY.
I CORINTHIANS 13:13

visual 13

True prophecies will be dependably fulfilled, but the special gifts of *prophecy* will be abolished, or rendered inactive, when they have served their purpose. Similarly, tongues-speaking by a special gift will fall silent, or *cease*, when it is no longer needed. And the gift of *knowledge,* or wisdom by special revelation, will be abolished (the same original word as the one applied to prophecy). All these are transitory, having been conveyed by the laying on of the apostles' hands, and designed for the infancy of the church.

LOVE'S ENDURANCE

Paul tells us that tongues shall cease. This we may believe is true of the tongues that were a gift of the Spirit in apostolic times. But even languages known and spoken by entire populations may become extinct. The language of the ancient inhabitants of Crete has so far vanished that the written material on buildings and monuments is only partially understood. The writings of the Mayan cultures of Central America are only now being partially and painfully restored. It is not so with love.

Human love has lightened peoples' lives in every age. Christian love has endured wherever it has been expressed. It passes from life to life—blessing, helping, lifting, brightening all who give and all who receive it.   —J. G. V. B.

9. For we know in part, and we prophesy in part.

Unlike the fruit of the Spirit—notably love, which is the possession of every member in the body of Christ—the spectacular gifts were bestowed on individual members here and there. Moreover, no one person was given the whole revelation of God's truth. To each was given a facet of knowledge, a piece of revelation, a part of understanding.

B. What Is Complete Will Last
(vv. 10-12)

10. But when that which is perfect is come, then that which is in part shall be done away.

That which is perfect—what is complete, whole, mature in Christianity will leave no need for what is found in bits and pieces. If by *that which is perfect* we mean the visible presence of Christ, we are talking of His appearance for the final judgment. If we mean fullness of the revealed Word, we are talking of the completed New Testament Scriptures, at the end of the first Christian century. If we are talking of maturity in the church, it may relate to the inclusion of Jew and Gentile—all kinds of persons—in the body of Christ (Galatians 3:26-29). If we are speaking of mature Christian character, we must refer to Ephesians 4:11-16 and the "perfect man . . . the measure of the stature of the fulness of Christ." The coming of the perfect, the mature, the complete, leaves no need for the gifts of prophecy, tongues, and knowledge. They are abolished—again we see the word that is used of prophecy and knowledge in verse 8.

11. When I was a child, I spake as a child, I understood as a child, I thought as a child: but when I became a man, I put away childish things.

It is natural and right for a child to be childlike in all things, including speech, understanding, and patterns of thinking. So there was a time in the church for spectacular patterns of speech, and for exciting displays of knowledge, and for being tremendously impressed with signs and wonders. But the mature church becomes increasingly focused on the person of Christ and the prospect of His coming in glorious judgment. So also does the mature Christian.

12. For now we see through a glass, darkly, but then face to face: now I know in part; but then shall I know even as also I am known.

Now we are invited to turn from the earthbound present to Heaven's boundless future. Our present acquaintance with Heaven is mediated through human language. It is imperfect, as even the best image mediated through a mirror is only an imperfect reflection of the reality. What we learn of God's infinite glory must be perceived, moreover, through the limits of the finite mind! It is like trying to solve a riddle. No wonder we look for something better, when we shall see our Lord as He is (1 John 3:2), and we shall know the things of eternity as fully as the eternal God knows us now. Love is our lasting link with that blessed forever.

Home Daily Bible Readings

Monday, May 22—Jesus' Commandment: Love One Another (John 15:9-17)

Tuesday, May 23—The Way of Love (1 Corinthians 13:1-7)

Wednesday, May 24—Love Is Above All Spiritual Gifts (1 Corinthians 13:8-13)

Thursday, May 25—Empowered by Christ's Love (Ephesians 3:14-20)

Friday, May 26—Love Your Enemies (Matthew 5:43-48)

Saturday, May 27—Love Your Neighbor (Luke 10:29-37)

Sunday, May 28—Love Shows No Partiality (James 2:1-8)

IV. Love Is Supreme (1 Corinthians 13:13)

13. And now abideth faith, hope, charity, these three; but the greatest of these is charity.

Christian love is built on *faith* in God's love as revealed in the gospel. That faith is quieter and more lasting than the faith that empowered miracles. Love's activity looks with confident *hope* to the fulfillment of God's promises. You can't have one of the trio without the others.

Some distinction must be made, however, among the elements in the cluster; and love is the one supremely valuable. Love, rather than faith or hope, is the quality of God. Love gives; faith and hope receive. Love keeps faith and hope from becoming selfish; it motivates and purifies their finest expressions. Love, moreover, will blossom increasingly in Heaven, whereas faith will merge into realization, and hope will ripen into fulfillment.

Conclusion
A. Follow Through With Love

The chapter before us is remarkable in many ways including this: it does not contain any plain exhortation! It is filled with practical implications, but nowhere does it say clearly, "Do this" or "Don't do that"! The opening verse of chapter 14, however, supplies the need: "Follow the way of love and eagerly desire spiritual gifts" (*New International Version*). Love is wholly constructive. It does not set aside anything of value. But when love becomes the most important feature on the agenda, it adds value to every good thing. And it gets better as it goes. "Ye . . . are taught of God to love one another. And indeed ye do it toward all the brethren . . . but we beseech you, brethren, that ye increase more and more" (1 Thessalonians 4:9, 10). And the outreach of love does not stop at the church door: "As we have therefore opportunity, let us do good unto all men, especially unto them who are of the household of faith" (Galatians 6:10). We shall never lack opportunity to wear the love badge of Christian discipleship!

B. Lord, Teach Me to Love

Open my eyes, God, to see; and open my heart to understand the instructions of love that are to be found in Your being and in Your Book. Thank You for every demonstration of divine love. Help me to be like my loving Lord. Amen.

C. Thought to Remember

"Let us not love in word, neither in tongue; but in deed and in truth"—1 John 3:18.

Learning by Doing

This page contains an alternate lesson plan emphasizing learning activities. Classes desiring such student involvement will find these suggestions helpful.

Learning Goals

After this lesson students will be able to:

1. Define and differentiate among several different kinds of love, and especially understand the love described in this text.

2. Evaluate their depth of *agape* based upon the characteristics found in 1 Corinthians 13.

3. List things that they sometimes substitute for the giving of love.

Into the Lesson

Collect magazines and bring them to class. Distribute them so that each person has two or three from which to choose. Ask students to search through the magazines and tear out things that are often used as love substitutes in personal relationships. Have each person find two or three things. (For example, a picture of a diamond ring, an expensive car, and a pet.)

Allow a few people to share their findings and explanations for choosing those particular things. Explain that God intended us to love people and use things, but that some people have reversed that. Lead into the Scripture by saying that the church at Corinth had become enamored, not of material things, but of abilities given to them. In doing so they had ignored the most excellent way, love.

Into the Word

Point out that there is great danger in studying this familiar passage. It is so familiar that much of its meaning is sometimes overlooked. Begin by having the entire chapter read aloud antiphonally by the class and you. You as teacher read verses 1, 3, 5, 7, 9, 11, and have the class read the alternating verses. Conclude by having everyone read verse 13. At the end, direct the students to close their Bibles and answer the following questions without looking at the text. (The questions are in the student book.)

1. What are seven characteristics of love according to this chapter? (Patient, kind, beareth all things, believeth all things, hopeth all things, endureth all things, never fails.)

2. What are some things love does not do? (Envy, boast, be proud, be rude, be self-seeking, be easily angered, keep a record of wrongs, rejoice in evil.)

3. Recall all the heroic and admirable things Paul listed as being desirable behavior but of no value unless accompanied by love. (Speaking in tongues, gifts of prophecy and knowledge, faith, give away everything, give body to be burned.)

Read the answers aloud and have people check their written responses. Ask if anyone got every answer correct by memory. Point out that we forget very easily and need to refresh ourselves periodically and also delve ever deeper into the meaning of the passage. To this end, discuss these questions:

1. Why will some spiritual gifts cease to be given? (They pass from the scene when they are no longer needed. For example, speaking in tongues was needed as a sign of authenticity in the early church; but when the authentic message was recorded in the New Testament, such signs were no longer needed.)

2. Why will love always continue? (It is the greatest commandment of all, Matthew 22:34-40; it is one of God's outstanding attributes, 1 John 4:8, 16. We need to be like Him always.)

3. Why does love need to be patient and long-suffering in our work place? (When frustrations and failures come at work, the Christian's response should be different from the pagan's.)

Into Life

Pass out the evaluation form below and ask each person to fill it out. Lead a time of preparatory prayer, using words similar to these: Father, we want to grow in the kind of love we have been studying. Help us not to be blind to our shortcomings, but to see them so as to ask Your grace in overcoming them. (The form is in the student book.)

HOW'S YOUR LOVE QUOTIENT?

Circle your present level of excellence in giving love through these particular characteristics. (Ten is the highest.)

PATIENT	1 2 3 4 5 6 7 8 9 10
KIND	1 2 3 4 5 6 7 8 9 10
REJOICE WITH TRUTH	1 2 3 4 5 6 7 8 9 10
TRUST	1 2 3 4 5 6 7 8 9 10
HOPE	1 2 3 4 5 6 7 8 9 10
PERSEVERE	1 2 3 4 5 6 7 8 9 10

Direct everyone to choose the characteristic in which he rated lowest, and ask God to help him grow in that area.

Let's Talk It Over

The questions on this page are designed to encourage review of the lesson Scriptures and to promote discussion of the lesson by the class. The answers provided are only discussion starters. Let your class talk it over from there.

1. Aside from the matter of tongues-speaking, the way people often use the word *love* in our society qualifies "as sounding brass, or a tinkling cymbal." How is this so?

"Love" is used to express attachment to a certain kind of food, or a specific form of recreation or a particular possession. It is employed to describe an emotional attraction or physical act between two persons, without any mutual commitment. Even in the church we say we love one another, but the shallowness of what we feel is often demonstrated by selfish squabbling. There is no handy replacement for the word *love*, so we must work at restoring its rich biblical meaning. It is often suggested that one can test the validity of his love by substituting his name for the word *charity* or *love* in 1 Corinthians 13:4-7.

2. Love "is not rude" (1 Corinthians 13:5, *New International Version*). Why does this attribute of love need to be stressed today?

We could almost say that rudeness has become an art form. On many television shows a common "humorous" device is the rude remarks family members make to one another. People who regularly watch such shows may copy such rudeness in their own conversation. There is a place for humorous teasing of one another in the home and in the church, but this rudeness goes beyond mere teasing with its disrespectful and discourteous character. Our love should be such as to lead us to speak respectfully *to* one another and *of* one another.

3. Real love will not allow us to hold onto bitter memories of slights we have suffered and injuries that have been inflicted on us. How does love work to remove such memories?

Love looks beyond the injury to the reasons why it was inflicted. It is often true that people who hurt us are themselves hurting. Out of the pain they are carrying in their own hearts they deal out angry, cutting words or injurious actions. What they do is wrong, but just as God has dealt with us lovingly in spite of our sins (Romans 5:6-8), even so we must do. When we see the cause of the sin, we can respond with compassion and love. Another way love works to eliminate bitter memories is by focusing on what

is good. If we concentrate on a person's admirable attributes and help him or her to develop them more fully, those troublesome negative associations will tend to fade in importance.

4. The lesson writer states that "love accepts the risk of giving another the benefit of the doubt." Can you think of some examples of how love works in this way?

Gossip may be unavoidable, but what we do about the gossip we hear is something we can control. We give another person the benefit of the doubt when we refuse to accept the accuracy of mere rumor about him and refuse to spread the unconfirmed "NEWS" to others. Consider also the matter of a sharp disagreement with another person. We may believe so strongly in our side of the disagreement that we blind ourselves to the other individual's viewpoint. But we give him the benefit of the doubt when we acknowledge his sincerity and carefully consider his position in the matter. In a more general way we give others the benefit of the doubt regarding some displeasing word they have spoken or action they have taken by keeping in mind the circumstances that may have caused them to speak or act in that way.

5. "Love . . . will blossom increasingly in Heaven, whereas faith will merge into realization, and hope will ripen into fulfillment." In this way the lesson writer aptly describes the enduring superiority of love. What may be involved in love's blossoming increasingly in Heaven?

Heaven will surely be a place in which we can express our love without the limitations imposed on us here. We are busy in this life with the responsibilities of earning a living, rearing a family, and discharging our obligations as citizens. Such duties make so many demands on our time and energy that they often keep us from speaking of our love and actively demonstrating our love to others. It seems safe to say that the priorities in Heaven will be different. As we are free to proclaim our love for God, Christ, and our fellow saints, and as we are unhindered in doing deeds of love for these, we will certainly experience the fullness and richness of a love such as we can now only dimly perceive.

Summer Quarter, 1995

Theme: A Nation Turns From God

Special Features

Lessons

Unit 1. The Price of Power

Unit 2. The Approaching Judgment

Unit 3. The Judgment Arrives

About these lessons

The lessons of the Summer Quarter span two centuries of the history of Israel, from the death of Solomon to the fall of the northern kingdom in 722/721 B.C. The violation of Israel's covenant with God, injustice, and the oppression of the poor and weak by the rich and powerful characterized these times. This period witnessed the ministries of many of God's prophets, among whom were Elijah, Elisha, Amos, Hosea, Micah, and Isaiah. Some of the actions and pronouncements of these prophets are presented in this study.

Jun 4

Jun 11

Jun 18

Jun 25

Jul 2

Jul 9

Jul 16

Jul 23

Jul 30

Aug 6

Aug 13

Aug 20

Aug 27

Quarterly Quiz

The questions on this page may be used in several ways: as a pretest at the beginning of the quarter; as a review at the end of the quarter; or as a review after each lesson. The questions are based on the Scripture text of each lesson (King James Version). ***The answers are on page 344.***

Lesson 1

1. Solomon's son ____ succeeded him as king of Israel. *1 Kings 12:6*
2. The new king favored the counsel of his ____ advisers over that of the ____ men who had advised Solomon. *1 Kings 12:8*
3. What was the result of the king's decision to treat the people harshly? *1 Kings 12:16.*

Lesson 2

1. Which of God's prophets contested with the prophets of Baal on Mount Carmel? *1 Kings 18:30*
2. How many barrels (large jars) of water did God's prophet have poured on the altar he built? *1 Kings 18:33, 34*

Lesson 3

1. Who owned a vineyard, which King Ahab desired to have? *1 Kings 21:1, 2*
2. Who charged Ahab with the murder of the vineyard's owner? *1 Kings 21:17-19*
3. Predicting Ahab's death, the prophet said dogs would do what? *1 Kings 21:19*

Lesson 4

1. During a siege of Samaria, the famine was so severe that four ____, hoping to save their lives, decided to surrender to the Syrians. *2 Kings 7:3, 4*
2. What did the four discover when they came to the Syrian camp? *2 Kings 7:5*

Lesson 5

1. Amos said God would send a ____ upon Judah to devour Jerusalem's palaces. *Amos 2:5*
2. Amos said that Israel would be punished because they sold the righteous for ____, and they sold the poor for what? *Amos 2:6*

Lesson 6

1. Speaking through Amos, God told Israel that He hated and despised their ____ ____. *Amos 5:21*
2. God wanted Israel to let ____ run down as waters, and ____ as a mighty stream. *Amos 5:24*

Lesson 7

1. Who was Hosea's wife? *Hosea 1:3*
2. Name the sons and daughters Hosea's wife bore unto him. *Hosea 1:3, 4, 6, 8, 9*

3. Hosea's kindness toward an adulterous woman was a picture of God's forgiving love toward unfaithful ____. *Hosea 3:1*

Lesson 8

1. When Israel was a ____, God loved him and called His son out of Egypt. *Hosea 11:1*
2. Israel refused to return to God. Therefore, the ____ would be his king. *Hosea 11:5*
3. Sorrowing over Israel's coming punishment, God said His ____ was turned within Him and His ____ were kindled together. *Hosea 11:8*

Lesson 9

1. Micah charged that the leaders of Israel abhorred (mercy, widows and orphans, judgment) and perverted all equity. *Micah 3:9*
2. Because of the leaders' evil, Zion would be ____ as a field. *Micah 3:12*

Lesson 10

1. Isaiah was in the temple when he had a vision of God. What year was it? *Isaiah 6:1*
2. In the vision, one of the seraphim touched Isaiah's lips with what? *Isaiah 6:6, 7*
3. Through Isaiah God said His people's hands were full of what? *Isaiah 1:15*

Lesson 11

1. During Isaiah's ministry King (Jothan, Ahaz, Hezekiah) feared an attack by the combined powers of Syria and Israel. *Isaiah 7:3, 4*
2. When Isaiah met with the king to tell him not to fear an attack, who did the prophet take with him? *Isaiah 7:3*

Lesson 12

1. Woe is pronounced on those who rise early in the morning to follow what? *Isaiah 5:11*
2. Isaiah pronounced woe on those who call evil ____, and ____ evil. *Isaiah 5:20*
3. Isaiah pronounced woe on those who are ____ in their own eyes. *Isaiah 5:21*

Lesson 13

1. The king of what nation captured Samaria and dispersed the defeated Israelites to various parts of his empire? *2 Kings 17:6*
2. In one sentence explain why the nation of Israel was overthrown. *2 Kings 17:7-14*

"History Is Bunk!"

by John W. Wade

"HISTORY IS BUNK!" Henry Ford once exclaimed. Ironically, even as he made that statement he was making history by introducing the assembly line technique that revolutionized automobile production.

Many people share Mr. Ford's evaluation of history. Perhaps one reason so many feel this way is that history is often taught as an endless series of persons, places, events, and dates that really don't have much meaning. History does have meaning, however. A sizable part of the Old Testament is given over to history—it deals with persons, places, events, and dates. The divinely inspired writers, while they recorded historical facts, saw beyond these data to give us a glimpse of what they meant. Beyond the ongoing collision of events that comprise human experience, these writers saw the hand of God interwoven and involved in them. In Israel's prosperity they saw God extending blessings; in the disaster that befell the nation, they saw Him exacting justice from an erring people.

If God had abandoned His world, if He had ceased to intervene in human events, we might be justified in concluding that history is nothing more than an academic exercise of interest to only a few scholars. At the very heart of our Christian faith, however, is the belief that God has not abandoned the world, that instead He cares about us and is involved in our activities. Therefore, we of all people ought to be interested in history.

The Old Testament gives us ample opportunity to see God at work. We can see how He blessed those who were righteous. We can also begin to understand the intricate pattern of events that He used to bring judgment upon His people when they fell into sin and rejected Him. We study this history in order to know how to use the blessings He gives us. We also study history in order to avoid the types of mistakes that brought the Hebrew people to repeated disasters. If we fail to study history, we are, as George Santayana once remarked, doomed to repeat it. The tragic fact is that ancient Israel failed to learn important lessons from her history, and that failure led to her dismal end.

The lessons studied this quarter, beginning with the division of the kingdom in 931 B.C. and concluding with the fall of the northern kingdom in 722/721 B.C., chronologically follow the lessons of the September-November 1994 quarter. That quarter's lessons began with the conquest of the promised land and ended with Israel at the peak of its glory during the reigns of David and Solomon.

The Price of Power
Unit 1—June

The title for this quarter's lessons is "A Nation Turns From God." Unit 1, entitled "The Price of Power," gives us a very good opportunity to see the dangers of power when it is used unwisely or maliciously.

Lesson 1 introduces us to Rehoboam, who was thrust into a position of power at the death of his father, Solomon. It was a critical time in the life of the nation, and a change in leadership, as it often does, brought things to a head. Solomon's building extravagances had created problems for the people, who were demanding a change. The problems were compounded by the fact that young Rehoboam had not been adequately prepared for the heavy burdens he had to assume. When he took bad advice from his young advisors, the kingdom was divided, a division that was never mended.

Lesson 2 deals with Elijah's dramatic confrontation with the false prophets of Baal on Mount Carmel. When Jeroboam, the first king of the northern kingdom, erected golden calves as elements of worship at Dan and Bethel, he opened the door to out-and-out apostasy. That apostasy was not long in coming. Solomon had already set a bad example of marrying foreign wives and allowing them to bring their pagan religions with them. In marrying Jezebel, daughter of the king of Sidon, Ahab was following a precedent already established. Jezebel was a follower of Baal with missionary zeal. She quickly began a campaign to convert Ahab and Israel to her faith. She had remarkable success until God sent Elijah to confront her and her false prophets.

Lesson 3 shows how a false religion leads to moral corruption. Ahab was thwarted in his effort to secure the vineyard of Naboth; but Jezebel, who knew no moral restraints, did not hesitate to use perjury and murder to gain the vineyard. Once more it was Elijah who announced God's judgment. The lesson reminds us that God, who is no respecter of persons, will not let sin in high places go unpunished.

Lesson 4, the final lesson of this unit, sounds a happier note. In the days of Elisha, successor of Elijah, the city of Samaria was besieged by the Syrians and reduced to the level of dire want. The king, seeking a scapegoat for his problems, tried to blame Elisha. The prophet, however, informed him that the siege would soon be lifted. The king didn't believe this report, and so it was left to four lepers, who ventured into the Syrian camp, to bring back the good news that the enemy had fled. This lesson may suggest to us that God uses all kinds of people to deliver His good news.

The Approaching Judgment
Unit 2—July

The second unit of the quarter calls our attention to the fact that ominous clouds were beginning to darken Israel's future. The events discussed in this unit all take place in the eighth century B.C.

Lesson 5 relates Amos's pronouncement of God's judgment on both Judah and Israel for their rejection of Him and His laws. Amos reminded the people of the blessings God had showered on them in the past, but he assured them that God would shower judgment upon them if they did not change their ways.

Lesson 6 also centers on Amos. The recipients of the prophet's message recorded in chapters 4 and 5 were the people of the northern kingdom. They were regularly involved in worship, but their efforts were nothing more than vain gestures that covered their corrupt hearts. Their worship was unacceptable to God because it did not translate into lives of justice and mercy. The application to our own times is obvious.

Lesson 7 introduces us to Hosea, who also delivered God's warnings and entreaties of repentance to the people of the northern kingdom. In the view of many Bible students, Hosea used the tragedy of his own marriage as an object lesson to illustrate how Israel had rejected God. Out of the depths of his own sorrow, he cried out for the people to repent and turn back to God. This lesson can be used to remind us that even personal tragedy can be used of God as a means of conveying His love for His wayward people.

Lesson 8 focuses on Hosea's picture of God as a loving parent, tenderly rearing His child, Israel. But Israel rebelled, turning away from God in pursuit of selfish interests. Yet God didn't give up, but continued to reach out to His erring child. While this lesson is directed to the people as a nation, it can touch the heart of parents who have been disappointed by their children.

Lesson 9, the final lesson of Unit 2, introduces us to Micah, whose messages were addressed to both Israel and Judah. This lesson carries Micah's denunciation of the dishonest priests and false prophets who were lining their own pockets, even as they misled the people. He also took aim at the political leaders who perverted justice and resorted to violence for their own gain. Many of the problems that he addressed seem so contemporary that we can almost believe we are studying the morning's newspaper as we discuss them.

The Judgment Arrives
Unit 3—August

The final unit of the quarter, "The Judgment Arrives," emphasizes the inevitable result of Israel's rebellious course of action. Three of these lessons are based on passages from Isaiah, the greatest of the eighth-century prophets.

Lesson 10 highlights Isaiah's dramatic call to his ministry to Judah. In a vision that brought him into the presence of a holy God, he was overwhelmed, and confessed his own unworthiness. After receiving forgiveness of sins, he was sent on a mission to his people. Like Amos, Hosea, and Micah, Isaiah pleaded with His people to stop their evil doing and return to God, but the people would not hear.

Lesson 11 deals with Judah's confrontation by enemies to the north. In this crisis Isaiah was sent to stubborn King Ahaz with a message of hope. A sign was given to the king, carrying the assurance that this hope would be realized. This sign had far-reaching implications, for it also tells us of the virgin-born Son, who would bring hope to the whole world.

Lesson 12 is full of woes, for it emphasizes Isaiah's pronouncement of woe on the people of Judah for their sins. He singled out the rich who enhanced their wealth at the expense of the poor, those who became inflamed with wine, those who perverted justice, and those who set their own standards of morality.

Lesson 13, the final lesson of the quarter, paints the tragic picture of the end of a nation that shunned the messengers God had sent. The irony of the destruction of the northern kingdom is that it came at the hands of Assyria, a nation even more wicked than Israel. Among other things, this lesson illustrates that God requires much from those to whom He has given much.

Conclusion

To help your students gain a better understanding of these lessons, prepare a large, historical time line of this period and display it in your classroom. Such a time line may be found in most Bible dictionaries. This series of lessons should convince your students that history is indeed bunk, but only to those who refuse to study it.

Warning Unheeded

by Keith P. Keeran

WE HAVE BEEN THE RECIPIENTS of the choicest bounties of heaven. We have been preserved, these many years, in peace and prosperity. We have grown in numbers, wealth and power, as no other nation has ever grown. But we have forgotten God. We have forgotten the gracious hand which preserved us in peace, and multiplied and enriched and strengthened us; and we have vainly imagined, in the deceitfulness of our hearts, that all these blessings were produced by some superior wisdom and virtue of our own. Intoxicated with unbroken success, we have become too self-sufficient to feel the necessity of redeeming and preserving grace, too proud to pray to the God that made us! It behooves us, then, to humble ourselves before the offended Power, to confess our national sins, and to pray for clemency and forgiveness."

With these words, on April 30, 1863, President Abraham Lincoln proclaimed a National Day of Fasting, Humiliation, and Prayer.

While President Lincoln was not a prophet, the words of the prophets of ancient Israel must have been ringing in his ears as he thought about his own nation. Our generation needs to listen to the prophets as never before. These messengers of God were sent specifically to Israel and Judah, but the truths they preached are timeless.

The tragic story of Israel's apostasy and eventual destruction is carefully chronicled in the pages of the Old Testament. Following the death of Solomon, the nation's downward slide accelerated. The oppressive demands of Solomon's son and successor, Rehoboam, and his advisers tore the fabric of the Davidic dynasty. Where there had been one nation, now there were two: Israel in the north, Judah in the south.

Israel and Judah would each be led by kings (about twenty each) whose walk with God would determine their direction and their destiny. When the kings drifted from God, the people also strayed. But, because it is God's nature to be gracious and long-suffering, He sent prophets to turn them from their evil ways. Occasionally they listened, but mostly they ignored and persecuted the messengers of God and refused to heed their warnings. The justice of God demanded that He not withhold His judgment.

In his first epistle to the Corinthians, Paul drew attention to that glorious time when the nation of Israel was miraculously led out of Egyptian bondage. Then he reminded his readers of Israel's subsequent overthrow in the wilderness. Paul gives two reasons why God detailed the story of Israel's failure: (1) Their actions are examples to keep us from lusting after evil things as they did, and (2) Israel's example is to serve as a warning for us (1 Corinthians 10:6, 11).

Someone has said, "The only thing one learns from history is that no one ever learned anything from history." If this statement is accurate, the fault lies not in the absence of lessons to be learned, but in the failure of students to take God seriously.

If God's judgment on our nation is to be averted, we must give heed to those unchanging truths that His messengers proclaimed to His chosen people. The Sovereign Ruler of the universe is ready to extend His mercy to the nation that submits to Him and walks in the ways of righteousness.

Three thousand years ago the Lord appeared to Solomon and said, "If my people, which are called by my name, shall humble themselves, and pray, and seek my face, and turn from their wicked ways; then will I hear from heaven, and will forgive their sin, and heal their land" (2 Chronicles 7:14). Even before Israel and Judah became separate nations and apostasy began to sweep the land, God had provided a means for them to be restored to Him. If they would have only listened, judgment could have been averted. Will we learn anything from their mistakes?

Perhaps there has never been a time when our nation needed to seek God and cry out for mercy more than it does now. Now is the time for us to cooperate with God and rebuild the foundations of our society that have been destroyed. If we are wise we will hear and heed the warnings that the ancient prophets delivered to Israel and Judah.

What lessons can we learn from them? They are many, but we will consider only two.

The Need for a Bold Prophetic Voice

Many believe that preachers should stay out of the affairs of state. They say that elected officials should run the government, and ministers should attend to church affairs. It is said that "religion and politics don't mix." If this is so, then we should tear out of the Bible most of the preaching of the Old Testament prophets!

Prophets sometimes were criticized as "political preachers" and were asked to desist.

Amaziah, the priest of Bethel, charged the prophet Amos with raising a conspiracy against Jeroboam, king of Israel. Amaziah said, "Get out, you seer! Go back to the land of Judah. . . . do your prophesying there. Don't prophesy anymore at Bethel, because this is the king's sanctuary" (Amos 7:12, 13, *New International Version*). But Amos would not be silenced!

The prophet Elijah was not timid about opposing King Ahab and Queen Jezebel concerning the introduction of idolatry into the northern kingdom. Our country needs such prophets today!

The church must promote and support the kind of ministry that will penetrate the conscience of our nation's leaders. When there is no prophet in the land in the time of crisis, the days are dark for that nation.

Those who would be the conscience of a nation will have little concern about their own personal safety or well-being. They are willing to sacrifice everything for the greater good. Consider Jesus Christ, the greatest prophet of all. (See Philippians 2:7, 8.)

Men of deep spiritual conviction like Amos and Elijah are required in times such as we are presently experiencing. Where is the man (or group of men) who will stand in the stead of the prophets of old and call our nation back to God? Where is the church that will become the social conscience of the community and speak with bold prophetic voice?

The prophets were patriotic, but they were not narrow nationalists. All of the prophets of Israel believed that their nation was chosen of God to be the spiritual light to other nations, the harbinger of godliness and peace for the world. Is this not true of any nation that God allows to rise to world leadership? "Blessed is the nation whose God is the Lord" (Psalm 33:12). Condemned is the nation who forgets its Maker!

No Substitute for Personal Holiness

All through the time of the prophets the people of Israel remained very religious. At first glance one might be impressed, but their religion was empty of spiritual substance. They had substituted the forms of worship for the substance of pure religion. While outwardly appearing religious, they were in fact spiritually corrupt. Prophet after prophet denounced God's people for their unfaithfulness to Him and their callous mistreatment of the weak and helpless in their society.

The people of Amos's day kept the holy days, but they couldn't wait for them to end so they could resume their dishonest business practices (see Amos 8:4-6). The greed of these people aroused the indignation of the prophets. God's spokesmen denounced those avaricious leaders who took advantage of the poor of the land to such an extent that they were reduced to slavery. The poor and the needy had become the object of scorn and abuse. The rich looked after only their own interests. The greed and heartlessness of Israel's rich and powerful toward the disadvantaged among them evoked God's wrath and assured the nation's destruction (vv. 7-14).

Earlier, when Ahab used his authority as king to have Naboth stoned in order to get possession of his vineyard, Elijah's righteous indignation led him to bitterly denounce the iniquity of the king and to prophesy Ahab's destruction (1 Kings 21). Such is the judgment that will fall on any person or nation characterized by greed.

A person today may go through the motions of worship and call it religion, but that person is deceived. James doesn't even speak of worship forms when he defines pure and undefiled religion. He says, "This is pure and undefiled religion in the sight of our God and Father, to visit orphans and widows in their distress, and to keep oneself unstained by the world" (James 1:27, *New American Standard Bible*). Selfless service to others, and the maintaining of personal purity and holiness is the very essence of godliness.

If the prophetic warnings go unheeded, our own personal futures and those of our families and our nation are decided already. Let us avoid the arrogance that convinces us that we are somehow immune to the consequences of sins both personal and national. They are foolish who believe that superior knowledge and advanced technology can save us from the consequences of moral and spiritual bankruptcy. Paul asked, "Where is the wise man? Where is the scribe? Where is the debater of this age? Has not God made foolish the wisdom of the world?" (1 Corinthians 1:20, *New American Standard Bible*).

On the night of April 14, 1912, the "unsinkable" *Titanic* was steaming through the foggy North Atlantic when it collided with an enormous iceberg and sank, claiming more than fifteen hundred lives.

A tragic, though often untold story about that night concerns one man on another ship, less than twenty miles away from the *Titanic*. That ship could have come to the rescue of the sinking liner, if only someone had heard its cry for help. But the radio operator had fallen asleep while on duty!

It's past time for our nation to wake up, if we would avert disaster. Like a clarion call, the words of the prophets are still echoing through the corridors of time. Will their warning go unheeded? Is anyone listening?

The Strength of a Nation

by Mark Reed

A S WE MOVE toward the twenty-first century, what will preserve our nation, keep it stable, and increase its strength? It seems that every group or party has an answer to that question, particularly something in line with its own political agenda. The Bible's answer, however, has little to do with politics. God has allowed nations and kingdoms and empires to exist under different forms of government, and He has brought about their rise and fall regardless of what party has held power.

A nation's muscle may be found in political wisdom, financial strength, or military might, but those attributes can fade away. From experience King Solomon discovered that a nation's success had far more to do with its heart than its muscle (Proverbs 14:34).

Solomon observed a principle that governs nations as well as individuals: *moral attitude can lead a nation to glory or disgrace.* That glory, as Solomon proved, can include widespread influence, success, and domination. The disgrace, his descendants discovered, can include humiliation, oppression, and destruction.

God's Case Study

Solomon built on the spiritual foundation of his father, David, and brought Israel to the pinnacle of glory as a nation. Israel expanded her borders, dominated her enemies, and became wealthier than any people on earth. David and Solomon cultivated righteousness among their people, focusing attention on the worship of Jehovah and eventually bringing that focus to the construction of the temple.

Righteousness involves right relationship. To be righteous is to act in accord with God's spiritual and moral laws; hence, it means that a person is in a right relationship with God and people. When David and Solomon cultivated right relationships, God exalted their nation.

The scene changed when Solomon allowed wrong relationships to develop. First, he married foreign women (daughters of dignitaries given to him in alliance) who worshiped false gods. Second, he tolerated his wives' idols, allowing their shrines in Israel, and eventually even building them himself (1 Kings 11:7, 8). The Israelites followed their king's example and began to accept and worship idols. After Solomon's death the nation divided and plunged into a downward spiral of idol worship and injustice that ended in bitter destruction. Both the northern kingdom (Israel) and the southern kingdom (Judah) allowed themselves to be drawn into this downward spiral.

As these people became unfaithful in their relationship with God, they increased in unrighteousness toward one another. The rich oppressed the poor. Judges took bribes and denied justice to the needy. Immorality became flagrant. Honest and righteous persons were despised. (See Amos 2:4-16; 5:10-12.)

God gave them warning signs: famine, drought, plagues, locusts, destructive war, poverty (Amos 4:6-11). He punished the nations around them while His prophets predicted the same for any nation who disobeyed, especially His chosen, Judah and Israel. Judah listened and made some effort to change, and as a result the nation continued for more than a century after Israel's destruction. Then Judah, too, fell.

Have you noticed that the prophets did not call for a particular political method or agenda? They called for righteousness. "Seek ye me, and ye shall live," God pleaded through Amos (5:4). "What doth the Lord require of thee," asked Micah, "but to do justly, and to love mercy, and to walk humbly with thy God?" (6:8). Over and over God issued this call for righteousness, offering forgiveness for past sins and promising *exalted nation status.*

The Downward Spiral

Sin became a reproach to both Judah and Israel, and it does the same for any nation. Those who choose unrighteous relationships plummet into the downward spiral. Sin diminishes a nation's influence, reputation, and effectiveness. If uninterrupted, that spiral leads deeper into immorality and disgrace, and ends in destruction.

Our generation has witnessed the collapse of the Soviet Union and other Communist nations. The reasons for their failure surely are many and varied. Chief among them, however, is the fact that belief in God had largely disappeared from the life of those societies. Those nations, which but a few years earlier appeared so formidable, fell because of the lack of a spiritual and moral infrastructure.

When the successor to King Saul was being chosen, God said to Samuel, "but the Lord looketh on the heart" (1 Samuel 16:7). That is true not only of persons, but nations as well.

The Upward Spiral

The influence of a nation's leaders cannot be underestimated regarding the spiritual and moral condition of the people. Have you ever noticed that in the Biblical records concerning Israel and Judah (included in the books of Kings and Chronicles), each king is introduced either as having walked in the sins of his father or as having done what was right in the eyes of God? As went the king, so went the nation.

God preserved Judah for a century longer than Israel because eight of her nineteen kings pursued righteousness, and that temporarily reversed the downward spiral. The northern kingdom never saw a righteous king—and her destruction came sooner.

Many people may agree with Solomon's proverb concerning righteousness and the exalting of a nation, but define *righteousness* in a way foreign to Solomon. In our time standards of righteousness have become a matter of individual interpretation. People change the rules to fit their life-styles and their choices of behavior. The only way to clear the confusion is to maintain the definition of righteousness as the Bible presents it—"right relationship to God and others." Right relationship to God means that we will follow His standards for right relationships with others. This leads to the upward spiral of blessing for both an individual and a nation.

The Need

The spiritual and moral weaknesses of one's nation may be apparent. And some may think it sufficient simply to accuse and protest and complain about the situation. It is more difficult to attempt to right the wrongs, to live according to God's standards regardless of how others live, and to commit oneself to being part of the strengthening moral fabric of a nation. As Christians, however, we are called to do just that.

Christians are to be salt that will preserve human society. Jesus built His kingdom not as a political power, but as a spiritual and moral force that would permeate every level of society, shedding the light of God to drive out spiritual darkness wherever it exists. He intends His citizens to be the moral conscience of society, to be examples of righteousness, to provide a haven for recovery from the results of unrighteousness, to administer the balm of forgiveness, and to broadcast a beacon of warning.

Christians can't expect others to do what they themselves have been called by God to do. A righteous heart for this nation or any other nation cannot be legislated. Nor can the media be expected to educate the citizenry on proper moral values. The church must issue the call for righteousness, because righteousness is of God and does not issue from human government or from worldly wisdom. When the church preaches the gospel it makes available that which preserves human society.

What can Christians do to be the salt of the earth and the light of the world? We can speak up for the cause of righteousness. We can conduct our daily lives in a godly manner so as to be examples to our fellowmen. We can take a stand on moral issues that affect our communities.

We must *climb* the staircase of the upward spiral; it is not an escalator ride. It is an effort to which we must give primary attention throughout our lives. With the apostle Paul may we say, "I press on toward the goal for the prize of the upward call of God in Christ Jesus" (Philippians 3:14, *New American Standard Bible*).

Hoping and praying that legislators will make decisions based on Christian values is not enough to preserve our nation. Every Christian must be involved in teaching, sharing, and living the righteousness that God demands.

Through Solomon God said, "Righteousness exalteth a nation: but sin is a reproach to any people" (Proverbs 14:34). That principle was illustrated in Israel and Judah, in ancient Greece and Rome, and it will stand as long as the earth lasts. Let us seek God's righteousness. Let us maintain a right relationship with Him, and deal rightly with all persons. In so doing we will contribute to the strength of our nation.

Answers to Quarterly Quiz
on page 338

Lesson 1—1. Rehoboam. 2. young, old. 3. the kingdom was divided. **Lesson 2**—1. Elijah. 2. twelve. **Lesson 3**—1. Naboth. 2. Elijah. 3. Lick Ahab's blood. **Lesson 4**—1. lepers. 2. the Syrian army had deserted the camp. **Lesson 5**—1. fire. 2. silver, a pair of shoes. **Lesson 6**—1. feast days. 2. judgment, righteousness. **Lesson 7**—1. Gomer. 2. Jezreel and Loammi (sons); Loruhamah (daughter). 3. Israel. **Lesson 8**—1. child. 2. Assyrian. 3. heart, repentings. **Lesson 9**—1. judgment. 2. plowed. **Lesson 10**—1. the year King Uzziah died. 2. a live coal. 3. blood. **Lesson 11**—1. Ahaz. 2. His son Shear-jashub. **Lesson 12**—1. strong drink. 2. good, good. 3. wise. **Lesson 13**—1. Assyria. 2. they rejected God and His laws to worship and serve idols.

When Power Is Misused

DEVOTIONAL READING: **Psalm 14.**

LESSON SCRIPTURE: **1 Kings 11:26—12:24.**

PRINTED TEXT: **1 Kings 12:6-11, 16, 17.**

1 Kings 12:6-11, 16, 17

6 And king Rehoboam consulted with the old men, that stood before Solomon his father while he yet lived, and said, How do ye advise that I may answer this people?

7 And they spake unto him, saying, If thou wilt be a servant unto this people this day, and wilt serve them, and answer them, and speak good words to them, then they will be thy servants for ever.

8 But he forsook the counsel of the old men, which they had given him, and consulted with the young men that were grown up with him, and which stood before him:

9 And he said unto them, What counsel give ye that we may answer this people, who have spoken to me, saying, Make the yoke which thy father did put upon us lighter?

10 And the young men that were grown up with him spake unto him, saying, Thus shalt thou speak unto this people that spake unto thee, saying, Thy father made our yoke heavy, but make thou it lighter unto us; thus shalt thou say unto them, My little finger shall be thicker than my father's loins.

11 And now whereas my father did lade you with a heavy yoke, I will add to your yoke: my father hath chastised you with whips, but I will chastise you with scorpions.

· · · · · · · · · · · · ·

16 So when all Israel saw that the king hearkened not unto them, the people answered the king, saying, What portion have we in David? neither have we inheritance in the son of Jesse: to your tents, O Israel: now see to thine own house, David. So Israel departed unto their tents.

17 But as for the children of Israel which dwelt in the cities of Judah, Rehoboam reigned over them.

GOLDEN TEXT: If thou wilt be a servant unto this people this day, and wilt serve them, and answer them, and speak good words to them, then they will be thy servants for ever.—1 Kings 12:7.

A Nation Turns From God
Unit 1: The Price of Power
(Lessons 1-4)

Lesson Aims

As a result of studying this lesson the students should:

1. Have a better understanding of the events that led to the division of the kingdom of Israel.

2. Be more willing to listen to people who believe they have grievances.

3. Have greater resolve to heed sound advice when they receive it.

Lesson Outline

INTRODUCTION
    A. Becoming a Man
    B. Lesson Background
I. GOOD ADVICE REJECTED (1 Kings 12:6-8a)
    A. Consultation With the Old Men (v. 6)
    B. The Old Men's Advice (v. 7)
    C. Rejection of Advice (v. 8a)
       Age Discrimination
II. BAD ADVICE ACCEPTED (1 Kings 12:8b-11)
    A. Consultation With the Young Men
       (vv. 8b, 9)
    B. The Young Men's Advice (vv. 10, 11)
III. TRAGIC RESULTS (1 Kings 12:16, 17)
    A. Rebellion of the Northern Tribes (v. 16)
    B. Reduced Kingdom in the South (v. 17)
CONCLUSION
    A. Heeding Sound Advice
    B. "Pride Goeth Before Destruction"
    C. Let Us Pray
    D. Thought to Remember

Visual 1 of the visuals packet is a chart of the kings and prophets of Israel and Judah. Visual 14 is a map of the divided kingdom. Both visuals will be useful throughout the quarter.

Introduction

A. Becoming a Man

A couple of generations ago when a young boy was given his first pair of long trousers, he felt that he had become a man, or at least was well on his way to becoming a man. Jeremy and his younger sister, Ruth, had been reared in a Christian home, and each morning before they left for school they would pray a brief prayer that God would help them and bless them that

day. But on the day that Jeremy wore his long trousers for the first time, he refused to pray with his sister. "After all," he said, "I am a man now and I don't need God's help."

After school that day Jeremy flew his kite. As he did so, the string broke and the kite fell into a tree. He climbed up into the tree to retrieve it, but as he reached out for it he slipped and fell to the limb below, where his foot became wedged in a fork. Try as he might, he couldn't free himself. Becoming frightened, he began to cry. Just then Ruth appeared and asked what was the matter. "Oh, Ruthie, I need help. Please pray for me," he said.

"I thought you said this morning that you didn't need God's help," she said.

"That was this morning," he replied. "But I need Him now." And so they prayed. Their prayer was soon answered when a neighbor saw Jeremy's plight and helped him out of the tree.

When Rehoboam became the new king of Israel, he was like Jeremy with his first pair of long trousers. He was a man now, and he didn't need God's advice or help. Unlike Jeremy, he didn't learn his folly until it was too late.

B. Lesson Background

The forty-year reign of Solomon had come to an end, and the powerful king now "slept with his fathers" (1 Kings 11:42, 43). In his stead reigned his son Rehoboam, who began his rule in 931 B.C. at the age of forty-one. We are told that his mother was Naamah, who was an Ammonite, but we know little else about his childhood or youth (1 Kings 14:21).

Rehoboam inherited a substantial kingdom that stretched from the Euphrates River in the northeast to Egypt in the southwest. This kingdom had been built by the military conquests of David and the political alliances forged by Solomon. The strategic location of Israel had allowed Solomon to control a number of trade routes, which brought considerable wealth to his kingdom. With this wealth he had carried out large building programs that included the temple, his own palace, and numerous military fortifications. Thus Rehoboam fell heir to a rich and powerful kingdom, but it was also a kingdom that had some serious problems. One was that the people had been heavily taxed to maintain Solomon's program. A more serious problem was that Solomon, as a result of his many foreign marriages, had allowed the worship of pagan gods to enter his kingdom.

The immediate background of our lesson text for today is found in verses 1-5 of 1 Kings 12. The time for Rehoboam's coronation had come, and Shechem was chosen as the place for it.

This is surprising because Solomon had firmly established Jerusalem as his capital. It may have been that Schechem, which is located about thirty miles north of Jerusalem near Mount Gerizim, was chosen to attempt to conciliate the northern tribes, who were showing increasing signs of discontent.

When the people assembled at Shechem for the coronation, they used the occasion to air their grievances. Their spokesman was Jeroboam, who had earlier opposed Solomon and had been forced to flee to Egypt to save his life. With the death of Solomon, Jeroboam felt it safe to return to Israel and had become the leader of the people. They were willing to serve the new king, but their condition was that he relieve the heavy tax burden that Solomon had laid upon them. Rehoboam asked for three days to consider a reply.

I. Good Advice Rejected (1 Kings 12:6-8a)

A. Consultation With the Old Men (v. 6)

6. And king Rehoboam consulted with the old men, that stood before Solomon his father while he yet lived, and said, How do ye advise that I may answer this people?

Rehoboam wisely turned to the older men who had counseled Solomon during his reign. Although they had not been able to prevent Solomon from making some foolish decisions, at least they had a good understanding of the conditions that had led to the present crisis.

B. The Old Men's Advice (v. 7)

7. And they spake unto him, saying, If thou wilt be a servant unto this people this day, and wilt serve them, and answer them, and speak good words to them, then they will be thy servants for ever.

The old men, who had watched Solomon develop his extravagant programs, urged Rehoboam to listen to the complaints of the people. They counseled him to be a servant to the people *this day*. The demands of the people were reasonable, and these older counselors felt that it would be wise and to Rehoboam's long-term good if, on this one occasion, he gave in to their wishes. These men realized that the people had been under a heavy burden, and to gain their support Rehoboam needed to give them some relief. Modern politicians realize that a promise of tax cuts will win more votes than a promise to increase taxes.

Ancient monarchs ruled with a heavy hand, and the thought of becoming a servant to his people undoubtedly did not appeal to Rehoboam, even if it involved putting their interests ahead of his own personal desires on this one occasion only. Rehoboam had grown up in the household of his father, Solomon, a fabulously wealthy and mighty potentate. Now Rehoboam was king, and he was only beginning to enjoy his position with all its rights and privileges. He was not inclined to relinquish his hold on any of them, and he was unable to see that to make a concession to his suffering people at the beginning of his reign would have increased their loyalty to him for many years.

C. Rejection of Advice (v. 8a)

8a. But he forsook the counsel of the old men, which they had given him.

The advice the older counselors had given Rehoboam, that if he served the people they in turn would become his servants forever, just did not seem reasonable to the young king. It is hard for the world to realize that the bonds of love are stronger than the heaviest steel chains. Yet millions of Christians through the centuries have learned the truth of this, and it is still true today. That isn't what Rehoboam wanted to hear. Most of us, when we get advice that we don't like, are inclined to reject it. That is exactly what Rehoboam did.

AGE DISCRIMINATION

Senior citizens sometimes are discriminated against, particularly in vocational settings. Otherwise-qualified job applicants may be rejected in favor of younger candidates. Though retirement may not be mandatory at age sixty-five, many employees who are near that age frequently are removed from service by the subtle offer of monetary concessions they can hardly turn down.

Older doesn't always mean *wiser*, but older people do possess awareness and understanding that come only by virtue of experience. Many in the current "youth culture" discount such wisdom. They stereotype anyone past age forty as "out of touch" with things as they are in the nineties.

Even so, a few companies are recognizing the value of counsel from retired executives, and

---

VISUALS FOR THESE LESSONS

The *Adult Visuals/Learning Resources* packet contains classroom-size visuals designed for use with the lessons in the Summer Quarter. The packet is available from your supplier. Order no. 492.

have put them "on retainer" for occasional business advice. Rehoboam was not that smart. "He forsook the counsel of the old men" who had advised Solomon, in favor of the *unwisdom* of the young men in his peer group.

Not all of the ideas of young people are bad; nor is all advice from older folk necessarily wise. Maturity and wisdom are not exclusively linked to chronological age. But youth demonstrate wisdom when they seek counsel from their elders.   —R. W. B.

II. Bad Advice Accepted
(1 Kings 12:8b-11)

A. Consultation With the Young Men
(vv. 8b, 9)

8b, 9. And consulted with the young men that were grown up with him, and which stood before him: and he said unto them, What counsel give ye that we may answer this people, who have spoken to me, saying, Make the yoke which thy father did put upon us lighter?

The "old men" had been counselors of Solomon. One almost gets the feeling that Rehoboam had sought their advice just out of courtesy to them, already knowing what they would advise. Then, having gone through the motions of listening to them, he could turn to his own friends. They had been his constant companions as he grew up, and they knew exactly what he wanted to hear. Courtiers and sycophants know how to answer their superiors, for their jobs and sometimes even their lives depend upon their answers. And so they gave him the answer he wanted.

In speaking to the two different groups, Rehoboam addressed them differently. To the old men he asked, "How do ye advise that *I* may answer this people?" On the other hand, he identified with the young men when he asked, "What counsel give ye that *we* may answer this people?"

B. The Young Men's Advice (vv. 10, 11)

10, 11. And the young men that were grown up with him spake unto him, saying, Thus shalt thou speak unto this people that spake unto thee, saying, Thy father made our yoke heavy, but make thou it lighter unto us; thus shalt thou say unto them, My little finger shall be thicker than my father's loins. And now whereas my father did lade you with a heavy yoke, I will add to your yoke: my father hath chastised you with whips, but I will chastise you with scorpions.

The answer that the young men proposed revealed a complete lack of understanding of the situation and a complete lack of compassion for the burdens that the people had had to bear under Solomon. Their response smacks of the isolation and arrogance that are so often displayed by those of privilege who live out of touch with the common people. Their contempt for the people can be felt in their words, and the complete lack of concern that their answer reveals could only serve to fan the spark of anger that had been just a smoldering ember during Solomon's reign.

The young men's answer rejected the requests of the people as almost an act of rebellion. In their view the best way to put down a rebellion was not by making concessions to the rebels but by dealing with them with a heavy hand. Every tyrant in history has thought like this. If the people thought Solomon's yoke was heavy, then add to it. If Solomon's overseers had beaten them with whips (and perhaps they had), then scourge them with scorpions. This may be a figure of speech simply meaning a more severe beating. Some commentators think it refers to a whip that had barbed points on it that would bite into the skin like the sting of a scorpion.

The verses that follow tell us that Rehoboam accepted the advice of these young men, and when the people, led by Jeroboam, returned after three days, the king gave them his decision. He "answered the people roughly" (v. 13). It should not surprise us that the people, already in a sullen mood, reacted in a violent manner to the king's speech.

III. Tragic Results
(1 Kings 12:16, 17)

A. Rebellion of the Northern Tribes
(v. 16)

16. So when all Israel saw that the king hearkened not unto them, the people answered the king, saying, What portion have we in David? neither have we inheritance in the son of Jesse: to your tents, O Israel: now see to thine own house, David. So Israel departed unto their tents.

How to Say It

ADORAM. Uh-*doe*-rum.
AMMONITE. *Am*-un-ite.
EUPHRATES. U-*fray*-teez.
GERIZIM. *Gair*-ih-zim or Guh-*rye*-zim.
JEROBOAM. Jair-o-*bo*-um.
NAAMAH. *Nay*-uh-muh.
REHOBOAM. Re-ho-*bo*-um.
SHECHEM. *Shee*-kem or *Shek*-em.

If there was anything praiseworthy in Rehoboam's answer to the people's request, it could only be that he gave them an honest answer. Unlike some modern politicians, who lie to the people or coat their threatening words with honey, the king gave it to them straight out. *The people answered the king.* We are not told explicitly, but probably the leaders of the northern tribes consulted among themselves after the king announced his decision. *All Israel* was in agreement when the northern tribes responded to Rehoboam. It seems apparent that tribal jealousies had simmered beneath the surface as far back as the time of the judges. Following the death of King Saul, civil war raged between the house of Saul and the house of David. For seven and one-half years David reigned as king over the tribe of Judah. The elders of the northern tribes then came to David and agreed to recognize him as king over their tribes as well. Now that unity was threatened; the earlier feelings of partisanship were resurfacing. If we have trouble understanding how God's people could divide, we need only to look to the area that was once Yugoslavia. Ethnic and religious differences have completely shattered that country. For that matter, we need look no further than to some of our churches where Christian brothers and sisters have divided over matters of less importance.

What portion have we in David? The people of the north proclaimed that they were not part of David's tribe. The implication of this statement and the parallel statement that follows it—*neither have we inheritance in the son of Jesse*—is that they were receiving nothing from David's son, so why should they give anything to him? Thus the northern tribes harshly rejected the ruling house that David had founded. In less than two generations his heirs squandered the trust and goodwill that he had built up in the nation.

See to thine own house, David. Their meaning was, "Rule the house of Judah, Rehoboam, and don't interfere in our affairs."

To your tents, O Israel. This may have simply been a call for the people to return to their homes, but it may have had a more ominous meaning—a call to take the field in their tents to prepare for battle.

B. Reduced Kingdom in the South (v. 17)

17. But as for the children of Israel which dwelt in the cities of Judah, Rehoboam reigned over them.

Left to be ruled by Rehoboam were the tribe of Judah and those persons of other Israelite tribes who had settled in the territory of Judah. It appears that the tribe of Benjamin also accept-

visual 1

ed him, for when Rehoboam prepared to go to war against the northern tribes, the tribe of Benjamin stood with him (v. 21).

A great tragedy had befallen the people of God. Yet even this tragedy was within God's oversight. Because Solomon had allowed the people to drift away from God and into idolatry, God took the northern tribes away from Solomon's son. God's prophet had previously announced to Jeroboam this division of the kingdom (1 Kings 11:28-39). Even though Rehoboam acted out of his own free will in dealing harshly with the people, God used that action to accomplish His purpose.

Conclusion

A. Heeding Sound Advice

How often heartache and disaster come when persons fail to follow sound advice! A young person has been flooded with good advice about avoiding drugs, but he fails to heed that advice and soon finds himself trapped in addiction. A young woman is swept off her feet by a dashing, handsome young man. Against the advice of her parents and friends she marries him, only to awake from her dream to find that he is lazy and unfaithful. A scam artist appears on the scene with a surefire get-rich-quick scheme. The entranced victim flies in the the face of common sense and good advice and takes the bait, only to find himself poorer for it.

Why is it that so many people in our society today, like Rehoboam, fail to take the good advice that is offered them? There are several possible reasons.

Often good advice goes contrary to what we want to do; it requires us to make some sacrifice, take on some burdensome duty, or give up some cherished pleasure. All of us are guilty on occasion of taking the easy way out and ignoring what we know to be sound advice.

There are times when we are persuaded by our friends not to take good advice. We may do what we know is wrong or foolish because we are afraid of offending our friends or we are afraid of being different.

At times we may question the motives of those who give us good advice. We may be led to believe that they are seeking to control our lives or deny us our freedom. How often young people believe that parents or teachers lay down restrictions because these people actually dislike them or want to do them harm!

We may fail to follow good advice because we fear that we don't have the resources or courage to see the matter through. Lack of self-confidence may cause us to follow the path of least resistance, which means that we don't follow the best advice available.

Many of the problems we face in our society are extremely complex, forcing us to rely on experts to provide the answers we need. On certain issues, however, Christians are, or should be, experts. Science cannot provide answers to moral issues, nor can psychology, nor sociology, nor medicine. We must turn to the Bible to find those answers. In order to do that, we must know the Bible, and to know the Bible, we must study it diligently.

B. "Pride Goeth Before Destruction"

Perhaps the most frequent reason we fail to take good advice is that it goes against our pride. It is ironic that these words of Solomon, "Pride goeth before destruction" (Proverbs 16:18), should find their embodiment in the life of his son Rehoboam. While the Scriptures do not provide any details about the life of this young prince as he was growing up, we can imagine what it must have been like. With his many wives and concubines, Solomon must have had many sons. Undoubtedly, this led to all kinds of conflicts and bitterness as each son struggled to gain a favorable position in that competition. We have no idea why Rehoboam was chosen from among all of the other sons to become the next king.

One virtue Rehoboam did not learn as he grew up was humility. When Solomon came to the throne, he at least did so humbly, acknowledging that he was "but a little child" (1 Kings 3:7). Not Rehoboam! He had been born to the purple, and in no way was he willing to become a servant to his people. That arrogance almost cost him his life. Soon after the incident recorded in our text, Rehoboam sent Adoram, the head taskmaster, to the rebels, perhaps to collect taxes or to round up workers for the king's service. Thus the king would let the people know that he gave no heed to their words. This added insult to injury, and the people took out their wrath on Adoram, stoning him to death. When Rehoboam learned what had happened, he realized that his own life was in jeopardy. Quickly he got into his chariot and sped back to the safety of Jerusalem.

Pride had cost Rehoboam much of his kingdom and had almost cost him his life. Yet, instead of repenting of his arrogance and trying to make amends for the damage he had done, he sought to gather his forces and launch an attack against the rebelling tribes. Before Rehoboam could carry out this plan, God sent His messenger to stop him.

How often we behave like Rehoboam! Pride leads a person to take an unwise course. Even when it becomes obvious that such a course can end only in disaster, one's pride keeps him from admitting his folly and making proper amends.

Pride causes us all to go astray from God. If we continue in such a course, the disaster that will ultimately befall us will be worse than any we can imagine in this life. The kingdom of God is reserved for those who will humble themselves before Him (Matthew 18:3, 4). Let us cast off our pride, humble ourselves before God, and submit to the lordship of Christ. In so doing, blessings will attend our way, and it will lead us to eternal life.

C. Let Us Pray

Almighty God, who watches over the destinies of men and of nations, we come to You humbly acknowledging our complete dependence on You. Teach us to avoid the folly of Rehoboam by learning to walk humbly with You and to obey Your commandments. In Jesus' name we pray. Amen.

D. Thought to Remember

Pride goes before a fall.

Home Daily Bible Readings

Monday, May 29—A Wise Person Seeks God's Help (Psalm 14)

Tuesday, May 30—Prophecy That Jeroboam Will Succeed Solomon (1 Kings 11:26-40)

Wednesday, May 31—Israel's Appeal for a Lightened Load (1 Kings 12:1-5)

Thursday, June 1—King Rehoboam Rejects the People's Appeal (1 Kings 12:6-11)

Friday, June 2—Israel Withdraws Allegiance From Rehoboam (1 Kings 12:12-17)

Saturday, June 3—Jeroboam Is Made King Over Israel (1 Kings 12:18-24)

Sunday, June 4—A Wise Person Uses Good Judgment (Proverbs 16:16-25)

Learning by Doing

This page contains an alternate lesson plan emphasizing learning activities. Classes desiring such student involvement will find these suggestions helpful.

Learning Goals

This study will enable the students to:

1. Analyze Rehoboam's use of power as recorded in 1 Kings 12.

2. Understand that individuals in positions of power are to use that power to serve others.

Into the Lesson

Begin the session by giving each class member a three-by-five card (or distribute the student books, which have this activity). Write the following on your chalkboard:

An individual in a position of power who used that power to serve others.

An individual in a position of power who used that power to serve self.

Say to the class, "Today we are considering the use of power. I'd like for each of you to jot down the name of a person who fits the first category on the chalkboard, and another person who fits the second category."

Allow about sixty seconds for your students to think of individuals. Then ask volunteers to tell whom they selected for each category. Have them indicate how each person they named demonstrated that particular use of power.

Lead into the Bible study by saying, "Power is a fact of life. Certain individuals are in positions of power. That power can be used for good or for evil, to benefit others or to promote one's selfish interests. In this lesson we will learn about a king who was presented with the option of using his power to serve others, or to serve himself. Let's seek to learn what we can about the appropriate use of power."

Into the Word

Present a brief lecture to establish the background of today's study. Use the thoughts included in the Lesson Background section on page 346 for this. The lecture should last only about three or four minutes.

Have a class member whom you have asked ahead of time read 1 Kings 12:1-20 aloud to the class at this point. Then have the class form groups of four to six people. Appoint a leader for each group, and give each leader a copy of the following questions to discuss.

1. What did the people request of Rehoboam?

2. What different kinds of advice did Rehoboam receive regarding this issue?

3. Put yourself in Rehoboam's place. You have received conflicting advice from the elders and from the young men, and you must make a decision. The following four questions seem to be logical ones to consider. Discuss them in your group.

- What are the pros for the advice from the elders?
- What are the cons for the advice from the elders?
- What are the pros for the advice from the young men?
- What are the cons for the advice from the young men?

4. What were the consequences of Rehoboam's choice?

Allow the groups about fifteen minutes to discuss the questions. Then have the groups reassemble as a class. Ask, "What were the most important observations made in your group?"

Allow for comments. Then ask, "From this incident, what do we learn about the use of power?"

We have seen that Rehoboam failed miserably in his first test as a leader. Ask the class to give reasons for his failure.

Option

Have a volunteer read 1 Kings 12:1-20 aloud to the class. Present a brief lecture on the background of the lesson, as suggested in the first paragraph of the "Into the Word" section. Then have the class break into groups of four students each. Provide each group with a pen and several sheets of paper. Give the following assignment: "Put yourself in Rehoboam's place in this narrative. Write a brief journal entry revealing your thoughts and concerns at each of these points: (1) vv. 1-5; (2) vv. 6-8a; (3) vv. 8b-11; (4) vv. 12-20."

Allow a few minutes. Then ask each group to read its journal entries to the rest of the class.

Into Life

Conclude by discussing these questions:

1. On the basis of the incident in the lesson text, what qualities do you think a person in authority should have to be a successful leader?

2. In seeking advice, is it wise to go only to people in our "own crowd"?

3. How can we decide from whom to seek advice?

Let's Talk It Over

The questions on this page are designed to encourage review of the lesson Scriptures and to promote discussion of the lesson by the class. The answers provided are only discussion starters. Let your class talk it over from there.

1. What are some reasons that would lead you to value the advice of an older person? What are some reasons why you would question the advice of an older person?

We generally expect that an older person has the wisdom born of experience. Whether a person succeeds or fails at some endeavor, it is to be hoped that he or she learns something valuable that can be passed on to those who come along later. Those who are older should also possess the wisdom that comes from observation. One gains from observing the experiences of others over the years. On the negative side, some older people may not have stayed in touch with life as it is being lived by the younger generation. Their experience may be so dated that it does not include prevailing factors of today's world. The passing of years may also have rendered them too timid to take risks that they would have considered reasonable in their younger days

2. Why was Rehoboam unwilling to accept the counsel of the old men? Does setting aside rights in the interest of service make a leader appear weak or strong? Why?

Rehoboam was being crowned king of all Israel. Power and wealth were within his grasp. Perhaps he had looked forward to this day for a long time. Now was his opportunity to make his mark, and to enjoy the privileges of power. But he was being asked to make concessions. He may have felt threatened. He may have worried about his prestige as king. He may have believed that to give in to a demand of the people would cause him to appear weak and unfit to rule. Actually, a benevolent leader who seeks the good of those he leads will generally be admired, and will have the grateful support of the people he serves.

3. Rehoboam asked for advice until he heard what pleased him. How can we evaluate advice we receive?

We can consider the source. Rehoboam had conflicting counsel from two sources—the experienced older men, and the friends his own age. The magnitude of the issue before Rehoboam should have caused him to give careful consideration to those who counseled him. We can also consider the possible outcomes of following the advice we receive. What is the upside potential if the prescribed course of action succeeds? What is the downside risk if it fails? Finally, we can evaluate advice in terms of the personal cost of following it. Try applying these tests to the two sets of advice Rehoboam received. Rehoboam appeared unprepared for the swift and drastic reaction of the ten tribes that withdrew. Evidently he had not evaluated very thoroughly the advice given to him.

4. What word could be used to characterize the response of Rehoboam's young counselors? How would "wisdom" have answered? How would "compassion" have answered?

The response of the young men could be described with a number of one-word characterizations, all of them negative. It was cruel, selfish, greedy, irresponsible, heartless. "Wisdom" may have answered the people much as the old men advised. At the very least, it would have acknowledged the heavy burden the people had been under and would have shown some sympathy for their situation, even if continued high taxes were deemed necessary. "Compassion" would have caused the king to consider their interests above his personal ambitions and pride, and would have moved to relieve their plight.

5. In conflict situations the persons involved may concede, contend, compromise, or collaborate. Which of these is the preferred option for resolving conflicts? How might Rehoboam have achieved that?

If we consider that collaboration is the win-win resolution that gives all parties what they desire, then that is the option that should be pursued first. In this case the people wanted relief from the burden of supporting the king's many ambitions. Rehoboam wanted to be regarded as a powerful ruler, and he wanted to reign in no less splendor than his father, Solomon. If reducing what was required from the people was unacceptable to Rehoboam, he could have offered them more benefits in return for what they were giving. Instead of building and spending for his own pleasure and glory, he could have applied the resources of the kingdom toward that which would have both benefited the people and strengthened the kingdom.

The Danger of False Religion

DEVOTIONAL READING: Deuteronomy 6:5-15.

LESSON SCRIPTURE: 1 Kings 18.

PRINTED TEXT: 1 Kings 18:30-39.

1 Kings 18:30-39

30 And Elijah said unto all the people, Come near unto me. And all the people came near unto him. And he repaired the altar of the LORD that was broken down.

31 And Elijah took twelve stones, according to the number of the tribes of the sons of Jacob, unto whom the word of the LORD came, saying, Israel shall be thy name:

32 And with the stones he built an altar in the name of the LORD: and he made a trench about the altar, as great as would contain two measures of seed.

33 And he put the wood in order, and cut the bullock in pieces, and laid him on the wood, and said, Fill four barrels with water, and pour it on the burnt sacrifice, and on the wood.

34 And he said, Do it the second time. And they did it the second time. And he said, Do it the third time. And they did it the third time.

35 And the water ran round about the altar; and he filled the trench also with water.

36 And it came to pass at the time of the offering of the evening sacrifice, that Elijah the prophet came near, and said, LORD God of Abraham, Isaac, and of Israel, let it be known this day that thou art God in Israel, and that I am thy servant, and that I have done all these things at thy word.

37 Hear me, O LORD, hear me, that this people may know that thou art the LORD God, and that thou hast turned their heart back again.

38 Then the fire of the LORD fell, and consumed the burnt sacrifice, and the wood, and the stones, and the dust, and licked up the water that was in the trench.

39 And when all the people saw it, they fell on their faces: and they said, The LORD, he is the God; the LORD, he is the God.

GOLDEN TEXT: How long halt ye between two opinions? if the LORD be God, follow him.
—1 Kings 18:21.

A Nation Turns From God
Unit 1: The Price of Power
(Lessons 1-4)

Lesson Aims

As a result of studying this lesson, the students should:

1. Have a higher regard for the influence one person can have on others.

2. Appreciate the uncompromising courage of Elijah in the face of those who promoted the worship of false gods.

3. Have courage to obey God when they are faced with a choice between good and evil.

Lesson Outline

INTRODUCTION
   A. "Here I Stand"
   B. Lesson Background
I. GOD'S ALTAR REPAIRED (1 Kings 18:30-32)
   A. Invitation to the People (v. 30)
   B. Construction of the Altar (vv. 31, 32)
II. A SACRIFICE PREPARED (1 Kings 18:33-35)
   A. Careful Arrangement (v. 33a)
   B. Convincing Precautions (vv. 33b-35)
      The Work of a Prophet
III. ELIJAH'S PRAYER AND ITS ANSWER (1 Kings 18:36-38)
   A. Request of God's Prophet (vv. 36, 37)
   B. Revelation of God's Power (v. 38)
IV. THE PEOPLE'S RESPONSE (1 Kings 18:39)
   A. Acknowledgment of the Miracle (v. 39a)
   B. Affirmation of Jehovah (v. 39b)
      Seeing Is Believing?
CONCLUSION
   A. The Indispensable Man
   B. The Danger of Compromise
   C. Let Us Pray
   D. Thought to Remember

Visual 2 of the visuals packet illustrates the superiority of the Bible to human philosophies. The visual is shown on page 356.

Introduction

A. "Here I Stand"

In 1517 Martin Luther nailed his famous Ninety-five Theses to the church door in Wittenberg. This document attacked many of the corruptions of the Roman Catholic Church. The reaction to it shook both the Roman Church and the Holy Roman Empire to its foundations. To quell this growing rebellion, Emperor Charles V summoned Luther to appear before the Imperial Diet to be held in Worms. The emperor planned to demand that Luther recant his teachings or face the consequences. The consequences, Luther was reminded, would likely be the same that John Hus had received a century earlier. This Bohemian reformer, haled before the Council of Constance, had refused to recant his beliefs and was burned at the stake.

Standing before the Diet, Luther refused to recant his writings, and boldly proclaimed: "Unless I am convinced by Scripture or by right reason, for I trust neither in popes nor in councils since they have often erred and contradicted themselves—unless I am thus convinced, I am bound by the texts of my Bible. My conscience is captive to the Word of God; I neither can nor will recant anything, since it is neither right nor safe to act against conscience. Here I stand! I can do no other! God help me!"

In the same way, Elijah, in challenging the false prophets of Baal, placed his life in jeopardy. But, in the face of a life-and-death choice, he did not flinch. Like Luther, he said, "Here I stand! I can do no other! God help me!"

B. Lesson Background

Ahab, the son of Omri, became the king of the northern kingdom about 875 B.C. Omri had been a wicked king, but Ahab outdid his father: "Ahab the son of Omri did evil in the sight of the Lord above all that were before him" (1 Kings 16:30). To compound his wickedness, Ahab married Jezebel, the daughter of the king of Sidon. Jezebel imported into Israel the worship of Baal, along with many priests to serve this false god. As a result, God, using Elijah as His spokesman, proclaimed a prolonged drought upon the land (1 Kings 17:1).

After the land suffered three and one-half years (Luke 4:25), God sent Elijah back to speak to Ahab. When they met, Ahab charged Elijah with being the troubler of Israel, but Elijah returned the charge, labeling Ahab as the real troubler of the nation. Elijah then challenged the prophets of Baal and the prophets "of the groves" to a contest on Mount Carmel (1 Kings 18:7-19).

In the contest that followed, each side was to prepare an altar and offer a bullock as a sacrifice. The prophets of Baal were supposed to call upon their god to send down fire and consume the sacrifice.

Elijah would make the same request of Jehovah. Whichever one answered the prayer by fire would be recognized as the true God.

The prophets of Baal cried out to their god from morning until noon. When no answer came, they cried out more loudly, leaped about the altar frantically, and even cut themselves, but their god did not answer. It is at this point that our lesson text begins.

I. God's Altar Repaired
(1 Kings 18:30-32)
A. Invitation to the People (v. 30)

30. And Elijah said unto all the people, Come near unto me. And all the people came near unto him. And he repaired the altar of the LORD that was broken down.

The prophets of Baal had had their chance to demonstrate the power of their god, but they had failed, and understandably so. The god they worshiped was one of their own imagining. He could not respond because he simply did not exist outside of the minds of those who proclaimed him a god.

Now it was the prophet Elijah's turn. The people who were witnessing this contest probably had been standing around the altar to Baal, waiting for something to happen. Elijah called them to come near to him so they could watch carefully as he repaired the altar to Jehovah. Elijah encouraged the group to watch so that they could be credible witnesses of the event later on.

Elijah began to repair the altar that had either fallen into disrepair or been deliberately destroyed by Ahab's forces (1 Kings 19:10). This involved assembling the stones that had been used in its initial construction.

B. Construction of the Altar
(vv. 31, 32)

31, 32. And Elijah took twelve stones, according to the number of the tribes of the sons of Jacob, unto whom the word of the LORD came, saying, Israel shall be thy name: and with the stones he built an altar in the name of the LORD: and he made a trench about the altar, as great as would contain two measures of seed.

The stones that Elijah used were probably not shaped stones but merely rough stones one might pick up on a mountain ridge. Of those available, he chose only twelve. In this action he may have been giving a reminder of the essential unity of God's people, even though the tribes had been divided into two separate kingdoms. He also reminded them that God had spoken to their father Jacob and had given him a new name—*Israel* (Genesis 32:28).

After building the altar, Elijah dug a trench around it. This action must have surprised the crowd, for they would have had no idea what purpose it could serve. *Two measures of seed.* Literally this reads "two seahs of seed." The seah was a dry measure equal to about a third of a bushel. One normally describes a trench by its depth, so the meaning may be that this trench was as deep as the measure containing two seahs of grain. Thus it would not have been a very deep trench, but it would have been adequate to hold the excess water that was to be poured over the sacrifice.

II. A Sacrifice Prepared
(1 Kings 18:33-35)
A. Careful Arrangement (v. 33a)

33a. And he put the wood in order, and cut the bullock in pieces, and laid him on the wood.

In preparing the sacrifice, Elijah apparently followed the instructions set forth in Leviticus 1:3-9. In following the procedure set forth in the law, Elijah may have been visually reminding the people that they were still subject to the law of Jehovah. Normally, the next step would be to kindle a fire under the sacrifice; what Elijah did, however, was unheard of and obviously very much unexpected.

B. Convincing Precautions
(vv. 33b-35)

33b-35. And said, Fill four barrels with water, and pour it on the burnt sacrifice, and on the wood. And he said, Do it the second time. And they did it the second time. And he said, Do it the third time. And they did it the third time. And the water ran round about the altar; and he filled the trench also with water.

Fill four barrels with water. When we think of barrels today, we are likely to think of fifty-five-gallon drums. The vessels mentioned in this verse were not nearly that large, however. Most modern translations render this "jars," referring to the vessels women balanced on their heads to carry water. Since a drought lasting three and one-half years had preceded this incident, one might wonder where this water was obtained. We are not told, and so we can only conclude

---

How to Say It

BAAL. *Bay*-ul.
JEHU. *Jee*-hew.
JEZEBEL. *Jez*-uh-bel.
OMRI. *Ahm*-rye.
SINAI. *Sye*-nay-eye or *Sye*-nye.

that the water came from a nearby spring that was supplied by an aquifer ample enough to keep flowing in spite of the drought.

Some ancient altars were constructed with holes beneath them so that concealed priests could ignite the wood, leading the worshipers to believe that their god had started the fire. Elijah took precautions against any charge of fraud. First, he called for the people to come near to him, and he built the altar right before their eyes so that they could know there were no secret hiding places beneath it (v. 30). Then, by drenching the sacrifice, the wood, and the altar, he completely excluded any possibility of being charged with deception.

Three times he called for four jars of water to be brought—thus twelve jars in all were poured on the sacrifice and the wood. As a consequence, the altar and everything on and around it were thoroughly soaked, and the excess water flowed into the trench that had been dug around it. Then, additional jars of water were poured into the trench, filling it to the brim.

THE WORK OF A PROPHET

Some of us remember the comic TV character whose famous line, spoken with heavy accent, was, "Tha's not my yob!" Who knows how many viewers have used that quip to communicate to superiors, "What you're asking me to do is not a part of my job description."

Wise employers make certain that workers know the boss's expectations. Job descriptions make for fewer misunderstandings and better efficiency.

Who would have guessed that a prophet of God would be required to build altars and slaughter cattle? Elijah either did that work or supervised it; he could have balked at all that menial labor. He might have said, "Why can't I just pray for fire to consume these animal sacrifices lying whole on the ground? Lord, can't You prove Your existence and power without all this human effort?"

visual 2

It seems that God most often chooses to work through human agency. Elijah set the stage for a dramatic demonstration of divine power. Such assistance was part of his *unwritten* job description, and it is part of ours, too.

What can you do to help God's miracles of love and grace happen?

The hymn writer Frances R. Havergal said it well:

> Take my hands, and let them move
> At the impulse of Thy love.

—R. W. B.

III. Elijah's Prayer and Its Answer (1 Kings 18:36-38)

A. Request of God's Prophet (vv. 36, 37)

36. And it came to pass at the time of the offering of the evening sacrifice, that Elijah the prophet came near, and said, LORD God of Abraham, Isaac, and of Israel, let it be known this day that thou art God in Israel, and that I am thy servant, and that I have done all these things at thy word.

The words *the time of* and *evening* were supplied by the translators of the *King James Version*. The Hebrew text at the beginning of this verse may literally be translated, "And it came to pass at the offering of the sacrifice," which would have no time reference. However, the translators may be correct in supposing that Elijah offered this sacrifice at the time when the second of two daily sacrifices was being offered in the temple in Jerusalem, probably about three o'clock in the afternoon.

Elijah addressed God as *Lord*, Jehovah or Yahweh, the distinct name for God. This would remind the people of the covenant they had made with Jehovah when they came out of Egypt. It is He who had guided them and watched over them from the time of *Abraham, Isaac, and of Israel* (Jacob) right down to their own time. *Let it be known.* The prophet then asked that God in a dramatic way demonstrate to the people not only that He was God but that he, Elijah, was God's spokesman.

37. Hear me, O LORD, hear me, that this people may know that thou art the LORD God, and that thou hast turned their heart back again.

The object of the miracle about to be performed was to convince the people that Jehovah was indeed the true God. But more than that, it was to turn their hearts back to Him. The language anticipates the people's conversion from Baal to Jehovah, and also indicates that their hearts were already being turned even while Elijah was praying.

B. Revelation of God's Power (v. 38)

38. Then the fire of the LORD fell, and consumed the burnt sacrifice, and the wood, and the stones, and the dust, and licked up the water that was in the trench.

Zap! In a split second God demonstrated His power. A flash of fire fell, and everything was consumed—the sacrifice, the wood, the stones, the dust, and even the water in the trench about the altar. Right before their eyes everything vanished. This was no sleight of hand magic; it was God's might revealed. Some commentators have suggested that this was a bolt of lightning. If so, it would have been out of a perfectly clear sky, a miracle indeed. That it was a cloudless sky is evident when later even a cloud the size of a man's hand could attract attention (1 Kings 18:44). It is interesting that some who hesitate to accept the miraculous will offer explanations that also require the miraculous.

IV. The People's Response (1 Kings 18:39)

A. Acknowledgment of the Miracle (v. 39a)

39a. And when all the people saw it, they fell on their faces.

The people immediately fell on their faces, acknowledging the miracle. In our culture we do not often assume the prone position, but in the culture of ancient Israel such a posture indicated fear, reverence, awe, and worship. It is likely that the people felt all of these emotions. They did not need an involved theological explanation for them to understand that God had intervened. He had not only revealed His own mighty power, but He had also accredited Elijah's claim that he was God's messenger.

B. Affirmation of Jehovah (v. 39b)

39b. And they said, The LORD he is the God; the LORD, he is the God.

Before this experience on Mount Carmel, the hearts of many of these people were divided. They were attempting to give allegiance both to Jehovah and to Baal. They did not want to break away from the worship of Jehovah, neither did they want to give up the sensuousness of the Baal worship. When Elijah arrived on Mount Carmel this day, he indicated that such a division of allegiance should not exist and challenged the people to make a choice between the two (1 Kings 18:21). Some today may think they can be a part of Christ's body, receive the blessings He bestows, and still participate in all the pleasures the world offers. It cannot be! We too must make a choice. Jesus must be Lord of all, or not at all.

In affirming that Jehovah is God, the people were saying that He is more than just one god among many, more even than the chief god. He is the *only* God! No longer would they go limping between Jehovah and Baal.

Now the people were ready to do the bidding of God and His spokesman, Elijah. The prophet's first order was that the prophets of Baal be executed. Without hesitation the people carried out that order.

SEEING IS BELIEVING?

Wouldn't it have been exciting to live in an era when God often revealed His presence and power by supernatural phenomena? Wouldn't faith have come easier in those days?

When the prophet Elijah's contemporaries saw fire from heaven consume the altar and everything *on and around* it—sure, they believed that Jehovah is God. Why not? Baal offered no such sensational evidence of existence or might. Seeing is believing!

But Jesus was frustrated by people who demand to see before they will believe: "Why does this generation ask for a miraculous sign? I tell you the truth, no sign will be given to it" (Mark 8:12, *New International Version*).

Remember also what the risen Christ told Thomas: "Because you have seen me, you have believed; blessed are those who have not seen and yet have believed" (John 20:29, *New International Version*). Christian faith is the "evidence of things *not seen*" (Hebrews 11:1).

Daily sunrises and sunsets, sowing/reaping cycles, the birth of a child, the spiritual transformation of those who are "born again"—for most of us these will have to suffice for sensational evidence of God in this era. Yet, we know it is true: "The Lord, He is God! The Lord, He is God!"

—R. W. B.

Conclusion

A. The Indispensable Man

In a very real sense, no person is indispensable. Even those who may seem to be so for a time eventually retire or die, and life somehow goes on without them. If nothing else, this fact should keep us humble.

Yet, in another sense, some people have been indispensable if a certain course was to be followed or if a certain goal was to be attained. Such a person was Elijah. The people of Israel were in a sorry state. For some time they had followed a zigzag course, claiming loyalty to God on the one hand and trying to serve Baal on the other. The faithful followers of God had become a small minority in the nation—seven thousand, we are told (1 Kings 19:18). The path the nation was following was leading to certain destruction. Then, without any prior notice, Elijah appeared on the scene. Sent by God to salvage what he could of the nation while there was still time, Elijah followed a course that was both stern and uncompromising. The times called for such a leader.

When Elijah confronted the people, he gave them a simple, clear-cut choice—Jehovah or Baal. The people were hesitant to make a decision until God revealed himself so dramatically on Mount Carmel. When they finally saw the truth, they turned their anger against the false prophets of Baal. Later, Elijah was sent to anoint Jehu who would eventually become king and in the process wipe out the house of Ahab, including the wicked Jezebel.

No doubt, God in His own way would have accomplished His purpose for Israel even if Elijah had not been on the scene. Yet Elijah was there, and because he was willing to be used of God, judgment was brought upon the house of Ahab. In this sense, Elijah was indispensable. Each of us can have a part in the fulfilling of God's ultimate plans for mankind. To do so we must be willing to submit ourselves to Him, and then as did Elijah, have the faith and courage to do the work that is set before us.

B. The Danger of Compromise

Jehovah God is a jealous God. He is not willing to accept a half-way commitment. He made this clear when he gave the law to Moses on Mount Sinai (Exodus 20:4, 5). Unfortunately, the Israelites forgot this, and thought they could serve both Baal and Jehovah. It seems obvious that the fathers failed to teach their children as instructed in Deuteronomy 6:4-12.

Because their fathers had not taught well, the Israelites were not very well prepared to resist the allurement of pagan deities when it came. The worship of pagan gods had been a problem to the Israelites since the time of the judges.

People often become involved in religious compromise when they are swept along by what is happening around them. It is likely that worshiping Baal became the "in" thing in ancient Israel. They may not have had popularity polls to determine what was the latest rage, but even in that society word got around. Add to this the pressures that came from friends and family who were into Baalism, and the result was that many people were swept along with the tide without really being aware of where they were going or what they were doing.

Does all this sound familiar? It should, for things haven't changed much in the nearly three thousand years that have passed since the time of Ahab and Elijah. Oh, of course, we moderns don't bow down before idols, but many are guilty of more subtle forms of idolatry—the all-consuming pursuit of possessions, popularity, and pleasure—to name just a few. Television programs and the movies have been allowed to erode our nation's long-standing moral standards and family values. Almost inundated by a sea of clever advertising, people today continually lust for things.

The loss of our standards has not come overnight. That loss has occurred gradually, a little bit here and a little bit there. We justify these compromises by speaking in glowing terms of the importance of tolerating other people's views. We insist on personal freedom and the right of choice, even as these things are destroying the very fabric of our society. If we are to stem this tide that is sweeping our nation, we must return to standards that are clear and absolute. Only the Bible provides these standards. In our homes and in our congregations we must turn to careful and thorough study of the Bible if we are to save our land.

C. Let Us Pray

O Jehovah, You alone are God. Let us never forget that You are a jealous God, demanding our complete allegiance. Help us to understand that we cannot serve You while seeking what the world has to offer. May our decision to serve You be followed by full commitment to Your way and to Your will. In Jesus' name, amen.

D. Thought to Remember

"The Lord, he is the God."

Home Daily Bible Readings

Monday, June 5—Third Year of Israel's Drought (1 Kings 18:1-6)
Tuesday, June 6—Obadiah Carries Elijah's Message to Ahab (1 Kings 18:7-16)
Wednesday, June 7—Command to Gather at Mount Carmel (1 Kings 18:17-21)
Thursday, June 8—Baal's Prophets Fail the Test (1 Kings 18:22-29)
Friday, June 9—Elijah Prepares the Burnt Offering (1 Kings 18:30-35)
Saturday, June 10—God's Fire Consumes Elijah's Offering (1 Kings 18:36-40)
Sunday, June 11—God Ends the Drought (1 Kings 18:41-46)

Learning by Doing

*This page contains an alternate lesson plan emphasizing learning activities. Classes
desiring such student involvement will find these suggestions helpful.*

Learning Goals

Seek to lead your class members to:

1. Conclude that God insists that we follow Him wholeheartedly.

2. Identify specific "gods" to whom they may be tempted to give allegiance.

3. Worship God alone.

Into the Lesson

Write this statement on the chalkboard: *You can't have it both ways.*

Point out that in some situations in life a person may be presented with more than one option, but accepting one excludes the others. For example, a single man may be attracted to two women, but he can marry only one. Ask your class to mention some other situations in which the choice of one option automatically excludes another option. (If students have difficulty coming up with ideas, suggest one of these to get them started: having a diet of rich foods and losing weight; saving money and buying everything you see.)

Allow two minutes for discussion. Then lead into the Bible study by saying, "The most important area of life in which this principle applies (point to the statement on the chalkboard) is in our spiritual life, specifically in our choice of the God to whom we would give our allegiance. At the time of the incident in today's lesson, Israel's loyalty was divided. The prophet Elijah informed them, however, that that could not continue. They could serve but one God. Our lesson text tells of an incident that guided them in their choice."

Into the Word

If your class is large enough, read 1 Kings 18:1-40 as a narrative. In the week before class ask various class members to read the words spoken by these in the text: God, Elijah, Obadiah, Ahab, at least two for the prophets of Baal, and at least two for the people. Another person should read the narrative portion.

After the Scripture reading, have your class form groups of six to discuss the questions below. Give each group a copy of the questions and appoint a leader for each group. Allow the groups twenty minutes for their Scripture exploration.

1. How were the Israelites in Elijah's day trying to "have it both ways"?

2. How did Elijah emphasize that they couldn't have it both ways?

3. Why was Elijah so dramatic in his confrontation with the prophets of Baal?

4. What does each passage below say about a person's dividing his loyalty between Jehovah and any other god?

Exodus 34:14-16

Deuteronomy 6:13-15

Deuteronomy 13:6-11

Joshua 24:14, 15, 19, 20, 23

Matthew 6:24

Luke 14:26, 27, 33

After time has expired, bring the groups together. Ask, "Which passage in question 4 do you think is the most powerful in teaching that we must worship God alone?"

Option

Have your class participate in the narrative reading as described above. Then have them form groups of four. Provide each group with paper and a pen, and appoint a leader. Ask each group to write what it considers to be the three most important questions about this passage (1 Kings 18:1-40). Allow about ten minutes for this. Then exchange questions with another group. Then have each group discuss the questions given them.

Into Life

Say to the class, "A tendency of humans is to combine different forms of belief or practice from two or more religious faiths to create a religious system of one's own liking. This is called 'syncretism.'

"The Israelites in today's passage had been practicing syncretism of sorts—mixing worship of God with worship of Baal. Let's consider how Christians today might be tempted to practice syncretism."

Lead your class in discussing these questions:

1. How have others' beliefs and values invaded the church today?

2. Why might Christians today be tempted to mix and match beliefs and values from the Bible with beliefs and values from other sources?

3. How can you keep from compromising your faith in God with other beliefs and values?

4. What will you do to remain wholeheartedly committed to worshiping God alone?

Let's Talk It Over

The questions on this page are designed to encourage review of the lesson Scriptures and to promote discussion of the lesson by the class. The answers provided are only discussion starters. Let your class talk it over from there.

1. The Israelites were lured away from God by the appeal of Baal worship. What are some of today's gods that weaken and may undermine a believer's loyalty to God?

Idol worship, as such, holds little threat to one's commitment to God in our day. But activities or things that are harmless themselves can become idols if we allow them to compete with God for our devotion. It may be a car, a house, a boat, a job, a hobby, or even a friendship. A good test might be to ask, "Is this interest contributing to God's will in my life, or is it crowding Him out?"

2. If you wanted to be a modern-day Elijah, what could you do to bring glory to God?

Some believers are choosing to go head-to-head with the powers of darkness in the courts, in legislative bodies, and even in the marketplace. These efforts may prove effective, but perhaps the most remarkable victories for God today occur when lives are changed by the gospel. The testimony of men, women, and young people who have experienced the transforming grace of God is compelling evidence of the authenticity of the gospel message. If we will pray fervently and work diligently for the conversion of unbelievers, their transformation will bring glory to God.

3. What was Elijah's motive in praying as he did? How does that compare with the motive behind many of our fervent prayers?

Elijah earnestly desired that his people would repent of their spiritual infidelity and turn back to God. He knew what an offense it was for them to be worshiping the false god Baal. He prayed as he did, not so he would be recognized as a great miracle worker, but so the people might be drawn back to Jehovah. When Jesus taught His disciples to pray, He indicated that the focus of our prayers should be on God and His will: "Thy will be done in earth, as it is in heaven." If we examine our prayers, we may find that our motive most often is to get God to do our will. We ask favors that are important to us, without always giving thought to what God's will may be. At other times it may be that we do not receive what we request because our motive is impure (see James 4:3).

4. What is the significance in the fact that not only the sacrifice, but also the wood, the stone altar, and the water were consumed when the fire of the Lord fell on them? What similarity do you see in this miracle and Jesus' resurrection?

God answered Elijah's prayer in a remarkable way, which left no doubt among the witnesses about the source of this miracle. No one could argue that Elijah had accomplished this by some clever trick. The fact that the people came near to Elijah while he constructed the altar gave assurance that there could not have been an accomplice hidden under the altar to ignite the sacrifice at the proper moment. The fact that the wood was water-soaked made the outcome even more convincing. There could be no excuse for disbelief that day.

Compare the triumph of God in Jesus' resurrection. Jesus was dead when He was put in the grave. Before He died, however, His body had suffered great harm. He had been beaten at His trial before Caiaphas, and brutally scourged by the Romans. Add to this the puncture of His body by the spikes driven into His hands and feet at His crucifixion and by the spear thrust into His side. The tomb was sealed and guarded by Roman soldiers. All of the facts clearly indicate that any kind of deception on the part of Jesus or His followers was impossible. In spite of all the obstacles, however, God overcame by bringing Jesus forth alive and well. God is "able to do exceeding abundantly above all that we ask or think" (Ephesians 3:20).

5. How can we demonstrate our loyalty to God above all competing idols?

The most obvious mark of loyalty to God has always been obedience. Deuteronomy 6 contains a clear statement of God's expectation of the Israelites, namely, love illustrated by obedience. "Thou shalt love the Lord thy God with all thine heart . . . .Ye shall not go after other gods. . . . Ye shall diligently keep the commandments of the Lord your God, and his testimonies, and his statutes, which he hath commanded thee" (vv. 5, 14, 17). Jesus echoed the thought that loyalty and love are demonstrated in obedience: "He that hath my commandments, and keepeth them, he it is that loveth me. . . . If a man love me, he will keep my words" (John 14:21, 23).

When Justice Is Corrupted

DEVOTIONAL READING: Micah 6:6-13.

LESSON SCRIPTURE: 1 Kings 21.

PRINTED TEXT: 1 Kings 21:1-4, 15-20.

1 Kings 21:1-4, 15-20

1 And it came to pass after these things, that Naboth the Jezreelite had a vineyard, which was in Jezreel, hard by the palace of Ahab king of Samaria.

2 And Ahab spake unto Naboth, saying, Give me thy vineyard, that I may have it for a garden of herbs, because it is near unto my house: and I will give thee for it a better vineyard than it; or, if it seem good to thee, I will give thee the worth of it in money.

3 And Naboth said to Ahab, The LORD forbid it me, that I should give the inheritance of my fathers unto thee.

4 And Ahab came into his house heavy and displeased because of the word which Naboth the Jezreelite had spoken to him: for he had said, I will not give thee the inheritance of my fathers. And he laid him down upon his bed, and turned away his face, and would eat no bread.

. . . .

15 And it came to pass, when Jezebel heard that Naboth was stoned, and was dead, that Jezebel said to Ahab, Arise, take possession of the vineyard of Naboth the Jezreelite, which he refused to give thee for money: for Naboth is not alive, but dead.

16 And it came to pass, when Ahab heard that Naboth was dead, that Ahab rose up to go down to the vineyard of Naboth the Jezreelite, to take possession of it.

17 And the word of the LORD came to Elijah the Tishbite, saying,

18 Arise, go down to meet Ahab king of Israel, which is in Samaria: behold, he is in the vineyard of Naboth, whither he is gone down to possess it.

19 And thou shalt speak unto him, saying, Thus saith the LORD, Hast thou killed, and also taken possession? And thou shalt speak unto him, saying, Thus saith the LORD, In the place where dogs licked the blood of Naboth shall dogs lick thy blood, even thine.

20 And Ahab said to Elijah, Hast thou found me, O mine enemy? And he answered, I have found thee: because thou hast sold thyself to work evil in the sight of the LORD.

GOLDEN TEXT: Thou hast sold thyself to work evil in the sight of the LORD.
—1 Kings 21:20.

A Nation Turns From God
Unit 1: The Price of Power
(Lessons 1-4)

Lesson Aims

As a result of studying this lesson, a student should:

1. Be aware of the corrupting effect of power.

2. Have increased concern for justice in our time.

3. Be able to suggest ways that he or she can work for justice in our times.

Lesson Outline

INTRODUCTION
    A. No Elijah
    B. Lesson Background
 I. AHAB'S DESIRE FOR NABOTH'S VINEYARD
      (1 Kings 21:1-4)
    A. Ahab's Offer (vv. 1, 2)
    B. Naboth's Refusal (v. 3)
      Heritage Not for Sale
    C. Ahab's Disappointment (v. 4)
 II. AHAB'S JUDGMENT (1 Kings 21:15-20)
    A. The Vineyard Available (v. 15)
    B. Possession at Last! (v. 16)
    C. Pronouncement of Judgment (vv. 17-19)
    D. Confrontation of Prophet and King (v. 20)
      Accessories to Sin
CONCLUSION
    A. Above the Law
    B. Souls at a Bargain Basement Price
    C. The Power Behind the Throne
    D. Justice Corrupted
    E. Let Us Pray
    F. Thought to Remember

Visual 3 of the visuals packet speaks to the sin of covetousness. The visual is pictured on page 365.

Introduction
A. No Elijah

During the California gold rush of 1849, thousands of people streamed into that state hoping to strike it rich. Some actually did find gold, and when they did, they went to the land office to register their claim. In one area an unscrupulous mining company made a deal with the local surveyor and the clerk who recorded the claims. When a prospector registered a claim, they would survey it and record the claim incorrect-ly. Then they would record the correct claim information in the name of the mining company. When the unsuspecting prospector later tried to sell his claim, he found that the company already had a deed to it. When this happened, there was no Elijah to greet the crooked mining officials when they showed up to take possession of the claim.

B. Lesson Background

Last week's lesson was about Elijah's tremendous victory over the false prophets of Baal. God's prophet had little time to celebrate that victory, however. First Kings 19 records the ensuing events.

As soon as word got back to Queen Jezebel about what had happened, she vowed to even the score by killing Elijah. As soon as he heard this, he ran for his life, not stopping until he reached the Judean wilderness south of Beersheba. Fearful, disappointed, and exhausted, he cried out for God to let him die; but God wasn't through with him yet.

After Elijah had eaten and rested, he then proceeded farther southward in the Sinai peninsula, to the area of Mount Horeb. There God spoke to him. Elijah was instructed to stand upon the mountain while God passed by. Subsequently there was a series of natural phenomena: a great wind, an earthquake, and fire. But God was in none of these. Instead, He revealed himself in a "still small voice" (1 Kings 19:12). God ordered Elijah to visit Syria and anoint Hazael king over that country. Then he was to anoint Jehu, a military leader, to be king over Israel. Next, he was to find Elisha and anoint him to be his successor as God's prophet.

Elijah next appears in the biblical record when God sends him to confront Ahab in Naboth's vineyard, where that wicked king had gone to take possession of it.

I. Ahab's Desire for Naboth's Vineyard (1 Kings 21:1-4)
A. Ahab's Offer (vv. 1, 2)

1. And it came to pass after these things, that Naboth the Jezreelite had a vineyard, which was in Jezreel, hard by the palace of Ahab king of Samaria.

After these things refers to a series of events recorded in 1 Kings 20. Ben-hadad, king of Syria, invaded Israel and besieged Samaria. With God's help, Ahab and his forces were able to defeat the Syrian forces and lift the siege. In a later conflict God enabled Ahab's outnumbered army to shatter completely Ben-hadad's forces, causing the Syrian king to plead for mercy.

Because he agreed to spare Ben-hadad in spite of the fact that God had condemned the Syrians to "utter destruction" (1 Kings 20:42), Ahab came under God's condemnation. An unnamed prophet brought the message of condemnation to Ahab: "Thy life shall go for his life, and thy people for his people" (v. 42). Ahab then returned to Samaria "heavy and displeased" (v. 43). It may be that he sought Naboth's vineyard as a diversion for the frightening news of his own coming death.

2. And Ahab spake unto Naboth, saying, Give me thy vineyard, that I may have it for a garden of herbs, because it is near unto my house: and I will give thee for it a better vineyard than it; or, if it seem good to thee, I will give thee the worth of it in money.

Ahab's capital was at Samaria, but he maintained another palace in Jezreel, which was located about twenty miles north of Samaria. Naboth owned a vineyard next to Ahab's palace in Jezreel. We are not told how large the plot of ground was, but if it was within the walls of the city, it could not have been large. Ahab wanted the plot for a kitchen garden where herbs could be grown for the royal table. He made Naboth what seemed to him a reasonable offer. He promised Naboth a better vineyard than the one he had, or if he preferred, he would buy it outright from him.

B. Naboth's Refusal (v. 3)

3. And Naboth said to Ahab, The LORD forbid it me, that I should give the inheritance of my fathers unto thee.

Naboth was a man of both courage and integrity. He had the courage to reject an offer from the king, and the courage to confess his faith in God before King Ahab, who worshiped Baal (1 Kings 16:31). The source of his courage was his faith in God, and his integrity is seen in his adherence to the laws God had given that governed the sale and transfer of land. The ancient law of the land bound property to a family (see Leviticus 25:23; Numbers 36:7). Naboth refused to sell his property to the king because he felt it was wrong for him to do so.

HERITAGE NOT FOR SALE

A certain widow was left with more real estate than she knows what to do with—at least, more than she can use. Her house has two stories, with several add-on ells. There are outbuildings, also, and multiple acres of land.

Well situated in a resort area, the property would bring a sizeable price. But it is not for sale. Too many memories live there. That is where she and her groom settled in a honey-

---

How to Say It

BEERSHEBA. Be-er-*she*-buh.
HAZAEL. *Haz*-uh-el or Haz-*zay*-el.
JEHU. *Jee*-hew.
JEZEBEL. *Jez*-uh-bel.
JEZREEL. *Jez*-re-el.
JEZREELITE. *Jez*-re-el-ite.
NABOTH. *Nay*-both (short "o" as in "*odd*").
THYATIRA. *Thy*-uh-*tie*-ruh (strong accent on *tie*, *th* as in *thin*).

moon cottage. They constructed the current residence practically with their bare hands, room by room by room. They enjoyed nearly forty years of married life in that spot.

We understand the widow's feelings, and we understand Naboth's, too. His vineyard was property inherited from cherished ancestors. It is likely that they sacrificed to provide it, and had worked endless hours to develop and maintain it. Such an inheritance is much more than a mere piece of real estate; it is an invaluable heritage, a link to past generations, a repository of blessed memories. What price tag could begin to reflect its worth?

Some treasures are simply not for sale.

—R. W. B.

C. Ahab's Disappointment (v. 4)

4. And Ahab came into his house heavy and displeased because of the word which Naboth the Jezreelite had spoken to him: for he had said, I will not give thee the inheritance of my fathers. And he laid him down upon his bed, and turned away his face, and would eat no bread.

Even though Ahab had strayed far from Jehovah, yet he respected the ancient laws enough that he would not use force to take the vineyard from Naboth. We know people in our times who, while abandoning the Christian faith, still have considerable respect for the ethical standards that that faith requires. The problem is that under pressure those standards give way because they are not based upon a solid foundation.

At Naboth's refusal, Ahab showed his immaturity by going home (probably his palace in the capital city, Samaria) and pouting like a spoiled child. This was no small pout, for he lay on his bed, turned his face to the wall, and refused to eat. Before we are too harsh on Ahab for his childishness, however, we need to take a look at some of our own actions. At times we are guilty of getting "out of sorts" over matters even more trivial than the disappointment that caused

Ahab's pout. Have we ever acted childishly when we haven't gotten our way in some matter in the church, or when we haven't received the recognition that we felt due us?

II. Ahab's Judgment
(1 Kings 21:15-20)

In verses 5 through 14 we learn the outcome of Ahab's effort to secure the vineyard. When Jezebel learned the reason for her husband's pout, she chided him for being such a weakling. When it became obvious that Ahab would not take action, Jezebel said, "Arise, and eat bread, and let thine heart be merry: I will give thee the vineyard of Naboth the Jezreelite."

Unconcerned about breaking any Israelite laws, Jezebel began to unfold a shameless plan that would accomplish her goal. She sent letters in Ahab's name to the leaders of Jezreel, instructing them to proclaim a fast and to set Naboth before the people. To proclaim a fast was to create the impression that the city was somehow disgraced. To set Naboth before the people was to bring him into the court of justice, as if he were the cause of the problem. Then the city leaders were to bring in two false witnesses who would testify that Naboth was guilty of blasphemy. The penalty for blasphemy was death by stoning (Leviticus 24:10-16), and this penalty was carried out once the guilty verdict was brought in against poor Naboth.

A. The Vineyard Available (v. 15)

15. And it came to pass, when Jezebel heard that Naboth was stoned, and was dead, that Jezebel said to Ahab, Arise, take possession of the vineyard of Naboth the Jezreelite, which he refused to give thee for money: for Naboth is not alive, but dead.

When the wicked deed was completed, Jezebel informed Ahab that the vineyard was his. She seemed to gloat over the fact that Naboth, who was too foolish to sell the plot of land to the king, ended up paying for it with his life. Second Kings 9:26 seems to indicate that not only was Naboth killed, but his sons as well. With any heirs out of the way, there would be no one to challenge Ahab's control of the vineyard. So often one sin leads to another.

B. Possession at Last! (v. 16)

16. And it came to pass, when Ahab heard that Naboth was dead, that Ahab rose up to go down to the vineyard of Naboth the Jezreelite, to take possession of it.

We can imagine that Ahab went down to the garden like some child who had just gotten a toy that had previously been denied him. It is likely that a sizeable entourage accompanied the king as he marched triumphantly down to the vineyard to claim his victory. A self-centered person such as Ahab would want to enjoy his victory in the presence of others. By possessing the property he would be demonstrating to his subjects that he was indeed king.

C. Pronouncement of Judgment
(vv. 17-19)

17-19. And the word of the LORD came to Elijah the Tishbite, saying, Arise, go down to meet Ahab king of Israel, which is in Samaria: behold, he is in the vineyard of Naboth, whither he is gone down to possess it. And thou shalt speak unto him, saying, Thus saith the LORD, Hast thou killed, and also taken possession? And thou shalt speak unto him, saying, Thus saith the LORD, In the place where dogs licked the blood of Naboth shall dogs lick thy blood, even thine.

We don't know where Elijah was when all this was happening. It is likely that he was in hiding, for he still feared the wrath of Jezebel. However, he could not have been far from Jezreel, because he was able to reach the vineyard only shortly after Ahab, coming, presumably, from Samaria, arrived there. Since Elijah traveled by foot, he must have been only a few miles away.

The message that Elijah was to deliver was short and to the point. Ahab was guilty of two sins—he had committed murder and he had taken property illegally. Both of these were serious crimes, and it is clear that God intended to deal with them. The punishment God pronounced would fit the crime. The dogs would lick the blood of Ahab just as they had licked the blood of Naboth. This judgment was fulfilled later, after Ahab was mortally wounded in battle. His blood flowed out into his chariot, and when the chariot was washed, the blood was licked up by dogs (1 Kings 22:34-38).

D. Confrontation of Prophet and King
(v. 20)

20. And Ahab said to Elijah, Hast thou found me, O mine enemy? And he answered, I have found thee: because thou hast sold thyself to work evil in the sight of the LORD.

At the moment of Ahab's celebration, suddenly Elijah appeared. At that moment the possession he had longed for and sulked about turned to ashes instantly. Ahab didn't need to ask why Elijah was there. He knew! His previous confrontations with Elijah had ended disastrously, and there was no reason to believe that this one would end any differently. Ahab's immediate response was to blame Elijah for his troubles. He tried to make it seem that Elijah was his enemy carrying out a personal vendetta against him. It is always easier to blame the messenger than it is to accept the message. Ahab refused to recognize the prophet as God's spokesman; instead, he viewed Elijah as an enemy trying to do him in. Actually, Elijah was the best friend Ahab had, one who tried to steer him aright; but Ahab refused to recognize that truth.

Elijah would not allow Ahab's personal attack to turn him aside from the message he had come to deliver. Ahab had sold himself to do evil, and for that reason anyone who opposed him was his enemy. How cheaply this wicked king had sold himself! For a vineyard, which couldn't have been more than a few square yards, he had sold his integrity, and worse, his eternal destiny. Even if we grant that Ahab was not directly involved in the murder of Naboth and the corruption of the officials who carried it out, nevertheless, he was willing to accept the fruits of the evil deeds of Jezebel.

The verses that follow the lesson text tell that the words of judgment had a profound impact upon Ahab. He "rent his clothes, and put sackcloth upon his flesh, and fasted, and lay in sackcloth, and went softly" (v. 27). The arrogant king, who had entered the garden so triumphantly to claim his ill-gotten possession, now left it in abject humility. This clearly was not just a public display that Ahab put on to impress those about him. It is obvious that his repentance was sincere, for God delayed part of the announced punishment (vv. 28, 29). The house of Ahab would fall, not in Ahab's days, but in the days of his son.

ACCESSORIES TO SIN

Indicted in the infamous Watergate case were more suspects than those who actually burglarized the offices of the Democratic party's headquarters. Several public officials, who were merely accessories to the crime, were convicted. They had knowledge of it and consented to it, if only by their silence. Even the president is not above the law that implicates accessories in such cases.

Jezebel wrote the letters that "put out a contract" on Naboth. But she signed Ahab's name, and affixed Ahab's seal to them. So Ahab became a consenting, if unwitting, partner in the assassination of his neighbor. Jezebel engineered the crime, and verse 23 following indicates the judgment that would fall on her. Ahab's hands, however, were not clean in this sordid affair. He was guilty as an accessory.

visual 3

Thou Shalt Not Covet

Is it possible that we too may be unwitting and silent accessories to sin? The church at Thyatira was rebuked by Jesus for tolerating "that woman Jezebel . . . to teach and to seduce my servants to commit fornication" (Revelation 2:20). The church is obligated to confront Christians with the errors of their ways, to call them to repentance, and to attempt to reclaim them for Christ by speaking the truth in love.

—R. W. B.

Conclusion

A. Above the Law

Many years ago an European nobleman, in order to impress some visiting noblemen, pointed out a man working in the courtyard below them. Then he took a gun and deliberately shot and killed the man. Some of the guests were appalled and insisted that when the king heard about it, he would have the nobleman brought to trial. The man snorted at the idea. "I'm too powerful for the king. He can't touch me!"

When the king heard about the incident, he was furious. There was nothing much that he could do, however, for he lacked the military strength to challenge the wicked nobleman. Then he had an idea. He issued an order that gave an automatic pardon to anyone who killed the nobleman. The man knew that he was almost universally hated, and he became so fearful for his life that he was afraid to leave his castle. Soon he was afraid of even his own servants, and before long his fear and isolation killed him.

Ahab was rather like this nobleman, thinking that he could live above the law. And he was above the law as far as his subjects were concerned. What he did not realize was that he would not be tried before a jury of his subjects but by the divine judge. There was no way that he could escape that court.

In our own times we have seen men and women, both in government service and in private life, who have acted as if they were above the law. They have stolen from the public till with apparent impunity, or they have flouted the standards of decency and morality of a shocked public. And they have gotten away with it—almost!

We may have no modern Elijahs to confront these arrogant evildoers in the midst of their wickedness, but God in Heaven holds high the sword of justice, and in His own time He will wield it with might.

B. Souls at a Bargain Basement Price

Facing Ahab in the ill-gotten vineyard, Elijah accused the king of having sold himself to work evil. He had sold himself as a slave to Satan. And how cheaply he had sold himself! For a few square feet of land that he wanted for an herb garden, he had mortgaged his soul. What about Judas? For thirty pieces of silver he had been willing to betray Jesus.

What about us? Have we ever entered into such an arrangement with Satan for some worthless trinket, for a fleeting moment in the spotlight, for a few minutes of pleasure? Yes, all of us at one time or another have mortgaged our souls to Satan at a bargain basement price. Thank God for Jesus, who paid the price of our redemption.

C. The Power Behind the Throne

Of the two, Ahab and Jezebel, Jezebel was clearly the more strong-willed. Brought up in the idolatrous culture of Phoenicia, she was not hindered by the ethical standards that every now and then seemed to hold Ahab in check. If she had ever had a conscience, it had long since been seared into total insensitivity. It didn't bother her a bit to forge letters to the public offi-cials in Jezreel and seal them with Ahab's seal. She didn't hesitate to corrupt these officials nor to bribe some wicked men to perjure them-selves. And if she ever had the slightest twinge of conscience about sending an innocent man and his sons to death, she never showed it.

Even though Ahab was a moral weakling, he cannot be let off the hook so easily. Far too often in our own times we have excused people of heinous behavior by allowing them to blame it on their neglected childhood or their inadequate education or their poverty. God did not excuse Ahab just because he had a wicked wife. God knew that Ahab had the power to say no at every step he took that drew him closer to moral disaster. That he didn't say no made him as guilty as Jezebel.

D. Justice Corrupted

Lord Acton once observed that "absolute power corrupts absolutely." The reign of Ahab illustrates that axiom very well. When Ahab couldn't get what he wanted, Jezebel took mat-ters in her own hands and, using the power of the throne, caused the courts of Jezreel to con-vict and execute an innocent man.

With the collapse of the Soviet Union and its satellites, we have been shocked at the reports of corruption and the abuse of power that existed in the countries behind the Iron Curtain. Even with all the checks and balances that are built into our system of government to protect us from this abuse of power, we have not been able to escape corruption. Every branch of our gov-ernment—executive, legislative, and judicial—has suffered from the corroding effects of greed and a lust for power.

We today may not have a call from God to right the wrongs of our society in the manner that Elijah did. But we do have in our hands powerful weapons that we can wield against the corruption we see about us—the freedoms of speech, press, and religion. Further, we have the power of the ballot box. Certainly we have a mandate from God to use this power to provide the best leadership possible for our nation.

E. Let Us Pray

Almighty God, we come to You concerned about the corruption we see on every hand. Keep us from becoming disheartened in our struggle against evil. Show us how we can use the tools we have to make a consistent witness for truth. In Jesus' name we pray. Amen.

F. Thought to Remember

One who has sold himself to do evil knows few restraints.

Home Daily Bible Readings

Monday, June 12—God Requires Justice and Faithfulness (Micah 6:6-13)

Tuesday, June 13—Naboth Refuses to Sell His Vineyard (1 Kings 21:1-7)

Wednesday, June 14—Jezebel Causes Naboth's Death (1 Kings 21:8-14)

Thursday, June 15—Ahab Seizes Naboth's Vineyard (1 Kings 21:15-19)

Friday, June 16—Elijah Judges Ahab and Jezebel (1 Kings 21:20-24)

Saturday, June 17—Ahab's Repentance Brings Temporary Reprieve (1 Kings 21:25-29)

Sunday, June 18—Evildoers Do Not Rever-ence God (Psalm 36)

Learning by Doing

This page contains an alternate lesson plan emphasizing learning activities. Classes desiring such student involvement will find these suggestions helpful.

Learning Goals

Lead your class members to do the following:
1. Determine God's attitude toward injustice.
2. Explore how Christians can promote justice in our nation.

Into the Lesson

Give copies of these statements to your students.

1. Christians in our nation aren't very concerned about justice.

2. Christians have a responsibility to take a stand against injustice.

3. Generally speaking, our national leaders are more concerned with personal gain than standing up for justice.

4. Generally speaking, Christians in our nation are more concerned with personal gain than standing up for justice.

5. There is very little that Christians can do to rid our nation of injustice.

Have students read each statement and put a plus sign (+) in front of the statement they agree with the most, and a minus sign (-) in front of the statement they disagree with the most. Allow a few seconds for them to decide. Then read each statement aloud and ask how many put a plus sign, and how many put a minus sign, for each. Ask why they selected the ones they did.

Help your class see the connection between this activity and today's Bible passage by saying, "In our study today we will consider a king who mocked justice, and we will see God's response. Let's look for some principles that God wants us to apply today."

Into the Word

Have your students form three groups. If you have more than twenty, form groups of six and give some duplicate assignments.

Using the four questions immediately following this paragraph, each group is to prepare an imaginary interview of the biblical person assigned to it. When the groups have done that, each group is to present its interview for the rest of the class.

Select a leader for each group to keep things moving. Each group is to select one person to be the interviewer, and one person to play the part of the assigned biblical character, when the group's interview is presented to the class. In their groups the students are to read 1 Kings 21:1-24 and then write answers they think their assigned person might have given to each question. The Biblical characters to be assigned are Ahab, Jezebel, and Elijah. Here are the questions:

1. From your perspective, what happened to Naboth? Why did it happen?

2. From your viewpoint, what were the results?

3. As you see it, how just was the situation?

4. What do you think God's opinion of the situation is?

Following the interviews, lead the class in discussing these questions: 1. What is justice? 2. Why does God demand that we deal justly and fairly with one another?

Option

Have a volunteer (or several volunteers) read 1 Kings 21:1-24 aloud to the class. Then lead the class in a discussion of these questions:

1. Was anything wrong with Ahab's original request of Naboth? (See verses 1-3.) Explain.

2. Jezebel plotted the injustice done to Naboth. Why was Ahab also condemned for it?

3. Based upon verses 17-24, how does God regard the perversion of justice?

4. How do these passages speak to the situation in 1 Kings 21; Jeremiah 22:3-5, 11-17; Micah 6:8?

5. Why does God demand that we deal justly and fairly with one another?

Into Life

Read Micah 6:6-8. Say, "It is clear from this passage and others that God abhors the unjust treatment of human beings. For a nation to please God, it must stand for justice. Its leaders must promote justice. Its courts must dispense justice. Its citizens must deal fairly with one another."

Our nation is committed to the just treatment of all its citizens. But we are not perfect in that regard. Have your students gather in their previous groups. Ask them to write some newspaper headlines one might read if existing injustices were removed from our society. Let the groups share their headlines with the class.

Ask, "What can Christians do to promote justice in our nation?" Allow discussion. Then close with prayer, asking God to help us be just in all our dealings.

Let's Talk It Over

The questions on this page are designed to encourage review of the lesson Scriptures and to promote discussion of the lesson by the class. The answers provided are only discussion starters. Let your class talk it over from there.

1. How can the sin of covetousness be a problem for affluent persons? How can we gain victory over covetousness?

One is inclined to suppose that persons with few material possessions would be greatly troubled by covetousness. One might also suspect that wealthy persons would have little reason to covet. In truth, however, covetousness is an attitude that can afflict both rich and poor. A person with the ability or resources to acquire many "wants," may be less prepared to handle the frustration of being denied. In the rich or poor, covetousness is linked with ingratitude. If a Christian focuses on being thankful for what he has, with emphasis on Christ's presence and the hope of eternal life, he will be less likely to covet (see Philippians 4:11; 1 Timothy 6:6-9).

2. What do we know about Naboth's value system? What are some principles a Christian should consider when making financial or business decisions?

Evidently Naboth did not value money more highly than everything else. From a strictly financial perspective, Naboth had good reason to accept King Ahab's offer for his vineyard. The king offered to give him a better vineyard for it, or a cash settlement, whichever Naboth preferred. But the value Naboth placed on his vineyard could not be measured tangibly. This parcel was part of his family's portion when the Israelites first settled the land. Having been passed down from generation to generation of his descendants, the land was his inheritance. He considered that it would dishonor God and his family to sell the land.

In financial decisions a Christian must consider the principle of stewardship. That simply means we recognize that everything belongs to God, and we are only managers of what He puts in our hands. Since all is His, our use of what is His—our spending, our investing, our giving— should honor Him. Our financial dealings, therefore, should be marked by honesty, frugality, and charity, not just shrewdness.

3. We have all heard the statement, "Every person has his price," meaning that when offered a large enough amount of money, or material gain, or carnal pleasure, every person will abandon his moral or ethical standards. What do you think of the accuracy of this statement?

The statement is false, but Satan would like for us to believe it is true. The Bible contains a number of examples of persons who maintained their faith and integrity, who held to their moral principles, in the face of strong temptation to do otherwise. Joseph, Moses, and Daniel and his three friends immediately come to mind. They would not sell their moral integrity. We today can make the same choice, and many do.

4. God's spokesman in Ahab's day was Elijah, and he did not shrink from exposing evil and prodding conscience. What is a Christian's responsibility in this regard?

Jesus is described as the light that God sent into the world to lead men out of spiritual darkness (John 3:16-19). In that passage we see that one purpose of the light is to reveal or expose the deeds of men (v. 20). Jesus has called His followers to share in that work, to be "the light of the world" (Matthew 5:14). Christians are to live such godly lives that the contrast between godliness and evil will be clearly seen by all. Even though we may agree on this responsibility, we may not agree on the most expedient way of fulfilling it. For some it may mean the positive, consistent witness of a life lived in obedience and reverence to God. Others may feel compelled to picket, boycott, demonstrate, launch petition drives etc., in exposing evil. If we fail to lift a voice of warning in some way, however, we have little cause to complain about the injustices of the Ahabs and Jezebels around us. We are responsible for the warning, not for the response to the warning. See Ezekiel 33:7-9.

5. Ahab referred to Elijah as his enemy. Was Elijah an enemy to Ahab? Why or why not?

Elijah was God's messenger, a voice for truth and justice. As such he was an enemy of wickedness and injustice. Elijah pointed out Ahab's sin, but not because he hated Ahab. If Ahab had responded with repentance and humility from the beginning, he could have been blessed. Then he would have realized that Elijah, instead of being his enemy, in reality was his friend. (See Proverbs 27:6.)

A Day of Good News

DEVOTIONAL READING: 1 Thessalonians 5:8-18.

LESSON SCRIPTURE: 2 Kings 6:24—7:20.

PRINTED TEXT: 2 Kings 7:1-9.

2 Kings 7:1-9

1 Then Elisha said, Hear ye the word of the LORD; Thus saith the LORD, Tomorrow about this time shall a measure of fine flour be sold for a shekel, and two measures of barley for a shekel, in the gate of Samaria.

2 Then a lord on whose hand the king leaned answered the man of God, and said, Behold, if the LORD would make windows in heaven, might this thing be? And he said, Behold, thou shalt see it with thine eyes, but shalt not eat thereof.

3 And there were four leprous men at the entering in of the gate: and they said one to another, Why sit we here until we die?

4 If we say, We will enter into the city, then the famine is in the city, and we shall die there: and if we sit still here, we die also. Now therefore come, and let us fall unto the host of the Syrians: if they save us alive, we shall live; and if they kill us, we shall but die.

5 And they rose up in the twilight, to go unto the camp of the Syrians: and when they were come to the uttermost part of the camp of Syria, behold, there was no man there.

6 For the LORD had made the host of the Syrians to hear a noise of chariots, and a noise of horses, even the noise of a great host: and they said one to another, Lo, the king of Israel hath hired against us the kings of the Hittites, and the kings of the Egyptians, to come upon us.

7 Wherefore they arose and fled in the twilight, and left their tents, and their horses, and their asses, even the camp as it was, and fled for their life.

8 And when these lepers came to the uttermost part of the camp, they went into one tent, and did eat and drink, and carried thence silver, and gold, and raiment, and went and hid it; and came again, and entered into another tent, and carried thence also, and went and hid it.

9 Then they said one to another, We do not well: this day is a day of good tidings, and we hold our peace: if we tarry till the morning light, some mischief will come upon us: now therefore come, that we may go and tell the king's household.

GOLDEN TEXT: This day is a day of good tidings . . . come, that we may go and tell.
—2 Kings 7:9.

A Nation Turns From God
Unit 1: The Price of Power
(Lessons 1-4)

Lesson Aims

As a result of studying this lesson, each student should:

1. Understand that God works in the affairs of nations.

2. Share the good news of salvation in Christ with someone who does not know it.

Lesson Outline

Visual 4 of the visuals packet emphasizes man's duty to share lifesaving news. The visual is shown on page 373.

Introduction

A. Good News

In late 1814 a large British force entered the Gulf of Mexico and headed toward New Orleans. Their objective was to capture that city, a major port for Americans living in what was then the West, and close off their shipping and receiving of supplies via the Mississippi River. The force landed and proceeded toward New Orleans, but they were met by an American army led by General Andrew Jackson. A fierce battle ensued. The Americans, fighting from behind a makeshift fortress built of bales of cotton, repulsed the British, inflicting severe losses upon them.

Ironically, this battle need never have been fought. The Treaty of Ghent, signed two weeks before the battle, had already ended the War of 1812. Because neither the telegraph nor the radio had been invented yet, the good news of the war's end did not reach New Orleans in time to prevent the battle.

As Christians we have good news for those locked in deadly battle with Satan. That good news is that Christ died to give men and women the victory over the powers of evil. What if we don't deliver that good news? Or what if we deliver it too late? Our lesson touches on good news and how we should deal with it.

B. Lesson Background

Upon the completion of his earthly ministry the prophet Elijah was taken up into Heaven, and his prophetic mantle fell on Elisha. Elisha continued the ministry that Elijah conducted in the kingdom of Israel. War between Israel and Syria had broken out once again. The Syrians under Ben-hadad had besieged Samaria, the capital of Israel. (In some modern translations the Syrians are called Arameans.) This siege had reduced the people to starvation, causing some of them even to resort to cannibalism (2 Kings 6:24-29). Learning of this, Jehoram, who was king of Israel, rent his garments and donned sackcloth as a sign of contrition. Blaming Elisha for the horrible conditions that existed, the king ordered the execution of the prophet and sent one of his court officers to carry it out. Relenting, it seems, from his hasty decision, the king himself came to Elisha's home (vv. 30-33).

I. Elisha's Prophecies
(2 Kings 7:1, 2)

A. Plenty by Tomorrow (v. 1)

1. Then Elisha said, Hear ye the word of the LORD: Thus saith the LORD, Tomorrow about this time shall a measure of fine flour be sold for a shekel, and two measures of barley for a shekel, in the gate of Samaria.

Even as Elisha spoke up, his life hung in the balance. The man whom the king had sent to kill Elisha was still there, and the king had not revoked his order to the man. The prophet's fate depended on how the king responded to his words. Elisha made it clear that the words he uttered were the *word of the Lord.*

The message was one of hope. Tomorrow, food would be available for the starving city. The *measure* is actually a "seah," which seems to have been nearly two gallons. In this period the *shekel* was not a coin, but a measure of weight, probably of silver. It is impossible to give an exact value for it. Most commentators indicate that a shekel was a high price to pay for a measure of flour, but it would be much less than the prices then current during the siege (see 2 Kings 6:25). The point is that food would be available this same time the next day. The famine would have ended. Elisha's obvious meaning was that the siege of the city was soon to be lifted. It was a common practice for business transactions to take place *in the gate.*

B. Prophecy Rejected (v. 2a)

2a. Then a lord on whose hand the king leaned answered the man of God, and said, Behold, if the LORD would make windows in heaven, might this thing be?

A lord on whose hand the king leaned. The word *lord* here is often translated "captain," a military officer who accompanied the king. The king did not immediately reply to Elisha, and so the officer spoke up. "Even if God opened the windows of Heaven," he insisted, "this could not happen!" Thus the officer expressed his disbelief in Elisha's prediction, and in the power of God.

C. Further Prediction (v. 2b)

2b. And he said, Behold, thou shalt see it with thine eyes, but shalt not eat thereof.

Elisha's prediction about the coming availability of food was precise. His prediction about what would befall this officer, however, is vague, perhaps deliberately so. If the officer would see the rising of the siege but not eat any of the food that would become available as a result, then obviously Elisha was predicting his death. Verses 17-20 of this chapter tell us of the outcome of this prophecy. After it was discovered that the Syrians had fled, the king appointed the officer to be in charge of the gate. At the news that there was food outside the walls of the city, the hungry people inside the city panicked and stampeded through the gate, trampling the officer to death.

WINDOWS IN HEAVEN

"When God shuts a door, He often opens a window." If the death of a loved one slams life's door in your face, God opens a window of comfort. When a door of opportunity closes, God opens a window of hope. Just as doors sometimes swing shut on today's dreams, God's window lets in the light of tomorrow's possibilities.

God seemed to have closed the door on His people in Samaria when the Syrians besieged the city. The gates were literally shut against enemy attacks. Inside, famine had reduced some citizens to cannibalism. Most were convinced that they would starve to death.

Then God opened a window of hope! Through His prophet Elisha, an imminent miracle was announced. The siege would end, and food would once more be available to even the poorest people of the city.

The king's aide was cynical. "In your dreams!" he seemed to say. He had lost all hope for the city. By God's miracle, however, the windows of Heaven did open, and the blessings of deliverance poured forth. It was as if the unwitting prophecy of the sarcastic aide was being fulfilled.

Faith, *hope* and *love* are the names of God's windows in Heaven. His light of life dispels disappointment, doubt, and despair.   —R. W. B.

II. Four Lepers' Decision
(2 Kings 7:3, 4)

A. Facing the Future (v. 3)

3. And there were four leprous men at the entering in of the gate: and they said one to another, Why sit we here until we die?

The law prohibited lepers to live inside a city (Leviticus 13:45, 46; Numbers 5:1-4). So they would gather about the city gate, where, presumably, their friends inside the city would bring food for them. Because of the siege of Samaria and the accompanying famine, the plight of these four lepers was worse than usual.

B. Decision to Act (v. 4)

4. If we say, We will enter into the city, then the famine is in the city, and we shall die there: and if we sit still here, we die also. Now therefore come, and let us fall unto the host of Syrians: if they save us alive, we shall live; and if they kill us, we shall but die.

The lepers' choices were limited. Even if they could sneak into the city, what good would it

---

How to Say It

ARAMEANS.   *Ar*-uh-*me*-unz (strong accent on *me*).
BEN-HADAD.   Ben-*hay*-dad.
ELISHA.   Ee-*lye*-shuh.
HITTITES.   *Hit*-ites or *Hit*-tites.
PHARAOH.   *Fair*-o or *Fay*-ro.
SAMARIA.   Suh-*meh*-ri-uh.
SYRIANS.   *Sear*-ee-unz.

do? The famine was there, no less than on the outside of the city, and they would die there. Or they could remain where they were and die from starvation. Their third option, and the one they chose, was to leave the gate and surrender to the Syrian army, which surrounded the city. They probably believed that the Syrians would kill them. If that happened, at least they would not suffer a long, lingering death. They even may have entertained a glimmer of hope that the Syrians might spare them. If the Syrians had heard about the healing of Naaman (2 Kings 5:8-14), perhaps they might remember it and extend them mercy.

NOTHING TO LOSE

A young couple and their baby were trapped by a mountain blizzard miles from civilization. Their car was immobilized. They took shelter in a small cave, but after several hours there, this courageous father made a decision. "We can all stay here and die, or I can try to make it down the mountain for help." Struggling through blinding snow in freezing temperatures, this young hero managed to trudge more than fifty miles to a ranger station. Rescuers soon found the mother and child, alive and without serious injury.

Their story is one that is truly inspiring. The husband/father told everyone how he came to make his hard decision. "There was nothing to lose. I decided not to let my family die without trying to save us."

The lepers at the gate of Samaria made a similar decision. "We have nothing to lose, and perhaps we'll live," they reasoned as they ventured into the enemy camp. They too survived, along with all Israel, rescued by God.

We who have chosen to follow Christ in this life know we have nothing to lose (and everything to gain). We know that our physical lives must end, but we trust Christ, who promises, "Whosoever liveth and believeth in me shall never die" (John 11:26). We stake our eternal destiny on that truth.   —R. W. B.

III. The Lepers' Discovery (2 Kings 7:5-8)

A. Empty Camp (v. 5)

5. And they rose up in the twilight, to go unto the camp of the Syrians: and when they were come to the uttermost part of the camp of Syria, behold, there was no man there.

In the twilight. The lepers may have waited until after sunset to avoid being seen deserting to the enemy and consequently being shot by archers on the walls of the city.

The uttermost part of the camp of Syria. This was the most advanced part of Syria's forces, the part nearest the city of Samaria. The lepers would have come to it first. Imagine their surprise and joy when, expecting mistreatment or even death, they found the camp abandoned!

B. Explanation (vv. 6, 7)

6. For the LORD had made the host of the Syrians to hear a noise of chariots, and a noise of horses, even the noise of a great host: and they said one to another, Lo, the king of Israel hath hired against us the kings of the Hittites, and the kings of the Eyptians, to come upon us.

Clearly this was a miracle. As darkness approached (v. 7), the Lord caused the sound of a mighty, advancing army to fall on the ears of the Syrian forces, an army they did not want to meet in combat. The Syrians' first thought was that the king of Israel had hired Hittite and Egyptian mercenaries to come to his rescue. The Hittites were located north of Syria. Both the Hittites and the Egyptians had centuries of experience in chariot warfare, and were considered skilled in the use of this weapon. Pharaoh of Egypt had used chariots in an attempt to prevent the Israelites from escaping (Exodus 14:7, 9, 17).

7. Wherefore they arose and fled in the twilight, and left their tents, and their horses, and their asses, even the camp as it was, and fled for their life.

This chaotic rout of the Syrian army occurred also in the twilight. It seems, therefore, that not long before the lepers entered the camp on the side nearest the city, the Syrians had fled the camp, going out the opposite side. In their haste the Syrians even left their animals tethered where they were (v. 10). The animals would not have had saddles or bridles on, and to equip them for riding would have taken more time than the frightened men dared take. They *fled for their life.*

C. Food and Treasure (v. 8)

8. And when these lepers came to the uttermost part of the camp, they went into one tent, and did eat and drink, and carried thence silver, and gold, and raiment, and went and hid it; and came again, and entered into another tent, and carried thence also, and went and hid it.

When the four lepers entered the camp, the only sign of life they saw in the gathering darkness was the animals—they neither saw nor heard any soldier. When it became obvious that the Syrians had abandoned the camp, the men satisfied their immediate need—food. After they had eaten their fill, they began to look over the wealth that had been left behind.

visual 4

For years, perhaps, these men had lived in abject poverty. Now they were surrounded by tents in which were all kinds of treasure. Since they could not carry with them all the wealth they found, they *hid it*, probably in the ground. Their plan, no doubt, was to come back later and retrieve it.

IV. Sharing Good News
(2 Kings 7:9)

9. Then they said one to another, We do not well: this day is a day of good tidings, and we hold our peace: if we tarry till the morning light, some mischief will come upon us: now therefore come, that we may go and tell the king's household.

It may be, as some suggest, that the lepers' consciences were pricked when they stopped to realize that they were keeping this good news to themselves, all the while people inside the city were starving to death. It also seems that they were concerned about what would happen to them if they didn't share this good news. *Some mischief will come upon us.* The *New International Version* translates this, "punishment will overtake us." This suggests that the lepers began to think that if they kept quiet about this good news and spent the whole night gratifying only themselves, they would be found out when the morning came and would suffer punishment for what they had done.

In some respects we who are Christians are like these lepers. We have come upon a vast treasure—the wonderful news that Christ saves sinful men. We should, of course, rejoice in that fact. At the same time, however, we have a moral obligation to share it with others. More than that, we have a divine mandate to do so. The lepers knew that they would be punished if they didn't do what was right. Dare we neglect the Lord's mandate?

Once the men realized the situation they were in, they returned to the city with the good news. At first, the king was skeptical, fearing that the Syrians were setting an ambush for him. So he sent out scouts, who, when they returned, confirmed the word of the lepers. Word quickly swept through the city, and the people rushed out to gather the food and wealth the Syrians had left behind. In the process two of Elisha's prophecies were fulfilled. A measure of fine flour did sell for a shekel, and two measures of barley for a shekel (v. 16). Further, the officer who had ridiculed Elisha's prophecy was trampled under foot by the people as they rushed out of the gate (v. 20).

GO AND TELL

What a relief finally to hear some good news! *Communism No Longer a Threat! Spiritual Revival in Russia! Israelis and Arabs Come to the Peace Table! Divorce Rate Declines!*

Such headlines as these are good news, indeed. To suppress word of these positive happenings and trends would be unthinkable. Good news is for sharing.

The lepers who discovered that the Syrian camp was deserted had some mighty good news to share. Even in the middle of the night, they knew that the mystifying departure of the enemy troops must be reported. Motivated by both privilege and obligation, they returned to Samaria and told the gatekeepers, who told the king, who told advisers—and so the news spread quickly.

Christians have incredibly good news to share—the gospel of Jesus Christ. It is a privilege to report that God has delivered mankind from sin and death. It also is an obligation to tell the lost of God's love, and of His plan for our redemption. Like the friends of Jesus who first discovered the empty tomb, let us "go and tell" that He is risen from the dead, that He can save, that He is Lord!   —R. W. B.

Conclusion
A. Just Suppose

Just suppose that the four lepers had remained in the Syrian camp, gathering up the treasures the fleeing enemy had left behind. Just suppose they had worked throughout the night on this self-aggrandizing mission and had waited until the next day to report to those trapped in the city what they had found.

The four might have gotten away with it—at least for a while. Since no one had seen them, there would have been no reason for accusing them of wrongdoing. However, there may have been serious consequences for the people within the city had the men not reported the good news. For some inside the city on the verge of starvation, even the delay of a few hours might have brought death. Others may have been driven to violence by their hunger, and may have robbed or even killed to get food.

What about the lepers themselves? Suppose they had worn some of the expensive garments they had taken from the Syrians' tents. Wouldn't someone have begun to ask questions? It isn't likely that lepers ordinarily wore new, expensive clothing. Suppose they had tried to spend some of the gold or silver they had hidden away. Wouldn't this have raised further questions? The simple fact is that they couldn't have enjoyed the fruits of their venture very long before someone would have become suspicious and found out the truth.

"Be sure your sin will find you out" (Numbers 32:23). How often this is true, even with the person who thinks he has committed the perfect crime! But does one ever really get away with it? Even if one goes to his grave without being caught, he has to live with his own conscience. That can be a more severe judge than any earthly judge. Suppose, however, that one has so dulled his conscience that he never feels its pangs—and some have done that! The grave does not end it all. Beyond this life one must face the divine Judge, who not only knows all the facts, but who will deal with them according to His eternal laws.

B. "No Man Is an Island"

John Donne once observed that "no man is an island . . . every man is part of the main." In an age that stresses individualism to the point of selfishness, many seem to have forgotten that fact. Certainly, every one of us is an individual, and each person must bear individual responsibility for his or her actions. No one can repent for another person who sins, and no one can stand before God in another's stead.

Home Daily Bible Readings

Monday, June 19—A Prayer for God's Help (Psalm 86:1-7)

Tuesday, June 20—God Does Wondrous Things (Psalm 86:8-17)

Wednesday, June 21—Syria's Siege Brings Famine in Samaria (2 Kings 6:24-29)

Thursday, June 22—Elisha's Assurance of Imminent Relief (2 Kings 6:30—7:2)

Friday, June 23—Lepers Find the Syrian Camp Abandoned (2 Kings 7:3-8)

Saturday, June 24—The Lepers Report the Good News (2 Kings 7:9-15)

Sunday, June 25—Relief From Siege and Famine (2 Kings 7:16-20)

Our individual responsibilities notwithstanding, we have responsibilities that go beyond our own immediate concern. We owe a great debt to our parents, who brought us into this world and sustained us through our fragile years. We owe thanks to those who across the centuries have sacrificed and worked that we may enjoy the blessings of freedom and affluence. Most of all, we owe a debt to our Savior, who left His heavenly home to bring us salvation.

What have we done to pay back some of this debt we owe? Too often we're like the four lepers. We become so busy stashing away treasure for ourselves that we forget others who need what we are hiding away. These men finally came to their senses and thought about the people in the besieged city, who needed some of the things they were hiding. Let us be alert to the needs of others and do what we can for them.

C. The Best News

For those starving survivors trapped in Samaria, there could have been no better news than that which the lepers brought them—food was available. Hearing this good news, they stampeded through the city streets and out the gate to the vacated Syrian camp. We who are Christians have better news—nay, the best news: Christ died to save sinful men. All about us people are starving spiritually. Jesus Christ, who is the bread of life, alone can satisfy their souls' hunger. Are we tarrying to take this good news to them? Or are we too busy seeking and hiding away the treasures that never can completely satisfy? Could it be that we are not quite sure in our own mind that the Bread of Life will sustain?

Someone has observed that we ought to share the good news of the gospel with all the intensity of one starving beggar telling another starving beggar where bread can be found. Let us not "tarry till the morning light," but let us, as did the lepers, hurry to the starving people and let them know that this is a day of good tidings.

D. Let Us Pray

Dear Father, help us not to forget those who are needy. May we share our physical blessings with them, but more important, may we share the good news of salvation with those all about us. Give us a passion for lost souls. Give us the courage to seek them out. Show us how to share with them the greatest news of all—that You loved us so much that You gave Your Son to die for us. In His name we pray. Amen.

E. Thought to Remember

"Woe is unto me, if I preach not the gospel!" (1 Corinthians 9:16).

Learning by Doing

*This page contains an alternate lesson plan emphasizing learning activities. Classes
desiring such student involvement will find these suggestions helpful.*

Learning Goals

In this session you will seek to lead your students to do the following:

1. Analyze the decision of the four lepers in 1 Kings 7 who shared their newly acquired provisions.

2. Become more aware of the needs of others and more willing to meet those needs.

Into the Lesson

Write the following incomplete statement on the chalkboard before class begins:

Most people would be more generous if—

Begin this session by asking your class members to pair off. Give each pair a pen and a sheet of paper and ask them to complete the sentence in at least five ways. Allow two minutes for the pairs to complete this activity.

After two minutes call time. Ask for volunteers to share several of their completions and discuss these as necessary. Then make the transition into the lesson by saying, "Our study today will introduce us to four men who chose to be generous rather than hoard the much-needed supplies that came into their possession."

Option

Bring to class several pages of newspaper comics. Have the class form groups of three. Distribute one page of comics to each group. Obviously you will need to bring a page for every three persons whom you anticipate will be in class. It may be necessary for you to ask several class members to bring a page of comics so you will have enough.

Ask half of the groups to look for cartoon strips that illustrate selfishness or acquiring things. Ask the other half to look for comic strips that illustrate generosity. Allow several minutes for the groups to do their searching. Then ask for volunteers to share the illustrations they found.

Into the Word

In order for your students to gain the full significance of the events recorded in the Scripture text assigned for this lesson, it is necessary that they understand the historical background of the passage. This may be found in 2 Kings 6:24-33. Present a brief lecture (three to five minutes in length) based on these verses. Refer also to the comments included in the Lesson Background section of the commentary portion of the lesson material. After you have established the background, ask a volunteer (whom you contacted during the week before class) to read the lesson's printed text aloud to the class. Then lead your class in discussing the following questions based on the text (2 Kings 7:1-9).

1. Elisha prophesied that within a day the siege of Samaria would be lifted (v. 1). The "lord" (that is, the king's officer) who was standing in Elisha's presence, would see it but would not eat of the food that would become available (v. 2). What was Elisha's meaning? (See verses 17-20.)

2. What was the condition of the four men at the city gate? (v. 3)

3. What were their options? (v. 4)

4. What change in the situation of these men took place? (vv. 5-8).

5. What was their response to their incredible find? (v. 9)

6. What arguments might these four men have used for not sharing the good news of their find? (See question 4 in "Let's Talk It Over" on page 376.)

7. What principles do we need to learn from these four men?

Into Life

Point out to the class that the four men refused to keep their good news to themselves, and they refused to hoard the provisions God had given them. They were willing to sacrifice for the good of others.

Lead your class members in discussing the following questions to help them make personal application of the principles we have seen illustrated by the four men in the lesson text.

1. What do we have that we could share with others? (Time, skills, material resources.)

2. How generous does God want us to be with what we have?

3. What causes us sometimes to be less than generous with our resources?

4. How can we develop a more generous heart?

5. The good news that every Christian has to share is the gospel of Christ. What one step can we take this coming week to share the news of salvation with someone who needs to hear it?

Let's Talk It Over

The questions on this page are designed to encourage review of the lesson Scriptures and to promote discussion of the lesson by the class. The answers provided are only discussion starters. Let your class talk it over from there.

1. When the promises of God run against circumstances or conventional wisdom, what can we do to strengthen our faith in Him?

Elisha's prophecy that flour and barley would be readily available in Samaria the next day must have seemed preposterous. The only apparent reason for believing it was confidence in Elisha as a prophet of God. Elisha had already demonstrated the power of God in several ways. Therefore anyone familiar with his reputation might trust his credibility.

Some of the promises given to Christians stretch credulity. "Seek ye first the kingdom of God, and his righteousness; and all these things shall be added unto you" (Matthew 6:33). "Whosoever will save his life shall lose it; but whosoever shall lose his life for my sake and the gospel's, the same shall save it" (Mark 8:35). The amount of trust we put in these promises depends upon the credibility we attribute to their Author. The more we know of Jesus, the more we know of His power to deliver on His promises, the stronger our faith becomes.

2. One who scoffed at Elisha's prophecy was told he would see it come to pass but would not personally benefit from it. Are unbelievers today missing out on blessings that believers in Christ enjoy? Name some blessings promised to believers.

Eternal life is promised to those who believe in Christ (John 3:16, 36). Other blessings promised to believers are answered prayer (John 15:7), help in trouble (Hebrews 4:16), forgiveness (1 John 1:9), and personal peace (Philippians 4:6, 7), to name a few. How great is the personal loss of not believing in Jesus!

3. God caused the Syrians to be overcome with fear. Have you ever withdrawn from a situation because of fears that you now believe were unfounded? How could you have faced down your fears?

Far too often we withdraw early from challenges or conflicts because we imagine we will fail or lose, and we are afraid of the prospect. We will never know what is possible if we surrender before we are put to the test. It may be participating in sports or academic competition, choosing a college or career, asking that special person for a date, or deciding to start a business, to adopt a child, or to volunteer at a local mission. We can face our fears by asking for an objective assessment of our chances of success. Accept the counsel of trusted advisers. Try to subdivide the challenge into smaller parts that can be tackled one at a time. Success in the first increments gives one courage to go further. Be sure to count all your resources, including divine help for worthy goals.

4. What statements might the lepers have offered to justify hoarding the wealth left by the Syrians? How does that compare with the way people justify selfishness today? What is wrong with their arguments?

"Finders keepers." "We have been poor all our lives; we deserve this now." "God must have meant for us to have it." "We took the risk . . . ." Today we hear similar attempts to defend selfish hoarding: "I work hard for my money . . . ," "I sacrificed to go to college so I could get this job . . . ," "God has rewarded me with wealth, and I am going to enjoy it." Overlooked in these statements is God's claim upon all that we are and all that we have. Yes, we may work hard and we may be brilliant; but where did we get our strength, our health, our intelligence, our opportunities, our resources? Most of what we take pride in can be attributed to the circumstances of our birth. In the final analysis, we owe everything to God. He allows us to manage varying portions of His wealth.

5. What motivated the lepers to go to the king with their discovery? What should motivate us to share the good news of salvation?

First, the lepers realized that their discovery was too wonderful to keep to themselves. People who could be saved by this news were dying. Second, they realized that they could be punished if it was discovered later that they withheld this news.

The gospel is good news that can save people and bring an end to suffering. It is news we ought to share out of compassion for those who are perishing. It is news we are commanded to share (Mark 16:15). Failing to do so could cause us to be judged "wicked and slothful" (Matthew 25:26-30).

Condemnation for National Wrongdoing

DEVOTIONAL READING: Psalm 82.

LESSON SCRIPTURE: Amos 1:1—3:2.

PRINTED TEXT: Amos 2:4-8; 3:1, 2.

Amos 2:4-8

4 Thus saith the LORD; For three transgressions of Judah, and for four, I will not turn away the punishment thereof; because they have despised the law of the LORD, and have not kept his commandments, and their lies caused them to err, after the which their fathers have walked:

5 But I will send a fire upon Judah, and it shall devour the palaces of Jerusalem.

6 Thus saith the LORD; For three transgressions of Israel, and for four, I will not turn away the punishment thereof; because they sold the righteous for silver, and the poor for a pair of shoes;

7 That pant after the dust of the earth on the head of the poor, and turn aside the way of the meek: and a man and his father will go in unto the same maid, to profane my holy name:

8 And they lay themselves down upon clothes laid to pledge by every altar, and they drink the wine of the condemned in the house of their god.

Amos 3:1, 2

1 Hear this word that the LORD hath spoken against you, O children of Israel, against the whole family which I brought up from the land of Egypt, saying,

2 You only have I known of all the families of the earth: therefore I will punish you for all your iniquities.

GOLDEN TEXT: You only have I known of all the families of the earth: therefore I will punish you for all your iniquities.—Amos 3:2.

A Nation Turns From God
Unit 2: The Approaching Judgment
(Lessons 5-9)

Lesson Aims

After this lesson, each student should:

1. Understand that the actions of a nation have consequences.

2. Understand that the actions of a nation are determined by the actions of its citizens.

3. Appreciate the importance of having absolute standards to govern human conduct.

Lesson Outline

INTRODUCTION
    A. An Avalanche of Sin
    B. Lesson Background
  I. JUDGMENT UPON JUDAH (Amos 2:4, 5)
    A. Their Sins Were Multiplied (v. 4a)
    B. They Despised the Law (v. 4b)
      Three or Four National Sins
    C. A Judgment of Fire Upon Judah (v. 5)
 II. JUDGMENT UPON ISRAEL (Amos 2:6-8)
    A. Their Sins Were Multiplied (v. 6a)
    B. They Were Unjust (v. 6b)
    C. They Were Greedy (v. 7a)
    D. They Engaged in Sexual Sins (v. 7b
      Profanity
    E. They Became Drunk (v. 8)
III. THEY FORGOT GOD'S BLESSINGS (Amos 3:1, 2)
    A. God's Word Was Spoken Against Them
      (v. 1a)
    B. They Had Forgotten the Exodus (v. 1b)
    C. They Had Been Greatly Blessed (v. 2)
      Tough Love
CONCLUSION
    A. Amos, Our Contemporary
    B. Seeking a Plumbline
    C. Let Us Pray
    D. Thought to Remember

Visual 5 of the visuals packet shows behaviors that bring God's punishment on nations. This chart is pictured on page 380.

Introduction

A. An Avalanche of Sin

Several years ago in the Alps a heavy snowfall accumulated high on a mountainside. Something disturbed the snow near the top of the mountain, and it started to slide. Soon a mighty avalanche thundered down the slope, carrying rocks and trees with it. The snow and the debris swept across a narrow valley, blocking a small stream. This barrier effectively dammed the stream, and water began to build up behind the barrier. Before long a sizable lake had formed. After a while the water burst through the dam, and a mighty flood swept down the valley to the village below, destroying everything before it.

The situation in Judah and Israel was rather like this. Like the heavy snowfall, their sins has been growing and accumulating. God delayed His judgment for a time, but eventually His justice would prevail. It came first upon Israel, the northern kingdom. Like a mighty avalanche, Assyria swept down upon that nation and destroyed it. Judgment was delayed awhile for Judah, but finally that nation came to feel God's wrath at the hands of the Babylonians.

Through Amos and other prophets, God gave the people a chance to repent and turn back before it was too late. But they were so entrapped in their sins that they did not heed the word of the Lord. Would Amos get a better hearing among us today if he should come back with the same message?

B. Lesson Background

Both Israel and Judah were enjoying prosperity and freedom from external threats. Egypt was in a period of decline, Assyria was also in a temporary decline, and Babylonia had not yet come on the scene as a major power.

Both Israel and Judah squandered the wealth that this respite brought them. The rich were becoming richer at the expense of the poor, who were becoming poorer. Not only did the rich often gain their wealth underhandedly, they frequently wasted it on luxuries and riotous living. Both nations were on their way to becoming prodigals, storing up for themselves God's righteous indignation.

God sent a warning before He sent judgment. His messenger was Amos, a shepherd from the remote village of Tekoa, about seven miles south of Bethlehem. Amos had no special training for the ministry to which he was called (Amos 7:14), yet he was a powerful proclaimer

How to Say It

AMMON. *Am*-mun.
ASSYRIA. Uh-*sear*-ee-uh.
CANAANITES. *Kay*-nan-ites.
JEROBOAM. Jair-o-*bo*-um.
SINAI. *Sye*-nay-eye or *Sye*-nye.
TEKOA. Tee-*koe*-uh.

of God's message. Although he was a native of Judah, his prophetic ministry was to the northern kingdom. While we cannot precisely date his ministry, we know it occurred when Jeroboam II was king of Israel and Uzziah was king of Judah, about 750 B.C. or a bit earlier.

I. Judgment Upon Judah
(Amos 2:4, 5)

A. Their Sins Were Multiplied (v. 4a)

4a. Thus saith the LORD; For three transgressions of Judah, and for four, I will not turn away the punishment thereof.

The book of Amos opens with denunciations directed at Israel's neighbors: Damascus, Gaza, Tyrus, Edom, Ammon, and Moab. No doubt his audience, the citizens of the northern kingdom, greeted these denunciations with loud amens, because all of the people mentioned were their enemies. Then Amos turned his attention to Judah, the southern kingdom. He probably got some strong amens for this too, because Israel and Judah had often been at odds.

B. They Despised the Law (v. 4b)

4b. Because they have despised the law of the LORD, and have not kept his commandments, and their lies caused them to err, after the which their fathers have walked.

The denunciation of Israel's other neighbors came because of their cruel and violent acts committed in war, including acts against Israel. But while Judah may have been guilty of similar violence, her condemnation was on a different basis. She was denounced because she had *despised the law of the Lord:* that is, she had broken the covenant God had made with His people at Mount Sinai. The audience must have taken special delight in this denunciation, because Judah had always claimed that she was the defender of the covenant while Israel was accused of being the covenant breaker. We can almost savor their delight as they heard Judah being denounced by one of her own citizens.

Not only had the people of Judah broken the covenant, but they had done so by chasing after false gods. Thus the *New International Version* translates this portion of the verse: "They have been led astray by false gods, the gods their ancestors followed."

THREE OR FOUR NATIONAL SINS

Headlines on scandal sheets are sometimes amusing (for example, "Two-Headed Two-Year-Old Quarrels Alone"), often disgusting, usually ridiculous, and almost always fictitious. Thinking people rarely take them seriously. Television counterparts to such yellow journalism may be a bit more credible, but still cater to the public appetite for sensationalism.

"Investigative reporting" seems to delight in digging up dirt about dignitaries. Wouldn't it be a surprise if any of them featured the *Sins of Our Nation*? Headline: *Four Vilest Sins of America.* The hard part would be deciding which national disgrace is the worst.

When God condemned Judah and Israel for their sins, He was specific; retribution was certain. God didn't have to manufacture sensationalized accounts; Amos spoke the tragic truth, listing three or four sins that God hated.

What sins of America does God hate most? Adultery? Pornography? Homosexuality? Pride? Apathy? Greed? Prostitution? Abortion? Humanism? Materialism? Satanism? Would only three or four make the top of His list? "Sin is a reproach to any people" (Proverbs 14:34).

—R. W. B.

C. A Judgment of Fire Upon Judah (v. 5)

5. But I will send a fire upon Judah, and it shall devour the palaces of Jerusalem.

Although Judah's sins had been different, she would receive the same punishment that the other nations would receive: God would *send a fire upon Judah.* God would punish other nations at the hands of Assyria. Judah would indeed suffer the wrath of Assyria; but her final punishment, including the destruction of Jerusalem, would come at the hands of the Babylonians nearly two hundred years after Amos spoke these words.

II. Judgment Upon Israel
(Amos 2:6-8)

A. Their Sins Were Multiplied (v. 6a)

6a. Thus saith the LORD; For three transgressions of Israel, and for four, I will not turn away the punishment thereof.

Up to this point, Amos' pronouncements of punishment upon Israel's neighbors were welcome news. People of Israel readily agreed that those neighbors deserved the punishment God would mete out to them. But now they found themselves the subjects of Amos' pronouncements. One cannot avoid the feeling that the prophet had carefully chosen this roundabout approach in order to capture and hold the attention of his audience. Israel's sins that Amos enumerated were not sins of violence and atrocities in war. Israel may on occasion have been guilty of these, but Amos spoke of social sins of Israelite against Israelite, neighbor against neighbor.

B. They Were Unjust (v. 6b)

6b. Because they sold the righteous for silver, and the poor for a pair of shoes.

The greed of some knew few limits. The righteous, sometimes because they were righteous and refused to cheat or take advantage of others, fell into debt and were being sold into slavery. The law allowed a debtor to serve his creditor, but he was to serve as a hired servant, not as a slave (Leviticus 25:39-43). Some commentators believe that the creditors were able to enslave their fellow citizens by bribing the judges. The bribe is the *silver* or the *pair of shoes*. Others suggest that the greed of the creditor is the point here, that he would sell a debtor into slavery for such a trivial sum as a piece of silver or a pair of shoes. Whichever interpretation we accept, it is obvious that this sin must have been fairly common, otherwise Amos would not have used it as his first charge against the people.

C. They Were Greedy (v. 7a)

7a. That pant after the dust of the earth on the head of the poor, and turn aside the way of the meek.

The greedy were so eager to acquire land that they did not hesitate to use whatever means necessary to gain it. Amos satirized this greed by charging that they were so land hungry that they even panted after the dust that had accumulated on the heads of the poor. The greed for land seems to arise in every generation. We see the same sin today in our society. Men use all kinds of devious ways, some legal and some not so legal, to acquire land. But legal or not, this greed is immoral.

They *turn aside the way of the meek.* This suggests that the rich were taking advantage of the poor in every way they could. They did all they could to prevent the down-and-outers from taking the steps they needed to take in order to relieve their poverty.

D. They Engaged in Sexual Sins (v. 7b)

7b. And a man and his father will go in unto the same maid, to profane my holy name.

An incestuous relationship in which a father married his son's widow or a son married his father's widow was forbidden by the law (Leviticus 18:1-18). But that may not be the situation here. Both father and son may have been going to the same concubine or prostitute. If this was the case, the father was setting a terrible example for his son. *To profane my holy name* may suggest that they were going to a sacred prostitute in a pagan temple. Thus they were guilty of a double sin: violating God's laws against sexual

immorality and becoming involved in worshiping a pagan god. We who live in a sex-saturated society know very well how destructive such activity can be.

PROFANITY

My mother heard me swear at a dog when I was still in diapers. She said she had no idea where I learned the word; no one in our household used such language.

As far as I know, that incident was my only experiment with cussing. Early on I was taught never to "take the name of the Lord thy God in vain."

Even people who profess few religious convictions know the Third Commandment. On the other hand, God's name is spoken profanely more and more in movies and television shows. What most folk don't understand are the far-reaching implications of the prohibition against profanity. God's name is profaned in more ways than just by swearing. Taking God's name in vain also means wearing His name (professing to be His child) while disgracing Him with a sinful life-style. Israel had profaned the holy name of God with sexual immorality, as well as by other transgressions.

Does anyone really believe that America is a Christian nation anymore? Our culture's profanity belies the name. We must confess with Isaiah, "Woe is me! . . . I dwell in the midst of a people of unclean lips" (Isaiah 6:5).   —R. W. B.

E. They Became Drunk (v. 8)

8. And they lay themselves down upon clothes laid to pledge by every altar, and they drink the wine of the condemned in the house of their god.

The *clothes* were the large outer garments that were worn as cloaks during the day and used as bedding at night. A person in dire poverty might give up his cloak as a pledge against a loan; but according to the law, it was to be returned to him at night so that he would not be without

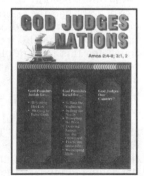

visual 5

bedding (Exodus 22:26, 27; Deuteronomy 24:12, 13). In this action the rich were violating the law and oppressing the poor. They were using the cloaks as bedding as they worshiped at *every altar,* presumably the altars that had been set up at Dan and Bethel. Since the only divinely authorized altar was in Jerusalem, their worship was improper at these altars. They were further condemned because they were engaged in drunken debauchery even as they worshiped. This kind of worship under these circumstances was more akin to the Baal worship of the Canaanites than the worship of Jehovah God. The *New International Version* renders the last part of this verse "they drink wine taken as fines," perhaps meaning unjust fines levied by corrupt judges.

III. They Forgot God's Blessings (Amos 3:1, 2)

A. God's Word Was Spoken Against Them (v. 1a)

1a. Hear this word that the LORD hath spoken against you, O children of Israel, against the whole family.

Amos attempted to get their attention by pointing out that his message was not his own, but had come from God. It carried authority far beyond anything that mere men could utter. It is worth remembering that God's authority is still found in His Word, the Scriptures, which carry far greater weight than the words of human wisdom. This message was not just against the citizens of the northern kingdom, but against the *whole family,* that is, Judah as well as Israel.

B. They Had Forgotten the Exodus (v. 1b)

1b. Which I brought up from the land of Egypt, saying.

Hundreds of years earlier, God had established His covenant with His people. But they forgot so easily. One way of reminding them of who they were was to remind them of their history and how God had worked mightily on their behalf. Their miraculous escape from enslavement in Egypt is a recurring theme in the Old Testament. It was indelibly imprinted upon their memories, and again and again it served to unite the people and carry them through difficult times.

C. They Had Been Greatly Blessed (v. 2)

2. You only have I known of all the families of the earth: therefore I will punish you for all your iniquities.

God knew all the families of the earth, but He knew only Israel as His own. They had been selected to be the channel through which God would send His Son. They had not been selected because they were more deserving than others. Their selection is an example of God's grace that is poured out, not on the basis of merit, but because He in His infinite wisdom knows best.

But there is a flip side to the coin. "For unto whomsoever much is given, of him shall be much required" (Luke 12:48). Because the Israelites had received so much from God, He would in turn require much from them. Amos had denounced the sins of the nations surrounding Israel; but they had often sinned in ignorance, not having the blessings of the light that came from God's revelation. The Israelites, however, had sinned in spite of the light they had and the blessings they had received.

If God made greater moral demands upon the Israelites because He gave them greater blessings, how will He deal with us who have received even greater blessings? In material things we have been blessed beyond the wildest imagination of even King Solomon. But our spiritual blessings have been infinitely greater. We have been privileged to receive further revelation in the New Testament, revelation that points us to our Lord and Savior.

TOUGH LOVE

Conscientious parents discipline their children out of love. And though kids don't believe it, the punishment often is harder on the parent than on the child. Some children have kids of their own before they understand that "tough love" is tough on both generations of the family. Genuine parental love, however, is not permissive. Father and mother must rear sons and daughters with the "iron hand" of authority in the "velvet glove" of tenderness.

God loves His children—all of His children, all of the time. He loved Israel before they were a nation, when they were slaves in Egypt. He loved Israel, even when they complained during their wilderness wanderings. He loved Israel when they prospered in Canaan. And He loved them still when they disobeyed and disgraced Him. In these latter cases, as today's text illustrates, God demonstrated His love with disciplinary punishment.

Nothing can separate us from the love of God (Romans 8:38, 39), not even ungodly behavior. But as all children of loving parents must suffer certain consequences of rebelling against authority, so we, the children of God, also must expect just retribution for wrongdoing. God is not a doting grandparent. He brings us to repentance when we sin. That is tough love.

—R. W. B.

Conclusion

A. Amos, Our Contemporary

In today's lesson text and in other passages from Amos, it is quite clear that one purpose of his ministry was to arouse the people to the social injustices found in Israel in his day. It was a society in which the rich were getting richer while the poor were becoming poorer. Worse still, the rich gained their wealth, not by hard work and frugality, but by using illegal methods to exact their toll from the poor. Further, they used their ill-gotten wealth, not in a responsible way, but to secure luxuries and to make a public display. For example, they built "houses of ivory" (Amos 3:15) and lay upon "beds of ivory" (Amos 6:4). Since ivory was imported and very expensive, its use spoke of great extravagance even as the poor went without food. Archaeologists working at the site of ancient Samaria have found ivory plaques that apparently adorned the walls of the houses of the rich, and they have found ivory works that were inlaid in furniture, giving ample evidence of the truthfulness of Amos' charges.

Persons who use material wealth in an irresponsible fashion are likely to be careless in other areas of their lives. Such was the case in ancient Israel. Amos accused them of sexual immorality, of drunkenness, and of going through the motions of meaningless worship.

Does not this all sound embarrassingly contemporary? To read the prophet's listing of the evils of his day is almost like reading the daily newspaper. Because Israel refused to heed Amos' call to repentance, she fell within a generation after the prophet delivered his message. We are foolish indeed if we do not observe Israel's tragic fate and learn from it.

B. Seeking a Plumbline

A theme runs through the book of Amos that expresses the authority with which he spoke. Again and again we read such expressions as "thus saith the Lord," "hear the word that the Lord hath spoken," "The Lord saith thus," and "the Lord commandeth." Amos spoke with conviction and without compromise because he spoke with divine authority. The standard he held the people to was not his own, but God's. In one vision he saw the Lord with a plumbline in the midst of the people, measuring them with His standard (Amos 7:7, 8).

Many in our society seem to have rejected all absolute standards. It is almost as if we were back in the times of the judges when "every man did that which was right in his own eyes" (Judges 21:25). Because God's standards are no longer widely recognized, our elected leaders disregard the Word of God, our legislative bodies pass laws that violate its teachings, and our judges ignore it. Even our citizens, when they vote on referendums, often ignore what the Bible teaches.

Rather pessimistic, you may say. Yes, but certainly not hopeless. So long as we have the Bible as our guide and so long as God continues to intervene in the affairs of man, no situation is hopeless. Further, we do not have to wait until God calls us from tending sheep in Tekoa as He did with Amos. We do not need some new revelation to give us direction. The Bible provides all the direction and motivation that we need.

But if we are to do God's bidding, we must know what His will for us is. His standards are laid out for us rather clearly in the Bible. But we must study the Bible if it is to become the standard that we follow. We must share our understanding of the Bible with others. We have a special obligation to pass it on to our children. While the church offers us vehicles for Christian education—Sunday school, Vacation Bible School, Christian camps, and other methods—yet the greater responsibility rests on us as parents and grandparents to get the job done.

C. Let Us Pray

Dear God, we thank You for the life and message of the prophet Amos. We thank You that that message has been preserved for us in the Scriptures. May we find in his message the strength and courage to speak to our age as he did to his. In Jesus' name we pray. Amen.

D. Thought to Remember

"Righteousness exalteth a nation: but sin is a reproach to any people" (Proverbs 14:34).

Home Daily Bible Readings

Monday, June 26—God Wants Justice in the World (Psalm 82)

Tuesday, June 27—Amos Announces God's Judgment on Syria (Amos 1:1-5)

Wednesday, June 28—Judgment on Philistia, Tyre, and Edom (Amos 1:6-12)

Thursday, June 29—Judgment on the Ammonites and Moab (Amos 1:13—2:3)

Friday, June 30—Unexpected Judgment on Judah and Israel (Amos 2:4-8)

Saturday, July 1—God's Mercy Has Been Ignored (Amos 2:9-13)

Sunday, July 2—Punishment for Abusing God's Favor (Amos 2:14—3:2)

Learning by Doing

This page contains an alternate lesson plan emphasizing learning activities. Classes desiring such student involvement will find these suggestions helpful.

Learning Goals

As you lead this lesson, concentrate on helping your students do the following:

1. Identify some of the sins for which God would judge Judah and Israel as noted in Amos 2 and 3.

2. Consider what their own role is for helping their nation turn to God.

3. Commit themselves to influence their nation to turn to righteousness.

Into the Lesson

Distribute the student books and have your students look at the word scramble included there. If you don't use the student book, write the following words on the chalkboard:

nation to is sin a people righteousness but exalts any a disgrace

Have students work in groups of three to unscramble the words. Allow two minutes, then ask for the unscrambled sentence.

It is "Righteousness exalts a nation, but sin is a disgrace to any people" (Proverbs 14:34, *New International Version*).

Lead into the Bible study by saying, "God has always demanded righteousness from nations. Today we will examine God's warning to the nations of Israel and Judah."

Into the Word

Have the class members form groups of four to six. Have one group complete Assignment One below, another group complete Assignment Two. All of the other groups should complete Assignment Three.

Assignment One

Read Amos 2:4-8; 3:1, 2. Use the helps provided to study the background of the book of Amos. Who was Amos? When did he minister? What prompted him to write this book? What are the main points of his book? Be prepared to report your observation.

Assignment Two

Using the commentaries provided, research Amos 2:4-8 and 3:1, 2. What sins would Israel be punished for? Prepare a brief commentary to read to the rest of the class.

Assignment Three

Read Amos 2:4-8; 3:1, 2. Discuss the questions below and jot down answers.

What is God looking for in a nation?	How is our nation doing in this regard?
2:4	
2:6	
2:7	
2:8	

Provide the group doing Assignment One with Bible dictionaries or encyclopedias, Bible handbooks such as Halley's or Eerdmans'. The group doing Assignment Two will need several commentaries on Amos. The groups doing Assignment Three will need copies of the chart.

Allow twenty-five minutes for the projects, then let the groups report.

Option

Divide the class into groups of four to six. Have them complete the chart above (which is in the student book). Discuss these questions:

1. How will God deal with Judah (2:5)? With Israel (3:1, 2)?

2. According to Amos, what is the solution for Israel's problem? See Amos 5:6, 14, 15.

Into Life

Lead your class in discussing these questions:

1. How can our church make a difference in helping our nation turn toward righteousness?

2. How can you make a difference in helping this nation turn toward righteousness?

Ask each student to write a prayer, asking God to help him make a difference.

Option

Distribute paper and pencils. Have students look up 2 Chronicles 7:14 and rewrite it in their own words. Discuss these questions:

1. What would happen to our nation if a significant number of Christians were to repent of their sins and pray fervently for the nation?

2. What is one thing you will do to help turn our nation back to God?

Let's Talk It Over

The questions on this page are designed to encourage review of the lesson Scriptures and to promote discussion of the lesson by the class. The answers provided are only discussion starters. Let your class talk it over from there.

1. What evidence is there in the New Testament that what Amos said to Israel applies to us today?

The very social responsibilities that Israel ignored are among the things that Jesus stressed in His ministry. Jesus' teachings are constantly punctuated with words and demonstrations of concern for the poor and needy, the forgotten and abused. Likewise, the letters of Paul speak frequently of kindness and concern for people in need. Paul seemed to stress very strongly that service to others indicated the reality of faith in Jesus. Such concern for people in need must characterize those today who claim to follow the Master. Surely the biggest difference for Christians, though, is that we see these responsibilities not as a response to law but as an opportunity to serve Jesus himself through people in need (Matthew 25:31-46).

2. What role do individuals play in determining the righteousness of a nation?

Many of those who preached in Old Testament times made it plain that personal sins affected all of society. Samuel did it in confronting Saul. Nathan stressed it in singling out David's sin. Micah verbally blasted the people of his day—and that very message was remembered a century later when Jeremiah was on trial for saying the same kind of thing. These preachers made it plain that the sins of individuals collectively spelled ruin for the nation. When the people take seriously the application of spiritual truth in their lives, it makes a difference in the direction of the nation. Many credit John Wesley's preaching in the 1700s with preventing a social upheaval in England comparable to the French Revolution in 1789. Christians so affected the pagan empire of Rome that its emperor declared himself a Christian barely three centuries after a Roman governor crucified Jesus. Individuals *do* make a difference!

3. How much does God still work through history to raise or bring low nations according to their righteousness or sinfulness?

This is such a subjective issue that historians and commentators will answer on the basis of their own faith or their personal point of view. It is easy for any of us to see our own riches and opportunities as blessings or rewards, but we are not so quick to see our losses as judgments and punishments.

Even when we trust God's Word and try to follow Him, we may not be able always to sort out historical events in terms of righteousness. Except for those rare prophets in Scripture, people have never been very good at accurately reading history while it is happening. It usually takes a century or two before we can look back and appraise the events in a particular nation or civilization. Up to this time, sin has taken its toll on every civilization; and it surely must be doing the same with ours. What we know assuredly is that God has told us how to live. We can begin there to try to make our own nation a lasting testimony of the joy of serving Him.

4. What specific connections are there between social sins and social unrest? May the violent problems of a society reflect its lack of attention to the needs of its poorest and most despised?

As the kids say, "It doesn't take a rocket scientist" to see that prejudice and discrimination (whether racial, ethnic, social, or economic) encourage resentment and anger, an attitude of hopelessness, and even a willingness to strike back in retaliation. That connection certainly does not excuse violence or lawlessness, but neither does it excuse tolerating the injustice that preceded it. Surely if more Christians were watching to correct the latter, a good measure of the former would evaporate.

Jesus, the prophets, and even the psalms of the Old Testament all spoke frequently about God's caring for the poor and the outcast. If we take this seriously, can we help to defuse some of the powder kegs of our society? Too often if "we" have jobs, no concern is given to the numerous problems of the unemployed; if "we" have good cars, opposition to taxing for public transportation is automatic. There is so much poverty and distress in the world that we feel unable to do anything about it. Maybe we don't know what differences our strong stand for the right might make because we take such a stand so seldom and sometimes so halfheartedly. Reading Amos—or the Gospels—can make us very uncomfortable sometimes!

A Call for Justice and Righteousness

DEVOTIONAL READING: Amos 5:6-15.

LESSON SCRIPTURE: Amos 4, 5.

PRINTED TEXT: Amos 4:4, 5; 5:18-24.

Amos 4:4, 5

4 Come to Bethel, and transgress; at Gilgal multiply transgression; and bring your sacrifices every morning, and your tithes after three years:

5 And offer a sacrifice of thanksgiving with leaven, and proclaim and publish the free offerings: for this liketh you, O ye children of Israel, saith the Lord GOD.

Amos 5:18-24

18 Woe unto you that desire the day of the LORD! to what end is it for you? the day of the LORD is darkness, and not light.

19 As if a man did flee from a lion, and a bear met him; or went into the house, and leaned his hand on the wall, and a serpent bit him.

20 Shall not the day of the LORD be darkness, and not light? even very dark, and no brightness in it?

21 I hate, I despise your feast days, and I will not smell in your solemn assemblies.

22 Though ye offer me burnt offerings and your meat offerings, I will not accept them; neither will I regard the peace offerings of your fat beasts.

23 Take thou away from me the noise of thy songs; for I will not hear the melody of thy viols.

24 But let judgment run down as waters, and righteousness as a mighty stream.

GOLDEN TEXT: Let judgment run down as waters, and righteousness as a mighty stream.—Amos 5:24.

A Nation Turns From God
Unit 2: The Approaching Judgment
(Lessons 5-9)

Lesson Aims

Following this lesson, each student should:

1. Have a better understanding of the social and religious situation in Amos's day.

2. Understand that the day of the Lord can be a day of judgment, not of blessings.

3. Have a growing appreciation for the importance of sincere worship that leads to righteous lives.

4. Be able to point out problems we face today in our worship.

Lesson Outline

INTRODUCTION
    A. Hay and Worship
    B. Lesson Background
 I. AMOS'S IRONIC CRITICISM (Amos 4:4, 5)
    A. Come to Worship and Sin (v. 4a)
    B. Bring Sacrifices (vv. 4b, 5)
       Lost in the Writing
 II. THE DAY OF THE LORD (Amos 5:18-20)
    A. The Day of the Lord Is Dark (v. 18)
    B. Dangers of the Day of the Lord (v. 19)
    C. Nature of the Day Reaffirmed (v. 20)
       From Frying Pan to Fire
III. EMPTY WORSHIP NOT ENOUGH (Amos 5:21-24)
    A. God Hates Their Feast Days (v. 21)
    B. Offerings Not Acceptable (v. 22)
    C. Music Not Acceptable (v. 23)
    D. An Appeal for Righteousness (v. 24)
       "This Ye Ought to Have Done"
CONCLUSION
    A. "In Spirit and in Truth"
    B. Our Solemn Assemblies
    C. Let Us Pray
    D. Thought to Remember

Visual 6 of the visuals packet illustrates the Golden Text of this lesson. The visual is shown on page 389.

Introduction

A. Hay and Worship

A church in a large city erected a new sanctuary that was impressive both for its size and for its strikingly modern architecture. When the building was dedicated, Christians from the surrounding area were invited to share in the service. A farmer and his family accepted the invitation and attended the meeting. After the service the wife commented to her husband, "Wasn't the huge organ exciting? The sound just sent shivers down my spine."

"I didn't notice," replied the husband.

"What did you think of the choir? Such singing we don't get in our church!" she said.

"I guess it was all right," responded he.

"And what a powerful sermon!"

"I didn't catch much of it."

"For goodness' sake, Pa, didn't you pay attention to anything?"

"Not really. I was too busy trying to figure how many bales of hay I could store in a building like that."

We must admit that at times we are just about as preoccupied with things of the world as that farmer was. This was one of the problems that Amos had to deal with as he brought God's message to the people of Israel.

B. Lesson Background

Amos, a native of the southern kingdom, was called by God to bring a message of judgment upon the northern kingdom. As he entered into this important ministry, he had at least three barriers to overcome.

First, he was a southerner who had to face the national prejudices of the citizens of the northern kingdom. After the kingdom had divided in 931 B.C. at the beginning of Rehoboam's reign, the two nations had experienced a stormy relationship that often led to open hostilities. Although relations between the two states were better than they had been, yet ethnic and national bitterness lasts a long time. We in our times have seen it in Northern Ireland and the area that was formerly Yugoslavia.

Second, Jeroboam II was king of Israel when Amos began his ministry about 760 B.C. Under this strong king, Israel, or at least the wealthy merchant class, was enjoying unprecedented prosperity. For Amos to appear at this time and bring a message of doom was certain to antagonize his hearers.

Finally, Amos had no formal preparation for the prophetic ministry to which he had been called. He readily acknowledged that he was but a humble shepherd and a "gatherer of sycamore fruit" (Amos 7:14). Ordinarily when God calls a person to a ministry, He calls one who is prepared. But we need to realize that one can become prepared through other than the normal channels, and this certainly was the case with Amos. During those long and lonely hours as he watched over his flock, the word of the Lord came to him in ways that we may not understand. But there was no doubt in the heart of the prophet about the authenticity of the message that he brought.

I. Amos's Ironic Criticism (Amos 4:4, 5)

A. Come to Worship and Sin (v. 4a)

4a. Come to Bethel, and transgress; at Gilgal multiply transgression.

In the verses before this, Amos prophesies that the people of Samaria will be defeated and taken captive like fish taken on hooks. Now he uses irony to drive home his point. He encourages them to continue their sin at Bethel and Gilgal. More than a century and a half earlier, Jeroboam I had set up a place of worship at Bethel, about a dozen miles north of Jerusalem, where he erected a golden calf (1 Kings 12:28, 29). He did this to prevent the people from going to Jerusalem to worship, knowing that he would have trouble maintaining their loyalty if they went to Judah to worship.

Gilgal was located west of the Jordan River. It was here that the twelve stones were set up as a memorial to the Israelites' crossing of the Jordan (Joshua 4:19-24). Apparently Gilgal, like Bethel, had become a center for worship. One can sense the biting sarcasm in Amos' voice as he urges the people to continue their false worship, thus piling up their sins.

B. Bring Sacrifices (vv. 4b, 5)

4b, 5. And bring your sacrifices every morning, and your tithes after three years: and offer a sacrifice of thanksgiving with leaven, and proclaim and publish the free offerings: for this liketh you, O ye children of Israel, saith the Lord God.

Every morning the Israelites brought their sacrifices. *After three years* is "every three days" in some more recent versions. Some commentators suggest that Amos means the people were paying their tithes more often than the law required. The *sacrifice of thanksgiving*, or thank offering, and the *free offerings* or freewill offering were offerings that went beyond the minimum. The people were doing more than was prescribed by the law. Yet the thanksgiving offering was *with leaven,* a clear violation of the law. The people were making these offerings in an apparently generous fashion, yet they were doing it their way, not God's way. *Proclaim and publish* seems to mean that they were making a public display of their worship, calling attention to their generosity. Jesus spoke in a similar fashion about the hypocrites in the synagogues who sounded a trumpet before them as they gave their alms (Matthew 6:2).

The point that Amos is making is that even though the people were going through the motions of worship, their efforts were not acceptable to God. All their empty worship would not avert God's judgment, which Amos describes in the verses that follow. God had sent famine, drought, pestilence, and war upon them, yet they had not repented. Now even worse suffering would be their lot.

They came under God's condemnation for at least three reasons. First, the legitimate place of worship was Jerusalem, not Bethel or Gilgal. Second, they had a golden calf as the center of their worship, a clear violation of the Second Commandment, which forbade the worship of images. In the third place, while they went through the motions of worship, they failed to display righteousness in their lives.

LOST IN THE WRITING

Sarcasm can be an effective figure of speech—*speech* being the key word here. Tone and inflection must be heard to identify sarcasm immediately and accurately. Written down, sarcastic comments lack that sound, and thus can be misunderstood. That is why good writers who create sarcastic dialogue add clues such as ". . . he said sarcastically," or ". . . she said with a sneer in her voice."

Israel couldn't miss the sarcasm in Amos's voice as he spoke for God. But in print, the tone and inflection is lost, so readers can become confused. God, of course, would never literally instruct people to sin—not in Bethel or Gilgal or anywhere. The prophet is speaking sarcastically to point out Israel's foolishly presumptuous behavior.

Amos was rebuking the Israelites for presuming upon God's grace, for thinking that religious ceremonies could atone for their sin. What he, and God, really wanted them to do is expressed in Amos 5:5, 6: "Do not seek Bethel, do not go to Gilgal . . . Seek the Lord and live" (*New International Version*).

Careful Bible study considers the context of each passage, and requires readers to "tune in" to the tone of the rhetoric for correct interpretation and understanding.   —R. W. B.

How to Say It

GILGAL. *Gil*-gal.
JEROBOAM. Jair-o-*bo*-um.
REHOBOAM. Re-ho-*bo*-um.

II. The Day of the Lord
(Amos 5:18-20)

A. The Day of the Lord Is Dark (v. 18)

18. Woe unto you that desire the day of the LORD! to what end is it for you? the day of the LORD is darkness, and not light.

Many in Israel longed for *the day of the Lord.* They thought Jehovah then would lead His people in triumph over their enemies. Because they were children of the covenant, they thought the day of the Lord would be a day of light, of victory for Israel. They must have been shocked when Amos announced that it would be just the opposite, a day of darkness, not of light.

B. Dangers of the Day of the Lord (v. 19)

19. As if a man did flee from a lion, and a bear met him; or went into the house, and leaned his hand on the wall, and a serpent bit him.

The prophet illustrates his point by examples from life. A man fleeing from a lion thinks he has escaped, but just at that moment he comes face to face with a bear, which some believe was a greater threat than a lion. Or a man has worked all day in the fields where he has faced all kinds of dangers. At last he enters his own home, expecting to find safety, only to be bitten by a snake.

C. Nature of the Day Reaffirmed (v. 20)

20. Shall not the day of the LORD be darkness, and not light? even very dark, and no brightness in it?

When Amos announced that the day of the Lord would be darkness, no doubt there were mutterings of unbelief and rejection, not only because it was a new idea, but because it contradicted what the hearers wanted to believe. The prophet assures them that their ears were not deceiving them: he really had said the day of the Lord would be darkness. Indeed, it would be *very dark, and no brightness in it.* In the verses that follow, Amos once again denounces their empty and hypocritical worship, assuring them that these acts will not save them from God's judgment.

FROM FRYING PAN TO FIRE

Sometimes a preacher escapes problems in a congregation by moving to serve another church. Often, however, he finds difficulties in the new place that equal or surpass those he left behind. Running is rarely the best way to resolve conflict. Changing schools, changing climates, changing marriage partners—all of these involve a risk that the latter situation will be worse than the former. (That explains why the rate of divorce among second time-arounders is higher than among those who are married to their first mates.)

Millions gamble away happiness by choosing what seems to be greener grass, only to find they have jumped from the frying pan into the fire. Those familiar metaphors may not mix well, but the meaning is clear enough.

Amos warned the people of Israel that they were deluding themselves if they thought "the day of the Lord" would bring them happiness and light. The unholy and disobedient cannot hope to be delivered from frustration, boredom, fear, and despair when the world ends. They will be held accountable for their wickedness, and thus be condemned to destruction that lasts forever. The "frying pan" of earth's trials is but a light affliction compared to divine punishment of the ungodly (Revelation 21:7, 8).   —R. W. B.

III. Empty Worship Not Enough
(Amos 5:21-24)

A. God Hates Their Feast Days (v. 21)

21. I hate, I despise your feast days, and I will not smell in your solemn assemblies.

The *feast days* were the great annual feasts—Passover, Pentecost, and Tabernacles—and some more frequently observed days such as Sabbaths and new moon festivals. The people were not neglecting these feast days, but their practices did not meet God's approval because the people's lives did not demonstrate the righteousness that true worship should produce. God would *not smell* the smoke of their burnt offerings and their incense. In other words, God refused to accept these offerings.

B. Offerings Not Acceptable (v. 22)

22. Though ye offer me burnt offerings and your meat offerings, I will not accept them; neither will I regard the peace offerings of your fat beasts.

Burnt offerings involved the burning of various animals on the altar. Such offerings symbolized the consecration of the worshiper. *Meat offerings* is translated as "grain offerings" in many versions because this offering was of flour or meal and oil, not animal flesh. The *peace offerings,* translated "fellowship offerings" in the *New International Version,* were offerings in which certain parts of a sacrificed animal were burned on the altar, while other parts were eaten by the priests and worshipers in a common meal. This is the reason for translating it "fellowship offering."

All of these offerings were presented, but they were not acceptable to God because they were not offered with the right motives or with the proper spirit.

C. Music Not Acceptable (v. 23)

23. Take thou away from me the noise of thy songs; for I will not hear the melody of thy viols.

Music was important in the praise of God in the Old Testament. The book of Psalms is ready testimony to this fact, for it was a hymnbook for Jewish worship. While we do not have a detailed description of music used in worship, it is generally agreed that singing to the accompaniment of stringed instruments was a part of that worship. The *viols*, sometimes translated "harps," were stringed instruments like small harps or lyres.

In the previous verse, Amos proclaims God's rejection of the people's sacrifices. In this verse he adds God's rejection of their praise. The reason was not that the people sang off key or used the wrong kind of music. God rejected their songs because they did not present them in the right spirit.

D. An Appeal for Righteousness (v. 24)

24. But let judgment run down as waters, and righteousness as a mighty stream.

Some commentators take this to mean that Amos is calling for God's judgment to overwhelm the sinful people like a disastrous flood. Others understand this to be Amos' call for the people to repent, to turn from their worldliness and wickedness to righteousness. This latter interpretation seems best to fit the situation here. The prophet is calling for the people to remove the barriers and take away the hindrances and let justice cover the land as an overwhelming flood.

The people of Israel were people of the covenant. They had agreed to serve God fully, but they had failed in that commitment. Would we call a businessman honest if he, while honest in most of his dealings, cheated once or twice a month? Of course not! What would we think of

"Let justice roll on like a river, righteousness like a never failing stream!"

visual 6

a husband who boasted of faithfulness to his marriage covenant and yet occasionally committed adultery? Obviously, the man is an adulterer. It was the same with the Israelites. They worshiped regularly, but in their daily living and even in their worship they violated the requirements of the covenant. No matter how much they protested, they were covenant breakers.

"THIS YE OUGHT TO HAVE DONE"

Did Jesus condemn Pharisees for tithing? He said, "Woe unto you . . . hypocrites! for ye pay tithe of mint and anise and cummin" (Matthew 23:23). These religious leaders were meticulous about giving a tenth of everything, even their kitchen spices, in temple offerings. But Christ did not rebuke them for their faithful stewardship. Rather, He told them not to leave such giving undone.

Jesus was indignant, not about tithing, but because *justice*, *mercy* and *faith* were being ignored. He said, "These ought ye to have done, and not to leave the other undone."

During the prophetic ministry of Amos, Israel made some similar mistakes. Despite their flagrant disobedience, they continued to fast and feast and sacrifice and sing praises to Jehovah. God didn't condemn their worship activities *per se;* He rebuked them for idolatry and other sins of affluence. Rituals and ceremonies are fraudulant and meaningless without righteousness in attitude and behavior.

James defined "pure religion" in terms of benevolence and morality (James 1:27). He also insisted that faith be accompanied by works (James 2:14-26). We can be certain that philanthropy without morality is not acceptable. Christianity involves the whole person, both heart and hand.   —R. W. B.

Conclusion

A. "In Spirit and in Truth"

In His conversation with the Samaritan woman at the well, Jesus stated that "the hour cometh, and now is, when the true worshippers shall worship the Father in spirit and in truth" (John 4:23). At least two things are suggested in this passage. First of all, to worship "in spirit" means to worship in harmony with God, who is spirit. To worship in spirit, one's worship must be free of hypocrisy. To pretend to worship God while allowing oneself to be in bondage to Satan would be a clear violation of this principle. Further, to go through the motions of worship in order to impress others comes under this condemnation. Jesus had strong words for those who took all kinds of measures to make their religious devotion more obvious to their fellow-men (Matthew 23:5-7).

The second basic principle of worship is that it must be "in truth." This means that it must be as God asks. Since God ruled out all forms of idolatry, the use of any figure or symbol that even suggested idolatry was wrong. Jeroboam, when he led the northern tribes to separate from the southern tribes, erected golden calves to be used in the worship at Dan and Bethel. He probably argued that this was not idolatry because the images actually represented God, and the people were worshiping God, not the images. Clearly this violated the Second Commandment. In actual practice, many people did not distinguish between worshiping God through the image and actually worshiping the image. As a result, many people were led astray even as they sought to worship in truth.

Amos condemned the people's worship because it violated both of these principles. They were going through the motions of worship, but their actions revealed that their worship was empty and meaningless. Even as they worshiped, they were plotting ways to cheat their neighbors and pervert the judicial process to their own advantage. In addition, they had erected sanctuaries in various places when the law established only one. They had added both plans and practices that were not authorized by the law. As the years passed, these innovations had come to be accepted as normal. No one questioned them. It is little wonder that the people were shocked when the prophet harshly criticized them.

B. Our Solemn Assemblies

Suppose Amos were to visit one of our worship services. What criticisms might he level at us? First of all, he would need to recognize that we no longer live under the law, that the detailed regulations that covered worship in the tabernacle and the temple do not apply to us. Other than to stipulate that true worship must be "in spirit and in truth," the New Testament gives us few specific directions. From the examples of worship that we read about in the New Testament, we learn that the apostles' doctrine or preaching and teaching, fellowship, the breaking of bread or the Lord's Supper, and prayers were elements of that worship (Acts 2:42). Other passages teach the singing of "psalms and hymns and spiritual songs" (Ephesians 5:19; Colossians 3:16). It seems proper to include them in our meetings for worship. The New Testament leaves us free to incorporate other elements if they do not violate the principles of "in spirit and in truth."

Today if one visits from congregation to congregation, he finds a great variety of activities included in worship services. Some involve formal and exacting rituals; others are spontaneous and informal. It is easy for us to become critical of any worship service that does not conform to our own accustomed practices. Today we hear much argument about the choice of music used in worship. Some prefer the majestic music of the classics and the stately lyrics of the traditional hymns. Others would adapt the beat, the volume, and repetitive lyrics of contemporary music to our worship. Controversies over worship have raged across the centuries, and so it should not surprise us that we still have these arguments with us.

The real issue is the bottom line. What happens when the last amen is said and we leave the sanctuary to face the world outside? That's what Amos' message is all about. God hated the feast days and the noise of the people's songs because justice and righteousness did not prevail in their lives after they left the sanctuary. Since much of what we do in worship is subjective and cannot be readily measured, the most effective test of our worship is what happens in our lives. Would our lives pass the test?

C. Let Us Pray

Dear God, as we approach You in worship, let us never forget that You are high and holy. Teach us to worship in spirit and truth, and may our lives reflect the fact that we have been in Your presence in our worship. Amen.

D. Thought to Remember

"The true worshippers shall worship the Father in spirit and in truth; for the Father seeketh such to worship him" (John 4:23).

Home Daily Bible Readings

Monday, July 3—Israel's Vain Piety Will Be Punished (Amos 4:1-5)

Tuesday, July 4—God's Warnings Have Been Ignored (Amos 4:6-11)

Wednesday, July 5—God's Punishment Is at Hand (Amos 4:12—5:3)

Thursday, July 6—There Is Still Time for Repentance (Amos 5:4-9)

Friday, July 7—Warning and Call to Seek God (Amos 5:10-15)

Saturday, July 8—The Day of the Lord: Judgment (Amos 5:16-20)

Sunday, July 9—God Wants Justice and Righteousness (Amos 5:21-27)

Learning by Doing

This page contains an alternate lesson plan emphasizing learning activities. Classes desiring such student involvement will find these suggestions helpful.

Learning Goals

As a result of this lesson your students should:

1. Identify a correlation between worshiping God and living righteously.

2. Evaluate the quality of their own worship.

Into the Lesson

Before class, write these two headings on the chalkboard:

God accepts worship that—

God doesn't accept worship that is—

To begin, have the class form groups of four. Provide each group with a sheet of paper and a pencil. Assign half of the groups to brainstorm answers to the first heading above, and half to do the same for the second heading. Allow two minutes. Then ask each group to report their suggestions as you write them on the chalkboard.

Connect this activity with today's passage by saying, "The nation of Israel in Amos' time was very religious. They had a high level of worship activity. And yet God was totally disgusted with their worship. Let's discover why."

Into the Word

Review the background of Amos in a brief lecture. Utilize the material in the introductions for today's lesson and last week's lesson.

Ask a volunteer to read Amos 4:4, 5; 5:18-24. Then lead your class in discussing these questions, which are in the student book:

1. In Amos 4:4, 5 God speaks sarcastically to Israel. What is the point of His sarcastic words?

2. Reread Amos 5:18-20. What will the "day of the Lord" hold for Israel?

3. In what ways did the Israelites worship God? (5:21-23)

4. Why were these acts of worship unacceptable? (5:21-24; 2:6, 7; 4:1; 5:7, 11, 12; 8:4-6).

5. What would it require for the nation of Israel to "let justice roll on like a river" (v. 24, *New International Version*)?

6. Why isn't it enough to participate in worship activities? What else does God require? (See Isaiah 1:10-20; 58:1-11; Hosea 6:6; Micah 6:6-8.)

Into Life

Point out that acceptable worship involves a number of aspects, including these: (1) It must be based upon truth about God. (2) It must be practiced according to God's instruction. (3) It must be approached with the right attitude and motive. (4) It must result in righteous living.

Write those four principles on the chalkboard. (They are also written in the student book.) Then have your class form at least four groups with groups no larger than six.

Assign one of the principles to each group. If you have more than four groups, you will need to duplicate some of the principles. Ask the groups to create questions that they can ask themselves to see if they are practicing that principle of worship. Here is an example for each of the four principles: (1) Am I worshiping God as the Bible describes Him, or am I worshiping Him as I want Him to be? (2) Am I more interested in worshiping God in a way that makes me feel good than I am in following His instructions for worship? (3) When I worship God, are my thoughts and desires focused on pleasing Him? (4) When I worship God, does it lead me to be kinder to those around me?

Appoint a discussion leader and provide each group with paper, a pencil, a sheet of poster board, and a felt-tip marker. Encourage them to have a secretary for the group, who will write down the questions they create. After they have compiled their list, they are to write the questions on the poster board large enough to be seen by the class. Allow about twelve minutes.

When time has expired, ask each group's leader to present its poster board to the class and read the questions out loud. Suggest to the class that they write the questions on paper and place them in their Bibles for periodic review.

Option

Suggest the four principles of acceptable worship under "Into Life." Then have the class form groups of four to six. Provide each group with paper and a pencil. Say to the class, "I'd like you to work in your groups to write a letter to an imaginary new Christian. You are trying to teach and encourage him to develop a life of worship, but you want to make sure he is worshiping God in an acceptable way. Be sure to utilize some of the Scriptures we have studied today, as well as others you think might apply."

Allow the groups twelve to fifteen minutes to compose their letters. When time has expired, bring the groups together and let a spokesperson for each group read their letter to the class.

Let's Talk It Over

The questions on this page are designed to encourage review of the lesson Scriptures and to promote discussion of the lesson by the class. The answers provided are only discussion starters. Let your class talk it over from there.

1. The thought of fragrant incense for God to smell and enjoy suggests that worship is presented as a gift to God. What will help us to make our worship a present pleasing to Him?

Chapters 4 and 5 of Revelation picture all creatures bowing before God, and twenty-four elders casting their crowns before Him. This suggests giving to God the best we have, which is what Old Testament law demanded. But Christians give their best because they want to, not because the law demands it.

Even as we give our best, we should be aware that God does not really *need* what we give. Our worship is not so much a favor to Him as a necessity because of who He is and who we are. Worship is not a good deed done to earn credit with God or admiration from men; it is coming to God with deepest admiration because we cannot do otherwise! The people of Israel missed that point, and today we are in the danger of missing it too.

2. As we take the Lord's Supper in memory of Jesus, are we aware that it is also a sharing with others, and therefore calls for a right attitude toward them?

People of Israel were going through rituals of worship, but that did not keep them from mistreating each other. At the Lord's table we focus strongly on Jesus at the cross, and that is right. But 1 Corinthians 10:16, 17 emphasizes that we who share the Lord's Supper are one body, and 1 Corinthians 11:20, 21 says we should treat one another well. Though Jesus spoke before the Lord's Supper was instituted, we may well think what He said about leaving your gift at the altar till you are reconciled with your brother (Matthew 5:23, 24).

3. Do we evaluate worship on the basis of what we like (hymns, gospel songs, choruses), rather than seeking what pleases God? Can we use a variety of music styles and still maintain a right spirit in worship?

About a century ago some Christians were disturbed by songs we now call old favorites. They thought those tunes were too much like popular love songs. In the sixteenth century some people objected to Luther's songs, but now we call them classics. Tastes vary and styles change, but God is always the same. Do you suppose He appreciates more musical styles than some of us do? Certainly He values sincerity of heart more than the sound of a tune.

Could a music committee have members with various tastes? Could they blend various kinds of music in a worship service pleasing to God and men?

4. How can we help a "mighty stream" of righteousness to become a way of life? How can we work for "justice for all" while strongly asserting our "liberty"?

Again we see the connection between worship and daily living. It is important to avoid hypocrisy and never worship for show, in part because genuine worship has the power to change lives. In other words, the best source of right living is right worship. As we are confronted by God's Word and the revelation of His love in Jesus we are impelled to go forth and live for Him. As we realize that Jesus died for us when we were not worthy (Romans 5:8), we are moved to seek what is right for all those for whom Jesus has such love. Christ has made us free, and we shall be free indeed as we align ourselves with His cause and purpose. That includes His concern for all mankind.

5. How can we strengthen the connection between what we do and say in worship and how we serve God during the week?

The Lord's Supper provides one time for introspection and good resolution. As we think of our need of forgiveness and the wonder of God's grace, we are moved to shape our lives according to His will.

Another helpful time is the time of invitation that calls for consecration in response to the message from Scripture. This is a time for specific commitment, for a resolve to live out our faith in the days ahead.

In every worship service we need to participate in worship, not merely to observe. We need to sing from our hearts, to give attention to Bible reading and sermon, even to take notes, and to think about applying God's Word to our life.

Our greatest need is for the *desire* to apply worship to life. God's Word and God's Spirit will help us find ways, if we really want to serve.

A Prophet Who Lived His Message

DEVOTIONAL READING: Romans 5:1-11.

LESSON SCRIPTURE: Hosea 1:1—3:5.

PRINTED TEXT: Hosea 1:2-9; 3:1-5.

Hosea 1:2-9

2 The beginning of the word of the LORD by Hosea. And the LORD said to Hosea, Go, take unto thee a wife of whoredoms and children of whoredoms: for the land hath committed great whoredom, departing from the LORD.

3 So he went and took Gomer the daughter of Diblaim; which conceived, and bare him a son.

4 And the LORD said unto him, Call his name Jezreel; for yet a little while, and I will avenge the blood of Jezreel upon the house of Jehu, and will cause to cease the kingdom of the house of Israel.

5 And it shall come to pass at that day, that I will break the bow of Israel in the valley of Jezreel.

6 And she conceived again, and bare a daughter. And God said unto him, Call her name Loruhamah: for I will no more have mercy upon the house of Israel; but I will utterly take them away.

7 But I will have mercy upon the house of Judah, and will save them by the LORD their God, and will not save them by bow, nor by sword, nor by battle, by horses, nor by horsemen.

8 Now when she had weaned Loruhamah, she conceived, and bare a son.

9 Then said God, Call his name Loammi: for ye are not my people, and I will not be your God.

Hosea 3:1-5

1 Then said the LORD unto me, Go yet, love a woman beloved of her friend, yet an adulteress, according to the love of the LORD toward the children of Israel, who look to other gods, and love flagons of wine.

2 So I bought her to me for fifteen pieces of silver, and for a homer of barley, and a half homer of barley:

3 And I said unto her, Thou shalt abide for me many days; thou shalt not play the harlot, and thou shalt not be for another man: so will I also be for thee.

4 For the children of Israel shall abide many days without a king, and without a prince, and without a sacrifice, and without an image, and without an ephod, and without teraphim:

5 Afterward shall the children of Israel return, and seek the LORD their God, and David their king; and shall fear the LORD and his goodness in the latter days.

GOLDEN TEXT: I will betroth thee . . . in righteousness, and in judgment, and in loving-kindness, and in mercies.—Hosea 2:19.

A Nation Turns From God
Unit 2: The Approaching Judgment
(Lessons 5-9)

Lesson Aims

As a result of studying this lesson, each student should:

1. Have a better understanding of God's love for Israel, and for us.

2. Consider his or her own love and compare it with God's love.

3. Be better able to give, receive, and respond to love in his or her own life.

Lesson Outline

The elements of sound and happy covenant relationships are highlighted by visual 7 of the visuals packet. Display the visual throughout the class session. It is shown on page 397.

Introduction

A. Restored Treasure

Several years ago while browsing in a cluttered second-hand store, a London art dealer found a dingy painting in a battered frame. Examining it closer his trained eye could see a gleam of greatness through the grime. He bought the picture for thirty-five shillings and took it to his studio, where he used all his expertise to clean it without damaging the paint. Then he took it to an expert for evaluation. It was a genuine work of the famous Rubens! Now it was worth thousands of pounds.

People too can become dingy and apparently worthless, and so can nations. But the expert eye of God can see value behind the dirt, and the expert hand of God can clear away the grime to reveal hidden beauty. In our lesson for today we see a dingy nation in need of cleansing, and we see a dingy person presented as a symbol of that nation.

B. Lesson Background

The prophet Hosea began his ministry when Jeroboam II was king of north Israel, which Hosea sometimes refers to as Ephraim. It was a time of prosperity for the rich, but they built their prosperity by cheating the poor. With such prosperity came greed, corruption, drunkenness, and sexual sins, as we have seen in our studies from Amos. A unique feature of Hosea's work is the way he illustrated his teaching in his life and his family.

I. The Prophet's Wife
(Hosea 1:2, 3)

A. The Lord's Command (v. 2)

2. The beginning of the word of the LORD by Hosea. And the LORD said to Hosea, Go, take unto thee a wife of whoredoms and children of whoredoms: for the land hath committed great whoredom, departing from the LORD.

The Lord had not been giving messages by Hosea before: this was *the beginning* of His speaking *by Hosea.* He began with a command, and it sounds as if He ordered Hosea to marry a prostitute who had children by her prostitution. Some students think that was exactly what the command meant. Imagine how Hosea must have felt if it was.

It does seem very strange, however, that a holy God would give such a command to a good man called to be His spokesman. Many students therefore wonder if the command should be understood in some other way. One possible way is suggested by the reason that follows: *for the land hath committed great whoredom, departing from the Lord.*

This presents a figure of speech that appears repeatedly in the Old Testament. In this figure, the nation of Israel is represented as married to Jehovah. Any worship of another god then is considered adultery. If Israel expects to gain any profit or pleasure by such worship, the adultery is *whoredom,* prostitution.

It is possible, then, to conclude that Hosea's wife was not a prostitute in the literal and physical sense, but only in the spiritual sense: she was a worshiper of false gods. Some students go a step further: they conclude that she was not a prostitute in any sense. Because the nation as a whole was far gone in great whoredom, any woman of that nation could be called a woman of whoredom even if she herself were pure.

B. The Prophet's Obedience (v. 3)

3. So he went and took Gomer the daughter of Diblaim; which conceived, and bare him a son.

Whatever the command meant, it seems clear that Hosea understood it perfectly and obeyed it exactly. About Gomer and her father we know only what we learn from this book.

In view of the uncertainties noted in verse 2, we can see various possibilities in verse 3. We may suppose Hosea walked down the street and took the first prostitute he met, or that he saw many prostitutes and chose the one he liked best. We may suppose he ignored the literal prostitutes and chose a worshiper of false gods, or he chose a worshiper of the true God out of a nation that worshiped false gods. We may suppose that God specifically directed Hosea to a particular woman. That is not stated in the text, but neither is it denied. We may even suppose that Hosea was already in love with Gomer, but had been delaying marriage for some reason. Two things are quite clear: Hosea took a wife, and in due time she *bare him a son.*

II. The Prophet's Children (Hosea 1:4-9)

A. Jezreel (vv. 4, 5)

4. And the LORD said unto him, Call his name Jezreel; for yet a little while, and I will avenge the blood of Jezreel upon the house of Jehu, and will cause to cease the kingdom of the house of Israel.

The house of Jehu then was the ruling family of Israel. The king was Jeroboam II (Hosea 1:1). About sixty years before he became king, his great-grandfather, Jehu, had destroyed the former ruling family in a bloody massacre beginning near the city of Jezreel (2 Kings 9:14—10:7). Many students think that massacre was *the blood of Jezreel* that God was going to avenge *upon the house of Jehu.* However, God himself had authorized that massacre before it began and had approved it after it was done (2 Kings 9:1-10; 10:30). Can we think He was going to avenge it now by punishing the descendants of Jehu? Perhaps there was some later bloodshed, some unjust bloodshed, either in the city of Jezreel or in the plain of the same name. For that unjust killing the Lord promised vengeance. That

How to Say It

ASSYRIA. Uh-*sear*-ee-uh.
DIBLAIM. *Dib*-lay-im or Dib-*lay*-im.
EPHRAIM. *Ee*-fray-im.
GOMER. *Go*-mer.
HOSEA. Ho-*zay*-uh or Ho-*zee*-uh.
HOSHEA. Ho-*she*-uh.
JEHU. *Jee*-hew.
JEROBOAM. Jair-o-*bo*-um.
JEZREEL. *Jez*-re-el.
LO-AMMI. Lo-*am*-my.
LO-RUHAMAH. Lo-roo-*hay*-muh or Lo-roo-*hah*-muh.
ZACHARIAH. Zack-uh-*rye*-uh.

promise was not fulfilled in the time of King Jeroboam, but in the time of the next king. Jeroboam's son Zachariah ruled only half a year before he was killed by a rebel who then took the throne (2 Kings 15:8-10). Thus the rule of Jehu's house came to an end.

The last part of verse 4 looks even farther into the future. About forty years after the end of Jehu's house came the end of *the kingdom of the house of Israel* (2 Kings 17:1-6).

5. And it shall come to pass at that day, that I will break the bow of Israel in the valley of Jezreel.

The bow of Israel means the nation's military power. Second Kings 17:1-6 tells how it was broken. The king of Assyria invaded the country with an overwhelming army. In the light of this prophecy, we can suppose the army of Israel was crushed in a decisive battle *in the valley of Jezreel.* King Hoshea was taken captive. Then the Assyrians besieged the capital city, Samaria, and starved out the people living there.

So the name *Jezreel* came into the prophecy at two points. First, bloodshed at Jezreel was to be avenged when Jehu's family would lose the kingdom. Second, the valley of Jezreel would be the scene of the decisive battle in the campaign that would end the kingdom of Israel.

The meaning of the name *Jezreel* supplies yet another link with the prophecy of Hosea. It means "God will scatter." That must have given Hosea many opportunities to repeat his warning. Wondering people would ask, "Why in the world did you name the boy 'God will scatter'?" Hosea would reply, "Because that is exactly what God will do if the people of Israel don't straighten up and do right. God will take them from their homes and scatter them in foreign lands." A prophecy similar to that appears in Hosea 9:17, and 2 Kings 17:6 records the fulfillment of that prophecy.

Since wheat or barley is planted by scattering it, *Jezreel* means also "God will plant." After scattering the people of Israel in faraway lands, God was going to plant them again in their own country. This is foretold in Hosea 1:11. See also Hosea 2:14-23; 14:4-8.

B. Lo-ruhamah (vv. 6, 7)

6. And she conceived again, and bare a daughter. And God said unto him, Call her name Lo-ruhamah: for I will no more have mercy upon the house of Israel; but I will utterly take them away.

Lo-ruhamah is literally translated, "She received no mercy." What a name to give a little girl! People would be sure to ask about it. Then Hosea could reply, "She is like Israel. For many years Israel did receive mercy in spite of many sins, but the time of mercy is coming to an end. Soon God will withdraw His mercy from our people, and *will utterly take them away.* Then everybody will say of Israel, 'Lo-ruhamah: she received no mercy.'"

7. But I will have mercy upon the house of Judah, and will save them by the LORD their God, and will not save them by bow, nor by sword, nor by battle, by horses, nor by horsemen.

Hosea lived long after the big kingdom of Solomon was divided. The north part was called Israel. From it God's mercy soon would be withdrawn; its people would be taken away (v. 6). The south part was *Judah.* God would continue to have mercy on that kingdom. The hordes of Assyria would attack it too, but God would save Judah. He would do it by His own power, not by Judah's military strength. Second Kings 19:35, 36 tells how this prophecy was fulfilled. The angel of the Lord killed 185,000 of the Assyrian troops in a single night. The rest quickly went home, leaving Judah in peace.

KNOWING YOUR OWN STRENGTH

Did you ever try to loosen lug nuts (when changing a tire) that had been tightened by someone else who didn't know his own strength? Pneumatic torque wrenches have complicated that problem. The power that has been added to human strength by well-engineered tools is amazing.

Knowing one's strength is important; knowing the source of one's strength is *more important.* Before David challenged Goliath, he told King Saul, "The Lord that delivered me out of the paw of the lion, and out of the paw of the bear, he will deliver me out of the hand of this Philistine" (1 Samuel 17:37). David knew from whence came his help. Well might he sing, "My help cometh from the Lord, which made heaven and earth" (Psalm 121:2).

God's people must be reminded from whom our strength comes. God told Hosea that Judah would be saved, "not . . . by bow, nor by sword, nor by battle, by horses, nor by horsemen" (Hosea 1:7). God told Zerubbabel, "Not by might, nor by power, but by my Spirit" (Zechariah 4:6). The *enemies* of God's people also should know.

We who are Christians need to know our own weakness and the source of our strength. Paul knew. He wrote, "I can do all things through Christ which strengtheneth me" (Philippians 4:13).   —R. W. B.

C. Lo-ammi (vv. 8, 9)

8. Now when she had weaned Lo-ruhamah, she conceived, and bare a son.

In those days a baby might be breast-fed for three years before being weaned, so Lo-ruhamah may have been four years old when her baby brother was born.

9. Then said God, Call his name Lo-ammi: for ye are not my people, and I will not be your God.

Lo-ammi means "not my people." It was another name that would surely arouse interest and bring questions. "Why do you call your son 'not my people'?" "Because that is what the Lord God Almighty is saying to all of us. For centuries we have been His people, blessed with His special care and protection. But we have not acted like people of the Lord. We have been disobedient for a long time. Now our sins have piled up so high that the Lord is about to disown us. No longer will He protect us and provide for us. He will leave us to depend on our own resources, and we shall be destroyed."

Still the prophecy of doom was followed by a prophecy of restoration. Israel again would be innumerable; in the very place where God disowned her, He would claim her again, "for great shall be the day of Jezreel," the day when Israel would be planted again in her own land, the day when the valley of Jezreel would not be a place of conflict and defeat, but a fruitful field for peaceful production (vv. 10, 11).

III. Loving Restoration
(Hosea 3:1-5)

A. Restoring a Fallen Woman (vv. 1-3)

1. Then said the LORD unto me, Go yet, love a woman beloved of her friend, yet an adulteress, according to the love of the LORD toward the children of Israel, who look to other gods, and love flagons of wine.

The Lord sent His prophet to give loving care to *an adulteress.* Hosea bought her (v. 2), so it is evident that her adulteries had brought her misery and slavery instead of happiness. Most men would scorn such a woman, but Hosea was told to love her and help her. Thus he would picture *the love of the Lord toward the children of Israel.* The Israelites' devotion to other gods was adultery in a spiritual sense. It was going to bring them nothing but misery and slavery; but God's love would continue, and He would lift Israel out of misery and bondage.

Most Bible students today agree that this depraved woman was Hosea's wife, Gomer. It is supposed that she had decided to leave Hosea to live in adultery, that her paramours failed her, and so she finally became a prostitute and a slave. This opinion is so prevalent that the *New International Version* boldly writes it into the text. It quotes God as saying, "Go, show your love to your wife again."

However, not all students agree that the adulteress was Gomer. Some think there is not enough evidence to convict Hosea's wife of adultery, and she should be considered innocent till she is proved to be guilty. Gomer's name does not appear in this text from the third chapter, neither is the woman said to be Hosea's wife. Whether this depraved woman was Gomer or some other, the message of the text is the same. It focuses on the love of God, not the identity of the adulteress.

2. So I bought her to me for fifteen pieces of silver, and for a homer of barley, and a half homer of barley.

Footnotes in the *New International Version* estimate the purchase price as about six ounces of silver and ten bushels of barley. Exodus 21:32 indicates that a slave was worth thirty shekels of silver. Some students conclude that Hosea paid that price, but paid half of it in produce instead of silver.

3. And I said unto her, Thou shalt abide for me many days; thou shalt not play the harlot, and thou shalt not be for another man: so will I also be for thee.

Whether this woman was Gomer or not, she was not now to live with Hosea as his wife. She was to *abide,* to wait, for *many days.* She was not allowed to engage in prostitution. She was not to be *for a man.* The *King James Version* says *for another man,* but the word *another* is printed in italics, meaning that it is not in the original writing. The woman was to have no sexual relations at all, neither with Hosea nor with anyone else. Hosea likewise would abstain from sexual relations with her. The meaning of this is explained in the verses that follow.

B. Application to Israel (vv. 4, 5)

4. For the children of Israel shall abide many days without a king, and without a prince, and without a sacrifice, and without an image, and without an ephod, and without teraphim.

As the woman had left her husband for another man or for other men, so Israel had left the Lord for false gods. As the woman had become enslaved, so Israel had found herself enslaved by the many sins that go with false worship. As the woman was freed from her slavery but left without any sex life at all, so Israel was going to be freed from her present enslavement by being deported to foreign lands, but she would be without any national life or religious life at all. Scattered throughout foreign lands the people of Israel would no longer be a nation, so they would have no *king* or *prince.* They could not get together to offer *sacrifice* either to the Lord or to imaginary gods. They would have no *image* such as idolaters worship, and no *ephod* such as the priest wore when he conducted the proper worship of Jehovah. *Teraphim* were little idols kept at home, but the scattered Israelites would not even have them. They would no longer be able to worship idols, but neither would they be able to worship the Lord in the way prescribed by His law. This condition would continue for *many days,* for a long time.

This prophecy of scattering was fulfilled when the Assyrians overran Israel and took her people to other countries, as we have noted earlier in this lesson (Hosea 1:5, 6; 2 Kings 17:1-6). God saved Judah from the Assyrians (Hosea 1:7), but in later years Judah also sank so deep in sin that God abandoned her as well. Then the Babylonians destroyed Jerusalem and took most of the surviving people of Judah into captivity (2 Kings 25:8-12). It was about 722 B.C. when Israel fell to Assyria. It was about 586 B.C. when the Babylonians destroyed Jerusalem, and it was about fifty years later when the Jews were allowed to go back home (Ezra 1:1-4). They were

visual 7

indeed many days without a national life or a national religion. Those days added up to about 186 years.

5. Afterward shall the children of Israel return, and seek the LORD their God, and David their king; and shall fear the LORD and his goodness in the latter days.

The children of Israel would be deprived of nation and religion for a long time, but not forever. They would *return*. Again they would give their allegiance to *the Lord their God, and David their king*. The books of Ezra and Nehemiah record how people of Judah came back from captivity in Babylon. No doubt many of the scattered Israelites joined them in the years that followed. But Hosea's prophecy looks far beyond that. David would not be back in person, but with the New Testament to guide us, we know that the Israel of God includes not only people of Israel and Judah, but also people of all nations who give their allegiance to the Son of David, Jesus Christ. With reverence and awe, the people of this real Israel *fear the Lord and his goodness* now and forever.

TWICE OWNED BY GOD

The women's movement, in the last two or three decades has made a change in male/female relationships. Much of that change has been positive progress, affirming the personhood and rights of women. Most men no longer consider wives to be their personal property. Most wives have made it clear: "You don't own me!"

Gomer was in a different situation, as well as in a different culture. She was not only Hosea's wife, but Hosea had actually bought her back from the world of pimps, "Johns," and "tricks." At God's command, the prophet had married

her, then he redeemed her from unfaithfulness. So Gomer now belonged to Hosea by virtue of both the marriage covenant and the price of her redemption.

Israel belonged to God by virtue of both covenant and deliverance. Christians, too, are twice-owned: God made us; then He bought us. We are like the toy sailboat made by a boy, who later lost it. When finally he spied the boat in a pawnshop window, he bought it back. When we were lost in sin, God purchased our redemption with the blood of His only begotten Son.

None of us can say to God, "You don't own me!" "For ye are bought with a price: therefore glorify God in your body, and in your spirit, which are God's" (1 Corinthians 6:20).

—R. W. B.

Conclusion

A. Family Values

In recent political campaigns in the United States, much has been said about family values. Everyone seems to agree that we need to emphasize such values, but who knows exactly what they are? In a democracy, should we vote on what is good, and accept the majority opinion? No, in a diverse culture such as ours, that would result only in confusion.

God knows what is good, and He shares His knowledge with us. "He hath showed thee, O man, what is good; and what doth the Lord require of thee, but to do justly, and to love mercy, and to walk humbly with thy God?" (Micah 6:8).

Obeying God's Word is good for a family, and equally good for an individual or a nation. Justice, mercy, humility before God—these are right, and they will bring good results. Greed, mistreatment of others, ignoring God—these are wrong, and they will be punished. But God is as merciful as He wants us to be. If we leave our wicked ways and obey Him, He is ready to forgive and restore, for He loves us. Hosea strongly reaffirms the ringing call of Amos: "Let justice roll on like a river, righteousness like a never-failing stream!" (Amos 5:24, *New International Version*).

B. Let Us Pray

Dear God, teach us the paths of righteousness that we may walk in them. Make us aware of our own weakness that we may walk humbly. Teach us to show mercy and understanding to all those about us. In Jesus' name we pray. Amen.

C. Thought to Remember

There, but for the grace of God, go I.

Home Daily Bible Readings

Monday, July 10—Peace With God Through Christ (Romans 5:1-11)

Tuesday, July 11—God's Call to Hosea (Hosea 1:1-5)

Wednesday, July 12—Israel Compared With Hosea's Unfaithful Wife (Hosea 1:6—2:1)

Thursday, July 13—Public Shame and Hardship for Israel (Hosea 2:2-13)

Friday, July 14—God Will Woo Israel Back (Hosea 2:14-23)

Saturday, July 15—God Will Restore Israel (Hosea 3:1-5)

Sunday, July 16—Praise for God's Steadfast Love (Psalm 115:1-13)

Learning by Doing

This page contains an alternate lesson plan emphasizing learning activities. Classes desiring such student involvement will find these suggestions helpful.

Learning Goals

In this lesson you will lead your students to:

1. See how Hosea and his family illustrated God's relationship with Israel.

2. Determine what is involved for Christians and the church to live faithfully to God in the 1990s.

Into the Lesson

Before class, write the word *Betrayed* on the chalkboard. Ask students to form groups of four or five. Provide each group with paper and a pen. Ask them to list five situations in which a person might feel betrayed. (Some examples may include a spouse having an affair; a friend gossiping about him; a teen running away from parents.) A space is provided in the student book for writing suggestions.

Allow two to three minutes for groups to complete their discussions. Then ask each group to report the situations they listed. Write these on the chalkboard.

Lead students in exploring the feelings of betrayal by discussing these questions:

1. What kind of emotions tend to accompany being betrayed?

2. How does being betrayed tend to affect our ability to function?

After leading several minutes of discussion, make this transition into today's Scripture study: "I doubt that anyone can make it through life without feeling betrayed. People let us down. They hurt us.

"We need to realize that God himself has experienced constant betrayal. Our lesson today includes a vivid, real-life illustration of how God has been betrayed. We will consider the fact that we too can betray God. And we will explore what it means to live faithfully to Him in our generation."

Into the Word

Present a brief lecture on the background of Hosea. Use the information in the Introduction to this lesson as well as a Bible handbook or commentary or study Bible.

Ask students to form their groups again. Provide each group with a copy of the questions and assignment below. (These are found in the student book.) Provide each group with a sheet of poster board and felt-tip markers.

Before they discuss the questions, assign to each group one of the references printed with question 3. Ask each group to circle the one they are to discuss. (If you have more than four groups, two groups will be assigned the same passage. If you have fewer than four groups, don't worry about covering all the passages.)

Here are the questions and assignment, which are also in the student book:

After reading Hosea 1:1-9 and 3:1-5, discuss these questions and complete your assignment:

1. In what way was Hosea betrayed? How might that have affected him?

2. In what ways was God betrayed? How might that have affected Him?

3. How had the nation of Israel been unfaithful to God? Read your assigned passage in Hosea to discuss this question.

2:8, 13; 4:1, 2; 8:1-4; 10:4, 12, 13

4. Using the poster board and felt-tip markers, create a stick figure cartoon to illustrate how Israel had been unfaithful. Base your cartoon on your passage in question 3. Your cartoon can have as many frames as you desire.

Allow groups twenty minutes to complete their assignments. Then bring the groups together. Ask each one to present its cartoon with a brief explanation.

Lead students in discussing these questions:

1. How did Hosea serve as a living illustration?

2. Though Israel would be punished, what hope did God give the nation in 1:10, 11 and 3:4, 5?

Into Life

Help your students see the implications of Hosea for their lives by asking, "In what ways might we live unfaithfully to God without realizing it?" Allow for discussion.

Provide each student with a sheet of paper and a pencil. Ask students to write a brief essay on one of these two topics:

What it Means for the Christian to Be Faithful to God in the 1990s.

What it Means for the Church to Be Faithful to God in the 1990s.

Give your class five minutes to write their brief essays. When time has expired ask volunteers to read their essays to the class.

Close with students in their small groups. Ask them to pray that God will help them be faithful.

Let's Talk It Over

The questions on this page are designed to encourage review of the lesson Scriptures and to promote discussion of the lesson by the class. The answers provided are only discussion starters. Let your class talk it over from there.

1. With Hosea God worked in unusual ways to make His will known. May we sometimes fail to see and understand God's working because He works in ways we do not expect?

We know much about what God has done through the centuries of history, but that does not mean He can never do anything in a new way. Remember how the religious experts of Jesus' time opposed and crucified the Christ because He did not do what they expected Him to do.

We may reasonably assume that God will never contradict His written Word. We can be sure He will always be as Jesus represented Him. But that does not mean He will never surprise us.

All of us want to do our best in the Lord's work. When someone suggests a new method or program, some of us are quick to ask, "Has it ever been done?" A better question is, "Is it consistent with God's nature and will and purpose?"

2. Instead of thanking the Lord for their blessings, the people of Israel looked to other gods (Hosea 3:1). Do we also rob God of due credit and give it to others?

Just listen any day to the credit that is given to "Mother Nature," or "my lucky stars," or even "the weather man." Politicians are eager to take credit for prosperity, while denying any responsibility for recession. And who does not like to attribute success to his own efforts and blame failure on someone else?

We know God gives the sunshine and rain (Matthew 5:45), along with "every good gift and every perfect gift" (James 1:17). We know our physical and mental abilities are gifts from the Lord (1 Corinthians 4:7). Why are we so slow to give credit where credit is due?

3. Does God thwart our plans by putting obstacles in our path when we are going the wrong way? When everything is going smoothly, does that mean we are on the right road?

Obstacles may sometimes stop us when we are doing wrong, but sometimes they strengthen us when we are doing right (James 1:2-4). It is wise to consider circumstances and make use of opportunities, but we cannot depend on circumstances for a clear indication of what God wants

us to do. The easiest way may be the worst (Matthew 7:13, 14). God's Word is a better guide. Of course it does not give specific answers to all our problems, but it has clear principles to help us. The advice of good Christian friends may help, and circumstances also are to be considered.

But anything that violates the teaching of Scripture is wrong. We can be sure of that.

4. Would you find it hard to love someone who spurned everything you hold dear, including yourself and your love, and then nearly destroyed herself with wrongdoing?

Hosea's story is fascinating because of the depth of love he demonstrated in rescuing a woman that most people would call worthless. But the best part of that fascinating story is that it pictures God's love for us. In our selfish and self-destructive sinning we have rejected not only God's way, but the Father himself. The marvel is that God can love us so patiently and persistently through all our waywardness and stupidity. And Jesus told His disciples to love one another as He loved them. Obeying that word is a clear indication that we belong to Him (John 13:34, 35).

5. How can we expect biblical standards of morality to prevail when we allow freedom of religion to all, even atheists, witches, and Satan worshipers?

Obviously there is no way to compel non-Christians to act like Christians. We cannot even compel Christians to act as they ought to act. Freedom of religion is not just a principle of law; it is a fact of life. This would be true even if the church were in complete control of the government and was determined to make everyone a Christian by law. A Satan worshiper will worship Satan still, even if he is compelled to join a church. An atheist baptized against his will is no more a Christian than is an atheist who was never baptized.

How can we make biblical standards more influential in our country? By persuading people to turn to God and obey Him. God has already done His part by extending His love to all the world (John 3:16). Our part is to let all of the world know about it.

God's Love for Israel

DEVOTIONAL READING: Psalm 103:6-14.

LESSON SCRIPTURE: Hosea 11.

PRINTED TEXT: Hosea 11:1-9.

Hosea 11:1-9

1 When Israel was a child, then I loved him, and called my son out of Egypt.

2 As they called them, so they went from them: they sacrificed unto Baalim, and burned incense to graven images.

3 I taught Ephraim also to go, taking them by their arms; but they knew not that I healed them.

4 I drew them with cords of a man, with bands of love: and I was to them as they that take off the yoke on their jaws, and I laid meat unto them.

5 He shall not return into the land of Egypt, but the Assyrian shall be his king, because they refused to return.

6 And the sword shall abide on his cities, and shall consume his branches, and devour them, because of their own counsels.

7 And my people are bent to backsliding from me: though they called them to the Most High, none at all would exalt him.

8 How shall I give thee up, Ephraim? how shall I deliver thee, Israel? how shall I make thee as Admah? how shall I set thee as Zeboim? mine heart is turned within me, my repentings are kindled together.

9 I will not execute the fierceness of mine anger, I will not return to destroy Ephraim: for I am God, and not man; the Holy One in the midst of thee: and I will not enter into the city.

GOLDEN TEXT: I will heal their backsliding, I will love them freely: for mine anger is turned away from him.—Hosea 14:4.

A. Nation Turns From God
Unit 2: The Approaching Judgment
(Lesson 5-9)

Lesson Aims

After this lesson, each student should:

1. Have a better understanding of God's love for Israel.

2. Appreciate the fact that God still exercises love for mankind.

3. Be better able to extend unconditional love to others.

Lesson Outline

INTRODUCTION

God's faithfulness to Israel is the subject of visual 8 of the visuals packet. This visual is pictured on page 405.

Introduction

A. Condemnation and Forgiveness

Dwight L. Moody, that popular evangelist of the last century, brought thousands of people under conviction before God by his thunderous denunciation of sin and sinners. But Moody's message was not entirely of judgment and doom. He also offered God's love and forgiveness. On one occasion the governor asked him to deliver a pardon to a prisoner then in the state prison. Moody was delighted to carry out the assignment. At a chapel service he preached a powerful sermon about the righteous judgment of God, but in his conclusion he told of God's forgiveness. Then just before the benediction, he called the fortunate prisoner forward and presented him with the pardon.

Hosea's ministry was rather like this. Much of his message was one of condemnation for Israel's sins and of God's judgment upon the nation. But he also brought a message of hope and restoration to the people.

B. Lesson Background

Last week's lesson provided the historical background for the ministry of Hosea. He began his ministry when Israel was enjoying great prosperity, but accompanying this prosperity was a great falling away from God's laws. It became the prophet's painful duty to bring a message of condemnation for the sins of the people. His burden was made the more painful by the tragedy of his own marriage, which typified God's relationship with Israel.

He had to speak of the punishment that would come to Israel through Assyria. This violent nation would soon take Syria, which was to the north of Israel. Then in 722 B.C. it would capture Israel's capital, Samaria, and take many of the citizens away into bondage. But God gave Hosea the prophetic vision to see beyond these disasters. He could see a God who would not give up on Ephraim (Israel), and who would not execute the fierceness of His anger upon His people. Once the people had turned from their idolatry, God would restore them.

I. The Richness of God's Love (Hosea 11:1-4)

A. God's Love for Israel in Egypt (v. 1)

1. When Israel was a child, then I loved him, and called my son out of Egypt.

God remembered Israel even while they were trapped in the agony of the Egyptian bondage. *Israel was a child:* that is, they were just in the early stages of their development as God's people. But they were children in another sense. They were completely helpless to deliver themselves from their Egyptian tyrants. God did not love them because they had done anything to deserve His love. Indeed, like a true parent, He loved them precisely because they were helpless and unworthy. *I . . . called my son out of Egypt.* This reminds us of the words of Moses before Pharaoh: "Thus saith the Lord, Israel is my son, even my firstborn" (Exodus 4:22).

We often take our blessings for granted, forgetting what they cost our forefathers. We enjoy our Thanksgiving turkey with scarcely a thought about the suffering the early Pilgrims bore. We celebrate our freedom without ever thinking of how it was hammered out on the bitter anvil of Valley Forge and sustained by the bloodshed at Gettysburg.

B. The Rejection of God's Love (v. 2)

2. As they called them, so they went from them: they sacrificed unto Baalim, and burned incense to graven images.

As they called them probably has reference to the numerous calls God had made to His people through Moses, the judges, kings like David, and the prophets. God had not made just one call to the people while they were in bondage in Egypt, but had continued through a variety of spokesmen to remind them again and again of the covenant He had made with them on Mount Sinai. These frequent reminders were necessary because the people soon forgot.

They sacrificed unto Baalim. When the Israelites entered the promised land, they came into contact with the Canaanites, who were followers of Baal. Thus from the beginning they were tempted by this false god. *Baalim* is plural because he was worshiped under different forms in different places. The worship of Baal often involved sexual orgies, and even infant sacrifice.

The people *burned incense to graven images,* indicating their commitment to a pagan god represented by an idol. While burning incense was not as vile as some of the other acts of worship, it was plainly condemned by God.

C. God as a Loving Parent (vv. 3, 4)

3. I taught Ephraim also to go, taking them by their arms; but they knew not that I healed them.

Ephraim was the name of one of the more powerful tribes of the northern kingdom and was sometimes used to signify the whole northern kingdom. The picture is of a parent teaching a child to walk. God as a parent had been beside Israel to guide and protect him as he took his first steps. *Taking them by their arms* pictures God holding their arms to guide and protect them during their first halting and unsteady steps. The *Revised Standard Version* has "I took them up in my arms," suggesting an even more tender and loving God who embraced them and comforted them when they fell and hurt themselves.

They knew not that I healed them. This was the tragedy of the situation. Even though God had comforted them when they had been hurt and healed their bruises when they had fallen, yet they had not acknowledged their benefactor. Such behavior is unnatural, for a small child will normally turn to his parents when he is

---

How to Say It

ADMAH. *Ad*-muh.
ASSYRIA. Uh-*sear*-ee-uh.
BAAL. *Bay*-ul.
BAALIM. *Bay*-uh-lim.
BAALISM. *Bay*-uh-lism.
CANAANITES. *Kay*-nan-ites.
EPHRAIM. *Ee*-fray-im.
GOMORRAH. Guh-*mor*-uh.
HOSHEA. Ho-*she*-uh.
SINAI. *Sye*-nay-eye or *Sye*-nye.
SODOM. *Sod*-um.
SYRIA. *Sear*-ee-uh.
ZEBOIM. Ze-*bo*-im.

---

hurting or discouraged. This is a theme God's spokesmen often used—that Israel's rejection of God was unnatural.

4. I drew them with cords of a man, with bands of love: and I was to them as they that take off the yoke on their jaws, and I laid meat unto them.

I drew them with cords of a man. Hosea now changes the figure. He portrays Israel as a stubborn young calf. Anyone who has worked with young calves knows that they can be about as stubborn as any animal, and their strength makes them hard to control. Sometimes about the only way to handle such an animal when it sets its heels is with a firm tug on a strong rope about its neck. On occasion God had to resort to such not-so-gentle treatment. More often, however, He guided them with the less harsh bands of love. A parent might use a soft harness and a leash to guide and protect a child; we would hardly expect a loving parent to use a heavy, abrasive rope for this purpose. On one occasion Jesus said, "I, if I be lifted up from the earth, will draw all men unto me" (John 12:32). Ultimately, love is far more powerful than threats and violence.

I was to them as they that take off the yoke on their jaws. God is now depicted as a farmer who removes the heavy wooden yoke from the neck of the oxen at the end of a busy day. This yoke may specifically refer to the Egyptian bondage, but it may also include several other occasions when the people were subjugated by their neighbors. Each time God had removed this heavy burden.

I laid meat unto them. This has reference to any food, not just edible animal flesh. The *New International Version* renders this "I . . . bent down to feed them." The picture of a parent patiently feeding his or her child adds another gentle touch to this view of God.

UNGRATEFUL KIDS

Most parents are thrilled when their children take first steps. Lots of hugging and picture-taking usually accompany the event. Such moments make happy memories.

Have your kids ever thanked you for teaching them to walk? Probably not. Parental help and support is taken for granted by children. And parents don't expect to be thanked by toddlers for acts of love and caring. Our reward comes in seeing children develop skills and make achievements.

Gratitude doesn't come naturally for children. It is a learned response that grows out of experience and example. Ephraim behaved as ingrates, but they were old enough to know better. They had experienced the love, care, protection, and encouragement of Father Jehovah for centuries. Gratitude should have expressed itself in Israel's obedience and faithfulness. They should have matured enough to live lives that said, "Thank You, God."

Now, we are a new generation of God's children. He has given every skill, talent, and resource. He has helped us with every accomplishment. Have we acknowledged His support and guidance? Do our work, worship, and service say, "Thank You, Lord"?   —R. W. B.

II. God's Continued Love
(Hosea 11:5-9)

A. Punishment for Rejecting God's Love
(vv. 5, 6)

5. He shall not return into the land of Egypt, but the Assyrian shall be his king, because they refused to return.

From speaking of God's love and concern for His people, Hosea turns abruptly to speak of His judgment, which would soon fall upon those people. Assyria posed a growing threat to Israel. Some feel that the mention of Egypt is a reference to the efforts that some were making to work out an alliance with Egypt to help fend off the Assyrians. It may be better that the Israelites would not be returning to bondage in Egypt, but would fall under the heavy hand of Assyria. As devastating as the Egyptian bondage had been, the Assyrian conquest would be worse. This disaster would come upon them because they had refused to return to God.

6. And the sword shall abide on his cities, and shall consume his branches, and devour them, because of their own counsels.

The fate of Israel would be even more painful than the Egyptian bondage, for the Assyrians would bring war to the land with all its death and suffering. In such times the people normally fled to the cities, hoping to find protection behind their walls. Sometimes this was a wise action, but it did not work against the Assyrians. Archaeologists have provided convincing evidence of the efficiency of the Assyrian war machine. Using battering rams and siege towers, they were able to overwhelm even the best fortified cities. Once a breach was made in a city wall, the Assyrian soldiers would rush in and finish their bloody task with swords. *Branches* is translated "bars of their gates" in some modern versions.

The reason for this terrible judgment upon Israel was that they had followed *their own counsels.* The leaders and the people had followed false prophets. Some of this bad advice had led the people to turn to Baal and other pagan gods. This bad advice may also have referred to the activities of King Hoshea, who reigned from about 732 to 722 B.C. He sought assistance from the pharaoh of Egypt against the Assyrians. When the Assyrians learned of this, they increased the pressure on Israel, captured Hoshea, and laid siege to Samaria, its capital (2 Kings 17:1-6).

B. Israel's Proneness to Backsliding
(v. 7)

7. And my people are bent to backsliding from me: though they called them to the Most High, none at all would exalt him.

The Hebrew text poses some difficulties in this verse. As a result, many later versions give a reading that differs from the *King James Version.* Regardless of the version we choose to follow, the verse makes certain points. First of all, God has not rejected His people. He still refers to them as *my people.* The second point is that their rejection of God is not just an occasional departure from His teaching. Rather, it reflects a deeply ingrained tendency to backslide. Their apostasy took two forms. It was sometimes theological: that is, they turned from Jehovah to pagan deities. It was often moral, in that they turned from the ethical teachings of the covenant to worldly behavior.

DOGS AND HOGS

Dogs have long enjoyed a reputation of being "man's best friend." Cat-lovers have argued otherwise. In recent years, many folk have found *hogs* to be quite friendly pets. Regardless of your preference, most animals have one or two obnoxious habits. The apostle Peter quotes this proverb: "The dog is turned to his own vomit again; and the sow that was washed to her wallowing in the mire" (2 Peter 2:22).

God was grieved at Israel's "bent to backsliding." He had delivered them, protected them, and provided for them. Yet they repeatedly turned to other gods. Such unfaithfulness breaks the heart of the Lord.

The dog-and-hog proverb illustrates the human tendency to regress to old habits. "You can take the hog out of the mud," Peter could have said, "but you can't take the mud out of the hog." Though animals can hardly be held accountable for instinctive behavior, humans have conscience and power to choose. Christ not only can take us out of sin, but He also *can take sin out of us.* When saved people choose to disobey, "the latter end is worse . . . than the beginning" (2 Peter 2:20).   —R. W. B.

C. God's Mercy Toward Israel (vv. 8, 9)

8. How shall I give thee up, Ephraim? how shall I deliver thee, Israel? how shall I make thee as Admah? how shall I set thee as Zeboim? mine heart is turned within me, my repentings are kindled together.

The previous verses brought a message of judgment. Now the prophet brings words of mercy. He shows that God's judgment is not dealt out whimsically or from a desire to see the people suffer. Rather, he shows God deliberating between His justice on one hand and His mercy on the other. God's love is a holy love that requires satisfaction when it is violated. Yet it is also a compassionate love that seeks to salvage the fallen Ephraim. The people deserved to be punished, and yet God did not desire to turn them over to their enemies. In a sense God faced and still faces a dilemma that can be solved only through the sacrificial death of His Son (Romans 3:24-26).

Admah . . . Zeboim. These two cities were located near Sodom and Gomorrah, probably at the southern end of the Dead Sea. They had suffered the same fate as these two infamous cities (Deuteronomy 29:23). Down through the centuries these cities have become a symbol of God's righteous judgment. Ephraim deserved a similar judgment, but the nation could still be spared if it heeded the prophet.

Mine heart is turned within me, my repentings are kindled together. Even as God contemplated the punishment that Ephraim rightly deserved, His compassion stirred within Him. On more than one occasion, the Scriptures speak of God's repenting. For example, when God looked upon the earth in the time of Noah, we are told that "it repented the Lord that he had made man on the earth" (Genesis 6:6). However, we are not to think of this as being the same thing as human repentance. It certainly does not imply a moral

visual 8

"I taught Ephraim also to go, taking them by their arms"

change on God's part; it is an attempt to express in human language God's actions.

9. I will not execute the fierceness of mine anger, I will not return to destroy Ephraim: for I am God, and not man; the Holy One in the midst of thee: and I will not enter into the city.

God would indeed punish His wayward children, but He would not utterly destroy them. God is not human: He would not go too far, as an angry man might do. *I will not enter into the city* for the purpose of destroying it. Although God's punishment would fall upon Ephraim, it would be tempered by His mercy. The following verses explain that their punishment, exile at the hands of the Assyrians, would eventually be followed by their restoration.

Anthropocentricity

"God created man in his own image" (Genesis 1:27), and we tend to think of God in *our* own image. Though we know He is spirit, we generally think of Him as having human characteristics: hands, ears, feet, and face.

Many of our ideas about God are *anthropocentric*—centered in what we know about human traits. For example, divine mercy is difficult to understand because our idea of justice is drawn from humanity's imperfect examples.

In light of Israel's gross unfaithfulness, we might think that God's response would be angry vengeance. Yet God says, "I will not return to destroy Ephraim: for I am God, and not man."

Aren't we lucky that God is God? We are quick to condemn and slow to forgive, but He "looks beyond our fault and sees our need." "The Lord . . . is long-suffering to us-ward, not willing that any should perish, but that all should come to repentance" (2 Peter 3:9).   —R. W. B.

Conclusion

A. Assured Mercy

The children of Israel had a unique relationship with God. In a very real sense they were the chosen people, chosen as a means of bringing God's plan of salvation to the entire human race.

The Israelites had not been chosen because they had special qualifications that others lacked. Trapped in grinding slavery in Egypt, they seemed to have little chance of ever making any significant contribution to the world. Yet God in His marvelous grace led them out of that bondage into a land that they could claim as their own. Step by halting step He led them to independence and prosperity.

That progress had not been easy. Again and again the people had strayed from Jehovah, seeking other gods and abandoning the paths of righteousness He had set before them. Hosea wrote as Israel stood poised on the brink of national catastrophe. The instrument of that disaster, the Assyrians, were already threatening. Hosea did not draw back from announcing this impending doom. Yet even as he brought God's word of judgment, he also offered hope, hope based upon God's love for His people.

We speak of America as being a Christian nation, but as a nation we cannot claim the special relationship that Israel enjoyed with God. It is true that for most of our history we have been guided by, or at least we have paid lip service to, Christian values. But in a proper sense only individuals can be Christians, not nations. We must gratefully acknowledge that God has richly blessed our nation, in part at least because we have followed Christian principles.

Suppose God were to send Hosea to America today. What kind of a message would he bring? Certainly he would be appalled because he would see so many parallels between his time and ours: crime rampant not only in the highways but in high places, sexual promiscuity openly flaunted, homes shattered, and personal morality considered out of date. His message would assuredly reverberate with the somber sounds of judgment.

Yet there would also be words of mercy—the unflagging love of a husband for an adulterous wife, the love of God the Father for His erring child. Make no mistake. Our nation rapidly approaches the precipice of moral disaster. If we are to be spared God's wrath, we must turn from our worldly ways, cease our backsliding, and turn once more to God. When we do return to Him we can do so with the assurance that His mercy is still available.

B. Hold It Steady

Beside his shop my grandfather had a big grindstone that was turned by a crank. My cousin and I would occasionally try to sharpen our knives on the stone. But try as we might, we never could get a sharp edge on our knives. Granddad offered good advice: "Boys, if you want a keen edge on your blade, you have to hold it steady against the stone."

That was good advice for sharpening a knife, and it is also good advice for maintaining our proper relationship with God. In a way God's commandments are like a grindstone, which, when properly used, can bring our lives to a keen moral edge. To accomplish this desired end, we have to hold our lives steady against God's laws. This is not an easy task and sometimes it is even painful. If one does not use a grindstone properly, he can ruin a knife. In the same way, if we misunderstand God's laws or misapply them, we can do serious damage to our lives. If we are not willing to work at it, our lives will never have the keen, cutting edge that they must have if we are to be pleasing to God. But by God's grace, we can become morally keen and useful if we hold our lives steady against His commandments.

That is the only way our nation can be spared. Good laws will help, of course, and we must work for good laws. But in the end, only a dedicated citizenry whose lives are honed to a keen edge can save our nation.

C. Let Us Pray

Almighty God, help us learn from these ancient prophets how to walk humbly with You in obedience to Your commandments. Let us never forget that You are a righteous God who demands that we become holy. Let us also never forget that You are a merciful God who will forgive us and restore us and set our feet on the right pathway if we but turn to You. Amen.

D. Thought to Remember

"Whom the Lord loveth he chasteneth" (Hebrews 12:6).

Home Daily Bible Readings

Monday, July 17—Mercy for Those Who Love God (Psalm 103:6-14)

Tuesday, July 18—Punishment for Israel's Unfaithfulness (Hosea 10:9-15)

Wednesday, July 19—God's Love Has Been Rejected (Hosea 11:1-7)

Thursday, July 20—God's Anger Is Restrained by Compassion (Hosea 11:8-12)

Friday, July 21—Israel Urged to Return to God (Hosea 14)

Saturday, July 22—A Prayer for God's Forgiveness (Psalm 79:8-13)

Sunday, July 23—God Forgives and Restores (Psalm 130)

Learning by Doing

This page contains an alternate lesson plan emphasizing learning activities. Classes desiring such student involvement will find these suggestions helpful.

Learning Goals

Seek to lead the students to:

1. Explore the nature of God's love to unfaithful Israel.

2. Celebrate God's love for them.

Into the Lesson

Write the following sentence on the chalkboard before class:

If it weren't for God's love—

Give a sheet of paper and a pencil to each student. Or, if you use the student book, distribute copies. Ask each student to write at least three ways of completing the sentence.

Ask your class to form groups of four to six. In their groups they should allow volunteers to share how they completed the sentence.

Allow several minutes. Then say to the class, "We often take God's love for granted. According to the Bible, however, God doesn't owe us His love. In fact, if we got what we deserve, we would be in a terrible condition. We can be thankful that God has not treated us as we deserve. In our study today we will see this illustrated in the nation of Israel."

Into the Word

Present a brief lecture to review last week's Scripture text and to set the background for today's passage. You will find some helpful information in the introduction to this week's commentary.

Your students should remain in their groups. They are to study the specified passages in Hosea and discuss the questions below. These questions are included in the student book:

1. Read Hosea 11:1-9. How had God shown His love to Israel? (vv. 1, 3, 4) Note: Israel is also called Ephraim.

2. How had Israel been unfaithful to God? (vv. 2, 7)

3. What would happen to Israel because the people refused to repent? (vv. 5, 6)

4. Verses 8 and 9 indicate that though God would punish Israel, God still had compassion on His people. Paraphrase these two verses as a group.

5. Read Hosea 14:1-4. God wanted Israel to return to Him, but with more than empty words. What would it take for Israel to return to God according to verse 2? According to verse 3?

Allow students about fifteen minutes for discussion. Then bring the groups together. Ask the class: "What did Israel deserve from God?" Allow for discussion. (The clear teaching of Scripture is that Israel deserved severe punishment and rejection from God.) Then say, "God wanted to overwhelm Israel with goodness and kindness even though Israel needed punishment. So He determined to soften the punishment and give Israel a chance to return. This is passionately expressed in Hosea 11:8, 9, which each group paraphrased."

Ask each group to read their paraphrase. Then read Psalm 103:1-12. Ask, "What phrases from this passage are illustrated in Hosea?" Allow for comments.

Options

Have students continue in the groups they began in. Give the groups a choice of how to explore Hosea 11:1-9. The options are:

1. Discuss the questions above, which are also in the student book.

2. Read Hosea 11:1-9. As a group prepare a pantomime to depict the passage. Be prepared to present the pantomime to the class.

3. Create a mural to depict what is said in Hosea 11:1-9. The mural should contain several scenes that are expressed in the passage.

Provide groups doing number 1 with a copy of the questions, and groups doing number 3 with newsprint, pencils, and felt-tip markers.

Allow fifteen to twenty minutes for groups to complete. Then bring the groups together and allow each group to present its work to the class.

Into Life

Lead your class in celebrating God's amazing love. Provide each student with a hymnal. Ask students to look for hymns that focus on God's love. They may look in the topical index, perhaps under God's love or Christ's love.

Ask them to note phrases that especially help them appreciate God's love. After about three minutes, ask students to read from some of the hymns they found moving. If the class knows the song, ask a talented member to lead in singing it.

Close with a praise time. Ask the class to worship God by completing this sentence, spoken to God: Father, Your love is —

Let's Talk It Over

The questions on this page are designed to encourage review of the lesson Scriptures and to promote discussion of the lesson by the class. The answers provided are only discussion starters. Let your class talk it over from there.

1. How can we keep from forgetting God's blessings as Israel did?

Most of us have "good forgetters." Our tendency seems to be a lapse of memory of how God has redeemed us and worked for good in our lives. Would that we could as easily forget all slights and hurts from other people!

Such forgetfulness is not new, and certainly God is aware of it. Think how Jesus instituted the Lord's Supper "in remembrance." We do need reminders, and perhaps visible ones do the most good.

God's written Word is one obvious help, not just as a visible symbol, a decoration on the coffee table, but as a help made effective by daily reading and meditation. The weekly meeting of the church is another help. If we neglect these reminders, very likely we will follow the path that Israel chose—with the same results.

2. How has God patiently and lovingly guided and healed our nation, even when we did not recognize and acknowledge His help?

When we look honestly at the material blessings we enjoy in the United States, we can hardly deny that they are more than we deserve, and those blessings are shared by most of the countries where this book is read. Those of us who put our faith in God are convinced that He is the source of our blessings. Our forefathers held that same conviction, and it is reflected in many patriotic songs and writings. Christians ought to be leading in the effort to make everybody aware of God's help and be grateful for it, and they ought to be leading in the effort to make sure all people are treated fairly and have equal opportunities. God's goodness to our nation, besides His grace in bringing forgiveness and life to believers, leads us to work for the healing of all relationships.

3. Does God's perspective differ from ours because He is able to see the future as well as the past? How can we keep from being too shortsighted?

God does see things differently (Isaiah 55:8, 9), but He has given us His Spirit and His Word so we can approach life from His point of view rather than ours. We can see much more than the world sees, if we are earnestly trying to see

God's way and follow it. The old adage about counting to ten may well be replaced by a call to take time to pray.

Can we train ourselves to think of fellow Christians as players on the same team and having the same desire to win that we have? Then when one of them does something wrong we can realize that he did not intend to do wrong—and most of us realize that the next wrong-doing may be our own. If God can be so gracious as to forgive us, surely we can extend that kind of grace to those around us. That does not condone sin—it treats it in the way God does.

4. Try to understand God's dilemma: He has to punish sin and destroy evil, yet He loves people and wants them to be free to choose and to respond to Him by their own wish, not by compulsion. How does Jesus' death resolve that dilemma?

Glibly we talk about hating sin and loving the sinner, but God really does it. On one hand we can see why Hell is a reality; it is needed because of God's goodness and the need for evil to be destroyed. On the other hand, we can see that God has given us the awesome responsibility of loving and serving Him. The same choice was given to Adam and Eve, and to every person. Because of many bad choices, God has answered our terrible need with a gift we don't deserve: forgiveness of sin and life eternal, made available through Jesus' death on the cross. When we respond to our Father's call, His love impells us to share the good news and urge others to respond as well.

5. John the Baptist challenged people to "bring forth therefore fruits worthy of repentance," and then went on to specify what he meant. What would he specify for our generation?

John focused on several areas: sharing with the poor, dealing honestly (spoken to tax officials), not abusing the powerless (directed to soldiers), being moral in life (aimed at King Herod) (Luke 3:10-14, 19). Would he signal the same call to people of today? John spoke sternly to religious people who ought to know God's way (Luke 3:7-9); would he have similar words for some of us churchgoers?

Greedy Leaders Denounced

DEVOTIONAL READING: Micah 2:1-7.

LESSON SCRIPTURE: Micah 1—3.

PRINTED TEXT: Micah 3:5-12.

Micah 3:5-12

5 Thus saith the LORD concerning the prophets that make my people err, that bite with their teeth, and cry, Peace; and he that putteth not into their mouths, they even prepare war against him:

6 Therefore night shall be unto you, that ye shall not have a vision; and it shall be dark unto you, that ye shall not divine; and the sun shall go down over the prophets, and the day shall be dark over them.

7 Then shall the seers be ashamed, and the diviners confounded: yea, they shall all cover their lips; for there is no answer of God.

8 But truly I am full of power by the Spirit of the LORD, and of judgment, and of might, to declare unto Jacob his transgression, and to Israel his sin.

9 Hear this, I pray you, ye heads of the house of Jacob, and princes of the house of Israel, that abhor judgment, and pervert all equity.

10 They build up Zion with blood, and Jerusalem with iniquity.

11 The heads thereof judge for reward, and the priests thereof teach for hire, and the prophets thereof divine for money: yet will they lean upon the LORD, and say, Is not the LORD among us? none evil can come upon us.

12 Therefore shall Zion for your sake be plowed as a field, and Jerusalem shall become heaps, and the mountain of the house as the high places of the forest.

Jul
30

GOLDEN TEXT: Then shall they cry unto the LORD, but he will not hear them: he will even hide his face from them at that time, as they have behaved themselves ill in their doings.—Micah 3:4.

A Nation Turns From God
Unit 2: The Approaching Judgment
(Lessons 5-9)

Lesson Aims

As a result of studying this lesson, each student should:

1. Understand more fully the problems created by corrupt leaders.

2. Have a growing commitment to personal integrity.

3. Be able to suggest one or more ways in which he or she can help to improve the dedication of leaders not only in the church but also in our society.

Lesson Outline

INTRODUCTION
 A. A Nineteenth-Century Micah
 B. Lesson Background
 I. THE FALSE PROPHETS (Micah 3:5-7)
 A. They Lead People Astray (v. 5a)
 B. They Are Greedy (v. 5b)
 C. They Will Be Confounded (vv. 6, 7)
 1-900-HIS WORD
 II. THE TRUE PROPHET (Micah 3:8-12)
 A. He Proclaims His Authority (v. 8)
 Power and Light Company
 B. He Condemns the Rulers (vv. 9, 10)
 C. He Condemns the Judges, Priests, and Prophets (v. 11)
 Ministerial Mercenaries
 D. He Pronounces Doom Upon Jerusalem (v. 12)
CONCLUSION
 A. We Need a Modern Micah
 B. Like Priest, Like People
 C. Let Us Pray
 D. Thought to Remember

The divine inspiration of God's prophets sent to Israel is asserted by visual 9 of the visuals packet. The visual is shown on page 413.

Introduction

A. A Nineteenth-Century Micah

In 1825 Alexander Campbell wrote a biting satire he called the *Third Epistle of Peter*, which he directed against the clergy of his day. It reminds us so much of Micah's writing that it bears repeating.

"In all of your gettings get money! Now, therefore, when ye go forth on your ministerial journey, go where there are silver and gold, and where each man will pay according to his measure. For verily I say ye must get your reward...

"And when ye shall have fleeced your flock, and shall know of another call, and if the flock be greater, or rather if the fleece be greater, then greater be also unto you the call....

"And the more that the people give you the more will they honor you; for they shall believe that 'in giving to you they are giving to the Lord'; for behold their sight shall be taken from them, and they shall be blind as bats, and 'shall know not what they do.'...

"And ye shall wax richer and richer, and grow greater and greater, and you shall be lifted up in your own sight, and exalted in the eyes of the multitude; and *lucre* shall be no longer *filthy* in your sight. And verily ye shall have your reward...."

As they say on television, "Only the names have been changed." If these charges were true one hundred seventy years ago in Campbell's day and true twenty-seven hundred years ago in Micah's day, what assurance do we have that we don't still have the problem today?

B. Lesson Background

Micah, whose ministry was carried on in the latter part of the eighth century B.C. was a contemporary of Hosea and Isaiah. We know little about him personally except that he came from the town of Moresheth, about twenty miles southwest of Jerusalem.

When he began his ministry during the reign of Jotham, both Judah and Israel were enjoying prosperity; but that was soon to end. Already Assyria, the great power from the northeast, was beginning to make itself felt. Soon Syria fell, and then in 722 B.C. Samaria, the capital of the northern kingdom, was captured and thousands of its citizens were carried off into captivity. Before Micah's ministry ended, Judah also was to feel the wrath of the Assyrian marauders. Sennacherib, who ruled Assyria from 705 B.C. to 681 B.C., boasted about taking forty-six towns and walled cities in Judah.

Micah, although he grew up in a rural area, was quite aware of the evils that beset the society of Judah. His message echoes the messages of Amos and Hosea that we have already studied. He spoke out against corrupt leaders, greedy priests, and injustices that oppressed the poor. He foretold the judgment that God would bring upon Judah through the Babylonians, but he also looked forward to the time when God would heal His people and restore their land.

I. The False Prophets
(Micah 3:5-7)

A. They Lead People Astray (v. 5a)

5a. Thus saith the Lord concerning the prophets that make my people err, that bite with their teeth, and cry, Peace.

In the previous verses Micah has already condemned the "heads of Jacob" and the "princes of the house of Israel" for oppressing the people. Now he turns to the religious leaders, the prophets and priests. These should have had an even greater responsibility to protect the people. Where there is good money, counterfeit money often arises. In the same way, because there are true prophets, false prophets appear. Since there were true prophets like Micah and Isaiah, others, not sent by God nor inspired by His Holy Spirit, sought to cash in on prophetic work. The result was that the people were led into error. When the blind lead the blind, both are likely to fall into the ditch. Micah's personal involvement is obvious as he speaks of *my people*, an expression that he uses several other times. Like any good shepherd, he makes the welfare of his flock his primary concern.

That bite with their teeth, perhaps suggesting the attack of wolves on a flock of sheep, indicates the harm they do to the people. They *cry, Peace,* even as the Assyrian enemy was preparing to invade the land. Instead of warning the people of the impending danger, they gave them the false assurance that the peace and prosperity that they were enjoying would continue. It is bad to warn of danger when none exists, but it is much worse not to warn of danger when it is impending.

B. They Are Greedy (v. 5b)

5b. And he that putteth not into their mouths, they even prepare war against him.

The false prophets had a price tag on their services. They expected to be fed when they brought their prophecies. They remind us of the false teacher that Paul mentions in Philippians 3:18, 19: "For many walk, of whom I have told you often, and now tell you even weeping, that they are the enemies of the cross of Christ: whose end is destruction, whose God is their belly, and whose glory is in their shame, who mind earthly things."

They prepare war against any who refuse to pay the bribes. This may mean that they actually threatened them with physical violence. It is more likely, however, that they would prophesy evil against those who refused to pay. In a culture that held prophets in high regard, this was a frightening threat.

C. They Will Be Confounded (vv. 6, 7)

6. Therefore night shall be unto you, that ye shall not have a vision; and it shall be dark unto you, that ye shall not divine; and the sun shall go down over the prophets, and the day shall be dark over them.

God's message was of coming judgment; but this was a very unpopular message. These so-called prophets gave instead a message that people liked and would pay for, a message of continuing prosperity. Such prophets would *not have a vision:* that is, they would not receive any revelation from God. The sun would go down; darkness would fall upon them; they would be ignorant of the truth.

7. Then shall the seers be ashamed, and the diviners confounded: yea, they shall all cover their lips; for there is no answer of God.

God gives *no answer* to mercenary prophets who care more for money than for truth. In time their lies will prove to be lies, and then they will be *confounded* and *ashamed.* In disgrace they will *cover their lips* and speak no more.

1-900-His Word

"Psychic Hotlines" seem to be the newest craze in telephone scams. Just call that 900 number, and you can connect yourself to some phony fortuneteller who, with a very sexy voice, will predict your future.

Imagine the devastating blow to a caller's self-esteem, if, when he dialed a sexy psychic, he was put "on hold," or if no one answered at all!

Micah pronounced God's judgment on mercenary seers, proclaiming that they would receive no answer from God. Divine truth and wisdom are not to be commercialized. God's supernatural gifts cannot be bought, nor are they to be sold. Simon, the sorcerer of Samaria, had to learn that lesson too (Acts 8:9-24).

Prophesying for money is selfish and shameful. Truly, "The love of money is the root of all evil" (1 Timothy 6:10). Basic greed is behind every contract that sinners sign with Satan. God's servants are not immune to such temptations. Nor are Christians nonsusceptible to the seduction of psychics. The lure of knowing the future is most enticing.

How to Say It

Assyrian. Uh-*sear*-ee-un.
Micah. *My*-kuh.
Sennacherib. Sen-*nack*-er-ib.

But all of the future we need to know is revealed in the Scriptures. God prophesies through His Word—and it doesn't cost two dollars a minute!   —R. W. B.

II. The True Prophet
(Micah 3:8-12)

A. He Proclaims His Authority (v. 8)

8. But truly I am full of power by the Spirit of the LORD, and of judgment, and of might, to declare unto Jacob his transgression, and to Israel his sin.

Micah contrasts his ministry with that of the false prophets. First of all, he presents the basis for his authority. His prophecies are not rooted in his imagination, nor do they come out of his desire to make money by pleasing the crowd. Rather, he is full of power *by the Spirit of the Lord.* He does not tell us how God's revelation came to him, whether it came as an audible voice, as a vision, in a dream, or in some other form; but he leaves no doubt that his word did come from God. This Spirit-filled quality makes the Bible unique among all the literature in the world. "All Scripture is given by inspiration" or literally, "All Scripture is God-breathed" is the way Paul expresses it in 2 Timothy 3:16 (*New International Version*).

The second point Micah makes is that the message he delivered was full *of judgment.* Unlike others who claimed prophetic powers, he did not tailor his message to fit the whims of his hearers. His prophetic blessings were not available to the highest bidders. Instead, he fearlessly pointed out to *Jacob his transgressions, and to Israel his sin.* As a faithful servant of the Lord, he could not protect his beloved countrymen from the harsh words of condemnation that he had to deliver. He was no politician seeking some kind of a popular consensus; he was a fearless spokesman delivering God's indictment without compromise.

POWER AND LIGHT COMPANY

One of the most impressive technological innovations in modern missionary enterprise is the solar-energy pack, developed to bring electric power for projected visual aids to primitive villages in third-world countries. Here's the way it works: A missionary carries a battery pack on his back as he travels on foot or by cycle to an out-back bush community to share the gospel. As he goes, sunlight generates energy through small solar panels to charge the batteries. When the missionary arrives in the village, he hangs a sheet, connects a projector to the battery pack, and shows a movie about Jesus. Thousands of unreached peoples have received the good news by this ingenious and effective method.

Prophets need power and light. Genuine spokesmen for God are energized and enlightened by His Spirit. The truth and courage of forthtellers comes from above. Micah had it; the mercenary "clergy" of his day did not.

Christians have received the Son-light of Jesus Christ. Even without a special gift of prophecy, we are empowered to declare "good tidings unto the meek . . . to proclaim liberty to the captives . . . to proclaim the acceptable year of the Lord, and the day of vengeance of our God" (Isaiah 61:1, 2).   —R. W. B.

B. He Condemns the Rulers (vv. 9, 10)

9. Hear this, I pray you, ye heads of the house of Jacob, and princes of the house of Israel, that abhor judgment, and pervert all equity.

Micah next turns his attention to the rulers of Judah, who are called *heads of the house of Jacob, and princes of the house of Israel.* During the time of the divided kingdom, the north part usually was called Israel and the south part was called Judah. However, in this case it seems that the southern kingdom is called Israel and Jacob, which is Israel's other name. Possibly this prophecy was given after the northern kingdom was destroyed. The south part then was all that was left of Israel.

Justice may be perverted in several ways. Illegal actions can be carried out so secretly that no one ever discovers them. Or laws may be passed that make certain actions legal even when they are obviously immoral. Or some activities may be practiced so long that they become accepted without challenge even though they are unjust. It is likely that all of these factors were at work in ancient Judah. They became starkly visible only when Micah focused God's spotlight upon them. Some of the evils this spotlight revealed were idolatry (1:7; 5:13), covetousness (2:2), witchcraft (5:12), using wicked balances and deceitful weights (6:11), and lying (6:12).

10. They build up Zion with blood, and Jerusalem with iniquity.

Here *Zion* means Jerusalem. When Micah says it was built *with blood,* he may mean this literally. We recall how Jezebel and Ahab plotted the death of Naboth so they could seize his vineyard (1 Kings 21:1-19). On the other hand, Micah often uses forceful language to drive home a point, and so he may be using the expression in a figurative sense to indicate that the rich built the city by extortion and deceit. The rulers may have levied taxes on the people, confiscating

"I am full of power by the Spirit of the Lord, and of judgment, and might, to declare unto ... Israel his sin."

Elijah
Elisha
Amos
Hosea
Micah
Isaiah

visual 9

their very livelihood, reducing them to beggars, and shortening their life-span. In either case, the activities of the rulers came under Micah's scathing denunciation.

C. He Condemns the Judges, Priests, and Prophets (v. 11)

11. The heads thereof judge for reward, and the priests thereof teach for hire, and the prophets thereof divine for money: yet will they lean upon the LORD, and say, Is not the LORD among us? none evil can come upon us.

Not only were the rulers corrupt; so were the judges, priests, and prophets. In ancient Judah, when the judges dispensed justice, they were looked upon as representatives of God. Yet they were perverting this high honor by taking bribes. The law specifically forbade such practices: "Thou shalt take no gift: for the gift blindeth the wise, and perverteth the words of the righteous" (Exodus 23:8).

The priests also came under Micah's indictment. The priests were not condemned because they were paid for their services. Jesus makes it clear that teachers may be compensated for their teaching (Luke 10:7). Paul agrees (1 Timothy 5: 17, 18). The problem was that these priests were perverting their teachings to please the people, hoping thereby to be rewarded. Paul foresaw a similar practice among Christians (2 Timothy 4:3, 4). The priests were looked to as interpreters of the law, and it is likely they collaborated with the corrupt judges to subvert justice.

Nor do the prophets escape Micah's condemnation. Faithful prophets often stood outside the system, serving as God's independent spokesmen against the establishment that broke God's laws. They were often rejected and mistreated, endangering their lives to be faithful spokesmen for God. We think immediately of Elijah, or Micaiah, or Amos, or Jeremiah, who prophesied a century after Micah. But many who claimed to be prophets were victims of the same contagion that afflicted other leaders—greed. They divined *for money.*

None of these leaders would ever admit that they had done wrong. Indeed, they did just the opposite! They arrogantly insisted that the Lord was with them, and that He was blessing them in their activities. They were quite certain that the punishment Micah was predicting would not fall upon them.

MINISTERIAL MERCENARIES

Jim Bakker is in prison convicted of misappropriating supporters' contributions; but still gospel hawkers of every description crowd the airwaves.

The contemporary situation is hardly different from the circumstances surrounding Micah's prophecy. Israel's judges, priests, and prophets sold their ministries to the highest bidder. Their greed doomed Jerusalem, and the entire nation, to defeat and destruction. And their sin was compounded by their presumption upon God's grace. They actually thought Jehovah would continue to bless them, despite their shameless materialism.

Not all ministerial mercenaries have radio or TV programs. The love of money can motivate the poor as well as the rich. Each of us needs to examine his personal attitudes toward material resources. All Christians are ministers in some capacity, and Christian service never is to be for sale. "You cannot serve both God and Money" (Matthew 6:24, *New International Version*).

—R. W. B.

D. He Pronounces Doom Upon Jerusalem (v. 12)

12. Therefore shall Zion for your sake be plowed as a field, and Jerusalem shall become heaps, and the mountain of the house as the high places of the forest.

Micah and his generation saw the destruction of north Israel by the Assyrians, and they should have learned their lesson. But they didn't. Even when Jerusalem was besieged by the Assyrians and saved by divine intervention (2 Kings 19:35), they still didn't learn. Micah's prophecy was fulfilled a century later when the Babylonians brought destruction to Jerusalem.

Plowed as a field. The destruction of the city would be so complete that a peasant might plant crops where it had been. *The mountain of the house* refers to Mount Moriah, upon which the temple was built. It would become covered with trees and underbrush.

Conclusion

A. We Need a Modern Micah

Reading the book of Micah reminds us that corrupt leadership, whether political or religious, did not first appear on the scene in the

1960s or 1970s. Indeed, it is nearly as old as the human race. But the time since World War II seems to have experienced more than its share of scandals among its leaders. We have seen local leaders proved guilty of serious immoralities and convicted of crimes against the public. Nor have our congressmen and senators been immune to these problems. For that matter, even some of the residents of the White House have not lived lives above reproach. Even more stunning to church members has been the moral failure of many religious leaders. As one scandal has followed another, it has become painfully apparent that no religious group is immune from this problem.

Are our times worse than earlier days? Not if we understand anything about the ministry of Micah, who devoted much of his effort to condemning the same failings that trouble us today. If these problems have always existed, why do our times seem so much worse? For one thing, the modern media, for all of their faults, have made it more difficult to conceal our misdeeds. At times the media seem to revel in exposing human imperfections, and the profit motive is often all too obvious in their actions. And yet their searchlight on our foibles makes us painfully aware of the serious task we have before us.

We would do well to examine reasons for so many moral failures. We must certainly recognize that greed is a significant factor. Materialism permeates every aspect of our society. Our very social structure is largely defined by possessions. We categorize people as lower, middle, or upper class, not on the basis of moral character, but on what they possess.

We live in a sex-saturated society. On every hand—on television, in the movies, in the printed media—sex is served up and exploited. In such an atmosphere it should not surprise us that sexual purity is so hard to maintain. Short of living on some remote mountaintop completely isolated from the rest of the world, there is little we can do to avoid all these pervasive influences. But we can avoid some of them and protect our families from some of them by controlling the switch on the TV, censoring what we read, and avoiding persons and places where contamination is rampant.

In all of this we must not overlook the part that ego plays. Positions of leadership feed our egos and give us power over other people. To enhance our power over others, we are often tempted to take moral shortcuts. Sins of sex and greed are easier to detect in others and in our own lives than is the lust for power. Some religious leaders seem especially blind to this sin as they labor in the vineyard of the Lord. Like the religious leaders in Micah's day, they say, "Is not the Lord among us?"

B. Like Priest, Like People

It is certainly true that leaders shape the people they lead, whether the leaders are secular or religious. Leaders set the standards and become the models for their followers. For this reason, leaders bear a very great responsibility for their words and their actions.

But in a situation where leaders are selected by a democratic process, we might reverse this and say instead, *like people, like priest.* After all, we do elect our leaders, and often they are but reflections of ourselves, including our weaknesses. Most of the time we deserve the leaders we get.

In our churches too we have a voice in selecting our leaders. In other words, we deserve the leaders we get. If some of our well-known leaders have been careless or worse about their finances or their personal lives, we must bear some of the responsibility because we supported them. Let us, then, use great care and seek divine guidance in selecting those who will lead us and those whom we will follow.

C. Let Us Pray

O gracious God, give us wisdom as we select our leaders. Help us prepare men and women and boys and girls for positions of leadership. Teach us to lead with humility and to follow our faithful leaders with grace. In all of these things may Your name be glorified. In the name of the Servant of servants we pray. Amen.

D. Thought to Remember

"He that is greatest among you shall be your servant."   —Matthew 23:11.

Home Daily Bible Readings

Monday, July 24—Judgment for Israel's Sins (Micah 1:1-7)

Tuesday, July 25—Lamentation for the Judgment on Israel (Micah 1:8-16)

Wednesday, July 26—Woe to Those Who Oppress Others (Micah 2:1-5)

Thursday, July 27—Israel's Moral Uncleanness (Micah 2:6-11)

Friday, July 28—Restoration After Punishment for Evil Deeds (Micah 2:12—3:4)

Saturday, July 29—Evil Rulers and Lying Prophets Denounced (Micah 3:5-12)

Sunday, July 30—Retribution for Wickedness Is Certain (Psalm 37:1-15)

Learning by Doing

This page contains an alternate lesson plan emphasizing learning activities. Classes desiring such student involvement will find these suggestions helpful.

Learning Goals

Seek to lead your students to:

1. Pinpoint evidence of corruption in the leaders during Micah's time.

2. Emphasize the necessity of righteousness, truth, and integrity for leaders.

3. Commit themselves to be people who live in righteousness, truth, and integrity.

Into the Lesson

Prepare a copy of the statements below for each student. (Students can find this activity in their student book.)

1. A church or nation will not rise above the character level of its leaders.

2. Most churches or nations deserve the leaders they select.

3. Corrupt leaders will usually lead their people into corruption.

4. Leaders should be expected to live with higher integrity than others.

5. Being a leader makes it more difficult to live with integrity than not being a leader.

Give a copy of the statements and a pencil to each student. Ask class members to read each statement and write *A* in front of each statement they agree with. They should write *D* in front of the statements they disagree with.

After about three minutes, take a tally on each statement. For each one ask volunteers to explain why they chose their opinions. Allow for brief discussion on the most controversial ones.

Say to your class, "We have been focusing on the nation of Israel in recent weeks. Unfortunately, the nation failed to follow God's instructions and brought God's displeasure. In our lesson today we will see that God pinned a lot of the responsibility for the dismal spiritual condition on the leaders."

Into the Word

Prepare your class for their Scripture study by briefly lecturing on the background of Micah. Zero in on the Introduction in the commentary on page 410 .

Ask a volunteer to read Micah 3:1-12. Then involve your students in a large-group discussion of these questions, which can be found in the student book:

1. What complaints are made against the leaders (national and spiritual) of Israel?

2. What will happen to the leaders, according to verse 4? Verse 6? Verse 7?

3. What will happen to the nation (Zion) because of the leaders? See verse 12.

4. Spiritual leaders were tempted to tell people what they wanted to hear rather than what God wanted them to hear. Compare these passages: Micah 3:5; Jeremiah 6:13, 14; 23:17, 22; 2 Timothy 4:1-4. What does each passage say about corrupt teachers or teaching that tells people what they want to hear, not what God wants them to be told?

Into Life

Help students connect the Scripture with the issues of today. Have students discuss the questions below in groups of six:

1. Righteousness. Integrity. Truth. God requires these of both political and spiritual leaders. In what ways have we witnessed corruption in leadership in the past several decades?

2. Are people becoming more tolerant of corruption in leadership? Support your answer.

3. In what ways may churches today be tempted to tell people what they want to hear rather than what God wants them to hear?

4. We ought to be as good as we want our leaders to be. Discuss these questions:

*In what ways are you tempted to compromise regarding truth or righteousness?

*How can you build a life of integrity?

Allow ten to fifteen minutes for discussion. Give a sheet of paper to each student to write a personal prayer committing himself to live in righteousness, truth, and integrity.

Option

Ask each group to think of a situation in which Christians might be tempted to compromise regarding truth or righteousness. (Examples may include: reporting income on tax forms; church publicity committee preparing a newspaper ad that promises people more than the church can deliver.) Each group is to develop a skit to illustrate the situation.

Allow each group to perform its skit. Following each one ask, "How would the situation have been approached if the people had been committed to integrity?"

Conclude by asking students to write prayers as described in the activity above.

Let's Talk It Over

The questions on this page are designed to encourage review of the lesson Scriptures and to promote discussion of the lesson by the class. The answers provided are only discussion starters. Let your class talk it over from there.

1. How can you know whether leaders or speakers today are really speaking for God, or are more concerned with "feathering their own nests" or "feeding themselves"?

It would be good if we could say no leader in a religious group ever had wrong motives, but we all know that cannot be believed. Satan can penetrate followers of Jesus today just as he entered Judas (Luke 22:3-6).

The best criterion to check authenticity is still God's Word, both the Word written in Scripture and the example of the living Word who became flesh and dwelt among us (John 1:14).

It is also appropriate to note the effect of following a human leader. Does it bring us toward the likeness of Christ? Before using this criterion as a club against current leaders, however, we need to pray much about the question and seek earnestly to encourage our leaders to move toward the way of Christ.

2. How can leaders and speakers withstand the pressure to say only what people want to hear?

We ought to give godly leaders such support and encouragement that they will never see a threat to their position because they speak firmly for Christ. We should encourage such speaking the more if some in the church or community are pushing a popular message rather than the Word of God. Surrounded by people who love the Lord, who spend time with His Word, who earnestly try to bring others to Him, leaders and speakers will find their zeal growing and even their skills improving. Too often we jump forth with criticism instead of kneeling in prayer and speaking with encouragement.

3. In a free and democratic society, we still see instances of evil, dishonesty, and immorality in high places. What can righteous people do about it?

When an election is near, there is likely to be more "mudslinging" than clear and sober discussion of facts and issues. We can raise our voices for truth and goodness, but our voices may be drowned in the cacophony of those who substitute noise for truth.

One thing we can do as Christians is to live in such a way that people around us will see the contrast and think about what makes the difference. That is what Peter urged on Christians in the first century: live for Christ even if it brings suffering, and people will note the living testimony to Christ (1 Peter 3:8-17).

4. What do you do when even the news media and popular advertisements portray evil as good?

This is indeed the same portrayal that was presented to Eve in the Garden of Eden, and to Jesus in the temptations that preceded His ministry. The example of Jesus, of course, is better than that of Eve. Easily we see that He used Scripture to correct the picture.

Constantly we need to take what the world tells us and hold it up beside the standard we find in God's Word. But around us many are being misled because they don't consider the standard God has given. It seems appropriate for us to speak out and warn the innocent and uninformed—but always in a way that reflects the spirit and the message of our Lord.

5. When people persuade themselves that evil is good or that God's will doesn't matter, what can be done to change their view? How can society's values be altered?

When we see a need to change great numbers of people and to turn a bad situation around, political action often seems appealing. In some situations it may help. But Jesus did not organize a political party or send out ward chairwomen or precinct committeemen. He sent out disciples to make more disciples. After nearly two thousand years His disciples are still doing that. When it is done faithfully, there is no more effective way.

6. In the face of the present great passion for personal gain and material wealth, how can we help the next generation to set proper values for their lives?

Our own example speaks more eloquently than any words we can utter. We can put our own priorities in such order that our children and others affected by us will at least have a good choice to consider. Of course we cannot really control what grown children decide or do, so we must rely much on prayer.

Isaiah's Call and Message

DEVOTIONAL READING: Isaiah 55:6-11.

LESSON SCRIPTURE: Isaiah 6, 1.

PRINTED TEXT: Isaiah 6:1-8; 1:14-17.

Isaiah 6:1-8

1 In the year that king Uzziah died I saw also the Lord sitting upon a throne, high and lifted up, and his train filled the temple.

2 Above it stood the seraphim: each one had six wings; with twain he covered his face, and with twain he covered his feet, and with twain he did fly.

3 And one cried unto another, and said, Holy, holy, holy, is the LORD of hosts: the whole earth is full of his glory.

4 And the posts of the door moved at the voice of him that cried, and the house was filled with smoke.

5 Then said I, Woe is me! for I am undone; because I am a man of unclean lips, and I dwell in the midst of a people of unclean lips: for mine eyes have seen the King, the LORD of hosts.

6 Then flew one of the seraphim unto me, having a live coal in his hand, which he had taken with the tongs from off the altar:

7 And he laid it upon my mouth, and said, Lo, this hath touched thy lips; and thine iniquity is taken away, and thy sin purged.

8 Also I heard the voice of the Lord, saying, Whom shall I send, and who will go for us? Then said I, Here am I; send me.

Isaiah 1:14-17

14 Your new moons and your appointed feasts my soul hateth: they are a trouble unto me; I am weary to bear them.

15 And when ye spread forth your hands, I will hide mine eyes from you; yea, when ye make many prayers, I will not hear: your hands are full of blood.

16 Wash ye, make you clean; put away the evil of your doings from before mine eyes; cease to do evil;

17 Learn to do well; seek judgment, relieve the oppressed, judge the fatherless, plead for the widow.

Aug
6

GOLDEN TEXT: I heard the voice of the Lord, saying, Whom shall I send, and who will go for us? Then said I, Here am I; send me.—Isaiah 6:8.

<table>
</table>

> A Nation Turns From God
> Unit 3: The Judgment Arrives
> (Lessons 10-13)

Lesson Aims

As a result of studying this lesson, each student should:

1. Have a better understanding of the circumstances surrounding Isaiah's call.

2. Appreciate Isaiah's sense of total inadequacy in the presence of God's holiness.

3. Realize that we must be cleansed before we can be at our best in God's service.

4. Be able to enumerate ways he or she can serve in the Lord's kingdom.

Lesson Outline

INTRODUCTION
  A. Opening the Lines of Communication
  B. Lesson Background
 I. VISION IN THE TEMPLE (Isaiah 6:1-4)
  A. The Vision of the Lord (v. 1)
  B. The Vision of the Seraphim (vv. 2, 3)
  C. The Impact of the Praise (v. 4)
 II. CALL TO SERVICE (Isaiah 6:5-8)
  A. Isaiah's Unworthiness (v. 5)
   You Are What You Say
  B. His Cleansing (vv. 6, 7)
  C. His Response (v. 8)
 III. DEMAND FOR REFORM (Isaiah 1:14-17)
  A. Empty Worship Rejected (vv. 14, 15)
   "Churchianity"
  B. Worshipers Must Be Cleansed (v. 16)
  C. They Must Reform Their Lives (v. 17)
   Don'ts and Dos
CONCLUSION
  A. "Here Am I; Send Me"
  B. Let Us Pray
  C. Thought to Remember

Responding to the holy God of the Bible is the theme of visual 10 of the visuals packet. The visual is shown on page 420.

Introduction

A. Opening the Lines of Communication

A severe summer thunderstorm swept across the city, knocking out the electrical power for many of its residents. Even before the storm had completely subsided, a utility truck carrying several workers pulled up to a corner and stopped. Lightning had knocked out a transformer on a utility pole at the corner, and the men had come to repair it.

One man climbed the pole, inspected the transformer, and began to shout instructions to the men standing below. But the noise of the traffic made it impossible for him to be heard. Finally he climbed back down, put on a headset, and climbed the pole again. One of the other men also put on a headset. What they were using was a special radio system that allowed them to communicate. The man on the pole began to give instructions, and soon with a rope he was pulling up the tools and pieces of equipment he needed to make repairs on the transformer.

It was somewhat like this for Isaiah. God wanted to instruct him and prepare him for service, but because of the busy world about him with all of its sin, he did not hear the instructions. Only after he was cleansed was he prepared to hear the Lord and obey Him. All of us are like Isaiah. We live in a society that is drowning in sin, and we have been corrupted by our surroundings. To serve the Lord we must first hear His call.

B. Lesson Background

The prophet Isaiah lived in the second half of the eighth century B.C., a contemporary of Hosea and Micah. His long ministry, conducted in Judah, the southern kingdom, fell in the reigns of four kings—Uzziah, Jotham, Ahaz, and Hezekiah. Isaiah was called to minister in difficult times. Judah had enjoyed considerable prosperity during the reign of Uzziah, in part because of the decline of Assyria's power, but that was about to end. In the tumultuous times that followed, Assyria once more moved westward, capturing Damascus, Syria's capital, and then Samaria, Israel's capital. Soon the Assyrian hordes were at the gates of Jerusalem, and only God's divine intervention spared that city (2 Kings 19).

We know little about Isaiah's personal life. His father was Amoz (not to be confused with Amos the prophet), and he had a wife who bore him two sons. His name means "Jehovah saves." Tradition has it that he was a member of the royal family, or at least a noble family. This is borne out by the fact that he had ready access to the royal court.

Many acclaim Isaiah as the greatest of the writing prophets. His elevated literary style, his sweeping vision of God acting in history, his eloquent denunciation of Judah's sins, but most of all his messianic prophecies give him a just claim to this title.

I. Vision in the Temple
(Isaiah 6:1-4)

A. The Vision of the Lord (v. 1)

1. In the year that king Uzziah died I saw also the Lord sitting upon a throne, high and lifted up, and his train filled the temple.

The reign of Uzziah, sometimes called Azariah, was long and prosperous. Although near the end of his reign he was smitten by leprosy because he tried to offer incense in the temple contrary to the law, he was on the whole a good king. His death was perhaps in 736 B.C. Isaiah's vision occurred *in the year that king Uzziah died,* whether before or after his death we are not told. Many commentators believe this was Isaiah's initial call to the prophetic ministry. Others, seeing that his call is in chapter 6, believe that his prophetic ministry had begun earlier and that this call was to a new and more specific ministry. They argue that the death of Uzziah marked the beginning of new and more serious threats to Judah, requiring a new commission for the prophet.

I saw also the Lord. Since no man has seen God at any time (John 1:18), we take this to mean a vision of God. Probably Isaiah had gone to the temple to worship when the vision occurred.

In this vision Isaiah saw God on the throne, indicating His power and authority. Presumably He appeared as a human being, dressed in a flowing robe—but much larger than an ordinary human. The word used for *Lord* in this verse is *adonay,* which seems to stress His might and sovereignty, rather than *Yahweh,* the personal name of Israel's God, which is used in verses 3 and 5. *His train,* that is, the skirt of his robe, was so expansive that it *filled the temple.* This imagery —the elevated throne and the flowing robe— obviously presents a picture of an earthly king of that day, but on a larger scale.

B. The Vision of the Seraphim
(vv. 2, 3)

2. Above it stood the seraphim: each one had six wings; with twain he covered his face, and with twain he covered his feet, and with twain he did fly.

Seraphim is plural. In some editions of the Bible *s* is added incorrectly: *seraphims.* These beings are mentioned only here in the Scriptures. Mention of *face* and *feet* suggests they had a human form, but each one had six wings. With four of these he humbly shielded himself from the divine glory; with the other two he *did fly,* hovering in the air over the outspread robe.

Because we know little about the seraphim, anything we conclude about them must be mostly speculation. Even the origin of the name is disputed by some scholars, although many hold that it means fiery or burning. Perhaps they were bright and shining. From this passage we can conclude that their function was to praise God and act as His servants and messengers.

3. And one cried unto another, and said, Holy, holy, holy, is the LORD of hosts: the whole earth is full of his glory.

Across the ages men have assigned many different attributes to God. For some He is the creator and sustainer of the universe. For others He is all wisdom and all knowledge. Some see Him as a stern and demanding judge, while others view Him as a loving and merciful Father. Jehovah God is all of these, but He is more. He is *holy!* No description of God is complete unless it makes reference to His holiness. When ascribed to man, holiness conveys the idea of being set apart, especially set apart or dedicated to God. It also includes the idea of a degree of moral purity. This idea of holiness, however, is inadequate when it is applied to God. God is holy in the sense that He is completely separate from and exalted above His creation. Our language is inadequate to express all that is involved in God's holiness, nor do we have the intellectual capacity to understand it even if we could express it.

Holy, holy, holy. The repetition is for emphasis. Some commentators suggest that the seraphim were arranged behind the divine throne as a heavenly choir. As one of the seraphim led, the others responded antiphonally.

C. The Impact of the Praise (v. 4)

4. And the posts of the door moved at the voice of him that cried, and the house was filled with smoke.

The volume and the tone of the chorus reverberated so thunderously that they shook *the posts of the door* or *the foundations of the thresholds* (*American Standard Version*). It must have been

---

How to Say It

AHAZ. *A*-haz.
AMOZ. *A*-mahz.
ASSYRIA. Uh-*sear*-ee-uh.
AZARIAH. Az-uh-*rye*-uh.
HEZEKIAH. Hez-ih-*kye*-uh.
ISAIAH. Eye-*zay*-uh.
JOTHAM. *Jo*-tham.
SERAPHIM. *sair*-uh-fim.
UZZIAH. Uh-*zye*-uh.

like a mighty church organ whose deep bass notes make the whole building vibrate. *The house was filled with smoke,* indicating the divine presence (Exodus 19:18; 20:18).

II. Call to Service
(Isaiah 6:5-8)

A. Isaiah's Unworthiness (v. 5)

5. Then said I, Woe is me! for I am undone; because I am a man of unclean lips, and I dwell in the midst of a people of unclean lips: for mine eyes have seen the King, the LORD of hosts.

It may surprise us that Isaiah was so completely overwhelmed by this experience. If he already had uttered the strong condemnations recorded in the first five chapters, then he had been the Lord's faithful spokesman, carrying out his proper duty. Why should he feel undone?

First of all, we need to recognize that any mere mortal ushered into the presence of almighty God will be utterly overwhelmed (Exodus 33:20).

Further, Isaiah was honest enough to recognize that even though he had faithfully delivered God's message of judgment, yet he had not completely escaped the sins he had condemned. No matter how carefully one makes his way through a coal mine, he is certain to pick up some coal dust on his clothing or shoes. So it is with a sinful society. Even a righteous man like Isaiah was bound to suffer some contamination just by living in such a society. We today face a similar problem, and we must honestly face up to it.

Like anyone who sincerely seeks to minister to a people, Isaiah identified with his people. His own lips, like those of his people, were unclean, suggesting that their utterances betrayed the corruption within. In sharing with his people, Isaiah indicated his willingness to share their punishment with them. This is the mark of a true shepherd.

YOU ARE WHAT YOU SAY

Sam (twenty-five) was trying to make conversation with his cousin Andrew (nine) at a family reunion. "Whatta ya say, Andrew?" said Sam in friendly greeting. Without hesitation, Andrew replied with Pavlovian predictability: "Thank you!" He obviously had been coached repeatedly in the social grace of gratitude, coached with the familiar parental prompt, "What do you say, Andrew?" So his learned response was triggered even by a rhetorical version of the question.

The conversation starter, *Whatta ya say?* may be more significant than it appears. It means everything from "How do you feel?" to "What do you think?" to "Where do you stand?" It is an invitation to share at least part of your character and personality. What you say reveals who you are.

When Isaiah bemoaned his and the nation's "unclean lips," he was confessing more than specific sins of speech, like lying and profanity. *Lips* stood for life. "Woe is me," he might have said, "for we are people of unclean thoughts, unclean habits, and unclean behavior. We are thoroughly sinful, totally unfaithful."

Speech can reveal character. That is why James taught that the tongue "defileth the whole body" (James 3:6). *Conversation* in King James English means *life-style,* not just dialogue. So, "Be careful, little lips, what you say."

—R. W. B.

B. His Cleansing (vv. 6, 7)

6, 7. Then flew one of the seraphim unto me, having a live coal in his hand, which he had taken with the tongs from off the altar: and he laid it upon my mouth, and said, Lo, this hath touched thy lips; and thine iniquity is taken away, and thy sin purged.

Isaiah stood before the throne of God as a penitent sinner, confessing his guilt. He made no attempt to plead his case or to claim extenuating circumstances. In the presence of almighty God no defense was possible. All he could ask for was mercy; but before he could even ask for it, God took action. One of the seraphim took tongs, lifted a live coal from the altar, and flew to Isaiah. Then he touched the coal to his lips, symbolically purging him from sin. Fire can have a purifying power. It can be used to burn away infected flesh, cauterizing a wound so that it can heal. Here the sin-infected lips were figuratively burned away, that they might be healed and once more become useful. Such a dramatic figure would leave no doubt in Isaiah's mind that he was cleansed, no longer having to carry about a burden of guilt.

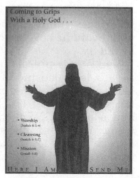

visual 10

C. His Response (v. 8)

8. Also I heard the voice of the Lord, saying, Whom shall I send, and who will go for us? Then said I, Here am I; send me.

Up to this point, the Lord had not uttered a word. Now as the prophet stood before Him, cleansed of his sins, he heard His voice for the first time. *Whom shall I send, and who will go for us?* God's call to service was quite general. God sought a messenger, but neither his destination nor his specific duties were mentioned. In a sense, this is the way everyone who becomes a Christian is called. We are called to service, and only later may we learn the specific nature of that service. Isaiah didn't hesitate an instant in responding to the call. He didn't ask any questions about what God wanted him to do, nor did he insist upon any conditions before he would accept the call. He responded out of a joy that came from a deep sense of gratitude because God had cleansed him from sin.

III. Demand for Reform
(Isaiah 1:14-17)

Some believe that these words were uttered early in Isaiah's ministry, before he received his special call recorded in chapter 6. Others believe that they came after his call and were typical of the message he was to carry to his people. If this is the case, we can readily understand why God warned him that the people would close their eyes and ears to the message (Isaiah 6:9, 10). After all, it was a message of condemnation and judgment, not of pious and pleasant platitudes.

A. Empty Worship Rejected
(vv. 14, 15)

14, 15. Your new moons and your appointed feasts my soul hateth: they are a trouble unto me; I am weary to bear them. And when ye spread forth your hands, I will hide mine eyes from you; yea, when ye make many prayers, I will not hear: your hands are full of blood.

Isaiah condemned his people because they were going through the motions of worshiping Jehovah, but that was the problem—they were just going through the motions. Their lives did not show that their worship was sincere.

In the previous verses Isaiah has indicated God's dissatisfaction with the people's sacrifices, burnt offerings, new moons, sabbaths, and solemn assemblies. In this verse, he concentrates on *new moons* and *appointed feasts.* The festival of the new moon came on the first day of each lunar month. Special sacrifices and feasting accompanied this day. The appointed feasts were the regular annual religious observances such as Passover, Pentecost, Tabernacles, and the Day of Atonement. The people were observing these, and so it must have come as a shock to hear their actions denounced in such strong terms.

God refused even to hear prayers that were offered hypocritically and perfunctorily. Sometimes people become so alienated from Him that He will not answer their prayers (Proverbs 1:28).

"CHURCHIANITY"

Church Growth is the buzz word of preference among Christians in this last decade of the century. Congregations are pulling out all the stops to coax greater numbers into highly mortgaged sanctuaries. Telemarketing, direct mail, sensational programming, entertainment spectaculars, "visitor friendly" formats, and culture-accommodating schedules—all are accepted means to the end that more and more warm bodies fill the pews. This caution is valid: "What people are won *by* is what they are won *to.*"

Big crowds of worshipers are one worthy goal for a church. But genuine conversion of sinners to authentic Christianity must be our first priority. The nation of Judah appeared to be faithful in attendance at temple rituals and ceremonies. God rejected their formal worship, though, because their hearts were empty of sincere faith, and their hands were full of guilty blood.

Is it possible that many modern worshipers are practicing *churchianity* instead of *Christianity?* Many simply go through the motions of church attendance without applying the gospel to daily living. Could you be guilty, too? The instruction of the apostle Paul is well taken: "Let a man examine himself" (1 Corinthians 11:28).

—R. W. B.

B. Worshipers Must Be Cleansed (v. 16)

16. Wash ye, make you clean; put away the evil of your doings from before mine eyes; cease to do evil.

Their first step, if they would become pleasing to God, was to turn away from their evil ways. There was no way they could cover over their sins or hide them. They had to repent and quit doing them. This included not only their empty worship services, but also acts of violence such as mentioned in verse 15: "your hands are full of blood." God stands always ready to welcome the wayward sinner to Him, but repentance must always come first. Repentance involves a sincere sorrow for past sins, but it also requires a resolve to turn away from those sins.

C. They Must Reform Their Lives (v. 17)

17. Learn to do well; seek judgment, relieve the oppressed, judge the fatherless, plead for the widow.

Now come the positive requirements. To be pleasing to God, one must not only refrain from evil activities; he must also be involved in doing good. The specific things that Isaiah mentions give a clue about some of the more serious problems besetting the society of his day. To *seek judgment* is to give justice in the courts, where bribery and shady deals seem to have been prevalent. The *oppressed* were the poverty-stricken who were taken advantage of by the rich. The *fatherless* and the *widow,* because they lack men to protect them, seem always to be ready victims of oppression. Isaiah's words echo those of his contemporary, Micah, who wrote that the Lord requires His people "to do justly, and to love mercy, and to walk humbly with thy God" (Micah 6:8).

DON'TS AND DOS

A nearby church has developed a sad situation: these folk are trying to live in a vacuum of negativism. They are well-versed in what they are against—graded Sunday school, church dinners, a trained ministry, etc. Their mistake is not in opposing what they consider to be extra biblical practices; but their negative emphasis has produced a melancholy, lifeless, shrinking congregation of legalistic, sour-spirited drudges. They know all the "don'ts" of their persuasion, but they are not accentuating the positive "dos" of Christian discipleship.

Isaiah issued a two-pronged exhortation to Judah: "Cease to do evil; learn to do well." There's both a *don't* and a *do.* Paul wrote the

same admonition: "Abhor that which is evil; cleave to that which is good" (Romans 12:9).

Giving up our bad habits is fine, but *good* habits must replace them. The Scriptures are replete with "Thou shalts" as well as with "Thou shalt nots." Righteousness is demonstrated by our active good works as much as by our abstinence from wickedness. Christianity is not neutrality; it is taking a stand for positive convictions, acting rightly toward God and toward all of our neighbors.   —R. W. B.

Conclusion

A. "Here Am I; Send Me"

Once Isaiah had been confronted by God and purged of his sins, he was ready to be used of God. Thus prepared, he did not hesitate when God asked for a volunteer. He did not even raise any questions about the kind of service God was calling him to. Then when God began to explain to him that his mission was to carry a message of judgment to his people, a message the people would reject, he did not begin to make excuses or try to back out of his commitment.

Every day God throws out similar invitations to us. He challenges us when we first become Christians. We are not called into a life of ease but a life of service. At that point we may not be adequately prepared to serve, and so He calls us to study and prepare ourselves so that we can serve more effectively.

The lesson for today gives us an opportunity to examine our lives to see how we are responding to God's call to cleansing and to service. Some need to be challenged to make that initial commitment to serve. Others, already serving faithfully, need to be challenged to step out and prepare themselves so that they can serve even more effectively.

In either situation, today's Scripture makes it clear that cleansing must precede commitment. Without that cleansing, our service will become exactly like that of the Israelites whom Isaiah condemned—empty and hypocritical, a kind of service that wearies God.

B. Let Us Pray

Almighty God, as we come before You, let us never forget that You are high and holy and lifted up. Let us never approach You casually or hypocritically. Open our hearts and our ears to your call to service. May we, like Isaiah, respond readily when that call comes. In the name of the Servant of servants we pray. Amen.

C. Thought to Remember

"Here am I; send me" (Isaiah 6:8).

Home Daily Bible Readings

Monday, July 31—Isaiah's Call and Plea of Unworthiness (Isaiah 6:1-5)

Tuesday, Aug. 1—A Forgiven Isaiah Accepts His Call (Isaiah 6:6-13)

Wednesday, Aug. 2—God's Message to Judah Through Isaiah (Isaiah 1:1-6)

Thursday, Aug. 3—Judah's Desolate Condition (Isaiah 1:7-11)

Friday, Aug. 4—Superficial Religion Is Offensive to God (Isaiah 1:12-17)

Saturday, Aug. 5—God Expects Justice and Righteousness (Isaiah 1:18-23)

Sunday, Aug. 6—Sinful Rebellion Must Be Punished (Isaiah 1:24-31)

Learning by Doing

This page contains an alternate lesson plan emphasizing learning activities. Classes desiring such student involvement will find these suggestions helpful.

Learning Goals

This session will focus on God's holiness and our response to His holiness. Lead your students to do the following:

1. Grasp that God is holy.

2. Explain a connection between worshiping God, seeking cleansing from God, and being committed to God's calling to mission.

3. Determine to be people who are saturated with worshiping a holy God.

Into the Lesson

Begin by asking your class to sing the familiar hymn, "Holy, Holy, Holy." You might ask a musically inclined class member ahead of time to lead the class. The words are found in the student book. If you do not use the student book, have hymnals available for the class to sing all four stanzas.

After singing, lead the class to discuss these questions:

1. What does it mean that God is holy?

2. How important do you think God's holiness is to Christians today?

Into the Word

Lead into the Bible study by presenting a brief background of Isaiah, using information in the introduction to the commentary on page 418.

Then point out that God's holiness has two primary aspects. First, God is holy in that He is separate and exalted above everything else. Nothing can compare to Him. Second, God is holy in a moral sense. That means that He is separate from sin or error or flaw.

Everything God is and does is holy. His love is a holy love. His wrath is a holy wrath. His wisdom is a holy wisdom. Nothing in God and nothing He does is unholy.

Have your class form at least three groups. If you have more than twenty in class, create more than three, making sure each group has about six. More than one group then will receive the same assignment. Give each group one of the assignments below and allow twenty-five minutes for discussion:

Assignment One

Focus on worship as a response to God's holiness. Read Isaiah 6:1-8. Then discuss these questions:

1. How is God's holiness shown in verses 1-4?

2. What in this passage suggests that worshiping God is serious business?

3. Compare Isaiah 6:1-8 with Revelation 4:1-11; Isaiah 57:15; and Psalm 96:9. Discuss these questions based on these passages:

What do you learn about God's holiness?

What do you learn about how to worship?

4. God is holy. Based upon your study, what difference should that make in our lives?

Assignment Two

Focus on personal cleansing as a response to God's holiness. Read Isaiah 6:1-8 and discuss these questions:

1. What convicted Isaiah of his uncleanness?

2. How did he react to his uncleanness?

3. How was he symbolically cleansed?

4. Compare Isaiah 6:1-8 with Psalm 51:1-4, 10-17; Hebrews 10:19-22; and James 4:7-10. Then discuss these questions:

How are we cleansed?

What role does worship play in cleansing us?

5. God is holy. Based upon your study, what difference should that make in our lives?

Assignment Three

Focus on participation in God's mission as a response to His holiness. Read Isaiah 6:1-8. Then discuss:

1. To what mission did God call Isaiah? How did Isaiah respond?

2. How may the following have contributed to Isaiah's willingness to accept God's mission?

Seeing God in His holiness

Coming to grips with his own uncleanness?

Having his sins taken away

3. Being involved in God's mission is a natural companion of true worship of God. How do these passages support that statement: Isaiah 6:1-8; Matthew 28:16-20; Acts 13:1-4?

4. God is holy. Based upon your study, what difference should that make in our lives?

After groups have completed their study, bring them together and let each group report.

Into Life

Read Isaiah 6:1-8 and Revelation 4:1-11 again. Have students sing "Holy, Holy, Holy" again, meditatively. Then ask them to pray silently about how they can grow in worship.

Let's Talk It Over

The questions on this page are designed to encourage review of the lesson Scriptures and to promote discussion of the lesson by the class. The answers provided are only discussion starters. Let your class talk it over from there.

1. When we meet for worship, is there a sense of the holiness and majesty of God? What can be done before, during, or after the service to enhance that?

Several people may agree to encourage one another to limit Saturday-night activities and get a good night's rest. Some churches have a pre-service time of prayer for leaders and others. This can be good if it does not add to an already hectic schedule, and if there is good child care. People seated before the service begins can meditate on hymns and Scriptures that will be used. Silent prayer for a right attitude can go a long way to prepare hearts.

During worship we can focus on pleasing and praising God, thinking of how we need His grace, and listening for His call to service.

After worship, joyful and committed service is appropriate. It may start with hospitality to visitors or loners in the meeting. All through the week we can walk with the Lord and anticipate our next meeting.

2. Do we lose a sense of awe and reverence in our effort to be friendly, to make announcements, to report on the sick? How can we all be aware of God's holiness, and yet have a warm and friendly service?

Can you imagine the drama of Isaiah being interrupted to announce a picnic? Perhaps we should first plan reverent worship, and then plan what to do with other items. Some churches confine making the announcements to the opening moments before worship begins or to the closing moments after it is completed. Some print them in a bulletin for the worshipers, and tell about the sick just before the morning prayer is offered.

3. Does worship require a sense of sinfulness? Does today's "positive thinking" require that services be always "upbeat"? On what should we focus our worship?

Probably Isaiah did not go to the temple expecting to feel unworthy. That just happened when he saw the holy God. We need not try to continue a feeling of sinfulness, though it may come when we are face to face with the Almighty. Let us focus our worship on Him and plan everything to honor Him.

4. Does the Lord's Supper provide a dramatic cleansing experience in our worship?

With a growing interest in renewing drama in worship, many of us have missed the drama always present when we reenact the breaking of bread and the sharing of the cup. If the songs don't happen to be our favorites, if the sermon fails to "ring a bell," if the pews are not comfortable enough, and the temperature is not quite right, still that moment of Communion tells us again how deeply Jesus loves us. Long ago He died to atone for our sins; today "if we confess our sins, he is faithful and just to forgive us our sins, and to cleanse us from all unrighteousness" (1 John 1:9).

5. Should every worship service include a call to action in response to God's holiness, our unworthiness, and God's provision for our cleansing? What actions are called for?

Many churches close every service with an invitation to accept Christ. Being commissioned to make disciples, we must not think lightly of such a call.

Worship calls for responses from Christians too—perhaps for personal self-control for the sake of holiness, perhaps participation in united Christian action by the church. Worship does call for action, and leaders of worship can provide guidance in specific actions.

6. Is it possible that emotional worship may bring impulsive responses that are ill-considered and inappropriate? How can we merge thoughtful resolution with grateful exhuberance?

There is danger in impulsive response to emotional worship, but that does not mean we should shun emotion and impulsiveness altogether. Faith without feeling is a cold thing indeed. If we know we are likely to "go overboard" in emotional moments, we can postpone our decision till we consult family or friends. If we are too unemotional, we need to consider how freely Jesus let His emotions show (Matthew 23:37-39; John 2:13-17; 11:35). Prayer and continuous communication with God will do much to keep us from swinging an emotional pendulum too far in either way, and will help us to put genuine feelings with action.

When a Nation Is in Danger

DEVOTIONAL READING: Psalm 125:1-5.

LESSON SCRIPTURE: Isaiah 7; 2 Kings 16.

PRINTED TEXT: Isaiah 7:2-6, 10-17.

Isaiah 7:2-6, 10-17

2 And it was told the house of David, saying, Syria is confederate with Ephraim. And his heart was moved, and the heart of his people, as the trees of the wood are moved with the wind.

3 Then said the LORD unto Isaiah, Go forth now to meet Ahaz, thou, and Shearjashub thy son, at the end of the conduit of the upper pool, in the highway of the fuller's field;

4 And say unto him, Take heed, and be quiet; fear not, neither be faint-hearted for the two tails of these smoking firebrands, for the fierce anger of Rezin with Syria, and of the son of Remaliah.

5 Because Syria, Ephraim, and the son of Remaliah, have taken evil counsel against thee, saying,

6 Let us go up against Judah, and vex it, and let us make a breach therein for us, and set a king in the midst of it, even the son of Tabeal.

. . . .

10 Moreover the LORD spake again unto Ahaz, saying,

11 Ask thee a sign of the LORD thy God; ask it either in the depth, or in the height above.

12 But Ahaz said, I will not ask, neither will I tempt the LORD.

13 And he said, Hear ye now, O house of David; Is it a small thing for you to weary men, but will ye weary my God also?

14 Therefore the Lord himself shall give you a sign; Behold, a virgin shall conceive, and bear a son, and shall call his name Immanuel.

15 Butter and honey shall he eat, that he may know to refuse the evil, and choose the good.

16 For before the child shall know to refuse the evil, and choose the good, the land that thou abhorrest shall be forsaken of both her kings.

17 The LORD shall bring upon thee, and upon thy people, and upon thy father's house, days that have not come, from the day that Ephraim departed from Judah; even the king of Assyria.

GOLDEN TEXT: Take heed, and be quiet; fear not.—Isaiah 7:4.

A Nation Turns From God
Unit 3: The Judgment Arrives
(Lessons 10-13)

Lesson Aims

After this lesson, each student should:

1. Have a better understanding of the political situation in the time of King Ahaz.

2. Appreciate Isaiah's courage in criticizing the king.

3. Trust in God rather than in political and military alliances.

Lesson Outline

INTRODUCTION

    A. He Holds the Future

    B. Lesson Background

  I. ISAIAH REASSURES AHAZ (Isaiah 7:2-6)

    A. Ahaz and the People Troubled (v. 2)

    B. Isaiah Sent to Meet Ahaz (v. 3)

    C. Isaiah Encourages Ahaz (v. 4)

      "I Shall Not Be Moved"

    D. Judah's Enemies' Plans (vv. 5, 6)

 II. THE LORD SPEAKS TO AHAZ (Isaiah 7:10-13)

    A. Ahaz Told to Ask for a Sign (vv. 10, 11)

    B. Ahaz Refuses to Ask (vv. 12, 13)

      ID

III. THE SIGN TO BE GIVEN (Isaiah 7:14-17)

    A. A Virgin Shall Bear a Son (vv. 14, 15)

    B. Judah Will Be Spared (vv. 16, 17)

      Good News/Bad News

CONCLUSION

    A. God Still Speaks

    B. We Need an Isaiah

    C. Immanuel

    D. Let Us Pray

    E. Thought to Remember

"Where do you place your trust?" is the question raised by visual 11 of the visuals packet. The visual is pictured on page 429.

Introduction

A. He Holds the Future

A train filled with vacationers lost its brakes as it came down a long mountain grade. The passengers at first were not aware of any problem, but soon the increasing speed showed that something was wrong. Some began to scream and others to cry as they realized the danger. During all the noise and commotion, one little lad sat calmly, apparently quite unaware of the danger. Ahead was an especially sharp curve, and those who knew about it began to cry out all the louder. But then the train slowed and made the turn safely.

After the crisis, a lady asked the boy, "Weren't you afraid the train was going to wreck?"

"No, ma'am, I wasn't afraid," he replied.

"But the train could have wrecked and all of us could have been killed," said the lady.

"No, ma'am, my daddy's the engineer, and he can take care of everything." This lad could view the future with calm assurance because he knew who was in charge.

When Isaiah came to visit King Ahaz, the king was as frightened as the tourists on that train, and for good reason. Syria and Israel were about to gang up on him, and he knew that Judah could never withstand their onslaught. Isaiah assured him that Judah would be saved from these two enemies, but Ahaz still was fearful. He refused even to ask for a sign that would give him assurance. Isaiah gave him a sign anyway, because he knew the future; and more importantly, he knew who was in charge of the future.

Many today face the future with fear. Unfortunately, we have no modern-day Isaiahs to reassure us. But even if we don't know what the future holds, at least we know who holds the future, and that ought to bring assurance enough.

B. Lesson Background

Last week's lesson introduced us to Isaiah and his dramatic call to the prophetic ministry. Things did not go well for Judah after that call. King Uzziah was succeeded by his son, Jotham. Jotham tried to serve Jehovah, but "the people did yet corruptly" (2 Chronicles 27:1, 2). Also, the nation was threatened by the rising Assyrian power to the north. Jotham died about 732 B.C., leaving the throne to his son, Ahaz, who soon proved to be a bad king. Syria and Israel wanted him to join them in a coalition against Assyria. When he refused, they turned on him. Ahaz knew little Judah did not have the strength to fend them off, and he became quite fearful. It was at this point that Isaiah came to him with reassuring words from Jehovah.

I. Isaiah Reassures Ahaz (Isaiah 7:2-6)

A. Ahaz and the People Troubled (v. 2)

2. And it was told the house of David, saying, Syria is confederate with Ephraim. And his heart was moved, and the heart of his people, as the trees of the wood are moved with the wind.

The *house of David* included King Ahaz, and other members of his family who may have been assembled when the word arrived of the threat to Judah. Ahaz was guilty of serious departures from the ways of his father and grandfather. "He did not that which was right in the sight of the Lord." Among other sins, he made "molten images for Baalim," offered incense to pagan gods, and even "burnt his children in the fire" (2 Chronicles 28:1-3). As a result of these sins, he was delivered into the hands of Syria and then Israel, both of whom defeated his troops with great slaughter. Judah was so seriously weakened by these defeats that she was easy prey for the Philistines and the Edomites (2 Chronicles 28:5-19)

Now the news that frightened Ahaz was that *Syria* and *Ephraim*, that is, Israel, were coming again. They had joined forces to attack Jerusalem, depose Ahaz, and install a king who would join them in the struggle against Assyria. Ahaz and his people were so frightened that their hearts were shaking like trees in a wind.

B. Isaiah Sent to Meet Ahaz (v. 3)

3. Then said the LORD unto Isaiah, Go forth now to meet Ahaz, thou, and Shear-jashub thy son, at the end of the conduit of the upper pool, in the highway of the fuller's field.

At this critical moment God spoke to Isaiah, sending him to meet the king. Accompanying Isaiah was his son whose unusual name meant "a remnant will return." This was seen as a message of hope: at least some of the people would survive the coming crisis.

Ahaz was out examining the defenses of the city when Isaiah found him. Probably he was hoping to protect Jerusalem's water supply when the city was besieged.

C. Isaiah Encourages Ahaz (v. 4)

4. And say unto him, Take heed, and be quiet; fear not, neither be faint-hearted for the two tails of these smoking firebrands, for the fierce anger of Rezin with Syria, and of the son of Remaliah.

Isaiah's message to the king was to be calm in the face of this threat. If he would put his trust in God, he would have nothing to fear. Trusting God was not easy for Ahaz. Already he had suffered at the hands of Syria and Israel, sent by God to punish him for his evil ways. He had not repented, but had continued in his wickedness. In sending Isaiah, God was giving him another chance. *Rezin* was the king of *Syria*, and *the son of Remaliah* was Pekah, who had murdered his predecessor to become the king of Israel. These two firebrands need not be feared; they were only smoking embers about to be extinguished.

"I SHALL NOT BE MOVED"

Ship travel is the ultimate luxury. Thirty years ago, a transatlantic crossing took a full week—seven days of leisure, only occasionally interrupted by rough waters. Our tour director organized a passenger talent show, so four of us formed a quartet. We sang in the ship's theater, just in front of a stage curtain. We happened to be in the midst of a storm, and the curtain was visibly swinging and swaying with the pitch and roll of the vessel. Our song selection was appropriate: "I Shall Not Be Moved."

King Ahaz needed the message of that song. The refrain says, "Just like a tree that's planted by the waters, I shall not be moved." The hearts of Ahaz and Judah were *moved* (*shaken* in the *New International Version*) "as the trees of the wood are moved with the wind." But Isaiah communicated God's encouragement: "Fear not, neither be faint-hearted." The winds of war are disturbing, but not always destructive.

Storms of fear and trouble can bend our branches, but never uproot our faith if we plant it by the living water Jesus gives. There our roots grow deep and strong. We continue to produce fruit of the Spirit, never withering and always prospering (Psalm 1:3). We shall not be moved!

—R. W. B.

D. Judah's Enemies' Plans (vv. 5, 6)

5, 6. Because Syria, Ephraim, and the son of Remaliah, have taken evil counsel against thee, saying, Let us go up against Judah, and vex it, and let us make a breach therein for us, and set a king in the midst of it, even the son of Tabeal.

The earlier defeat of Judah by Syria and Israel gave Ahaz good reason to fear another attack. In that first victory the two allies had not been able to take Jerusalem, but now they seemed determined to breach the wall and take the city. Then their plan was to depose Ahaz and replace him with the *son of Tabeal*, who would cooperate with them. We know nothing more about this man.

II. The Lord Speaks to Ahaz (Isaiah 7:10-13)

A. Ahaz Told to Ask for a Sign (vv. 10, 11)

10, 11. Moreover the LORD spake again unto Ahaz, saying, Ask thee a sign of the LORD thy God; ask it either in the depth, or in the height above.

God did not speak to Ahaz directly, but through his prophet, Isaiah. He had already told Ahaz that the coalition against him would fail

How to Say It

AHAZ. *A*-haz.
ASSYRIA. Uh-*sear*-ee-uh.
EPHRAIM. *Ee*-fray-im.
IMMANUEL. Ih-*man*-you-el.
ISAIAH. Eye-*zay*-uh.
JOTHAM. *Jo*-tham.
PEKAH. *Pee*-kuh.
REMALIAH. Rem-ah-*lye*-ah.
REZIN. *Re*-zin.
SHEAR-JASHUB. *She*-are-ja*y*-shub (strong accent on *jay*).
TABEAL. *Tay*-be-al.
UZZIAH. Uh-*zye*-uh.

(vv. 7-9), but the king was not willing to trust God's assurance. Perhaps a few days or even weeks elapsed between verses 7-9 and verses 10 and 11. Since Ahaz had rejected the first message, Isaiah returned, this time encouraging him to ask for a sign that the message was true. Sometimes asking for a sign can be the wrong thing to do. For example, the Pharisees asked Jesus for a sign, but He rejected their request because He knew they had hardened their hearts against believing in Him (Matthew 12:38, 39). A dozen signs wouldn't have changed their minds. On the other hand, when Gideon asked for a sign for reassurance, God answered his request because He knew that Gideon's heart was right (Judges 6:36-40).

Ahaz was given a wide choice of possible signs. He could ask for something from the depths or something from the heights. Obviously, anything between would be equally appropriate. The signs that God gives are not always miraculous, but in this situation He seemed ready to offer a miraculous sign.

B. Ahaz Refuses to Ask (vv. 12, 13)

12, 13. But Ahaz said, I will not ask, neither will I tempt the LORD. And he said, Hear ye now, O house of David; Is it a small thing for you to weary men, but will ye weary my God also?

Ahaz refused to ask because he had decided to seek help from Assyria instead of God. Trying to appear pious, he said asking a sign would be tempting God, testing Him. That was forbidden (Deuteronomy 6:16). Of course Ahaz should have trusted God without a sign; but of course it would not be wrong to ask a sign when God invited him to do so.

The Lord's reply was addressed to the *house of David*: not only Ahaz, but his whole family, even future generations of that family. Isaiah's

patience was just about exhausted. He had grown very weary of Ahaz's arrogance and obstinance, and he made it clear that even God was getting tired of it.

ID

Most of us have become accustomed to showing proof of personal identity every time we write a check. We are surprised when it is not required. I have been patronizing the same dry cleaners for fifteen years, and they still insist on seeing my driver's license when I write them a check. It's routine; obviously a store policy with no exceptions.

Business loss due to bad checks has made ID proof a necessity in our corrupt society. But Ahaz should have trusted God with or without a sign, and so should we. Over the centuries, Jehovah has established unimpeachable credibility with His people. Jesus condemned some who demanded evidence of God's presence and power: "An evil and adulterous generation seeketh after a sign" (Matthew 12:39).

Some Christians still "put out a fleece," as Gideon did (Judges 6:36-40), to determine God's will, to see if God's guidance is really His. It is like asking the King of the universe for ID, proof of identity and integrity. Isaiah would chide, "Will ye weary my God also?" And he would exhort, "Trust ye in the Lord for ever (Isaiah 26:4). The only ID God needs is, "I AM THAT I AM" (Exodus 3:14).   —R. W. B.

III. The Sign to Be Given (Isaiah 7:14-17)

A. A Virgin Shall Bear a Son (vv. 14, 15)

14. Therefore the Lord himself will give you a sign; Behold, a virgin shall conceive, and bear a son, and shall call his name Immanuel.

This particular verse has sparked a great deal of controversy. Space in this book does not allow a discussion of the arguments, and neither does time in a Sunday school session. We shall try merely to state the two main opinions as briefly as possible.

Opinion one: This birth was to be a sign to Ahaz. Therefore it must occur during his lifetime. The Hebrew word translated *virgin* may mean a young woman who is not a virgin. Isaiah was saying that some young woman known to Ahaz would soon conceive, bear a son, and name him Immanuel. However, in the same words Isaiah was also foretelling the virgin birth of Jesus. This is clear in Matthew 1:18-23.

Opinion two: The word translated *virgin* does mean virgin. This is shown by the quotation of it in Matthew 1:18-23. Verse 13 of our text shows that Isaiah turned from Ahaz to address the house of David. The virgin birth was not to be a sign to Ahaz, but to the house of David seven hundred years later. The prophecy of Isaiah 7:14 is fulfilled only in Jesus. No one else has been born of a virgin; no one else can so fittingly be called Immanuel, God with us.

15. Butter and honey shall he eat, that he may know to refuse the evil, and choose the good.

Most students now agree that this should be translated *cottage cheese* rather than *butter,* and some versions have *when he shall know* or *till he shall know* instead of *that he may know.*

If we choose the first of the two opinions cited above, of course we take verse 15 to mean the child soon to be born. Armies of Syria and Israel would steal the harvests in Judah so there would be no bread, but a farmer could hide a cow or a few goats to provide milk and cottage cheese for his son. Honey would be taken from wild bees.

If we think verse 14 refers to Jesus only, verse 15 is not so simple. Possibly it means Jesus would live on simple fare because He would be in a poor family. Possibly only verse 14 refers to Jesus, while verse 15 refers to a child of Ahaz's time, but not some particular child. *Butter and honey shall he eat:* any child of that time in Judah will have that limited diet.

B. Judah Will Be Spared (vv. 16, 17)

16. For before the child shall know to refuse the evil, and choose the good, the land that thou abhorrest shall be forsaken of both her kings.

Now we come to the reassuring message for King Ahaz, and it is the same whether we have been thinking of a particular child soon to be born, or just any child born in those days, or of Jesus to be born much later. The message is that the kings of Israel and Syria will both be removed. That will happen soon, within the few years required for a child to grow old enough to know good from bad.

17. The LORD shall bring upon thee, and upon thy people, and upon thy father's house, days that have not come, from the day that Ephraim departed from Judah; even the king of Assyria.

Even though Ahaz refused to trust and obey, the Lord was going to save Judah from Israel and Syria. That is the promise of verse 17. But there was worse to come. The days ahead would be more troublesome than any time had been in the two hundred years since the big kingdom of Solomon was divided into *Ephraim,* or Israel in

visual 11

the north, and *Judah* in the south. That trouble would come with *the king of Assyria,* from whom Ahaz was asking help.

That was exactly what happened. Ahaz went on with his plan to seek help from Assyria. He paid heavily for help, but got none (2 Chronicles 28:16-21). And a few decades later, the Assyrians invaded Judah with terrible results (2 Kings 18:13-16). But again the Lord came to the rescue (2 Kings 19:35, 36).

GOOD NEWS/BAD NEWS

We are all familiar with "good news/bad news" jokes. The question incorporated in the joke usually is, "Which do you want to hear first, the good news or the bad news?"

Quite often, good news is tainted by negative implications. We are somewhat conditioned, it seems, when we hear announcements that make us glad, to listen for "the other shoe to drop." Phrases such as, *"on the other hand,"* or *"the other side of the coin"* or even a simple *"but"* are clues that not-so-good news will follow.

Prophets foretold both good and bad futures. Isaiah predicted for Ahaz that both Israel and Syria would soon lose their kings, and thus no longer be a threat to Judah. That was good news to Ahaz. With his next breath, however, Isaiah warned that the king of Assyria would bring incomparable grief to Judah, due to their sin and rebellion.

I prefer to receive my good news last, as in Romans 6:23: "For the wages of sin is death; *but the gift of God is eternal life through Jesus Christ our Lord.*"
                                                    —R. W. B.

Conclusion

A. God Still Speaks

The same holy God who confronted Isaiah in the temple is seen in today's lesson confronting King Ahaz. Two aspects of this confrontation are different. First, in this confrontation God did not speak to Ahaz in a vision as He had spoken to Isaiah. Instead, He spoke through Isaiah. In the second place, Ahaz did not respond in the same way that Isaiah had. Isaiah was overwhelmed by the experience, readily confessing his own sinfulness and the sinfulness of the people. Once he was cleansed he was ready to serve God. On the other hand, Ahaz never acknowledged his sin and never experienced a cleansing, nor did he offer himself for service.

Most of us would have difficulty identifying with either Isaiah or Ahaz. Not many of us feel as pious as Isaiah, nor do many of us believe we are as wicked as Ahaz. We certainly do not expect to experience a vision in which we are brought directly into the presence of Jehovah. Nor is it likely that we will be confronted by an inspired prophet like Isaiah. Yet we cannot escape being confronted regularly by God. That confrontation comes through his holy Word. As we read and study the Bible, we read of His standards that should govern our conduct, or we draw guidance from reading about a historical situation in which God intervened.

As we read the Bible reverently and expectantly, we find guidance for our lives. Most of us do not live on a heroic plane, nor are we great leaders whose decisions affect the lives of thousands. But whether we live in a king's palace or are homeless, God expects us to live in accordance with His will. Finding His will in our complicated times may be difficult, yet we must seek it diligently. Once we have found it, we must follow it courageously. A holy God can demand nothing less.

B. We Need an Isaiah

For many decades now we have suffered through tumultuous times both in our personal lives and as a nation. To protect the security of our nation, our leaders have resorted to huge expenditures for armaments and have entered numerous military alliances. We may debate about which decisions were wise, but we know for certain that they have not brought the security we hoped for.

In Ahaz's day, he made most of the decisions for his country. The citizens could do little more than try to live with these decisions. But it is different for us who live in a democracy. We choose our leaders and we have a hand in the decisions that they make. We must accept some of the responsibility for these decisions. To refuse to participate in the democratic process is in effect to make a decision. Since we don't have an Isaiah to give us direction as we make decisions, let us learn to make them prayerfully, intelligently, and in the light of God's Word.

C. Immanuel

Immanuel! It is not likely that Isaiah understood the full implications of this name when he spoke to King Ahaz. Of course, he knew that it meant "God with us," and in a sense that was true in Isaiah's time. In spite of Ahaz's sinful behavior, God had not abandoned His people. He would deliver them from the threat of Judah's neighbors to the north.

But the birth of a son named Immanuel carried more than just a promise for the deliverance of Judah within the space of two or three years. Only as we read Matthew 1:20-23 do we begin to plumb the depth of meaning conveyed in Isaiah 7:14. This verse and other passages in Isaiah gave assurance that God in His own good time would intersect history in a new and dramatic fashion. In Isaiah's day God spoke through the prophets; but seven hundred years after Isaiah lived, God spoke with finality through His Son, who was born of a virgin. It is unfortunate that about the only time we give attention to this important fact is at Christmastime. We need to be reminded every day that God is still with us, that He will provide us light for our darkest times.

D. Let Us Pray

Almighty God, we come before You recognizing that in Your hands You hold the destinies of men and of nations. We feel the need of Your presence when life comes crashing down around us; but may we also realize our needs when all seems to be going well. Show us how to understand and accept the guidance You give us through the Scriptures. Let us find assurance in the words of our Savior that He will be with us to the end of time. In the name of Immanuel we pray. Amen.

E. Thought to Remember

Immanuel, God with us.

Home Daily Bible Readings

Monday, Aug. 7—Isaiah Advises Ahaz to Trust God (Isaiah 7:1-9)

Tuesday, Aug. 8—A Sign for the Fearful King (Isaiah 7:10-17)

Wednesday, Aug. 9—Ahaz's Actions Will Bring Hard Times (Isaiah 7:18-25)

Thursday, Aug. 10—Ahaz Turns Away From God (2 Kings 16:1-6)

Friday, Aug. 11—Ahaz Buys Help From Assyria (2 Kings 16:7-11)

Saturday, Aug. 12—Ahaz's New Altar (2 Kings 16:12-18)

Sunday, Aug. 13—God Will Judge Unrighteousness (Psalm 75)

Learning by Doing

This page contains an alternate lesson plan emphasizing learning activities. Classes desiring such student involvement will find these suggestions helpful.

Learning Goals

In this lesson you will lead your students to do the following:

1. Explore the issue of reliance on human resources vs. reliance upon God.

2. Pinpoint their own tendencies to rely upon human resources instead of God.

3. Seek to rely upon God for security.

Into the Lesson

Bring a number of magazines to class. As the class session begins, ask students to form groups of four. In these groups they are to browse through magazines and cut out pictures. The pictures they are to look for are ones that suggest reliance upon something other than God. For example, they might select a picture of someone drinking alcohol, or someone with a fancy new car. As they select pictures they should discuss how each picture symbolizes reliance upon a human resource.

Allow about five minutes. Then bring the groups together and ask volunteers to display their pictures and briefly explain what they represent.

Lead into the Scripture study by saying, "The Bible instructs us to trust in God, not human resources. In fact, many of the Scriptures are focused upon this very issue. In our lesson today we will observe a king who was challenged to trust God, not military might."

Option

Write the following three sentences on the chalkboard:

Sometimes it is easier for people to trust in _____ than to trust in God.

Sometimes it is easier for nations to trust in _____ than to trust in God.

Sometimes it is easier for churches to trust in _____ than to trust in God.

Have your class form groups of three or four. Provide paper and pencils for each. Ask one third of the groups to work on the first sentence, one third to work on the second, and one third to work on the third. Ask each of the groups to think of three to five ways to fill in the blank in its sentence.

Allow about two minutes. Then ask each group to report its answers to the rest of the class.

Into the Word

Ask a volunteer to read Isaiah 7:2-17. Explain the background of this passage, using the commentary in this book. Then have the students continue in their groups to discuss these questions, which are in the student book:

1. What was Ahaz's predicament?

2. How did the king and people of Judah react to the predicament?

3. What encouragement did Isaiah give Ahaz?

4. How did God emphasize He is in control?

5. Did Ahaz put his trust in God? What evidence supports your answer?

6. How do these two passages relate to Ahaz's situation: Psalm 20:7 and 33:17, 18?

Option

Ask a volunteer to read Isaiah 7:2-17. Then present a brief lecture on the background and on the passage. The lecture should be about ten minutes and cover the main ideas of the passage.

Then have the class members meet again in the groups they formed earlier. In their groups they are to write a poem about relying on the Lord based upon Isaiah 7:2-17. Students need not worry about the quality of the poem. They can be serious or humorous. They may or may not want their poems to rhyme.

Allow fifteen to twenty minutes for the groups to work on their poetry. Then ask each group to present its poem to the rest of the class.

Into Life

Lead your class in discussing these questions:

1. What is the difference between using a human resource and relying upon it?

2. What clues can we look for to tell us if we are relying on human resources instead of God?

3. How does God teach us to rely upon Him instead of His resources?

4. What are you personally tempted to rely upon instead of God?

Allow time for this final portion of the lesson. Write on the chalkboard the words of Zechariah 4:6, "'Not by might nor by power, but by my Spirit,' says the Lord Almighty" (*New International Version*).

Point out that this verse teaches that God accomplishes His will, not through human strength or human efforts, but through His Holy Spirit.

Close with group prayers.

Let's Talk It Over

The questions on this page are designed to encourage review of the lesson Scriptures and to promote discussion of the lesson by the class. The answers provided are only discussion starters. Let your class talk it over from there.

1. Do modern countries still rely on military power, even when the cold war is over? If so, what can be done to change the pattern?

Of course nations have armies and police to protect themselves and their citizens from wrong. No doubt citizens will continue to disagree about when or if such power should be used to protect other countries or their citizens too. But most adults can think of recent times when military power has been used to inflict wrong, not to prevent it. Both nations and factions within nations have been guilty of this.

The United Nations represents one kind of effort to settle disputes by reason and right rather than force, but continuing warfare shows how difficult that task can be. Another move in the right direction is the outpouring of help to victims of natural disasters or of warfare. An even finer example is presented as the church reaches out to all the world with the news of God's love and of salvation in Jesus.

2. Are today's leaders in government willing to listen to God's message about values or moral choices? If so, how do we speak up so we will be heard when we stand for the right?

Most of us can recall one or more times when an official of government has taken a stand for truth and right, perhaps because of the pressure of good people more than because of his own moral convictions. Officials do listen when many people study the issues and the Scriptures enough to be able to speak clearly and firmly for the right. Knowledge of the right comes from God's Word; but when both leaders and people are overeager to avoid any entanglement of government with religion, it may be best to present the right simply as right, not with quotations from Scripture. But we will do well if we think through social and legal issues in terms of what God has said and how it applies to current events. The present trend to encourage "open forums" and "town meetings" offers excellent opportunities to present our positions if we have thought them through carefully and can speak them clearly.

3. Do God's signs always have to be miraculous? Are there signs today to confirm the truth of God's message?

God has given so many miraculous signs that the word *sign* sometimes seems to be a synonym for *miracle*. Jesus' birth from a virgin certainly was a tremendous miracle, a sign that He is truly the Son of God.

Still, the word *sign* merely means something that points out or indicates. Many signs are not miracles. Circumcision was a sign of God's covenant with Abraham (Genesis 17:11). Our version says "a token," but the Hebrew word is the same one that is translated "sign" in Isaiah 7:14. The Sabbath also was a sign of the covenant (Exodus 31:12, 13). Without using the word *sign*, Psalm 19:1-6 makes it clear that the sky is a sign of God's glory and power. Romans 1:20 likewise shows that the creation is a sign of the Creator's "eternal power and Godhead."

These signs in earth and sky are still before us. Besides, the truth revealed in Scripture has been corroborated many times in history. Evil does get punished eventually, and righteous living brings its ultimate reward. A conclusive sign for our generation is presented when Christian people put into practice what Jesus has taught.

4. Does God give special signs to individuals now? If so, how? May a passage of Scripture have a special message for you personally?

A tenant farmer had an opportunity to buy the land he was using. The price was low, and he could easily borrow the money. Still, he decided not to apply for a loan because the Bible says, "Owe no man any thing." Neighbors admired his loyalty to the Bible, but most of them thought he misapplied Romans 13:8.

There is danger in drawing a bit of Scripture out of its context and giving it a meaning not intended by the writer in order to find guidance in some personal problems. In all honesty and with due respect to Scripture, we need to consider who spoke or wrote those words, to whom he addressed them, and for what purpose. When we understand the original meaning of a passage, then we are ready to consider if and how it can be applied in different circumstances. If "Owe no man any thing" is applied to financial dealings, it does not necessarily mean not to borrow money. It can as reasonably be taken to mean to make each payment when it is due.

Judgment Comes On Israel

DEVOTIONAL READING: **Psalm 2.**

LESSON SCRIPTURE: **Isaiah 9:8—10:4; 5.**

PRINTED TEXT: **Isaiah 5:8-12, 18-23.**

Isaiah 5:8-12, 18-23

8 Woe unto them that join house to house, that lay field to field, till there be no place, that they may be placed alone in the midst of the earth!

9 In mine ears said the LORD of hosts, Of a truth many houses shall be desolate, even great and fair, without inhabitant.

10 Yea, ten acres of vineyard shall yield one bath, and the seed of a homer shall yield an ephah.

11 Woe unto them that rise up early in the morning, that they may follow strong drink; that continue until night, till wine inflame them!

12 And the harp and the viol, the tabret and pipe, and wine, are in their feasts: but they regard not the work of the LORD, neither consider the operation of his hands.

. . . .

18 Woe unto them that draw iniquity with cords of vanity, and sin as it were with a cart rope:

19 That say, Let him make speed, and hasten his work, that we may see it: and let the counsel of the Holy One of Israel draw nigh and come, that we may know it!

20 Woe unto them that call evil good, and good evil; that put darkness for light, and light for darkness; that put bitter for sweet, and sweet for bitter!

21 Woe unto them that are wise in their own eyes, and prudent in their own sight!

22 Woe unto them that are mighty to drink wine, and men of strength to mingle strong drink:

23 Which justify the wicked for reward, and take away the righteousness of the righteous from him!

GOLDEN TEXT: Put away the evil of your doings from before mine eyes; cease to do evil; learn to do well; seek judgment, relieve the oppressed, judge the fatherless, plead for the widow.—Isaiah 1:16, 17.

A Nation Turns From God
Unit 3: The Judgment Arrives
(Lessons 10-13)

Lesson Aims

As a result of studying this lesson, each student should:

1. Have a better understanding of the social and political situation in the time of Isaiah.

2. Recognize that some of the moral evils that Isaiah dealt with are similar to those that we must deal with today.

3. Have a growing appreciation for the dangers of strong drink.

4. Be able to mention a specific way of applying the lesson to our situation.

Lesson Outline

INTRODUCTION
    A. Woe and Whoa
    B. Lesson Background
 I. DANGER OF COVETOUSNESS (Isaiah 5:8-10)
    A. The Results of Greed (v. 8)
    B. The Punishment of Greed (vv. 9, 10)
 II. DANGER OF STRONG DRINK (Isaiah 5:11, 12)
    A. Strong Drink Inflames (v. 11)
       Why Ask Why?
    B. Strong Drink Dominates Feasts (v. 12)
 III. DANGERS OF SIN (Isaiah 5:18-23)
    A. Sin Becomes a Burden (v. 18)
    B. Sin Leads to Arrogance (v. 19)
    C. Sin Has Its Own Standards (vv. 20, 21)
       Confused Values
    D. Sin Perverts Justice (vv. 22, 23)
CONCLUSION
    A. The Times They Are NOT A-changin'
    B. Greed, Ancient and Modern
    C. Let Us Pray
    D. Thought to Remember

Visual 12 of the visuals packet warns against the deliberate confusing of good and evil. Display it throughout the class session. The visual is shown on page 436.

Introduction

A. Woe and Whoa

Isaiah uses the word *woe* a number of times in today's lesson text. In each case he is pronouncing God's judgment upon a particular sin of the people. In verse 8 he condemns their greed for real estate. In verse 11 he condemns their drunkenness. In verse 18 he speaks out against those who have allowed themselves to become enmeshed in sin. In verse 20 woe is pronounced upon those who set up their own standards of right and wrong. Their spiritual arrogance is denounced in verse 21. In verse 22 their indulgence in strong drink is condemned for the second time.

Several years ago when we still worked our farms with horses, we yelled the word *whoa* when we wanted them to stop. Horses that were well trained would stop immediately when they were given that command. When the prophet Isaiah condemned a particular sin of his people with a strong *woe*, he also intended to convey the idea of *whoa*, stop it. It's a pity that the people of Israel were not as well trained as our horses.

B. Lesson Background

Scholars differ about the exact date when the oracles that serve as today's lesson text were proclaimed. Some hold that they come early in Isaiah's ministry, before his call recorded in chapter 6. In this case the prophet was addressing the conditions that existed during the reign of Uzziah. It is plain that sin was rampant among the people even while that good king was promoting true worship and righteous living. If, on the other hand, these oracles were uttered after his special call, then they dealt with the conditions that occurred during the reign of Jotham or Ahaz, or somewhere after about the year 740 B.C.

In either event, it was a time of prosperity for the nation of Judah, perhaps the most prosperous time since the days of King Solomon. Prosperity, unfortunately, breeds certain kinds of sins, and these were plainly evident in that society. But the international scene soon would be changing. Assyria, under Tiglath-pileser, regained the power it had lost and began to extend its influence over Syria, Israel, and Judah. Syria and Israel formed an alliance to resist Assyria and tried to force Judah to join the alliance. When King Ahaz refused, the two threatened to replace him with a puppet of their own choosing. In desperation, Ahaz appealed to Tiglath-pileser for help. As a result, he was forced to pay tribute to the Assyrians.

All of this was still on the horizon when Isaiah addressed some of the serious evils of his nation. He clearly saw that moral decay in Judah was the reason for the disaster about to come upon her. But it didn't have to happen. If they would only repent, this catastrophe could be easily avoided.

I. Danger of Covetousness
(Isaiah 5:8-10)

A. The Results of Greed (v. 8)

8. Woe unto them that join house to house, that lay field to field, till there be no place, that they may be placed alone in the midst of the earth!

Woe is a strong word. It is more than a slap on the wrist or an expression of mild disapproval. It suggests divine condemnation. Greed drove the rich to accumulate houses and land. Both Amos and Micah, writing near the same time, condemn the same sin (Amos 8:4; Micah 2:2). By joining *house to house* a rich man would acquire a whole row of houses along a street; and by laying *field to field* he would add land to what he already had. As a result, poor people were reduced to the level of impoverished peasants. The Mosaic law required that the title to land revert to the original owners in the jubilee year (every fifty years), but the rich had ways to subvert this law. A rich man sought to *be placed alone in the midst of the earth*, owning all the property he could see. In his greed he seized poor people's houses and lands with injustice and violence (Micah 2:2). His own gain was more important to him than the very livelihood of the poor people.

B. The Punishment of Greed (vv. 9, 10)

9. In mine ears said the LORD of hosts, Of a truth many houses shall be desolate, even great and fair, without inhabitant.

Isaiah made sure the greedy ones would understand that the message of doom came from the *Lord of hosts* and was not the prophet's own idea. God spoke in his ear in such a way that he could not misunderstand. The rich would not be able to enjoy their ill-gotten gain. The houses would be left desolate, the inhabitants would be gone. Apparently all of this desolation would result from the war that was about to fall upon the land.

10. Yea, ten acres of vineyard shall yield one bath, and the seed of a homer shall yield an ephah.

An acre was the amount of land a yoke of oxen could plow in a day. A *bath* probably was about five and a half gallons. Such a pitiful yield from such a large vineyard would indicate an almost total crop failure. The exact volume of a *homer* is disputed, with estimates ranging from six and a half bushels to about fourteen bushels. An *ephah* was a tenth of a homer. The desolation of the land was obvious, when a farmer got back only a tenth of the seed he planted. Whether these crop failures came as a result of bad weather, ravenous insects, or invading armies, Isaiah does not tell us. The point that Isaiah was making was that God would see to it that greed did not pay.

II. Danger of Strong Drink
(Isaiah 5:11, 12)

A. Strong Drink Inflames (v. 11)

11. Woe unto them that rise up early in the morning, that they may follow strong drink; that continue until night, till wine inflame them!

The second woe is pronounced upon those who drink to an excess. Their pursuit of strong drink was carried out with all the enthusiasm and energy generally reserved for more worthy causes. Those *that rise up early in the morning* ordinarily do so because they are hard-working, industrious people. These did so because they were hard-drinking. Further, their drinking bouts continued all day long and into the evening. Obviously, these people had to be rich to be able to engage in such prolonged debaucheries. Such behavior on the part of those who have to work daily for a living would soon leave them in poverty.

WHY ASK WHY?

Isn't it surprising that society has become so smoke-conscious? Public smoking seems on its way to being banned everywhere—even in baseball stadiums! Thousands give up cigarettes each year, and thousands more push for antismoking statutes to reduce the hazard of inhaling "second-hand smoke." Frankly, it is surprising to see so many making such good sense!

Now, a logical question occurs to thinking people: Why isn't similar good sense being demonstrated in regard to alcohol? Why no warning labels on beer cans and liquor bottles? Has no one determined that imbibing alcohol can be dangerous to one's health?

Obviously, distillers and brewers have a strong lobby in Washington. And media marketers are reluctant to forfeit the billions of dollars of advertising revenue realized from beer and wine ads. But there's another bottom line to this question. *People like to drink.* They like to depress their inhibitions and dull their pain. Never mind the jeopardy to health, home, jobs, relationships, and eternal salvation. If inebriation feels good, drinkers will consider those risks worth taking, if they give it any consideration at all. Jeremiah was right: "The heart is . . . desperately wicked" (Jeremiah 17:9).   —R. W. B.

B. Strong Drink Dominates Feasts
(v. 12)

12. And the harp and the viol, the tabret and pipe, and wine, are in their feasts: but they regard not the work of the LORD, neither consider the operation of his hands.

The strains of various musical instruments enhanced their drunken revelries. The variety of instruments used gives an indication of the revelers' wealth. There is a good deal of confusion about musical instruments mentioned in the Old Testament. The *harp* mentioned in this verse was probably a lyre, a stringed instrument that could be held in the hand. The *viol* was a stringed instrument; the Hebrew word is sometimes rendered *harp* or *lyre* in modern translations. The *tabret* was a small percussion instrument. The word is sometimes translated *tambourine*. The *pipe* may have been a wind instrument like a flute. The impression one gets is that professional musicians were employed to perform at these feasts, a further indication that only the rich were involved in these drinking orgies. Whether other entertainers were present we are not told. Perhaps these feasts were not as sophisticated as our modern night clubs, but the parallels are obvious.

These people, consumed by their drinking, gave little thought to the *work of the Lord*. They were not interested in how God had called the Israelites to become His own people and how He had blessed them across the centuries. Assuredly, they gave no thought to how their own wealth came from Him. The wine had dulled their senses so they could not discern God's work in history, and it had destroyed their gratitude for all He had done for them. Isaiah's message still confronts a similar problem in our society today.

III. Dangers of Sin
(Isaiah 5:18-23)

A. Sin Becomes a Burden (v. 18)

Verses 13-17 announce the judgment that is about to fall upon those who have blatantly ignored God. Verse 13 tells of the coming captivity of the people. The tragedy is that many of those who would suffer as a result of this captivity were innocent of the excesses that brought it on. But that is often the case. One of the terrible aspects of sin is that the innocent often have to suffer along with the guilty. We see this in the current AIDS epidemic. Little children and others who have not been guilty of violating God's laws have been made to suffer right along with the guilty.

Verse 14 states that hell (actually sheol, or death) will be enlarged, indicating that multitudes will die as a result of this captivity. Verses 15 and 16 inform us that the proud will be humbled and that God will be exalted. In verse 17 we learn that the land will become desolate, fit only for a pasture, where the "lambs feed after their manner."

18. Woe unto them that draw iniquity with cords of vanity, and sin as it were with a cart rope.

In this third woe, Isaiah uses a striking figure to make his point. The exact meaning of this figure may not be clear, but the point the prophet is making is evident enough. He indicates that the people had willfully engaged in a sinful lifestyle. With a thrust of sarcasm, he points out that their sins had become a heavy cart that they unwittingly pulled behind them. They had willingly accepted the yoke of sin without looking back to see what they were hitched to. Truly, "the way of transgressors is hard" (Proverbs 13:15).

B. Sin Leads to Arrogance (v. 19)

19. That say, Let him make speed, and hasten his work, that we may see it: and let the counsel of the Holy One of Israel draw nigh and come, that we may know it!

Those who reject the word of the Lord often do so with brazen arrogance, or at least they put up a bold front that reflects a defiant attitude. In effect, they were saying, "OK, so God is at work in history. But right now we don't see any evidence of His work. Let Him show us, and then we will believe." They remind us of Jesus' enemies who said, "If thou be the Son of God, come down from the cross" (Matthew 27:40). But unbelief was so deeply ingrained in their hearts that no demonstration, regardless of how dramatic it might be, would convince them.

This attitude is not that of blatant atheism. It is, rather, the attitude of persons who believe in a God who is so remote that He doesn't make any difference in their lives. These ancient skeptics have their modern counterparts. Surveys indicate that few people in our society boldly

"Woe unto them that call evil good, and good evil; that put darkness for light, and light for darkness."

visual 12

deny the existence of God. When asked, they may affirm that they believe in God, but then they proceed to live as if He didn't exist. At least they live that way until they face a crisis in their lives. That crisis came in ancient Judah, and we are foolish to suppose that we can forever avoid crises in our lives.

C. Sin Has Its Own Standards
(vv. 20, 21)

20. Woe unto them that call evil good, and good evil; that put darkness for light, and light for darkness; that put bitter for sweet, and sweet for bitter!

When people who have known the will of God fall into sin, they experience a sense of guilt because they know they are doing wrong. Unwilling to mend their ways, they seek a means of relieving the irritation that a guilty conscience brings. One way to do this is to confuse the issue by changing definitions. If they can make bad look good, then the wrong they are doing appears to be right. Those who approve of homosexuality now refer to it as "an alternate lifestyle," as if changing terms will somehow change the way God looks at it. To avoid the burden of guilt that comes from destroying life still in the womb, some no longer talk about aborting babies. Rather, babies have become "fetuses," and all sense of guilt is removed. Isaiah does not hesitate to pronounce a woe upon this moral sleight of hand.

CONFUSED VALUES

Thousands of babies are killed each day by abortion, which is considered by many to reflect a good choice by mothers with unwanted pregnancies. Condoms are freely distributed by some schools to protect sexually active students. This is viewed as a good approach to curbing teenage pregnancies and sexually transmitted diseases. Homosexuals are allowed to join our armed forces, and even the ministry of some churches. This is seen as a good interpretation of the "equal rights" guaranteed by the Constitution.

Prayer, Bible reading, and nativity scenes are banned from public schools in America, for such expressions of religion are viewed by some as politically wrong. Sexual abstinence and morality are not taught, because such lessons are considered by liberal educators to be socially inhibitive. Homemaking careers are viewed by feminists as less than fulfilling (at least), and a bad choice by modern women who should work outside the home instead.

This confused culture needs to hear the warning of Isaiah: "Woe unto them that call evil good, and good evil." Values are so confused today that many people have little idea of what is right and what is wrong. What will prevent God's wrath from being kindled against America, just as it was against Judah?   —R. W. B.

21. Woe unto them that are wise in their own eyes, and prudent in their own sight!

Those who subvert God's laws often develop a proud complacency that blinds them to their moral condition. They set their own standards, and since they are able to meet these human standards, they feel quite comfortable. They proclaim woe to those who dare threaten their comfort. Such persons are likely to be labeled as "narrowminded," "legalists," "bigots," or even "hypocrites." But that's not the way Isaiah sees it. His woe is reserved for the moral compromisers whose complacency ought to be disturbed.

Wisdom and prudence are often extolled in the Old Testament as virtues. The question is by what standard or by whose standard are wisdom and prudence determined. Some had created their own standards, and by these standards they appeared quite wise. Upon such persons Isaiah pronounces a forceful woe. One of Satan's tricks is to convince us that we are better than we really are, and we often fall for the bait. Self-deceit is a dangerous weakness, because when we are self-deceived, we refuse to listen to advice.

D. Sin Perverts Justice (vv. 22, 23)

22, 23. Woe unto them that are mighty to drink wine, and men of strength to mingle strong drink: which justify the wicked for reward, and take away the righteousness of the righteous from him!

This is the sixth of Isaiah's woes. At first glance it may seem that he is simply repeating the woe he had earlier pronounced against strong drink. The word here translated *mighty* is translated *heroes* in several modern translations. It was often used to describe those who had proven themselves outstanding in military combat. Here it is used in a less positive sense to describe champions in drinking bouts.

They are singled out here for the prophet's condemnation, not just because they could drink everyone else under the table, but because their drinking led to serious injustices in society. They were guilty of justifying *the wicked for reward*. In other words, they were using their positions in the courts to gain bribes, which in turn were spent on strong drink. It was bad enough to spend on strong drink the money one had earned by hard work. It was far worse to pervert justice in order to finance one's drinking habit. In the process the wicked won court decisions while the righteous were denied justice.

Conclusion

A. The Times They Are NOT A-changin'

Many things were different in Isaiah's day. Most of us would not feel comfortable about these differences. We take for granted so many of our physical comforts—heating and air conditioning, a rich variety of plentiful foods, household conveniences. We enjoy our comfortable cars and good highways and the electronic magic that makes communication so excellent and so easy.

Yet, in spite of these differences, some things haven't changed; or, if they have changed, it is for the worse. We speak of the excessive use of alcoholic beverages that in Isaiah's day inflamed the hearts of the imbibers and today still produces the same results. The situation in many respects is worse today. Alcoholic beverages are more readily available than they were twenty-seven hundred years ago. Further, our beverages are available with a much higher alcoholic content than that of ancient wine.

Our government spends billions of dollars a year fighting the so-called hard drugs—marijuana, heroin, cocaine. Yet alcohol creates more havoc in the form of broken homes, crime, ruined health, and death than all the hard drugs combined. The hard drugs we attempt to stamp out; alcohol we make legal. Obviously, our logic isn't any better than in Isaiah's day.

Even though the cost of alcohol is high, it has gained general acceptance in our society. The outcry against liquor that once sounded forth from our pulpits has largely been muted. Churches that once led the crusade against strong drink now champion other causes. The International Sunday School Lessons years ago designated one lesson a quarter as a temperance lesson. Of course many lessons, such as today's, still point out the dangers of strong drink, but the topic is no longer given specific emphasis each quarter. No doubt many factors have contributed to this change of emphasis, but certainly the advertising campaign carried on by the liquor interests has been one of these factors. Because alcoholic beverages have become so generally acceptable, Christians need to become more involved in warning against alcohol's dangers and providing help for those who have become its victims.

B. Greed, Ancient and Modern

The sin of greed is most pervasive. It ignores the boundaries of time, culture, and socio-economic classes. It engulfed the society of ancient Judah when Isaiah lived, and it has penetrated every level of our society. The prophet pronounced woe upon those who joined "house to house" and laid "field to field," thus gaining a real-estate monopoly. Isaiah did not condemn them because they were rich, but because they used this monopoly to oppress the poor.

We have seen similar things in our own times. The scandals that have rocked the saving and loan institutions and our banks came about because of greed. Junk bonds and stock market manipulations are other symptoms of the epidemic of greed that has swept across our land. We are bombarded continuously by advertisements that stimulate our desire for things and more things. So clever are these enticements that all of us are affected to some degree. Even if we do not succumb to these blandishments, we become more tolerant of them, muting the objections we ought to be raising against this blatant materialism.

God created a world that is rich in resources, resources that He intends us to use and enjoy. But He intends us to use them wisely, frugally, and unselfishly. Only then can we experience the joy that comes from responsible stewardship of all these good things.

C. Let Us Pray

Bountiful Father, we give You thanks for the many things You have entrusted to us. Help us to avoid the temptations of greed. We pray for those who have become trapped in the throes of alcohol and other drugs. Show us how to help them. Keep us from the same snares. In our Master's precious name we pray. Amen.

D. Thought to Remember

"Wine is a mocker, strong drink is raging: and whosoever is deceived thereby is not wise" (Proverbs 20:1).

Home Daily Bible Readings

Monday, Aug. 14—Punishment for Proud and Corrupt Leaders (Isaiah 9:8-17)
Tuesday, Aug. 15—Moral Decay and Injustice Are Judged (Isaiah 9:18—10:4)
Wednesday, Aug. 16—Israel and Judah as a Vineyard (Isaiah 5:1-7)
Thursday, Aug. 17—Judgment on Greed and Selfish Indulgence (Isaiah 5:8-12)
Friday, Aug. 18—God's Judgment Is Just (Isaiah 5:13-17)
Saturday, Aug. 19—Judgment on Arrogant Immorality (Isaiah 5:18-23)
Sunday, Aug. 20—Destruction Awaits the Wicked (Isaiah 5:24-30)

Learning by Doing

This page contains an alternate lesson plan emphasizing learning activities. Classes desiring such student involvement will find these suggestions helpful.

Learning Goals

Focus on leading your students to do the following through this session:

1. Identify sins for which God condemned His people in Isaiah 5.

2. Wrestle with this issue: Should we approach a sinful world in a positive manner or in a negative manner?

Into the Lesson

Ask two volunteers to participate in a role play, assuming a role and making up their conversation and activity spontaneously.

Give a copy of the following instructions to each of the volunteers:

The role play will involve two Christians discussing a radio preacher.

The first Christian complains that the preacher is too negative. He is always harping on sin. This person suggests that the preacher needs to take a more positive approach.

The second Christian disagrees. He believes society is under God's judgment and needs to be warned. And many Christians are lukewarm and need to be shaken from complacency.

Give both players about a minute to think through their roles. Then ask them to play it out. Allow about three minutes for class discussion. Then cut off the role play. Be sure to thank both players.

Ask the rest of the class, "Which points did you agree with the most?" Allow some time for discussion.

Relate this activity to the Bible study by saying, "A positive approach usually is welcome. That makes it difficult for us to understand why God was frequently negative in dealing with the sins of His people. Today in our lesson we will consider another message from one of God's prophets, and it was a message of condemnation. God used this approach for a reason, and He put it in Scripture for a reason too. Let's try to figure out why God focused so much on condemnation."

Into the Word

Read Isaiah 5:8-12, 18-23.

Briefly summarize the background for today's passage. Then pass out copies of the outline below to your students, one per person. You can find this outline in the student book.

What is condemned?		What is the solution?
vv. 8-10		1 Timothy 6:6-10
vv. 11, 12, 22		Ephesians 5:18
vv. 18-20		1 Thessalonians 5:21, 22
v. 21		James 4:6-10
v. 23		Amos 5:24

Ask students to form groups of four and fill in the column under "What is condemned?" They should not discuss the solution unless they are finished before the other groups. Allow about eight minutes for the groups to complete the first column. (Note: they can finish the second column at home. This will encourage them to dig deeper into the lesson on their own.)

Ask the groups for their observations in the first column. Write these on the chalkboard. Then ask the question, "Why did God take the negative approach when dealing with His wayward people?" Allow for discussion.

Into Life

Write these situations on the chalkboard:

1. A person with a serious illness.

2. A person on a sinking ship.

3. A person in a house on fire.

Ask these questions for each situation:

1. What hope would a person in this situation want to hear?

2. What bad news would the person have to agree with before receiving hope?

Then say, "The gospel is good news, but the positive message cannot be received until a person has accepted the bad news that we deserve God's wrath unless we are forgiven in Christ."

Then lead a discussion of these questions:

1. In what ways should we be negative in dealing with the world?

2. In what ways should we be positive?

3. What should be our attitude when we have to deal negatively with the world? Why?

4. What negative message from God do you personally need to pay attention to?

5. What positive message from God do you need to cling to?

Encourage students to complete the chart, dealing with the solutions, at home. Close with prayer.

Let's Talk It Over

The questions on this page are designed to encourage review of the lesson Scriptures and to promote discussion of the lesson by the class. The answers provided are only discussion starters. Let your class talk it over from there.

1. How does greed affect the economy? Was Isaiah predicting a mere recession, or something more? Does God still work in the economy?

Recessions seem to be natural economic phenomena, but Isaiah was warning of a greater disaster (v. 10). He was not talking about mistakes in economic policy; he was warning about the results of a degenerate life-style supported by greed and injustice. These will still bring disaster in our time. God has built in certain laws of cause and effect, and with all our sophistication we cannot evade them. Gravity pulls downward, fire destroys, and greed also has results that we cannot escape.

2. The costs of alcohol consumption are high—purchase costs, health-care costs, time lost from work, families disrupted, lives lost by accidents and violence. What appeals can be made to people who try to justify drinking?

Appeals to common sense can be made, and can be effective with some people. Perhaps the current surgeon general can be persuaded to attack drinking as a former one has attacked smoking. The example of clean Christian living may have more effect than we know, and the good news of salvation in Jesus may be the most effective appeal of all.

3. What excuses do we use for actions, habits, or attitudes that God condemns?

Excuses may vary as much as fingerprints, and they have been used ever since Adam and Eve (Genesis 3). We may claim that a wrong is too small to matter, that we don't do it often, that it's just for fun with no evil intent, that we're going to stop it soon. But no one yet has found an excuse that is good enough.

4. How can the local church help alcoholics or people injured by alcoholism in the family?

Alcoholics Anonymous is based on the conviction that addiction can be combated only with divine help, and many Christians are comfortable working with that organization. Some churches provide meeting places for AA gatherings. Other churches form support groups of their own. These can be very effective if members are unstinting with their time and effort.

5. The liquor traffic is legal almost everywhere and so is abortion. Gambling is becoming legal in more and more places, and even prostitution is legal in some. It is argued that such activities will continue, whether they are legal or not, so it is better to legalize them and benefit from the taxes they pay. What can be done at the local level to make such businesses less profitable?

We may admire Carrie Nation, who used to go into saloons and smash the furniture with a hatchet; but most Christians agree that bombing abortion clinics or other places of business is not the best way to serve Christ. True, Jesus removed crooked businesses from the temple, but not many of us claim to have the kind of authority He had. Christians are taught to live within the law (Romans 13:1-7), and it is hard to justify illegal violence against legal wrongs.

If we want to reduce the profits of an evil business, probably the best way is to reduce the demand for its product. This is done by changing the desires, the thinking, the way of life of those who might be customers of the evil business. Persons are thus transformed when we win them to Christ and teach them to obey Him. Do you remember how Paul hurt the business of the idol makers in Ephesus? He did it by preaching the gospel (Acts 19:23-41).

6. In your class and your church, is stewardship being taught as a way of life, not just a way to raise money?

Too many churches talk of stewardship only when it is time to ask for financial pledges. Stewardship is being faithful managers of whatever God has put in our charge. It encompasses all of life all through the year.

We contribute a share of our incomes to the church because the church is Christ's body, doing His work in the community and in the world. But it is no less important to use the rest of our incomes in ways that He approves. If you have not become aware of that, read 2 Corinthians 8 and 9 and see if there are some blessings that you have been missing. As Jesus pointed out, "Where your treasure is, there will your heart be also" (Matthew 6:21). What better place can there be to make an investment than in the kingdom of God?

The End of a Nation

DEVOTIONAL READING: Deuteronomy 8:11-20.

LESSON SCRIPTURE: 2 Kings 17:1-23.

PRINTED TEXT: 2 Kings 17:6-14.

2 Kings 17:6-14

6 In the ninth year of Hoshea the king of Assyria took Samaria, and carried Israel away into Assyria, and placed them in Halah and in Habor by the river of Gozan, and in the cities of the Medes.

7 For so it was, that the children of Israel had sinned against the LORD their God, which had brought them up out of the land of Egypt, from under the hand of Pharaoh king of Egypt, and had feared other gods,

8 And walked in the statutes of the heathen, whom the LORD cast out from before the children of Israel, and of the kings of Israel, which they had made.

9 And the children of Israel did secretly those things that were not right against the LORD their God, and they built them high places in all their cities, from the tower of the watchmen to the fenced city.

10 And they set them up images and groves in every high hill, and under every green tree:

11 And there they burnt incense in all the high places, as did the heathen whom the LORD carried away before them; and wrought wicked things to provoke the LORD to anger:

12 For they served idols, whereof the LORD had said unto them, Ye shall not do this thing.

13 Yet the LORD testified against Israel, and against Judah, by all the prophets, and by all the seers, saying, Turn ye from your evil ways, and keep my commandments and my statutes, according to all the law which I commanded your fathers, and which I sent to you by my servants the prophets.

14 Notwithstanding, they would not hear, but hardened their necks, like to the neck of their fathers, that did not believe in the LORD their God.

GOLDEN TEXT: The LORD testified against Israel, and against Judah, by all the prophets, and by all the seers, saying, Turn ye from your evil ways, and keep my commandments and my statutes.—2 Kings 17:13.

Aug
27

A Nation Turns From God
Unit 3. The Judgment Arrives
(Lessons 10-13)

Lesson Aims

As a result of studying this lesson, each student should:

1. Have a better understanding of the political situation at the time Israel fell.

2. Have a better understanding of how Israel sinned against God.

3. Have a growing appreciation for the fact that disobedience to God's commandments has dire consequences.

4. Be able to point out sins in our nation that can lead to our downfall.

Lesson Outline

INTRODUCTION
  A. Neglect Brings Disaster
  B. Lesson Background
 I. ISRAEL FALLS TO ASSYRIA (2 Kings 17:6)
  A. Samaria Is Captured (v. 6a)
  B. The Captives Are Deported (v. 6b)
II. REASONS FOR ISRAEL'S FALL (2 Kings 17:7-12)
  A. They Had Sinned Against God (v. 7)
    Paradise Lost
  B. They Had Followed Pagan Laws (v. 8)
  C. They Had Worshiped Pagan Gods
    (vv. 9-12)
III. ISRAEL HAD BEEN WARNED (2 Kings 17:13, 14)
  A. Prophets and Seers Had Warned Them
    (v. 13)
  B. They Had Rejected the Warnings (v. 14)
    Mulish Heritage
CONCLUSION
  A. While There Is Still Time
  B. Prophets and Seers
  C. Let Us Pray
  D. Thought to Remember

Visual 13 proclaims that those who persist in rebelling against God eventually will be punished. The visual is shown on page 445.

Introduction

A. Neglect Brings Disaster

Several years ago Joe bought a new car. With it came a manual that explained how the car should be cared for to keep it in good running condition. But Joe was more interested in driving his new car than he was in maintaining it, and so he ignored the manual. He didn't worry about keeping the tires properly inflated, he didn't check the radiator coolant, and he didn't change the oil regularly. The car ran well for a while, but eventually little things began to go wrong. Joe had repairs made to keep his car running, but he still paid little attention to proper maintenance. He ignored friends who kept telling him that he would ruin the engine if he didn't change the oil. Then one day it happened. The engine blew up, throwing a rod through the side of the block. Joe no longer had a car to drive, and he had no one but himself to blame.

This sounds rather like the situation in ancient Israel. God had placed them in the land of promise and given them instructions about what they were to do so they could continue to enjoy its blessings. But they had ignored these instructions. Again and again God had sent His spokesmen to warn them of the dangers they faced if they didn't change their ways. But they rejected these messengers and continued on their reckless way. Then it happened. As a result of moral decay within and Assyrian aggression from without, the nation was swept away—and it had only itself to blame.

B. Lesson Background

During the reigns of Jeroboam II of the northern kingdom and Uzziah of the southern kingdom, Israel and Judah had enjoyed great prosperity. In part this prosperity came because the power of Assyria had declined. But all this was to change when Tiglath-pileser came to the throne of Assyria in 745 B.C. Once he had gained firm control over his kingdom, he turned

---

How to Say It

ASSYRIA. Uh-*sear*-ee-uh.
BEN-HADAD. Ben-*hay*-dad.
CANAANITE. *Kay*-nun-ite.
GOZAN. *Go*-zun.
HABOR. *Hay*-bor.
HALAH. *Hay*-luh.
HOSHEA. Ho-*she*-uh.
JEROBOAM. Jair-o-*bo*-um.
NINEVEH. *Nin*-uh-vuh.
OMRI. *Ahm*-rye.
PEKAH. *Pee*-kuh.
SARGON. *Sar*-gon.
SHALMANESER. *Shal*-man-*ee*-zer (strong accent on *ee*).
TIGLATH-PILESER. *Tig*-lath-pih-*lee*-zer (strong accent on *lee*).
UZZIAH. Uh-*zye*-uh.

his attention to the west, forcing Syria, Israel, and Judah to pay him tribute.

In 731 B.C. Hoshea assassinated Pekah, the king of Israel, and made himself king. At first he paid tribute to Shalmaneser, who had succeeded Tiglath-pileser as king of Assyria. But when Hoshea later withheld the tribute, Shalmaneser marched against Israel, determined to punish her. Apparently he ravaged the countryside, and then in 725 laid siege to Samaria, the capital. After three years Samaria fell. Some records indicate that by this time Shalmaneser had been succeeded by Sargon II, who takes credit for the capture of Israel's capital. The fall of Samaria brought an end to Israel, which never again appears as a nation separate from Judah.

I. Israel Falls to Assyria
(2 Kings 17:6)

A. Samaria Is Captured (v. 6a)

6a. In the ninth year of Hoshea the king of Assyria took Samaria.

Samaria was located in the hill country of central Palestine, about forty miles north of Jerusalem. The city, built by Omri about 880 B.C., was situated on a readily defended height, which is apparently the reason that Omri chose to make it his capital. On one occasion Benhadad, king of Syria, besieged the city and was able to bring the people almost to the point of starvation (2 Kings 6:24, 25). Yet he was not able to breach the walls or enter the city. The Assyrians had perfected the art of warfare. Few cities could stand against them when they brought their battering rams and their siege towers into play. Yet Samaria was able to hold out for three years, attesting to its formidable defenses. But after three years it fell in 722 B.C., probably because its food supplies were exhausted.

B. The Captives Are Deported (v. 6b)

6b. And carried Israel away into Assyria, and placed them in Halah and in Habor by the river of Gozan, and in the cities of the Medes.

When the Assyrians captured a city, it was not unusual for them to put to death all the able-bodied men, often subjecting them to terrible cruelty in the process. While some may have been killed at Samaria, apparently many of the inhabitants were spared and sent back to Assyria. In the Assyrian records that have been recovered, King Sargon II boasts of deporting 27,290 prisoners. The deportees were sent to several different places. *Halah* has been identified with a town northeast of Nineveh. Some translations indicate that *Habor* was a river that ran through the area of *Gozan* and emptied into

the Euphrates River. The Medes lived in an area northeast of the Tigris River in what is now Iran.

This deportation served two purposes. First, it provided the Assyrians with a good supply of slaves. Further, it is likely that those who were selected for deportation were the most capable people, those who might lead a revolt in the future. By depriving the Israelites of their natural leaders and by settling foreigners among those who remained, the Assyrians were trying to prevent another uprising.

II. Reasons for Israel's Fall
(2 Kings 17:7-12)

A. They Had Sinned Against God (v. 7)

7. For so it was, that the children of Israel had sinned against the LORD their God, which had brought them up out of the land of Egypt, from under the hand of Pharaoh king of Egypt, and had feared other gods.

The first six verses in this chapter tell of the destruction that came upon Israel. This verse introduces an explanation of why it happened. The *children of Israel* had sinned against God, though they owed Him their gratitude and obedience because He had delivered them out of Egypt. The nation that God had formed and called out of Egypt was now going back into bondage and would lose her identity. The cycle that we see in the book of Judges—Israel falling into sin, God sending punishment upon them, the people repenting, and then God restoring them to favor—would not be repeated this time. Their great sin, one they had repeated time and again, was that they worshiped *other gods*.

PARADISE LOST

Eve and Adam were removed from God's garden because they sinned against the Lord. They ate forbidden fruit, so they lost paradise. They were separated from God by their disobedience, and punished by pain, sorrow, toil, and death.

The nation of Israel was removed from God's promised land because "Israel had sinned against the Lord their God." These "chosen people" were rebellious and disobedient. So God allowed them to be defeated by enemies who displaced them to foreign lands and cultures.

Sin still separates us from God, but "we were reconciled to God by the death of his Son" (Romans 5:10). So Christians again possess the promise of paradise (Revelation 2:7).

What we must learn from the experiences of Adam and Israel is that God's promise is *conditional*. "Be thou faithful unto death, and I will give thee a crown of life" (Revelation 2:10).

—R.W.B.

B. They Had Followed Pagan Laws (v. 8)

8. And walked in the statutes of the heathen, whom the LORD cast out from before the children of Israel, and of the kings of Israel, which they had made.

It is not possible for one to separate his religion from his daily life. When the Israelites abandoned Jehovah to worship various pagan gods, they also became involved in immoralities that Jehovah considered abominations—human sacrifice, for example, and sexual orgies. These activities of pagan worship were reflected in everyday matters. Human sacrifice devalued human life, increasing the likelihood of violent crimes, and sexual orgies undermined the sanctity of marriage and family life.

From Canaanite neighbors they learned to walk *in the statutes* of the heathen. God had ordered them to drive the Canaanites out of the land, but they had never completely carried out this order. The Canaanites who remained infected the Israelites with their false religion. But this was not the only source of infection. On occasion their own kings, Ahab, for example, imported pagan religion and encouraged the people to become involved in it.

C. They Had Worshiped Pagan Gods
(vv. 9-12)

9. And the children of Israel did secretly those things that were not right against the LORD their God, and they built them high places in all their cities, from the tower of the watchmen to the fenced city.

The tower of the watchmen was any one of the many towers that were built in fields and vineyards to help the owners guard their crops against thieves. *The fenced city* was a town with a massive stone wall. The historian is saying that *high places* were built all over the country, from the most remote rural area to the big city. These high places were places of worship on hilltops and artificial mounds. It seems that false worship in these places was open and blatant, so it is hard to see what is meant by *did secretly*. Possibly some people pretended to worship Jehovah, but secretly worshiped other gods. Some students think *did secretly* means *covered* or *hid*. Possibly it means the worship of Jehovah was buried and lost in the mass of words or *things that were not right*—the ceremonies of pagan worship. Or could the meaning possibly be that the people of Israel were secretly committing other crimes in addition to building high places for false worship?

10. And they set them up images and groves in every high hill, and under every green tree.

The making of an image to be worshiped was strictly forbidden by the Second Commandment, which is so clear and specific that there was no reason for anyone to misunderstand it. The people had so compromised their faith that they had no trouble violating such a plain commandment. If we find this hard to understand, we need only to look at our own times. The Scriptures have some quite specific teachings about homosexuality, and yet some church groups have completely ignored these teachings.

Images and groves is translated *pillars and Asherim* in the *American Standard* and the *Revised Standard Versions*. The *pillars* were stone obelisks that undoubtedly had some significance in idolatrous worship. Asherah (the plural form is *Asherim*) was the Canaanite fertility goddess. Her symbol was often a trunk of a tree, hence the reference to *groves*. The fact that she was the fertility goddess gives a clue to the licentious sex acts that went on in the name of worship.

11, 12. And there they burnt incense in all the high places, as did the heathen whom the LORD carried away before them; and wrought wicked things to provoke the LORD to anger: for they served idols, whereof the LORD had said unto them, Ye shall not do this thing.

Burning incense symbolized prayer, and so in this act they were praying to pagan gods just as the heathen had done before them. Because of their wickedness, the heathen had been driven out. Now the Israelites were guilty of the same offense, and as a result they would soon have to suffer the same punishment. *Wicked things* may refer to the sexual activities involved in the worship, or perhaps to human sacrifice. Both of these were abominations to the Lord. Involvement in idolatry disobeyed God's direct commands against it, making their offense all the more wicked.

III. Israel Had Been Warned
(2 Kings 17:13, 14)

A. Prophets and Seers Had Warned Them
(v. 13)

13. Yet the LORD testified against Israel, and against Judah, by all the prophets, and by all the seers, saying, Turn ye from your evil ways, and keep my commandments and my statutes, according to all the law which I commanded your fathers, and which I sent to you by my servants the prophets.

Incorporated in the law of Moses were prohibitions that should have kept the people from the idolatry into which they had fallen. But God's warnings did not stop with these prohibitions. Again and again He sent His spokesmen to

visual 13

MULISH HERITAGE

"Like father, like son!" Children have proved through the ages that offspring inherit not only physical characteristics, but temperament and personality, too.

No one knows for certain if stubbornness is a genetic or learned trait, but often stubborn parents have at least one stubborn child. And when an "immovable object" lives under the same roof with an "irresistible force," troubled times are inevitable.

The stubbornness of mules is legendary. Some people are so mulish one might think of them as evidence of a new theory of evolution. Apparently several generations of both Judah and Israel were like that. They "hardened their necks" and refused to believe in Jehovah. They were stubbornly wicked. In fact, they acted both stubbornly and stupidly.

A case could be made for stubbornness when it is channelled for righteous causes. Tenacity can be a good quality when rightly used.

But stiffnecked sinners cannot be justified. When personal pride and wanton selfishness preclude repentance, stubbornness is totally detrimental and self-destructive. God wants us to give in to goodness and receive His grace, for He is "not willing that any should perish" (2 Peter 3:9).
—R. W. B.

bring further warnings. The term *prophets* covers a great variety of people who spoke for God, including Abram and Aaron. Specifically, we think of the writing prophets such as Isaiah, Jeremiah, and the so-called minor prophets. Some of these whom we have studied this quarter directed their messages specifically at some of the sins that were dragging Israel down to destruction. The term *seer* is sometimes used synonymously with *prophet*; however, it carries the idea of one who sees beyond what a person can ordinarily see. God gave the power to see not only the future, but also a deeper meaning in ordinary events.

God had sent these special messengers over a period of many years. He was unwilling to give His people up at their first offense, but patiently and lovingly tried to bring them back to Him. God is "long-suffering to us-ward, not willing that any should perish, but that all should come to repentance" (2 Peter 3:9).

B. They Had Rejected the Warnings (v. 14)

14. Notwithstanding, they would not hear, but hardened their necks, like to the neck of their fathers, that did not believe in the LORD their God.

The people of Israel certainly had heard the messages the Lord had sent, but they *would not hear* in the sense that they would not heed the messages God had sent. When Isaiah was called to speak to God's people, God warned him that his preaching would "make the heart of this people fat, and make their ears heavy, and shut their eyes" (Isaiah 6:10). The very message that could save them would only harden their hearts. They *hardened their necks* like stubborn oxen that refused to be turned from the wrong way. They *did not believe in the Lord*, that is, they did not trust in Him. They were like many today who say they believe in God, but their lives clearly show that they do not trust Him to provide direction for their lives.

Conclusion

A. While There Is Still Time

Nearly four centuries ago a few hardy venturers left the shores of England to find homes in the New World. Many came out of deep religious conviction, hoping to find the freedom to worship God that they felt was denied them in their native land. They hoped to build a "city built on a hill" that would serve as a model to the whole world. The Old Testament law, tempered by the teachings of the New Testament, served as their constitution and their guide for daily living.

Not all who came to the New World shared this Puritan faith. Some came in search of gold or wealth in other forms. Some came with religious convictions that differed from the convictions of the Puritans. Some arrived in chains, victims of the horrible slave system. Yet, regardless of how they came or what they believed when they came, they were all in one way or another influenced by the Puritans.

It is popular today to sneer at the Puritans, rejecting them as narrow-minded bigots whose main purpose in life was to keep people from enjoying themselves. Or they are simply ignored in our history texts, or their contributions are greatly minimized. Of course, not all of their actions can be justified. Their intolerance of dissent is a black mark on their record, and so is the hanging of a number of alleged witches. Nevertheless, their stern ethic made a lasting impact on American history. Their commitment to God and their dedication to hard work, combined with the rich natural resources God had placed in the land, allowed America eventually to become the richest country in the world.

But America faced some of the same problems that ancient Israel encountered. With wealth came temptations that over the years gradually eroded the firm convictions of these stalwart pioneers. The Pilgrims were not able to pass on their convictions to their children and their children's children. If they were to return today, they would surely be shocked to see what has happened to their dreams of building the kingdom of God on earth. On every hand they would see crime, drug abuse, political corruption, adultery, abortion, and religious apathy. No doubt they would tremble as they contemplated the wrath of God that certainly will fall upon such a nation if it continues to sink deeper into wrongdoing.

All of us to some extent have been beneficiaries of these Pilgrim fathers. In the Old Testament they found guidelines that helped shape their theology. We too can learn from ancient Israel and Judah. They were God's chosen people; yet when they departed from His ways, He did not withhold His judgment from them. We also have been richly blessed by God, and someday He will call for an accounting. God is still on His throne, and He still demands righteousness of a nation.

We have an obligation to speak out against the evils we see about us. We need to enlist others to join us in that mission. Most of all, we must impart to our children the faith that can yet save us.

B. Prophets and Seers

When God gave Moses the law on Mount Sinai, He did not leave the people without further guidance. After they entered the promised land, it was not long before they began to go astray. God sent judges to deliver them from their enemies and bring them back to Him. He used great heroes like Samuel and David to provide guidance for His people. Then came prophets and seers. In the exercise of their office these men were both foretellers and forthtellers. In some cases God gave them the vision to pull aside the curtains and catch a glimpse of the future. With this divine insight they could bring warnings of impending doom that threatened the nation if the people did not change their ways. As forthtellers they told of God's righteousness and His requirements that the people live up to His law. This quarter we have studied the lives and messages of several of these prophets. Even after twenty-five hundred years or more, their messages strike a responsive chord in our hearts. They brought God's condemnation of wrong in their societies, a judgment that is still needed today.

We do not have prophets and seers in the same sense that they did in those days. No one today can proclaim Holy Spirit inspired messages as they did. But we no longer need such inspired messengers because we have God's inspired Word, the holy Scriptures. That puts a responsibility on the shoulders of each one of us. If the Bible is to speak to us today, we must read it and study it and heed it. Each one of these steps takes effort on our part. That's why it is important that students in your class be regular in their attendance and participate in the learning activities.

C. Let Us Pray

Dear God and heavenly Father, use these lessons from ancient Israel to open our eyes to the dangers that our nation faces. Give us the wisdom to bring Your Word to bear on the moral problems that we face. Teach us that Your mercy is still available to those who repent and turn to You. In the precious name of our Savior we pray. Amen.

D. Thought to Remember

"The Lord your God ye shall fear" (2 Kings 17:39).

Home Daily Bible Readings

Monday, Aug. 21—A Warning to Keep God's Commandments (Deuteronomy 8:11-20)

Tuesday, Aug. 22—Israel Falls, the People Are Deported (2 Kings 17:1-6)

Wednesday, Aug. 23—Israel's Sins Caused Its Fall (2 Kings 17:7-12)

Thursday, Aug. 24—Israel Scorned God and Worshiped Idols (2 Kings 17:13-18)

Friday, Aug. 25—Jeroboam's Leadership Started Israel's Decline (2 Kings 17:19-23)

Saturday, Aug. 26—The Land Resettled With Other Peoples (2 Kings 17:24-28)

Sunday, Aug. 27—The End of the Nation Israel (2 Kings 17:29-34)

Learning by Doing

*This page contains an alternate lesson plan emphasizing learning activities. Classes
desiring such student involvement will find these suggestions helpful.*

Learning Goals

Students should be able to:

1. Determine a correlation between obedience
and God's blessing, and between rebellion and
God's punishment for a nation.

2. Evaluate where his own nation is on a continuum between God's blessing and God's punishment.

3. Suggest principles to help our nation turn
to God and receive His favor.

Into the Lesson

Write these two sentences on the chalkboard,
or distribute the student books and call attention to these sentences there:

Obeying God brings His blessing.

Rebellion against God brings punishment.

Ask your class members to brainstorm examples that illustrate both of these principles. The
examples can be from Scripture, from other history, or just common examples from life.

Then say to the class, "This is the final lesson
in this quarter. In the history of nations and
their leaders, we have observed a strong correlation between rebelling against God and receiving God's judgment. The opposite is also true.
Nations that seek God and obey Him receive His
blessing. Today we will see God's judgment
against His northern kingdom, Israel."

Into the Word

Explain the background to today's text. Then
ask a volunteer to read 2 Kings 17:6-20. Have
your class form groups of six to discuss the
questions below, which can be found in the student book. If you do not use the student book,
be sure to copy these questions for each group:

1. Why was Israel (also called Samaria) punished, according to:

verses 7-13

verses 14, 15

verses 16, 17

verses 18-20

2. How was Israel punished?

3. How had God tried to prevent this punishment?

4. What does this passage teach you about—
Human nature?
God?

5. According to Jeremiah 18:7-11, how can a
wicked nation prevent punishment from God?

Option

Explain the passage background and ask a
volunteer to read 2 Kings 17:6-20. Have class
members form groups of six.

In their groups they are to imagine they are
prosecuting attorneys in a courtroom trial of the
nation of Israel. They are seeking to prove that
Israel is guilty and should be punished. Based
upon 2 Kings 17:6-20 they should prepare a
closing argument to present to the jury.

Appoint a leader for each group and provide
paper and pens. Inform groups that they have
twenty minutes to compile their arguments.
They should appoint someone from the group to
present the closing argument to the rest of the
class, who will serve as the jury.

After the time has elapsed, allow each group
to present its case.

Then have the class read Jeremiah 18:7-11.
Ask, "Based on this passage, how can a wicked
nation prevent God's punishment?" Allow time
for discussion.

Into Life

Write the following on the chalkboard:

Blessing 1 2 3 4 5 6 7 8 9 10 Punishment

Provide pen and paper for each student. Ask
each to write the scale on his paper. Then ask
him to circle the number that best represents
where he thinks our nation is in relation to
God's blessing or punishment.

Take a tally and try to get an average score.
Explain that this obviously is only an opinion,
and only God knows where our nation is in relation to His favor or rejection.

Have class members form their small groups
again. Then ask the groups to discuss and identify what they believe are the three most important things our nation needs to change in order
to gain God's continual blessing. After five minutes, ask the groups to report their conclusions.

Ask each class member to write down what
he thinks are the three most important things for
him to do individually to help our nation gain
God's blessing. He can write these on the paper
he received earlier.

Finally, close in small group prayer, asking
students to pray that they and their country will
live righteously for God.

Let's Talk It Over

The questions on this page are designed to encourage review of the lesson Scriptures and to promote discussion of the lesson by the class. The answers provided are only discussion starters. Let your class talk it over from there.

1. How much do other people influence what we do and the values we hold?

When the people of Israel came to the promised land, they were told to drive out or destroy the depraved heathen who lived there. That seems terribly harsh till we see the result of failure to do it. Israel itself was destroyed because it fell into the pagan style of worship and life.

What about us? Should we destroy pagans? No, Jesus has called us to be salt, light, and leaven in a lost world. Because we are commissioned to make disciples of all peoples, we can neither destroy them nor avoid them. But we must take care not to adopt their values or participate in their sins. It is good for the church to be in the world, but disastrous for the world to be in the church.

2. What kinds of secret paganism can Christians sometimes engage in?

King Jeroboam I introduced idolatry in a sneaky way. Calling Israel to worship golden calves, he said, "Behold thy gods, O Israel, which brought thee up out of the land of Egypt" (1 Kings 12:28). In other words, he tried to pretend the calves represented Jehovah even while they violated Jehovah's Second Commandment (Exodus 20:4, 5). Centuries later the people were still pretending to honor Jehovah even while they were pagan in worship and life-style.

When we rely on social trends, or even time-honored traditions, we may be running away from what God has taught us in His Word. When church people engage in harmful gossip, jealousy, or party dissension, it indicates the creeping presence of sin, even if "everybody" is doing it. Pagan values are reflected in "the works of the flesh," but Christians treasure "the fruit of the Spirit" (Galatians 5:19-26).

3. What messengers does God use today to call us to repentance? How can we know whom to believe?

The most obvious messenger of God is the Holy Bible, and a person is worthy of belief when he faithfully presents God's Word. But God has never been limited. He may use a surprising array of people and events to get His message to us. Paul's physical ailment was "the messenger of Satan," but God used even that to draw the apostle closer to Him (2 Corinthians 12:7-10). Paul then could testify "that in all things God works for the good of those who love him" (Romans 8:28, *New International Version*).

If we are attentive, God communicates with us in a multitude of ways: through the sky above and the earth around us, through blessings and punishments, through good examples and bad examples. But His supreme messenger is Jesus (Hebrews 1:1-4). Every message and messenger must be in agreement with Him.

4. If we trust God, what evidence should our lives give to verify our trust?

The Old Testament prophets called in vain for Israel and Judah to show evidence of their faith in God. The lack of such evidence showed that faith itself was lacking. Both nations were destroyed because the people were like their ancestors "that did not believe in the Lord their God" (2 Kings 17:14).

We say we believe in God and Jesus, but people around us may be asking, "Where is the evidence of your faith?" Several studies have indicated that there doesn't seem to be much difference between the way Christians act and the way non-Christians act. That is a serious indictment, for Jesus said a tree is known by its fruit (Matthew 12:33). Are we affected by our culture more than by our Lord?

5. Sometime the promised punishment will come; and there will be no more time to reform. What are we doing to make people aware of that and to bring about changes while there is time?

Destroyed by Assyria, Israel ceased to exist as a nation. For that northern kingdom there were no more second chances. Someday that will be true for the whole world. As long as Jesus has not returned, there is still time before the Judgment Day—but not for everyone. Every day some are dying unprepared to face judgment.

What are we doing with the time we have left? What priority are we giving to evangelism and missions? What share do they have of our money, our prayer, our concern? Time was limited for Israel. Time is limited for people who do not know Jesus as Lord. Time is limited for the church to be about the Father's business.